Election 2010

The Official Results

Election 2010

The Official Results

Compiled by

Colin Rallings & Michael Thrasher

First published in Great Britain in 2011 by
Biteback Publishing Ltd
Westminster Tower
3 Albert Embankment
London
SE1 7SP

ISBN 978-1-84954-090-2

10 9 8 7 6 5 4 3 2 1

A CIP catalogue record for this book is available from the British Library.

Typeset in Times New Roman by Dawn Cole
Printed and bound in Great Britain by TJ International, Padstow, Cornwall

Contents

Overview

The Official Results

Overview

1   The General Election 2010

The 2010 general election held on Thursday 6ᵗʰ May gave the United Kingdom its first hung parliament since February 1974. The Conservatives gained over 100 additional seats and nearly 2 million more votes compared with 2005, but fell short of an overall majority. Labour polled less than 30% of the vote for only the second time since the war, but still managed to win more than four in 10 seats in the House of Commons. The Liberal Democrats attracted more support than in 2005, but won five fewer seats.

The election in one of the 650 parliamentary constituencies, Thirsk and Malton, was postponed until 27ᵗʰ May following the death of the UKIP candidate. This is the second election in succession that a parliamentary election has been postponed in this way. The previous occurrence in 2005 was the first for more than 50 years. In this report both the commentary and Tables *include* the result for Thirsk and Malton. Tables summarising the outcome by country and region, together with a wealth of other lists and statistical information, can be found following the detailed listing of constituency results.

The total number of seats is four more than were contested at the previous general election. This followed the implementation of the review of constituency boundaries in England which increased its representation from 529 to 533 seats. Similar boundary reviews in Wales and Northern Ireland led to no change in the number of seats, 40 and 18 respectively. A review of Scotland's representation had already been implemented prior to the 2005 general election. This reduced Scotland's seats in the Westminster parliament from 72 to 59.

The headline figures are that the Conservatives won 306 seats –twenty less than required for a House of Commons majority. Estimates are that they would have won 210 seats if the 2010 boundaries had existed at the time of the 2005 general election, meaning a net gain of 96 seats for the party. Labour captured 258 seats (a net loss of 91) and the Liberal Democrats 57 (a net loss of five seats). Other parties plus The Speaker account for the remaining 29 (4.5%) seats.

The strategic situation at the conclusion of the 2010 general election is summarised in Table 1. The first column shows the winning party and each row identifies the party that finished in the runner-up position. The Table highlights how far the Liberal Democrats are now a key feature of the electoral landscape. Although they actually lost seats in 2010, they occupy more second places (243) than either of their major party rivals –and thus pose a potential threat to either of them depending on the mood swing of the country. The Conservatives are second to Labour in 147 of its 258 seats while the Liberal Democrats are second in 76. The position in Conservative controlled constituencies is that Labour and the Liberal Democrats are second in 137 and 167 seats respectively.

Table 1: The distribution of first and second places at the 2010 general election

1st	2nd										
	Con	Lab	LD	SNP	PC	UCUNF	SF	DUP	SDLP	Ind/Other	Total 1st
Con		137	167							2	**306**
Lab	147		76	28	5					2	**258**
LD	38	16		2	1						**57**
DUP						5	2		1		**8**
SNP	4	2									**6**
SF								2	2	1	**5**
SDLP							2	1			**3**
PC	1	2									**3**
APNI								1			**1**
Speaker										1	**1**
Green		1									**1**
Ind						1					**1**
Total 2nd	**190**	**158**	**243**	**30**	**6**	**6**	**4**	**4**	**3**	**6**	**650**

A record total of 4,150 candidates contested the election – a rise of 596 candidates compared to the previous election in 2005. Some 1,893 candidates (46%) failed to win five per cent of their constituency vote and forfeited their deposit. The number of registered parties choosing to contest the election also reached an all-time high. Excluding the Speaker, Independent candidates and candidates who fought without any description on the ballot paper, there were 132 parties represented by at least one candidate compared with 113 parties in 2005.

The battle for votes

In the UK as a whole nearly 29.7 million valid votes were cast from a total eligible electorate of almost 45.6 million. Two and a half million additional votes were cast in 2010 than in 2005. The Conservatives' share of the UK vote was 36.1% and that for Labour 29.0% - a combined two-party vote of just 65.1%. This is the lowest combined Conservative/Labour share at a UK election since Labour was established as a national party in 1918. The Liberal Democrats finished in third place, receiving support from almost one in four voters (23%). The fourth-placed party in the nationwide vote was the United Kingdom Independence Party (UKIP) which received 3.1%.

The broad analysis that follows concentrates mainly on the situation in Great Britain. Although the Conservative and Ulster Unionist parties contested the election in Northern Ireland together as the Ulster Conservatives and Unionists New Force (UCUNF), neither Labour nor the Liberal Democrats fielded candidates there. The case of Northern Ireland is therefore discussed separately alongside country-specific analyses for the other nations of the UK.

Across Britain, Conservative candidates won 36.9% of the popular vote, an increase of 3.7 points. This was better than the 36.1% Labour achieved in 2005, but whereas Labour emerged from that election with an overall majority of 66 seats, the Conservatives fell 19 seats short of that threshold[1]. Although the Conservatives polled nearly two million more votes than five years previously, their total of 10.7 million pales into insignificance compared with the more than 14 million votes they won in 1992: itself a record for any party in Britain.

The Labour party finished in second place overall in votes and seats, and led on both measures in Scotland and Wales. However, fewer than one in three voters (29.7%) in Britain supported the party as it lost more than six percentage points and a million votes compared with 2005. Labour's share was its third lowest ever as a national party, after 1918 and 1983. The party was saved from greater humiliation by the large number of very safe seats it was defending (more than 200 with majorities in excess of 15%) and by an above average performance in London and Scotland. Together they helped it to win four in ten seats in the House of Commons with less than 30% of the vote.

---

[1]   This assumes that the Speaker and his three deputies (one Conservative and two Labour MPs) do not vote.

The Liberal Democrat share of the vote increased for the third election running, this time by just less than one percentage point to 23.6%. This was the largest third party share since the Liberal/SDP Alliance peaked at 26.0% at the 1983 election. However, the party's recent success in improving its vote/seat ratio was damaged by the net loss of five seats even as it polled 850,000 more votes than in 2005.

The nationalist parties in Scotland and Wales, the Scottish National Party (SNP) and Plaid Cymru, maintained their parliamentary representation of six and three respectively. The SNP increased its vote share by 2.3% to regain second place in the popular vote which it had surrendered to the Liberal Democrats in 2005. Nonetheless the party still attracted fewer than half as many votes as Labour. Plaid Cymru's share of the vote in Wales fell (by 1.3%) for the second election in succession, although it did win the new Arfon seat of which it had been notionally deprived following boundary changes. The comparative support base of the two nationalist parties can be gauged from the fact that the SNP retained its deposit in every seat whereas Plaid lost its in 11 out of 40 cases.

The most popular of the remaining parties was the United Kingdom Independence Party (UKIP) which won over nine hundred thousand votes or 3.2% of the total cast in Britain. When compared to the previous election UKIP's vote rose by 0.9 percentage points. Almost one in six of its candidates successfully saved their deposit but none were elected. The Greens fielded 331 candidates who between them won over a quarter million votes or 1.0% of the total. Although the Greens' share was down compared with 2005 despite having more than 100 additional candidates, the party had the substantial consolation of winning its first ever Westminster seat. Caroline Lucas's victory in Brighton Pavilion followed an 8.5% swing from Labour. The party also registered a large increase in its vote share in Norwich South (7.5% up). It remained in fourth place there, but probably contributed to former Home Secretary Charles Clarke's narrow defeat by the Liberal Democrats. The British National Party fielded nearly three times as many candidates as in 2005, 338 compared with 119, and saw its vote share rise correspondingly from 0.7% to 1.9%. However, the party's average share in seats contested actually declined. In Barking, where leader Nick Griffin hoped to build on the party's best result from 2005, its share fell from a notional 16.3% to 14.6%.

The other more than 800 Independent and small party candidates polled fewer than half a million votes between them and all but 24 lost their deposit. Respect fielded 11 candidates compared with 26 in 2005, and lost its only seat following George Galloway's decision to contest Poplar and

Limehouse rather than Bethnal Green and Bow where he was the sitting member. Neither he nor his successor in Bethnal Green could do better than third place. The two other seats on the British mainland held by candidates outside the party political mainstream were also lost. Health campaigner Dr Richard Taylor faced a Liberal Democrat opponent in Wyre Forest for the first time and was beaten by the Conservatives; Dai Davies, who had won a by-election in Blaenau Gwent following the death of the sitting Independent in 2006, could only manage a distant second as Labour re-established hegemony in the successor seat to Aneurin Bevan and Michael's Foot's Ebbw Vale stronghold. Two sitting MPs who were initially elected as Conservatives contested their 'own' seats and retained their deposits. Andrew Pelling polled 6.5% as an Independent in Croydon Central and Robert Spink came second to the Conservative in Castle Point with 27% for the vote. Labour's deselected Frank Cook was less successful in Stockton North winning a mere 4% share. Eighty eight parties in all each attracted fewer than a thousand votes

Country specific analysis

England

A large majority (86.2%) of the UK electorate is registered to vote in England, which has 533 constituencies or 82% of the total. More than 25 million votes were cast from an eligible electorate of just over 38 million. A total of 3,425 candidates contested the English constituencies - on average more than six candidates for each constituency. However, almost half the candidates in England -1,638 or 47.8%- lost their deposit, thereby contributing some £819,000 towards defraying the costs of the election.

The Conservatives had narrowly won the popular vote in England in 2005, but still finished some 90 seats behind Labour. This time their victory was decisive. They polled 39.5% of the vote (+3.7%) to Labour's 28.1% (-7.4%) and secured 297 seats -106 ahead. Nonetheless the fact that they did not benefit more directly from the sharp decline in Labour support was an important contributing factor in their failure to win an overall majority. They had to share the spoils with the Liberal Democrats –up 1.3 points in vote share but down four to 43 seats, UKIP (+0.9), and the BNP (+1.3). The Liberal Democrats lost 11 seats to the Conservatives compared with three gains from them, but took five seats from Labour in exchange for a single loss. Their most dramatic victory was in Redcar, unaffected by boundary changes, where there was a near 22% swing from Labour.

Examining the pattern of voting across the English regions it becomes clear that the decline in Labour's vote was relatively uniform with one major and one minor exception. In London, where the party had suffered a more than 8-point fall in 2005, its further loss in share was held to just over two percentage points. Indeed the higher turnout meant that Labour actually polled more votes in the capital than five years previously. Outside London the smallest drop in Labour support, and smallest Lab/Con swing, was in the North West. It is interesting to compare the change in vote share for the major parties since Tony Blair's 2001 election landslide –see Table 2. The Labour vote has collapsed everywhere, but only in the South East and South West regions have the Conservatives outpaced the Liberal Democrats. Moreover, only in the South East have the Conservatives picked up even 40% of the lapsed Labour support. The aggregate data match the story of the opinion polls: England has rejected Labour since 2001, but has yet to embrace the Conservatives.

Table 2: Regional change in vote share 2001-10

	Con	*Lab*	*LD*
East Midlands	3.9	-15.3	5.4
East of England	5.3	-17.1	6.6
London	4.0	-10.7	4.6
North East	2.4	-15.9	6.9
North West	2.4	-11.3	4.7
South East	6.3	-13.1	2.5
South West	4.3	-11.5	2.2
West Midlands	4.5	-14.2	5.8
Yorkshire & The Humber	2.6	-14.2	5.8

Scotland

Nearly two and a half million votes were cast in Scotland from an eligible electorate of almost four million. A total of 349 candidates challenged in 59 constituencies but almost a third (32.1%) lost their deposit. In contrast to the rest of the country Labour's fortunes rose in 2010. The party's share increased by 3.1% to 42.0% as it recovered much of the ground lost in 2005. It won back its two by-election losses in Dunfermline and Fife West and in Glasgow East, as well as retaining Glasgow North East which had been held by Speaker Martin in 2005. No other seats changed hands. Labour candidates were successful in 41 out of the 59 constituencies, more than two-thirds of the total. The Liberal Democrats on the other hand fell back by 3.7% and into third place. They nonetheless retained all 11 of their seats. The SNP fell far short of the level achieved at the 2007 Scottish Parliament elections, but managed to increase their vote share by a modest 2.3% despite the potential handicap of being in power at Holyrood. They comfortably retained all six seats being defended, but made no headway in their few marginal targets. In Ochil and South Perthshire, for example, there was a 4.4% swing to Labour. The Conservatives, the only party ever to win an absolute majority of votes cast at a general election in Scotland (in 1955), received only a small increase in support (+0.9%) taking their vote share to 16.7%. This is just over half of what it was as recently as the 1979 general election. As in 2001 and 2005 the Scottish party is represented by just a single MP at Westminster and remains in fourth place. No other party fielded candidates in more than half the seats. The Scottish Socialist party contested just 10 constituencies compared with 58 in 2005 and mustered little more than 3,000 votes in total. In fact Scotland is something of an exception to the march of minor parties with all but 2.5% of the vote there cast for one of the 'big four'

Wales

In Wales nearly one and a half million votes were cast by almost 2.3 million eligible electors. Although there are only 40 seats available in Wales some 268 candidates contested – a ratio of almost seven candidates per seat. A large proportion of those, 114 or 42.5%, polled less than one in twenty votes and thereby forfeited their £500 deposit. Labour's share declined by over six points (-6.5%) but it remains more than 10 points ahead of its nearest rival, the Conservatives. The electoral system operates very much in Labour's favour, a position exaggerated still further when so many candidates compete and vote share is distributed across more parties. Although Labour secured just 36.2% of the valid votes, it won 26 seats (65% of the total). The Conservatives posted their highest vote since 1992. Their 26.1% share was nearly five points better than in 2005 and helped them achieve a swing of 5.6% from Labour and the gain of five seats for a total of eight. The Liberal Democrat vote rose again to just over 20% (+1.7%), but they lost Montgomeryshire in one of the biggest shocks of the night; Lembit Opik saw his 7,000 vote majority wiped out by a more than 13% swing to the Conservatives. As noted above, the vote for nationalist candidates declined. Plaid Cymru's share of 11.3% saw it rooted in fourth place, although its strength in north west Wales enabled it to take better advantage of the first past the post system than some of its rivals. Plaid and the Liberal Democrats both have three seats at Westminster despite the latter securing almost twice as many votes.

Northern Ireland

The electoral battle in Northern Ireland, although quite different to the rest of the UK, provided considerable interest. The 18 seats attracted 108 candidates and nearly 700,000 of 1.17 million eligible electors voted. The Democratic Unionist Party (DUP) was once again the largest party in terms of seats (8), but its share of the vote (25.0%) was more than eight percentage points lower than in 2005 and it polled over 3,500 fewer votes than Sinn Fein. The DUP also provided one of the upsets of the election as First Minister Peter Robinson lost his Belfast East Westminster seat to the Alliance Party's Naomi Long. Following an electoral alliance with the Conservative party the Ulster Unionists contested the election as Ulster Conservatives and Unionists –New Force (UCUNF). The change did them little electoral good. The new party's share of the vote fell behind that of the Social Democratic and Labour Party (SDLP), and it lost its only seat at Westminster following Lady Sylvia Hermon's decision to contest Down North as an Independent. She won by a landslide. A new unionist party, Traditional Unionist Voice, contested 10 seats, with its best result being a distant second in Antrim North. Sinn Fein retained five seats and topped the popular vote. It attracted support from more than one in four voters (25.5%) and increased its share (by 1.2 points) for the fourth election in succession. The SDLP, by contrast, continues to suffer a decline in support. It did overtake UCUNF, but polled 15,000 fewer votes than in 2005 and its share of 16.5% was a further point down. For the first time the Alliance party fielded a candidate in every seat. This, together with its victory in Belfast East, contributed to an increase in vote share from 3.9% in 2005 to 6.3% in 2010.

Changes in seats and proportionality

Changes in seats take account of the revised boundaries that increased the number of parliamentary constituencies by four between 2005 and 2010 and of estimates of what the outcome would have been had the 2005 general election been fought on the new boundaries[2]. On this basis Labour had a net loss of 91 seats in 2010 –see Table 3. These overwhelmingly comprised 87 defeats at the hands of Conservatives. Other parties to incur net losses were the Liberal Democrats, the DUP, and UCUNF. The Conservatives made a net gain of 97 seats. The net figure is arrived at by subtracting the party's three losses to the Liberal Democrats from its 100 gains. The Liberal Democrats' losses were almost entirely to the Conservatives, whereas they

---

[2]   See Colin Rallings and Michael Thrasher, Media Guide to the New Parliamentary Constituencies, Plymouth, 2007.

gained five former Labour seats. Plaid Cymru 'gained' the Arfon seat in Wales which had been notionally allocated to Labour. The two seats to change hands in Northern Ireland are detailed above.

Table 3: Seat change matrix 2005-10

	Con	*Lab*	*LD*	*SNP/PC*	*Other*	*Total*
Con	-	87	12	-	1	100
Lab	-	-	1	-	2	3
LD	3	5	-	-	-	8
SNP/PC	-	1	-	-	-	1
Other	-	1	-	-	2*	3
Total	3	**94**	**13**	-	**5**	
Net gains/losses	+97	-91	-5	+1	-2	

Note: Gains to be read across; losses down. *Speaker excluded. Seats in Northern Ireland – see below.

	DUP	*SDLP*	*SF*	*UU*	*Total*
DUP	-	-	-	-	0
SDLP	-	-	-	-	0
SF	-	-	-	-	0
UU	-	-	-	-	0
APNI	1	-	-	-	1
Ind	-	-	-	1	1
Total	1	-	-	**1**	
Net gains/losses	-1	-	-	-1	

A party benefits from the operation of the electoral system when its seats to votes ratio exceeds one as a result of its share of seats being greater than its vote share. Of course, there may be different reasons for this. Larger parties tend to have favourable seat/vote ratios because of electoral system effects under 'first past the post'. Smaller parties may also have a favourable ratio simply because their support is concentrated across a relatively small geographical area, rather than fragmented across the country. When the seat/vote ratio lies below one then a party has won a lower share of seats than its vote share.

Table 4 shows some seat/vote ratios for the 2010 election. Both Labour and the Conservatives enjoyed a 'large party' advantage. The Liberal Democrats, on the other hand, suffered most from the operation of the voting system (they would need to have won another 93 seats to achieve parity!). Plaid Cymru, whose vote tends to be concentrated in a small number of constituencies even within Wales, fared better than the SNP who have wider but often shallower appeal across Scotland. The SNP polled 20% of the vote or better in 25 of Scotland's 59 constituencies; Plaid matched that in only 7 of the 40 seats in Wales. The contrast in the relationship between votes and seats is stark amongst the parties competing in Northern Ireland. While the DUP enjoys a hugely favourable ratio, neither Sinn Fein nor SDLP are disadvantaged by the translation of votes into seats. The same cannot be said of the new Ulster Conservatives and Unionists however whose 15% share of the vote yielded not a single seat.

Table 4: Seats/Votes ratio for selected political parties in 2010

Party	*Seats/Votes*
Labour	1.4
Conservative	1.3
Liberal Democrat	0.4
SNP	0.5
PC	0.8
DUP	1.8
UCUNF	0.0
SF	1.1
SDLP	1.0
APNI	0.9

* The calculations take account of the fact that some parties are present only in parts of the UK.

One useful method for assessing the electoral outcome in terms of seat/vote relationships and overall proportionality is to employ a measure such as the Loosemore-Hanby index. This index first measures the absolute difference (i.e. ignores negative or positive signs) between each party's share of votes and seats. The differences are then summed and the total divided by two, leaving the index of proportionality as a single summary statistic. An index score of zero would indicate complete equality between each party's seat and vote shares, although even in the most demanding system of proportional representation that would be rare. An index score of

10 or below normally indicates a reasonably proportional outcome. When applied to the results of the 2010 general election the index measures 21.3. The comparable figure for the previous election was 20.7, suggesting a slightly less proportional outcome this time.

Candidates

The mean number of candidates fighting each constituency was 6.4 – almost a whole candidate more than the average of 5.5 per seat that contested in 2005. To provide greater historical perspective on the continuing growth in competition it is worth noting that in 1966 the average was 2.7 candidates per seat and in October 1974, when the Liberal party fielded a full slate of candidates, 3.5. The previous highest candidate/seat ratio was in 1997 when the Referendum Party helped boost the average to 5.7 candidates per seat.

In 2010 there was just a single constituency, Birkenhead, featuring three candidates compared with 21 constituencies in 2005. There were a further 43 seats with four candidates (136 in 2005). At the opposite extreme, although nowhere could compete with the 15 candidates who stood in then Prime Minister Tony Blair's Sedgefield seat last time, there were 25 constituencies where candidate numbers stretched into double figures with Hackney South and Shoreditch and Luton South each having twelve.

The large scale retirement of members of the 2005 parliament meant that only 496 incumbents stood for re-election compared with 571 in 2005. They accounted for just 11.9% of all candidates. However 419 incumbents were successfully re-elected - 84.5% of all those standing. Nearly two-thirds of the new House of Commons comprise former incumbents.

Men comprised more than three-quarters of candidates in 2010 (3,276, 78.9%). For the third election in succession there was a one percentage point rise in the proportion of women candidates (19.2% in 2001; 20.3% in 2005) contesting the general election. Within England women candidates could be found in larger numbers in London (25.4%), whilst there was a particularly low proportion in the East Midlands region (17.5%).

Among the major parties, Labour and the Conservatives both fielded a record proportion of women candidates. Almost one in three Labour candidates were women -30.3% compared with 26.5% in 2005, as were more than a quarter of Conservatives -26.5% compared with 19.4%. The Liberal Democrat proportion slipped however from 23.0% to 21.2%. Of the smaller parties that fielded more than 25 candidates in total, there were three (the Christian Party, Greens, and the SNP) where women made up

28% or more of candidates. In Northern Ireland six of the eighteen Alliance Party candidates was a woman. By contrast, there was not a single woman among the 16 DUP representatives standing for election.

A total of 143 women (22.0%) were elected at the 2010 general election compared with 128 in 2005. Once again, Labour has the most women; 81 were elected, 31.4% of the parliamentary party. The number of female Conservative MPs almost trebled from 17 to 49. Taking the party's increased overall representation into account, this amounts to a near doubling of their proportion in the parliamentary party from 8.6% to 16.0%. Liberal Democrat retirements and seat losses had an impact with just 7 women elected -12.2% of the parliamentary party compared with 16.1% in 2005.

The proportion of incumbents seeking re-election who were women exactly replicated their representation in the Commons elected in 2005 (19.8%). However those women that remained to fight another election did fare rather worse than their male counterparts. A total of 27 women incumbents were defeated (27.8%) while 49 men (12.3%) suffered the same fate.

Electorate and Turnout

The electorate for the 2010 general election was, at almost 45.6 million, the largest ever –see Table 5. It showed an increase of over 1.35 million or 3.1% compared with 2005; the bulk of the rise being concentrated in southern England. Some of the volatility in electorate numbers can be accounted for by those taking advantage of the so-called '11 day rule' (which was introduced by the 2006 Electoral Administration Act) and choosing to register after the election was called. It appears that more than half a million people registered to vote in the weeks leading up to May 6th.

There was a modest increase in turnout across all parts of Great Britain, although that in Northern Ireland fell back for the second election in succession. Nevertheless, and despite the growth in the electorate, fewer than 30 million valid votes were cast: a long way short of the record of 33.6 million votes at the 1992 general election. Indeed the adjusted (that is, valid vote) turnout of 65.1% was just 3.7 percentage points higher than in 2005 and was the third lowest figure since universal male suffrage in 1918. Among the English regions turnout was once again highest in the South West, and jumped particularly sharply in London where London borough council elections were held on the same day as a general election for the first time ever.

Table 5: Turnout at the 2010 general election

	Electorate 2010	Valid votes 2010	Adjusted % turnout 2010	%Change 2005-10
UK	45,597,461	29,687,804	65.1	+3.7
GB	44,428,277	29,013,933	65.3	+4.0
England	38,300,110	25,081,468	65.5	+4.2
N. Ireland	1,169,184	673,871	57.6	-5.3
Scotland	3,863,042	2,465,780	63.8	+3.0
Wales	2,265,125	1,466,685	64.8	+2.2
English regions				
East Midlands	3,332,058	2,224,279	66.8	+4.1
Eastern	4,257,453	2,878,997	67.6	+3.6
London	5,276,910	3,401,268	64.5	+6.7
North East	1,948,281	1,189,925	61.1	+3.7
North West	5,255,192	3,272,990	62.3	+5.0
South East	6,298,261	4,294,227	68.2	+3.5
South West	4,020,915	2,773,443	69.0	+2.5
West Midlands	4,084,007	2,640,572	64.7	+4.0
Yorkshire & The Humber	3,827,033	2,405,567	62.9	+3.8

The turnout figures are broadly the same whether the total vote, the mean (average) turnout across constituencies, or the turnout in the median (or middle) constituency in each geographical unit is considered – see Table 6.

Table 6: Turnout in 2010 using different statistical measures

2010	Aggregate turnout	Mean turnout	Median turnout
UK	65.1	65.0	65.4
GB	65.3	65.2	65.5
England	65.5	65.4	65.8
N. Ireland	57.6	57.5	57.0
Scotland	63.8	63.7	63.8
Wales	64.8	64.8	64.2

Turnout at the constituency level reflected the general pattern of a modest increase since 2005 –see Table 7. A total of 139 constituencies had turnouts in excess of 70% (37 in 2005), and just 6 had a turnout of less than 50% (39 in 2005). The overwhelming majority of constituencies in Great Britain (600 out of 632) saw increases in turnout and, of the remainder, turnout dropped by greater than one percentage point in only 19 instances.

Once more Northern Ireland was the exception. Leaving aside the postponed election in Thirsk and Malton, 14 of the 19 biggest falls in turnout were in Northern Ireland. Individual constituency figures for England, Wales and Northern Ireland do need to be treated with caution because turnouts for 2005 are only estimates following boundary changes. However, it appears that there were sizeable increases in turnout in some London constituencies, with 14 of them featuring among the 23 nationwide where turnout rose by 10 percentage points or more. It may also be worth pointing out that turnout rose by an average of 5 percentage points in constituencies in England with coincident local elections, but only by 4 points where there were no such contests.

Table 7: Constituency level turnout and turnout change, 2010

	Highest turnout 2010		*Lowest turnout 2010*	
England	Westmorland & Lonsdale	76.9	Manchester Central	44.3
Northern Ireland	Fermanagh & S, Tyrone	68.9	Antrim East	50.7
Scotland	Renfrewshire East	77.3	Glasgow North East	49.1
Wales	Cardiff North	72.7	Swansea East	54.6
	Biggest increase in turnout 2005-10		*Biggest fall in turnout 2005-10*	
England	Hackney N. & Stoke Newington	+13.5	Derby South	-6.7
Northern Ireland	Belfast East	+0.9	Tyrone West	-11.7
Scotland	Glasgow North	+7.1	Dundee East	-0.5
Wales	Cardiff West	+7.1	Blaenau Gwent	-4.4

*   Calculations exclude postponed elections in Staffordshire South (2005) and Thirsk and Malton (2010).

There are interesting variations in turnout depending on the political status and marginality of the constituency –see Table 8. As is usual, turnout was lower in safe as opposed to marginal seats, although the gap seems to have narrowed compared with 2005. Turnout did remain sharply lower in constituencies won (held) by Labour than in those won by either the Conservatives or the Liberal Democrats, although these seats also showed the largest mean increase in turnout. In constituencies gained by the Conservatives mean change in turnout was only fractionally higher than in those the party held.

Table 8: Turnout by political status of constituency

% majority 2005	Mean turnout 2010	Change 2005-10
0 to 4.99	67.9	+3.6
5 to 9.99	66.9	+4.3
10 to 19.99	66.7	+4.1
20+	62.8	+3.9
Winning party 2010		
Con seats	68.3	+3.9
Lab seats	61.1	+4.9
LD seats	67.5	+3.6
Con gains	67.0	+4.0

We are also able to examine turnout taking into account those electors who tried to vote but whose postal vote returns and/or ballot papers were rejected –see Table 9. 'Minimal unadjusted turnout' includes all electors whose ballot papers, whether valid or invalid, were scrutinised at the count. 'Maximal unadjusted turnout' adds those whose postal vote returns were deemed invalid and therefore not forwarded to the count. Each adjustment has the effect of fractionally increasing the proportion of the electorate who participated. The largest proportion of rejected ballots appears to be in Northern Ireland (see later section).

Table 9 'Adjusted' and 'unadjusted' turnout 2010

	Adjusted	'Minimal' unadjusted	'Maximal' unadjusted
UK	65.1	65.3	65.8
GB	65.3	65.5	66.0
England	65.5	65.7	66.2
N. Ireland	57.6	58.0	58.1
Scotland	63.8	63.9	64.3
Wales	64.8	64.9	65.5

Postal voting – uptake and turnout

The proportion of electors with postal votes trebled from 4% to 12.1% between 2001 and 2005. This year it increased again to 15.3% despite the new legislative requirement for those wishing to vote by post to apply afresh and provide evidence of identity in the form of a signature and date of birth both on application and when returning their ballot paper –see Table 10.

The only exception to this pattern was Northern Ireland where different rules are in force and where postal voting declined once again to now minuscule levels.

Postal voting in Scotland remains less prevalent than in England and Wales, but the number of Scots registered to vote by post rose by more than half compared with 2005. All the English regions saw further increases in postal voters with more than one in seven electors now registered to vote in this way in seven of the nine regions. The four regions which had had all postal ballots at the 2004 European Parliament elections continue to top the league table. In the North East, where there had also been an all-postal referendum in November 2004, more than a quarter now vote by post -an increase of greater than seven percentage points since 2005.

Table10: Postal voting in 2010

	Total Postal ballots issued	*%electors with postal ballot*	*Change 2005-10*
UK	6,996,006	15.3	+3.2
GB	6,980,005	15.7	+3.3
England	6,096,006	15.9	+3.1
N. Ireland	16,001	1.4	-1.0
Scotland	511,413	13.2	+5.1
Wales	372,586	16.4	+3.7

English regions	*% electors with postal ballot*	*Change 2005-2010*
East Midlands*	16.2	+2.7
Eastern	14.5	+2.4
London	13.8	+2.9
North East*	26.7	+7.4
North West*	17.7	+5.0
South East	14.6	+2.3
South West	15.7	+1.9
West Midlands	12.8	+2.1
Yorkshire & The Humber*	18.0	+3.8

*All-postal voting at the 2004 European parliament elections.

The individual constituencies at the top of the North East-dominated postal vote league table similarly reflect the importance of previous all-postal vote experience in stimulating registration – see Table 11. Newcastle upon Tyne North also had the largest proportion of postal voters in 2005, although notional calculations suggest the overall figure has declined by about five percentage points since then. In Sunderland, on the other hand, postal voting has nearly trebled in both number and proportion since the last general election. Those at the bottom confirm that local authorities as well as political parties play a part in encouraging (or not) postal voting. All three constituencies in Hull are once again rooted at the foot despite the city's previous all-postal voting history. However the range covered by those 20 constituencies with the lowest proportion of postal voters has risen from 3.1%-5.4% in 2005 to 5.9%-8.7% now. Postal electors accounted for 15.7% of the total in the mean constituency in Great Britain (12.4% in 2005), with a standard deviation of 4.94 about the mean.

Table 11: The extent of postal vote take-up in individual constituencies

Top and bottom 20 postal vote take-up 2010 – % of electorate (G.B. only)

——————— Top ———————		——————— Bottom ———————	
Newcastle Upon Tyne North*	40.6	Airdrie & Shotts	8.7
Houghton & Sunderland South*	38.9	Glasgow East	8.7
Sunderland Central*	37.4	Barrow & Furness*	8.6
Washington & Sunderland West*	37.2	Glasgow North	8.5
South Shields*	36.2	Halton*	8.4
Jarrow*	35.3	Oxford East	8.3
Blyth Valley*	34.8	Birmingham Selly Oak	8.2
Stevenage*	34.5	Coatbridge, Chryston & Bellshill	8.2
Newcastle Upon Tyne Central*	34.5	Glasgow Central	8.1
Telford*	31.8	Birmingham Ladywood	7.9
Rushcliffe*	31.8	Brent Central	7.7
Wrekin, The*	31.7	Birmingham Erdington	7.7
Blaydon*	31.6	Motherwell & Wishaw	7.5
Don Valley*	31.4	Birmingham Perry Barr	7.4
Chorley*	31.0	Cambridgeshire North East	7.4
Newcastle Upon Tyne East*	29.8	Ealing North	7.1
Doncaster Central*	29.2	Hull West & Hessle*	7.1
Gateshead*	27.9	Lewisham West & Penge	6.8
Doncaster North*	27.9	Hull East*	6.7
Altrincham & Sale West*	27.9	Hull North*	5.9

Top 20 percentage point change in % of electorate with postal votes 2005-10 (G.B. only)

Houghton & Sunderland South*	23.9	Harrow East	9.5
Sunderland Central*	23.0	Paisley & Renfrewshire North	9.2
Washington & Sunderland West*	21.5	Redcar*	9.1
Wansbeck*	15.0	Penistone & Stocksbridge*	9.0
Easington*	13.1	Southport*	9.0
Blyth Valley*	12.1	Wyre & Preston North*	8.9
Doncaster Central*	12.0	Tyneside North*	8.9
Sedgefield*	11.6	Liverpool West Derby*	8.9
Durham, City of *	10.2	Worsley & Eccles South*	8.5
Inverclyde	9.8	Llanelli	8.5

*All-postal vote at one or more elections 2002-4 inclusive.

There was remarkable uniformity across Great Britain in the turnout of postal voters with over 83% returning their ballots in each nation. The figure in Northern Ireland was just a little less –see Table 12. Compared with 2005 there was a small overall increase from 2.5% to 3.8% in the proportion of postal ballots rejected before being forwarded to the count. A total of more than 200,000 individual ballots were rejected. In about half the cases this was because a signature or date of birth (or both) were mismatched; in another quarter because the elector omitted to enclose either the ballot paper or the postal vote statement (or both). Given the new rules covering the validity of postal votes this increase is perhaps not surprising.

Table 12: Invalid postal vote returns 2010

2010	% Postal ballots returned	Invalid returns	Invalid as % of returned	Change 2005-10
UK	83.2	221,988	3.8	+1.3
GB	83.2	220,628	3.8	+1.3
England	83.2	192,103	3.8	+1.4
N. Ireland	78.1	1,360	10.9	+5.7
Scotland	83.6	15,368	3.6	+1.5
Wales	83.1	13,157	4.2	-0.4

The increase in the take up of postal votes had an inevitable impact on the proportion of total votes cast in that way. Across the United Kingdom nearly 19% of all the votes counted were postal ballots –see Table 13. In England and Wales the figure was even higher. In the North East postal votes comprised more than a third of the total.   In Newcastle upon Tyne North and in all three constituencies in Sunderland, a majority of all votes were cast by post. Postal votes accounted for 19.2% of votes counted in the mean constituency in Great Britain, with a standard deviation of 6.31 about the mean.

Turnout among postal electors was again significantly higher than that among in-person voters, although both groups showed an increase compared with 2005 –see Table 14. It is interesting that the new regulations have had no adverse effect in Great Britain on either the level of applications for or the use of postal votes. In the North East, for example, whereas 82.5% of the very large number of postal voters returned their ballots in line with the national average, only a little over half (54.5%) of those who did not take up this facility attended in person - a proportion little changed from 2005. The extension of postal voting has certainly helped to boost overall participation, but is far from a panacea for the problem of low turnout.

Table 13: Postal votes as % of votes at count

	postal votes as % of votes at count	Change 2005-10
UK	18.8	+3.8
GB	19.2	+3.8
England	19.4	+3.4
Northern Ireland	1.6	-1.4
Scotland	16.7	+6.5
Wales	20.2	+4.6
English regions		
East Midlands*	19.9	+3.2
Eastern	17.4	+3.1
London	15.9	+2.2
North East*	34.8	+9.7
North West*	22.0	+4.7
South East	17.7	+2.9
South West	18.9	+2.4
West Midlands	15.9	+2.6
Yorkshire & The Humber*	22.8	+4.2

*2004 all-postal pilot regions

Table 14: Turnout among postal and in-person electors 2010

	'Minimal unadjusted' turnout (postal electors)		'Minimal unadjusted turnout' (in-person electors)	
	2010	Change 2005-10	2010	Change 2005-10
UK	83.2	+4.6	62.6	+3.1
GB	83.2	+4.6	62.8	+3.4
England	83.2	+4.6	63.0	+3.7
Northern Ireland	78.1	-9.3	57.8	-5.2
Scotland	83.6	+4.2	61.4	+3.0
Wales	83.1	+4.9	62.0	+1.3

Proxy voting

It was expected that easier access to postal voting would lead to a decrease in the number of electors wishing or having the need to appoint proxies. This was indeed the case in 2005 when fewer than 100,000 proxy votes were issued compared with nearly 250,000 in 2001. This year, however, there was an increase in proxy voting in Great Britain, itself perhaps reflecting greater interest in the election as evidenced by the higher overall turnout – see Table 15. More than 500 proxy votes were issued in 22 constituencies, with Newbury and Devon South West topping the table with over 700 each. Proxy voting in Northern Ireland fell again and it is now even less common than in the rest of the UK having once been much higher. On average about a third of one per cent of electors now rely on a proxy to cast their vote.

Table 15: Proxy voting 2010

	Proxy votes cast	*as % of electorate*	*Change 2005-10*
UK	143,801	0.32	+0.10
GB	141,692	0.32	+0.10
England	124,125	0.32	+0.10
N. Ireland	2,109	0.18	-0.41
Scotland	11,384	0.29	+0.10
Wales	6,183	0.27	+0.08

* Data missing for 15 English constituencies.

Rejected ballots

The number of ballot papers rejected at the count continues to be but a small fraction of the total cast (0.28%), and is hardly changed compared with 2010 – see Table 16. The bulk of these are because the voter has either not marked the ballot paper or made their intention clear. In just over a quarter of cases voters have chosen more than one candidate in a single-member election. The latter instance was especially noticeable in London this year where almost all electors were also voting in multi-member council wards. An above average 0.5% of votes was disallowed with 'voting more than once' the single biggest reason for general election votes being rejected. Northern Ireland once more provides something of an exception. An overall greater proportion of votes are rejected, more than half for voting more than once. It is likely that this is caused by confusion among electors used to voting in elections where they are invited to cast a preference vote for candidates on the ballot paper. The Single Transferable Vote (STV) method is used for European Parliament, Assembly, and local council elections in Northern Ireland.

Table 16: Rejected ballot papers 2010

	Ballot papers rejected at the count	% of ballots at count	Change 2005-10
UK	81,868	0.28	-0.03
GB	77,803	0.27	-0.03
England	70,580	0.28	-0.03
N. Ireland	4,003	0.60	-0.25
Scotland	4,524	0.18	-0.02
Wales	2,699	0.18	-0.08

Reasons for rejection*

	No official mark (%)	Voting more than once (%)	Voter could be identified (%)	Void or uncertain (%)	Rejected in part (%)
UK	640 (0.8)	21,888 (26.7)	2,520 (3.1)	50,866 (62.1)	1,788 (2.2)
GB	638 (0.8)	19,871 (25.5)	2,407 (3.1)	48,933 (62.2)	1,788 (2.3)
England	628 (0.9)	18,261 (25.9)	2,183 (3.1)	43,915 (62.9)	1,788 (2.5)
N. Ireland	9 (0.2)	2,017 (49.6)	96 (2.8)	1,933 (47.6)	-
Scotland	1 (0.0)	805 (17.8)	128 (2.1)	3,317 (73.3)	-
Wales	2 (0.0)	805 (29.8)	113 (4.7)	1,701 (63.0)	-

* Not all constituencies provided this breakdown.

Once again there is considerable variation between constituencies in both the number and proportion of ballot papers rejected, and in the reasons for rejection. In Blackburn over 1,700 ballots (nearly 4% of the total) were rejected; in Buckingham, where the Speaker stood for re-election with no major party opposition, more than 1,000 ballots were disqualified. In London a total of nearly 800 votes were ruled out for voting more than once in the two Tower Hamlets seats of Bethnal Green and Bow, and Poplar and Limehouse alone. At the other extreme, in 24 constituencies fewer than 50 votes were rejected, including 35 in Filton and Bradley Stoke and 36 in its South Gloucestershire council neighbour Kingswood. It is likely both that returning officers differ in their judgements about the admissibility of ballots, and that electors in some constituencies may be more prone to making errors than those in others.

Correlates of turnout

Turnout at general elections has long been correlated with both the socio-economic character and political marginality of a constituency. 2010 was no exception to this pattern, although marginality appears to have played a lesser role than previously. In part this may be explained by new constituency boundaries making the exact electoral arithmetic uncertain for parties and voters alike. Nonetheless, indices of deprivation such as the proportion unemployed and the proportion of single parents with dependent children in a constituency show especially strong negative correlations with turnout and all the relationships in Table 17 are statistically significant. The basic rule still holds: the more affluent the area and/or the more marginal the seat before the election, the higher the turnout is likely to be.

Table 17: Correlates of turnout 2005 and 2010*

	Correlation with % turnout 2005	*Correlation with % turnout 2010*
% prof/managerial workers	0.43	0.50
% owner-occupiers	0.72	0.64
% aged 18-24	-0.47	-0.41
% aged 65+	0.42	0.30
% degree	0.47	0.34
% lone parents with children	-0.80	-0.77
% unemployed	-0.76	-0.75
% non-white	-0.41	-0.29
% majority post-election	-0.51	-0.15
% majority pre-election	-0.72	-0.48

* Englland and Wales only for census variables..

Correlates of postal voting

It was clear in analysis of the 2005 general election that there was a positive relationship between increased postal vote registration and *less* affluent and/or politically *less* marginal areas. This ran contrary to the media emphasis on the importance accorded by political parties at that election to maximising postal votes in marginal seats, but did make sense in terms of the kinds of places where all-postal pilots had been most prevalent. The list of constituencies in Table 11 suggests this pattern has continued. One interesting by product of the spread of postal voting and the high turnout among such electors is demonstrated in Table 18. The expected relationships are still present, but they are much less strong than historically and weaker too than the correlations shown for the propensity of 'in-person' voters to turn out.

In particular constituency marginality appears to be much less of a driver for those with a postal vote.

Table 18: Correlates of turnout by postal and 'in-person' voters 2010

	Correlation with % turnout by postal voters	*Correlation with % turnout by 'in-person' voters*
% prof/managerial workers	0.10	0.53
% owner-occupiers	0.46	0.59
% aged 18-24	-0.26	-0.37
% aged 65+	0.32	0.24
-% degree	0.00	0.38
% lone parents with children	-0.48	-0.72
% unemployed	-0.46	-0.70
% non-white	-0.37	-0.18
% majority post-election	-0.13	-0.12
% majority pre-election	-0.29	-0.47

* England and Wales only for census variables.

Prospects for 2015

Although the indecisive outcome of the 2010 general election had been widely forecast, it still took many commentators by surprise. It was well known that the Conservatives had to achieve an historic high swing of nearly 7% from Labour and a lead in the popular vote of over 10% just to achieve an overall majority. Few polls conducted through the election campaign suggested they were on course to do so.   In the event David Cameron has perhaps not received due credit for the result he did secure. Although the Conservative share rose by less than Labour's fell and although it was scarcely better than at the October 1974 election which the party lost, the Conservatives had not gained as many seats at a single election since 1931. The swing from Labour of 5.1% eclipsed that achieved by Edward Heath in 1970 and was only a little less than the one which put Mrs Thatcher in Downing Street in 1979.

The brutal fact remains though that the Conservatives are in a minority at Westminster and the electoral arithmetic still seems stacked against them. Even the review of constituency boundaries proposed by the coalition will do no more than mitigate the disadvantages the party suffers. With turnout systematically lower in Labour than Conservative supporting areas, Labour picks up more seats for any given share of the vote. At the next election the Conservatives need a swing of almost 2% and a lead over Labour of 11% to win a clear majority. On current boundaries the key seat is Gedling which

Labour retained by 1,859 votes in May following a below average 3% swing to the Conservatives. By contrast, Labour could become the largest party in the Commons following a 2% swing away from the Conservatives and despite still being in second place in the popular vote – with another East Midlands seat, Corby, currently marking the spot. A Labour overall majority would require a 5% swing and a less than 3% lead in the popular vote or, put another way, victory in all its target seats up to and including Jacob Rees-Mogg's Somerset North East. Any outcome between the two extremes - a 2% Labour to Conservative or a 5% Conservative to Labour swing - and another hung parliament will result. The continued presence of a large number of 'third party' MPs and the erosion in the number of marginal seats can only enhance such a possibility.

Underlying such calculations is an assumption that the Liberal Democrats will continue to secure a fifth or more of the vote and around 50 seats or more in the House as they have done ever since 1997. However, as junior partners in the coalition, there is even more uncertainty than usual about their role in the crucial seats/votes conundrum. A collapse in Liberal Democrat votes and seats, for example, might make it easier for the Conservatives to beat Labour. According to our seat projection grid *(see page 398)*, the Conservatives could win an overall majority by being six points ahead of Labour if the Liberal Democrats were to poll just 13% of the vote. Equally, though, Labour itself could govern alone even following a tie with the Conservatives in the popular vote under a similar scenario.

Colin Rallings and Michael Thrasher

The Official Results

2   Introduction

Explanatory Notes

All constituencies in the United Kingdom are listed in alphabetical order following the practice of the Press Association and the major broadcasting organisations. Compass point references usually follow the substantive name. Thus Aberavon is number 1 and Yorkshire East number 650.

A general review of constituency boundaries was enacted before the 2010 general election in England, Wales, and Northern Ireland. An 'index of change' list, providing a guide to how far the boundaries of a new constituency differ from that of the old constituency from which it was drawn, can be found on page 36. The further the figure exceeds 0.0, the more the constituency has experienced boundary changes.

Under the name of each constituency are seven columns:

1. Electors   The number of electors eligible to vote on 6 May 2010.

2. Turnout   The number of valid votes cast expressed as a percentage of the eligible electorate.

3. Candidate   The surname and initials of the candidate. All women are listed as 'Ms.'; those candidates who were members of the 2005-10 Parliament are denoted by a *.

4. Party   The party affiliation of the candidate.

5. Vote   The number of votes polled by the candidate.

6. Share   The number of votes polled by the candidate expressed as a percentage of the total valid votes cast. An asterisk indicates a forfeited deposit.

7. Change   The percentage change in the share of the vote for the party since the 2005 general election. In the case of constituencies with new boundaries, change is based on 'notional' results calculated as if those constituencies had been in existence in 2005. Detailed figures can be found in C. Rallings and M. Thrasher (eds), *The Media Guide to the New Parliamentary Constituencies*.

At the foot of each set of voting figures appears the majority of the successful candidate and this is also expressed as a percentage. (The rounding of percentages originally calculated to two decimal places sometimes results in the percentage majority figure differing by ±0.1% from that obtained by subtracting the share of the first placed party from that of the second placed party.) The party which actually or 'notionally' won the seat at the 2005 general election is also noted.

By-Elections

The boundary changes came into effect with the dissolution of parliament. All by-elections in the 2005-10 Parliament were fought on the old boundaries and are NOT listed here. Table 10 in the current volume describes the subsequent fate of candidates elected at by-elections between 2005 and 2010.

Change of Party Allegiance

In a number of cases MPs changed their party allegiance following election in 2005. These are listed below:

Clare Short (Birmingham Ladywood) – from Labour to Independent Labour (2006)

Quentin Davies (Grantham & Stamford) – from Conservative to Labour (2007)

Robert Wareing (Liverpool West Derby) – from Labour to Independent (2007)

Andrew Pelling (Croydon Central) – Conservative whip suspended (2007)

Derek Conway (Old Bexley & Sidcup) – Conservative whip withdrawn (2008)

Bob Spink (Castle Point) – resigned the Conservative whip (March 2008) joined UKIP (April 2008) then became an Independent (November 2008)

Ian Gibson (Norwich North) – resigned from the Labour Party and House (2009)

David Chaytor (Bury North) – suspended from Labour Party (2010)

Jim Devine (Livingstone) - suspended from Labour Party (2010)

Elliot Morley (Scunthorpe) - suspended from Labour Party (2010)

Sylvia Hermon (North Down) – from Ulster Unionist to Independent (2010)

Hermon was re-elected for North Down in 2010; Pelling and Spink stood unsuccessfully in their former constituencies.

Electorate Statistics

Under the terms of the Representation of the People Act 2000, a system of 'rolling registration' was introduced to allow eligible persons to register to vote at any time of the year. Subsequently, the 2006 Electoral Administration Act provided for electors to apply to be registered to vote up to 11 working days before polling day. These procedures have led to electoral registers being updated more frequently and to the numbers on the register at the time of an election differing from those both 'as first published' and when the election is called.

The constituency electorates used here are 'on the day' figures as supplied by Returning Officers and have *not* been subject to the formula used in previous volumes in the Britain Votes series to calculate the electorate on any given date. For an explanation of that formula see Colin Rallings and Michael Thrasher (eds), *British Electoral Facts, 1832-2006* (Biteback, 2009).

Forfeited Deposits

A candidate forfeited a deposit of £500 if he or she was not elected and did not poll more than one-twentieth of the valid votes cast.

General Election Polling Date

Polling took place on 6 May 2010.

Surnames and Initials

The surnames and initials of candidates are based on returns made to the authors on behalf of the Electoral Commission by Returning Officers. Only initials and titles which can be derived from these sources are listed.

Voting Statistics

The number of votes cast for candidates are based on returns made to the authors on behalf of the Electoral Commission by Returning Officers.

Registered Party Labels and Abbreviations

Abbrev.	Party	No. of candidates
AC	Animals Count	1
AD	Apolitical Democrats	1
AGS	Alliance for Green Socialism	6
APNI	Alliance Party	18
APP	Animal Protection Party	4
AWL	Alliance for Workers Liberty	1
AWP	Anticapitalists -Workers' Power	1
BB	A Better Britain for All	1
BCD	Buckingham Campaign for Democracy	1
Bean	New Millennium Bean	1
Best	The Best of a Bad Bunch	2
BGPV	Blaenau Gwent People's Voice	1
BIB	Bushra Irfan of Blackburn	1
BIC	Bromsgrove Independent Conservative	1
Blue	Blue Environment Party	1
BNP	British National Party	338
BP Elvis	Bus-Pass Elvis Party	1
C28	Clause 28, Children's Protection Christian Democrats	1
Cam Soc	Cambridge Socialists	1
CG	The Common Good	1
Ch M	Christian Movement for Great Britain	2
Ch P	Christian Party	71
CIP	Campaign for Independent Politicians	1
CITY	City Independent	1
CNPG	Community Need Before Private Greed	1
Comm	Communist Party of Britain	6
Comm L	Communist League	2
Con	Conservative Party	631
Cor D	Cornish Democrats	1
CPA	Christian Peoples Alliance	17
CSP	Common Sense Party	2
CTDP	Cut the Deficit Party	1
CURE	Citizens for Undead Rights and Equality	4
DDP	Direct Democracy Party	1
D Lab	Democratic Labour Party	1
D Nat	Democratic Nationalist	2
DUP	Democratic Unionist Party	16
ED	English Democrats	107
EIP	English Independence Party	1
EPA	Equal Parenting Alliance	2
FAWG	Fight for an Anti-War Government	1

Abbrev.	Party	No. of candidates
FDP	Fancy Dress Party	1
FFR	For Freedom and Responsibility	1
Gm	Green Party	335
GSOT	Get Snouts Out The Trough	1
Hum	Humanity	1
ICHC	Independent Community and Health Concern	1
IEAC	Independent Ealing Acton Communities Public Services	1
IFED	Independents Federation UK	4
ILEU	Independent Leave The EU Alliance	1
Ind	Independent	307
Impact	Impact Party	3
IPT	Independent People Together	1
ISGB	Independent Save Our Green Belt	1
ISQM	Independents to Save Queen Mary's Hospital	1
IUK	Integrity UK	1
IVH	Independent Voice for Halifax	1
IZB	Islam Zinda Baad Platform	1
JAC	Justice & Anti-Corruption Party	2
JBNF	Jannen will put Brent North First	1
Joy	The Joy of Talk	1
JP	Justice Party	1
Lab	Labour Party	631
Land	Land is Power	1
LD	Liberal Democrat	631
Lib	Liberal	5
Libert	Libertarian Party	2
LIND	Lincolnshire Independents	3
LLPB	Local Liberals People Before Politics Party	1
LTT	Lawfulness Trustworthiness and Transparency	1
MACI	The Macclesfield Independent	1
MCP	Magna Carta Party	3
MEDI	Medway Independent	1
MEP	Middle England Party	1
MIF	Mansfield Independent Forum	1
MK	Mebyon Kernow	6
MPEA	A Vote Against MP Expense Abuse	1
MRLP	Monster Raving Loony Party	27
MRP	Money Reform Party	1
Nat Lib	National Liberal	1
NCDV	No candidate deserves my vote	1
ND	Candidates who gave No Description	24
New	The New Party	1
NF	National Front	17

Abbrev.	Party	No. of candidates
NFP	Nationwide Reform Party	1
NICF	New Independent Conservative Chelsea and Fulham	1
Nobody	Nobody Party	1
NSPS	Northampton - Save Our Public Services	1
PBP	People Before Profit	1
PC	Plaid Cymru	40
Pirate	Pirate Party UK	9
PNDP	People's National Democratic Party	1
Poet	The True English (Poetry) Party	1
PPBF	Putting the People of Battersea First	1
PPE	Peoples Party Essex	1
PPNV	Peace Party, non-violence, justice, environment	3
Reform	Reform 2000	1
Respect	Respect Party	11
Rest	The Restoration Party	1
RRG	Radical Reform Group	1
RTBP	Reduce Tax on Beer Party	1
SACL	Scotland Against Crooked Lawyers	1
Sci	The Science Party	1
SDLP	Social Democratic & Labour Party	18
SEP	Socialist Equality Party	2
SF	Sinn Fein	17
SIG	Staffordshire Independent Group	1
SJP	Scottish Jacobite Party	2
SKGP	Save King George Hospital	1
Soc Alt	Socialist Alternative Party	4
Soc Dem	Social Democratic Party	2
Soc Lab	Socialist Labour Party	23
SMA	Scrap Members Allowances	2
SMRA	Solihull and Meriden Residents' Association	2
SNP	Scottish National Party	59
Soc	Socialist Party	1
South	All The South Party	1
Speaker	Speaker	1
SSP	Scottish Socialist Party	10
TF	Tendring First	1
TOC	Tamsin Omond to the Commons	1
Trust	Trust	2
TUSC	Trade Unionist and Socialist Coalition	37
TUV	Traditional Unionist Voice	10
UCUNF	Ulster Conservatives and Unionists New Force	17
UKIP	United Kingdom Independence Party	558
UPS	Unity for Peace and Socialism	1

Abbrev.	Party	No. of candidates
UV	United Voice	1
VCCA	Virtue Currency Cognitive Appraisal Party	1
Vote	Go Mad and Vote For Yourself Party	1
WR	Wessex Regionalist	1
WRP	Workers' Revolutionary Party	7
You	You Party	2
Youth	Youth Party	1
YRDPL	Your Right to Democracy Party Limited	3

A total of 43 Labour candidates, jointly sponsored by the Co-operative Party, are described in the results as 'Lab'. The following constituencies had Lab/Co-op candidates:

Barrow and Furness
Basildon
Bermondsey & Old Southwark
Brighton Kemptown
Cardiff South & Penarth
Corby
Croydon Central
Dumfriesshire, Clydesdale & Tweeddale
Dunbartonshire West
Edinburgh North
Edmonton
Feltham and Heston
Glasgow South West
Gravesham
Hackney South
Halifax
Harrow West
Heywood and Middleton
Huddersfield
Ilford South
Islwyn

Kilmarnock & Loudon
Liverpool Riverside
Liverpool Wavertree
Liverpool West Derby
Loughborough
Luton South
Milton Keynes North
Morley and Outwood
Norwich North
Nottingham East
Plymouth Sutton & Devonport
Portsmouth North
Preston
Rutherglen and Hamilton West
Sheffield Heeley
Stalybridge and Hyde
Stevenage
Stroud
Swansea West
The Wrekin
Walthamstow
West Bromwich West

List of Constituencies by Press Association number & Index of Change

PA	Constituency	Index of change	PA	Constituency	Index of change
1	Aberavon	None	53	Beverley & Holderness	3.9
2	Aberconwy	45.4	54	Bexhill & Battle	18.8
3	Aberdeen North	n/a	55	Bexleyheath & Crayford	21.0
4	Aberdeen South	n/a	56	Birkenhead	11.0
5	Aberdeenshire West & Kincardine	n/a	57	Birmingham Edgbaston	12.0
6	Airdrie & Shotts	n/a	58	Birmingham Erdington	1.7
7	Aldershot	16.1	59	Birmingham Hall Green	105.9
8	Aldridge-Brownhills	5.6	60	Birmingham Hodge Hill	47.4
9	Altrincham & Sale West	2.5	61	Birmingham Ladywood	51.2
10	Alyn & Deeside	None	62	Birmingham Northfield	38.0
11	Amber Valley	9.0	63	Birmingham Perry Barr	23.7
12	Angus	n/a	64	Birmingham Selly Oak	100.7
13	Antrim East	8.2	65	Birmingham Yardley	39.5
14	Antrim North	3.7	66	Bishop Auckland	0.0
15	Antrim South	19.9	67	Blackburn	1.0
16	Arfon	85.1	68	Blackley & Broughton	46.2
17	Argyll & Bute	n/a	69	Blackpool North & Cleveleys	42.3
18	Arundel & South Downs	20.2	70	Blackpool South	14.8
19	Ashfield	1.7	71	Blaenau Gwent	None
20	Ashford	5.1	72	Blaydon	7.1
21	Ashton Under Lyne	10.3	73	Blyth Valley	None
22	Aylesbury	32.4	74	Bognor Regis & Littlehampton	5.1
23	Ayr, Carrick & Cumnock	n/a	75	Bolsover	4.2
24	Ayrshire Central	n/a	76	Bolton North East	3.3
25	Ayrshire North & Arran	n/a	77	Bolton South East	14.0
26	Banbury	4.5	78	Bolton West	27.1
27	Banff & Buchan	n/a	79	Bootle	33.3
28	Barking	38.4	80	Boston & Skegness	2.8
29	Barnsley Central	61.5	81	Bosworth	4.9
30	Barnsley East	114.6	82	Bournemouth East	22.9
31	Barrow & Furness	4.5	83	Bournemouth West	43.5
32	Basildon & Billericay	84.4	84	Bracknell	19.4
33	Basildon South & Thurrock East	66.8	85	Bradford East	27.2
34	Basingstoke	12.6	86	Bradford South	8.2
35	Bassetlaw	41.7	87	Bradford West	20.9
36	Bath	9.4	88	Braintree	74.9
37	Batley & Spen	27.2	89	Brecon & Radnorshire	None
38	Battersea	4.0	90	Brent Central	106.6
39	Beaconsfield	25.8	91	Brent North	43.4
40	Beckenham	66.8	92	Brentford & Isleworth	4.4
41	Bedford	0.9	93	Brentwood & Ongar	5.8
42	Bedfordshire Mid	3.7	94	Bridgend	9.0
43	Bedfordshire North East	4.5	95	Bridgwater & Somerset West	5.2
44	Bedfordshire South West	None	96	Brigg & Goole	3.3
45	Belfast East	26.2	97	Brighton Kemptown	9.2
46	Belfast North	22.9	98	Brighton Pavilion	9.5
47	Belfast South	15.1	99	Bristol East	52.1
48	Belfast West	8.2	100	Bristol North West	77.8
49	Bermondsey & Old Southwark	3.6	101	Bristol South	3.4
50	Berwick-upon-Tweed	0.8	102	Bristol West	52.5
51	Berwickshire, Roxburgh & Selkirk	n/a	103	Broadland	72.3
52	Bethnal Green & Bow	11.3	104	Bromley & Chislehurst	43.9

PA	Constituency	Index of change	PA	Constituency	Index of change
105	Bromsgrove	None	162	Cornwall North	29.8
106	Broxbourne	None	163	Cornwall South East	14.3
107	Broxtowe	1.7	164	Cotswolds, The	6.0
108	Buckingham	20.4	165	Coventry North East	2.8
109	Burnley	None	166	Coventry North West	3.9
110	Burton	6.3	167	Coventry South	4.7
111	Bury North	8.0	168	Crawley	None
112	Bury South	8.4	169	Crewe & Nantwich	4.5
113	Bury St Edmunds	2.3	170	Croydon Central	7.3
114	Caerphilly	6.6	171	Croydon North	2.6
115	Caithness, Sutherland & Easter Ross	n/a	172	Croydon South	5.0
116	Calder Valley	0.5	173	Cumbernauld, Kilsyth & Kirkintilloch E.	n/a
117	Camberwell & Peckham	33.7	174	Cynon Valley	8.7
118	Camborne & Redruth	52.3	175	Dagenham & Rainham	84.3
119	Cambridge	7.8	176	Darlington	1.0
120	Cambridgeshire North East	7.4	177	Dartford	4.4
121	Cambridgeshire North West	6.9	178	Daventry	76.5
122	Cambridgeshire South	15.9	179	Delyn	None
123	Cambridgeshire South East	7.3	180	Denton & Reddish	11.1
124	Cannock Chase	3.8	181	Derby North	74.9
125	Canterbury	2.6	182	Derby South	58.7
126	Cardiff Central	None	183	Derbyshire Dales	36.9
127	Cardiff North	None	184	Derbyshire Mid	105.3
128	Cardiff South & Penarth	5.1	185	Derbyshire North East	11.5
129	Cardiff West	8.3	186	Derbyshire South	23.0
130	Carlisle	6.2	187	Devizes	40.1
131	Carmarthen East & Dinefwr	2.5	188	Devon Central	121.2
132	Carmarthen W. & Pembrokeshire S.	3.4	189	Devon East	62.1
133	Carshalton & Wallington	3.2	190	Devon North	5.3
134	Castle Point	None	191	Devon South West	4.0
135	Ceredigion	0.7	192	Devon West & Torridge	20.6
136	Charnwood	5.7	193	Dewsbury	66.9
137	Chatham & Aylesford	13.6	194	Don Valley	18.9
138	Cheadle	14.1	195	Doncaster Central	9.8
139	Chelmsford	44.0	196	Doncaster North	66.3
140	Chelsea & Fulham	83.9	197	Dorset Mid & Poole North	39.0
141	Cheltenham	12.9	198	Dorset North	35.2
142	Chesham & Amersham	21.8	199	Dorset South	None
143	Chester, City of	1.3	200	Dorset West	None
144	Chesterfield	7.5	201	Dover	1.6
145	Chichester	7.9	202	Down North	None
146	Chingford & Woodford Green	None	203	Down South	8.0
147	Chippenham	97.4	204	Dudley North	14.3
148	Chipping Barnet	13.0	205	Dudley South	8.4
149	Chorley	10.8	206	Dulwich & West Norwood	40.2
150	Christchurch	18.4	207	Dumfries & Galloway	n/a
151	Cities of London & Westminster	17.0	208	Dumfriesshire, Clydesdale & Tweeddale	n/a
152	Clacton	26.5	209	Dunbartonshire East	n/a
153	Cleethorpes	None	210	Dunbartonshire West	n/a
154	Clwyd South	4.9	211	Dundee East	n/a
155	Clwyd West	3.3	212	Dundee West	n/a
156	Coatbridge, Chryston & Bellshill	n/a	213	Dunfermline & Fife West	n/a
157	Colchester	7.9	214	Durham, City of	None
158	Colne Valley	4.6	215	Durham North	0.0
159	Congleton	None	216	Durham North West	0.0
160	Copeland	15.6	217	Dwyfor Meirionnydd	86.1
161	Corby	None	218	Ealing Central & Acton	77.1

PA	Constituency	Index of change	PA	Constituency	Index of change
219	Ealing North	14.4	276	Great Grimsby	None
220	Ealing Southall	25.9	277	Great Yarmouth	None
221	Easington	1.2	278	Greenwich & Woolwich	36.8
222	East Ham	6.0	279	Guildford	4.4
223	E. Kilbride, Strathaven & Lesmahagow	n/a	280	Hackney North & Stoke Newington	13.0
224	East Lothian	n/a	281	Hackney South & Shoreditch	12.6
225	Eastbourne	3.1	282	Halesowen & Rowley Regis	7.5
226	Eastleigh	3.2	283	Halifax	0.5
227	Eddisbury	9.6	284	Haltemprice & Howden	1.8
228	Edinburgh East	n/a	285	Halton	7.7
229	Edinburgh North & Leith	n/a	286	Hammersmith	83.4
230	Edinburgh South	n/a	287	Hampshire East	82.9
231	Edinburgh South West	n/a	288	Hampshire North East	64.9
232	Edinburgh West	n/a	289	Hampshire North West	3.1
233	Edmonton	27.9	290	Hampstead & Kilburn	65.3
234	Ellesmere Port & Neston	1.3	291	Harborough	1.4
235	Elmet & Rothwell	40.3	292	Harlow	2.8
236	Eltham	31.7	293	Harrogate & Knaresborough	12.5
237	Enfield North	27.4	294	Harrow East	17.4
238	Enfield Southgate	17.3	295	Harrow West	50.2
239	Epping Forest	6.4	296	Hartlepool	None
240	Epsom & Ewell	2.5	297	Harwich & Essex North	47.8
241	Erewash	12.5	298	Hastings & Rye	5.6
242	Erith & Thamesmead	28.9	299	Havant	0.7
243	Esher & Walton	None	300	Hayes & Harlington	12.9
244	Exeter	9.3	301	Hazel Grove	10.6
245	Falkirk	n/a	302	Hemel Hempstead	1.7
246	Fareham	None	303	Hemsworth	6.4
247	Faversham & Kent Mid	9.1	304	Hendon	4.1
248	Feltham & Heston	4.9	305	Henley	5.8
249	Fermanagh & South Tyrone	None	306	Hereford & Herefordshire South	3.7
250	Fife North East	n/a	307	Herefordshire North	15.0
251	Filton & Bradley Stoke	97.7	308	Hertford & Stortford	0.9
252	Finchley & Golders Green	15.9	309	Hertfordshire North East	4.3
253	Folkestone & Hythe	5.7	310	Hertfordshire South West	1.7
254	Forest of Dean	None	311	Hertsmere	None
255	Foyle	6.6	312	Hexham	0.8
256	Fylde	14.5	313	Heywood & Middleton	6.3
257	Gainsborough	2.5	314	High Peak	7.8
258	Garston & Halewood	34.7	315	Hitchin & Harpenden	1.1
259	Gateshead	100.9	316	Holborn & St Pancras	25.9
260	Gedling	4.3	317	Hornchurch & Upminster	39.3
261	Gillingham & Rainham	3.5	318	Hornsey & Wood Green	None
262	Glasgow Central	n/a	319	Horsham	10.9
263	Glasgow East	n/a	320	Houghton & Sunderland South	85.7
264	Glasgow North	n/a	321	Hove	0.4
265	Glasgow North East	n/a	322	Huddersfield	10.6
266	Glasgow North West	n/a	323	Hull East	7.2
267	Glasgow South	n/a	324	Hull North	8.0
268	Glasgow South West	n/a	325	Hull West & Hessle	0.4
269	Glenrothes	n/a	326	Huntingdon	6.1
270	Gloucester	8.9	327	Hyndburn	1.5
271	Gordon	n/a	328	Ilford North	2.1
272	Gosport	None	329	Ilford South	None
273	Gower	0.0	330	Inverclyde	n/a
274	Grantham & Stamford	8.6	331	Inverness, Nairn, Badenoch & Strathspey	n/a
275	Gravesham	None			

PA	Constituency	Index of change	PA	Constituency	Index of change
332	Ipswich	5.4	389	Manchester Withington	2.1
333	Isle of Wight	None	390	Mansfield	14.0
334	Islington North	None	391	Meon Valley	88.4
335	Islington South & Finsbury	None	392	Meriden	9.2
336	Islwyn	8.8	393	Merthyr Tydfil & Rhymney	None
337	Jarrow	24.6	394	Middlesbrough	2.4
338	Keighley	None	395	Middlesbrough S. & Cleveland E.	2.3
339	Kenilworth & Southam	109.9	396	Midlothian	n/a
340	Kensington	73.5	397	Milton Keynes North	34.3
341	Kettering	19.6	398	Milton Keynes South	33.8
342	Kilmarnock & Loudoun	n/a	399	Mitcham & Morden	1.8
343	Kingston & Surbiton	0.9	400	Mole Valley	None
344	Kingswood	53.5	401	Monmouth	None
345	Kirkcaldy & Cowdenbeath	n/a	402	Montgomeryshire	2.8
346	Knowsley	96.1	403	Moray	n/a
347	Lagan Valley	10.3	404	Morecambe & Lunesdale	0.8
348	Lanark & Hamilton East	n/a	405	Morley & Outwood	67.6
349	Lancashire West	None	406	Motherwell & Wishaw	n/a
350	Lancaster & Fleetwood	71.5	407	Na h-Eileanan an Iar (Western Isles)	n/a
351	Leeds Central	45.7	408	Neath	0.0
352	Leeds East	41.7	409	New Forest East	4.1
353	Leeds North East	11.0	410	New Forest West	4.1
354	Leeds North West	23.8	411	Newark	48.3
355	Leeds West	9.8	412	Newbury	1.5
356	Leicester East	6.4	413	Newcastle-under-Lyme	None
357	Leicester South	0.1	414	Newcastle upon Tyne Central	74.7
358	Leicester West	6.5	415	Newcastle upon Tyne East	57.4
359	Leicestershire North West	None	416	Newcastle upon Tyne North	15.6
360	Leicestershire South	1.1	417	Newport East	None
361	Leigh	74.0	418	Newport West	None
362	Lewes	4.8	419	Newry & Armagh	None
363	Lewisham Deptford	18.6	420	Newton Abbot	30.4
364	Lewisham East	50.6	421	Norfolk Mid	106.1
365	Lewisham West & Penge	81.9	422	Norfolk North	16.5
366	Leyton & Wanstead	2.3	423	Norfolk North West	9.0
367	Lichfield	7.4	424	Norfolk South	19.4
368	Lincoln	7.8	425	Norfolk South West	27.0
369	Linlithgow & Falkirk East	n/a	426	Normanton, Pontefract & Castleford	24.0
370	Liverpool Riverside	27.2	427	Northampton North	17.6
371	Liverpool Walton	31.6	428	Northampton South	51.0
372	Liverpool Wavertree	34.5	429	Northamptonshire South	82.5
373	Liverpool West Derby	33.2	430	Norwich North	19.6
374	Livingston	n/a	431	Norwich South	8.1
375	Llanelli	None	432	Nottingham East	10.6
376	Londonderry East	7.7	433	Nottingham North	12.9
377	Loughborough	1.3	434	Nottingham South	11.2
378	Louth & Horncastle	5.1	435	Nuneaton	28.4
379	Ludlow	None	436	Ochil & South Perthshire	n/a
380	Luton North	0.4	437	Ogmore	5.5
381	Luton South	0.4	438	Old Bexley & Sidcup	4.7
382	Macclesfield	0.4	439	Oldham East & Saddleworth	18.5
383	Maidenhead	8.3	440	Oldham West & Royton	16.2
384	Maidstone & The Weald	9.2	441	Orkney & Shetland	n/a
385	Makerfield	50.8	442	Orpington	15.1
386	Maldon	69.2	443	Oxford East	9.9
387	Manchester Central	36.7	444	Oxford West & Abingdon	13.9
388	Manchester Gorton	18.3	445	Paisley & Renfrewshire North	n/a

PA	Constituency	Index of change	PA	Constituency	Index of change
446	Paisley & Renfrewshire South	n/a	503	Sheffield Brightside & Hillsborough	38.1
447	Pendle	None	504	Sheffield Central	59.5
448	Penistone & Stocksbridge	81.2	505	Sheffield Hallam	54.0
449	Penrith & The Border	10.5	506	Sheffield Heeley	11.1
450	Perth & North Perthshire	n/a	507	Sheffield South East	10.0
451	Peterborough	8.9	508	Sherwood	9.3
452	Plymouth Moor View	14.7	509	Shipley	9.5
453	Plymouth Sutton & Devonport	15.8	510	Shrewsbury & Atcham	None
454	Pontypridd	14.0	511	Shropshire North	None
455	Poole	18.6	512	Sittingbourne & Sheppey	5.7
456	Poplar & Limehouse	41.5	513	Skipton & Ripon	11.7
457	Portsmouth North	11.4	514	Sleaford & North Hykeham	12.2
458	Portsmouth South	9.6	515	Slough	5.1
459	Preseli Pembrokeshire	1.7	516	Solihull	8.9
460	Preston	28.3	517	Somerset North	0.3
461	Pudsey	12.5	518	Somerset North East	26.2
462	Putney	2.1	519	Somerton & Frome	3.3
463	Rayleigh & Wickford	59.0	520	South Holland & The Deepings	3.4
464	Reading East	2.2	521	South Ribble	25.9
465	Reading West	2.0	522	South Shields	12.6
466	Redcar	None	523	Southampton Itchen	7.9
467	Redditch	3.0	524	Southampton Test	10.6
468	Reigate	2.9	525	Southend West	2.0
469	Renfrewshire East	n/a	526	Southport	None
470	Rhondda	None	527	Spelthorne	None
471	Ribble Valley	69.4	528	Stafford	3.4
472	Richmond (Yorks)	11.5	529	Staffordshire Moorlands	36.9
473	Richmond Park	1.0	530	Staffordshire South	4.0
474	Rochdale	19.2	531	Stalybridge & Hyde	1.3
475	Rochester & Strood	15.9	532	Stevenage	2.5
476	Rochford & Southend East	2.6	533	Stirling	n/a
477	Romford	23.2	534	Stockport	17.7
478	Romsey & Southampton North	31.3	535	Stockton North	4.6
479	Ross, Skye & Lochaber	n/a	536	Stockton South	4.1
480	Rossendale & Darwen	2.5	537	Stoke-on-Trent Central	7.0
481	Rother Valley	28.2	538	Stoke-on-Trent North	39.5
482	Rotherham	31.5	539	Stoke-on-Trent South	3.3
483	Rugby	49.6	540	Stone	8.9
484	Ruislip, Northwood & Pinner	91.5	541	Stourbridge	10.0
485	Runnymede & Weybridge	None	542	Strangford	30.4
486	Rushcliffe	13.5	543	Stratford-on-Avon	36.1
487	Rutherglen & Hamilton West	n/a	544	Streatham	7.7
488	Rutland & Melton	0.3	545	Stretford & Urmston	2.5
489	Saffron Walden	51.6	546	Stroud	5.2
490	St Albans	0.3	547	Suffolk Central & Ipswich North	5.5
491	St Austell & Newquay	95.5	548	Suffolk Coastal	1.0
492	St Helens North	7.2	549	Suffolk South	0.3
493	St Helens South & Whiston	32.2	550	Suffolk West	2.6
494	St Ives	14.3	551	Sunderland Central	81.7
495	Salford & Eccles	95.6	552	Surrey East	None
496	Salisbury	17.7	553	Surrey Heath	None
497	Scarborough & Whitby	None	554	Surrey South West	4.5
498	Scunthorpe	3.6	555	Sussex Mid	7.3
499	Sedgefield	2.2	556	Sutton & Cheam	3.4
500	Sefton Central	72.5	557	Sutton Coldfield	0.7
501	Selby & Ainsty	35.6	558	Swansea East	None
502	Sevenoaks	4.6	559	Swansea West	None

PA	Constituency	Index of change	PA	Constituency	Index of change
560	Swindon North	6.9	617	Weston-Super-Mare	0.2
561	Swindon South	1.5	618	Wigan	18.9
562	Tamworth	None	619	Wiltshire North	62.9
563	Tatton	1.4	620	Wiltshire South West	33.3
564	Taunton Deane	4.7	621	Wimbledon	1.9
565	Telford	6.2	622	Winchester	53.7
566	Tewkesbury	23.0	623	Windsor	35.8
567	Thanet North	21.2	624	Wirral South	4.7
568	Thanet South	22.8	625	Wirral West	17.0
569	Thirsk & Malton	63.0	626	Witham	93.1
570	Thornbury & Yate	20.7	627	Witney	3.8
571	Thurrock	6.0	628	Woking	None
572	Tiverton & Honiton	67.8	629	Wokingham	1.7
573	Tonbridge & Malling	None	630	Wolverhampton North East	5.5
574	Tooting	2.1	631	Wolverhampton South East	19.3
575	Torbay	9.4	632	Wolverhampton South West	6.4
576	Torfaen	None	633	Worcester	None
577	Totnes	21.3	634	Worcestershire Mid	3.4
578	Tottenham	None	635	Worcestershire West	9.2
579	Truro & Falmouth	80.2	636	Workington	18.0
580	Tunbridge Wells	6.6	637	Worsley & Eccles South	92.5
581	Twickenham	None	638	Worthing East & Shoreham	0.0
582	Tynemouth	12.6	639	Worthing West	0.0
583	Tyneside North	36.6	640	Wrekin, The	5.7
584	Tyrone West	None	641	Wrexham	None
585	Ulster Mid	None	642	Wycombe	39.9
586	Upper Bann	None	643	Wyre & Preston North	87.4
587	Uxbridge & Ruislip South	70.0	644	Wyre Forest	2.9
588	Vale of Clwyd	1.1	645	Wythenshawe & Sale East	None
589	Vale of Glamorgan	8.9	646	Yeovil	3.3
590	Vauxhall	9.8	647	Ynys Mon	None
591	Wakefield	73.2	648	York Central	12.4
592	Wallasey	3.5	649	York Outer	128.0
593	Walsall North	6.9	650	Yorkshire East	2.4
594	Walsall South	13.0			
595	Walthamstow	None			
596	Wansbeck	None			
597	Wantage	1.8			
598	Warley	9.9			
599	Warrington North	11.3			
600	Warrington South	11.1			
601	Warwick & Leamington	20.6			
602	Warwickshire North	11.1			
603	Washington & Sunderland West	135.9			
604	Watford	0.0			
605	Waveney	0.7			
606	Wealden	11.7			
607	Weaver Vale	12.0			
608	Wellingborough	7.3			
609	Wells	None			
610	Welwyn Hatfield	None			
611	Wentworth & Dearne	40.4			
612	West Bromwich East	2.8			
613	West Bromwich West	9.0			
614	West Ham	34.5			
615	Westminster North	47.8			
616	Westmorland & Lonsdale	4.3			

3 Constituency Results

Aberavon [1]

50,838	60.9	Francis, H.*	Lab	16,073	51.9	- 8.1
		Davies, K.	LD	5,034	16.3	+ 2.5
		Jones, C.Y. Ms.	Con	4,411	14.2	+ 4.1
		Nicholls-Jones, P.	PC	2,198	7.1	- 4.7
		Edwards, K.A.	BNP	1,276	4.1 *	
		Tutton, A.	Ind	919	3.0 *	
		Beany, C.	Bean	558	1.8 *	
		Callan, J.	UKIP	489	1.6 *	
2005: Lab				11,039	35.7	

Aberconwy [2]

44,593	67.2	Bebb, G.A.	Con	10,734	35.8	+ 6.8
		Hughes, R.A.	Lab	7,336	24.5	- 8.5
		Priestley, M.A.	LD	5,786	19.3	+ 0.2
		Edwards, P.R.	PC	5,341	17.8	+ 3.8
		Wieteska, M.B.	UKIP	632	2.1 *	+ 1.0
		Wynne-Jones, E.L. Ms.	Ch P	137	0.5 *	
2005: Lab				3,398	11.3	

Aberdeen North [3]

64,808	58.2	Doran, F.*	Lab	16,746	44.4	+ 2.0
		Strathdee, J.J. Ms.	SNP	8,385	22.2	- 0.1
		Chapman, K.T.	LD	7,001	18.6	- 5.3
		Whyte, S.N.G.	Con	4,666	12.4	+ 2.9
		Jones, R.D.	BNP	635	1.7 *	
		Robertson, E.J.	SSP	268	0.7 *	- 1.2
2005: Lab				8,361	22.2	

Aberdeen South [4]

64,031	67.2	Begg, A. Ms.*	Lab	15,722	36.5	- 0.2
		Sleigh, J.	LD	12,216	28.4	- 5.1
		Harvie, A. Ms.	Con	8,914	20.7	+ 3.6
		McDonald, M.	SNP	5,102	11.9	+ 2.0
		Ross, S. Ms.	BNP	529	1.2 *	
		Reekie, R. Ms.	Grn	413	1.0 *	- 0.9
		Green, R.	SACL	138	0.3 *	
2005: Lab				3,506	8.1	

Aberdeenshire West & Kincardine [5]

66,110	68.4	Smith, R.*	LD	17,362	38.4	- 7.9
		Johnstone, A.	Con	13,678	30.3	+ 1.9
		Robertson, D.	SNP	7,086	15.7	+ 4.4
		Williams, G.	Lab	6,159	13.6	+ 0.5
		Raikes, G.	BNP	513	1.1 *	
		Atkinson, A.N.G.	UKIP	397	0.9 *	
2005: LD				3,684	8.2	

Airdrie & Shotts [6]

62,364	57.5	Nash, P. Ms.	Lab	20,849	58.2		- 0.9
		Coyle, S. Ms.	SNP	8,441	23.5	+	7.0
		Whitfield, R. Ms.	Con	3,133	8.7		- 1.1
		Love, J.	LD	2,898	8.1		- 3.4
		McGeechan, J.	Ind	528	1.5 *		
2005: Lab				12,408	34.6		

Aldershot [7]

71,465	63.5	Howarth, J.G.D.*	Con	21,203	46.7	+	2.7
		Collett, A.P.	LD	15,617	34.4	+	5.5
		Slater, J.	Lab	5,489	12.1		- 9.6
		Snare, R.T.F.	UKIP	2,041	4.5 *	+	2.1
		Crowd, G.A.	EIP	803	1.8 *		
		Brimicombe, J. Ms.	Ch P	231	0.5 *		
2005: Con				5,586	12.3		

Aldridge-Brownhills [8]

58,909	65.6	Shepherd, R.C.S.*	Con	22,913	59.3	+11.1
		Hussain, A.	Lab	7,647	19.8	- 12.9
		Jenkins, I.C.	LD	6,833	17.7	+ 5.8
		McNaughton, K.R.	Grn	847	2.2 *	
		Gray, S. Ms.	Ch P	394	1.0 *	
2005: Con				15,266	39.5	

Altrincham & Sale West [9]

72,208	68.4	Brady, G.S.*	Con	24,176	48.9	+	1.9
		Brophy, J.E. Ms.	LD	12,581	25.5	+	3.6
		Ross, T.W.	Lab	11,073	22.4		- 7.0
		Bullman, K.	UKIP	1,563	3.2 *	+	1.5
2005: Con				11,595	23.5		

Alyn & Deeside [10]

60,931	65.5	Tami, M.R.*	Lab	15,804	39.6		- 9.2
		Gallagher, W.E.	Con	12,885	32.3	+	7.1
		Brighton, P.J.	LD	7,308	18.3	+	0.9
		Jones, M.	PC	1,549	3.9 *	+	0.2
		Walker, J.A.	BNP	1,368	3.4 *		
		Howson, J.W.	UKIP	1,009	2.5 *		- 0.1
2005: Lab				2,919	7.3		

Amber Valley [11]

70,171	65.5	Mills, N.J.	Con	17,746	38.6	+ 4.7
		Mallaber, J. Ms.*	Lab	17,210	37.4	- 9.0
		Snowdon, T.	LD	6,636	14.4	+ 2.1
		Clarke, M.J.	BNP	3,195	7.0	+ 4.1
		Ransome, S. Ms.	UKIP	906	2.0 *	+ 0.3
		Thing, S.	MRLP	265	0.6 *	
2005: Lab				536	1.2	

Angus [12]

62,860	60.4	Weir, M.F.*	SNP	15,020	39.6	+ 5.9
		Costa, A.C.	Con	11,738	30.9	+ 1.5
		Hutchens, K.	Lab	6,535	17.2	- 0.7
		Samani, S.R.	LD	4,090	10.8	- 6.7
		Gray, M.	UKIP	577	1.5 *	
2005: SNP				3,282	8.6	

Antrim East [13]

60,204	50.7	Wilson, S.*	DUP	13,993	45.9	- 1.0
		McCune, R.J.	UCUNF	7,223	23.7	
		Lynch, G.	APNI	3,377	11.1	
		McMullan, O.	SF	2,064	6.8	+ 1.4
		McCamphill, J.	SDLP	2,019	6.6	- 0.8
		Morrison, S.	TUV	1,826	6.0	
2005: DUP				6,770	22.2	

Antrim North [14]

73,338	57.8	Paisley , I.R.K.	DUP	19,672	46.4	- 10.4
		Allister, J.	TUV	7,114	16.8	
		McKay, D.	SF	5,265	12.4	- 1.8
		Armstrong, I.	UCUNF	4,634	10.9	
		O'Loan, D.	SDLP	3,738	8.8	- 2.2
		Dunlop, J. Ms.	APNI	1,368	3.2 *	
		Cubitt, L.	ND	606	1.4 *	
2005: DUP				12,558	29.6	

Antrim South [15]

63,054	53.9	McCrea, R.T.W.*	DUP	11,536	33.9	- 6.4
		Empey, R.	UCUNF	10,353	30.4	
		McLaughlin, M.	SF	4,729	13.9	+ 3.2
		Byrne, M. Ms.	SDLP	2,955	8.7	- 2.5
		Lawther, A.	APNI	2,607	7.7	
		Lucas, M.	TUV	1,829	5.4	
2005: DUP				1,183	3.5	

Arfon [16]

41,198	63.3	Williams, H.*	PC	9,383	36.0		+	3.9
		Pugh, A.J.	Lab	7,928	30.4		-	3.5
		Millar, R.J.	Con	4,416	16.9		+	0.5
		Green, S.L. Ms.	LD	3,666	14.1		-	1.7
		Williams, E.	UKIP	685	2.6	*	+	0.7
2005: Lab				1,455	5.6			

Argyll & Bute [17]

67,165	67.3	Reid, A.*	LD	14,292	31.6		-	4.9
		Mulvaney, G.	Con	10,861	24.0		+	0.5
		Graham, D.	Lab	10,274	22.7		+	0.3
		McKenzie, M.	SNP	8,563	18.9		+	3.4
		Morrison, E. Ms.	Grn	789	1.7	*		
		Doyle, G.	Ind	272	0.6	*		
		Black, J.A.	SJP	156	0.3	*		
2005: LD				3,431	7.6			

Arundel & South Downs [18]

76,835	72.9	Herbert, N.*	Con	32,333	57.8		+	7.4
		Deedman, D.R.	LD	15,642	27.9		+	1.4
		Lunnon, T.	Lab	4,835	8.6		-	8.7
		Bower, S.N.	UKIP	3,172	5.7		+	0.4
2005: Con				16,691	29.8			

Ashfield [19]

77,379	62.3	de Piero, G. Ms.	Lab	16,239	33.7		-	15.0
		Zadrozny, J.B.	LD	16,047	33.3		+	19.5
		Hickton, G.K.	Con	10,698	22.2		-	2.2
		Holmes, E.	BNP	2,781	5.8			
		Ellis, A.	ED	1,102	2.3	*		
		Coleman, T.G.	UKIP	933	1.9	*		
		Smith, E.I.	Ind	396	0.8	*		
2005: Lab				192	0.4			

Ashford [20]

81,271	67.9	Green, D.H.*	Con	29,878	54.1		+	2.7
		Took, C.J.	LD	12,581	22.8		+	7.2
		Clark, C.R.	Lab	9,204	16.7		-	9.7
		Elenor, J.	UKIP	2,508	4.5	*	+	1.4
		Campkin, S.R.	Grn	1,014	1.8	*	-	1.6
2005: Con				17,297	31.3			

Ashton Under Lyne [21]

67,714	56.8	Heyes, D.*	Lab	18,604	48.4	- 10.1
		Kennedy, S.L.G. Ms.	Con	9,510	24.7	+ 4.6
		Larkin, P.	LD	5,703	14.8	+ 3.2
		Lomas, D.G.	BNP	2,929	7.6	+ 1.7
		McManus, A. Ms.	UKIP	1,686	4.4 *	+ 2.3
2005: Lab				9,094	23.7	

Aylesbury [22]

77,844	68.3	Lidington, D.R.*	Con	27,736	52.2	+ 3.8
		Lambert, S.M.	LD	15,118	28.4	- 0.4
		White, K. Ms.	Lab	6,695	12.6	- 5.7
		Adams, C.M.	UKIP	3,613	6.8	+ 2.3
2005: Con				12,618	23.7	

Ayr, Carrick & Cumnock [23]

73,320	62.6	Osborne, S.C. Ms.*	Lab	21,632	47.1	+ 1.8
		Grant, B.	Con	11,721	25.5	+ 2.4
		Brodie, C.	SNP	8,276	18.0	+ 4.9
		Taylor, J.K.	LD	4,264	9.3	- 4.8
2005: Lab				9,911	21.6	

Ayrshire Central [24]

68,352	64.2	Donohoe, B.H.*	Lab	20,950	47.7	+ 1.3
		Golden, M.C.	Con	8,943	20.4	- 1.8
		Mullen, J.K.	SNP	8,364	19.0	+ 7.5
		Chamberlain, A.S.	LD	5,236	11.9	- 4.1
		McDaid, J.	Soc Lab	422	1.0 *	
2005: Lab				12,007	27.3	

Ayrshire North & Arran [25]

74,223	62.1	Clark, K. Ms.*	Lab	21,860	47.4	+ 3.5
		Gibson, P. Ms.	SNP	11,965	25.9	+ 8.0
		Lardner, P.	Con	7,212	15.6	- 2.7
		Cole-Hamilton, G. Ms.	LD	4,630	10.0	- 6.4
		McDaid, L. Ms.	Soc Lab	449	1.0 *	
2005: Lab				9,895	21.5	

Banbury [26]

84,379	66.7	Baldry, A.B.*	Con	29,703	52.8	+ 5.9
		Rundle, D.G.	LD	11,476	20.4	+ 2.9
		Sibley, L.F.	Lab	10,773	19.2	- 8.9
		Fairweather, D.S.	UKIP	2,806	5.0 *	+ 2.8
		White, A.T.	Grn	959	1.7 *	- 1.1
		Edwards, C.J.R. Ms.	Ind	524	0.9 *	
2005: Con				18,227	32.4	

Banff & Buchan [27]

64,300	59.8	Whiteford, E. Ms.	SNP	15,868	41.3	- 9.9
		Buchan, J.	Con	11,841	30.8	+11.4
		Reynolds, G.	Lab	5,382	14.0	+ 2.0
		Milne, G.	LD	4,365	11.3	- 2.0
		Payne, R.K.	BNP	1,010	2.6 *	
2005: SNP				4,027	10.5	

Barking [28]

73,868	61.4	Hodge, M.E. Ms.*	Lab	24,628	54.3	+ 4.7
		Marcus, S.J.S.	Con	8,073	17.8	+ 1.2
		Griffin, N.J.	BNP	6,620	14.6	- 1.7
		Carman, D.S.E.	LD	3,719	8.2	- 2.6
		Maloney, F.T.	UKIP	1,300	2.9 *	- 0.6
		Hargreaves, J.G.	Ch P	482	1.1 *	
		Forbes, J.E. Ms.	Grn	317	0.7 *	- 1.0
		Dowling, C.D.	MRLP	82	0.2 *	
		Darwood, T.F.	Ind	77	0.2 *	
		Sijuwola, D.	Rest	45	0.1 *	
2005: Lab				16,555	36.5	

Barnsley Central [29]

65,543	56.5	Illsley, E.*	Lab	17,487	47.3	- 10.4
		Wiggin, C.J.	LD	6,394	17.3	- 2.0
		Tempest, P.	Con	6,388	17.3	+ 2.5
		Sutton, I.	BNP	3,307	8.9	+ 4.4
		Silver, D.W.	UKIP	1,727	4.7 *	
		Wood, D.	Ind	732	2.0 *	
		Devoy, T.	Ind	610	1.6 *	
		Robinson, T.	Soc Lab	356	1.0 *	
2005: Lab				11,093	30.0	

Barnsley East [30]

68,435	56.1	Dugher, M.	Lab	18,059	47.0	- 23.9
		Brown, J.	LD	6,969	18.2	+ 4.1
		Hockney, J.A.	Con	6,329	16.5	+ 3.8
		Porter, C.	BNP	3,301	8.6	
		Watson, T.	UKIP	1,731	4.5 *	
		Hogan, K.M.J.	Ind	712	1.9 *	
		Devoy, E.	Ind	684	1.8 *	
		Capstick, K.	Soc Lab	601	1.6 *	
2005: Lab				11,090	28.9	

Barrow & Furness [31]

68,943	64.0	Woodcock, J.	Lab	21,226	48.1	+ 2.9
		Gough, J.	Con	16,018	36.3	+ 3.7
		Rabone, B.M.	LD	4,424	10.0	- 7.8
		Smith, J.N.	UKIP	841	1.9 *	- 0.1
		Ashburner, M.	BNP	840	1.9 *	
		Loynes, C.	Grn	530	1.2 *	
		Greaves, B.	Ind	245	0.6 *	
2005: Lab				5,208	11.8	

Basildon & Billericay [32]

65,515	63.4	Baron, J.C.*	Con	21,922	52.7	+ 6.7
		Davies, A.R.	Lab	9,584	23.1	- 11.7
		Hibbs, M.	LD	6,538	15.7	+ 2.5
		Bateman, I.L. Ms.	BNP	1,934	4.7 *	+ 1.1
		Broad, A.D.	UKIP	1,591	3.8 *	+ 1.4
2005: Con				12,338	29.7	

Basildon South & Thurrock East [33]

71,874	62.2	Metcalfe, S.	Con	19,624	43.9	+ 5.3
		Smith, A.E. Ms.*	Lab	13,852	31.0	- 9.7
		Williams, G.	LD	5,977	13.4	+ 2.8
		Smith, K.J.D.	UKIP	2,639	5.9	+ 3.3
		Roberts, C.	BNP	2,518	5.6	+ 0.8
		X, N.	ND	125	0.3 *	
2005: Lab				5,772	12.9	

Basingstoke [34]

75,473	67.1	Miller, M.F.L. Ms.*	Con	25,590	50.5	+ 11.7
		Shaw, J.D.	LD	12,414	24.5	+ 2.6
		Pepperell, F. Ms.	Lab	10,327	20.4	- 12.2
		Howell, S.H. Ms.	UKIP	2,076	4.1 *	+ 1.9
		Saul, S.	Ind	247	0.5 *	
2005: Con				13,176	26.0	

Bassetlaw [35]

76,513	64.8	Mann, J.*	Lab	25,018	50.5	- 2.5
		Girling, K.F.	Con	16,803	33.9	- 1.2
		Dobbie, D.P.	LD	5,570	11.2	- 0.7
		Hamilton, A. Ms.	UKIP	1,779	3.6 *	
		Whitehurst, G.M.	Ind	407	0.8 *	
2005: Lab				8,215	16.6	

Bath [36]

66,686	70.6	Foster, D.M.E.*	LD	26,651	56.6	+11.2
		Richter, F.F.	Con	14,768	31.4	- 0.5
		Ajderian, H.J. Ms.	Lab	3,251	6.9	- 7.5
		Lucas, E.P.	Grn	1,120	2.4 *	- 3.6
		Warrender, E.J.V.	UKIP	890	1.9 *	+ 0.2
		Hewett, S.P.	Ch P	250	0.5 *	
		Onymous, A.	ND	69	0.1 *	
		Geddis, S.A.	Ind	56	0.1 *	
		Craig, R.I.	South	31	0.1 *	
2005: LD				11,883	25.2	

Batley & Spen [37]

76,738	66.6	Wood, M.*	Lab	21,565	42.2	- 3.1
		Small, J.A. Ms.	Con	17,159	33.6	+ 1.9
		Bentley, N.D.	LD	8,095	15.8	+ 0.4
		Exley, D.A.	BNP	3,685	7.2	+ 1.2
		Blakeley, M.	Grn	605	1.2 *	- 0.5
2005: Lab				4,406	8.6	

Battersea [38]

74,311	65.7	Ellison, J.E. Ms.	Con	23,103	47.3	+ 7.5
		Linton, M.*	Lab	17,126	35.1	- 5.6
		Moran, L.M. Ms.	LD	7,176	14.7	+ 0.3
		Evans, G.	Grn	559	1.1 *	- 3.1
		MacDonald, C.P.	UKIP	505	1.0 *	+ 0.2
		Salmon, H.G.B.	PPBF	168	0.3 *	
		Fox, T.W.	Ind	155	0.3 *	
2005: Lab				5,977	12.2	

Beaconsfield [39]

74,982	70.0	Grieve, D.C.R.*	Con	32,053	61.1	+ 7.0
		Edwards, J.W.	LD	10,271	19.6	- 2.4
		Miles, J.	Lab	6,135	11.7	- 7.8
		Gray-Fisk, D.I. Ms.	UKIP	2,597	4.9 *	+ 0.5
		Bailey, J.	Grn	768	1.5 *	
		Cowen, A.	MPEA	475	0.9 *	
		Baron, Q.	Ind	191	0.4 *	
2005: Con				21,782	41.5	

Beckenham [40]

66,219	72.0	Stewart, R.A.	Con	27,597	57.9	- 1.8
		Jenkins, S.M.	LD	9,813	20.6	+ 4.5
		Egan, D.J.	Lab	6,893	14.5	- 4.9
		Brolly, O.G.M.	UKIP	1,551	3.3 *	+ 0.4
		Tonks, R.W.	BNP	1,001	2.1 *	
		Garrett, A.C. Ms.	Grn	608	1.3 *	
		Cheeseman, D.P.	ED	223	0.5 *	
2005: Con				17,784	37.3	

Bedford [41]

68,530	65.8	Fuller, R.Q.	Con	17,546	38.9	+ 5.4
		Hall, P.*	Lab	16,193	35.9	- 5.7
		Vann, H.P.	LD	8,957	19.9	- 2.0
		Adkin, M.	UKIP	1,136	2.5 *	+ 0.1
		Dewick, W.J.	BNP	757	1.7 *	
		Foley, B.	Grn	393	0.9 *	
		Bhandari, S.	Ind	120	0.3 *	
2005: Lab				1,353	3.0	

Bedfordshire Mid [42]

76,310	71.9	Dorries, N.V. Ms.*	Con	28,815	52.5	+ 5.9
		Jack, L.A. Ms.	LD	13,663	24.9	+ 1.4
		Reeves, D.P.	Lab	8,108	14.8	- 7.7
		Hall, B.	UKIP	2,826	5.1	+ 2.4
		Bailey, M.	Grn	773	1.4 *	- 1.2
		Cooper, J.	ED	712	1.3 *	
2005: Con				15,152	27.6	

Bedfordshire North East [43]

78,060	71.2	Burt, A.J.H.*	Con	30,989	55.8	+ 5.9
		Pitt, M.	LD	12,047	21.7	+ 0.8
		Brown, E.M.	Lab	8,957	16.1	- 9.1
		Capell, B.	UKIP	2,294	4.1 *	+ 0.1
		Seeby, I.J.	BNP	1,265	2.3 *	
2005: Con				18,942	34.1	

Bedfordshire South West [44]

76,559	66.3	Selous, A.E.A.*	Con	26,815	52.8	+ 4.5
		Cantrill, R.G.	LD	10,166	20.0	+ 3.2
		Bone, J. Ms.	Lab	9,948	19.6	- 10.6
		Newman, M.J.	UKIP	2,142	4.2 *	+ 0.0
		Tolman, M.C.	BNP	1,703	3.4 *	
2005: Con				16,649	32.8	

Belfast East [45]

59,007	58.4	Long, N. Ms.	APNI	12,839	37.2	
		Robinson, P.*	DUP	11,306	32.8	- 19.6
		Ringland, T.	UCUNF	7,305	21.2	
		Vance, D.	TUV	1,856	5.4	
		O'Donnghaile, N.	SF	817	2.4 *	- 0.1
		Muldoon, M. Ms.	SDLP	365	1.1 *	- 1.1
2005: DUP				1,533	4.4	

Belfast North [46]

65,504	56.5	Dodds, N.*	DUP	14,812	40.0	- 2.9
		Kelly, G.	SF	12,588	34.0	+ 7.1
		Maginness, A.A.	SDLP	4,544	12.3	- 4.5
		Cobain, F.	UCUNF	2,837	7.7	
		Webb, B.	APNI	1,809	4.9 *	
		McAuley, M.	Ind	403	1.1 *	
2005: DUP				2,224	6.0	

Belfast South [47]

59,524	57.4	McDonnell, A.*	SDLP	14,026	41.0	+10.9
		Spratt, J.	DUP	8,100	23.7	- 5.9
		Bradshaw, P.J. Ms.	UCUNF	5,910	17.3	
		Lo, A. Ms.	APNI	5,114	15.0	
		McGibbon, A.M.J.	Grn	1,036	3.0 *	
2005: SDLP				5,926	17.3	

Belfast West [48]

59,522	54.0	Adams, G.*	SF	22,840	71.1	+ 2.5
		Attwood, A.	SDLP	5,261	16.4	+ 0.3
		Humphrey, W.	DUP	2,436	7.6	- 3.3
		Manwaring, B.	UCUNF	1,000	3.1 *	
		Hendron, M. Ms.	APNI	596	1.9 *	
2005: SF				17,579	54.7	

Bermondsey & Old Southwark [49]

77,628	57.5	Hughes, S.H.W.*	LD	21,590	48.4	+ 0.7
		Shawcross, V. Ms.	Lab	13,060	29.2	- 2.4
		Morrison, L. Ms.	Con	7,638	17.1	+ 4.1
		Tyler, S.J.	BNP	1,370	3.1 *	
		Chance, T.	Grn	718	1.6 *	- 1.4
		Kirkby, A.D.	Ind	155	0.3 *	
		Freeman, S.	ND	120	0.3 *	
2005: LD				8,530	19.1	

Berwick-upon-Tweed [50]

56,578	67.9	Beith, A.J.*	LD	16,806	43.7	-	8.9
		Trevelyan, A.B. Ms.	Con	14,116	36.7	+	7.7
		Strickland, A.	Lab	5,061	13.2	-	5.2
		Weatheritt, M.	UKIP	1,243	3.2 *		
		Mailer, P.W.	BNP	1,213	3.2 *		
2005: LD				2,690	7.0		

Berwickshire, Roxburgh & Selkirk [51]

73,826	66.4	Moore, M.K.*	LD	22,230	45.4	+	3.5
		Lamont, J.R.	Con	16,555	33.8	+	4.9
		Miller, I.	Lab	5,003	10.2	-	5.7
		Wheelhouse, P.R.W.	SNP	4,497	9.2	+	0.6
		Fowler, S.M. Ms.	UKIP	595	1.2 *	-	0.1
		Black, C. Ms.	SJP	134	0.3 *		
2005: LD				5,675	11.6		

Bethnal Green & Bow [52]

81,243	62.4	Ali, R. Ms.	Lab	21,784	42.9	+	8.5
		Masroor, A.	LD	10,210	20.1	+	7.8
		Miah, A.	Respect	8,532	16.8		
		Khan, Z.H.	Con	7,071	13.9	+	2.0
		Marshall, J.C.	BNP	1,405	2.8 *		
		Bakht, F.	Grn	856	1.7 *	-	2.8
		Brooks, P.	Ind	277	0.5 *		
		Van Terheyden, A.R.	Pirate	213	0.4 *		
		Hikmat, H.	UV	209	0.4 *		
		Choudhury, M.	Ind	100	0.2 *		
		Malik, A.A.	Ind	71	0.1 *		
2005: Respect				11,574	22.8		

Beverley & Holderness [53]

79,318	67.1	Stuart, G.C.*	Con	25,063	47.1	+	6.2
		Dobson, C.	LD	12,076	22.7	+	3.0
		Saunders, I.	Lab	11,224	21.1	-	13.6
		Whitelam, N.	BNP	2,080	3.9 *		
		Horsfield, A.	UKIP	1,845	3.5 *	-	1.2
		Rigby, B.	Grn	686	1.3 *		
		Hughes, R.	Ind	225	0.4 *		
2005: Con				12,987	24.4		

Bexhill & Battle [54]

81,032	67.4	Barker, G.L.G.*	Con	28,147	51.6	- 2.6
		Varrall, M.E. Ms.	LD	15,267	28.0	+ 5.3
		Royston, J.W.	Lab	6,524	12.0	- 5.9
		Wheeler, J.S.	Trust	2,699	4.9 *	
		Jackson, N.P.	BNP	1,950	3.6 *	
2005: Con				12,880	23.6	

Bexleyheath & Crayford [55]

65,015	66.4	Evennett, D.A.*	Con	21,794	50.5	+ 3.9
		Dawber, H.	Lab	11,450	26.5	- 7.7
		Scott, K. Ms.	LD	5,502	12.7	- 0.4
		James, S.A.	BNP	2,042	4.7 *	+ 1.8
		Dunford, J.W.	UKIP	1,557	3.6 *	+ 0.4
		Griffiths, J.H.	ED	466	1.1 *	
		Ross, A.N.	Grn	371	0.9 *	
2005: Con				10,344	24.0	

Birkenhead [56]

62,773	56.3	Field, F.*	Lab	22,082	62.5	- 2.3
		Gilbert, A.N.	Con	6,687	18.9	+ 2.4
		Kelly, S.E.	LD	6,554	18.6	- 0.1
2005: Lab				15,395	43.6	

Birmingham Edgbaston [57]

68,573	60.6	Stuart, G.G. Ms.*	Lab	16,894	40.6	- 2.5
		Alden, D.C. Ms.	Con	15,620	37.6	- 1.5
		Harmer, R.K.	LD	6,387	15.4	+ 2.6
		Lloyd, T.S.	BNP	1,196	2.9 *	
		Warwick, G.J.G.	UKIP	732	1.8 *	- 0.4
		Simpson, P.	Grn	469	1.1 *	- 1.7
		Takhar, H.	Impact	146	0.4 *	
		Fernando, C.H.	Ch P	127	0.3 *	
2005: Lab				1,274	3.1	

Birmingham Erdington [58]

66,405	53.5	Dromey, J.	Lab	14,869	41.8	- 11.1
		Alden, R.J.C.	Con	11,592	32.6	+ 9.7
		Holtom, A.L. Ms.	LD	5,742	16.2	+ 0.3
		McHugh, K.	BNP	1,815	5.1	+ 0.4
		Foy, M.T. Ms.	UKIP	842	2.4 *	- 0.0
		Tomkins, T.	Ind	240	0.7 *	
		Williams, T.	NF	229	0.6 *	
		Gray, T.J.	Ch P	217	0.6 *	
2005: Lab				3,277	9.2	

Birmingham Hall Green [59]

76,580	63.6	Godsiff, R.D.*	Lab	16,039	32.9	- 9.4
		Yaqoob, S. Ms.	Respect	12,240	25.1	
		Evans, J.	LD	11,988	24.6	- 1.8
		Barker, J. Ms.	Con	7,320	15.0	+ 0.1
		Blumenthal, A.	UKIP	950	1.9 *	- 1.0
		Gardner, A.	Ind	190	0.4 *	
2005: Lab				3,799	7.8	

Birmingham Hodge Hill [60]

75,040	56.6	Byrne, L.*	Lab	22,077	52.0	+ 5.1
		Khan, T.A.	LD	11,775	27.7	- 2.1
		Parekh, S.	Con	4,936	11.6	+ 1.0
		Lumby, R.J.	BNP	2,333	5.5	+ 2.0
		Rafiq, W.	UKIP	714	1.7 *	- 1.1
		Johnson, P.F.	Soc Dem	637	1.5 *	
2005: Lab				10,302	24.3	

Birmingham Ladywood [61]

73,646	48.7	Mahmood, S. Ms.	Lab	19,950	55.7	+ 3.0
		Khan, A.	LD	9,845	27.5	- 1.9
		Ghani, N.M.	Con	4,277	11.9	+ 3.5
		Booth, C.	UKIP	902	2.5 *	- 3.0
		Beck, P.C.	Grn	859	2.4 *	+ 2.1
2005: Lab				10,105	28.2	

Birmingham Northfield [62]

71,338	58.6	Burden, R.*	Lab	16,841	40.3	-10.1
		Huxtable, K.S. Ms.	Con	14,059	33.6	+ 3.2
		Dixon, M.	LD	6,550	15.7	+ 3.3
		Orton, L.J.	BNP	2,290	5.5	+ 2.2
		Borthwick, J.H.	UKIP	1,363	3.3 *	+ 1.0
		Pearce, S. Ms.	Grn	406	1.0 *	
		Rodgers, D.	CG	305	0.7 *	
2005: Lab				2,782	6.7	

Birmingham Perry Barr [63]

71,304	59.0	Mahmood, K.*	Lab	21,142	50.3	+ 4.0
		Hamilton, K. Ms.	LD	9,234	22.0	- 4.1
		Norton, W.G.D.	Con	8,960	21.3	+ 4.0
		Ward, M.J.	UKIP	1,675	4.0 *	+ 1.6
		Tyrrell, J.	Soc Lab	527	1.3 *	
		Hey-Smith, D. Ms.	Ch P	507	1.2 *	
2005: Lab				11,908	28.3	

Birmingham Selly Oak [64]

74,805	62.2	McCabe, S.*	Lab	17,950	38.5		- 8.3
		Dawkins, N.D.	Con	14,468	31.1		+ 1.4
		Radcliffe, D.S.	LD	10,371	22.3		+ 4.9
		Orton, L.A. Ms.	BNP	1,820	3.9	*	
		Burgess, J.	UKIP	1,131	2.4	*	- 0.1
		Burn, J.	Grn	664	1.4	*	- 2.2
		Leeds, S.L.	Ch P	159	0.3	*	
2005: Lab				3,482	7.5		

Birmingham Yardley [65]

72,321	56.5	Hemming, J.A.M.*	LD	16,162	39.6		- 2.5
		Kelly, L.C. Ms.	Lab	13,160	32.2		- 2.5
		Jenkins, M.	Con	7,836	19.2		+ 8.6
		Lumby, T.J. Ms.	BNP	2,153	5.3		+ 1.4
		Duffen, G.M.	UKIP	1,190	2.9	*	+ 1.2
		Morris, P.E.	NF	349	0.9	*	
2005: LD				3,002	7.3		

Bishop Auckland [66]

68,368	60.2	Goodman, H.C. Ms.*	Lab	16,023	39.0		- 11.1
		Harrison, B.W. Ms.	Con	10,805	26.3		+ 3.4
		Wilkes, M.A.	LD	9,189	22.3		- 1.3
		Walker, A.	BNP	2,036	4.9	*	
		Zair, S.	LLPB	1,964	4.8	*	
		Brothers, D.J.	UKIP	1,119	2.7	*	- 0.7
2005: Lab				5,218	12.7		

Blackburn [67]

72,331	62.9	Straw, J.*	Lab	21,751	47.8		+ 5.7
		Law-Riding, M.J.	Con	11,895	26.1		+ 3.5
		English, P.A.	LD	6,918	15.2		- 5.4
		Evans, R.J.	BNP	2,158	4.7	*	- 0.7
		Irfanullah, B. Ms.	BIB	1,424	3.1	*	
		Anwar, B.	UKIP	942	2.1	*	- 0.2
		Astley, G.C. Ms.	Ind	238	0.5	*	
		Sharp, J. Ms.	Ind	173	0.4	*	
2005: Lab				9,856	21.7		

Blackley & Broughton [68]

69,489	49.2	Stringer, G.*	Lab	18,563	54.3		- 8.2
		Edsberg, J.	Con	6,260	18.3		+ 5.3
		Hobhouse, W.S.	LD	4,861	14.2		- 4.9
		Adams, D.G.	BNP	2,469	7.2		
		Phillips, K.A. Ms.	Respect	996	2.9	*	
		Willescroft, B.	UKIP	894	2.6	*	- 2.7
		Zaman, S.	Ch P	161	0.5	*	
2005: Lab				12,303	36.0		

Blackpool North & Cleveleys [69]

66,017	61.5	Maynard, P.C.	Con	16,964	41.8	+ 4.5
		Martin, P.A. Ms.	Lab	14,814	36.5	- 9.2
		Greene, W.L.	LD	5,400	13.3	- 0.4
		Hopwood, R.G.	UKIP	1,659	4.1 *	+ 0.7
		Clayton, J.A.	BNP	1,556	3.8 *	
		Davies, A.J.	MRLP	198	0.5 *	
2005: Lab				2,150	5.3	

Blackpool South [70]

63,027	55.8	Marsden, G.*	Lab	14,449	41.1	- 7.5
		Bell, R.	Con	12,597	35.8	+ 4.9
		Holt, D. Ms.	LD	5,082	14.4	- 0.7
		Goodwin, R.	BNP	1,482	4.2 *	+ 0.9
		Howitt, H.A.	UKIP	1,352	3.8 *	+ 1.7
		Tun, S.	IUK	230	0.7 *	
2005: Lab				1,852	5.3	

Blaenau Gwent [71]

52,442	61.8	Smith, N.D.J.	Lab	16,974	52.4	+20.1
		Davies, D.C.*	BGPV	6,458	19.9	
		Smith, M.G.	LD	3,285	10.1	+ 5.9
		Stevenson, E.E. Ms.	Con	2,265	7.0	+ 4.7
		Davies, R.	PC	1,333	4.1 *	+ 1.7
		King, A.D.J.	BNP	1,211	3.7 *	
		Kocan, M.K.	UKIP	488	1.5 *	+ 1.0
		O'Connell, A. Ms.	Soc Lab	381	1.2 *	
2005: Ind				10,516	32.5	

Blaydon [72]

67,808	66.2	Anderson, D.*	Lab	22,297	49.6	- 2.0
		Bradbury, N.	LD	13,180	29.3	- 8.5
		Hall, G.	Con	7,159	15.9	+ 7.9
		McFarlane, K.	BNP	2,277	5.1	
2005: Lab				9,117	20.3	

Blyth Valley [73]

62,900	61.3	Campbell, R.*	Lab	17,156	44.5	-10.5
		Reid, J.	LD	10,488	27.2	- 3.9
		Flux, B.M.	Con	6,412	16.6	+ 2.7
		Fairbairn, S.	BNP	1,699	4.4 *	
		Condon, J.	UKIP	1,665	4.3 *	
		Elliott, B.	Ind	819	2.1 *	
		White, A.	ED	327	0.8 *	
2005: Lab				6,668	17.3	

Bognor Regis & Littlehampton [74]

70,816	66.2	Gibb, N.J.*	Con	24,087	51.4	+ 6.3
		McDougall, S.E.	LD	11,024	23.5	+ 1.6
		Jones, M.G.	Lab	6,580	14.0	- 11.0
		Denny, D.E.	UKIP	3,036	6.5	- 1.5
		Moffat, A.J.	BNP	1,890	4.0 *	
		Briggs, M.L. Ms.	Ind	235	0.5 *	
2005: Con				13,063	27.9	

Bolsover [75]

72,766	60.5	Skinner, D.E.*	Lab	21,994	50.0	- 15.2
		Rowley, L.B.	Con	10,812	24.6	+ 7.3
		Hawksworth, D.E. Ms.	LD	6,821	15.5	- 2.0
		Radford, M.D.	BNP	2,640	6.0	
		Calladine, R.	UKIP	1,721	3.9 *	
2005: Lab				11,182	25.4	

Bolton North East [76]

66,846	64.7	Crausby, D.A.*	Lab	19,870	45.9	- 0.4
		Dunleavy, D.J. Ms.	Con	15,786	36.5	+ 2.2
		Ankers, P.J.	LD	5,624	13.0	- 3.1
		Johnson, N.D.	UKIP	1,815	4.2 *	+ 2.4
		Armston, N. Ms.	You	182	0.4 *	
2005: Lab				4,084	9.4	

Bolton South East [77]

69,499	57.0	Qureshi, Y. Ms.	Lab	18,782	47.4	- 8.3
		Morgan, A.P.	Con	10,148	25.6	+ 2.9
		O'Hanlon, D.	LD	6,289	15.9	- 2.2
		Spink, S.M. Ms.	BNP	2,012	5.1	
		Sidaway, I.D.	UKIP	1,564	3.9 *	+ 1.4
		Johnson, A.	Grn	614	1.6 *	
		Syed, N.	CPA	195	0.5 *	
2005: Lab				8,634	21.8	

Bolton West [78]

71,284	66.7	Hilling, J.A. Ms.	Lab	18,327	38.5	- 6.8
		Williams, S. Ms.	Con	18,235	38.3	+ 4.9
		Pearcey, J. Ms.	LD	8,177	17.2	- 1.8
		Lamb, H.	UKIP	1,901	4.0 *	+ 2.6
		Mann, R.E. Ms.	Grn	545	1.1 *	
		Jones, J.	Ind	254	0.5 *	
		Bagnall, D.	You	137	0.3 *	
2005: Lab				92	0.2	

Bootle [79]

71,422	57.8	Benton, J.E.*	Lab	27,426	66.4	- 4.6	
		Murray, J.	LD	6,245	15.1	- 1.4	
		Qureshi, S.	Con	3,678	8.9	+ 1.5	
		Nuttall, P.A.	UKIP	2,514	6.1	+ 2.8	
		Stewart, C.	BNP	942	2.3 *		
		Glover, P.	TUSC	472	1.1 *		
2005: Lab				21,181	51.3		

Boston & Skegness [80]

67,186	64.2	Simmonds, M.J.M.*	Con	21,325	49.4	+ 3.1	
		Kenny, P.R.	Lab	8,899	20.6	- 10.9	
		Smith, P.A.	LD	6,371	14.8	+ 5.4	
		Pain, C.	UKIP	4,081	9.5	+ 0.0	
		Owens, D.	BNP	2,278	5.3	+ 2.9	
		Wilson, P.H.	Ind	171	0.4 *		
2005: Con				12,426	28.8		

Bosworth [81]

77,296	70.2	Tredinnick, D.*	Con	23,132	42.6	+ 0.0	
		Mullaney, M.T.	LD	18,100	33.3	+ 11.7	
		Palmer, R.	Lab	8,674	16.0	- 15.9	
		Ryde, J.E.	BNP	2,458	4.5 *		
		Veldhuizen, D.	UKIP	1,098	2.0 *	- 1.9	
		Lampitt, J.A.	ED	615	1.1 *		
		Brooks, M.E.	Sci	197	0.4 *		
2005: Con				5,032	9.3		

Bournemouth East [82]

71,125	61.9	Ellwood, T.M.*	Con	21,320	48.4	+ 3.1	
		Northover, L.J.E. Ms.	LD	13,592	30.9	- 0.4	
		Stokes, D.	Lab	5,836	13.3	- 5.3	
		Hughes, D.N.	UKIP	3,027	6.9	+ 2.0	
		Humphrey, S.J.	Ind	249	0.6 *		
2005: Con				7,728	17.6		

Bournemouth West [83]

71,753	58.1	Burns, C.	Con	18,808	45.1	+ 5.6	
		Murray, A.J.	LD	13,225	31.7	- 0.2	
		Carr-Brown, S.L. Ms.	Lab	6,171	14.8	- 8.1	
		Glover, P.	UKIP	2,999	7.2	+ 1.6	
		Taylor, J.C.	Ind	456	1.1 *		
2005: Con				5,583	13.4		

Bracknell [84]

76,888	67.8	Lee, P.J.	Con	27,327	52.4	+ 2.6
		Earwicker, R.W.	LD	11,623	22.3	+ 4.5
		Piasecki, J.S.	Lab	8,755	16.8	-11.1
		Barter, M.P.	UKIP	2,297	4.4 *	+ 0.9
		Burke, M.A.	BNP	1,253	2.4 *	
		Young, D.H.	Grn	821	1.6 *	
		Haycocks, D.J.	SMA	60	0.1 *	
2005: Con				15,704	30.1	

Bradford East [85]

65,116	62.1	Ward, D.	LD	13,637	33.7	+ 3.9
		Rooney, T.*	Lab	13,272	32.8	-11.3
		Riaz, M.	Con	10,860	26.8	+ 9.4
		Poynton, N.	BNP	1,854	4.6 *	- 1.0
		Hussain, R.S.	Ind	375	0.9 *	
		Shields, P.T.	Ind	237	0.6 *	
		Robinson, G.	NF	222	0.5 *	
2005: Lab				365	0.9	

Bradford South [86]

63,580	59.8	Sutcliffe, G.*	Lab	15,682	41.3	- 7.0
		Palmer, M.J.S.	Con	11,060	29.1	+ 4.8
		Griffiths, A.O.	LD	6,948	18.3	+ 3.8
		Sutton, S. Ms.	BNP	2,651	7.0	- 1.2
		Illingworth, J.	UKIP	1,339	3.5 *	+ 2.0
		Lewthwaite, J.G.	D Nat	315	0.8 *	
2005: Lab				4,622	12.2	

Bradford West [87]

62,519	64.9	Singh, M.*	Lab	18,401	45.3	+ 5.6
		Iqbal, Z.	Con	12,638	31.1	- 0.2
		Hall-Matthews, D.N.J.	LD	4,732	11.7	- 7.4
		Sampson, J. Ms.	BNP	1,370	3.4 *	- 3.5
		Ali, A.	Respect	1,245	3.1 *	
		Ford, D.M.	Grn	940	2.3 *	- 0.7
		Smith, J.P.	UKIP	812	2.0 *	
		Craig, N.	D Nat	438	1.1 *	
2005: Lab				5,763	14.2	

Braintree [88]

71,163	69.1	Newmark, B.*	Con	25,901	52.6	+ 2.7
		Edwards, B.	Lab	9,780	19.9	- 10.8
		Jarvis, S.	LD	9,247	18.8	+ 5.2
		Ford, M.	UKIP	2,477	5.0	+ 2.6
		Hooks, P.S.	BNP	1,080	2.2 *	
		Blench, D.E.M. Ms.	Grn	718	1.5 *	- 1.5
2005: Con				16,121	32.8	

Brecon & Radnorshire [89]

53,589	72.5	Williams, R.H.*	LD	17,929	46.2	+ 1.3
		Davies, S. Ms.	Con	14,182	36.5	+ 1.9
		Lloyd, C.	Lab	4,096	10.5	- 4.5
		Davies, J.M. Ms.	PC	989	2.5 *	- 1.1
		Easton, C.G.	UKIP	876	2.3 *	+ 0.4
		Robinson, D.J. Ms.	Grn	341	0.9 *	
		Green, J.D.	Ch P	222	0.6 *	
		Offa, L.	MRLP	210	0.5 *	
2005: LD				3,747	9.6	

Brent Central [90]

74,046	61.2	Teather, S.L. Ms.*	LD	20,026	44.2	+13.1
		Butler, D. Ms.*	Lab	18,681	41.2	- 8.9
		Rajput, S.	Con	5,067	11.2	- 1.9
		Ali, S.	Grn	668	1.5 *	- 2.2
		Williams, E.A.	Ch P	488	1.1 *	
		Duale, A.	Respect	230	0.5 *	
		McCastree, D.	Ind	163	0.4 *	
2005: Lab				1,345	3.0	

Brent North [91]

83,896	62.3	Gardiner, B.*	Lab	24,514	46.9	- 2.5
		Patel, H.	Con	16,486	31.5	+ 2.2
		Allie, J.B.	LD	8,879	17.0	- 2.5
		Malik, A.	Ind	734	1.4 *	
		Francis, M.	Grn	725	1.4 *	
		Webb, S. Ms.	UKIP	380	0.7 *	
		Vamadeva, J.	JBNF	333	0.6 *	
		Tailor, A.A.	ED	247	0.5 *	
2005: Lab				8,028	15.4	

Brentford & Isleworth [92]

83,546	64.4	Macleod, M. Ms.	Con	20,022	37.2	+	6.5
		Keen, A. Ms.*	Lab	18,064	33.6	-	5.4
		Dakers, A.S.	LD	12,718	23.7	+	0.7
		Hargreaves, J.D.	UKIP	863	1.6 *		
		Hunt, J.G.	Grn	787	1.5 *	-	2.1
		Winnett, P.	BNP	704	1.3 *		
		Cunningham, D.B.	ED	230	0.4 *		
		Bhatti, A.J.	Ch P	210	0.4 *		
		Pillai, E. Ms.	CPA	99	0.2 *		
		Vanneck- Surplice, T.M. Ms.	Ind	68	0.1 *		
2005: Lab				1,958	3.6		

Brentwood & Ongar [93]

69,309	73.0	Pickles, E.J.*	Con	28,793	56.9	+	2.9
		Kendall, D.J.	LD	11,872	23.5	-	3.4
		Benzing, H.C. Ms.	Lab	4,992	9.9	-	4.9
		McGough, M.J.	UKIP	2,037	4.0 *	+	0.0
		Morris, P.	BNP	1,447	2.9 *		
		Barnecutt, J. Ms.	Grn	584	1.2 *		
		Tilbrook, R.C.W.	ED	491	1.0 *		
		Sapwell, J.W.A.	Ind	263	0.5 *		
		Attfield, D.	ND	113	0.2 *		
2005: Con				16,921	33.4		

Bridgend [94]

58,700	65.3	Moon, M. Ms.*	Lab	13,931	36.3	-	6.6
		Baker, H.L. Ms.	Con	11,668	30.4	+	5.4
		Morgan, W.	LD	8,658	22.6	+	0.5
		Thomas, N.H.	PC	2,269	5.9	-	1.0
		Urch, B.M.	BNP	1,020	2.7 *		
		Fulton, D.E.	UKIP	801	2.1 *	+	0.7
2005: Lab				2,263	5.9		

Bridgwater & Somerset West [95]

82,180	66.3	Liddell-Grainger, I.R.*	Con	24,675	45.3	-	0.1
		Butt Philip, T.J.	LD	15,426	28.3	+	5.7
		Pearce, K.E. Ms.	Lab	9,332	17.1	-	8.5
		Hollings, P.G.	UKIP	2,604	4.8 *	+	1.1
		Treanor, D. Ms.	BNP	1,282	2.4 *		
		Graham, R.C.	Grn	859	1.6 *	-	1.2
		Cudlipp, W.R.	Ind	315	0.6 *		
2005: Con				9,249	17.0		

Brigg & Goole [96]

67,345	65.1	Percy, A.	Con	19,680	44.9	+ 6.9
		Cawsey, I.A.*	Lab	14,533	33.1	- 12.7
		Nixon, R.A.	LD	6,414	14.6	+ 1.4
		Wright, N.J.	UKIP	1,749	4.0 *	+ 1.0
		Ward, S.J.	BNP	1,498	3.4 *	
2005: Lab				5,147	11.7	

Brighton Kemptown [97]

66,015	64.7	Kirby, S.G.	Con	16,217	38.0	+ 3.8
		Burgess, S.	Lab	14,889	34.9	- 4.1
		Williams, J. Ms.	LD	7,691	18.0	+ 1.1
		Duncan, B.	Grn	2,330	5.5	- 1.1
		Chamberlain-Webber, J.	UKIP	1,384	3.2 *	+ 1.3
		Hill, D.	TUSC	194	0.5 *	
2005: Lab				1,328	3.1	

Brighton Pavilion [98]

74,009	70.0	Lucas, C. Ms.	Grn	16,238	31.3	+ 9.4
		Platts, N. Ms.	Lab	14,986	28.9	- 7.5
		Vere, C. Ms.	Con	12,275	23.7	+ 0.4
		Millam, B. Ms.	LD	7,159	13.8	- 2.2
		Carter, N.D.	UKIP	948	1.8 *	+ 0.6
		Fyvie, I.C.	Soc Lab	148	0.3 *	
		Kara, S.A. Ms.	CURE	61	0.1 *	
		Atreides, L.	ND	19	0.0 *	
2005: Lab				1,252	2.4	

Bristol East [99]

69,448	64.8	McCarthy, K. Ms.*	Lab	16,471	36.6	- 8.9
		Shafi, A. Ms.	Con	12,749	28.3	+ 0.2
		Popham, M.	LD	10,993	24.4	+ 4.7
		Jenkins, B.T. Ms.	BNP	1,960	4.4 *	
		Collins, P.J.	UKIP	1,510	3.4 *	+ 0.7
		Vowles, G.R.	Grn	803	1.8 *	- 0.9
		Wright, S.M.	ED	347	0.8 *	
		Lynch, R. Ms.	TUSC	184	0.4 *	
2005: Lab				3,722	8.3	

Bristol North West [100]

73,469	68.5	Leslie, C.A. Ms.	Con	19,115	38.0	+ 5.5
		Harrod, P.	LD	15,841	31.5	+ 6.6
		Townend, S.	Lab	13,059	25.9	- 12.2
		Upton, R.	UKIP	1,175	2.3 *	+ 0.7
		Carr, R.	ED	635	1.3 *	
		Dunn, A.	Grn	511	1.0 *	
2005: Lab				3,274	6.5	

Bristol South [101]

78,579	61.6	Primarolo, D. Ms.*	Lab	18,600	38.4	- 10.1
		Wright, M.	LD	13,866	28.7	+ 4.9
		Lloyd Davies, M.T.	Con	11,086	22.9	+ 3.3
		Chidsey, C.R.	BNP	1,739	3.6 *	
		McNamee, C.	UKIP	1,264	2.6 *	- 0.5
		Bolton, C.N.	Grn	1,216	2.5 *	- 2.5
		Clarke, C.S.	ED	400	0.8 *	
		Baldwin, T.	TUSC	206	0.4 *	
2005: Lab				4,734	9.8	

Bristol West [102]

82,728	66.9	Williams, S.R.*	LD	26,593	48.0	+ 9.0
		Smith, P.	Lab	15,227	27.5	- 9.0
		Yarker, N.	Con	10,169	18.4	+ 2.0
		Knight, R.	Grn	2,090	3.8 *	- 1.9
		Lees, C.	UKIP	655	1.2 *	- 0.1
		Kushlick, D.	Ind	343	0.6 *	
		Baker, J.	ED	270	0.5 *	
2005: LD				11,366	20.5	

Broadland [103]

72,445	72.7	Simpson, K.R.*	Con	24,338	46.2	+ 2.8
		Roper, D.J.	LD	17,046	32.4	+ 2.9
		Barron, A.M. Ms.	Lab	7,287	13.8	- 9.8
		Agnew, J.S.	UKIP	2,382	4.5 *	+ 1.1
		Crowther, E. Ms.	BNP	871	1.7 *	
		Curran, S. Ms.	Grn	752	1.4 *	
2005: Con				7,292	13.8	

Bromley & Chislehurst [104]

65,427	67.3	Neill, R.J.M.*	Con	23,569	53.5	+ 8.5
		Webber, S.D.	LD	9,669	22.0	- 1.8
		Kirby, C.C.A.	Lab	7,295	16.6	- 7.9
		Jenner, E.	UKIP	1,451	3.3 *	+ 0.1
		Savage, R.L. Ms.	BNP	1,070	2.4 *	
		Robertson, R.T.S. Ms.	Grn	607	1.4 *	- 2.3
		Cheeseman, J.D.	ED	376	0.9 *	
2005: Con				13,900	31.6	

Bromsgrove [105]

73,036	70.7	Javid, S.	Con	22,558	43.7	- 7.3
		Burden, S.	Lab	11,250	21.8	- 8.1
		Ling, P.	LD	10,124	19.6	+ 4.6
		Morson, S.W.	UKIP	2,950	5.7	+ 1.7
		Kriss, A.D.	BIC	2,182	4.2 *	
		Wainwright, E.J. Ms.	BNP	1,923	3.7 *	
		France, M.A.	Ind	336	0.7 *	
		Wheatley, K.	Ind	307	0.6 *	
2005: Con				11,308	21.9	

Broxbourne [106]

71,391	64.0	Walker, C.A.R.*	Con	26,844	58.8	+ 4.9
		Watson, M.	Lab	8,040	17.6	- 7.9
		Witherick, A.S.M.	LD	6,107	13.4	+ 1.1
		McCole, S.	BNP	2,159	4.7 *	- 0.0
		Harvey, M.	UKIP	1,890	4.1 *	+ 0.5
		LeMay, D. Ms.	ED	618	1.4 *	
2005: Con				18,804	41.2	

Broxtowe [107]

72,042	73.2	Soubry, A.M. Ms.	Con	20,585	39.0	+ 1.8
		Palmer, N.D.*	Lab	20,196	38.3	- 3.4
		Watts, D.K.	LD	8,907	16.9	+ 0.8
		Shore, M.P.	BNP	1,422	2.7 *	
		Cobb, C.P.	UKIP	1,194	2.3 *	+ 0.8
		Mitchell, D.	Grn	423	0.8 *	- 1.1
2005: Lab				389	0.7	

Buckingham [108]

74,989	64.5	Bercow, J.S.*	Speaker	22,860	47.3	
		Stevens, J.C.C.	BCD	10,331	21.4	
		Farage, N.P.	UKIP	8,401	17.4	+13.9
		Phillips, F.P.S.	Ind	2,394	5.0 *	
		Martin, D.V. Ms.	Ind	1,270	2.6 *	
		Mozar, L. Ms.	BNP	980	2.0 *	
		Dale-Mills, C.	MRLP	856	1.8 *	
		Howard, W.G.	Ind	435	0.9 *	
		Hews, D.P.R.	Ch P	369	0.8 *	
		Watts, A.	Ind	332	0.7 *	
		Strutt, S.J.	CTDP	107	0.2 *	
2005: Con				12,529	25.9	

Burnley [109]

66,615	62.8	Birtwistle, G.	LD	14,932	35.7		+ 12.0
		Cooper, J.E. Ms.	Lab	13,114	31.3		- 7.1
		Ali, R.	Con	6,950	16.6		+ 5.8
		Wilkinson, S. Ms.	BNP	3,747	9.0		- 1.3
		Brown, A.	Ind	1,876	4.5	*	
		Wignall, J.	UKIP	929	2.2	*	+ 1.3
		Hennessey, A.	Ind	297	0.7	*	
2005: Lab				1,818	4.3		

Burton [110]

74,874	66.5	Griffiths, A.J.	Con	22,188	44.5		+ 7.2
		Smeeth, R.L. Ms.	Lab	15,884	31.9		- 10.2
		Rodgers, M.J.	LD	7,891	15.8		+ 3.4
		Hewitt, A.	BNP	2,409	4.8	*	+ 0.7
		Lancaster, P.A.	UKIP	1,451	2.9	*	+ 1.0
2005: Lab				6,304	12.7		

Bury North [111]

66,759	67.3	Nuttall, D.J.	Con	18,070	40.2		+ 3.4
		Khan, M. Ms.	Lab	15,827	35.2		- 6.6
		Baum, R.	LD	7,645	17.0		+ 1.9
		Maude, J.	BNP	1,825	4.1	*	- 0.3
		Evans, S.M.	UKIP	1,282	2.9	*	+ 1.8
		Brison, B.	Ind	181	0.4	*	
		Lambert, G.P.	Pirate	131	0.3	*	
2005: Lab				2,243	5.0		

Bury South [112]

73,544	65.6	Lewis, I.*	Lab	19,508	40.4		- 10.5
		Wiseman, M.J. Ms.	Con	16,216	33.6		+ 5.5
		D'Albert, V.	LD	8,796	18.2		+ 1.1
		Purdy, J.M. Ms.	BNP	1,743	3.6	*	
		Chadwick, P.	UKIP	1,017	2.1	*	- 0.5
		Morris, V. Ms.	ED	494	1.0	*	
		Heron, G.A.	Grn	493	1.0	*	
2005: Lab				3,292	6.8		

Bury St Edmunds [113]

84,716	69.3	Ruffley, D.L.*	Con	27,899	47.5		+ 1.2
		Chappell, D.E.	LD	15,519	26.4		+ 6.7
		Hind, K.R.C.	Lab	9,776	16.6		- 10.7
		Howlett, J.E.	UKIP	3,003	5.1		+ 1.6
		Ereira-Guyer, M.A.	Grn	2,521	4.3	*	+ 1.3
2005: Con				12,380	21.1		

Caerphilly [114]

62,122	62.3	David, W.*	Lab	17,377	44.9	- 10.5
		Caulfield, M.C. Ms.	Con	6,622	17.1	+ 2.4
		Whittle, L.	PC	6,460	16.7	- 1.4
		David, K. Ms.	LD	5,688	14.7	+ 4.7
		Reid, L.	BNP	1,635	4.2 *	
		Jenkins, T.	UKIP	910	2.4 *	
2005: Lab				10,755	27.8	

Caithness, Sutherland & Easter Ross [115]

47,263	60.9	Thurso, J.A.*	LD	11,907	41.4	- 9.1
		Mackay, J.	Lab	7,081	24.6	+ 3.7
		Urquhart, J. Ms.	SNP	5,516	19.2	+ 5.8
		Graham, A.	Con	3,744	13.0	+ 2.8
		Campbell, G.	Ind	520	1.8 *	
2005: LD				4,826	16.8	

Calder Valley [116]

76,903	67.3	Whittaker, C.	Con	20,397	39.4	+ 3.6
		Booth, S. Ms.	Lab	13,966	27.0	- 11.5
		Myers, H.A. Ms.	LD	13,037	25.2	+ 6.3
		Gregory, J.D.	BNP	1,823	3.5 *	- 0.4
		Burrows, G.	UKIP	1,173	2.3 *	
		Sweeny, K. Ms.	Grn	858	1.7 *	- 1.2
		Cole, T.	Ind	194	0.4 *	
		Greenwood, B.	Ind	175	0.3 *	
		Rogan, P.G.	ED	157	0.3 *	
2005: Lab				6,431	12.4	

Camberwell & Peckham [117]

78,627	59.3	Harman, H. Ms.*	Lab	27,619	59.2	- 4.1
		Blango, C.M.J.	LD	10,432	22.4	+ 1.9
		Stranack, A.J.	Con	6,080	13.0	+ 3.1
		Jones, J. Ms.	Grn	1,361	2.9 *	- 1.7
		Robby Munilla, J.M. Ms.	ED	435	0.9 *	
		Ogunleye, J.	WRP	211	0.5 *	
		Sharkey, M.M. Ms.	Soc Lab	184	0.4 *	
		Francis, D.S. Ms.	Ind	93	0.2 *	
		Robbins, S.	Ind	87	0.2 *	
		Knox, P.L. Ms.	ND	82	0.2 *	
		Mountford, J. Ms.	AWL	75	0.2 *	
2005: Lab				17,187	36.8	

Camborne & Redruth [118]

63,975	66.4	Eustice, C.G.	Con	15,969	37.6	+ 12.0
		Goldsworthy, J.A. Ms.*	LD	15,903	37.4	+ 1.6
		Robinson, J.C. Ms.	Lab	6,945	16.3	- 12.4
		Elliott, D.J.	UKIP	2,152	5.1	+ 0.3
		Jenkin, L.E.T. Ms.	MK	775	1.8 *	
		McPhee, E.C.	Grn	581	1.4 *	
		Hawkins, R.J.	Soc Lab	168	0.4 *	
2005: LD				66	0.2	

Cambridge [119]

74,699	67.1	Huppert, J.L.	LD	19,621	39.1	- 5.6
		Hillman, N.P.H.	Con	12,829	25.6	+ 8.3
		Zeichner, D.S.	Lab	12,174	24.3	- 8.2
		Juniper, A.T.	Grn	3,804	7.6	+ 4.7
		Burkinshaw, P.	UKIP	1,195	2.4 *	+ 1.0
		Booth, M.J.	Cam Soc	362	0.7 *	
		Old, H.	Ind	145	0.3 *	
2005: LD				6,792	13.5	

Cambridgeshire North East [120]

73,224	71.1	Barclay, S.P.	Con	26,862	51.6	+ 4.7
		Spenceley, L.H. Ms.	LD	10,437	20.0	+ 3.0
		Roberts, P.J.	Lab	9,274	17.8	- 12.8
		Talbot, R.L.	UKIP	2,791	5.4	+ 0.0
		Clapp, S.I. Ms.	BNP	1,747	3.4 *	
		Jordan, D. Ms.	Ind	566	1.1 *	
		Murphy, G.C.	ED	387	0.7 *	
2005: Con				16,425	31.5	

Cambridgeshire North West [121]

88,851	65.6	Vara, S.L.*	Con	29,425	50.5	+ 4.3
		Wilkins, K.	LD	12,748	21.9	- 1.0
		York, C.R.	Lab	9,877	16.9	- 8.7
		Brown, R.H.	UKIP	4,826	8.3	+ 3.0
		Goldspink, S.K.S.	ED	1,407	2.4 *	
2005: Con				16,677	28.6	

Cambridgeshire South [122]

78,995	74.8	Lansley, A.D.*	Con	27,995	47.4	+ 0.9
		Kindersley, S.G.M.	LD	20,157	34.1	+ 5.8
		Sadiq, M.T.	Lab	6,024	10.2	- 9.5
		Page, R.	Ind	1,968	3.3 *	
		Davies-Green, H.Y. Ms.	UKIP	1,873	3.2 *	+ 0.4
		Saggers, S.P.	Grn	1,039	1.8 *	- 1.0
2005: Con				7,838	13.3	

Cambridgeshire South East [123]

83,068	69.3	Paice, J.*	Con	27,629	48.0	+ 0.8
		Chatfield, J.P.	LD	21,683	37.6	+ 6.2
		Cowan, J.L.	Lab	4,380	7.6	- 13.8
		Monk, A.	UKIP	2,138	3.7 *	
		Sedgwick-Jell, S.D.F.	Grn	766	1.3 *	
		Woollard, G.L.	Ind	517	0.9 *	
		Bell, D.B.	CPA	489	0.8 *	
2005: Con				5,946	10.3	

Cannock Chase [124]

74,508	61.1	Burley, A.	Con	18,271	40.1	+10.1
		Woodward, S. Ms.	Lab	15,076	33.1	- 17.9
		Hunt, J.	LD	7,732	17.0	+ 3.0
		Majorowicz, T.	BNP	2,168	4.8 *	
		McKenzie, M.K.	UKIP	1,580	3.5 *	- 1.6
		Turville, R.	Ind	380	0.8 *	
		Jenkins, R.	GSOT	259	0.6 *	
		Walters, M.	Ind	93	0.2 *	
2005: Lab				3,195	7.0	

Canterbury [125]

74,121	66.4	Brazier, J.W.H.*	Con	22,050	44.8	+ 0.3
		Voizey, G.S.B.	LD	16,002	32.5	+11.1
		Samuel, G.M. Ms.	Lab	7,940	16.1	- 12.0
		Farmer, H.M.	UKIP	1,907	3.9 *	+ 1.9
		Meaden, G.J.	Grn	1,137	2.3 *	- 1.0
		Belsey, A.E.J. Ms.	MRP	173	0.4 *	
2005: Con				6,048	12.3	

Cardiff Central [126]

61,165	59.1	Willott, J.N. Ms.*	LD	14,976	41.4	- 8.4
		Rathbone, J.A. Ms.	Lab	10,400	28.8	- 5.5
		Robson, K. Ms.	Con	7,799	21.6	+12.3
		Williams, C.J.	PC	1,246	3.4 *	- 0.1
		Davies, S.M. Ms.	UKIP	765	2.1 *	+ 1.1
		Coates, S.	Grn	575	1.6 *	
		Saunders, R.	TUSC	162	0.4 *	
		Beech, M.W.	MRLP	142	0.4 *	
		Mathias, A.J.	Ind	86	0.2 *	
2005: LD				4,576	12.7	

Cardiff North [127]

65,553	72.7	Evans, J.P.	Con	17,860	37.5		+ 1.0
		Morgan, J. Ms.*	Lab	17,666	37.1		- 1.9
		Dixon, J.L.	LD	8,724	18.3		- 0.4
		Rhys, L.a.	PC	1,588	3.3 *		- 0.9
		Gwynn, L.D.	UKIP	1,130	2.4 *		+ 1.2
		von Ruhland, C.J.	Grn	362	0.8 *		
		Thomson, D.L.	Ch P	300	0.6 *		
2005: Lab				194	0.4		

Cardiff South & Penarth [128]

73,707	60.2	Michael, A.E.*	Lab	17,262	38.9		- 7.7
		Hoare, S.	Con	12,553	28.3		+ 4.4
		Hannigan, D.J.	LD	9,875	22.3		+ 2.4
		Aslam, F.T. Ms.	PC	1,851	4.2 *		- 1.1
		Zeigler, S.C.D.	UKIP	1,145	2.6 *		+ 1.2
		Burke, G.	Ind	648	1.5 *		
		Townsend, M.J.	Grn	554	1.2 *		- 0.6
		Bate, C.S.	Ch P	285	0.6 *		
		Griffiths, R.D.	Comm	196	0.4 *		
2005: Lab				4,709	10.6		

Cardiff West [129]

62,787	65.2	Brennan, K.D.*	Lab	16,894	41.2		- 3.6
		Jones-Evans, A. Ms.	Con	12,143	29.6		+ 7.0
		Hitchinson, R.E. Ms.	LD	7,186	17.5		+ 0.5
		Islam, M.S.	PC	2,868	7.0		- 5.9
		Hennessey, M.J.	UKIP	1,117	2.7 *		+ 0.6
		Griffiths, D.J.	Grn	750	1.8 *		
2005: Lab				4,751	11.6		

Carlisle [130]

65,263	64.7	Stevenson, A.J.	Con	16,589	39.3		+ 5.9
		Boaden, M.W.	Lab	15,736	37.3		- 9.6
		Hughes, N.	LD	6,567	15.6		- 1.0
		Stafford, P.B.	BNP	1,086	2.6 *		
		Owen, M.J.	UKIP	969	2.3 *		- 0.0
		Reardon, J.B.	Grn	614	1.5 *		
		Metcalfe, J.	TUSC	376	0.9 *		
		Howe, P.P.	ND	263	0.6 *		
2005: Lab				853	2.0		

Carmarthen East & Dinefwr [131]

52,385	72.6	Edwards, J.	PC	13,546	35.6	- 10.2
		Gwyther, C. Ms.	Lab	10,065	26.5	- 1.8
		Morgan, A.D.	Con	8,506	22.4	+ 8.7
		Powell, W.D.	LD	4,609	12.1	+ 2.4
		Atkinson, J.C.	UKIP	1,285	3.4 *	+ 1.7
2005: PC				3,481	9.2	

Carmarthen West & Pembrokeshire South [132]

58,108	69.7	Hart, S.A.	Con	16,649	41.1	+ 9.8
		Ainger, N.*	Lab	13,226	32.7	- 4.0
		Gossage, J.R.	LD	4,890	12.1	- 2.1
		Dixon, J.	PC	4,232	10.4	- 5.1
		Clarke, R.P.	UKIP	1,146	2.8 *	+ 1.4
		Langen, H.	Ind	364	0.9 *	
2005: Lab				3,423	8.5	

Carshalton & Wallington [133]

66,524	69.0	Brake, T.A.*	LD	22,180	48.3	+ 7.9
		Andrew, K.	Con	16,920	36.8	- 0.6
		Khan, S.I.	Lab	4,015	8.7	- 8.6
		Day, F.R.	UKIP	1,348	2.9 *	+ 0.3
		Lewis, C. Ms.	BNP	1,100	2.4 *	
		Dow, G.T.	Grn	355	0.8 *	- 1.4
2005: LD				5,260	11.5	

Castle Point [134]

67,284	66.9	Harris, R.E. Ms.	Con	19,806	44.0	- 4.3
		Spink, R.M.*	ISGB	12,174	27.0	
		Ware-Lane, J.G.S.	Lab	6,609	14.7	- 15.7
		D'Cruz, B.T.	LD	4,232	9.4	- 0.9
		Howell, P.D.	BNP	2,205	4.9 *	
2005: Con				7,632	17.0	

Ceredigion [135]

59,882	63.9	Williams, M.F.*	LD	19,139	50.0	+13.5
		James, P.	PC	10,815	28.3	- 7.6
		Evetts, L.	Con	4,421	11.6	- 0.8
		Boudier, R.	Lab	2,210	5.8	- 6.3
		Williams, E.W.	UKIP	977	2.6 *	
		Kiersch, L. Ms.	Grn	696	1.8 *	- 0.5
2005: LD				8,324	21.8	

Charnwood [136]

74,473	71.9	Dorrell, S.J.*	Con	26,560	49.6	+ 3.0
		Webber-Jones, R.	LD	11,531	21.5	+ 3.2
		Goodyer, E.	Lab	10,536	19.7	- 8.9
		Duffy, C.A.M. Ms.	BNP	3,116	5.8	+ 2.2
		Storier, M.E.	UKIP	1,799	3.4 *	+ 0.4
2005: Con				15,029	28.1	

Chatham & Aylesford [137]

67,964	64.5	Crouch, T.E.A. Ms.	Con	20,230	46.2	+ 9.4
		Shaw, J.R.*	Lab	14,161	32.3	-12.7
		McClintock, J.H.C.	LD	5,832	13.3	- 0.2
		McCarthy-Stewart, C.J.	BNP	1,365	3.1 *	
		Newton, S.W.	UKIP	1,314	3.0 *	+ 0.0
		Varnham, S.M.	ED	400	0.9 *	
		Arthur, D.	Grn	396	0.9 *	
		Smith, M.I. Ms.	Ch P	109	0.2 *	
2005: Lab				6,069	13.9	

Cheadle [138]

71,635	73.3	Hunter, M.J.*	LD	24,717	47.1	- 0.7
		Jeffreys, B.	Con	21,445	40.8	+ 0.5
		Miller, M.	Lab	4,920	9.4	- 0.5
		Moore, T.	UKIP	1,430	2.7 *	+ 1.5
2005: LD				3,272	6.2	

Chelmsford [139]

77,525	70.4	Burns, S.H.M.*	Con	25,207	46.2	+ 6.7
		Robinson, S.J.	LD	20,097	36.8	+ 6.6
		Dixon, P.A.	Lab	5,980	11.0	-16.0
		Wedon, K.A.E.	UKIP	1,527	2.8 *	- 0.6
		Bateman, M.R.	BNP	899	1.6 *	
		Thomson, A.J. Ms.	Grn	476	0.9 *	
		Tilbrook, C.E. Ms.	ED	254	0.5 *	
		Sherman, B.J.	RTBP	153	0.3 *	
2005: Con				5,110	9.4	

Chelsea & Fulham [140]

66,257	60.2	Hands, G.*	Con	24,093	60.5	+ 5.2
		Hilton, A.J.P.	Lab	7,371	18.5	- 6.9
		Hazell, D.	LD	6,473	16.2	+ 2.2
		Stephenson, J.C. Ms.	Grn	671	1.7 *	- 2.5
		Gittos, T.	UKIP	478	1.2 *	+ 0.1
		McDonald, B.	BNP	388	1.0 *	
		Courtenay, R.B.	NICF	196	0.5 *	
		Roseman, G.	ED	169	0.4 *	
		Spickernell, G.	Blue	17	0.0 *	
2005: Con				16,722	42.0	

Cheltenham [141]

78,998	66.8	Horwood, M.C.*	LD	26,659	50.5	+11.1
		Coote, M.S.	Con	21,739	41.2	+ 2.4
		Green, J.	Lab	2,703	5.1	- 6.7
		Bowman, P.	UKIP	1,192	2.3 *	+ 1.0
		Hanks, D.	MRLP	493	0.9 *	
2005: LD				4,920	9.3	

Chesham & Amersham [142]

70,333	74.6	Gillan, C.E.K. Ms.*	Con	31,658	60.4	+ 6.8
		Starkey, T.L.	LD	14,948	28.5	+ 2.3
		Gajadharsingh, A.G.	Lab	2,942	5.6	- 8.0
		Stevens, A.P.	UKIP	2,129	4.1 *	+ 0.9
		Wilkins, N.J.E.	Grn	767	1.5 *	- 2.0
2005: Con				16,710	31.9	

Chester, City of [143]

70,131	66.7	Mosley, S.J.	Con	18,995	40.6	+ 3.8
		Russell, C.M. Ms.*	Lab	16,412	35.1	- 3.9
		Jewkes, E.B. Ms.	LD	8,930	19.1	- 2.7
		Weddell, A.A.J.	UKIP	1,225	2.6 *	+ 0.9
		Abrams, R.E.	ED	594	1.3 *	
		Barker, M.T.	Grn	535	1.1 *	
		Whittingham, J.P.	Ind	99	0.2 *	
2005: Lab				2,583	5.5	

Chesterfield [144]

71,878	63.8	Perkins, T.	Lab	17,891	39.0	- 1.6
		Holmes, P.R.*	LD	17,342	37.8	- 9.1
		Abbott, C. Ms.	Con	7,214	15.7	+ 7.5
		Phillips, D.	UKIP	1,432	3.1 *	+ 0.9
		Jerram, I.L.	ED	1,213	2.6 *	
		Kerr, D.A.	Grn	600	1.3 *	
		Daramy, J.N.	Ind	147	0.3 *	
2005: LD				549	1.2	

Chichester [145]

81,576	69.6	Tyrie, A.*	Con	31,427	55.3	+ 7.4
		Lury, M.	LD	15,550	27.4	- 0.3
		Holland, S.	Lab	5,937	10.5	- 8.1
		Moncrieff, A.	UKIP	3,873	6.8	+ 1.0
2005: Con				15,877	28.0	

Chingford & Woodford Green [146]

64,831	66.5	Duncan Smith, I.*	Con	22,743	52.8	-	0.4
		Arakelian, C. Ms.	Lab	9,780	22.7	-	3.0
		Seeff, G.M.	LD	7,242	16.8	-	0.9
		Leppert, J.P.	BNP	1,288	3.0 *		
		Jones, N.	UKIP	1,133	2.6 *	-	0.2
		Craig, L. Ms.	Grn	650	1.5 *		
		Above, N.	Ind	202	0.5 *		
		White, B.J.	Ind	68	0.2 *		
2005: Con				12,963	30.1		

Chippenham [147]

72,106	72.6	Hames, D.J.	LD	23,970	45.8	+	3.3
		Emmanuel-Jones, W.	Con	21,500	41.0	+	3.3
		Lovell, G.S.	Lab	3,620	6.9	-	9.9
		Reid, J. Ms.	UKIP	1,783	3.4 *	+	0.3
		Simpkins, M.	BNP	641	1.2 *		
		Fletcher, S. Ms.	Grn	446	0.9 *		
		Maguire, J.P.	ED	307	0.6 *		
		Sexton, R.G.	Ch P	118	0.2 *		
2005: LD				2,470	4.7		

Chipping Barnet [148]

75,120	67.4	Villiers, T. Ms.*	Con	24,700	48.8	+	2.9
		Welfare, D.	Lab	12,773	25.2	-	8.6
		Barber, S.D.	LD	10,202	20.2	+	4.9
		Fluss, J.G.	UKIP	1,442	2.8 *	+	0.8
		Tansley, K. Ms.	Grn	1,021	2.0 *	-	0.8
		Clayton, P.G.	Ind	470	0.9 *		
2005: Con				11,927	23.6		

Chorley [149]

70,976	70.1	Hoyle, L.H.*	Lab	21,515	43.2	-	7.6
		Cullens, A.	Con	18,922	38.0	+	3.6
		Fenn, S.J.	LD	6,957	14.0	-	0.7
		Hogan, N.	UKIP	2,021	4.1 *		
		Curtis, C.	Ind	359	0.7 *		
2005: Lab				2,593	5.2		

Christchurch [150]

68,859	71.8	Chope, C.R.*	Con	27,888	56.4	+	1.1
		Hurll, M.J.	LD	12,478	25.3	+	1.2
		Deeks, R.W.I.	Lab	4,849	9.8	-	5.8
		Williams, D.J.	UKIP	4,201	8.5	+	3.4
2005: Con				15,410	31.2		

Cities of London & Westminster [151]

66,849	55.2	Field, M.C.*	Con	19,264	52.2	+ 3.9
		Rowntree, D.A.D.	Lab	8,188	22.2	- 3.1
		Smith, N. Ms.	LD	7,574	20.5	+ 2.0
		Chase, D.	Grn	778	2.1 *	- 2.2
		Weston, P.M.L.	UKIP	664	1.8 *	+ 0.7
		Roseman, F.	ED	191	0.5 *	
		Delderfield, D.W.	Ind	98	0.3 *	
		Nunn, J.S.	Pirate	90	0.2 *	
		Mad, C.	Ind	84	0.2 *	
2005: Con				11,076	30.0	

Clacton [152]

67,194	64.2	Carswell, J.D.W.*	Con	22,867	53.0	+ 8.6
		Henderson, I.J.	Lab	10,799	25.0	- 10.9
		Green, M.A.	LD	5,577	12.9	- 0.6
		Taylor, J.C.	BNP	1,975	4.6 *	
		Allen, E.T.	TF	1,078	2.5 *	
		Southall, C.J.	Grn	535	1.2 *	
		Humphrey, C.A.	Ind	292	0.7 *	
2005: Con				12,068	28.0	

Cleethorpes [153]

70,214	64.0	Vickers, M.J.	Con	18,939	42.1	+ 4.8
		McIsaac, S. Ms.*	Lab	14,641	32.6	- 10.8
		Morland, M.	LD	8,192	18.2	+ 3.5
		Harness, S.W.	UKIP	3,194	7.1	+ 2.5
2005: Lab				4,298	9.6	

Clwyd South [154]

53,748	64.5	Jones, S.E. Ms.	Lab	13,311	38.4	- 6.8
		Bell, J.	Con	10,477	30.2	+ 4.8
		Roberts, B.S.S.	LD	5,965	17.2	+ 1.7
		Ryder, J. Ms.	PC	3,009	8.7	- 0.8
		Hynes, S.A. Ms.	BNP	1,100	3.2 *	
		Powell, N.E.	UKIP	819	2.4 *	+ 0.4
2005: Lab				2,834	8.2	

Clwyd West [155]

57,913	65.8	Jones, D.I.*	Con	15,833	41.5	+ 5.4
		Hutton, D.E. Ms.	Lab	9,414	24.7	- 11.3
		Gruffydd, L.H.	PC	5,864	15.4	+ 4.5
		Jones, H.M. Ms.	LD	5,801	15.2	+ 1.9
		Nicholson, W.J.	UKIP	864	2.3 *	+ 0.8
		Griffiths, D.P.	Ch P	239	0.6 *	
		Blakesley, J.L.G.	Ind	96	0.3 *	
2005: Con				6,419	16.8	

Coatbridge, Chryston & Bellshill [156]

70,067	59.4	Clarke, T.*	Lab	27,728	66.6	+ 2.1
		McGlinchey, F.M. Ms.	SNP	7,014	16.8	+ 3.3
		Elder, K.C.	LD	3,519	8.5	- 3.6
		Houston, F. Ms.	Con	3,374	8.1	+ 0.9
2005: Lab				20,714	49.8	

Colchester [157]

74,064	62.3	Russell, R.E.*	LD	22,151	48.0	+ 0.3
		Quince, W.J.	Con	15,169	32.9	+ 0.8
		Newell, J.A.	Lab	5,680	12.3	- 7.9
		Pitts, J.	UKIP	1,350	2.9 *	
		Chaney, S.A.	BNP	705	1.5 *	
		Lynn, P.J.	Grn	694	1.5 *	
		Bone, E.	ED	335	0.7 *	
		Noble, G.H.S.	PPE	35	0.1 *	
		Shaw, P.R.	ND	20	0.0 *	
2005: LD				6,982	15.1	

Colne Valley [158]

80,060	69.1	McCartney, J.A.	Con	20,440	37.0	+ 4.1
		Turner, N. Ms.	LD	15,603	28.2	+ 3.7
		Abrahams, D.A. Ms.	Lab	14,589	26.4	- 9.0
		Fowler, B.	BNP	1,893	3.4 *	+ 0.6
		Roberts, M. Ms.	UKIP	1,163	2.1 *	
		Ball, C.	Grn	867	1.6 *	- 1.2
		Grunsell, J. Ms.	TUSC	741	1.3 *	
2005: Lab				4,837	8.7	

Congleton [159]

72,280	70.3	Bruce, F.C. Ms.	Con	23,250	45.8	+ 0.4
		Hirst, P.J.	LD	16,187	31.9	+ 5.0
		Bryant, D.J.	Lab	8,747	17.2	- 10.5
		Slaughter, L.W.	UKIP	2,147	4.2 *	
		Edwards, P.J.	Ind	276	0.5 *	
		Rothwell, P.	ND	94	0.2 *	
		Parton, A.R.	Ind	79	0.2 *	
2005: Con				7,063	13.9	

Copeland [160]

63,149	67.8	Reed, J.R.*	Lab	19,699	46.0	- 0.7
		Whiteside, C.J.	Con	15,866	37.1	+ 3.6
		Hollowell, F.G.	LD	4,365	10.2	- 3.7
		Jefferson, C.	BNP	1,474	3.4 *	
		Caley-Knowles, E.	UKIP	994	2.3 *	+ 0.0
		Perry, J.B. Ms.	Grn	389	0.9 *	
2005: Lab				3,833	9.0	

Corby [161]

78,024	69.5	Bagshawe, L.D. Ms.	Con	22,886	42.2	+	2.2
		Hope, P.I.*	Lab	20,991	38.7	-	4.4
		Wilson, P.C. Ms.	LD	7,834	14.4	+	1.7
		Davies, R.R.	BNP	2,525	4.7 *		
2005: Lab				1,895	3.5		

Cornwall North [162]

67,940	68.9	Rogerson, D.J.*	LD	22,512	48.1	+	5.7
		Flynn, S.P. Ms.	Con	19,531	41.7	+	6.3
		Damerell-					
		O'Connor, M.J. Ms.	UKIP	2,300	4.9 *	-	0.8
		Hulme, J.E. Ms.	Lab	1,971	4.2 *	-	8.3
		Willett, J.M.A. Ms.	MK	530	1.1 *		
2005: LD				2,981	6.4		

Cornwall South East [163]

71,373	69.5	Murray, S. Ms.	Con	22,390	45.1	+	10.1
		Gillard, K. Ms.	LD	19,170	38.6	-	8.1
		Sparling, M.H.	Lab	3,507	7.1	-	3.4
		McWilliam, S. Ms.	UKIP	3,083	6.2	+	1.1
		Creagh-Osborne, R.M.	Grn	826	1.7 *		
		Holmes, R.G.	MK	641	1.3 *		
2005: LD				3,220	6.5		

Cotswolds, The [164]

76,729	71.5	Clifton-Brown, G.R.*	Con	29,075	53.0	+	3.7
		Collins, M.J.D.	LD	16,211	29.6	+	1.5
		Dempsey, M.E.	Lab	5,886	10.7	-	7.9
		Blake, A.G.	UKIP	2,292	4.2 *	+	1.0
		Lister, K.J.	Grn	940	1.7 *		
		Steel, J.A.D.	Ind	428	0.8 *		
2005: Con				12,864	23.5		

Coventry North East [165]

73,035	59.4	Ainsworth, B.*	Lab	21,384	49.3	-	7.6
		Noonan, H. Ms.	Con	9,609	22.1	+	3.3
		Field, R.D.	LD	7,210	16.6	+	0.1
		Gower, T.	BNP	1,863	4.3 *		
		Nellist, D.	Soc Alt	1,592	3.7 *		
		Forbes, C.	UKIP	1,291	3.0 *	+	0.2
		Lebar, R.	Ch M	434	1.0 *		
2005: Lab				11,775	27.1		

Coventry North West [166]

72,871	63.9	Robinson, G.*	Lab	19,936	42.8		- 5.2
		Ridley, G.C.	Con	13,648	29.3		+ 2.7
		McKee, V.	LD	8,344	17.9		- 0.5
		Sheppard, E.J.	BNP	1,666	3.6 *		- 0.1
		Nattrass, M.	UKIP	1,295	2.8 *		+ 1.0
		Clarke, J.N.	Ind	640	1.4 *		
		Wood, J.	Grn	497	1.1 *		
		Downes, N. Ms.	Soc Alt	370	0.8 *		
		Sidhu, W.	Ch M	164	0.4 *		
2005: Lab				6,288	13.5		

Coventry South [167]

73,652	62.4	Cunningham, J.*	Lab	19,197	41.8		- 4.0
		Foster, K.J.	Con	15,352	33.4		+ 2.8
		Patton, B.D.	LD	8,278	18.0		+ 0.4
		Taylor, M.	UKIP	1,767	3.8 *		+ 1.8
		Griffiths, J. Ms.	Soc Alt	691	1.5 *		
		Gray, S.R.G.	Grn	639	1.4 *		
2005: Lab				3,845	8.4		

Crawley [168]

72,781	65.3	Smith, H.E.M.	Con	21,264	44.8		+ 5.8
		Oxlade, C.	Lab	15,336	32.3		- 6.8
		Vincent, J.W.	LD	6,844	14.4		- 1.1
		Trower, R.J.	BNP	1,672	3.5 *		+ 0.5
		French, C.	UKIP	1,382	2.9 *		+ 0.7
		Smith, P.P.	Grn	598	1.3 *		
		Khan, A.	JP	265	0.6 *		
		Hubner, A.P.	Ind	143	0.3 *		
2005: Lab				5,928	12.5		

Crewe & Nantwich [169]

79,728	64.1	Timpson, A.E.*	Con	23,420	45.8		+ 12.9
		Williams, D.A.	Lab	17,374	34.0		- 14.4
		Wood, R.J.	LD	7,656	15.0		- 3.7
		Clutton, J.R.	UKIP	1,414	2.8 *		
		Williams, P.	BNP	1,043	2.0 *		
		Parsons, M.	Ind	177	0.3 *		
2005: Lab				6,046	11.8		

Croydon Central [170]

76,349	65.1	Barwell, G.L.	Con	19,567	39.4	- 1.0
		Ryan, M.G.	Lab	16,688	33.6	- 7.5
		Lambell, P.J.	LD	6,553	13.2	+ 0.4
		Pelling, A.J.*	Ind	3,239	6.5	
		Le May, C.J.	BNP	1,448	2.9 *	
		Atkinson, R.S.	UKIP	997	2.0 *	- 0.2
		Golberg, B.C. Ms.	Grn	581	1.2 *	- 1.0
		Gitau, J.K.N.	Ch P	264	0.5 *	
		Cartwright, J.S.	MRLP	192	0.4 *	
		Castle, M.M.	Ind	138	0.3 *	
2005: Lab				2,879	5.8	

Croydon North [171]

85,216	60.6	Wicks, M.H.*	Lab	28,947	56.0	+ 2.4
		Hadden, J.M.	Con	12,466	24.1	+ 1.9
		Jerome, G.	LD	7,226	14.0	- 3.2
		Khan, S.	Grn	1,017	2.0 *	- 0.9
		Serter, J.N.	UKIP	891	1.7 *	- 0.0
		Williams, N.L. Ms.	Ch P	586	1.1 *	
		Shaikh, M.	Respect	272	0.5 *	
		Stevenson, B.	Comm	160	0.3 *	
		Seyed Mohamed, M.B.	Ind	111	0.2 *	
2005: Lab				16,481	31.9	

Croydon South [172]

81,303	69.3	Ottaway, R.G.J.*	Con	28,684	50.9	- 1.1
		Rix, S.	LD	12,866	22.8	+ 2.4
		Avis, J. Ms.	Lab	11,287	20.0	- 4.0
		Bolter, J.W.	UKIP	2,504	4.4 *	+ 2.3
		Ross, G.H.	Grn	981	1.7 *	
2005: Con				15,818	28.1	

Cumbernauld, Kilsyth & Kirkintilloch East [173]

64,037	64.3	McClymont, G.	Lab	23,549	57.2	+ 5.4
		Hepburn, J. Ms.	SNP	9,794	23.8	+ 1.6
		Ackland, R.	LD	3,924	9.5	- 5.3
		Fraser, S.M. Ms.	Con	3,407	8.3	+ 1.3
		O'Neill, W.	SSP	476	1.2 *	- 1.8
2005: Lab				13,755	33.4	

Cynon Valley [174]

50,650	59.0	Clwyd, A. Ms.*	Lab	15,681	52.5	- 10.5
		Davies, D.T.	PC	6,064	20.3	+ 6.8
		Thacker, L.N.	LD	4,120	13.8	+ 1.6
		Ash, J.K.C. Ms.	Con	3,010	10.1	+ 1.5
		Hughes, F.R.W.	UKIP	1,001	3.4 *	+ 0.7
2005: Lab				9,617	32.2	

Dagenham & Rainham [175]

69,764	63.4	Cruddas, J.*	Lab	17,813	40.3	- 8.9
		Jones, S.A.P.	Con	15,183	34.3	+ 0.9
		Barnbrook, M.J.	BNP	4,952	11.2	+ 6.8
		Bourke, J.G.	LD	3,806	8.6	- 0.4
		Litwin, C.J.	UKIP	1,569	3.5 *	- 0.4
		Kennedy, G.	Ind	308	0.7 *	
		Watson, P.D. Ms.	Ch P	305	0.7 *	
		Rosaman, D.A. Ms.	Grn	296	0.7 *	
2005: Lab				2,630	5.9	

Darlington [176]

68,168	62.9	Chapman, J. Ms.	Lab	16,891	39.4	- 12.9
		Legard, E.	Con	13,503	31.5	+ 5.4
		Barker, M.	LD	10,046	23.4	+ 5.0
		Foster, A.M. Ms.	BNP	1,262	2.9 *	
		Bull, C.E. Ms.	UKIP	1,194	2.8 *	+ 0.9
2005: Lab				3,388	7.9	

Dartford [177]

76,271	65.7	Johnson, G.A.	Con	24,428	48.8	+ 7.6
		Adams, J.P.	Lab	13,800	27.6	- 15.5
		Willis, J.M.	LD	7,361	14.7	+ 4.6
		Rogers, G.P.	ED	2,178	4.3 *	
		Palmer, R.F.	UKIP	1,842	3.7 *	+ 0.7
		Tindame, S.	Ind	264	0.5 *	
		Crockford, J.K.	FDP	207	0.4 *	
2005: Lab				10,628	21.2	

Daventry [178]

71,452	72.5	Heaton-Harris, C.	Con	29,252	56.5	+ 3.5
		McGlynn, C.G.	LD	10,064	19.4	+ 4.9
		Corazzo, P.A.	Lab	8,168	15.8	- 12.1
		Broomfield, P.J.	UKIP	2,333	4.5 *	+ 1.6
		Bennett-Spencer, A.	ED	1,187	2.3 *	
		Whiffen, S.J.	Grn	770	1.5 *	
2005: Con				19,188	37.1	

Delyn [179]

53,470	69.2	Hanson, D.G.*	Lab	15,083	40.8	- 4.9
		Sandbach, A.G.M. Ms.	Con	12,811	34.6	+ 8.5
		Brereton, W.D.	LD	5,747	15.5	- 2.4
		Ryder, P.	PC	1,844	5.0 *	- 2.4
		Matthys, J.A. Ms.	BNP	844	2.3 *	
		Haigh, A.M.	UKIP	655	1.8 *	+ 0.2
2005: Lab				2,272	6.1	

Denton & Reddish [180]

66,330	56.7	Gwynne, A.J.*	Lab	19,191	51.0	- 6.7
		Searle, J. Ms.	Con	9,360	24.9	+ 5.8
		Broadhurst, S.J.	LD	6,727	17.9	+ 1.6
		Robinson, W.	UKIP	2,060	5.5	+ 2.3
		Dennis, J.	Ind	297	0.8 *	
2005: Lab				9,831	26.1	

Derby North [181]

71,474	63.1	Williamson, C.	Lab	14,896	33.0	- 9.0
		Mold, S.	Con	14,283	31.7	+ 5.8
		Care, L.H. Ms.	LD	12,638	28.0	+ 0.5
		Cheeseman, P.	BNP	2,000	4.4 *	
		Ransome, E.L.C. Ms.	UKIP	829	1.8 *	- 0.2
		Gale, D.	Ind	264	0.6 *	
		Geraghty, D.	Pirate	170	0.4 *	
2005: Lab				613	1.4	

Derby South [182]

70,999	58.0	Beckett, M.M. Ms.*	Lab	17,851	43.3	- 9.8
		Perschke, J.	Con	11,729	28.5	+ 8.7
		Batey, D.R.	LD	8,430	20.5	- 3.7
		Fowke, S.	UKIP	1,821	4.4 *	+ 3.0
		Graves, A.	Ind	1,357	3.3 *	
2005: Lab				6,122	14.9	

Derbyshire Dales [183]

63,376	73.8	McLoughlin, P.A.*	Con	24,378	52.1	+ 5.6
		Naitta, H.S.J.	LD	10,512	22.5	- 1.9
		Swindell, C.	Lab	9,061	19.4	- 6.3
		Guiver, I.	UKIP	1,779	3.8 *	+ 1.3
		Stockell, J.	Grn	772	1.7 *	
		Delves, N.C.E.	MRLP	228	0.5 *	
		Y'mech, A.	Hum	50	0.1 *	
2005: Con				13,866	29.6	

Derbyshire Mid [184]

66,074	71.6	Latham, P.E. Ms.	Con	22,877	48.3	+ 1.1
		Dhindsa, H.S.	Lab	11,585	24.5	- 10.2
		McIntosh, S.A. Ms.	LD	9,711	20.5	+ 4.5
		Allsebrook, L.R.	BNP	1,698	3.6 *	
		Kay, T.	UKIP	1,252	2.6 *	+ 0.5
		Seerius, R.U.	MRLP	219	0.5 *	
2005: Con				11,292	23.9	

Derbyshire North East [185]

71,398	65.9	Engel, N. Ms.*	Lab	17,948	38.2	- 10.1
		Merriman, H.W.	Con	15,503	33.0	+ 7.0
		Bull, R.E.	LD	10,947	23.3	+ 1.8
		Bush, J.H.	UKIP	2,636	5.6	+ 1.2
2005: Lab				2,445	5.2	

Derbyshire South [186]

70,608	71.4	Wheeler, H.K. Ms.	Con	22,935	45.5	+ 8.1
		Edwards, M.M.	Lab	15,807	31.4	- 11.5
		Diouf, A.S.	LD	8,012	15.9	+ 3.0
		Jarvis, P.C.D.	BNP	2,193	4.3 *	+ 0.3
		Swabey, J.C.M.	UKIP	1,206	2.4 *	
		Liversuch, P.A.	Soc Lab	266	0.5 *	
2005: Lab				7,128	14.1	

Devizes [187]

67,379	68.8	Perry, C.L. Ms.	Con	25,519	55.1	+ 4.0
		Hornby, F.C. Ms.	LD	12,514	27.0	+ 4.7
		Ali, J.	Lab	4,711	10.2	- 12.2
		Bryant, P.A. Ms.	UKIP	2,076	4.5 *	+ 0.2
		Fletcher, M.	Grn	813	1.8 *	
		Houlden, M.J.	Ind	566	1.2 *	
		Coombe, N.	Libert	141	0.3 *	
2005: Con				13,005	28.1	

Devon Central [188]

71,203	75.7	Stride, M.J.	Con	27,737	51.5	+ 7.7
		Hutty, P.A.	LD	18,507	34.4	- 4.4
		Macdonald, M. Ms.	Lab	3,715	6.9	- 4.7
		Edwards, R.C.	UKIP	2,870	5.3	- 0.5
		Matthews, C.R.	Grn	1,044	1.9 *	
2005: Con				9,230	17.1	

Devon East [189]

73,109	72.6	Swire, H.G.W.*	Con	25,662	48.3	+	1.1
		Robathan, D.P.	LD	16,548	31.2	+	3.1
		Manson, G.T.	Lab	5,721	10.8	-	7.5
		Amor, M.J.	UKIP	4,346	8.2	+	2.6
		Pavey, S. Ms.	Grn	815	1.5 *		
2005: Con				9,114	17.2		

Devon North [190]

74,508	68.9	Harvey, N.B.*	LD	24,305	47.4	+	0.9
		Milton, P.J.	Con	18,484	36.0	+	0.3
		Crowther, S.J.	UKIP	3,720	7.2	+	2.0
		Cann, M.M.R.	Lab	2,671	5.2	-	3.7
		Knight, L.A. Ms.	Grn	697	1.4 *	-	2.3
		Marshall, G.L.	BNP	614	1.2 *		
		Cann, R.S.	Ind	588	1.1 *		
		Vidler, N.B.	ED	146	0.3 *		
		Sables, G.A.	Comm	96	0.2 *		
2005: LD				5,821	11.3		

Devon South West [191]

70,813	70.4	Streeter, G.N.*	Con	27,908	56.0	+	11.6
		Pascoe, A.K. Ms.	LD	12,034	24.1	+	0.3
		Pollard, L.	Lab	6,193	12.4	-	11.8
		Williams, H.M.	UKIP	3,084	6.2	-	1.3
		Brean, V.	Grn	641	1.3 *		
2005: Con				15,874	31.8		

Devon West & Torridge [192]

77,360	71.4	Cox, C.G.*	Con	25,230	45.7	+	3.4
		Symons, A.J.	LD	22,273	40.3	+	3.4
		Julian, R.	UKIP	3,021	5.5	-	0.9
		Jones, D.P.	Lab	2,917	5.3	-	5.3
		Simmons, C.H. Ms.	Grn	1,050	1.9 *	-	2.0
		Baker, N.P.	BNP	766	1.4 *		
2005: Con				2,957	5.4		

Dewsbury [193]

78,910	68.4	Reevell, S.J.	Con	18,898	35.0	+	3.3
		Malik, S.*	Lab	17,372	32.2	-	8.4
		Hutchinson, A.	LD	9,150	16.9	+	3.2
		Iqbal, K.	Ind	3,813	7.1		
		Roberts, R.	BNP	3,265	6.0	-	5.2
		Cruden, A.H.	Grn	849	1.6 *	-	0.5
		Felse, M.J.	ED	661	1.2 *		
2005: Lab				1,526	2.8		

Don Valley [194]

72,597	59.8	Flint, C.L. Ms.*	Lab	16,472	37.9		- 18.6
		Stephens, M.	Con	12,877	29.7		+ 2.7
		Simpson, E.H.	LD	7,422	17.1		+ 0.6
		Toseland, E.	BNP	2,112	4.9	*	
		Shaw, W.B.	UKIP	1,904	4.4	*	
		Aston, B. Ms.	ED	1,756	4.0	*	
		Williams, M.	Ind	877	2.0	*	
2005: Lab				3,595	8.3		

Doncaster Central [195]

72,985	57.2	Winterton, R. Ms.*	Lab	16,569	39.7		- 11.3
		Davies, G.M.	Con	10,340	24.8		+ 6.1
		Wilson, P.J.	LD	8,795	21.1		- 2.6
		Parramore, L.E.	ED	1,816	4.4	*	
		Bettney, J.	BNP	1,762	4.2	*	+ 0.9
		Andrews, M.	UKIP	1,421	3.4	*	- 0.0
		Pickles, S.A.	Ind	970	2.3	*	
		Williams, D.A.	CURE	72	0.2	*	
2005: Lab				6,229	14.9		

Doncaster North [196]

71,681	57.9	Miliband, E.*	Lab	19,637	47.3		- 3.8
		Brodie, S.R. Ms.	Con	8,728	21.0		+ 1.8
		Sanderson, E.	LD	6,174	14.9		- 0.8
		Chambers, P. Ms.	BNP	2,818	6.8		+ 2.8
		Crawshaw, W.	ED	2,148	5.2		
		Andrews, L. Ms.	UKIP	1,797	4.3	*	+ 2.1
		Rawcliffe, B.	TUSC	181	0.4	*	
2005: Lab				10,909	26.3		

Dorset Mid & Poole North [197]

64,660	72.4	Brooke, A.L. Ms.*	LD	21,100	45.1		- 4.9
		King, N.P.R.	Con	20,831	44.5		+ 7.7
		Brown, D.A.	Lab	2,748	5.9		- 4.2
		Evans, D.W.	UKIP	2,109	4.5	*	+ 1.4
2005: LD				269	0.6		

Dorset North [198]

73,741	73.4	Walter, R.J.*	Con	27,640	51.1		+ 4.6
		Gasson, E.J. Ms.	LD	20,015	37.0		- 0.9
		Bunney, M.	Lab	2,910	5.4		- 4.2
		Nieboer, J.C.S.	UKIP	2,812	5.2		+ 1.3
		Hayball, A.T. Ms.	Grn	546	1.0	*	- 1.3
		Monksummers, R.J.	MRLP	218	0.4	*	
2005: Con				7,625	14.1		

Dorset South [199]

73,360	68.6	Drax, R.	Con	22,667	45.1	+ 7.1
		Knight, J.*	Lab	15,224	30.3	- 11.4
		Kayes, R. Ms.	LD	9,557	19.0	+ 3.3
		Hobson, M.	UKIP	2,034	4.0 *	+ 0.8
		Heatley, B.	Grn	595	1.2 *	
		Kirkwood, A.	Vote	233	0.5 *	
2005: Lab				7,443	14.8	

Dorset West [200]

76,869	74.6	Letwin, O.*	Con	27,287	47.6	+ 1.1
		Farrant, S.R. Ms.	LD	23,364	40.7	- 1.2
		Bick, S.A.	Lab	3,815	6.7	- 1.1
		Chisholm, O.M.	UKIP	2,196	3.8 *	+ 1.8
		Greene, J.S. Ms.	Grn	675	1.2 *	- 0.6
2005: Con				3,923	6.8	

Dover [201]

71,833	70.1	Elphicke, C.B.A.	Con	22,174	44.0	+ 9.1
		Prosser, G.M.*	Lab	16,900	33.5	- 11.8
		Brigden, J.G.	LD	7,962	15.8	+ 0.0
		Matcham, V.P.	UKIP	1,747	3.5 *	+ 0.8
		Whiting, A.D.	BNP	1,104	2.2 *	
		Walters, M.P.	ED	216	0.4 *	
		Clark, D.R.	CPA	200	0.4 *	
		Lee-Delisle, E.G.	Ind	82	0.2 *	
2005: Lab				5,274	10.5	

Down North [202]

60,698	55.2	Hermon, S. Ms.*	Ind	21,181	63.3	
		Parsley, I.J.	UCUNF	6,817	20.4	
		Farry, S.	APNI	1,876	5.6	
		Kilpatrick, K. Ms.	TUV	1,634	4.9 *	
		Agnew, S.	Grn	1,043	3.1 *	
		Logan, L.	SDLP	680	2.0 *	- 1.1
		Parker, V.	SF	250	0.7 *	+ 0.1
2005: UU				14,364	42.9	

Down South [203]

70,784	60.2	Ritchie, M. Ms.	SDLP	20,648	48.5	+ 1.6
		Ruane, C. Ms.	SF	12,236	28.7	+ 1.7
		Wells, J.	DUP	3,645	8.6	- 7.6
		McCallister, J.	UCUNF	3,093	7.3	
		McConnell, I.	TUV	1,506	3.5 *	
		Enright, C.	Grn	901	2.1 *	
		Griffin, D.	APNI	560	1.3 *	
2005: SDLP				8,412	19.8	

Dudley North [204]

60,838	63.5	Austin, I.*	Lab	14,923	38.7	- 3.9
		Brown, G.H.	Con	14,274	37.0	+ 5.6
		Beckett, M.	LD	4,066	10.5	+ 0.0
		Davis, M.	UKIP	3,267	8.5	+ 3.9
		Griffiths, K.J.	BNP	1,899	4.9 *	- 6.0
		Inman, K.	NF	173	0.4 *	
2005: Lab				649	1.7	

Dudley South [205]

60,572	63.0	Kelly, C.	Con	16,450	43.1	+ 8.1
		Harris, R.N. Ms.	Lab	12,594	33.0	- 11.0
		Bramall, J.	LD	5,989	15.7	+ 3.0
		Rowe, P.A.	UKIP	3,132	8.2	+ 5.0
2005: Lab				3,856	10.1	

Dulwich & West Norwood [206]

72,817	66.2	Jowell, T.J.H. Ms.*	Lab	22,461	46.6	+ 2.3
		Mitchell, J.S.	LD	13,096	27.2	+ 4.0
		Adegoke, K. Ms.	Con	10,684	22.2	- 2.3
		Collins, W.S.	Grn	1,266	2.6 *	- 3.7
		Jones, E.E. Ms.	UKIP	707	1.5 *	+ 0.7
2005: Lab				9,365	19.4	

Dumfries & Galloway [207]

74,584	70.0	Brown, R.L.*	Lab	23,950	45.9	+ 4.8
		Duncan, P.J.	Con	16,501	31.6	- 3.7
		Wood, A.S.	SNP	6,419	12.3	+ 0.2
		Brodie, R.J.	LD	4,608	8.8	+ 0.5
		Wright, W.G.	UKIP	695	1.3 *	
2005: Lab				7,449	14.3	

Dumfriesshire, Clydesdale & Tweeddale [208]

66,627	68.9	Mundell, D.G.*	Con	17,457	38.0	+ 1.9
		Beamish, C.H. Ms.	Lab	13,263	28.9	- 3.4
		Bhatia, C.J.S. Ms.	LD	9,080	19.8	- 0.5
		Orr, A. Ms.	SNP	4,945	10.8	+ 1.6
		McKeane, S.	UKIP	637	1.4 *	+ 0.4
		Ballance, A.R.H. Ms.	Grn	510	1.1 *	
2005: Con				4,194	9.1	

Dunbartonshire East [209]

63,795	75.2	Swinson, J. Ms.*	LD	18,551	38.7	-	3.1
		Galbraith, M. Ms.	Lab	16,367	34.1	+	1.0
		Nolan, M.	Con	7,431	15.5	-	1.0
		White, I.R.	SNP	5,054	10.5	+	4.7
		Beeley, J.M.	UKIP	545	1.1 *		
2005: LD				2,184	4.6		

Dunbartonshire West [210]

66,086	64.0	Doyle, G. Ms.	Lab	25,905	61.3	+	9.4
		McCormick, T.G.	SNP	8,497	20.1	-	1.6
		Watt, H.D. Ms.	LD	3,434	8.1	-	6.3
		McIntyre, M.A.	Con	3,242	7.7	+	1.2
		Sorbie, M.	UKIP	683	1.6 *	+	0.8
		McGavigan, K.M. Ms.	Soc Lab	505	1.2 *		
2005: Lab				17,408	41.2		

Dundee East [211]

65,471	62.0	Hosie, S.*	SNP	15,350	37.8	+	0.6
		Murray, K.L. Ms.	Lab	13,529	33.3	-	2.9
		Bustin, C.	Con	6,177	15.2	+	2.4
		Sneddon, C.R.	LD	4,285	10.6	-	0.8
		Baird, S.E. Ms.	Grn	542	1.3 *		
		Arthur, M.J.	UKIP	431	1.1 *	+	0.3
		Gorrie, A. Ms.	SSP	254	0.6 *	-	0.7
2005: SNP				1,821	4.5		

Dundee West [212]

63,013	58.9	McGovern, J.*	Lab	17,994	48.5	+	3.9
		Barrie, J.	SNP	10,716	28.9	-	1.2
		Barnett, J.E.	LD	4,233	11.4	-	3.0
		Stewart, C.	Con	3,461	9.3	+	1.0
		McBride, A.	Ind	365	1.0 *		
		McFarlane, J.	TUSC	357	1.0 *		
2005: Lab				7,278	19.6		

Dunfermline & Fife West [213]

73,590	66.5	Docherty, T.	Lab	22,639	46.3	-	1.2
		Rennie, W.*	LD	17,169	35.1	+	14.9
		McCall, J.	SNP	5,201	10.6	-	8.3
		Hacking, B. Ms.	Con	3,305	6.8	-	3.6
		Inglis, O.	UKIP	633	1.3 *	-	0.2
2005: Lab				5,470	11.2		

Durham, City of [214]

68,832	67.2	Blackman- Woods, R.C. Ms.*	Lab	20,496	44.3	- 2.9
		Woods, C. Ms.	LD	17,429	37.7	- 2.1
		Varley, N.	Con	6,146	13.3	+ 3.9
		Musgrave, R.S.	BNP	1,153	2.5 *	
		Coghill-Marshall, N.R.	UKIP	856	1.9 *	
		Collings, J.C.	Ind	172	0.4 *	
2005: Lab				3,067	6.6	

Durham North [215]

67,544	60.7	Jones, K.D.*	Lab	20,698	50.5	- 13.6
		Skelton, D.J.	Con	8,622	21.0	+ 4.3
		Lindley, I.P.	LD	8,617	21.0	+ 1.9
		Molloy, P.	BNP	1,686	4.1 *	
		Reid, B.R.	UKIP	1,344	3.3 *	
2005: Lab				12,076	29.5	

Durham North West [216]

70,350	62.3	Glass, P. Ms.	Lab	18,539	42.3	- 11.6
		Temple, O.	LD	10,927	24.9	+ 5.0
		Tempest, M.E. Ms.	Con	8,766	20.0	+ 3.6
		Stelling, W.	Ind	2,472	5.6	
		Stewart, M.	BNP	1,852	4.2 *	
		McDonald, A.	UKIP	1,259	2.9 *	
2005: Lab				7,612	17.4	

Dwyfor Meirionnydd [217]

45,354	63.7	Llwyd, E.*	PC	12,814	44.3	- 6.4
		Baynes, S.R.M.	Con	6,447	22.3	+ 8.1
		Humphreys, A.	Lab	4,021	13.9	- 7.8
		Churchman, S.W.	LD	3,538	12.2	+ 1.3
		Hughes, L. Ms.	Ind	1,310	4.5 *	
		Wykes, F.C.	UKIP	776	2.7 *	+ 0.3
2005: PC				6,367	22.0	

Ealing Central & Acton [218]

70,251	67.2	Bray, A. Ms.	Con	17,944	38.0	+ 6.8
		Mahfouz, B.	Lab	14,228	30.1	- 3.2
		Ball, J.T.A.	LD	13,041	27.6	- 3.0
		Carter, J. Ms.	UKIP	765	1.6 *	
		Edwards, S.J. Ms.	Grn	737	1.6 *	- 3.3
		Fernandes, S. Ms.	Ch P	295	0.6 *	
		Akaki, S.	IEAC	190	0.4 *	
2005: Lab				3,716	7.9	

Ealing North [219]

73,104	65.2	Pound, S.*	Lab	24,023	50.4	+ 3.5
		Gibb, I.	Con	14,722	30.9	+ 2.6
		Lucas, C.	LD	6,283	13.2	- 6.0
		Furness, D.R.	BNP	1,045	2.2 *	
		De Wulverton, I.	UKIP	685	1.4 *	- 0.1
		Warleigh-Lack, C.B.	Grn	505	1.1 *	- 1.8
		Ljubisic, P.	Ch P	415	0.9 *	
2005: Lab				9,301	19.5	

Ealing Southall [220]

66,970	63.8	Sharma, V.K.*	Lab	22,024	51.5	- 5.8
		Singh, G.	Con	12,733	29.8	+10.8
		Bakhai, N.	LD	6,383	14.9	- 3.3
		Basu, S.	Grn	705	1.6 *	- 3.1
		Anil, M.	Ch P	503	1.2 *	
		Chaggar, S.	ED	408	1.0 *	
2005: Lab				9,291	21.7	

Easington [221]

63,879	54.7	Morris, G.M.	Lab	20,579	58.9	- 12.4
		Saville, T.J. Ms.	LD	5,597	16.0	+ 3.1
		Harrison, R.J.	Con	4,790	13.7	+ 3.0
		Dunn, C.A. Ms.	BNP	2,317	6.6	+ 3.4
		Aiken, M.D.	UKIP	1,631	4.7 *	
2005: Lab				14,982	42.9	

East Ham [222]

90,674	55.6	Timms, S.*	Lab	35,471	70.4	+16.8
		Shea, P.S.	Con	7,645	15.2	+ 1.4
		Brice, C.	LD	5,849	11.6	+ 0.8
		O'Connor, B.	ED	822	1.6 *	
		Maciejowska, J. Ms.	Grn	586	1.2 *	
2005: Lab				27,826	55.2	

East Kilbride, Strathaven & Lesmahagow [223]

76,534	66.6	McCann, M.	Lab	26,241	51.5	+ 2.8
		McKenna, J.	SNP	11,738	23.0	+ 5.1
		Simpson, G.	Con	6,613	13.0	+ 3.0
		Loughton, J.	LD	5,052	9.9	- 6.6
		Robb, K. Ms.	Grn	1,003	2.0 *	- 1.3
		Houston, J.	Ind	299	0.6 *	
2005: Lab				14,503	28.5	

East Lothian [224]

73,348	67.0	O'Donnell, F. Ms.	Lab	21,919	44.6	+ 3.1
		Veitch, M.G.	Con	9,661	19.7	+ 3.7
		Ritchie, S.	LD	8,288	16.9	- 8.0
		Sharp, A.	SNP	7,883	16.0	+ 2.9
		Mackenzie, J.N.G.	Grn	862	1.8 *	- 0.7
		Lloyd, J.	UKIP	548	1.1 *	+ 0.4
2005: Lab				12,258	24.9	

Eastbourne [225]

77,840	67.0	Lloyd, S.A.C.	LD	24,658	47.3	+ 5.6
		Waterson, N.C.*	Con	21,223	40.7	- 2.3
		Brinson, D.C.	Lab	2,497	4.8 *	- 6.0
		Shing, S.S.H.	Ind	1,327	2.5 *	
		Needham, R.A.	UKIP	1,305	2.5 *	- 0.0
		Poulter, C.	BNP	939	1.8 *	
		Baldry, M.R.	Ind	101	0.2 *	
		Gell, K.V.	Ind	74	0.1 *	
2005: Con				3,435	6.6	

Eastleigh [226]

77,436	69.3	Huhne, C.M.P.*	LD	24,966	46.5	+ 8.2
		Hutchings, M. Ms.	Con	21,102	39.3	+ 2.1
		Barraclough, L.D.	Lab	5,153	9.6	- 11.5
		Finch, R.T.	UKIP	1,933	3.6 *	+ 0.2
		Pewsey, T.S.	ED	249	0.5 *	
		Stone, D.R.	Ind	154	0.3 *	
		Low, K.	Nat Lib	93	0.2 *	
2005: LD				3,864	7.2	

Eddisbury [227]

72,100	63.0	O'Brien, S.R.*	Con	23,472	51.7	+ 4.8
		Thompson, R.J.	LD	10,217	22.5	+ 4.5
		Merrick, P.A. Ms.	Lab	9,794	21.6	- 10.5
		Dodman, C.W.H.	UKIP	1,931	4.3 *	+ 1.3
2005: Con				13,255	29.2	

Edinburgh East [228]

60,945	65.4	Gilmore, S. Ms.	Lab	17,314	43.4	+ 3.4
		Kerevan, G.	SNP	8,133	20.4	+ 3.4
		Hope, B. Ms.	LD	7,751	19.4	- 5.0
		Donald, M.	Con	4,358	10.9	+ 0.6
		Harper, R.	Grn	2,035	5.1	- 0.6
		Clark, G.P.	TUSC	274	0.7 *	
2005: Lab				9,181	23.0	

Edinburgh North & Leith [229]

69,207	68.4	Lazarowicz, M.*	Lab	17,740	37.5	+	3.2
		Lang, K.R.	LD	16,016	33.8	+	4.6
		McGill, I.	Con	7,079	14.9	-	3.7
		Cashley, C.P.	SNP	4,568	9.6	-	0.5
		Joester, K. Ms.	Grn	1,062	2.2 *	-	3.6
		Hein, J.	Lib	389	0.8 *		
		Black, W.	TUSC	233	0.5 *		
		Jacobsen, D.	Soc Lab	141	0.3 *		
		MacIntyre, C.J.	Ind	128	0.3 *		
2005: Lab				1,724	3.6		

Edinburgh South [230]

59,362	73.8	Murray, I.	Lab	15,215	34.7	+	1.5
		Mackintosh, F.	LD	14,899	34.0	+	1.7
		Hudson, N.	Con	9,452	21.6	-	2.5
		Howat, S.	SNP	3,354	7.7	+	1.5
		Burgess, S.	Grn	881	2.0 *	-	1.2
2005: Lab				316	0.7		

Edinburgh South West [231]

66,361	68.5	Darling, A.*	Lab	19,473	42.8	+	3.0
		Rust, J.G.	Con	11,026	24.3	+	1.0
		McKay, T.C.	LD	8,194	18.0	-	3.0
		Stewart, K. Ms.	SNP	5,530	12.2	+	1.6
		Cooney, C. Ms.	Grn	872	1.9 *	-	1.5
		Fox, C.A.	SSP	319	0.7 *	-	0.6
		Bellamy, C. Ms.	Comm L	48	0.1 *		
2005: Lab				8,447	18.6		

Edinburgh West [232]

65,159	71.3	Crockart, M.	LD	16,684	35.9	-	13.6
		Day, C.	Lab	12,881	27.7	+	9.1
		Geddes, S.	Con	10,767	23.2	+	3.7
		Cleland, S.M. Ms.	SNP	6,115	13.2	+	4.1
2005: LD				3,803	8.2		

Edmonton [233]

63,904	63.2	Love, A.*	Lab	21,665	53.7	-	2.3
		Charalambous, A.	Con	12,052	29.8	+	2.3
		Kilbane-Dawe, I.J.	LD	4,252	10.5	-	1.5
		Freshwater, R.A.	UKIP	1,036	2.6 *	+	0.3
		Johnson, J.G.	Grn	516	1.3 *	-	1.0
		Basarik, E.	Reform	379	0.9 *		
		Morrison, C.	Ch P	350	0.9 *		
		McLean, D.A.	Ind	127	0.3 *		
2005: Lab				9,613	23.8		

Ellesmere Port & Neston [234]

66,509	66.5	Miller, A.P.*	Lab	19,750	44.6	- 4.1
		Penketh, S.P.	Con	15,419	34.9	+ 2.1
		Aspinall, D.M.E. Ms.	LD	6,663	15.1	- 0.7
		Crocker, H.F.	UKIP	1,619	3.7 *	+ 0.8
		Starkey, J.C.	Ind	782	1.8 *	
2005: Lab				4,331	9.8	

Elmet & Rothwell [235]

77,724	71.8	Shelbrooke, A.	Con	23,778	42.6	+ 8.1
		Lewis, J.	Lab	19,257	34.5	-11.4
		Golton, S.	LD	9,109	16.3	- 1.0
		Clayton, S.M.	BNP	1,802	3.2 *	+ 0.9
		Oddy, D.P.	UKIP	1,593	2.9 *	
		Nolan, C.	Ind	250	0.4 *	
2005: Lab				4,521	8.1	

Eltham [236]

62,590	67.0	Efford, C.S.*	Lab	17,416	41.5	- 0.7
		Gold, D.S.	Con	15,753	37.5	+ 2.9
		Toole, S.T.	LD	5,299	12.6	- 4.7
		Woods, R.F.L. Ms.	BNP	1,745	4.2 *	+ 1.6
		Adams, R.	UKIP	1,011	2.4 *	- 0.4
		Hayles, A.	Grn	419	1.0 *	
		Tibby, M.	ED	217	0.5 *	
		Graham, A.	Ind	104	0.2 *	
2005: Lab				1,663	4.0	

Enfield North [237]

66,261	67.1	de Bois, N.	Con	18,804	42.3	- 0.8
		Ryan, J.M. Ms.*	Lab	17,112	38.5	- 2.3
		Smith, P.D.	LD	5,403	12.2	+ 0.7
		Avery, T.	BNP	1,228	2.8 *	+ 0.2
		Jones, M. Ms.	UKIP	938	2.1 *	+ 0.3
		Linton, B.	Grn	489	1.1 *	
		Williams, A.	Ch P	161	0.4 *	
		Weald, R. Ms.	ED	131	0.3 *	
		Athow, A.C. Ms.	WRP	96	0.2 *	
		Daniels, G. Ms.	Ind	91	0.2 *	
2005: Con				1,692	3.8	

Enfield Southgate [238]

64,139	69.1	Burrowes, D.J.B.*	Con	21,928	49.4	+ 5.7
		Charalambous, B.	Lab	14,302	32.2	- 8.8
		Khan, J.	LD	6,124	13.8	+ 2.7
		Krakowiak, P.J.	Grn	632	1.4 *	- 1.4
		Brock, B.	UKIP	505	1.1 *	- 0.1
		Mukhopadhyay, A.	Ind	391	0.9 *	
		Billoo, S.	Respect	174	0.4 *	
		Weald, B.	ED	173	0.4 *	
		Malakounides, M.	ND	88	0.2 *	
		Sturgess, J.B.	BB	35	0.1 *	
2005: Con				7,626	17.2	

Epping Forest [239]

72,186	64.5	Laing, E.F. Ms.*	Con	25,148	54.0	+ 1.2
		Haigh, A.M. Ms.	LD	10,017	21.5	+ 3.4
		Curtis, K.E. Ms.	Lab	6,641	14.3	- 7.2
		Richardson, P.H. Ms.	BNP	1,982	4.3 *	+ 0.2
		Smith, A.G.	UKIP	1,852	4.0 *	+ 1.7
		Pepper, S.B.	Grn	659	1.4 *	
		Sawyer, K. Ms.	ED	285	0.6 *	
2005: Con				15,131	32.5	

Epsom & Ewell [240]

79,908	68.8	Grayling, C.S.*	Con	30,868	56.2	+ 1.2
		Lees, J.	LD	14,734	26.8	+ 5.3
		Montgomery, C.	Lab	6,538	11.9	- 8.1
		Wallace, E. Ms.	UKIP	2,549	4.6 *	+ 1.1
		Ticher, P.	RRG	266	0.5 *	
2005: Con				16,134	29.4	

Erewash [241]

69,655	68.4	Lee, J.K. Ms.	Con	18,805	39.5	+10.4
		Pidgeon, C.J. Ms.	Lab	16,304	34.2	-10.5
		Garnett, M.C.	LD	8,343	17.5	+ 4.0
		Bailey, M.	BNP	2,337	4.9 *	+ 1.9
		Sutton, J.L. Ms.	UKIP	855	1.8 *	- 0.1
		Fletcher, L.C.	Grn	534	1.1 *	
		Wilkins, L.S.O.	Ind	464	1.0 *	
2005: Lab				2,501	5.2	

Erith & Thamesmead [242]

69,900	60.8	Pearce, T. Ms.	Lab	19,068	44.9	- 7.7
		Bloom, C.C.	Con	13,365	31.5	+ 5.0
		Cunliffe, A.M.	LD	5,116	12.0	- 0.8
		Saunders, K.	BNP	2,184	5.1	+ 0.9
		Perrin, P.M. Ms.	UKIP	1,139	2.7 *	- 1.1
		Williams, L.	ED	465	1.1 *	
		Akinoshun, A.	ND	438	1.0 *	
		Cordle, S.C.	CPA	379	0.9 *	
		Powley, M.D.A.	Grn	322	0.8 *	
2005: Lab				5,703	13.4	

Esher & Walton [243]

75,338	72.4	Raab, D.	Con	32,134	58.9	+13.2
		Blackman, L.F.	LD	13,541	24.8	- 4.7
		Eldergill, F.	Lab	5,829	10.7	- 8.8
		Collignon, B.M.	UKIP	1,783	3.3 *	- 0.0
		Popham, T.	Ind	378	0.7 *	
		Chinners,	MRLP	341	0.6 *	
		Kearsley, M.	ED	307	0.6 *	
		Lear, A.	Best	230	0.4 *	
2005: Con				18,593	34.1	

Exeter [244]

77,158	67.7	Bradshaw, B.P.J.*	Lab	19,942	38.2	- 4.0
		Foster, H.M. Ms.	Con	17,221	33.0	+ 8.1
		Oakes, G.J.	LD	10,581	20.3	- 0.7
		Crawford, K.M.	UKIP	1,930	3.7 *	+ 0.3
		Gale, C.G.	Lib	1,108	2.1 *	
		Black, P.J. Ms.	Grn	792	1.5 *	- 2.3
		Farmer, R.D.	BNP	673	1.3 *	
2005: Lab				2,721	5.2	

Falkirk [245]

81,869	62.0	Joyce, E.*	Lab	23,207	45.7	- 5.1
		McNally, J.	SNP	15,364	30.3	+ 8.9
		Mackie, K. Ms.	Con	5,698	11.2	+ 1.3
		Leach, K.A.	LD	5,225	10.3	- 5.7
		Goldie, B.	UKIP	1,283	2.5 *	
2005: Lab				7,843	15.4	

Fareham [246]

75,915	71.6	Hoban, M.G.*	Con	30,037	55.3	+ 5.6
		Bentley, A.M.	LD	12,945	23.8	+ 2.1
		Carr, J.W.	Lab	7,719	14.2	- 11.4
		Richards, S.A.	UKIP	2,235	4.1 *	+ 1.2
		Doggett, P.J.	Grn	791	1.5 *	
		Jenkins, J.A.	ED	618	1.1 *	
2005: Con				17,092	31.5	

Faversham & Kent Mid [247]

68,858	67.8	Robertson, H.M.*	Con	26,250	56.2	+ 6.1
		Naghi, D.S.	LD	9,162	19.6	+ 2.9
		Rehal, A.	Lab	7,748	16.6	- 12.5
		Larkins, S. Ms.	UKIP	1,722	3.7 *	+ 1.0
		Valentine, T.	Grn	890	1.9 *	
		Kemp, G.	NF	542	1.2 *	
		Davidson, H.K.	MRLP	398	0.9 *	
2005: Con				17,088	36.6	

Feltham & Heston [248]

81,058	59.9	Keen, A.*	Lab	21,174	43.6	- 4.5
		Bowen, M.	Con	16,516	34.0	+ 5.2
		Wilson, M.H. Ms.	LD	6,679	13.8	- 2.9
		Donnelly, J.	BNP	1,714	3.5 *	
		Shadbolt, J.	UKIP	992	2.0 *	+ 0.5
		Anstis, E. Ms.	Grn	530	1.1 *	- 1.2
		Tripathi, D.P.	Ind	505	1.0 *	
		Khaira, A.S.	Ind	180	0.4 *	
		Williams, R.	Ind	168	0.3 *	
		Linley, M.	WRP	78	0.2 *	
2005: Lab				4,658	9.6	

Fermanagh & South Tyrone [249]

67,908	68.9	Gildernew, M. Ms.*	SF	21,304	45.5	+ 7.3
		Connor, R.	Ind	21,300	45.5	
		McKinney, F.	SDLP	3,574	7.6	- 7.2
		Kamble, V. Ms.	APNI	437	0.9 *	
		Stevenson, J.B.	Ind	188	0.4 *	
2005: SF				4	0.0	

Fife North East [250]

62,771	63.8	Campbell, M.*	LD	17,763	44.3	- 7.8
		Briggs, M.	Con	8,715	21.8	+ 2.3
		Hood, M.	Lab	6,869	17.1	+ 4.4
		Campbell, R.A.M.	SNP	5,685	14.2	+ 3.8
		Scott-Hayward, M.	UKIP	1,032	2.6 *	+ 1.2
2005: LD				9,048	22.6	

Filton & Bradley Stoke [251]

69,003	70.0	Lopresti, J.	Con	19,686	40.8	+ 5.3
		Boulton, I.M.	Lab	12,772	26.4	- 7.4
		Tyzack, P.L.	LD	12,197	25.3	- 3.1
		Knight, J.W.	UKIP	1,506	3.1 *	+ 0.9
		Scott, D.J.	BNP	1,328	2.7 *	
		Lucas, J.	Grn	441	0.9 *	
		Johnson, R.M. Ms.	Ch P	199	0.4 *	
		Zero None of the Above, V.	ND	172	0.4 *	
2005: Con				6,914	14.3	

Finchley & Golders Green [252]

70,722	66.7	Freer, M.	Con	21,688	46.0	+ 6.2
		Moore, A. Ms.	Lab	15,879	33.7	- 5.4
		Edge, L.R. Ms.	LD	8,036	17.0	- 0.1
		Cummins, S. Ms.	UKIP	817	1.7 *	+ 0.6
		Lyven, D.E.	Grn	737	1.6 *	- 1.0
2005: Con				5,809	12.3	

Folkestone & Hythe [253]

78,005	67.7	Collins, D.N.	Con	26,109	49.4	- 4.5
		Beaumont, L. Ms.	LD	15,987	30.3	+ 0.7
		Worsley, D.R.	Lab	5,719	10.8	- 1.8
		McKenna, F.J.	UKIP	2,439	4.6 *	+ 3.3
		Williams, H.H.J.	BNP	1,662	3.1 *	
		Kemp, P.A. Ms.	Grn	637	1.2 *	- 0.3
		Plumstead, D.	Ind	247	0.5 *	
2005: Con				10,122	19.2	

Forest of Dean [254]

68,419	71.3	Harper, M.J.*	Con	22,853	46.9	+ 6.0
		Hogan, B.A.	Lab	11,789	24.2	- 12.4
		Coleman, C.	LD	10,676	21.9	+ 4.7
		Congdon, T.	UKIP	2,522	5.2	+ 2.8
		Greenwood, J.	Grn	923	1.9 *	- 0.2
2005: Con				11,064	22.7	

Foyle [255]

65,843	57.5	Durkan, M.*	SDLP	16,922	44.7	- 1.7
		Anderson, M. Ms.	SF	12,098	31.9	- 1.4
		Devenney, M.	DUP	4,489	11.8	- 2.2
		McCann, E.J.	PBP	2,936	7.7	
		Harding, D.	UCUNF	1,221	3.2 *	
		McGrellis, K.	APNI	223	0.6 *	
2005: SDLP				4,824	12.7	

Fylde [256]

65,926	66.3	Menzies, M.A.	Con	22,826	52.2	- 2.1
		Winlow, W.	LD	9,641	22.1	+ 6.2
		Robinson, L.J.	Lab	8,624	19.7	- 5.9
		Bleeker, M.	UKIP	1,945	4.5 *	
		Mitchell, P.A.	Grn	654	1.5 *	
2005: Con				13,185	30.2	

Gainsborough [257]

72,939	67.5	Leigh, E.J.E.*	Con	24,266	49.3	+ 5.4
		O'Connor, P.J.	LD	13,707	27.8	+ 1.8
		McMahon, J.	Lab	7,701	15.6	- 10.5
		Pearson, S.	UKIP	2,065	4.2 *	+ 0.1
		Porter, M.D.	BNP	1,512	3.1 *	
2005: Con				10,559	21.4	

Garston & Halewood [258]

71,312	60.1	Eagle, M. Ms.*	Lab	25,493	59.5	+ 1.6
		Keaveney, P. Ms.	LD	8,616	20.1	- 9.9
		Downey, R.M.	Con	6,908	16.1	+ 6.3
		Hammond, T.S.	UKIP	1,540	3.6 *	+ 1.8
		Raby, D.L. Ms.	Respect	268	0.6 *	
2005: Lab				16,877	39.4	

Gateshead [259]

66,492	57.5	Mearns, I.	Lab	20,712	54.1	- 7.3
		Hindle, F.	LD	8,163	21.3	+ 0.6
		Anderson, H. Ms.	Con	5,716	14.9	+ 4.8
		Scott, K.	BNP	1,787	4.7 *	+ 1.6
		Tennant, J.	UKIP	1,103	2.9 *	- 0.4
		Redfern, A.	Grn	379	1.0 *	
		Brunskill, E. Ms.	TUSC	266	0.7 *	
		Walton, D.	Ch P	131	0.3 *	
2005: Lab				12,549	32.8	

Gedling [260]

70,866	68.0	Coaker, V.R.*	Lab	19,821	41.1	- 5.5
		Laughton, R.B.	Con	17,962	37.3	+ 0.3
		Bateman, J. Ms.	LD	7,350	15.3	+ 1.5
		Adcock, S.	BNP	1,598	3.3 *	
		Marshall, D.M.	UKIP	1,459	3.0 *	+ 1.3
2005: Lab				1,859	3.9	

Gillingham & Rainham [261]

70,814	66.1	Chishti, A.	Con	21,624	46.2	+ 5.5
		Clark, P.G.*	Lab	12,944	27.7	- 13.1
		Stamp, A.	LD	8,484	18.1	+ 2.8
		Oakley, R.N.	UKIP	1,515	3.2 *	+ 0.6
		Ravenscroft, B.C.	BNP	1,149	2.5 *	
		Lacey, D.R.	ED	464	1.0 *	
		Marchant, P.A. Ms.	Grn	356	0.8 *	
		Bryan, G.C.	ND	141	0.3 *	
		Meegan, G.G.	MEDI	109	0.2 *	
2005: Lab				8,680	18.6	

Glasgow Central [262]

60,105	50.9	Sarwar, A.	Lab	15,908	52.0	+ 3.8
		Saeed, O.	SNP	5,357	17.5	+ 2.7
		Young, C.	LD	5,010	16.4	- 1.4
		Bradley, J.	Con	2,158	7.1	+ 0.8
		Whitelaw, A.	Grn	800	2.6 *	- 2.3
		Holt, I.	BNP	616	2.0 *	- 0.4
		Nesbitt, J.	SSP	357	1.2 *	- 2.8
		Urquhart, R.	UKIP	246	0.8 *	
		Archibald, F.	Pirate	128	0.4 *	
2005: Lab				10,551	34.5	

Glasgow East [263]

61,865	52.0	Curran, M.P. Ms.	Lab	19,797	61.6	+ 0.9
		Mason, J.*	SNP	7,957	24.7	+ 7.7
		Ward, K.	LD	1,617	5.0	- 6.8
		Khan, H. Ms.	Con	1,453	4.5 *	- 2.4
		Finnie, J.T.	BNP	677	2.1 *	
		Curran, F. Ms.	SSP	454	1.4 *	- 2.1
		Thackeray, A.M.	UKIP	209	0.6 *	
2005: Lab				11,840	36.8	

Glasgow North [264]

51,490	57.5	McKechin, A. Ms.*	Lab	13,181	44.5	+ 5.1
		Gordon, K. Ms.	LD	9,283	31.3	+ 3.9
		Grady, P.	SNP	3,530	11.9	- 1.0
		Boyle, E.M. Ms.	Con	2,089	7.1	- 1.7
		Bartos, M.	Grn	947	3.2 *	- 4.4
		Main, T.	BNP	296	1.0 *	
		McCormick, A. Ms.	TUSC	287	1.0 *	
2005: Lab				3,898	13.2	

Glasgow North East [265]

59,861	49.1	Bain, W.*	Lab	20,100	68.3	
		McAllister, B.	SNP	4,158	14.1	- 3.5
		Baxendale, E.J.G. Ms.	LD	2,262	7.7	
		Davidson, R. Ms.	Con	1,569	5.3	
		Hamilton, W.	BNP	798	2.7 *	- 0.5
		Campbell, G.	TUSC	187	0.6 *	
		McVey, K.	SSP	179	0.6 *	- 4.3
		Berrington, J.	Soc Lab	156	0.5 *	
2005: Speaker				15,942	54.2	

Glasgow North West [266]

60,997	58.3	Robertson, J.*	Lab	19,233	54.1	+ 4.9
		McKee, N. Ms.	LD	5,622	15.8	- 3.7
		Park, M. Ms.	SNP	5,430	15.3	+ 1.5
		Sullivan, R.A.	Con	3,537	9.9	+ 0.4
		Crawford, M. Ms.	Grn	882	2.5 *	- 1.4
		Mclean, S.	BNP	699	2.0 *	
		Livingstone, M.	Comm	179	0.5 *	
2005: Lab				13,611	38.3	

Glasgow South [267]

65,069	61.6	Harris, T.*	Lab	20,736	51.7	+ 4.5
		Fleming, M.	SNP	8,078	20.1	+ 7.5
		Mustapha, S. Ms.	LD	4,739	11.8	- 7.2
		Rankin, D.M. Ms.	Con	4,592	11.5	- 1.1
		Campbell, M. Ms.	Grn	961	2.4 *	- 2.0
		Coyle, M.A.	BNP	637	1.6 *	
		Smith, B.	TUSC	351	0.9 *	
2005: Lab				12,658	31.6	

Glasgow South West [268]

58,191	54.6	Davidson, I.*	Lab	19,863	62.5	+ 2.3
		Stephens, C.	SNP	5,192	16.3	+ 1.0
		Nelson, I. Ms.	LD	2,870	9.0	- 2.6
		Forrest, M.H. Ms.	Con	2,084	6.6	+ 0.8
		Sheridan, T.	TUSC	931	2.9 *	
		Orr, D.	BNP	841	2.6 *	
2005: Lab				14,671	46.2	

Glenrothes [269]

67,765	59.8	Roy, L.A.*	Lab	25,247	62.3	+10.4
		Alexander, D.	SNP	8,799	21.7	- 1.6
		Wills, H.	LD	3,108	7.7	- 5.0
		Low, S. Ms.	Con	2,922	7.2	+ 0.1
		Seunarine, K.	UKIP	425	1.0 *	- 0.1
2005: Lab				16,448	40.6	

Gloucester [270]

79,321	64.0	Graham, R.M.J.	Con	20,267	39.9		+	5.3
		Dhanda, P.S.*	Lab	17,847	35.2		-	12.4
		Hilton, J.E.	LD	9,767	19.2		+	5.6
		Smith, M.J.	UKIP	1,808	3.6	*	+	1.2
		Platt, A.A.	ED	564	1.1	*		
		Meloy, B.J.	Grn	511	1.0	*	-	0.7
2005: Lab				2,420	4.8			

Gordon [271]

73,420	66.4	Bruce, M.G.*	LD	17,575	36.0		-	9.0
		Thomson, R.G.	SNP	10,827	22.2		+	6.2
		Crockett, B.	Lab	9,811	20.1		-	0.1
		Thomson, R.	Con	9,111	18.7		+	1.0
		Edwards, S. Ms.	Grn	752	1.5	*		
		Jones, E.M. Ms.	BNP	699	1.4	*		
2005: LD				6,748	13.8			

Gosport [272]

72,816	64.5	Dinenage, C.J. Ms.	Con	24,300	51.8		+	7.0
		Hylands, R.L.	LD	9,887	21.1		+	4.5
		Giles, G.W.	Lab	7,944	16.9		-	14.5
		Rice, A.J.	UKIP	1,496	3.2	*	-	1.1
		Bennett, B.J.S.	BNP	1,004	2.1	*		
		Shaw, R.H.	ED	622	1.3	*		
		Smith, A.C.H. Ms.	Grn	573	1.2	*	-	1.7
		Smith, D.G.W.	Ind	493	1.1	*		
		Read, C.D.E.	Ind	331	0.7	*		
		Hart, B.	Ind	289	0.6	*		
2005: Con				14,413	30.7			

Gower [273]

61,696	67.5	Caton, M.P.*	Lab	16,016	38.4		-	4.0
		Davies, B.	Con	13,333	32.0		+	6.5
		Day, M.	LD	7,947	19.1		+	0.6
		Price, D.	PC	2,760	6.6		-	1.2
		Jones, A.	BNP	963	2.3	*		
		Triggs, G.W.	UKIP	652	1.6	*	-	1.6
2005: Lab				2,683	6.4			

Grantham & Stamford [274]

78,008	67.7	Boles, N.E.C.	Con	26,552	50.3	+ 3.4
		Bisnauthsing, H.	LD	11,726	22.2	+ 5.7
		Bartlett, M.F.	Lab	9,503	18.0	- 13.2
		Robinson, C.J.	BNP	2,485	4.7 *	
		Wells, A.B.	UKIP	1,604	3.0 *	- 0.2
		Horn, M.P.M.	LIND	929	1.8 *	
2005: Con				14,826	28.1	

Gravesham [275]

70,195	67.4	Holloway, A.J.H.*	Con	22,956	48.5	+ 4.8
		Smith, K.A. Ms.	Lab	13,644	28.8	- 13.4
		Arrowsmith, A.I. Ms.	LD	6,293	13.3	+ 2.6
		Clark, G.	UKIP	2,265	4.8 *	+ 2.9
		Uncles, S.T.	ED	1,005	2.1 *	
		Crawford, R.	Grn	675	1.4 *	
		Dartnell, A.S. Ms.	Ind	465	1.0 *	
2005: Con				9,312	19.7	

Great Grimsby [276]

61,229	53.8	Mitchell, A.V.*	Lab	10,777	32.7	- 14.4
		Ayling, V.C. Ms.	Con	10,063	30.5	+ 6.7
		de Freitas, A.	LD	7,388	22.4	+ 3.1
		Hudson, H.R.	UKIP	2,043	6.2	+ 2.4
		Fyfe, S.	BNP	1,517	4.6 *	+ 0.5
		Brown, E.A.	Ind	835	2.5 *	
		Howe, A.M.	PNDP	331	1.0 *	
2005: Lab				714	2.2	

Great Yarmouth [277]

70,315	61.2	Lewis, B.K.	Con	18,571	43.1	+ 5.0
		Wright, A.D.*	Lab	14,295	33.2	- 12.4
		Partridge, S.J.	LD	6,188	14.4	+ 3.3
		Baugh, A.J.	UKIP	2,066	4.8 *	+ 0.5
		Tann, B.L.	BNP	1,421	3.3 *	
		Biggart, L.P. Ms.	Grn	416	1.0 *	
		Morris, M. Ms.	LTT	100	0.2 *	
2005: Lab				4,276	9.9	

Greenwich & Woolwich [278]

65,489	62.9	Raynsford, N.*	Lab	20,262	49.2		- 3.3
		Drury, S.	Con	10,109	24.5		+ 7.0
		Lee, J.	LD	7,498	18.2		- 1.5
		Rustem, L.	BNP	1,151	2.8	*	
		Hewett, A.	Grn	1,054	2.6	*	- 1.9
		Adeleye, E.A.	Ch P	443	1.1	*	
		Wresniwiro, T.	ED	339	0.8	*	
		Kasab, O.M.	TUSC	267	0.6	*	
		Alingham, T.	Ind	65	0.2	*	
2005: Lab				10,153	24.7		

Guildford [279]

77,082	72.1	Milton, A.F. Ms.*	Con	29,618	53.3		+ 9.9
		Doughty, S.K. Ms.	LD	21,836	39.3		- 4.0
		Shand, T.J.C.	Lab	2,812	5.1		- 4.8
		Manzoor, M.	UKIP	1,021	1.8	*	+ 0.6
		Morris, J.H.	PPNV	280	0.5	*	
2005: Con				7,782	14.0		

Hackney North & Stoke Newington [280]

73,906	62.9	Abbott, D.J. Ms.*	Lab	25,553	55.0		+ 6.0
		Angus, K.	LD	11,092	23.9		+ 0.8
		Caplan, D.S.	Con	6,759	14.5		- 0.0
		Sellwood, M.W.	Grn	2,133	4.6	*	- 5.1
		Hargreaves, M. Ms.	Ch P	299	0.6	*	
		Moore, S.L. Ms.	ND	258	0.6	*	
		Knapp, K.	MRLP	182	0.4	*	
		Shaer, P.M.	Ind	96	0.2	*	
		Williams, A. Ms.	Ind	61	0.1	*	
		Pope-De-Locksley, J.	MCP	28	0.1	*	
2005: Lab				14,461	31.1		

Hackney South & Shoreditch [281]

72,841	58.8	Hillier, M. Ms.*	Lab	23,888	55.7		+ 3.0
		Raval, D.	LD	9,600	22.4		+ 1.1
		Nayyar, S.N.	Con	5,800	13.5		- 0.2
		Lane, P. Ms.	Grn	1,493	3.5	*	- 2.0
		King, M.	UKIP	651	1.5	*	
		Rae, B.	Lib	539	1.3	*	
		Williams, J.	Ch P	434	1.0	*	
		Sen, N.	DDP	202	0.5	*	
		Davies, P.M.	Comm L	110	0.3	*	
		De La Haye, D.	Ind	95	0.2	*	
		Tuckett, J.C. Ms.	Ind	26	0.1	*	
		Spinks, M.J.	Ind	20	0.0	*	
2005: Lab				14,288	33.3		

Halesowen & Rowley Regis [282]

63,693	69.0	Morris, J.G.	Con	18,115	41.2	+ 4.6
		Hayman, S. Ms.	Lab	16,092	36.6	- 9.7
		Tibbetts, P.S.	LD	6,515	14.8	+ 2.3
		Baddeley, D.	UKIP	2,824	6.4	+ 1.7
		Thompson, D.G.	Ind	433	1.0 *	
2005: Lab				2,023	4.6	

Halifax [283]

70,380	61.9	Riordan, L.J. Ms.*	Lab	16,278	37.4	- 4.5
		Allott, P.D.	Con	14,806	34.0	+ 0.9
		Wilson, E.M. Ms.	LD	8,335	19.1	+ 1.2
		Bates, T.	BNP	2,760	6.3	- 0.3
		Park, D. Ms.	IVH	722	1.7 *	
		Sangha, J.	UKIP	654	1.5 *	
2005: Lab				1,472	3.4	

Haltemprice & Howden [284]

70,254	69.4	Davis, D.M.*	Con	24,486	50.2	+ 3.2
		Neal, J.	LD	12,884	26.4	- 10.0
		Marten, D.	Lab	7,630	15.7	+ 2.2
		Cornell, J.E.	BNP	1,583	3.2 *	+ 1.6
		Robinson, J. Ms.	ED	1,485	3.0 *	
		Oakes, S. Ms.	Grn	669	1.4 *	
2005: Con				11,602	23.8	

Halton [285]

68,846	60.0	Twigg, D.*	Lab	23,843	57.7	- 5.4
		Jones, B.	Con	8,339	20.2	+ 0.3
		Harasiwka, F.	LD	5,718	13.8	- 3.2
		Taylor, A.A.	BNP	1,563	3.8 *	
		Moore, J.H.	UKIP	1,228	3.0 *	
		Craig, J.	Grn	647	1.6 *	
2005: Lab				15,504	37.5	

Hammersmith [286]

72,348	65.6	Slaughter, A.*	Lab	20,810	43.9	+ 1.5
		Bailey, S.	Con	17,261	36.4	+ 2.4
		Emmerson, M. Ms.	LD	7,567	15.9	- 3.0
		Miles, R.	Grn	696	1.5 *	- 2.6
		Crichton, V. Ms.	UKIP	551	1.2 *	+ 0.6
		Searle, J.	BNP	432	0.9 *	
		Brennan, S.	Ind	135	0.3 *	
2005: Lab				3,549	7.5	

Hampshire East [287]

72,262	71.0	Hinds, D.P.G.	Con	29,137	56.8	+	9.7
		Carew, A.S.	LD	15,640	30.5	-	3.5
		Edbrooke, A.J. Ms.	Lab	4,043	7.9	-	8.6
		McGuinness, G.H.	UKIP	1,477	2.9 *	+	0.3
		Williams, M.S.	ED	710	1.4 *		
		Jerrard, D.G.	JAC	310	0.6 *		
2005: Con				13,497	26.3		

Hampshire North East [288]

72,196	73.3	Arbuthnot, J.N.*	Con	32,075	60.6	+	7.5
		Coulson, D.	LD	13,478	25.5	-	1.6
		Jones, B.	Lab	5,173	9.8	-	6.8
		Duffin, R.L. Ms.	UKIP	2,213	4.2 *	+	0.9
2005: Con				18,597	35.1		

Hampshire North West [289]

76,695	69.5	Young, G.S.K.*	Con	31,072	58.3	+	7.8
		McCann, T.D.	LD	12,489	23.4	-	1.5
		Evans, S. Ms.	Lab	6,980	13.1	-	7.7
		Oram, S.	UKIP	2,751	5.2	+	1.4
2005: Con				18,583	34.9		

Hampstead & Kilburn [290]

80,373	65.7	Jackson, G. Ms.*	Lab	17,332	32.8	-	3.5
		Philp, C.	Con	17,290	32.7	+	9.8
		Fordham, E.	LD	16,491	31.2	-	4.0
		Campbell, B. Ms.	Grn	759	1.4 *	-	3.2
		Nielsen, M.	UKIP	408	0.8 *	+	0.1
		Moore, V. Ms.	BNP	328	0.6 *		
		Omond, T. Ms.	TOC	123	0.2 *		
		Alcantara, G.	Ind	91	0.2 *		
2005: Lab				42	0.1		

Harborough [291]

77,917	70.5	Garnier, E.H.*	Con	26,894	48.9	+	6.0
		Haq, Z.	LD	17,097	31.1	-	3.5
		McKeever, K.M.J.	Lab	6,981	12.7	-	6.6
		Dickens, G.W.	BNP	1,715	3.1 *		
		King, M.E.N. Ms.	UKIP	1,462	2.7 *	-	0.5
		Ball, D.P.	ED	568	1.0 *		
		Stephenson, J.	Ind	228	0.4 *		
2005: Con				9,797	17.8		

Harlow [292]

67,583	64.9	Halfon, R.H.	Con	19,691	44.9	+	4.1
		Rammell, W.E.*	Lab	14,766	33.7	-	7.7
		White, D.C.	LD	5,990	13.7	+	0.7
		Butler, E.M.	BNP	1,739	4.0 *		
		Croft, J.A.	UKIP	1,591	3.6 *	+	1.1
		Adeeko, O.	Ch P	101	0.2 *		
2005: Lab				4,925	11.2		

Harrogate & Knaresborough [293]

74,760	71.1	Jones, A.H.	Con	24,305	45.7	+	9.9
		Kelley, C.E. Ms.	LD	23,266	43.8	-	8.3
		McNerney, K.J.	Lab	3,413	6.4	-	2.7
		Gill, S.D.	BNP	1,094	2.1 *	+	1.1
		Upex, J.R.	UKIP	1,056	2.0 *	+	0.3
2005: LD				1,039	2.0		

Harrow East [294]

70,510	68.1	Blackman, B.	Con	21,435	44.7	+	6.1
		McNulty, T.*	Lab	18,032	37.6	-	7.9
		Boethe, N. Ms.	LD	6,850	14.3	+	0.1
		Pandya, A.P.G.	UKIP	896	1.9 *	+	0.1
		Atkins, M.C. Ms.	Grn	793	1.7 *		
2005: Lab				3,403	7.1		

Harrow West [295]

68,554	67.3	Thomas, G.*	Lab	20,111	43.6	-	5.0
		Joyce, R. Ms.	Con	16,968	36.8	+	6.4
		Noyce, C.D.	LD	7,458	16.2	-	2.5
		Crossman, H.W.	UKIP	954	2.1 *	+	0.8
		Langley, R.N.C.	Grn	625	1.4 *		
2005: Lab				3,143	6.8		

Hartlepool [296]

68,927	55.5	Wright, I.*	Lab	16,267	42.5	-	9.0
		Wright, A.	Con	10,758	28.1	+	16.7
		Clark, R.	LD	6,533	17.1	-	13.3
		Allison, S.	UKIP	2,682	7.0	+	3.5
		Bage, R.	BNP	2,002	5.2		
2005: Lab				5,509	14.4		

Harwich & Essex North [297]

70,743	69.3	Jenkin, B.C.*	Con	23,001	46.9	+ 4.3
		Raven, J.R.	LD	11,554	23.6	+ 4.3
		Barrenger, D.M.	Lab	9,774	19.9	- 10.9
		Anselmi, S.P.	UKIP	2,527	5.2	+ 1.5
		Robey, S.H.	BNP	1,065	2.2 *	
		Fox, C.J.	Grn	909	1.9 *	- 1.8
		Thompson Bates, P.M.P.	Ind	170	0.3 *	
2005: Con				11,447	23.4	

Hastings & Rye [298]

77,030	64.7	Rudd, A. Ms.	Con	20,468	41.1	+ 3.0
		Foster, M.J.*	Lab	18,475	37.1	- 3.5
		Perry, N.D.S.	LD	7,825	15.7	- 0.1
		Smith, A.B.F.	UKIP	1,397	2.8 *	+ 0.1
		Prince, N.A.P.	BNP	1,310	2.6 *	
		Bridger, R.W.	ED	339	0.7 *	
2005: Lab				1,993	4.0	

Havant [299]

69,662	63.0	Willetts, D.L.*	Con	22,433	51.1	+ 6.8
		Payton, A.C.B.	LD	10,273	23.4	+ 3.2
		Smith, R.J.	Lab	7,777	17.7	- 11.0
		Kerrin, G.J.	UKIP	2,611	5.9	+ 3.5
		Addams, F.	ED	809	1.8 *	
2005: Con				12,160	27.7	

Hayes & Harlington [300]

70,231	60.7	McDonnell, J.M.*	Lab	23,377	54.8	- 1.6
		Seaman-Digby, S.M.	Con	12,553	29.4	+ 1.7
		Khalsa, S.K. Ms.	LD	3,726	8.7	- 1.1
		Forster, C.W.C.	BNP	1,520	3.6 *	+ 1.3
		Cripps, A.M.	NF	566	1.3 *	
		Dixon, C.	ED	464	1.1 *	
		Lee, J.M. Ms.	Grn	348	0.8 *	- 0.6
		Shahzad, A.	Ch P	83	0.2 *	
2005: Lab				10,824	25.4	

Hazel Grove [301]

62,300	67.4	Stunell, A.*	LD	20,485	48.8	- 1.5
		Abercorn, A.G.	Con	14,114	33.6	+ 3.3
		Scorer, R.	Lab	5,234	12.5	- 3.6
		Whittaker, J.	UKIP	2,148	5.1	+ 1.9
2005: LD				6,371	15.2	

Hemel Hempstead [302]

72,752	68.0	Penning, M.*	Con	24,721	50.0	+ 9.9
		Grayson, R.	LD	11,315	22.9	+ 6.0
		Orhan, A. Ms.	Lab	10,295	20.8	- 18.9
		Price, J.D. Ms.	BNP	1,615	3.3 *	
		Alexander, D.J.	UKIP	1,254	2.5 *	- 0.7
		Young, M.	Ind	271	0.5 *	
2005: Con				13,406	27.1	

Hemsworth [303]

75,542	58.0	Trickett, J.H.*	Lab	20,506	46.8	- 11.9
		Myatt, A.E. Ms.	Con	10,662	24.3	+ 2.2
		Belmore, A.	LD	5,667	12.9	- 2.8
		Womersley, I.	Ind	3,946	9.0	
		Kitchen, I.A.	BNP	3,059	7.0	+ 6.8
2005: Lab				9,844	22.5	

Hendon [304]

72,943	63.6	Offord, M.J.	Con	19,635	42.3	+ 5.2
		Dismore, A.*	Lab	19,529	42.1	- 3.0
		Harris, M.F.	LD	5,734	12.4	- 1.7
		Lambert, R.	UKIP	958	2.1 *	+ 0.5
		Newby, A.J.	Grn	518	1.1 *	- 0.7
2005: Lab				106	0.2	

Henley [305]

73,123	73.2	Howell, J.M.*	Con	30,054	56.2	+ 3.0
		Crick, A.E.	LD	13,466	25.2	- 0.9
		McKenzie, R.M.	Lab	5,835	10.9	- 4.1
		Hughes, L.	UKIP	1,817	3.4 *	+ 0.9
		Stevenson, M.C.	Grn	1,328	2.5 *	- 0.8
		Bews, J.R.	BNP	1,020	1.9 *	
2005: Con				16,588	31.0	

Hereford & Herefordshire South [306]

72,021	67.2	Norman, A.J.	Con	22,366	46.2	+ 5.2
		Carr, S.J. Ms.	LD	19,885	41.1	- 2.3
		Roberts, P.L. Ms.	Lab	3,506	7.2	- 3.0
		Smith, V.J.	UKIP	1,638	3.4 *	+ 1.2
		Oliver, J.	BNP	986	2.0 *	
2005: LD				2,481	5.1	

Herefordshire North [307]

66,946	71.1	Wiggin, W.D.*	Con	24,631	51.8	- 0.7
		Hurds, L.A. Ms.	LD	14,744	31.0	+ 6.9
		Sabharwal, N.	Lab	3,373	7.1	- 8.4
		Oakton, J.P.	UKIP	2,701	5.7	+ 2.4
		Norman, F.M. Ms.	Grn	1,533	3.2 *	- 1.5
		King, E.J.	Ind	586	1.2 *	
2005: Con				9,887	20.8	

Hertford & Stortford [308]

78,459	70.6	Prisk, M.M.*	Con	29,810	53.8	+ 3.6
		Lewin, A.A.	LD	14,373	26.0	+ 7.5
		Terry, S.	Lab	7,620	13.8	-10.5
		Sodey, D.	UKIP	1,716	3.1 *	+ 1.0
		Harris, R.H.	BNP	1,297	2.3 *	
		Xenophontos, L.	Ind	325	0.6 *	
		Adams, M.P.	Ind	236	0.4 *	
2005: Con				15,437	27.9	

Hertfordshire North East [309]

72,200	69.8	Heald, O.*	Con	26,995	53.5	+ 5.5
		Annand, H.M.C.	LD	11,801	23.4	+ 3.1
		Kirkman, D.T.	Lab	8,291	16.4	-11.9
		Smyth, A.F. Ms.	UKIP	2,075	4.1 *	+ 0.8
		Bland, R.A. Ms.	Grn	875	1.7 *	
		Campbell, R.F.	Ind	209	0.4 *	
		Ralph, D.J.	YRDPL	143	0.3 *	
		Reichardt, J.P.C.	Ind	36	0.1 *	
2005: Con				15,194	30.1	

Hertfordshire South West [310]

78,248	72.5	Gauke, D.M.*	Con	30,773	54.2	+ 7.2
		Townsend, C.	LD	15,853	27.9	- 2.1
		Mann, H.	Lab	6,526	11.5	- 9.3
		Benson, M.	UKIP	1,450	2.6 *	+ 0.3
		Gates, D.A. Ms.	BNP	1,302	2.3 *	
		Hannaway, J.	Ind	846	1.5 *	
2005: Con				14,920	26.3	

Hertsmere [311]

73,057	64.7	Clappison, J.*	Con	26,476	56.0	+ 2.8
		Russell, S.	Lab	8,871	18.8	- 8.4
		Rowlands, A.F.	LD	8,210	17.4	- 1.0
		Rutter, D.	UKIP	1,712	3.6 *	
		Seabrook, D.	BNP	1,397	3.0 *	
		Krishna-Das, A.	Grn	604	1.3 *	
2005: Con				17,605	37.2	

Hexham [312]

60,360	72.0	Opperman, G.	Con	18,795	43.2	+ 0.8
		Duffield, A.	LD	13,007	29.9	+ 4.2
		Tinnion, A.	Lab	8,253	19.0	- 11.4
		Ford, S.	Ind	1,974	4.5 *	
		Hawkins, Q.J.	BNP	1,205	2.8 *	
		Moss, C.J.	Ind	249	0.6 *	
2005: Con				5,788	13.3	

Heywood & Middleton [313]

80,171	57.5	Dobbin, J.*	Lab	18,499	40.1	- 8.2
		Holly, M.C.	Con	12,528	27.2	+ 5.4
		Hobhouse, W. Ms.	LD	10,474	22.7	+ 2.5
		Greenwood, P.	BNP	3,239	7.0	+ 2.6
		Cecil, V.P.E. Ms.	UKIP	1,215	2.6 *	+ 0.7
		Lee, C.M. Ms.	Ind	170	0.4 *	
2005: Lab				5,971	12.9	

High Peak [314]

71,458	70.4	Bingham, A.R.	Con	20,587	40.9	+ 3.6
		Bisknell, C.J. Ms.	Lab	15,910	31.6	- 9.5
		Stevens, A.J.	LD	10,993	21.8	+ 2.4
		Hall, S. Ms.	UKIP	1,690	3.4 *	+ 1.2
		Allen, P.D.	Grn	922	1.8 *	
		Dowson, L.E.	Ind	161	0.3 *	
		Alves, A.J.	ND	74	0.1 *	
2005: Lab				4,677	9.3	

Hitchin & Harpenden [315]

73,851	74.1	Lilley, P.B.*	Con	29,869	54.6	+ 5.2
		Quinton, N.A.	LD	14,598	26.7	+ 0.2
		de Botton, O.T.	Lab	7,413	13.6	- 8.4
		Wilkinson, G.P.	UKIP	1,663	3.0 *	+ 1.3
		Wise, R.L.	Grn	807	1.5 *	
		Henderson, M.A. Ms.	Ind	109	0.2 *	
		Byron, S.J.	CURE	108	0.2 *	
		Hannah, E.W.	YRDPL	90	0.2 *	
		Rigby, P.E.	Ind	50	0.1 *	
2005: Con				15,271	27.9	

Holborn & St Pancras [316]

86,563	63.1	Dobson, F.*	Lab	25,198	46.1	+	1.0
		Shaw, J. Ms.	LD	15,256	27.9	+	1.8
		Lee, G.	Con	11,134	20.4	-	0.5
		Bennett, N.L. Ms.	Grn	1,480	2.7 *	-	4.8
		Carlyle, R.	BNP	779	1.4 *		
		Spencer, M.	UKIP	587	1.1 *		
		Chapman, J.	Ind	96	0.2 *		
		Susperregi, M.	ED	75	0.1 *		
		Meek, I.	Ind	44	0.1 *		
2005: Lab				9,942	18.2		

Hornchurch & Upminster [317]

78,547	68.0	Watkinson, A.E. Ms.*	Con	27,469	51.4	+	3.9
		McGuirk, K. Ms.	Lab	11,098	20.8	-	10.3
		Chilvers, K.L. Ms.	LD	7,426	13.9	+	5.4
		Whelpley, W.T.	BNP	3,421	6.4	+	1.4
		Webb, L.J.	UKIP	2,848	5.3	+	3.2
		Collins, M.J. Ms.	Grn	542	1.0 *	-	0.1
		Durant, D.W.	Ind	305	0.6 *		
		Olukotun, J.A.	Ch P	281	0.5 *		
2005: Con				16,371	30.7		

Hornsey & Wood Green [318]

78,748	69.9	Featherstone, L. Ms.*	LD	25,595	46.5	+	3.2
		Jennings, K. Ms.	Lab	18,720	34.0	-	4.3
		Merrin, R.J.	Con	9,174	16.7	+	4.0
		McAskie, P.	Grn	1,261	2.3 *	-	2.7
		De Roche, S.M.	Ind	201	0.4 *		
		Kapur, R.	Ind	91	0.2 *		
2005: LD				6,875	12.5		

Horsham [319]

77,564	72.0	Maude, F.A.A.*	Con	29,447	52.7	+	3.4
		Newman, G.	LD	17,987	32.2	+	4.5
		Skudder, A.C.	Lab	4,189	7.5	-	9.2
		Aldridge, H.C.	UKIP	2,839	5.1	+	0.4
		Fitter, N.	Grn	570	1.0 *		
		Lyon, S.	Ch P	469	0.8 *		
		Duggan, J.	PPNV	253	0.5 *		
		Kissach, D.A.	Ind	87	0.2 *		
2005: Con				11,460	20.5		

Houghton & Sunderland South [320]

68,729	55.3	Phillipson, B. Ms.	Lab	19,137	50.3	- 11.7
		Oliver, R.G.	Con	8,147	21.4	+ 5.2
		Boyle, C.P.	LD	5,292	13.9	- 0.6
		Wakefield, C.	Ind	2,462	6.5	
		Allen, K. Ms.	BNP	1,961	5.2	- 1.7
		Elvin, R.P.	UKIP	1,022	2.7 *	
2005: Lab				10,990	28.9	

Hove [321]

71,720	69.5	Weatherley, M.	Con	18,294	36.7	+ 0.3
		Barlow, C. Ms.*	Lab	16,426	33.0	- 4.5
		Elgood, P.	LD	11,240	22.6	+ 4.6
		Davey, I.A.	Grn	2,568	5.2	- 0.6
		Perrin, P.W.	UKIP	1,206	2.4 *	+ 1.1
		Ralfe, B.	Ind	85	0.2 *	
2005: Lab				1,868	3.7	

Huddersfield [322]

66,318	61.1	Sheerman, B.J.*	Lab	15,725	38.8	- 7.6
		Tweed, K. Ms.	Con	11,253	27.8	+ 6.7
		Blanchard, J.C.	LD	10,023	24.7	+ 0.6
		Cooper, A.V.	Grn	1,641	4.0 *	- 0.6
		Firth, R. Ms.	BNP	1,563	3.9 *	+ 0.9
		Cooney, P.F.	TUSC	319	0.8 *	
2005: Lab				4,472	11.0	

Hull East [323]

67,530	50.6	Turner, K.	Lab	16,387	47.9	- 8.1
		Wilcock, J.D.	LD	7,790	22.8	+ 2.6
		Mackay, C.A. Ms.	Con	5,667	16.6	+ 3.6
		Hookem, M.	UKIP	2,745	8.0	
		Uttley, J.	NF	880	2.6 *	
		Burton, M.	ED	715	2.1 *	
2005: Lab				8,597	25.1	

Hull North [324]

64,082	52.0	Johnson, D.R. Ms.*	Lab	13,044	39.2	- 13.1
		Healy, D.G.	LD	12,403	37.3	+ 11.3
		Aitken, V.A. Ms.	Con	4,365	13.1	- 0.2
		Mainprize, J.P.	BNP	1,443	4.3 *	+ 1.6
		Barlow, P.T.	UKIP	1,358	4.1 *	
		Deane, M.J.	Grn	478	1.4 *	- 1.6
		Cassidy, M.W.	ED	200	0.6 *	
2005: Lab				641	1.9	

Hull West & Hessle [325]

57,264	55.0	Johnson, A.*	Lab	13,378	42.5	- 12.6
		Ross, M.J.	LD	7,636	24.2	+ 3.2
		Shores, G.C.	Con	6,361	20.2	- 0.5
		Hordon, K.W.	UKIP	1,688	5.4	
		Scott, E.	BNP	1,416	4.5 *	
		Mawer, P.	ED	876	2.8 *	
		Gibson, K.A.	TUSC	150	0.5 *	
2005: Lab				5,742	18.2	

Huntingdon [326]

83,557	64.9	Djanogly, J.S.*	Con	26,516	48.9	- 1.9
		Land, M.G.	LD	15,697	28.9	+ 2.3
		Cox, A.J. Ms.	Lab	5,982	11.0	- 7.4
		Curtis, I.J.	UKIP	3,258	6.0	+ 1.8
		Salt, J.M.	Ind	1,432	2.6 *	
		Clare, J.D.W.	Grn	652	1.2 *	
		Jug, L.T.	MRLP	548	1.0 *	
		Holliman, C. Ms.	APP	181	0.3 *	
2005: Con				10,819	19.9	

Hyndburn [327]

67,221	63.5	Jones, G.P.	Lab	17,531	41.1	- 4.6
		Buckley, K.E. Ms.	Con	14,441	33.8	+ 1.9
		Rankine, A.	LD	5,033	11.8	- 2.6
		Shapcott, D.	BNP	2,137	5.0	- 1.2
		Barker, G.	UKIP	1,481	3.5 *	+ 1.6
		Logan, K.	CPA	795	1.9 *	
		Gormley, K. Ms.	Grn	463	1.1 *	
		Reid, C.A.	ED	413	1.0 *	
		Hall, C.I.	Ind	378	0.9 *	
2005: Lab				3,090	7.2	

Ilford North [328]

72,372	65.0	Scott, L.*	Con	21,506	45.7	+ 2.0
		Klein, S.N. Ms.	Lab	16,102	34.2	- 5.4
		Berhanu, A.	LD	5,966	12.7	- 1.1
		Warville, D.	BNP	1,545	3.3 *	
		van der Stighelen, H.	UKIP	871	1.9 *	- 0.3
		Allen, C.J. Ms.	Grn	572	1.2 *	
		Hampson, R.E.	CPA	456	1.0 *	
2005: Con				5,404	11.5	

Ilford South [329]

86,220	59.4	Gapes, M.J.*	Lab	25,301	49.4	+ 0.6
		Boutle, T.J.	Con	14,014	27.4	+ 0.1
		Al-Samerai, A. Ms.	LD	8,679	17.0	- 3.6
		Chowdhry, W.	Grn	1,319	2.6 *	
		Murray, T.P.	UKIP	1,132	2.2 *	+ 0.6
		Jestico, J.V.	SKGP	746	1.5 *	
2005: Lab				11,287	22.0	

Inverclyde [330]

59,209	63.4	Cairns, D.*	Lab	20,993	56.0	+ 5.2
		Nelson, I.	SNP	6,577	17.5	- 2.0
		Hutton, S.	LD	5,007	13.3	- 3.6
		Wilson, D.	Con	4,502	12.0	+ 1.8
		Campbell, P.P.G.	UKIP	433	1.2 *	
2005: Lab				14,416	38.4	

Inverness, Nairn, Badenoch & Strathspey [331]

72,528	64.9	Alexander, D.*	LD	19,172	40.7	+ 0.4
		Robb, M.	Lab	10,407	22.1	- 8.8
		Finnie, J.	SNP	8,803	18.7	+ 5.2
		Ferguson, J.	Con	6,278	13.3	+ 3.0
		Boyd, D.M.	Ch P	835	1.8 *	
		Macleod, D.	Grn	789	1.7 *	- 0.7
		Durance, R.S.	UKIP	574	1.2 *	
		MacDonald, G.	TUSC	135	0.3 *	
		Fraser, K.	Joy	93	0.2 *	
2005: LD				8,765	18.6	

Ipswich [332]

75,770	62.0	Gummer, B.M.	Con	18,371	39.1	+ 8.0
		Mole, C.D.*	Lab	16,292	34.7	- 8.2
		Dyson, M.H.	LD	8,556	18.2	- 2.9
		Streatfield, C.J.	UKIP	1,365	2.9 *	+ 0.2
		Boater, D.H.	BNP	1,270	2.7 *	
		Glover, T.R.	Grn	775	1.7 *	
		Christofi, K. Ms.	Ch P	149	0.3 *	
		Turtill, P.E.	Ind	93	0.2 *	
		Wainman, S. Ms.	Ind	70	0.1 *	
2005: Lab				2,079	4.4	

Isle of Wight [333]

109,922	63.9	Turner, A.J.*	Con	32,810	46.7		- 2.3
		Wareham, J.L. Ms.	LD	22,283	31.7		+ 2.2
		Chiverton, M.H.	Lab	8,169	11.6		- 5.6
		Tarrant, M.N.A.	UKIP	2,435	3.5 *		- 0.1
		Clynch, G.	BNP	1,457	2.1 *		
		Dunsire, I.M.	ED	1,233	1.8 *		
		Keats, R.J.	Grn	931	1.3 *		
		Martin, P.S.	MEP	616	0.9 *		
		Harris, P.J.	Ind	175	0.2 *		
		Randle-Jolliffe, P.D.	Ind	89	0.1 *		
		Corby, E.D.P.	Ind	66	0.1 *		
2005: Con				10,527	15.0		

Islington North [334]

68,119	65.4	Corbyn, J.B.*	Lab	24,276	54.5		+ 3.3
		Jamieson-Ball, R.I.	LD	11,875	26.7		- 3.2
		Berrill-Cox, A.L.	Con	6,339	14.2		+ 2.4
		Dixon, E.L. Ms.	Grn	1,348	3.0 *		- 4.1
		Lennon, D.J.	UKIP	716	1.6 *		
2005: Lab				12,401	27.8		

Islington South & Finsbury [335]

67,650	64.4	Thornberry, E. Ms.*	Lab	18,407	42.3		+ 2.4
		Fox, B.C. Ms.	LD	14,838	34.1		- 4.2
		Cox, A.M. Ms.	Con	8,449	19.4		+ 4.6
		Humphreys, J.W.	Grn	710	1.6 *		- 3.1
		McDonald, R. Ms.	UKIP	701	1.6 *		+ 0.1
		Dodds, J.	ED	301	0.7 *		
		Deboo, R.J.	AC	149	0.3 *		
2005: Lab				3,569	8.2		

Islwyn [336]

54,866	63.2	Evans, C.	Lab	17,069	49.2		- 15.1
		Thomas, D.	Con	4,854	14.0		+ 3.0
		Lewis, S.	PC	4,518	13.0		+ 0.6
		Ali, A.J.	LD	3,597	10.4		- 1.8
		Rees, D.	Ind	1,495	4.3 *		
		Voisey, J.R.	BNP	1,320	3.8 *		
		Crew, J.R.	UKIP	930	2.7 *		
		Taylor, P.	Ind	901	2.6 *		
2005: Lab				12,215	35.2		

Jarrow [337]

64,350	60.3	Hepburn, S.*	Lab	20,910	53.9	- 4.9
		Milburn, J.	Con	8,002	20.6	+ 7.8
		Appleby, T.	LD	7,163	18.5	- 4.0
		Swaddle, A.	BNP	2,709	7.0	
2005: Lab				12,908	33.3	

Keighley [338]

65,893	72.4	Hopkins, K.	Con	20,003	41.9	+ 7.7
		Thomas, J. Ms.	Lab	17,063	35.8	- 9.0
		Fekri, N.	LD	7,059	14.8	+ 3.0
		Brons, A.H.W.	BNP	1,962	4.1 *	- 5.0
		Latham, P.J.	UKIP	1,470	3.1 *	
		Smith, S.	NF	135	0.3 *	
2005: Lab				2,940	6.2	

Kenilworth & Southam [339]

64,362	75.2	Wright, J.P.*	Con	25,945	53.6	+ 3.2
		Rock, N.I.C.	LD	13,393	27.7	+ 5.6
		Milton, N.D.	Lab	6,949	14.3	- 11.2
		Moore, J.D.	UKIP	1,214	2.5 *	+ 0.4
		Harrison, J.N.	Grn	568	1.2 *	
		Rukin, J.	Ind	362	0.7 *	
2005: Con				12,552	25.9	

Kensington [340]

65,975	53.3	Rifkind, M.L.*	Con	17,595	50.1	+ 6.2
		Gurney, S.	Lab	8,979	25.5	- 4.1
		Meltzer, R.M.	LD	6,872	19.6	- 0.6
		Pearson, C. Ms.	UKIP	754	2.1 *	+ 1.0
		Ebrahimi-Fardouee, Z. Ms.	Grn	753	2.1 *	- 2.4
		Adams, E.	AGS	197	0.6 *	
2005: Con				8,616	24.5	

Kettering [341]

68,824	68.8	Hollobone, P.T.*	Con	23,247	49.1	+ 6.2
		Sawford, P.A.	Lab	14,153	29.9	- 12.7
		Nelson, C.R.	LD	7,498	15.8	+ 3.6
		Skinner, C.R.	BNP	1,366	2.9 *	
		Hilling, D.	ED	952	2.0 *	
		Bishop, D.L.	BP Elvis	112	0.2 *	
2005: Con				9,094	19.2	

Kilmarnock & Loudoun [342]

74,131	62.8	Jamieson, C. Ms.*	Lab	24,460	52.5	+ 5.3
		Leslie, G.	SNP	12,082	26.0	- 1.7
		McAlpine, J. Ms.	Con	6,592	14.2	+ 2.8
		Tombs, S.M.	LD	3,419	7.3	- 3.8
2005: Lab				12,378	26.6	

Kingston & Surbiton [343]

81,115	70.4	Davey, E.J.*	LD	28,428	49.8	- 1.3
		Whately, H.O.B. Ms.	Con	20,868	36.5	+ 3.5
		Freedman, M.O.	Lab	5,337	9.3	- 3.8
		Greensted, J.J.P.	UKIP	1,450	2.5 *	+ 1.2
		Walker, C.J.	Grn	555	1.0 *	
		Pope, P.R.	MRLP	247	0.4 *	
		May, A.J.	CPA	226	0.4 *	
2005: LD				7,560	13.2	

Kingswood [344]

66,361	72.2	Skidmore, C.	Con	19,362	40.4	+ 8.3
		Berry, R.L.*	Lab	16,917	35.3	- 10.6
		Fitzharris, S.A. Ms.	LD	8,072	16.8	- 1.2
		Dowdney, N.F.	UKIP	1,528	3.2 *	+ 0.8
		Carey, M.J.	BNP	1,311	2.7 *	
		Foster, N.	Grn	383	0.8 *	
		Blundell, M.	ED	333	0.7 *	
2005: Lab				2,445	5.1	

Kirkcaldy & Cowdenbeath [345]

73,534	62.3	Brown, G.*	Lab	29,559	64.5	+ 6.4
		Chapman, D.	SNP	6,550	14.3	- 0.2
		Mainland, J.	LD	4,269	9.3	- 3.7
		Paterson, L. Ms.	Con	4,258	9.3	- 1.0
		Adams, P.	UKIP	760	1.7 *	+ 0.4
		Archibald, S. Ms.	Ind	184	0.4 *	
		MacLaren of MacLaren, D.	Ind	165	0.4 *	
		Jackson, D.L.	Land	57	0.1 *	
2005: Lab				23,009	50.2	

Knowsley [346]

79,564	56.1	Howarth, G.E.*	Lab	31,650	70.9	- 0.9
		Clucas, H.F. Ms.	LD	5,964	13.4	- 0.4
		Dunne, D.J.	Con	4,004	9.0	- 2.3
		Greenhalgh, S.	BNP	1,895	4.2 *	+ 2.2
		Rundle, A.J.	UKIP	1,145	2.6 *	
2005: Lab				25,686	57.5	

Lagan Valley [347]

65,257	56.0	Donaldson, J.*	DUP	18,199	49.8	- 8.5
		Trimble, D. Ms.	UCUNF	7,713	21.1	
		Lunn, T.	APNI	4,174	11.4	
		Harbinson, K.	TUV	3,154	8.6	
		Heading, B.	SDLP	1,835	5.0	+ 1.5
		Butler, P.	SF	1,465	4.0 *	- 0.3
2005: DUP				10,486	28.7	

Lanark & Hamilton East [348]

74,773	62.3	Hood, J.*	Lab	23,258	50.0	+ 3.9
		Adamson, C. Ms.	SNP	9,780	21.0	+ 3.2
		McGavigan, C.	Con	6,981	15.0	+ 2.2
		Herbison, D.	LD	5,249	11.3	- 7.4
		McFarlane, D.M.	Ind	670	1.4 *	
		Sale, R.	UKIP	616	1.3 *	+ 0.3
2005: Lab				13,478	29.0	

Lancashire West [349]

73,835	65.7	Cooper, R.E. Ms.*	Lab	21,883	45.1	- 2.9
		Owens, A.E.	Con	17,540	36.2	+ 2.2
		Gibson, J.P.R.	LD	6,573	13.6	- 0.5
		Noone, D.E.	UKIP	1,775	3.7 *	+ 1.6
		Cranie, P.A.	Grn	485	1.0 *	
		Braid, D.O.	C28	217	0.4 *	
2005: Lab				4,343	9.0	

Lancaster & Fleetwood [350]

67,379	63.4	Ollerenshaw, E.	Con	15,404	36.1	+ 2.5
		Grunshaw, C.	Lab	15,071	35.3	- 7.1
		Langhorn, S.	LD	8,167	19.1	+ 3.5
		Dowding, G. Ms.	Grn	1,888	4.4 *	- 1.4
		McGlade, F.	UKIP	1,020	2.4 *	- 0.1
		Kent, D. Ms.	BNP	938	2.2 *	
		Riley, K.	Ind	213	0.5 *	
2005: Lab				333	0.8	

Leeds Central [351]

81,266	46.0	Benn, H.J.*	Lab	18,434	49.3	- 10.2
		Taylor, M.	LD	7,789	20.8	- 0.7
		Lamb, A.J.	Con	7,541	20.2	+ 7.5
		Meeson, K.	BNP	3,066	8.2	+ 4.7
		Procter, D.	Ind	409	1.1 *	
		One-Nil, W.	ND	155	0.4 *	
2005: Lab				10,645	28.5	

Leeds East [352]

64,698	58.4	Mudie, G.*	Lab	19,056	50.4	- 9.4
		Anderson, B.J.	Con	8,763	23.2	+ 1.6
		Tear, A.P.	LD	6,618	17.5	+ 0.3
		Brown, T.D.	BNP	2,947	7.8	
		Davies, M.F.	AGS	429	1.1 *	
2005: Lab				10,293	27.2	

Leeds North East [353]

67,899	70.0	Hamilton, F.*	Lab	20,287	42.7	- 3.0
		Lobley, M.	Con	15,742	33.1	+ 2.9
		Choudhry, A. Ms.	LD	9,310	19.6	- 2.1
		Hendon, W.	UKIP	842	1.8 *	
		Redmond, T.	BNP	758	1.6 *	
		Foote, C.E. Ms.	AGS	596	1.3 *	
2005: Lab				4,545	9.6	

Leeds North West [354]

65,399	66.5	Mulholland, G.*	LD	20,653	47.5	+ 10.6
		Mulligan, J. Ms.	Con	11,550	26.6	- 0.3
		Blake, J. Ms.	Lab	9,132	21.0	- 10.9
		Bulmer, G.J.	BNP	766	1.8 *	
		Thackray, M.A.	UKIP	600	1.4 *	
		Hemingway, M.F.	Grn	508	1.2 *	- 1.5
		Procter, A.	ED	153	0.4 *	
		Bavage, T.A.J.	AGS	121	0.3 *	
2005: LD				9,103	20.9	

Leeds West [355]

67,453	57.5	Reeves, R.J. Ms.	Lab	16,389	42.3	- 13.9
		Coleman, R. Ms.	LD	9,373	24.2	+ 6.8
		Marjoram, J.W.	Con	7,641	19.7	+ 5.6
		Beverley, J. Ms.	BNP	2,377	6.1	+ 2.8
		Blackburn, D.	Grn	1,832	4.7 *	- 2.5
		Miles, J.	UKIP	1,140	2.9 *	+ 1.1
2005: Lab				7,016	18.1	

Leicester East [356]

72,986	65.8	Vaz, K.*	Lab	25,804	53.8	- 5.0
		Hunt, J.M. Ms.	Con	11,722	24.4	+ 4.6
		Asghar, A.	LD	6,817	14.2	- 2.3
		Gilmore, C.R.	BNP	1,700	3.5 *	
		Taylor, M. Ms.	Grn	733	1.5 *	
		Ransome, F.E.E. Ms.	UKIP	725	1.5 *	
		Sadiq, A.	UPS	494	1.0 *	
2005: Lab				14,082	29.3	

Leicester South [357]

77,175	61.1	Soulsby, P.A.*	Lab	21,479	45.6	+ 6.2
		Gill, P.S.	LD	12,671	26.9	- 3.7
		Grant, R.I.	Con	10,066	21.4	+ 3.6
		Waudby, A.	BNP	1,418	3.0 *	
		Dixey, D.	Grn	770	1.6 *	- 1.6
		Lucas, C.J.	UKIP	720	1.5 *	
2005: Lab				8,808	18.7	

Leicester West [358]

64,900	55.2	Kendall, L. Ms.	Lab	13,745	38.4	- 12.4
		Harvey, C.J. Ms.	Con	9,728	27.2	+ 2.8
		Coley, P.	LD	8,107	22.6	+ 4.4
		Reynolds, G.	BNP	2,158	6.0	
		Ingall, S.M.	UKIP	883	2.5 *	
		Forse, G.	Grn	639	1.8 *	- 3.0
		Huggins, S.	Ind	181	0.5 *	
		Score, S.	TUSC	157	0.4 *	
		Dyer, S.	Pirate	113	0.3 *	
		Bowley, D.J.	Ind	108	0.3 *	
2005: Lab				4,017	11.2	

Leicestershire North West [359]

71,217	72.9	Bridgen, A.	Con	23,147	44.6	+ 8.6
		Willmott, R.	Lab	15,636	30.1	- 15.4
		Reynolds, P.	LD	8,639	16.6	+ 4.6
		Meller, I.	BNP	3,396	6.5	+ 3.4
		Green, M.	UKIP	1,134	2.2 *	- 1.1
2005: Lab				7,511	14.5	

Leicestershire South [360]

76,633	71.2	Robathan, A.R.G.*	Con	27,000	49.5	+ 4.1
		Ayesh, A.S.S.	LD	11,476	21.0	+ 2.0
		Gimson, S.L. Ms.	Lab	11,392	20.9	- 8.8
		Preston, P.M.	BNP	2,721	5.0 *	+ 1.5
		Williams, J.G.	UKIP	1,988	3.6 *	+ 1.2
2005: Con				15,524	28.4	

Leigh [361]

75,903	58.4	Burnham, A.M.*	Lab	21,295	48.0	- 9.8
		Awan, S. Ms.	Con	9,284	20.9	+ 4.5
		Blackburn, C.G.A.	LD	8,049	18.2	- 0.9
		Chadwick, G.C.	BNP	2,724	6.1	
		Lavelle, M.T. Ms.	UKIP	1,535	3.5 *	
		Bradbury, N.A.	Ind	988	2.2 *	
		Dainty, T.	Ind	320	0.7 *	
		Hessell, R.G.	Ch P	137	0.3 *	
2005: Lab				12,011	27.1	

Lewes [362]

68,708	72.9	Baker, N.J.*	LD	26,048	52.0	+ 0.5
		Sugarman, J.A.	Con	18,401	36.7	+ 2.1
		Koundarjian, H.	Lab	2,508	5.0	- 4.3
		Charlton, P.A.	UKIP	1,728	3.4 *	+ 1.2
		Murray, S.J. Ms.	Grn	729	1.5 *	- 0.8
		Lloyd, D.R.	BNP	594	1.2 *	
		Soucek, O.	Ind	80	0.2 *	
2005: LD				7,647	15.3	

Lewisham Deptford [363]

67,058	61.5	Ruddock, J. Ms.*	Lab	22,132	53.7	- 1.7
		Langley, T.E. Ms.	LD	9,633	23.4	+ 5.4
		Townsend, G.R. Ms.	Con	5,551	13.5	+ 0.8
		Johnson, D.P.	Grn	2,772	6.7	- 3.3
		Page, I.G.	Soc Alt	645	1.6 *	
		Martin, M.K.	CPA	487	1.2 *	
2005: Lab				12,499	30.3	

Lewisham East [364]

65,926	63.3	Alexander, H. Ms.	Lab	17,966	43.1	- 4.6
		Pattisson, P.	LD	11,750	28.2	+ 8.3
		Clamp, J.C.W.	Con	9,850	23.6	- 0.7
		Reed, R.A.	UKIP	771	1.8 *	- 0.4
		Cotterell, P.M. Ms.	Grn	624	1.5 *	- 2.7
		Rose, J.H.S.	ED	426	1.0 *	
		Hallam, R.G.	CNPG	332	0.8 *	
2005: Lab				6,216	14.9	

Lewisham West & Penge [365]

69,022	65.2	Dowd, J.P.*	Lab	18,501	41.1	- 5.2
		Feakes, A.D.	LD	12,673	28.1	+ 1.0
		Phillips, C.W.S.	Con	11,489	25.5	+ 3.9
		Staveley, P.	UKIP	1,117	2.5 *	- 0.1
		Phoenix, R.A.G. Ms.	Grn	931	2.1 *	- 0.3
		Hammond, S.C.	CPA	317	0.7 *	
2005: Lab				5,828	12.9	

Leyton & Wanstead [366]

63,541	63.2	Cryer, J.R.	Lab	17,511	43.6	- 2.2
		Qureshi, F.	LD	11,095	27.6	+ 2.9
		Northover, E.	Con	8,928	22.2	- 0.5
		Wood, G.R.	UKIP	1,080	2.7 *	+ 0.9
		Gunstock, A.	Grn	562	1.4 *	- 3.0
		Clift, J.	BNP	561	1.4 *	
		Bhatti, S.K. Ms.	Ch P	342	0.9 *	
		Levin, M.	IFED	80	0.2 *	
2005: Lab				6,416	16.0	

Lichfield [367]

72,586	71.0	Fabricant, M.L.D.*	Con	28,048	54.4	+ 5.7
		Jackson, I.A.	LD	10,365	20.1	+ 4.2
		Hyden, S.	Lab	10,230	19.8	- 12.4
		Maunder, K. Ms.	UKIP	2,920	5.7	+ 2.4
2005: Con				17,683	34.3	

Lincoln [368]

73,540	62.2	McCartney, K.I.	Con	17,163	37.5	+ 3.3
		Merron, G.J. Ms.*	Lab	16,105	35.2	- 8.5
		Shore, R.	LD	9,256	20.2	+ 1.9
		West, R.M.B.	BNP	1,367	3.0 *	
		Smith, N.	UKIP	1,004	2.2 *	- 1.5
		Coleman, E.C.	ED	604	1.3 *	
		Walker, G.R.	Ind	222	0.5 *	
2005: Lab				1,058	2.3	

Linlithgow & Falkirk East [369]

80,907	63.6	Connarty, M.*	Lab	25,634	49.8	+ 2.1
		Smith, T.	SNP	13,081	25.4	+ 1.9
		Glenn, S.	LD	6,589	12.8	- 2.5
		Stephenson, A. Ms.	Con	6,146	11.9	+ 0.1
2005: Lab				12,553	24.4	

Liverpool Riverside [370]

74,539	52.1	Ellman, L. Ms.*	Lab	22,998	59.3	+ 0.0
		Marbrow, R.	LD	8,825	22.7	- 0.6
		Wu, K. Ms.	Con	4,243	10.9	+ 1.9
		Crone, T.M.	Grn	1,355	3.5 *	- 1.7
		Stafford, P.J.	BNP	706	1.8 *	
		Gaskell, P. Ms.	UKIP	674	1.7 *	+ 0.1
2005: Lab				14,173	36.5	

Liverpool Walton [371]

62,612	54.8	Rotheram, S.	Lab	24,709	72.0	+ 0.2
		Moloney, P.	LD	4,891	14.2	- 2.7
		Marsden, A.	Con	2,241	6.5	+ 0.1
		Stafford, P.	BNP	1,104	3.2 *	
		Nugent, J.	UKIP	898	2.6 *	- 0.7
		Manwell, J.D.	CPA	297	0.9 *	
		Ireland, D.A.	TUSC	195	0.6 *	
2005: Lab				19,818	57.7	

Liverpool Wavertree [372]

62,518	60.6	Berger, L.C. Ms.	Lab	20,132	53.1	+	3.6
		Eldridge, C.W.	LD	12,965	34.2	-	6.4
		Garnett, A.D.	Con	2,830	7.5	+	1.0
		Miney, N.L.	UKIP	890	2.3 *	+	0.4
		Lawson, R. Ms.	Grn	598	1.6 *		
		Singleton, K. Ms.	Soc Lab	200	0.5 *		
		McEllenborough, S.	BNP	150	0.4 *		
		Dunne, F.	Ind	149	0.4 *		
2005: Lab				7,167	18.9		

Liverpool West Derby [373]

63,082	56.7	Twigg, S.	Lab	22,953	64.1	+	3.6
		Twigger, P.	LD	4,486	12.5	-	2.7
		Radford, S.	Lib	3,327	9.3		
		Hall, P.T. Ms.	Con	3,311	9.3	+	1.0
		Jones, H.J. Ms.	UKIP	1,093	3.1 *	+	1.1
		Andersen, K.	Soc Lab	614	1.7 *		
2005: Lab				18,467	51.6		

Livingston [374]

75,924	63.1	Morrice, G.	Lab	23,215	48.5	-	2.6
		Bardell, L. Ms.	SNP	12,424	25.9	+	4.4
		Dundas, C.	LD	5,316	11.1	-	4.3
		Adamson-Ross, A. Ms.	Con	5,158	10.8	+	0.6
		Orr, D.	BNP	960	2.0 *		
		Forrest, A.	UKIP	443	0.9 *		
		Hendry, A.	SSP	242	0.5 *	-	1.3
		Slavin, J.	Ind	149	0.3 *		
2005: Lab				10,791	22.5		

Llanelli [375]

55,637	67.3	Griffith, N. Ms.*	Lab	15,916	42.5	-	4.5
		Davies, M. Ms.	PC	11,215	29.9	+	3.5
		Salmon, C.	Con	5,381	14.4	+	0.7
		Edwards, O.M.	LD	3,902	10.4	-	2.5
		Marshall, A.I.	UKIP	1,047	2.8 *		
2005: Lab				4,701	12.5		

Londonderry East [376]

63,220	55.3	Campbell, G.*	DUP	12,097	34.6	-	6.3
		O hOisin, C.J.M.	SF	6,742	19.3	+	1.9
		Macaulay, L.A. Ms.	UCUNF	6,218	17.8		
		Conway, T.	SDLP	5,399	15.4	-	3.9
		Ross, W.	TUV	2,572	7.4		
		Fitzpatrick, B.	APNI	1,922	5.5		
2005: DUP				5,355	15.3		

Loughborough [377]

77,505	68.2	Morgan, N.A. Ms.	Con	21,971	41.6	+	4.3
		Reed, A.J.*	Lab	18,227	34.5	-	6.7
		Willis, M.J.	LD	9,675	18.3	+	0.4
		Stafford, K.	BNP	2,040	3.9 *		
		Foden, J.B.	UKIP	925	1.8 *	-	0.6
2005: Lab				3,744	7.1		

Louth & Horncastle [378]

77,650	65.0	Tapsell, P.H.B.*	Con	25,065	49.6	+	3.2
		Martin, F.M. Ms.	LD	11,194	22.2	+	1.6
		Mountain, P.W.	Lab	8,760	17.3	-	8.0
		Green, J.L. Ms.	BNP	2,199	4.4 *		
		Nurse, P.M. Ms.	UKIP	2,183	4.3 *	-	3.4
		Simpson, D.A.	LIND	576	1.1 *		
		Mair, C.E.D.	ED	517	1.0 *		
2005: Con				13,871	27.5		

Ludlow [379]

66,632	73.1	Dunne, P.M.*	Con	25,720	52.8	+	7.7
		Kidd, H.M. Ms.	LD	15,971	32.8	-	7.9
		Hunt, A.J.	Lab	3,272	6.7	-	4.0
		Gill, C.J.F.	UKIP	2,127	4.4 *	+	2.7
		Evans, C. Ms.	BNP	1,016	2.1 *		
		Morrish, J.M. Ms.	Grn	447	0.9 *	-	0.9
		Powell, A.J.	MRLP	179	0.4 *		
2005: Con				9,749	20.0		

Luton North [380]

65,645	65.5	Hopkins, K.*	Lab	21,192	49.3	+	0.7
		Brier, J.M.	Con	13,672	31.8	-	0.4
		Martins, R.	LD	4,784	11.1	-	4.5
		Brown, C.D.	UKIP	1,564	3.6 *	+	0.4
		Rose, S. Ms.	BNP	1,316	3.1 *		
		Hall, S.	Grn	490	1.1 *		
2005: Lab				7,520	17.5		

Luton South [381]

65,219	64.7	Shuker, G.	Lab	14,725	34.9	- 7.9
		Huddleston, N.P.	Con	12,396	29.4	+ 1.3
		Hussain, Q.	LD	9,567	22.7	+ 0.1
		Rantzen, E. Ms.	Ind	1,872	4.4 *	
		Blakey, T.	BNP	1,299	3.1 *	
		Lawman, C.S.	UKIP	975	2.3 *	- 0.1
		Rhodes, S.	Ind	463	1.1 *	
		Scheimann, M.	Grn	366	0.9 *	- 1.2
		Hall, J.	Ind	264	0.6 *	
		Choudhury, F.	Ind	130	0.3 *	
		Lathwell, S.P.	Ind	84	0.2 *	
		Sweeney, F.	WRP	75	0.2 *	
2005: Lab				2,329	5.5	

Macclesfield [382]

75,370	66.4	Rutley, D.H.	Con	23,503	47.0	- 2.7
		Barlow, R.J.	LD	11,544	23.1	+ 3.5
		Heald, A.	Lab	10,164	20.3	- 8.7
		Murphy, B.	MACI	2,590	5.2	
		Smith, J.M. Ms.	UKIP	1,418	2.8 *	
		Knight, J.A.	Grn	840	1.7 *	
2005: Con				11,959	23.9	

Maidenhead [383]

72,844	73.7	May, T.M. Ms.*	Con	31,937	59.5	+ 7.6
		Hill, A.C.	LD	15,168	28.2	- 8.0
		McDonald, P.S.	Lab	3,795	7.1	- 2.1
		Wight, K.J.	UKIP	1,243	2.3 *	+ 0.9
		Rait, T.S.	BNP	825	1.5 *	+ 0.1
		Forbes, P.M.	Grn	482	0.9 *	
		Prior, P.H.	FFR	270	0.5 *	
2005: Con				16,769	31.2	

Maidstone & The Weald [384]

71,041	68.9	Grant, H. Ms.	Con	23,491	48.0	- 3.8
		Carroll, P.	LD	17,602	36.0	+ 13.2
		Seeruthun, R.	Lab	4,769	9.7	- 12.6
		Kendall, G.A.	UKIP	1,637	3.3 *	+ 0.3
		Jeffery, S.R.	Grn	655	1.3 *	
		Butler, G.	NF	643	1.3 *	
		Simmonds, H.A. Ms.	Ch P	131	0.3 *	
2005: Con				5,889	12.0	

Makerfield [385]

73,813	59.3	Fovargue, Y.H. Ms.	Lab	20,700	47.3	- 14.8
		Ali, I. Ms.	Con	8,210	18.8	+ 5.2
		Crowther, D.	LD	7,082	16.2	+ 4.8
		Brierley, R.	Ind	3,424	7.8	
		Haslam, K.	BNP	3,229	7.4	+ 4.1
		Mather, J.M.	Ind	1,126	2.6 *	
2005: Lab				12,490	28.5	

Maldon [386]

68,777	69.6	Whittingdale, J.F.L.*	Con	28,661	59.8	+ 3.5
		Tealby-Watson, E.D.S. Ms.	LD	9,254	19.3	+ 4.3
		Nandanwar, S.D.	Lab	6,070	12.7	- 11.5
		Pryke, J.C.	UKIP	2,446	5.1	+ 0.6
		Blain, L.K.	BNP	1,464	3.1 *	
2005: Con				19,407	40.5	

Manchester Central [387]

90,110	44.3	Lloyd, T.*	Lab	21,059	52.7	- 6.6
		Ramsbottom, M.S.	LD	10,620	26.6	+ 5.6
		Rahuja, S.	Con	4,704	11.8	+ 1.3
		Trebilcock, T.	BNP	1,636	4.1 *	
		O'Donovan, G. Ms.	Grn	915	2.3 *	- 1.9
		Weatherill, N. Ms.	UKIP	607	1.5 *	- 0.3
		Sinclair, R.	Soc Lab	153	0.4 *	
		Cartwright, J.	Ind	120	0.3 *	
		Leff, J.	WRP	59	0.1 *	
		Skelton, R.	SEP	54	0.1 *	
2005: Lab				10,439	26.1	

Manchester Gorton [388]

75,933	50.5	Kaufman, G.B.*	Lab	19,211	50.1	- 3.0
		Afzal, Q.	LD	12,508	32.6	- 0.9
		Healy, C.F. Ms.	Con	4,224	11.0	+ 1.2
		Hall, J. Ms.	Grn	1,048	2.7 *	
		Zulfikar, M.	Respect	507	1.3 *	
		Reissmann, K.J. Ms.	TUSC	337	0.9 *	
		Harrison, P.	Ch P	254	0.7 *	
		Dobson, T.	Pirate	236	0.6 *	
2005: Lab				6,703	17.5	

Manchester Withington [389]

74,371	60.5	Leech, J.*	LD	20,110	44.7	+ 2.4
		Powell, L. Ms.	Lab	18,216	40.5	- 0.4
		Green, C.J.	Con	5,005	11.1	+ 0.8
		Candeland, B.	Grn	798	1.8 *	- 2.5
		Gutfreund-Walmsley, R.	UKIP	698	1.6 *	+ 0.4
		Zalzala, Y. Ms.	Ind	147	0.3 *	
		Farmer, M.	Ind	57	0.1 *	
2005: LD				1,894	4.2	

Mansfield [390]

80,069	60.4	Meale, J.A.*	Lab	18,753	38.7	- 11.4
		Critchlow, T. Ms.	Con	12,741	26.3	+ 7.6
		Wyatt, M.B.	LD	7,469	15.4	+ 1.4
		Camilleri, A.P.	MIF	4,339	9.0	
		Hamilton, D.	UKIP	2,985	6.2	
		Hill, R.E. Ms.	BNP	2,108	4.4 *	
2005: Lab				6,012	12.4	

Meon Valley [391]

70,488	72.7	Hollingbery, G.	Con	28,818	56.2	+ 10.4
		Leffman, L. Ms.	LD	16,693	32.6	- 8.4
		Linsley, H.J.	Lab	3,266	6.4	- 4.2
		Harris, S.A.	UKIP	1,490	2.9 *	+ 0.4
		Harris, P.	ED	582	1.1 *	
		Coats, S.N.A. Ms.	APP	255	0.5 *	
		Quar, G.B.	Ind	134	0.3 *	
2005: Con				12,125	23.7	

Meriden [392]

82,228	63.4	Spelman, C.A. Ms.*	Con	26,956	51.7	+ 4.0
		Williams, E.M.	Lab	10,703	20.5	- 11.7
		Slater, S.C.	LD	9,278	17.8	+ 1.0
		O'Brien, S.F.	BNP	2,511	4.8 *	
		Allcock, B.S.	UKIP	1,378	2.6 *	- 0.7
		Stanton, E.C.R. Ms.	Grn	678	1.3 *	
		Sinclaire, N. Ms.	SMRA	658	1.3 *	
2005: Con				16,253	31.2	

Merthyr Tydfil & Rhymney [393]

54,715	58.6	Havard, D.*	Lab	14,007	43.7	- 16.8
		Kitcher, A. Ms.	LD	9,951	31.0	+ 17.0
		Hill, M. Ms.	Con	2,412	7.5	- 1.4
		Tovey, C.	Ind	1,845	5.8	
		Jones, G.C.	PC	1,621	5.1	- 4.9
		Barnes, R.	BNP	1,173	3.7 *	
		Brown, A.	UKIP	872	2.7 *	+ 0.4
		Cowdell, A.B.	Soc Lab	195	0.6 *	
2005: Lab				4,056	12.6	

Middlesbrough [394]

65,148	51.4	Bell, S.*	Lab	15,351	45.9	- 11.7
		Foote-Wood, C.	LD	6,662	19.9	+ 1.2
		Walsh, J.P.P.	Con	6,283	18.8	+ 2.3
		McTigue, J. Ms.	Ind	1,969	5.9	
		Ferguson, M.S.	BNP	1,954	5.8	+ 3.3
		Parker, R.	UKIP	1,236	3.7 *	+ 1.3
2005: Lab				8,689	26.0	

Middlesbrough South & Cleveland East [395]

72,666	63.6	Blenkinsop, T.F.	Lab	18,138	39.2	- 11.1
		Bristow, P.	Con	16,461	35.6	+ 3.8
		Emmerson, N.P.	LD	7,340	15.9	+ 2.1
		Lightwing, S.W.	UKIP	1,881	4.1 *	+ 2.6
		Gatley, S.	BNP	1,576	3.4 *	+ 0.9
		Allen, M.J.	Ind	818	1.8 *	
2005: Lab				1,677	3.6	

Midlothian [396]

61,387	63.9	Hamilton, D.*	Lab	18,449	47.0	+ 1.5
		Beattie, C.	SNP	8,100	20.6	+ 3.7
		Laird, R.	LD	6,711	17.1	- 9.1
		Callander, J.E.	Con	4,661	11.9	+ 2.5
		Baxter, I.G.	Grn	595	1.5 *	
		Norrie, G.	UKIP	364	0.9 *	
		McCleery, G.	Ind	196	0.5 *	
		Duncan, W.C.	TUSC	166	0.4 *	
2005: Lab				10,349	26.4	

Milton Keynes North [397]

82,432	65.4	Lancaster, J.M.*	Con	23,419	43.5	+ 7.3
		Pakes, A.E.	Lab	14,458	26.8	- 11.1
		Hope, J.S. Ms.	LD	11,894	22.1	+ 1.4
		Phillips, M.S.	UKIP	1,772	3.3 *	+ 0.5
		Hamilton, R.J.M.	BNP	1,154	2.1 *	
		Francis, A.H.	Grn	733	1.4 *	- 0.8
		Lennon, J.F.	CPA	206	0.4 *	
		Fensome, M.	MRLP	157	0.3 *	
		Vyas, A.M.	Ind	95	0.2 *	
2005: Lab				8,961	16.6	

Milton Keynes South [398]

86,559	63.9	Stewart, I.A.	Con	23,034	41.6	+ 3.9
		Starkey, P.M. Ms.*	Lab	17,833	32.2	- 8.6
		Jones, P.M.	LD	9,787	17.7	+ 2.5
		Pinto, J.F.A.	UKIP	2,074	3.7 *	+ 0.2
		Tait, M.R.J.	BNP	1,502	2.7 *	
		Deacon, K.J. Ms.	Grn	774	1.4 *	- 1.3
		Nti, S.M. Ms.	CPA	245	0.4 *	
		Worth, J.P.	NFP	84	0.2 *	
2005: Lab				5,201	9.4	

Mitcham & Morden [399]

65,939	66.4	McDonagh, S.A. Ms.*	Lab	24,722	56.4	- 0.3
		Hampton, M.C.A. Ms.	Con	11,056	25.2	+ 0.6
		Coman, L.D. Ms.	LD	5,202	11.9	- 2.1
		Martin, T.L.	BNP	1,386	3.2 *	
		Mills, A.T.	UKIP	857	2.0 *	
		Roy, S.	Grn	381	0.9 *	- 2.6
		Alagaratnam, R. Ms.	Ind	155	0.4 *	
		Redgrave, E.A.	Ind	38	0.1 *	
2005: Lab				13,666	31.2	

Mole Valley [400]

72,297	75.1	Beresford, P.*	Con	31,263	57.5	+ 2.8
		Humphreys, A. Ms.	LD	15,610	28.7	- 1.7
		Dove, J.F.	Lab	3,804	7.0	- 3.7
		Jones, L.	UKIP	2,752	5.1	+ 2.1
		Sedgwick, R.P.	Grn	895	1.6 *	
2005: Con				15,653	28.8	

Monmouth [401]

64,538	72.1	Davies, D.T.C.*	Con	22,466	48.3	+ 1.4
		Sandison, H.R.	Lab	12,041	25.9	- 11.1
		Blakebrough, M.O.	LD	9,026	19.4	+ 6.6
		Clark, J.T.	PC	1,273	2.7 *	+ 0.6
		Rowe, D.J.	UKIP	1,126	2.4 *	+ 1.2
		Millson, S.	Grn	587	1.3 *	
2005: Con				10,425	22.4	

Montgomeryshire [402]

48,730	69.4	Davies, G.	Con	13,976	41.3	+ 13.8
		Opik, L.*	LD	12,792	37.8	- 12.5
		Fychan, H. Ms.	PC	2,802	8.3	+ 1.3
		Colbourne, N.	Lab	2,407	7.1	- 5.2
		Rowlands, D.W.L.	UKIP	1,128	3.3 *	+ 0.4
		Ellis, M.	NF	384	1.1 *	
		Lawson, B.	Ind	324	1.0 *	
2005: LD				1,184	3.5	

Moray [403]

65,925	62.2	Robertson, A.S.C.*	SNP	16,273	39.7	+ 3.1
		Ross, D.G.	Con	10,683	26.1	+ 4.1
		Green, K.R.N.	Lab	7,007	17.1	- 3.3
		Paterson, J.	LD	5,956	14.5	- 4.7
		Gatt, D.	UKIP	1,085	2.6 *	
2005: SNP				5,590	13.6	

Morecambe & Lunesdale [404]

69,576	62.4	Morris, D.	Con	18,035	41.5	+ 4.2
		Smith, G. Ms.*	Lab	17,169	39.5	- 9.5
		Jones, L.	LD	5,791	13.3	- 0.3
		Knight, M.A.	UKIP	1,843	4.2 *	
		Coates, C.	Grn	598	1.4 *	
2005: Lab				866	2.0	

Morley & Outwood [405]

74,891	65.2	Balls, E.*	Lab	18,365	37.6	- 8.4
		Calvert, A.J.	Con	17,264	35.3	+ 10.3
		Monaghan, J.	LD	8,186	16.8	+ 6.7
		Beverley, C.	BNP	3,535	7.2	- 0.6
		Daniel, D.	UKIP	1,506	3.1 *	
2005: Lab				1,101	2.3	

Motherwell & Wishaw [406]

66,918	58.5	Roy, F.*	Lab	23,910	61.1		+	3.6
		Fellows, M. Ms.	SNP	7,104	18.2		+	1.7
		Douglas, S.	LD	3,840	9.8		-	2.2
		Gilroy, P. Ms.	Con	3,660	9.4		+	0.1
		Gunnion, R.	TUSC	609	1.6	*		
2005: Lab				16,806	43.0			

Na h-Eileanan an Iar (Western Isles) [407]

21,780	67.6	MacNeil, A.B.*	SNP	6,723	45.7		+	0.8
		MacSween, D.J.	Lab	4,838	32.9		-	1.6
		Murray, M.A.	Ind	1,412	9.6			
		Davis, J. Ms.	LD	1,097	7.5		-	0.5
		Norquay, S. Ms.	Con	647	4.4	*	-	0.0
2005: SNP				1,885	12.8			

Neath [408]

57,295	64.8	Hain, P.*	Lab	17,172	46.3		-	6.3
		Llewelyn, A.	PC	7,397	19.9		+	2.8
		Little, F.	LD	5,535	14.9		+	0.6
		Owens, E. Ms.	Con	4,847	13.1		+	1.5
		Green, M.	BNP	1,342	3.6	*		
		Bevan, J.	UKIP	829	2.2	*		
2005: Lab				9,775	26.3			

New Forest East [409]

72,858	68.7	Lewis, J.M.*	Con	26,443	52.8		+	3.4
		Scriven, T.G.	LD	15,136	30.3		-	3.0
		Sopowski, P.W.J.	Lab	4,915	9.8		-	2.4
		Day, P.A.	UKIP	2,518	5.0		-	0.1
		Golden, B.J. Ms.	Grn	1,024	2.0	*		
2005: Con				11,307	22.6			

New Forest West [410]

68,332	69.6	Swayne, D.A.*	Con	27,980	58.8		+	2.9
		Plummer, M.I.	LD	11,084	23.3		+	4.1
		Hurne, J.C. Ms.	Lab	4,666	9.8		-	6.7
		Lyon, M.E.	UKIP	2,783	5.9		+	1.7
		Richards, J.E. Ms.	Grn	1,059	2.2	*	-	1.9
2005: Con				16,896	35.5			

Newark [411]

71,755	71.4	Mercer, P.*	Con	27,590	53.9		+	3.4
		Campbell, I.W.	Lab	11,438	22.3		-	6.0
		Jenkins, P. Ms.	LD	10,246	20.0		+	1.6
		Irvine, T.	UKIP	1,954	3.8	*	+	1.0
2005: Con				16,152	31.5			

Newbury [412]

79,144	74.0	Benyon, R.H.R.*	Con	33,057	56.4	+ 7.4
		Rendel, D.D.	LD	20,809	35.5	- 7.1
		Cooper, H. Ms.	Lab	2,505	4.3 *	- 1.7
		Black, D.M.	UKIP	1,475	2.5 *	+ 0.9
		Hollister, A.O.	Grn	490	0.8 *	
		Burgess, B.	Ind	158	0.3 *	
		Yates, D.E.	AD	95	0.2 *	
2005: Con				12,248	20.9	

Newcastle-under-Lyme [413]

69,433	62.2	Farrelly, P.*	Lab	16,393	38.0	- 7.4
		Jenrick, R.E.	Con	14,841	34.4	+ 9.4
		Jones, N.	LD	8,466	19.6	+ 0.7
		Nixon, D.E.	UKIP	3,491	8.1	+ 4.5
2005: Lab				1,552	3.6	

Newcastle upon Tyne Central [414]

60,507	56.5	Onwurah, C. Ms.	Lab	15,694	45.9	- 4.6
		Kane, G.	LD	8,228	24.1	- 3.4
		Holder, N.	Con	6,611	19.4	+ 2.8
		Booth, K.	BNP	2,302	6.7	
		Davies, M.	UKIP	754	2.2 *	
		Pearson, J.	Grn	568	1.7 *	- 2.2
2005: Lab				7,466	21.9	

Newcastle upon Tyne East [415]

64,487	58.7	Brown, N.H.*	Lab	17,043	45.0	- 7.7
		Taylor, W.B. Ms.	LD	12,590	33.3	+ 1.5
		Llewellyn, D.R.C.	Con	6,068	16.0	+ 3.0
		Spence, A.	BNP	1,342	3.5 *	
		Gray, A.	Grn	620	1.6 *	
		Levy, M.R.	Comm	177	0.5 *	
2005: Lab				4,453	11.8	

Newcastle upon Tyne North [416]

67,110	65.5	McKinnell, C. Ms.	Lab	17,950	40.8	- 9.0
		Beadle, R.W.A.	LD	14,536	33.1	+ 0.1
		Parkinson, S.G.	Con	7,966	18.1	+ 3.4
		Gibson, T.	BNP	1,890	4.3 *	
		Proud, I.	UKIP	1,285	2.9 *	
		Heyman, A. Ms.	Grn	319	0.7 *	
2005: Lab				3,414	7.8	

Newport East [417]

54,437	63.3	Morden, J.E. Ms.*	Lab	12,744	37.0	- 8.2
		Townsend, C.E.	LD	11,094	32.2	+ 8.5
		Parry, D. Ms.	Con	7,918	23.0	- 0.5
		Jones, K.M.	BNP	1,168	3.4 *	
		Cross, F.C. Ms.	PC	724	2.1 *	- 1.7
		Rowlands, D.J.	UKIP	677	2.0 *	- 1.0
		Screen, E.A. Ms.	Soc Lab	123	0.4 *	
2005: Lab				1,650	4.8	

Newport West [418]

62,111	64.0	Flynn, P.P.*	Lab	16,389	41.3	- 3.6
		Williams, M.R.	Con	12,845	32.3	+ 2.8
		German, V.K. Ms.	LD	6,587	16.6	- 1.3
		Windsor, T.J.	BNP	1,183	3.0 *	
		Moelwyn Hughes, H.	UKIP	1,144	2.9 *	+ 0.5
		Rees, J.	PC	1,122	2.8 *	- 0.8
		Bartolotti, P.J. Ms.	Grn	450	1.1 *	- 0.4
2005: Lab				3,544	8.9	

Newry & Armagh [419]

74,308	60.4	Murphy, C.*	SF	18,857	42.0	+ 0.6
		Bradley, D.	SDLP	10,526	23.4	- 1.7
		Kennedy, D.	UCUNF	8,558	19.1	
		Irwin, W.G.	DUP	5,764	12.8	- 5.5
		Frazer, W.	Ind	656	1.5 *	
		Muir, A.	APNI	545	1.2 *	
2005: SF				8,331	18.6	

Newton Abbot [420]

69,319	69.7	Morris, A.M. Ms.	Con	20,774	43.0	+ 8.0
		Younger-Ross, R.A.*	LD	20,251	41.9	- 3.6
		Canavan, P.	Lab	3,387	7.0	- 4.4
		Hooper, J.M. Ms.	UKIP	3,088	6.4	- 0.1
		Lindsey, C.J. Ms.	Grn	701	1.5 *	
		Sharp, K.H.	Ind	82	0.2 *	
2005: LD				523	1.1	

Norfolk Mid [421]

74,260	68.4	Freeman, G.	Con	25,123	49.5	+ 2.9
		Newman, D.I.	LD	11,267	22.2	+ 3.0
		Hughes, E.P. Ms.	Lab	8,857	17.4	- 12.8
		Coke, R.T.	UKIP	2,800	5.5	+ 1.5
		Birt, T.E.	Grn	1,457	2.9 *	
		Kelly, C.A. Ms.	BNP	1,261	2.5 *	
2005: Con				13,856	27.3	

Norfolk North [422]

67,851	73.2	Lamb, N.P.*	LD	27,554	55.5	+ 2.3
		Ivory, T.C.C.	Con	15,928	32.1	- 3.9
		Harris, P.A.	Lab	2,896	5.8	- 3.1
		Baker, M.J.M.	UKIP	2,680	5.4	+ 3.7
		Boswell, A.P.	Grn	508	1.0 *	
		Mann, S.E.	Ind	95	0.2 *	
2005: LD				11,626	23.4	

Norfolk North West [423]

73,105	65.4	Bellingham, H.C.*	Con	25,916	54.2	+ 4.3
		Summers, W.D.	LD	11,106	23.2	+ 8.5
		Sood, M.A.	Lab	6,353	13.3	- 18.3
		Gray, J.W.	UKIP	1,841	3.9 *	+ 0.2
		Fleming, D.A.	BNP	1,839	3.8 *	
		de Whalley, A.M.	Grn	745	1.6 *	
2005: Con				14,810	31.0	

Norfolk South [424]

76,179	72.2	Bacon, R.M.*	Con	27,133	49.3	+ 5.2
		Howe, J.A. Ms.	LD	16,193	29.4	- 1.3
		Castle, M.V.	Lab	7,252	13.2	- 9.0
		Heasley, E.	UKIP	2,329	4.2 *	+ 1.4
		Mitchell, H.M. Ms.	BNP	1,086	2.0 *	
		Willcott, J. Ms.	Grn	1,000	1.8 *	
2005: Con				10,940	19.9	

Norfolk South West [425]

73,758	66.6	Truss, E.M. Ms.	Con	23,753	48.3	+ 3.4
		Gordon, S.J.	LD	10,613	21.6	+ 2.4
		Smith, P.D.	Lab	9,119	18.6	- 11.4
		Hipsey, K. Ms.	UKIP	3,061	6.2	+ 1.5
		Pearce, D.	BNP	1,774	3.6 *	
		Allen, L. Ms.	Grn	830	1.7 *	
2005: Con				13,140	26.7	

Normanton, Pontefract & Castleford [426]

82,336	56.2	Cooper, Y. Ms.*	Lab	22,293	48.2	- 17.1
		Pickles, N.	Con	11,314	24.5	+ 7.9
		Rush, C.	LD	7,585	16.4	+ 5.3
		Thewlis-Hardy, G.G.	BNP	3,864	8.4	+ 4.4
		Allen, G.	Ind	1,183	2.6 *	
2005: Lab				10,979	23.7	

Northampton North [427]

61,850	65.1	Ellis, M.T.	Con	13,735	34.1		+ 4.4
		Keeble, S.C. Ms.*	Lab	11,799	29.3		- 9.4
		Simpson, A.S.J.	LD	11,250	27.9		+ 1.0
		Beasley, R.J.	BNP	1,316	3.3	*	
		Macarthur, M.	UKIP	1,238	3.1	*	+ 0.6
		Lochmuller, A.J.	Grn	443	1.1	*	
		Fitzpatrick, E.	Ind	334	0.8	*	
		Webb, T.S.D.	Ch P	98	0.2	*	
		Mildren, M.K.	Ind	58	0.1	*	
2005: Lab				1,936	4.8		

Northampton South [428]

63,105	61.8	Binley, B.A.R.*	Con	15,917	40.8		+ 3.0
		Loakes, C.W.	Lab	9,913	25.4		- 16.1
		Varnsverry, P.D.	LD	7,579	19.4		+ 5.9
		Clarke, A.R.	Ind	2,242	5.8		
		Clark, D.R.	UKIP	1,897	4.9	*	+ 2.8
		Sills, K.J.	ED	618	1.6	*	
		Hawkins, J.M. Ms.	Grn	363	0.9	*	
		Green, D.S.	NSPS	325	0.8	*	
		Willsher, K.R.J.	Ind	65	0.2	*	
		Costello, L.	SMA	59	0.2	*	
2005: Lab				6,004	15.4		

Northamptonshire South [429]

82,033	73.0	Leadsom, A.J. Ms.	Con	33,081	55.2		+ 3.7
		Collins, S.J.	LD	12,603	21.0		+ 3.9
		May, M.J.	Lab	10,380	17.3		- 11.4
		Mahoney, B.J.	UKIP	2,406	4.0	*	+ 1.4
		Tappy, T.	ED	735	1.2	*	
		Rock, M.C.	Grn	685	1.1	*	
2005: Con				20,478	34.2		

Norwich North [430]

64,814	65.7	Smith, C.R. Ms.*	Con	17,280	40.6		+ 10.1
		Cook, J.	Lab	13,379	31.4		- 15.7
		Stephen, J.D.	LD	7,783	18.3		+ 2.2
		Tingle, G.S.	UKIP	1,878	4.4	*	+ 2.1
		Goldfinch, J. Ms.	Grn	1,245	2.9	*	- 0.3
		Richardson, T.L.	BNP	747	1.8	*	
		Holden, B.	Ind	143	0.3	*	
		Holland, A.M.	Ch P	118	0.3	*	
2005: Lab				3,901	9.2		

Norwich South [431]

73,649	64.6	Wright, S.J.	LD	13,960	29.4		- 0.6
		Clarke, C.R.*	Lab	13,650	28.7		- 8.7
		Little, A.D.	Con	10,902	22.9		+ 1.1
		Ramsay, A.P.	Grn	7,095	14.9		+ 7.5
		Emmens, S.M.	UKIP	1,145	2.4	*	+ 0.9
		Heather, L.A.	BNP	697	1.5	*	
		Polley, G.A.C.	WRP	102	0.2	*	
2005: Lab				310	0.7		

Nottingham East [432]

58,705	56.4	Leslie, C.M.	Lab	15,022	45.4		- 1.3
		Boote, S.J.	LD	8,053	24.3		+ 2.5
		Lamont, A.E.	Con	7,846	23.7		+ 1.2
		Wolfe, P.A. Ms.	UKIP	1,138	3.4	*	+ 0.9
		Hoare, B.R.	Grn	928	2.8	*	- 2.4
		Sardar, P.A.	Ch P	125	0.4	*	
2005: Lab				6,969	21.0		

Nottingham North [433]

63,240	54.2	Allen, G.W.*	Lab	16,646	48.6		- 10.6
		Curtis, M.J.	Con	8,508	24.8		+ 6.7
		Ball, T.S.	LD	5,849	17.1		- 0.3
		Brindley, S.D.	BNP	1,944	5.7		
		Marriott, I. Ms.	UKIP	1,338	3.9	*	- 1.5
2005: Lab				8,138	23.7		

Nottingham South [434]

67,441	60.5	Greenwood, L.R. Ms.	Lab	15,209	37.3		- 8.6
		Holland, R.E. Ms.	Con	13,437	32.9		+ 6.2
		Sutton, T.B.	LD	9,406	23.1		- 0.4
		Woodward, A.R.	BNP	1,140	2.8	*	
		Browne, J.K.	UKIP	967	2.4	*	- 1.5
		Butcher, M.	Grn	630	1.5	*	
2005: Lab				1,772	4.3		

Nuneaton [435]

67,837	65.8	Jones, M.C.	Con	18,536	41.5		+ 4.6
		Innes, J.E. Ms.	Lab	16,467	36.9		- 9.8
		Jebb, C.R. Ms.	LD	6,846	15.3		+ 2.8
		Findley, M.R.	BNP	2,797	6.3		
2005: Lab				2,069	4.6		

Ochil & South Perthshire [436]

75,115	67.2	Banks, G.R.*	Lab	19,131	37.9	+ 6.5
		Ewing, A. Ms.	SNP	13,944	27.6	- 2.3
		Michaluk, G.R.G.	Con	10,342	20.5	- 1.0
		Littlejohn, G.	LD	5,754	11.4	- 1.9
		Bushby, D.	UKIP	689	1.4 *	+ 0.8
		Charles, H. Ms.	Grn	609	1.2 *	- 0.9
2005: Lab				5,187	10.3	

Ogmore [437]

55,527	62.4	Irranca-Davies, H.*	Lab	18,644	53.8	- 7.1
		Moore, E.S. Ms.	Con	5,398	15.6	+ 1.4
		Radford, J. Ms.	LD	5,260	15.2	+ 0.5
		Clark, D.	PC	3,326	9.6	- 0.6
		Thomas, K. Ms.	BNP	1,242	3.6 *	
		Passey, C.A. Ms.	UKIP	780	2.3 *	
2005: Lab				13,246	38.2	

Old Bexley & Sidcup [438]

65,699	69.2	Brokenshire, J.P.*	Con	24,625	54.1	+ 4.1
		Everitt, R.	Lab	8,768	19.3	- 8.7
		Borrowman, D.K.	LD	6,996	15.4	+ 1.5
		Brooks, R.J.	BNP	2,132	4.7 *	+ 1.8
		Coburn, D.A.	UKIP	1,532	3.4 *	- 1.2
		Cheeseman, E.F. Ms.	ED	520	1.1 *	
		Hemming-Clark, J.S.C.	ISQM	393	0.9 *	
		Rooks, J.S.	Grn	371	0.8 *	
		Dynamite, N.	MRLP	155	0.3 *	
2005: Con				15,857	34.9	

Oldham East & Saddleworth [439]

72,557	61.4	Woolas, P.J.*	Lab	14,186	31.9	- 10.7
		Watkins, E.	LD	14,083	31.6	- 0.5
		Ali, K.	Con	11,773	26.4	+ 8.7
		Stott, A.	BNP	2,546	5.7	+ 0.6
		Bentley, D.J.	UKIP	1,720	3.9 *	+ 1.8
		Nazir, G.	Ch P	212	0.5 *	
2005: Lab				103	0.2	

Oldham West & Royton [440]

72,359	59.3	Meacher, M.H.*	Lab	19,503	45.5	- 2.9
		Ghafoor, K.	Con	10,151	23.7	+ 2.6
		Alcock, M.	LD	8,193	19.1	- 2.1
		Joines, D.P.	BNP	3,049	7.1	+ 0.3
		Roberts, H. Ms.	UKIP	1,387	3.2 *	+ 0.7
		Miah, S.	Respect	627	1.5 *	
2005: Lab				9,352	21.8	

Orkney & Shetland [441]

33,085	58.5	Carmichael, A.M.*	LD	11,989	62.0	+ 10.5
		Cooper, M.	Lab	2,061	10.7	- 3.5
		Mowat, J.R.	SNP	2,042	10.6	+ 0.2
		Spencer Nairn, C.F.	Con	2,032	10.5	- 2.8
		Smith, R.W.	UKIP	1,222	6.3	+ 3.9
2005: LD				9,928	51.3	

Orpington [442]

67,732	72.2	Johnson, J.E.	Con	29,200	59.7	+ 8.5
		McBride, D.	LD	12,000	24.5	- 15.9
		Morgan, S.R.	Lab	4,400	9.0	+ 3.0
		Greenhough, J.M.	UKIP	1,360	2.8 *	+ 0.4
		Culnane, M.T. Ms.	BNP	1,241	2.5 *	
		Galloway, T.E. Ms.	Grn	511	1.0 *	
		Snape, C.K.	ED	199	0.4 *	
2005: Con				17,200	35.2	

Oxford East [443]

81,903	63.1	Smith, A.D.*	Lab	21,938	42.5	+ 6.5
		Goddard, S.H.	LD	17,357	33.6	- 1.6
		Argar, E.J.C.	Con	9,727	18.8	+ 1.5
		Dhall, S.D. Ms.	Grn	1,238	2.4 *	- 2.1
		Gasper, J.M. Ms.	UKIP	1,202	2.3 *	+ 0.6
		O'Sullivan, D.A.	SEP	116	0.2 *	
		Crawford, R.M.	EPA	73	0.1 *	
2005: Lab				4,581	8.9	

Oxford West & Abingdon [444]

86,458	65.3	Blackwood, N.C. Ms.	Con	23,906	42.3	+ 9.6
		Harris, E.*	LD	23,730	42.0	- 4.1
		Stevens, R.M.	Lab	5,999	10.6	- 5.2
		Williams, P.J.	UKIP	1,518	2.7 *	+ 1.2
		Goodall, C.	Grn	1,184	2.1 *	- 1.7
		Mann, K.J.	APP	143	0.3 *	
2005: LD				176	0.3	

Paisley & Renfrewshire North [445]

63,704	68.6	Sheridan, J.*	Lab	23,613	54.0	+ 8.3
		MacLaren, M. Ms.	SNP	8,333	19.1	+ 0.2
		Campbell, A.	Con	6,381	14.6	+ 1.0
		Dobson, R.	LD	4,597	10.5	- 7.7
		Pearson, G.	Ind	550	1.3 *	
		Rollo, C.	SSP	233	0.5 *	- 1.0
2005: Lab				15,280	35.0	

Paisley & Renfrewshire South [446]

61,197	65.4	Alexander, D.G.*	Lab	23,842	59.6	+	7.0
		Doig, A.	SNP	7,228	18.1	+	0.5
		McCaskill, G.A.	Con	3,979	9.9	+	1.5
		Ghai, A.	LD	3,812	9.5	-	8.1
		Mack, P.	Ind	513	1.3 *		
		Kerr, J.	SSP	375	0.9 *	-	1.1
		Hendry, W.	Ind	249	0.6 *		
2005: Lab				16,614	41.5		

Pendle [447]

66,422	67.8	Stephenson, A.	Con	17,512	38.9	+	7.1
		Prentice, G.*	Lab	13,927	30.9	-	6.2
		Anwar, M.A.	LD	9,095	20.2	-	3.0
		Jackman, J.D.M.	BNP	2,894	6.4	+	0.2
		Cannon, G.G.	UKIP	1,476	3.3 *	+	1.5
		Masih, R.E.	Ch P	141	0.3 *		
2005: Lab				3,585	8.0		

Penistone & Stocksbridge [448]

68,480	67.9	Smith, A. Ms.*	Lab	17,565	37.8	-	7.4
		Pitfield, S.	Con	14,516	31.2	+	7.5
		Cuthbertson, I.M.	LD	9,800	21.1	-	3.7
		James, P.	BNP	2,207	4.7 *	-	0.0
		French, G.	UKIP	1,936	4.2 *	+	2.5
		McEnhill, P.H.A.	ED	492	1.1 *		
2005: Lab				3,049	6.6		

Penrith & The Border [449]

64,484	69.9	Stewart, R.	Con	24,071	53.4	+	2.0
		Thornton, P.C.	LD	12,830	28.5	+	2.6
		Cannon, B.A. Ms.	Lab	5,834	12.9	-	6.1
		Stanyer, J.B.	UKIP	1,259	2.8 *	+	0.3
		Davidson, C.	BNP	1,093	2.4 *		
2005: Con				11,241	24.9		

Perth & North Perthshire [450]

72,141	66.9	Wishart, P.*	SNP	19,118	39.6	+	5.9
		Lyburn, P.J.	Con	14,739	30.5	+	0.2
		Glackin, J.	Lab	7,923	16.4	-	2.3
		Barrett, P.A.	LD	5,954	12.3	-	3.8
		Taylor, D.S.	Trust	534	1.1 *		
2005: SNP				4,379	9.1		

Peterborough [451]

70,278	63.9	Jackson, S.J.*	Con	18,133	40.4	- 2.9
		Murphy, E.P.	Lab	13,272	29.5	- 4.8
		Sandford, J.N.	LD	8,816	19.6	+ 2.9
		Fox, F.A. Ms.	UKIP	3,007	6.7	+ 3.5
		King, R.J.	ED	770	1.7 *	
		Radic, F.J. Ms.	Grn	523	1.2 *	
		Swallow, J.P.	Ind	406	0.9 *	
2005: Con				4,861	10.8	

Plymouth Moor View [452]

68,062	61.0	Seabeck, A.J. Ms.*	Lab	15,433	37.2	- 7.2
		Groves, M.P.	Con	13,845	33.3	+ 8.3
		Bonar, S.A.	LD	7,016	16.9	- 2.1
		Wakeham, B.	UKIP	3,188	7.7	- 0.0
		Cook, R.	BNP	1,438	3.5 *	
		Miller, W.M. Ms.	Grn	398	1.0 *	
		Marchesi, D.T.	Soc Lab	208	0.5 *	
2005: Lab				1,588	3.8	

Plymouth Sutton & Devonport [453]

72,938	60.2	Colvile, O.N.	Con	15,050	34.3	+ 4.7
		Gilroy, L. Ms.*	Lab	13,901	31.7	- 9.0
		Evans, J. Ms.	LD	10,829	24.7	+ 2.1
		Leigh, A.M.	UKIP	2,854	6.5	- 0.1
		Brown, A.M.	Grn	904	2.1 *	
		Gerrish, B.J.	Ind	233	0.5 *	
		Hawkins, R.O.	Soc Lab	123	0.3 *	
2005: Lab				1,149	2.6	

Pontypridd [454]

58,205	63.0	Smith, O.	Lab	14,220	38.8	- 15.4
		Powell, M.J.	LD	11,435	31.2	+ 11.2
		Gonzalez, L.G.	Con	5,932	16.2	+ 4.6
		Bellin, I.R.	PC	2,673	7.3	- 3.7
		Bevan, D.M.	UKIP	1,229	3.4 *	+ 0.8
		Parsons, S.	Soc Lab	456	1.2 *	
		Watson, D.W.E.	Ch P	365	1.0 *	
		Matthews, J.	Grn	361	1.0 *	
2005: Lab				2,785	7.6	

Poole [455]

72,641	65.3	Syms, R.A.R.*	Con	22,532	47.5	+ 4.1
		Eades, P.M.	LD	14,991	31.6	+ 2.5
		Sanderson, J.G.	Lab	6,041	12.7	- 10.0
		Wellstead, N.J.	UKIP	2,507	5.3	+ 1.8
		Holmes, H.D.	BNP	1,188	2.5 *	+ 1.2
		Northover, I.D.	Ind	177	0.4 *	
2005: Con				7,541	15.9	

Poplar & Limehouse [456]

74,955	62.3	Fitzpatrick, J.*	Lab	18,679	40.0	+ 4.7
		Archer, T.J.	Con	12,649	27.1	+ 2.6
		Galloway, G.*	Respect	8,160	17.5	
		Fryer, J.H.	LD	5,209	11.2	- 2.8
		Lochner, W.	UKIP	565	1.2 *	
		Osborne, A.D.	ED	470	1.0 *	
		Smith, C.D.	Grn	449	1.0 *	- 1.7
		Mahmud, K.	Ind	293	0.6 *	
		Hoque, M.A.	Ind	167	0.4 *	
		Thornton, J.D.	Ind	59	0.1 *	
2005: Lab				6,030	12.9	

Portsmouth North [457]

70,329	62.7	Mordaunt, P.M. Ms.	Con	19,533	44.3	+ 6.5
		McCarthy-Fry, S.L. Ms.*	Lab	12,244	27.8	- 10.8
		Sanders, D.	LD	8,874	20.1	- 0.2
		Fitzgerald, M.R.D.	UKIP	1,812	4.1 *	+ 0.7
		Knight, D.J.	ED	1,040	2.4 *	
		Maclennan, I.R.	Grn	461	1.0 *	
		Tosh, M.I.	TUSC	154	0.3 *	
2005: Lab				7,289	16.5	

Portsmouth South [458]

70,242	58.7	Hancock, M.T.*	LD	18,921	45.9	+ 4.2
		Drummond, F.J.B. Ms.	Con	13,721	33.3	- 0.4
		Ferrett, J.	Lab	5,640	13.7	- 8.7
		Martin, C.D.E.	UKIP	876	2.1 *	- 0.2
		Crompton, G.A.	BNP	873	2.1 *	
		Dawes, T.M.	Grn	716	1.7 *	
		DuCane, I.A.	ED	400	1.0 *	
		Cummings, L.P.	JAC	117	0.3 *	
2005: LD				5,200	12.6	

Preseli Pembrokeshire [459]

57,400	69.0	Crabb, S.*	Con	16,944	42.8	+ 6.4
		Rees, M. Ms.	Lab	12,339	31.2	- 3.7
		Tregoning, N.	LD	5,759	14.5	+ 1.5
		Jones-Davies, H.E.	PC	3,654	9.2	- 3.3
		Lawson, R.M.	UKIP	906	2.3 *	+ 1.0
2005: Con				4,605	11.6	

Preston [460]

61,187	53.1	Hendrick, M.P.*	Lab	15,668	48.2	- 0.5
		Jewell, M.G.	LD	7,935	24.4	+ 4.5
		Warner-O'Neill, N.E. Ms.	Con	7,060	21.7	+ 0.7
		Muirhead, R.F.	UKIP	1,462	4.5 *	+ 1.7
		Ambroze, G.	Ch P	272	0.8 *	
		Tayya, K.M.	Ind	108	0.3 *	
2005: Lab				7,733	23.8	

Pudsey [461]

69,257	70.9	Andrew, S.	Con	18,874	38.5	+ 4.8
		Hanley, J.	Lab	17,215	35.1	- 10.3
		Matthews, J.	LD	10,224	20.8	+ 2.7
		Gibson, I.	BNP	1,549	3.2 *	
		Dews, D.A.	UKIP	1,221	2.5 *	- 0.3
2005: Lab				1,659	3.4	

Putney [462]

63,371	64.4	Greening, J. Ms.*	Con	21,223	52.0	+ 9.7
		King, S.T.	Lab	11,170	27.4	- 10.2
		Sandbach, J.P.C.	LD	6,907	16.9	+ 0.6
		Mackenzie, B.W.	Grn	591	1.4 *	- 1.3
		Darby, P.	BNP	459	1.1 *	
		Wareham, F.H.J.	UKIP	435	1.1 *	+ 0.0
2005: Con				10,053	24.6	

Rayleigh & Wickford [463]

75,661	69.2	Francois, M.G.*	Con	30,257	57.8	+ 3.9
		Gaszczak, S. Ms.	LD	7,919	15.1	- 0.3
		Le-Surf, M.	Lab	7,577	14.5	- 12.0
		Hayter, J.	ED	2,219	4.2 *	
		Callaghan, T.	UKIP	2,211	4.2 *	+ 0.1
		Evennett, A.W.	BNP	2,160	4.1 *	
2005: Con				22,338	42.7	

Reading East [464]

74,929	66.7	Wilson, R.*	Con	21,269	42.6		+ 6.9
		Epps, G.D.	LD	13,664	27.3		+ 3.0
		Dodds, A.J. Ms.	Lab	12,729	25.5		- 8.5
		Pitfield, A.B.W.	UKIP	1,086	2.2 *		+ 0.2
		White, R.J.	Grn	1,069	2.1 *		- 1.4
		Lloyd, J.R. Ms.	Ind	111	0.2 *		
		Turberville, M.J.	Ind	57	0.1 *		
2005: Con				7,605	15.2		

Reading West [465]

72,120	65.9	Sharma, A.K.	Con	20,523	43.2		+ 9.6
		Sarkar, A.	Lab	14,519	30.5		- 14.5
		Benson, D. Ms.	LD	9,546	20.1		+ 4.3
		Hay, B.A.	UKIP	1,508	3.2 *		+ 0.4
		Thomas, H.	CSP	852	1.8 *		
		Windisch, A.	Grn	582	1.2 *		- 1.0
2005: Lab				6,004	12.6		

Redcar [466]

67,127	62.5	Swales, I.C.	LD	18,955	45.2		+ 25.0
		Baird, V. Ms.*	Lab	13,741	32.7		- 18.6
		Mastin, S.J.	Con	5,790	13.8		- 4.1
		Bulmer, M.G.	UKIP	1,875	4.5 *		+ 3.0
		Broughton, K.	BNP	1,475	3.5 *		+ 1.0
		Walter, H.R. Ms.	TUSC	127	0.3 *		
2005: Lab				5,214	12.4		

Redditch [467]

66,573	66.1	Lumley, K.E. Ms.	Con	19,138	43.5		+ 5.0
		Smith, J. Ms.*	Lab	13,317	30.3		- 13.4
		Lane, N.H.	LD	7,750	17.6		+ 3.2
		Davis, A.V. Ms.	UKIP	1,497	3.4 *		- 0.0
		Ingram, A.	BNP	1,394	3.2 *		
		White, K.	Grn	393	0.9 *		
		Schittone, V.	ED	255	0.6 *		
		Beverley, S.	Ch P	101	0.2 *		
		Swansborough, P.J.	Ind	100	0.2 *		
		Fletcher, D.	Nobody	73	0.2 *		
2005: Lab				5,821	13.2		

Reigate [468]

71,604	69.8	Blunt, C.J.R.*	Con	26,688	53.4	+ 4.8
		Kulka, J.N. Ms.	LD	13,097	26.2	+ 3.1
		Hull, R.	Lab	5,672	11.3	- 10.2
		Fox, J.B.	UKIP	2,089	4.2 *	- 0.3
		Brown, K.	BNP	1,345	2.7 *	
		Essex, J.C.A.	Grn	1,087	2.2 *	
2005: Con				13,591	27.2	

Renfrewshire East [469]

66,249	77.3	Murphy, J.*	Lab	25,987	50.8	+ 6.9
		Cook, R.E.	Con	15,567	30.4	+ 0.5
		Macdonald, G.	LD	4,720	9.2	- 9.0
		Archer, G.	SNP	4,535	8.9	+ 2.0
		MacKay, D.M.	UKIP	372	0.7 *	
2005: Lab				10,420	20.4	

Rhondda [470]

51,554	60.3	Bryant, C.J.*	Lab	17,183	55.3	- 12.8
		Davies, G.R.	PC	5,630	18.1	+ 2.2
		Wasley, P.J.	LD	3,309	10.6	+ 0.2
		Howe, P.	Ind	2,599	8.4	
		Henderson, J.M. Ms.	Con	1,993	6.4	+ 0.9
		John, P.N.	UKIP	358	1.2 *	
2005: Lab				11,553	37.2	

Ribble Valley [471]

77,789	67.2	Evans, N.M.*	Con	26,298	50.3	+ 5.4
		Foster, P.A.	Lab	11,529	22.0	- 7.8
		Knox, A.M.	LD	10,732	20.5	- 2.1
		Rush, S.P.	UKIP	3,496	6.7	+ 4.0
		Johnson, A.G.	ND	232	0.4 *	
2005: Con				14,769	28.2	

Richmond (Yorks) [472]

80,563	66.3	Hague, W.J.*	Con	33,541	62.8	+ 3.5
		Meredith, L.	LD	10,205	19.1	+ 2.2
		Driver, E. Ms.	Lab	8,150	15.3	- 5.3
		Rowe, L.A.	Grn	1,516	2.8 *	- 0.3
2005: Con				23,336	43.7	

Richmond Park [473]

77,751	76.2	Goldsmith, Z.	Con	29,461	49.7	+10.1
		Kramer, S.V. Ms.*	LD	25,370	42.8	- 3.8
		Tunnicliffe, E. Ms.	Lab	2,979	5.0	- 4.2
		Dul, P.J.	UKIP	669	1.1 *	+ 0.2
		Page, J.R.	Grn	572	1.0 *	- 1.7
		May, S.J. Ms.	CPA	133	0.2 *	
		Hill, C.	Ind	84	0.1 *	
2005: LD				4,091	6.9	

Rochdale [474]

78,952	58.1	Danczuk, S.C.	Lab	16,699	36.4	- 4.5
		Rowen, P.J.*	LD	15,810	34.4	- 6.1
		Dean, M.A.	Con	8,305	18.1	+ 7.6
		Jackson, C.	NF	2,236	4.9 *	
		Denby, C.	UKIP	1,999	4.4 *	+ 3.0
		Salim, M.	IZB	545	1.2 *	
		Whitehead, J.M.	Ind	313	0.7 *	
2005: Lab				889	1.9	

Rochester & Strood [475]

73,758	65.0	Reckless, M.J.	Con	23,604	49.2	+ 6.6
		Murray, T.M. Ms.	Lab	13,651	28.5	-13.1
		Juby, G.W.	LD	7,800	16.3	+ 3.9
		Sands, R.P.	ED	2,182	4.5 *	
		Marchant, S.P.	Grn	734	1.5 *	
2005: Con				9,953	20.7	

Rochford & Southend East [476]

71,467	58.3	Duddridge, J.*	Con	19,509	46.9	+ 1.5
		Bonavia, K.A.M.	Lab	8,459	20.3	-11.3
		Longley, G.E.	LD	8,084	19.4	+ 4.7
		Moyies, J.W.	UKIP	2,405	5.8	+ 0.9
		Strobridge, G.	BNP	1,856	4.5 *	
		Vaughan, A.J.	Grn	707	1.7 *	- 1.8
		Chytry, A.B.	Ind	611	1.5 *	
2005: Con				11,050	26.5	

Romford [477]

71,306	65.2	Rosindell, A.R.*	Con	26,031	56.0	- 1.7
		Voller, R.A. Ms.	Lab	9,077	19.5	- 9.5
		Duffett, H.A. Ms.	LD	5,572	12.0	+ 3.6
		Bailey, R.W.	BNP	2,438	5.2	+ 2.7
		Batten, G.J.	UKIP	2,050	4.4 *	+ 2.1
		Thorogood, P.B.	ED	603	1.3 *	
		Haines, G.L.	Grn	447	1.0 *	
		Hyde, P.J.	Ind	151	0.3 *	
		Sturman, D.L.	Ind	112	0.2 *	
2005: Con				16,954	36.5	

Romsey & Southampton North [478]

68,157	71.8	Nokes, C.F.E. Ms.	Con	24,345	49.7	+ 6.6
		Gidley, S.J. Ms.*	LD	20,189	41.3	- 2.4
		Beg, A.	Lab	3,116	6.4	- 4.6
		Meropoulos, J.	UKIP	1,289	2.6 *	+ 0.3
2005: LD				4,156	8.5	

Ross, Skye & Lochaber [479]

51,836	67.2	Kennedy, C.P.*	LD	18,335	52.6	- 6.1
		McKendrick, J.D.	Lab	5,265	15.1	+ 0.2
		Stephen, A.M.	SNP	5,263	15.1	+ 5.5
		Cameron, D.A.J.	Con	4,260	12.2	+ 2.2
		Scott, E.R. Ms.	Grn	777	2.2 *	- 1.1
		Anderson, P.A.	UKIP	659	1.9 *	+ 0.4
		Campbell, R.	Ind	279	0.8 *	
2005: LD				13,070	37.5	

Rossendale & Darwen [480]

73,229	64.4	Berry, J.	Con	19,691	41.8	+ 7.1
		Anderson, J. Ms.*	Lab	15,198	32.2	- 10.7
		Sheffield, B.	LD	8,541	18.1	+ 3.2
		Duthie, D.S.	UKIP	1,617	3.4 *	+ 1.8
		Bryan, K.A.	NF	1,062	2.3 *	
		Johnson, M.	ED	663	1.4 *	
		Melia, T.	Impact	243	0.5 *	
		Sivieri, M.	Ind	113	0.2 *	
2005: Lab				4,493	9.5	

Rother Valley [481]

72,847	64.2	Barron, K.J.*	Lab	19,147	40.9	- 10.6
		Donaldson, L. Ms.	Con	13,281	28.4	+ 5.3
		Paxton, W.	LD	8,111	17.3	+ 1.2
		Blair, W.R.	BNP	3,606	7.7	+ 2.7
		Dowdall, T.C. Ms.	UKIP	2,613	5.6	+ 1.3
2005: Lab				5,866	12.5	

Rotherham [482]

63,563	59.0	MacShane, D.*	Lab	16,741	44.6	- 13.1
		Whiteley, J. Ms.	Con	6,279	16.7	+ 3.4
		Taylor, R.E. Ms.	LD	5,994	16.0	- 0.4
		Guest, M. Ms.	BNP	3,906	10.4	+ 4.5
		Thirlwall, P.	Ind	2,366	6.3	
		Vines, C.	UKIP	2,220	5.9	+ 2.0
2005: Lab				10,462	27.9	

Rugby [483]

68,914	68.9	Pawsey, M.J.F.	Con	20,901	44.0	+ 5.7
		King, A.*	Lab	14,901	31.4	- 12.1
		Roodhouse, J.M.	LD	9,434	19.9	+ 4.9
		Badrick, M.	BNP	1,375	2.9 *	
		Sandison, R.L.	Grn	451	1.0 *	
		Milford, B.D.W.	UKIP	406	0.9 *	- 1.1
2005: Lab				6,000	12.6	

Ruislip, Northwood & Pinner [484]

70,873	70.8	Hurd, N.R.*	Con	28,866	57.5	+ 2.8
		McDonald, A.G. Ms.	Lab	9,806	19.5	- 4.5
		Papworth, T.J.	LD	8,345	16.6	+ 0.3
		Pontey, J.A.	UKIP	1,351	2.7 *	+ 1.2
		Costard, I.E.	NF	899	1.8 *	
		Lee, G.J.	Grn	740	1.5 *	- 0.0
		Akhtar, R. Ms.	Ch P	198	0.4 *	
2005: Con				19,060	38.0	

Runnymede & Weybridge [485]

72,566	66.4	Hammond, P.*	Con	26,915	55.9	+ 4.5
		Falconer, A.G.	LD	10,406	21.6	+ 3.8
		Greenwood, P.A.	Lab	6,446	13.4	- 9.6
		Micklethwait, A.R.	UKIP	3,146	6.5	+ 2.6
		Gould, J.N. Ms.	Grn	696	1.4 *	- 1.3
		Sammons, D.C.F.	Ind	541	1.1 *	
2005: Con				16,509	34.3	

Rushcliffe [486]

72,955	73.6	Clarke, K.H.*	Con	27,470	51.2	+ 3.1
		Khan, K.	LD	11,659	21.7	+ 4.4
		Clayworth, A.W.	Lab	11,128	20.7	- 6.7
		Faithfull, M.	UKIP	2,179	4.1 *	+ 1.6
		Mallender, R.	Grn	1,251	2.3 *	- 1.2
2005: Con				15,811	29.5	

Rutherglen & Hamilton West [487]

76,408	61.5	Greatrex, T.	Lab	28,566	60.8	+ 5.2
		Horne, G.	SNP	7,564	16.1	+ 2.2
		Robertson, I.	LD	5,636	12.0	- 6.4
		Macaskill, M.	Con	4,540	9.7	+ 1.3
		Murdoch, J. Ms.	UKIP	675	1.4 *	+ 0.4
2005: Lab				21,002	44.7	

Rutland & Melton [488]

77,185	71.5	Duncan, A.J.C.*	Con	28,228	51.1	- 0.1
		Hudson, G.F.G.	LD	14,228	25.8	+ 7.2
		Morgan, J.	Lab	7,893	14.3	-10.6
		Baker, P.C.J.	UKIP	2,526	4.6 *	+ 1.4
		Addison, K.P.	BNP	1,757	3.2 *	
		Higgins, L.F.	Ind	588	1.1 *	
2005: Con				14,000	25.4	

Saffron Walden [489]

76,035	71.5	Haselhurst, A.*	Con	30,155	55.5	+ 4.6
		Wilcock, P.A.	LD	14,913	27.4	- 2.2
		Light, B.A. Ms.	Lab	5,288	9.7	- 4.5
		Lord, R.G.	UKIP	2,228	4.1 *	+ 1.4
		Mitchell, C.M. Ms.	BNP	1,050	1.9 *	
		Hossain, R.	Grn	735	1.4 *	
2005: Con				15,242	28.0	

St Albans [490]

70,058	75.4	Main, A.M. Ms.*	Con	21,533	40.8	+ 3.5
		Walkington, A.S.B.	LD	19,228	36.4	+11.0
		Mills, R.A.C. Ms.	Lab	9,288	17.6	-16.7
		Stocker, J.F.	UKIP	2,028	3.8 *	+ 2.3
		Easton, J.E.	Grn	758	1.4 *	
2005: Con				2,305	4.4	

St Austell & Newquay [491]

75,284	62.7	Gilbert, S.D.J.	LD	20,189	42.7	- 4.5
		Righton, C.A. Ms.	Con	18,877	40.0	+ 5.1
		Jameson, L.C.	Lab	3,386	7.2	- 6.6
		Cole, R.M.	MK	2,007	4.2 *	
		Medway, C.	UKIP	1,757	3.7 *	- 0.4
		Fitton, J.	BNP	1,022	2.2 *	
2005: LD				1,312	2.8	

St Helens North [492]

74,985	59.4	Watts, D.L.*	Lab	23,041	51.7	- 5.6
		Greenall, P.V.	Con	9,940	22.3	+ 3.5
		Beirne, J.	LD	8,992	20.2	- 0.7
		Robinson, G.	UKIP	2,100	4.7 *	+ 1.8
		Whatham, S.B.	Soc Lab	483	1.1 *	
2005: Lab				13,101	29.4	

St Helens South & Whiston [493]

77,975	59.1	Woodward, S.A.*	Lab	24,364	52.9	- 2.7
		Spencer, B.T.	LD	10,242	22.2	- 6.6
		Allen, V.M. Ms.	Con	8,209	17.8	+ 5.7
		Winstanley, J.T.	BNP	2,040	4.4 *	
		Sumner, J.P.	UKIP	1,226	2.7 *	+ 0.8
2005: Lab				14,122	30.6	

St Ives [494]

66,944	68.6	George, A.H.*	LD	19,619	42.7	- 9.1
		Thomas, D.G.	Con	17,900	39.0	+11.7
		Latimer, P.J. Ms.	Lab	3,751	8.2	- 4.4
		Faulkner, M.P.	UKIP	2,560	5.6	+ 1.3
		Andrewes, T.H.	Grn	1,308	2.8 *	- 1.1
		Rogers, J.C.	Cor D	396	0.9 *	
		Reed, S.J.	MK	387	0.8 *	
2005: LD				1,719	3.7	

Salford & Eccles [495]

75,483	55.0	Blears, H.A. Ms.*	Lab	16,655	40.1	- 15.3
		Owen, N.J.	LD	10,930	26.3	+ 3.5
		Sephton, M.J.	Con	8,497	20.5	+ 3.6
		Wingfield, T.D. Ms.	BNP	2,632	6.3	
		O'Dwyer, D.B.	UKIP	1,084	2.6 *	- 2.3
		Henry, D.	TUSC	730	1.8 *	
		Morris, S.	ED	621	1.5 *	
		Carvath, R.	Ind	384	0.9 *	
2005: Lab				5,725	13.8	

Salisbury [496]

67,430	71.9	Glen, J.P.	Con	23,859	49.2	+ 2.8
		Radford, N.M.H.	LD	17,893	36.9	+10.0
		Gann, T.G.	Lab	3,690	7.6	- 11.0
		Howard, F.M. Ms.	UKIP	1,392	2.9 *	- 1.3
		Witheridge, S.	BNP	765	1.6 *	
		Startin, N.J.	Grn	506	1.0 *	- 2.4
		Pendragon, A.U.	Ind	257	0.5 *	
		Holme, J.	Ind	119	0.2 *	
2005: Con				5,966	12.3	

Scarborough & Whitby [497]

75,470	65.3	Goodwill, R.*	Con	21,108	42.8	+ 1.8
		David, A. Ms.	Lab	12,978	26.3	- 12.0
		Exley-Moore, T.C. Ms.	LD	11,093	22.5	+ 6.5
		James, M.J.	UKIP	1,484	3.0 *	+ 1.0
		Scott, P.A. Ms.	BNP	1,445	2.9 *	
		Cluer, D.V. Ms.	Grn	734	1.5 *	- 1.1
		Popple, P.G.	Ind	329	0.7 *	
		Boddington, J.M. Ms.	AGS	111	0.2 *	
2005: Con				8,130	16.5	

Scunthorpe [498]

63,089	58.7	Dakin, N.	Lab	14,640	39.5	- 12.5
		Johnson, C.E. Ms.	Con	12,091	32.6	+ 5.8
		Poole, N.	LD	6,774	18.3	+ 1.2
		Collins, J.M. Ms.	UKIP	1,686	4.6 *	+ 0.5
		Ward, D.N.	BNP	1,447	3.9 *	
		Hurst, N. Ms.	Grn	396	1.1 *	
2005: Lab				2,549	6.9	

Sedgefield [499]

64,728	62.1	Wilson, P.*	Lab	18,141	45.1	- 13.9
		Mahapatra, N.	Con	9,445	23.5	+ 9.3
		Thompson, A.	LD	8,033	20.0	+ 8.2
		Walker, M.	BNP	2,075	5.2	
		Gregory, B.J.	UKIP	1,479	3.7 *	+ 2.1
		Gittins, P.S.	ND	1,049	2.6 *	
2005: Lab				8,696	21.6	

Sefton Central [500]

67,511	71.8	Esterson, B.	Lab	20,307	41.9	- 3.7
		Jones, D. Ms.	Con	16,445	33.9	+ 0.4
		Clein, R.	LD	9,656	19.9	+ 0.7
		Harper, P.J.	UKIP	2,055	4.2 *	+ 3.5
2005: Lab				3,862	8.0	

Selby & Ainsty [501]

72,804	71.1	Adams, N.	Con	25,562	49.4		+ 2.3
		Marshall, J. Ms.	Lab	13,297	25.7		- 17.1
		Holvey, T.	LD	9,180	17.7		+ 7.7
		Haley, D.	UKIP	1,635	3.2	*	
		Lorriman, D.	BNP	1,377	2.7	*	
		Glynn, G.M.	ED	677	1.3	*	
2005: Con				12,265	23.7		

Sevenoaks [502]

69,591	71.0	Fallon, M.C.*	Con	28,076	56.8		+ 5.5
		Bullion, A.J.	LD	10,561	21.4		- 0.8
		Siddorn, G.J.	Lab	6,541	13.2		- 8.0
		Heath, C.D.L.	UKIP	1,782	3.6	*	+ 0.6
		Golding, P.A.	BNP	1,384	2.8	*	
		Uncles, L.A. Ms.	ED	806	1.6	*	
		Ellis, M.C.	Ind	258	0.5	*	
2005: Con				17,515	35.4		

Sheffield Brightside & Hillsborough [503]

67,740	57.4	Blunkett, D.*	Lab	21,400	55.0		- 14.6
		Harston, J.G.	LD	7,768	20.0		+ 6.9
		Sharp, J.	Con	4,468	11.5		+ 1.7
		Sheldon, J.	BNP	3,026	7.8		+ 3.2
		Sullivan, P. Ms.	UKIP	1,596	4.1	*	+ 1.1
		Bowler, M.	TUSC	656	1.7	*	
2005: Lab				13,632	35.0		

Sheffield Central [504]

67,554	61.4	Blomfield, P.	Lab	17,138	41.3		- 5.2
		Scriven, P.J.	LD	16,973	40.9		+ 9.5
		Lee, A.	Con	4,206	10.1		+ 1.0
		Creasy, J. Ms.	Grn	1,556	3.8	*	- 2.0
		Smith, T. Ms.	BNP	903	2.2	*	+ 0.6
		Shaw, J.S.	UKIP	652	1.6	*	- 0.1
		Rodgers, R.	Ind	40	0.1	*	
2005: Lab				165	0.4		

Sheffield Hallam [505]

68,798	74.3	Clegg, N.*	LD	27,324	53.4	+ 7.1
		Bates, N.S. Ms.	Con	12,040	23.5	- 6.6
		Scott, J.	Lab	8,228	16.1	- 1.7
		James, N.T.	UKIP	1,195	2.3 *	+ 1.0
		Barnard, S.	Grn	919	1.8 *	- 0.8
		Wildgoose, D.B.	ED	586	1.1 *	
		Fitzpatrick, M.	Ind	429	0.8 *	
		Green, R.	Ch P	250	0.5 *	
		Adshead, M.S.	MRLP	164	0.3 *	
2005: LD				15,284	29.9	

Sheffield Heeley [506]

65,571	62.3	Munn, M. Ms.*	Lab	17,409	42.6	- 11.5
		Clement-Jones, S.W.	LD	11,602	28.4	+ 7.0
		Crampton, A. Ms.	Con	7,081	17.3	+ 3.0
		Beatson, J.W.	BNP	2,260	5.5	+ 2.1
		Arnott, C.E. Ms.	UKIP	1,530	3.7 *	+ 1.4
		Roberts, G.	Grn	989	2.4 *	- 1.2
2005: Lab				5,807	14.2	

Sheffield South East [507]

67,068	61.7	Betts, C.J.C.*	Lab	20,169	48.7	- 11.6
		Smith, G. Ms.	LD	9,664	23.3	+ 6.4
		Bonson, N.S.	Con	7,202	17.4	+ 3.0
		Hartigan, C.N.	BNP	2,345	5.7	+ 1.6
		Arnott, J.W.	UKIP	1,889	4.6 *	+ 0.2
		Andrew, S.J.	Comm	139	0.3 *	
2005: Lab				10,505	25.4	

Sherwood [508]

71,443	68.5	Spencer, M.	Con	19,211	39.2	+ 5.8
		Oldknow, E.A. Ms.	Lab	18,997	38.8	- 10.6
		Moore, K.	LD	7,283	14.9	+ 1.4
		North, J.D.	BNP	1,754	3.6 *	
		Parker, M. Ms.	UKIP	1,490	3.0 *	- 0.7
		Swan, R.	Ind	219	0.4 *	
2005: Lab				214	0.4	

Shipley [509]

67,689	73.0	Davies, P.A.*	Con	24,002	48.6	+ 9.7
		Hinchcliffe, S.K. Ms.	Lab	14,058	28.4	- 9.4
		Harris, J.P.R.	LD	9,890	20.0	+ 4.8
		Warnes, K.R.	Grn	1,477	3.0 *	- 0.4
2005: Con				9,944	20.1	

Shrewsbury & Atcham [510]

75,446	70.3	Kawczynski, D.R.*	Con	23,313	43.9		+	6.3
		West, C.A.	LD	15,369	29.0		+	6.1
		Tandy, J.	Lab	10,915	20.6		-	13.5
		Lewis, P.M.	UKIP	1,627	3.1	*	+	0.4
		Whittall, J.	BNP	1,168	2.2	*		
		Whittaker, J.A.	Grn	565	1.1	*	-	1.2
		Gollins, J.G.	Impact	88	0.2	*		
2005: Con				7,944	15.0			

Shropshire North [511]

78,930	65.7	Paterson, O.W.*	Con	26,692	51.5		+	1.9
		Croll, I.P.	LD	10,864	20.9		+	1.2
		McLaughlan, I.P.	Lab	9,406	18.1		-	7.8
		List, S.A. Ms.	UKIP	2,432	4.7	*	-	0.1
		Reddall, P.R.	BNP	1,667	3.2	*		
		Boulding, S.C.	Grn	808	1.6	*		
2005: Con				15,828	30.5			

Sittingbourne & Sheppey [512]

75,855	64.0	Henderson, G.	Con	24,313	50.0		+	8.3
		Harrison, A. Ms.	Lab	11,930	24.6		-	17.1
		Nevols, K.S.	LD	7,943	16.4		+	3.6
		Davison, I.J.	UKIP	2,610	5.4		+	3.1
		Tames, L.A.	BNP	1,305	2.7	*		
		Young, M.J.	MRLP	319	0.7	*		
		Cassidy, D.P.	Ind	158	0.3	*		
2005: Con				12,383	25.5			

Skipton & Ripon [513]

77,381	70.7	Smith, J.R.	Con	27,685	50.6		+	0.6
		Flynn, H.C. Ms.	LD	17,735	32.4		+	5.8
		Hazelgrove, C. Ms.	Lab	5,498	10.0		-	8.2
		Mills, J.R.	UKIP	1,909	3.5	*	-	1.1
		Allen, B.A.	BNP	1,403	2.6	*		
		Bell, R.A.	Ind	315	0.6	*		
		Gilligan, D.	Youth	95	0.2	*		
		Leakey, R.D.	VCCA	84	0.2	*		
2005: Con				9,950	18.2			

Sleaford & North Hykeham [514]

84,806	70.2	Phillips, S.J.	Con	30,719	51.6		+ 1.0
		Harding-Price, D.	LD	10,814	18.2		+ 0.1
		Normington, J.A.	Lab	10,051	16.9		- 9.5
		Overton, M.J. Ms.	LIND	3,806	6.4		
		Doughty, R.	UKIP	2,163	3.6	*	- 1.3
		Clayton, M.P.	BNP	1,977	3.3	*	
2005: Con				19,905	33.4		

Slough [515]

77,473	61.6	Mactaggart, F.M. Ms.*	Lab	21,884	45.8		- 0.4
		Coad, D. Ms.	Con	16,361	34.3		+ 7.9
		Tucker, C.	LD	6,943	14.5		- 2.2
		Mason-Apps, P.W.	UKIP	1,517	3.2	*	- 0.5
		Kennet, M.F. Ms.	Grn	542	1.1	*	- 0.9
		Chaudhary, S.	Ch P	495	1.0	*	
2005: Lab				5,523	11.6		

Solihull [516]

76,288	72.3	Burt, L. Ms.*	LD	23,635	42.9		+ 3.5
		Throup, M.A. Ms.	Con	23,460	42.6		+ 2.9
		Merrill, S. Ms.	Lab	4,891	8.9		- 6.7
		Terry, A.	BNP	1,624	2.9	*	- 0.5
		Ison, J.P.	UKIP	1,200	2.2	*	+ 0.3
		Watts, N.J.	SMRA	319	0.6	*	
2005: Con				175	0.3		

Somerset North [517]

77,306	75.0	Fox, L.*	Con	28,549	49.3		+ 7.5
		Mathew, B.	LD	20,687	35.7		+ 5.5
		Parry-Hearn, S.C.	Lab	6,448	11.1		-10.6
		Taylor, S.E. Ms.	UKIP	2,257	3.9	*	+ 1.4
2005: Con				7,862	13.6		

Somerset North East [518]

67,881	75.4	Rees-Mogg, J.W.	Con	21,130	41.3		+ 2.2
		Norris, D.*	Lab	16,216	31.7		- 7.0
		Coleshill, G.M. Ms.	LD	11,433	22.3		+ 2.7
		Sandell, P.G.	UKIP	1,754	3.4	*	+ 1.2
		Jay, M.E.	Grn	670	1.3	*	
2005: Con				4,914	9.6		

Somerton & Frome [519]

81,548	74.3	Heath, D.W.S.*	LD	28,793	47.5	+ 3.8
		Rees-Mogg, A.M. Ms.	Con	26,976	44.5	+ 1.9
		Oakensen, D.A.	Lab	2,675	4.4 *	- 6.4
		Harding, B.F.	UKIP	1,932	3.2 *	+ 1.3
		Warry, T.N.	ILEU	236	0.4 *	
2005: LD				1,817	3.0	

South Holland & The Deepings [520]

76,243	65.8	Hayes, J.H.*	Con	29,639	59.1	+ 2.1
		Conroy, J.E. Ms.	LD	7,759	15.5	+ 2.6
		Gould, G.D.	Lab	7,024	14.0	- 10.5
		Fairman, R.G.	UKIP	3,246	6.5	+ 2.5
		Harban, R.	BNP	1,796	3.6 *	
		Baxter, A.J.	Grn	724	1.4 *	
2005: Con				21,880	43.6	

South Ribble [521]

75,822	67.9	Fullbrook, L. Ms.	Con	23,396	45.5	+ 6.6
		Borrow, D.S.*	Lab	17,842	34.7	- 9.6
		Fisher, P.	LD	7,271	14.1	- 0.6
		Duxbury, D.T.	UKIP	1,895	3.7 *	+ 1.5
		Gauci, R.C. Ms.	BNP	1,054	2.0 *	
2005: Lab				5,554	10.8	

South Shields [522]

64,084	57.0	Miliband, D.*	Lab	18,995	52.0	- 8.8
		Allen, K. Ms.	Con	7,886	21.6	+ 4.0
		Psallidas, S.A.	LD	5,189	14.2	- 5.0
		Watson, D. Ms.	BNP	2,382	6.5	
		Ford, S.F. Ms.	Grn	762	2.1 *	
		Kaikavoosi, S.	Ind	729	2.0 *	
		Thompson, V.	ND	316	0.9 *	
		Navabi, S.	Ind	168	0.5 *	
		Nettleship, R.	FAWG	91	0.2 *	
2005: Lab				11,109	30.4	

Southampton Itchen [523]

74,532	59.6	Denham, J.Y.*	Lab	16,326	36.8	- 11.5
		Smith, R.M.	Con	16,134	36.3	+ 9.0
		Goodall, D.I.	LD	9,256	20.8	+ 0.1
		Kebbell, A.J.	UKIP	1,928	4.3 *	+ 0.6
		Spottiswoode, J.C.T.	Grn	600	1.4 *	
		Cutter, T.G.F.	TUSC	168	0.4 *	
2005: Lab				192	0.4	

Southampton Test [524]

71,931	61.4	Whitehead, A.P.V.*	Lab	17,001	38.5	− 5.7
		Moulton, J.R.	Con	14,588	33.0	+ 8.0
		Callaghan, D.J.	LD	9,865	22.3	− 1.8
		Hingston, P. Ms.	UKIP	1,726	3.9 *	+ 0.9
		Bluemel, C.F.	Grn	881	2.0 *	− 1.6
		Sanderson, C.R.	Ind	126	0.3 *	
2005: Lab				2,413	5.5	

Southend West [525]

66,918	65.2	Amess, D.A.A.*	Con	20,086	46.1	− 0.1
		Welch, P.	LD	12,816	29.4	+ 5.4
		Flynn, T.	Lab	5,850	13.4	− 9.2
		Cockrill, G.L.	UKIP	1,714	3.9 *	+ 0.5
		Gladwin, T.	BNP	1,333	3.1 *	
		Bolton, B.G.	Grn	644	1.5 *	
		Vel, D.	Ind	617	1.4 *	
		Phillips, T.	ED	546	1.3 *	
2005: Con				7,270	16.7	

Southport [526]

67,200	65.1	Pugh, J.D.*	LD	21,707	49.6	+ 3.3
		Porter, B. Ms.	Con	15,683	35.8	− 1.2
		Conalty, J.	Lab	4,116	9.4	− 3.4
		Durrance, T.J.	UKIP	2,251	5.1	+ 3.3
2005: LD				6,024	13.8	

Spelthorne [527]

70,479	67.1	Kwarteng, K.A.A.	Con	22,261	47.1	− 3.4
		Chapman, M.R.	LD	12,242	25.9	+ 8.8
		Tyler-Moore, A.	Lab	7,789	16.5	−10.8
		Browne, C.A.	UKIP	4,009	8.5	+ 3.9
		Swinglehurst, I.A.	Ind	314	0.7 *	
		Littlewood, H.R.A.	Best	244	0.5 *	
		Couchman, P.D.	TUSC	176	0.4 *	
		Gore, J.S.	CIP	167	0.4 *	
		Leon-Smith, G.	IFED	102	0.2 *	
2005: Con				10,019	21.2	

Stafford [528]

70,667	71.1	Lefroy, J.	Con	22,047	43.9	+ 4.7
		Kidney, D.N.*	Lab	16,587	33.0	−10.2
		Stamp, B.	LD	8,211	16.3	+ 2.0
		Goode, R.	UKIP	1,727	3.4 *	+ 0.1
		Hynd, R.T.	BNP	1,103	2.2 *	
		Shone, M.	Grn	564	1.1 *	
2005: Lab				5,460	10.9	

Staffordshire Moorlands [529]

62,137	70.5	Bradley, K.A. Ms.	Con	19,793	45.2	+ 5.4
		Atkins, C.J.S. Ms.*	Lab	13,104	29.9	- 6.0
		Jebb, H.W.G.	LD	7,338	16.7	- 0.8
		Povey, S.F.	UKIP	3,580	8.2	+ 1.4
2005: Con				6,689	15.3	

Staffordshire South [530]

73,849	68.3	Williamson, G.A.	Con	26,834	53.2	+ 2.5
		McElduff, K.D.	Lab	10,244	20.3	+ 0.3
		Fellows, S.J. Ms.	LD	8,427	16.7	+ 3.3
		Nattrass, M.	UKIP	2,753	5.5	- 4.7
		Bradnock, D.	BNP	1,928	3.8 *	
		Morris, A.G.	Ind	254	0.5 *	
2005: Con				16,590	32.9	

Stalybridge & Hyde [531]

69,081	59.2	Reynolds, J.	Lab	16,189	39.6	- 10.1
		Adlard, R.	Con	13,445	32.9	+ 6.8
		Potter, J.J.	LD	6,965	17.0	+ 1.4
		Jones, A.D.	BNP	2,259	5.5	+ 1.6
		Cooke, J.	UKIP	1,342	3.3 *	+ 1.6
		Bergan, R. Ms.	Grn	679	1.7 *	- 1.4
2005: Lab				2,744	6.7	

Stevenage [532]

68,937	64.8	McPartland, S.A.	Con	18,491	41.4	+ 6.4
		Taylor, S.J. Ms.	Lab	14,913	33.4	- 9.7
		Davies, J.M. Ms.	LD	7,432	16.6	- 1.7
		Mason, M.A. Ms.	UKIP	2,004	4.5 *	+ 1.4
		Green, M.A.	BNP	1,007	2.3 *	
		Vickers, C.J.	ED	366	0.8 *	
		Phillips, S.J.	NCDV	327	0.7 *	
		Cox, D.	Ind	80	0.2 *	
		Ralph, A.J.	YRDPL	31	0.1 *	
2005: Lab				3,578	8.0	

Stirling [533]

66,080	70.9	McGuire, A.C. Ms.*	Lab	19,558	41.8	+ 5.8
		Dalrymple, R.H.	Con	11,254	24.0	- 1.1
		Lindsay, A.J. Ms.	SNP	8,091	17.3	+ 4.7
		Reed, G.R.	LD	6,797	14.5	- 6.2
		Ruskell, M.C.	Grn	746	1.6 *	- 1.4
		Henke, W.P.	UKIP	395	0.8 *	+ 0.4
2005: Lab				8,304	17.7	

Stockport [534]

62,879	62.2	Coffey, A. Ms.*	Lab	16,697	42.7	- 9.6
		Holland, S.A.	Con	9,913	25.3	+ 1.8
		Bodsworth, S.A.	LD	9,778	25.0	+ 3.6
		Warner, D.N.	BNP	1,201	3.1 *	
		Kelly, M.	UKIP	862	2.2 *	- 0.6
		Barber, P.J.	Grn	677	1.7 *	
2005: Lab				6,784	17.3	

Stockton North [535]

66,752	59.2	Cunningham, A.	Lab	16,923	42.8	- 12.0
		Galletley, I.P.	Con	10,247	25.9	+ 4.7
		Latham, P.R.	LD	6,342	16.1	- 2.6
		Macpherson, J.S.	BNP	1,724	4.4 *	+ 1.8
		Cook, F.*	Ind	1,577	4.0 *	
		Parkin, G.H.	UKIP	1,556	3.9 *	+ 1.2
		Saul, I.	ED	1,129	2.9 *	
2005: Lab				6,676	16.9	

Stockton South [536]

73,840	68.1	Wharton, J.S.	Con	19,577	38.9	+ 4.7
		Taylor, D.J. Ms.*	Lab	19,245	38.3	- 9.4
		Bell, J.D. Ms.	LD	7,600	15.1	- 1.0
		Sinclair, W.N.	BNP	1,553	3.1 *	
		Braney, P.B.T.	UKIP	1,471	2.9 *	+ 0.9
		Hossack, Y. Ms.	Ind	536	1.1 *	
		Strike, E.A.	Ch P	302	0.6 *	
2005: Lab				332	0.7	

Stoke-on-Trent Central [537]

61,003	53.2	Hunt, T.J.W.	Lab	12,605	38.8	- 13.6
		Redfern, J.P.	LD	7,039	21.7	+ 3.1
		Bhatti, N. Ms.	Con	6,833	21.0	+ 3.7
		Darby, S.	BNP	2,502	7.7	+ 0.1
		Lovatt, C. Ms.	UKIP	1,402	4.3 *	+ 1.1
		Breeze, P.D.	Ind	959	3.0 *	
		Elsby, G.	ND	399	1.2 *	
		Ward, B.	CITY	303	0.9 *	
		Walker, N.A.	Ind	295	0.9 *	
		Wright, M.S.	TUSC	133	0.4 *	
2005: Lab				5,566	17.1	

Stoke-on-Trent North [538]

72,054	55.8	Walley, J.L. Ms.*	Lab	17,815	44.3	- 11.5
		Large, A.W.	Con	9,580	23.8	+ 6.0
		Fisher, J.M.	LD	7,120	17.7	+ 4.2
		Baddeley, M.J. Ms.	BNP	3,196	8.0	+ 2.0
		Locke, G.L.E.	UKIP	2,485	6.2	+ 2.1
2005: Lab				8,235	20.5	

Stoke-on-Trent South [539]

68,032	58.6	Flello, R.C.D.*	Lab	15,446	38.8	- 8.1
		Rushton, J.S.	Con	11,316	28.4	+ 4.2
		Ali, Z.	LD	6,323	15.9	+ 0.8
		Coleman, M.	BNP	3,762	9.4	+ 0.4
		Barlow, M.H.	UKIP	1,363	3.4 *	+ 0.7
		Follows, T.	SIG	1,208	3.0 *	
		Breeze, M.	Ind	434	1.1 *	
2005: Lab				4,130	10.4	

Stone [540]

67,062	70.4	Cash, B.*	Con	23,890	50.6	+ 2.2
		Tinker, C.M. Ms.	LD	10,598	22.4	+ 3.8
		Lewis, J. Ms.	Lab	9,770	20.7	- 9.0
		Illsley, A.	UKIP	2,481	5.3	+ 2.0
		Hoppe, D.L.	Grn	490	1.0 *	
2005: Con				13,292	28.1	

Stourbridge [541]

69,637	67.8	James, M. Ms.	Con	20,153	42.7	+ 3.4
		Waltho, L. Ms.*	Lab	14,989	31.7	- 10.4
		Bramall, C.A.	LD	7,733	16.4	+ 0.4
		Westrop, M. Ms.	UKIP	2,103	4.5 *	+ 1.8
		Weale, R.	BNP	1,696	3.6 *	
		Duckworth, W.	Grn	394	0.8 *	
		Nicholas, A.R.	Ind	166	0.4 *	
2005: Lab				5,164	10.9	

Strangford [542]

60,539	53.7	Shannon, J.	DUP	14,926	45.9	- 8.8
		Nesbitt, M.	UCUNF	9,050	27.8	
		Girvan, D. Ms.	APNI	2,828	8.7	
		Hanna, C. Ms.	SDLP	2,164	6.7	- 1.8
		Williams, T.	TUV	1,814	5.6	
		Coogan, M.	SF	1,161	3.6 *	- 0.1
		Haig, B. Ms.	Grn	562	1.7 *	
2005: DUP				5,876	18.1	

Stratford-on-Avon [543]

69,517	72.7	Zahawi, N.	Con	26,052	51.5	+ 0.3
		Turner, M.M.	LD	14,706	29.1	+ 1.7
		Johnston, R.	Lab	4,809	9.5	- 6.0
		Parsons, B.R.	UKIP	1,846	3.7 *	+ 1.0
		Jones, G.A.	BNP	1,097	2.2 *	
		Basnett, N.W.	Ind	1,032	2.0 *	
		Varga, K.T. Ms.	Grn	527	1.0 *	- 2.2
		Bishop, F.J.	ED	473	0.9 *	
2005: Con				11,346	22.4	

Streatham [544]

74,532	62.8	Umunna, C.H.	Lab	20,037	42.8	- 4.2
		Nicholson, C.A.	LD	16,778	35.8	+ 6.3
		Bhansali, V.R.	Con	8,578	18.3	+ 2.0
		Findlay, R. Ms.	Grn	861	1.8 *	- 3.7
		Macharia, G.W.	Ch P	237	0.5 *	
		Polenceus, J.	ED	229	0.5 *	
		Lepper, P.R.	WRP	117	0.2 *	
2005: Lab				3,259	7.0	

Stretford & Urmston [545]

70,991	63.3	Green, K. Ms.	Lab	21,821	48.6	- 2.8
		Williams, A.	Con	12,886	28.7	- 1.4
		Cooke, S.	LD	7,601	16.9	+ 3.0
		Owen, D.	UKIP	1,508	3.4 *	+ 1.1
		Westbrook, M.E. Ms.	Grn	916	2.0 *	
		Jacob, S.A.	Ch P	178	0.4 *	
2005: Lab				8,935	19.9	

Stroud [546]

78,286	74.1	Carmichael, W.N.	Con	23,679	40.8	+ 2.5
		Drew, D.E.*	Lab	22,380	38.6	- 1.5
		Andrewartha, D.A.	LD	8,955	15.4	+ 1.5
		Whiteside, M.J.	Grn	1,542	2.7 *	- 3.0
		Parker, S.A.	UKIP	1,301	2.2 *	+ 0.3
		Lomas, A.E.	Ind	116	0.2 *	
2005: Lab				1,299	2.2	

Suffolk Central & Ipswich North [547]

75,786	70.5	Poulter, D.L.J.	Con	27,125	50.8	+ 6.2
		Aalders-Dunthorne, A.P.	LD	13,339	25.0	+ 4.7
		Joshi, B. Ms.	Lab	8,636	16.2	- 12.3
		Philpot, R.B.	UKIP	2,361	4.4 *	+ 0.9
		Stringer, A.G.	Grn	1,452	2.7 *	- 0.6
		Trevitt, W.H.	Ind	389	0.7 *	
		Vass, R.A.	New	118	0.2 *	
2005: Con				13,786	25.8	

Suffolk Coastal [548]

76,572	71.7	Coffey, T.A. Ms.	Con	25,475	46.4	+ 1.8
		Cooper, D. Ms.	LD	16,347	29.8	+ 7.7
		Leeder, A.J.	Lab	8,812	16.1	- 10.1
		Bush, S.F.	UKIP	3,156	5.7	+ 1.9
		Fulcher, R. Ms.	Grn	1,103	2.0 *	- 1.3
2005: Con				9,128	16.6	

Suffolk South [549]

72,498	70.9	Yeo, T.S.K.*	Con	24,550	47.7	+ 5.7
		Bennett, N.A.	LD	15,861	30.8	+ 2.4
		Bishton, E.J. Ms.	Lab	7,368	14.3	- 10.1
		Campbell Bannerman, D.	UKIP	3,637	7.1	+ 2.0
2005: Con				8,689	16.9	

Suffolk West [550]

74,374	64.7	Hancock, M.	Con	24,312	50.6	+ 1.7
		Brooks-Gordon, B.M. Ms.	LD	11,262	23.4	+ 6.2
		Ahmed, A.M.O.	Lab	7,089	14.7	- 14.2
		Smith, I.J.	UKIP	3,085	6.4	+ 1.5
		Johns, R.P.	BNP	1,428	3.0 *	
		Appleby, A.J.	Ind	540	1.1 *	
		Young, C.	CPA	373	0.8 *	
2005: Con				13,050	27.1	

Sunderland Central [551]

74,485	57.0	Elliott, J. Ms.	Lab	19,495	45.9	- 4.1
		Martin, L.	Con	12,770	30.1	+ 5.6
		Dixon, P.	LD	7,191	16.9	+ 0.1
		McCaffrey, J.V.	BNP	1,913	4.5 *	+ 1.4
		Featonby-Warren, P. Ms.	UKIP	1,094	2.6 *	
2005: Lab				6,725	15.8	

Surrey East [552]

76,855	71.1	Gyimah, S.	Con	31,007	56.7	+	0.6
		Lee, D.	LD	14,133	25.9	+	2.0
		Rodda, M.	Lab	4,925	9.0	-	5.8
		Windsor, H. Ms.	UKIP	3,770	6.9	+	2.5
		Hogbin, M.	MRLP	422	0.8 *		
		Pratt, S.	Ind	383	0.7 *		
2005: Con				16,874	30.9		

Surrey Heath [553]

78,107	69.6	Gove, M.A.*	Con	31,326	57.6	+	6.2
		Hilliar, A.R.	LD	14,037	25.8	-	3.0
		Willey, M.J.	Lab	5,552	10.2	-	6.5
		Stroud, M.	UKIP	3,432	6.3	+	3.3
2005: Con				17,289	31.8		

Surrey South West [554]

76,501	74.8	Hunt, J.*	Con	33,605	58.7	+	8.1
		Simpson, M.	LD	17,287	30.2	-	9.2
		Mollet, R.J.	Lab	3,419	6.0	-	1.9
		Meekins, R.	UKIP	1,486	2.6 *	+	0.8
		Allan, C.T. Ms.	Grn	690	1.2 *		
		Hamilton, H.J. Ms.	BNP	644	1.1 *		
		Leighton, L.K.C.	Pirate	94	0.2 *		
		Price, A.S.	ND	34	0.1 *		
2005: Con				16,318	28.5		

Sussex Mid [555]

77,199	72.4	Soames, N.*	Con	28,329	50.7	+	2.5
		Tierney, S. Ms.	LD	20,927	37.5	+	1.8
		Boot, D.T.	Lab	3,689	6.6	-	6.2
		Montgomery, M.D.	UKIP	1,423	2.5 *	-	0.7
		Brown, P.	Grn	645	1.2 *		
		Minihane, S.A.	BNP	583	1.0 *		
		Thunderclap, B.	MRLP	259	0.5 *		
2005: Con				7,402	13.3		

Sutton & Cheam [556]

66,658	72.8	Burstow, P.K.*	LD	22,156	45.7	-	1.2
		Stroud, P.C. Ms.	Con	20,548	42.4	+	1.7
		Allen, K. Ms.	Lab	3,376	7.0	-	4.9
		Clarke, J.J.	BNP	1,014	2.1 *		
		Pickles, D.J.	UKIP	950	2.0 *		
		Hickson, P.H.	Grn	246	0.5 *		
		Dodds, J.B.	ED	106	0.2 *		
		Connolly, M.B.	CPA	52	0.1 *		
		Cullip, M.J.	Libert	41	0.1 *		
		Hammond, B.R.	IFED	19	0.0 *		
2005: LD				1,608	3.3		

Sutton Coldfield [557]

74,489	67.9	Mitchell, A.J.B.*	Con	27,303	54.0	+	1.4
		Pocock, R.L.	Lab	10,298	20.4	-	5.5
		Brighton, R.A.	LD	9,117	18.0	+	1.4
		Grierson, R.J.	BNP	1,749	3.5 *		
		Siddall-Jones, E.	UKIP	1,587	3.1 *	-	1.8
		Rooney, J.	Grn	535	1.1 *		
2005: Con				17,005	33.6		

Swansea East [558]

59,823	54.6	James, S. Ms.*	Lab	16,819	51.5	-	5.1
		Speht, R.	LD	5,981	18.3	-	1.8
		Holliday, C.J.	Con	4,823	14.8	+	4.7
		Jones, D.	PC	2,181	6.7	-	0.2
		Bennett, C.	BNP	1,715	5.2	+	2.8
		Rogers, D.J.	UKIP	839	2.6 *	+	0.4
		Young, T.	Grn	318	1.0 *	-	0.6
2005: Lab				10,838	33.2		

Swansea West [559]

61,334	58.0	Davies, G.R.	Lab	12,335	34.7	-	7.2
		May, P.N.	LD	11,831	33.2	+	4.3
		Kinzett, R.H.	Con	7,407	20.8	+	4.8
		Roberts, H.	PC	1,437	4.0 *	-	2.5
		Bateman, A.	BNP	910	2.6 *		
		Jenkins, T.C.	UKIP	716	2.0 *	+	0.2
		Ross, K.M.	Grn	404	1.1 *	-	1.1
		McCloy, I.A.	Ind	374	1.1 *		
		Williams, R.	TUSC	179	0.5 *		
2005: Lab				504	1.4		

Swindon North [560]

78,384	64.2	Tomlinson, J.P.	Con	22,408	44.6	+ 5.7
		Agarwal, V.	Lab	15,348	30.5	- 14.6
		Lock, K.J. Ms.	LD	8,668	17.2	+ 4.4
		Halden, S.F.	UKIP	1,842	3.7 *	+ 1.4
		Bates, R.J.	BNP	1,542	3.1 *	
		Hughes, J.V.	Grn	487	1.0 *	
2005: Lab				7,060	14.0	

Swindon South [561]

72,619	64.9	Buckland, R.J.	Con	19,687	41.8	+ 4.9
		Snelgrove, A.C. Ms.*	Lab	16,143	34.3	- 6.2
		Hooton, D.J.	LD	8,305	17.6	+ 0.6
		Tingey, R.H.	UKIP	2,029	4.3 *	+ 2.1
		Miles, J.A. Ms.	Grn	619	1.3 *	- 1.6
		Kirk, A.J.	Ch P	176	0.4 *	
		Evans, K.	Ind	160	0.3 *	
2005: Lab				3,544	7.5	

Tamworth [562]

71,962	64.5	Pincher, C.	Con	21,238	45.8	+ 8.7
		Jenkins, B.D.*	Lab	15,148	32.7	- 10.3
		Pinkett, J. Ms.	LD	7,516	16.2	+ 2.1
		Smith, P.W.	UKIP	2,253	4.9 *	+ 2.1
		Detheridge, C.A. Ms.	Ch P	235	0.5 *	
2005: Lab				6,090	13.1	

Tatton [563]

66,746	67.8	Osborne, G.*	Con	24,687	54.6	+ 3.1
		Lomax, D.W.	LD	10,200	22.6	+ 0.8
		Jackson, R.A.	Lab	7,803	17.3	- 6.5
		Flannery, S.C. Ms.	Ind	2,243	5.0 *	
		Gibson, M.G.	Poet	298	0.7 *	
2005: Con				14,487	32.0	

Taunton Deane [564]

82,507	70.5	Browne, J.R.*	LD	28,531	49.1	+ 4.7
		Formosa, M.A.	Con	24,538	42.2	+ 1.1
		Jevon, M.L.P.	Lab	2,967	5.1	- 7.0
		McIntyre, T.	UKIP	2,114	3.6 *	+ 1.2
2005: LD				3,993	6.9	

Telford [565]

65,061	63.5	Wright, D.*	Lab	15,974	38.7	-	9.5
		Biggins, T.H.	Con	14,996	36.3	+	3.2
		Bennion, R.P.	LD	6,399	15.5	+	1.4
		Allen, D.G.	UKIP	2,428	5.9	+	1.2
		Spencer, P.W.	BNP	1,513	3.7 *		
2005: Lab				978	2.4		

Tewkesbury [566]

76,655	70.4	Robertson, L.A.*	Con	25,472	47.2	-	1.0
		Cameron, A.R.	LD	19,162	35.5	+	7.1
		Emmerson, S.	Lab	6,253	11.6	-	8.7
		Jones, B.A.	UKIP	2,230	4.1 *		
		Sidford, M.J.	Grn	525	1.0 *	-	2.2
		Ridgeon, G.F.	MRLP	319	0.6 *		
2005: Con				6,310	11.7		

Thanet North [567]

68,602	63.2	Gale, R.J.*	Con	22,826	52.7	+	4.7
		Britton, M.K.	Lab	9,298	21.5	-	11.1
		Murphy, L.J. Ms.	LD	8,400	19.4	+	3.8
		Parker, R.M. Ms.	UKIP	2,819	6.5	+	2.6
2005: Con				13,528	31.2		

Thanet South [568]

70,045	65.6	Sandys, L.J. Ms.	Con	22,043	48.0	+	6.8
		Ladyman, S.J.*	Lab	14,426	31.4	-	8.1
		Bucklitsch, P.J.	LD	6,935	15.1	+	2.9
		Shonk, T.L.	UKIP	2,529	5.5	+	0.7
2005: Con				7,617	16.6		

Thirsk & Malton [569]

76,416	49.9	McIntosh, A. Ms.*	Con	20,167	52.9	+	1.0
		Keal, H.	LD	8,886	23.3	+	4.5
		Roberts, J.	Lab	5,169	13.6	-	9.8
		Horton, T.	UKIP	2,502	6.6	+	3.5
		Clark, J.S.	Lib	1,418	3.7 *		
2005: Con				11,281	29.6		

Thornbury & Yate [570]

64,092	75.2	Webb, S.J.*	LD	25,032	51.9	-	2.4
		Riddle, M.R.	Con	17,916	37.2	+	6.3
		Egan, R.R. Ms.	Lab	3,385	7.0	-	3.8
		Knight, J. Ms.	UKIP	1,709	3.5 *	+	1.8
		Beacham, T.E.R.	IFED	126	0.3 *		
		Clements, A.G.A.	ND	58	0.1 *		
2005: LD				7,116	14.8		

Thurrock [571]

77,758	58.9	Doyle-Price, J. Ms.	Con	16,869	36.8	+ 3.6
		Morris, C.A.G.	Lab	16,777	36.6	- 9.6
		Davis, C. Ms.	LD	4,901	10.7	- 0.4
		Colgate, E.L. Ms.	BNP	3,618	7.9	+ 1.8
		Broad, C.H.	UKIP	3,390	7.4	+ 4.0
		Araba, A.I. Ms.	Ch P	266	0.6 *	
2005: Lab				92	0.2	

Tiverton & Honiton [572]

76,808	71.5	Parish, N.Q.G.	Con	27,614	50.3	+ 3.6
		Underwood, J.W.R.	LD	18,294	33.3	+ 4.2
		Whitlock, V.C.	Lab	4,907	8.9	- 4.4
		Stanbury, D.P.	UKIP	3,277	6.0	+ 1.2
		Connor, C.D. Ms.	Grn	802	1.5 *	- 1.3
2005: Con				9,320	17.0	

Tonbridge & Malling [573]

71,790	71.5	Stanley, J.P.*	Con	29,723	57.9	+ 5.0
		Simpson, L. Ms.	LD	11,545	22.5	+ 3.0
		Griffiths, D.	Lab	6,476	12.6	-11.3
		Waller, D.L.	UKIP	1,911	3.7 *	- 0.0
		Dawe, S.	Grn	764	1.5 *	
		Easter, M.	NF	505	1.0 *	
		Rogers, L. Ms.	ED	390	0.8 *	
2005: Con				18,178	35.4	

Tooting [574]

73,840	68.6	Khan, S.A.*	Lab	22,038	43.5	+ 0.8
		Clarke, M.A.	Con	19,514	38.5	+ 8.0
		Butt, N.M.	LD	7,509	14.8	- 4.8
		McDonald, S.D.	UKIP	624	1.2 *	+ 0.2
		Vickery, A.R.	Grn	609	1.2 *	- 2.9
		John-Richards, S. Ms.	Ind	190	0.4 *	
		Paul, S.H. Ms.	Ch P	171	0.3 *	
2005: Lab				2,524	5.0	

Torbay [575]

76,244	64.5	Sanders, A.M.*	LD	23,126	47.0	+ 5.2
		Wood, C.M.A.	Con	19,048	38.7	+ 2.9
		Pedrick-Friend, D.	Lab	3,231	6.6	- 7.9
		Parrott, J.H.	UKIP	2,628	5.3	- 2.7
		Conway, A.P. Ms.	BNP	709	1.4 *	
		Moss, S.A.	Grn	468	1.0 *	
2005: LD				4,078	8.3	

Torfaen [576]

61,183	61.5	Murphy, P.P.*	Lab	16,847	44.8	- 12.1
		Burns, J.H.	Con	7,541	20.0	+ 4.2
		Morgan, D.P.	LD	6,264	16.6	+ 0.9
		ab Elis, R.G.	PC	2,005	5.3	- 0.9
		Noble, J. Ms.	BNP	1,657	4.4 *	
		Wildgust, F.	Ind	1,419	3.8 *	
		Dunn, G.	UKIP	862	2.3 *	- 0.9
		Turner-Thomas, R.J.	Ind	607	1.6 *	
		Clarke, O.	Grn	438	1.2 *	
2005: Lab				9,306	24.7	

Totnes [577]

67,962	70.4	Wollaston, S. Ms.	Con	21,940	45.9	+ 3.0
		Brazil, J.C.M.	LD	17,013	35.6	- 1.5
		Whitty, C.A. Ms.	Lab	3,538	7.4	- 4.7
		Beer, J.S.	UKIP	2,890	6.0	- 1.5
		Somerville, L.H. Ms.	Grn	1,181	2.5 *	
		Turner, M.H.	BNP	624	1.3 *	
		Drew, S.B.	Ind	390	0.8 *	
		Hopwood, S.	Ind	267	0.6 *	
2005: Con				4,927	10.3	

Tottenham [578]

68,834	59.1	Lammy, D.*	Lab	24,128	59.3	+ 1.4
		Schmitz, D.R.	LD	7,197	17.7	+ 0.9
		Sullivan, S.	Con	6,064	14.9	+ 1.4
		Sutton, J. Ms.	TUSC	1,057	2.6 *	
		Gray, A.M. Ms.	Grn	980	2.4 *	- 2.2
		McKenzie, W.T.	UKIP	466	1.1 *	
		Watson, N.K.	IPT	265	0.7 *	
		Kadara, A. Ms.	Ch P	262	0.6 *	
		Thompson, S.G.L.	Ind	143	0.4 *	
		Carr, E.W.E.	Ind	125	0.3 *	
2005: Lab				16,931	41.6	

Truro & Falmouth [579]

70,598	69.1	Newton, S.L. Ms.	Con	20,349	41.7	+ 10.0
		Teverson, T.L. Ms.	LD	19,914	40.8	- 0.1
		Mackenzie, C. Ms.	Lab	4,697	9.6	- 9.4
		Blakeley, H.F.	UKIP	1,911	3.9 *	- 1.8
		Rich, L.J.	MK	1,039	2.1 *	
		Wright, I.N.	Grn	858	1.8 *	
2005: LD				435	0.9	

Tunbridge Wells [580]

73,855	68.1	Clark, G.D.*	Con	28,302	56.2	+ 5.6
		Hallas, D.M.	LD	12,726	25.3	+ 0.0
		Heather, G.F.J.	Lab	5,448	10.8	- 9.6
		Webb, V.C.	UKIP	2,054	4.1 *	+ 0.5
		Dawe, H.F. Ms.	Grn	914	1.8 *	
		McBride, A.	BNP	704	1.4 *	
		Bradbury, F.	Ind	172	0.3 *	
2005: Con				15,576	31.0	

Twickenham [581]

80,569	74.1	Cable, V.*	LD	32,483	54.4	+ 2.7
		Thomas, D.H. Ms.	Con	20,343	34.1	+ 1.7
		Tomlinson, B.	Lab	4,583	7.7	- 3.7
		Gilbert, B.P.	UKIP	868	1.5 *	- 0.0
		Roest, S.G.	Grn	674	1.1 *	- 1.7
		Hurst, C.	BNP	654	1.1 *	
		Cole, H.	CURE	76	0.1 *	
		Armstrong, P.	MCP	40	0.1 *	
2005: LD				12,140	20.3	

Tynemouth [582]

75,680	69.6	Campbell, A.*	Lab	23,860	45.3	- 3.0
		Morton, W. Ms.	Con	18,121	34.4	- 2.2
		Appleby, J.C.	LD	7,845	14.9	- 0.2
		Brooke, D. Ms.	BNP	1,404	2.7 *	
		Payne, N.R. Ms.	UKIP	900	1.7 *	
		Erskine, J.A. Ms.	Grn	538	1.0 *	
2005: Lab				5,739	10.9	

Tyneside North [583]

77,690	59.7	Glindon, M.T. Ms.	Lab	23,505	50.7	- 8.7
		Ord, D.	LD	10,621	22.9	+ 0.9
		Mohindra, G.	Con	8,514	18.3	- 0.3
		Burrows, J.	BNP	1,860	4.0 *	
		Blake, C. Ms.	UKIP	1,306	2.8 *	
		Batten, B.	NF	599	1.3 *	
2005: Lab				12,884	27.8	

Tyrone West [584]

61,148	61.0	Doherty, P.*	SF	18,050	48.4	+ 9.5
		Buchanan, T.E.	DUP	7,365	19.8	+ 2.0
		Hussey, R.	UCUNF	5,281	14.2	
		Byrne, J.	SDLP	5,212	14.0	+ 4.9
		Bower, M.J.	APNI	859	2.3 *	
		McClean, C.M.	Ind	508	1.4 *	
2005: SF				10,685	28.7	

Ulster Mid [585]

64,594	63.2	McGuinness, M.*	SF	21,239	52.0	+ 4.4
		McCrea, I.	DUP	5,876	14.4	- 9.1
		Quinn, T.	SDLP	5,826	14.3	- 3.2
		Overend, S. Ms.	UCUNF	4,509	11.0	
		Millar, W.E.	TUV	2,995	7.3	
		Butler, I.	APNI	397	1.0 *	
2005: SF				15,363	37.6	

Upper Bann [586]

74,732	55.4	Simpson, D.*	DUP	14,000	33.8	- 3.7
		Hamilton, H.	UCUNF	10,639	25.7	
		O'Dowd, J.F.	SF	10,237	24.7	+ 3.8
		Kelly, D. Ms.	SDLP	5,276	12.7	- 0.2
		Heading, B.J.	APNI	1,231	3.0 *	
2005: DUP				3,361	8.1	

Uxbridge & Ruislip South [587]

71,160	63.3	Randall, A.J.*	Con	21,758	48.3	+ 3.8
		Garg, S.	Lab	10,542	23.4	- 3.0
		Cox, M.F.	LD	8,995	20.0	- 2.7
		Neal, D.S. Ms.	BNP	1,396	3.1 *	+ 1.2
		Wadsworth, G.M.	UKIP	1,234	2.7 *	+ 1.1
		Harling, M.R.F.	Grn	477	1.1 *	- 1.1
		Cooper, R.	ED	403	0.9 *	
		McAllister, F.	NF	271	0.6 *	
2005: Con				11,216	24.9	

Vale of Clwyd [588]

55,781	63.7	Ruane, C.S.*	Lab	15,017	42.3	- 3.6
		Wright, M.G.	Con	12,508	35.2	+ 3.5
		Penlington, P.A.	LD	4,472	12.6	+ 0.7
		Wyn-Jones, C. Ms.	PC	2,068	5.8	- 1.4
		Si'Ree, I.J.	BNP	827	2.3 *	
		Turner, T.P.	UKIP	515	1.4 *	+ 0.3
		Butler, M.J.	AGS	127	0.4 *	
2005: Lab				2,509	7.1	

Vale of Glamorgan [589]

70,211	69.3	Cairns, A.H.	Con	20,341	41.8	+ 4.4
		Davies, A.E. Ms.	Lab	16,034	32.9	- 7.8
		Parrott, E.S. Ms.	LD	7,403	15.2	+ 2.0
		Johnson, I.J.	PC	2,667	5.5	+ 0.3
		Mahoney, K.	UKIP	1,529	3.1 *	+ 1.4
		Thomas, R.H.	Grn	457	0.9 *	
		Harrold, J.	Ch P	236	0.5 *	
2005: Lab				4,307	8.8	

Vauxhall [590]

74,811	57.7	Hoey, C.L. Ms.*	Lab	21,498	49.8	- 2.0
		Pidgeon, C.V. Ms.	LD	10,847	25.1	- 2.1
		Chambers, G.E.	Con	9,301	21.5	+ 7.0
		Healy, J.	Grn	708	1.6 *	- 2.8
		Navarro, J.W.	ED	289	0.7 *	
		Martin, L.J. Ms.	Ch P	200	0.5 *	
		Lambert, D.P.	Soc	143	0.3 *	
		Drinkall, J.B.	AWP	109	0.3 *	
		Kapetanos, J.	APP	96	0.2 *	
2005: Lab				10,651	24.7	

Wakefield [591]

70,812	62.8	Creagh, M.H. Ms.*	Lab	17,454	39.3	- 4.8
		Story, A.	Con	15,841	35.6	+ 9.1
		Smith, D.S.	LD	7,256	16.3	- 2.5
		Senior, I.	BNP	2,581	5.8	+ 0.1
		Hawkins, M. Ms.	Grn	873	2.0 *	+ 0.0
		Harrop, M.	Ind	439	1.0 *	
2005: Lab				1,613	3.6	

Wallasey [592]

65,915	63.2	Eagle, A. Ms.*	Lab	21,578	51.8	- 2.7
		Fraser, L. Ms.	Con	13,071	31.4	+ 0.9
		Pitt, S.	LD	5,693	13.7	+ 0.9
		Snowden, D.M.	UKIP	1,205	2.9 *	+ 0.6
		Mwaba, E.	Ind	107	0.3 *	
2005: Lab				8,507	20.4	

Walsall North [593]

64,034	56.5	Winnick, D.J.*	Lab	13,385	37.0	-11.2
		Clack, H. Ms.	Con	12,395	34.3	+ 6.8
		Fazal, N. Ms.	LD	4,754	13.1	+ 0.8
		Woodhall, C.J.	BNP	2,930	8.1	+ 2.1
		Hazell, E.A. Ms.	UKIP	1,737	4.8 *	+ 1.1
		Smith, P.E.	D Lab	842	2.3 *	
		Shakir, B.	Ch P	144	0.4 *	
2005: Lab				990	2.7	

Walsall South [594]

64,387	63.5	Vaz, V. Ms.	Lab	16,211	39.7	- 9.5
		Hunt, R.	Con	14,456	35.4	+ 6.9
		Sinha, M.	LD	5,880	14.4	+ 4.6
		Bennett, D.	UKIP	3,449	8.4	+ 3.6
		Khan, G.	Ch P	482	1.2 *	
		Mulia, M.M.	ND	404	1.0 *	
2005: Lab				1,755	4.3	

Walthamstow [595]

64,625	63.4	Creasy, S. Ms.	Lab	21,252	51.8	+	1.5
		Ahmed, F.	LD	11,774	28.7	+	1.6
		Hemsted, A.	Con	5,734	14.0	-	4.2
		Chisholm-Benli, J. Ms.	UKIP	823	2.0 *	-	0.3
		Perrett, D.P.	Grn	767	1.9 *		
		Taaffe, N. Ms.	TUSC	279	0.7 *		
		Mall, A.J.	Ch P	248	0.6 *		
		Warburton, P.	Ind	117	0.3 *		
2005: Lab				9,478	23.1		

Wansbeck [596]

61,782	61.9	Lavery, I.	Lab	17,548	45.8	-	9.3
		Reed, S.L.	LD	10,517	27.5	+	1.0
		Storey, C.	Con	6,714	17.5	+	2.6
		Finlay, S.	BNP	1,418	3.7 *		
		Stokoe, L. Ms.	UKIP	974	2.5 *		
		Best, N.	Grn	601	1.6 *	-	1.8
		Reid, M.	Ind	359	0.9 *		
		Flynn, M.	Ch P	142	0.4 *		
2005: Lab				7,031	18.4		

Wantage [597]

80,456	70.0	Vaizey, E.*	Con	29,284	52.0	+	8.9
		Armitage, A.E.	LD	15,737	27.9	+	0.3
		Mitchell, S.P.	Lab	7,855	13.9	-	10.0
		Jones, J.A.C. Ms.	UKIP	2,421	4.3 *	+	2.8
		Twine, A.	Grn	1,044	1.9 *	-	0.7
2005: Con				13,547	24.0		

Warley [598]

62,751	61.0	Spellar, J.F.*	Lab	20,240	52.9	-	2.0
		Parmar, J.S.	Con	9,484	24.8	+	1.9
		Keating, E.	LD	5,929	15.5	+	2.3
		Harvey, N.	UKIP	2,617	6.8	+	4.7
2005: Lab				10,756	28.1		

Warrington North [599]

70,473	62.7	Jones, H.M. Ms.*	Lab	20,135	45.5	-	7.3
		Campbell, P.T.	Con	13,364	30.2	+	5.9
		Eccles, D.	LD	9,196	20.8	+	2.1
		Scott, A.	Ind	1,516	3.4 *		
2005: Lab				6,771	15.3		

Warrington South [600]

79,182	69.3	Mowat, D.J.	Con	19,641	35.8	+	3.7
		Bent, N.	Lab	18,088	33.0	-	8.3
		Crotty, J. Ms.	LD	15,094	27.5	+	3.5
		Ashington, J.	UKIP	1,624	3.0 *	+	1.2
		Davies, S. Ms.	Grn	427	0.8 *		
2005: Lab				1,553	2.8		

Warwick & Leamington [601]

67,800	72.3	White, C.	Con	20,876	42.6	+	8.2
		Plaskitt, J.A.*	Lab	17,363	35.4	-	9.3
		Beddow, A.C.	LD	8,977	18.3	+	2.4
		Lenton, C.	UKIP	926	1.9 *	+	0.2
		Davison, I.	Grn	693	1.4 *	-	1.9
		Cullinane, J.	Ind	197	0.4 *		
2005: Lab				3,513	7.2		

Warwickshire North [602]

70,138	67.4	Byles, D.A.	Con	18,993	40.2	+	8.1
		O'Brien, M.*	Lab	18,939	40.1	-	7.3
		Martin, E.S.	LD	5,481	11.6	-	1.9
		Holmes, J.	BNP	2,106	4.5 *	+	0.1
		Fowler, S.	UKIP	1,335	2.8 *	+	0.2
		Lane, D.	ED	411	0.9 *		
2005: Lab				54	0.1		

Washington & Sunderland West [603]

68,910	54.2	Hodgson, S. Ms.*	Lab	19,615	52.5	-	16.2
		Cuthbert, I.M.	Con	8,157	21.8	+	6.9
		Andras, P.	LD	6,382	17.1	+	0.9
		McDonald, I.	BNP	1,913	5.1		
		Hudson, L. Ms.	UKIP	1,267	3.4 *		
2005: Lab				11,458	30.7		

Watford [604]

80,798	68.3	Harrington, R.	Con	19,291	34.9	+	5.3
		Brinton, S.V. Ms.	LD	17,866	32.4	+	1.1
		Ward, C.M. Ms.*	Lab	14,750	26.7	-	6.8
		Emerson, A.	BNP	1,217	2.2 *		
		Eardley, G.	UKIP	1,199	2.2 *	-	0.4
		Brandon, I.	Grn	885	1.6 *	-	1.4
2005: Lab				1,425	2.6		

Waveney [605]

78,532	65.1	Aldous, P.	Con	20,571	40.2		+	6.9
		Blizzard, R.J.*	Lab	19,802	38.7		-	6.6
		Dean, A.	LD	6,811	13.3		-	1.8
		Tyler, J.A.	UKIP	2,684	5.2		+	1.5
		Elliott, G.J.	Grn	1,167	2.3	*	-	0.1
		Barfe, L.F.	Ind	106	0.2	*		
2005: Lab				769	1.5			

Wealden [606]

76,537	71.8	Hendry, C.*	Con	31,090	56.6		+	6.1
		Bowers, C.A.	LD	13,911	25.3		+	0.6
		Blackmore, J.L. Ms.	Lab	5,266	9.6		-	7.1
		Docker, D.M.	UKIP	3,319	6.0		+	2.2
		Jonas, D.	Grn	1,383	2.5	*	-	1.8
2005: Con				17,179	31.3			

Weaver Vale [607]

67,269	65.4	Evans, G.T.	Con	16,953	38.5		+	6.9
		Stockton, J.R.	Lab	15,962	36.3		-	9.4
		Hampson, P.J.	LD	8,196	18.6		-	1.1
		Marsh, C.B.	BNP	1,063	2.4	*		
		Remfry, P.M.	UKIP	1,018	2.3	*	-	0.5
		Thorp, H.G.	Grn	338	0.8	*		
		Cooksley, M.J.	Ind	270	0.6	*		
		Reynolds, T.P.C.	Ind	133	0.3	*		
		Charlton, W.M.	Ind	57	0.1	*		
2005: Lab				991	2.3			

Wellingborough [608]

76,846	67.2	Bone, P.W.*	Con	24,918	48.2		+	5.5
		Buckland, J.C. Ms.	Lab	13,131	25.4		-	16.0
		Barron, K.C.	LD	8,848	17.1		+	5.6
		Haynes, A.J.	UKIP	1,636	3.2	*	+	0.9
		Walker, M.R.	BNP	1,596	3.1	*		
		Spencer, T.A.W.	ED	530	1.0	*		
		Hornett, J.T.	Grn	480	0.9	*		
		Crofts, P.J.	TUSC	249	0.5	*		
		Donaldson, G.A.	Ind	240	0.5	*		
		Lavin, M.J.	Ind	33	0.1	*		
2005: Con				11,787	22.8			

Wells [609]

79,432	70.3	Munt, T.J. Ms.	LD	24,560	44.0	+ 6.1
		Heathcoat-Amory, D.*	Con	23,760	42.5	- 1.0
		Merryfield, A.	Lab	4,198	7.5	- 8.1
		Baynes, J.	UKIP	1,711	3.1 *	+ 0.1
		Boyce, H.	BNP	1,004	1.8 *	
		Briton, C.	Grn	631	1.1 *	
2005: Con				800	1.4	

Welwyn Hatfield [610]

72,058	68.0	Shapps, G.*	Con	27,894	57.0	+ 7.4
		Hobday, M.J.	Lab	10,471	21.4	- 14.9
		Zukowskyj, P.M.	LD	8,010	16.4	+ 2.2
		Platt, D.S.	UKIP	1,643	3.4 *	
		Weston, P.J. Ms.	Grn	796	1.6 *	
		Parker, N.R.	Ind	158	0.3 *	
2005: Con				17,423	35.6	

Wentworth & Dearne [611]

72,586	58.0	Healey, J.*	Lab	21,316	50.6	- 11.2
		Donelan, M.E.M. Ms.	Con	7,396	17.6	+ 3.8
		Love, N.	LD	6,787	16.1	- 0.1
		Wilkinson, J.	UKIP	3,418	8.1	+ 4.6
		Baldwin, W.G.	BNP	3,189	7.6	+ 2.9
2005: Lab				13,920	33.1	

West Bromwich East [612]

62,668	60.6	Watson, T.A.*	Lab	17,657	46.5	- 9.2
		Thompson, A.J.	Con	10,961	28.9	+ 6.1
		Garrett, I.A.G.	LD	4,993	13.2	+ 0.8
		Lewin, T.J.	BNP	2,205	5.8	- 0.6
		Cowles, M.A.	ED	1,150	3.0 *	
		Grey, S.G.	UKIP	984	2.6 *	+ 0.9
2005: Lab				6,696	17.6	

West Bromwich West [613]

64,859	55.8	Bailey, A.E.*	Lab	16,263	45.0	- 8.7
		Hardie, A.D.	Con	10,612	29.3	+ 6.6
		Smith, S.L. Ms.	LD	4,336	12.0	+ 1.8
		Green, R.D.	BNP	3,394	9.4	- 1.5
		Ford, M.J.	UKIP	1,566	4.3 *	+ 1.8
2005: Lab				5,651	15.6	

West Ham [614]

85,313	55.0	Brown, L. Ms.*	Lab	29,422	62.7		+10.9
		Morris, V. Ms.	Con	6,888	14.7		+ 2.6
		Pierce, M.	LD	5,392	11.5		+ 1.3
		Gain, S.	CPA	1,327	2.8	*	
		Malik, K.	Ind	1,245	2.7	*	
		Davidson, M.	NF	1,089	2.3	*	
		Gandy, K.E. Ms.	UKIP	766	1.6	*	+ 0.6
		Lithgow, J.A. Ms.	Grn	645	1.4	*	- 1.6
		Agbogun-Toko, G. Ms.	Ind	177	0.4	*	
2005: Lab				22,534	48.0		

Westminster North [615]

66,739	59.3	Buck, K.P. Ms.*	Lab	17,377	43.9		+ 4.0
		Cash, J.C. Ms.	Con	15,251	38.5		+ 5.2
		Blackburn, M.	LD	5,513	13.9		- 5.7
		Smith, T.J.L.	Grn	478	1.2	*	- 3.5
		Curry, S.	BNP	334	0.8	*	
		Badzak, J. Ms.	UKIP	315	0.8	*	- 0.4
		Bahaijoub, A.	Ind	101	0.3	*	
		Roseman, E.	ED	99	0.3	*	
		Fajardo, G. Ms.	Ch P	98	0.2	*	
		Dharamsey, A.J.	Ind	32	0.1	*	
2005: Lab				2,126	5.4		

Westmorland & Lonsdale [616]

66,988	76.9	Farron, T.*	LD	30,896	60.0		+14.1
		McKeever, G.	Con	18,632	36.2		- 8.1
		Todd, J.W.	Lab	1,158	2.2	*	- 5.6
		Mander, J.M.	UKIP	801	1.6	*	+ 0.2
2005: LD				12,264	23.8		

Weston-Super-Mare [617]

78,487	67.2	Penrose, J.D.*	Con	23,356	44.3		+ 4.0
		Bell, M.	LD	20,665	39.2		+ 3.1
		Bradley, D.A.	Lab	5,772	10.9		- 7.7
		Spencer, P.D.	UKIP	1,406	2.7	*	+ 0.2
		Parsons, P.W.	BNP	1,098	2.1	*	+ 0.5
		Peverelle, C.J.	ED	275	0.5	*	
		Satchwell, S.C.	Ind	144	0.3	*	
2005: Con				2,691	5.1		

Wigan [618]

75,407	58.5	Nandy, L.E. Ms.	Lab	21,404	48.5	- 9.6
		Winstanley, M.W.	Con	10,917	24.7	+ 5.8
		Clayton, R.M.	LD	6,797	15.4	- 1.5
		Freeman, A.	UKIP	2,516	5.7	+ 2.3
		Mather, C.E.	BNP	2,506	5.7	
2005: Lab				10,487	23.8	

Wiltshire North [619]

66,315	73.4	Gray, J.W.*	Con	25,114	51.6	+ 1.9
		Evemy, M.S.	LD	17,631	36.2	+ 1.8
		Hughes, J.P.	Lab	3,239	6.7	- 5.3
		Bennett, C.A.	UKIP	1,908	3.9 *	+ 1.2
		Chamberlain, P.C.	Grn	599	1.2 *	
		Allnatt, P.G.	Ind	208	0.4 *	
2005: Con				7,483	15.4	

Wiltshire South West [620]

71,647	68.4	Murrison, A.W.*	Con	25,321	51.7	+ 2.5
		Carbin, T.W.	LD	14,954	30.5	+ 0.3
		Rennison, R.L. Ms.	Lab	5,613	11.5	- 5.7
		Cuthbert-Murray, M.A.	UKIP	2,684	5.5	+ 2.0
		Black, C.N.	Ind	446	0.9 *	
2005: Con				10,367	21.1	

Wimbledon [621]

65,723	72.1	Hammond, S.W.*	Con	23,257	49.1	+ 7.7
		Sheehan, S. Ms.	LD	11,849	25.0	+ 6.8
		Judge, A.J.	Lab	10,550	22.3	- 13.4
		McAleer, M.T.	UKIP	914	1.9 *	+ 1.0
		Thacker, R.K.	Grn	590	1.2 *	- 1.9
		Martin, D.L.	Ch P	235	0.5 *	
2005: Con				11,408	24.1	

Winchester [622]

73,805	75.8	Brine, S.	Con	27,155	48.5	+ 11.2
		Tod, M.	LD	24,107	43.1	- 7.0
		Davies, P.	Lab	3,051	5.5	- 3.9
		Penn-Bull, J.F.D.	UKIP	1,139	2.0 *	- 0.2
		Lancaster, M.	ED	503	0.9 *	
2005: LD				3,048	5.4	

Windsor [623]

69,511	71.3	Afriyie, A.*	Con	30,172	60.8	+ 11.4
		Tisi, J.P.	LD	11,118	22.4	- 4.7
		Jhund, A.S.	Lab	4,910	9.9	- 8.0
		Rye, J.	UKIP	1,612	3.3 *	+ 0.6
		Phillips, P.F.	BNP	950	1.9 *	
		Wall, D.N.	Grn	628	1.3 *	- 1.1
		Hooper, P.J.	Ind	198	0.4 *	
2005: Con				19,054	38.4	

Wirral South [624]

56,099	71.1	McGovern, A. Ms.	Lab	16,276	40.8	- 1.7
		Clarke, J.	Con	15,745	39.5	+ 6.3
		Saddler, J.R.	LD	6,611	16.6	- 5.0
		Scott, D.A.	UKIP	1,274	3.2 *	+ 1.6
2005: Lab				531	1.3	

Wirral West [625]

55,050	71.5	McVey, E. Ms.	Con	16,726	42.5	+ 0.7
		Davies, P.L.	Lab	14,290	36.3	- 4.0
		Reisdorf, P.T.C.	LD	6,630	16.8	+ 0.5
		Griffiths, P.W.B.	UKIP	899	2.3 *	+ 1.1
		Kirwan, D.S.	Ind	506	1.3 *	
		James, D.	CSP	321	0.8 *	
2005: Con				2,436	6.2	

Witham [626]

66,969	69.9	Patel, P. Ms.	Con	24,448	52.2	+ 2.5
		Phelps, M.M. Ms.	LD	9,252	19.8	+ 4.6
		Spademan, J.	Lab	8,656	18.5	- 13.9
		Hodges, D.	UKIP	3,060	6.5	+ 3.8
		Abbott, J.E.	Grn	1,419	3.0 *	
2005: Con				15,196	32.4	

Witney [627]

78,766	73.3	Cameron, D.W.D.*	Con	33,973	58.8	+ 9.4
		Barnes, D.C. Ms.	LD	11,233	19.4	- 3.1
		Goldberg, J.D.	Lab	7,511	13.0	- 9.4
		Macdonald, S.	Grn	2,385	4.1 *	+ 1.0
		Tolstoy-Miloslavsky, N.	UKIP	2,001	3.5 *	+ 0.9
		Hope, A.	MRLP	234	0.4 *	
		Wesson, P.G.	Ind	166	0.3 *	
		Cook, J.P.M.	Ind	151	0.3 *	
		Bex, C.R.	WR	62	0.1 *	
		Barschak, A.A.	Ind	53	0.1 *	
2005: Con				22,740	39.4	

Woking [628]

73,837	71.5	Lord, J.G.C.	Con	26,551	50.3	+	2.9
		Sharpley, R. Ms.	LD	19,744	37.4	+	4.3
		Miller, T.A.C.	Lab	4,246	8.0	-	8.3
		Burberry, R.J.	UKIP	1,997	3.8 *	+	0.9
		Roxburgh, J. Ms.	PPNV	204	0.4 *		
		Temple, R. Ms.	MCP	44	0.1 *		
2005: Con				6,807	12.9		

Wokingham [629]

76,386	71.4	Redwood, J.A.*	Con	28,754	52.7	+	4.6
		Bray, P. Ms.	LD	15,262	28.0	-	4.7
		Davidson, G.H.	Lab	5,516	10.1	-	4.9
		Ashwell, M.A.	Ind	2,340	4.3 *		
		Zebedee, A.P. Ms.	UKIP	1,664	3.1 *	+	0.9
		Bisset, M.D. Ms.	Grn	567	1.0 *		
		Owen, T.C.	MRLP	329	0.6 *		
		Smith, R.	Ind	96	0.2 *		
2005: Con				13,492	24.7		

Wolverhampton North East [630]

58,931	59.2	Reynolds, E.E. Ms.	Lab	14,448	41.4	-	13.3
		Rook, J.A. Ms.	Con	11,964	34.3	+	4.7
		Ross, C.A.	LD	4,711	13.5	+	1.9
		Patten, S.G.	BNP	2,296	6.6		
		Valdmanis, P.	UKIP	1,138	3.3 *	-	0.8
		Bhatoe, S.S.	Soc Lab	337	1.0 *		
2005: Lab				2,484	7.1		

Wolverhampton South East [631]

59,884	58.0	McFadden, P.B.*	Lab	16,505	47.6	-	12.0
		Wood, K.W.	Con	9,912	28.6	+	5.6
		Whitehouse, R.F.	LD	5,277	15.2	+	2.9
		Fanthom, G.E.	UKIP	2,675	7.7	+	2.5
		Handa, S.I.	Ind	338	1.0 *		
2005: Lab				6,593	19.0		

Wolverhampton South West [632]

58,845	68.2	Uppal, P.S.	Con	16,344	40.7	+	2.6
		Marris, R.*	Lab	15,653	39.0	-	4.5
		Lawrence, R.T.	LD	6,430	16.0	+	2.5
		Mobberley, A. Ms.	UKIP	1,487	3.7 *	+	1.2
		Barry, R.J.	EPA	246	0.6 *		
2005: Lab				691	1.7		

Worcester [633]

72,835	67.2	Walker, R.C.	Con	19,358	39.5		+ 4.4
		Foster, M.J.*	Lab	16,376	33.4		- 8.4
		Alderson, J.L. Ms.	LD	9,525	19.4		+ 3.2
		Bennett, J.H.A.	UKIP	1,360	2.8	*	+ 0.4
		Kirby, S.L.	BNP	1,219	2.5	*	+ 0.4
		Stephen, L.J.S.	Grn	735	1.5	*	- 0.5
		Robinson, A.P.	Pirate	173	0.4	*	
		Sandland-Nielsen, P.E.	Ind	129	0.3	*	
		Christian-Brookes, A.J.	Ind	99	0.2	*	
2005: Lab				2,982	6.1		

Worcestershire Mid [634]

72,145	70.6	Luff, P.J.*	Con	27,770	54.5		+ 3.2
		Rowley, A.M. Ms.	LD	11,906	23.4		+ 3.1
		Lunn, R.C.	Lab	7,613	14.9		- 9.1
		White, J.	UKIP	3,049	6.0		+ 1.6
		Matthews, G.E.	Grn	593	1.2	*	
2005: Con				15,864	31.1		

Worcestershire West [635]

72,807	74.3	Baldwin, H.M.M. Ms.	Con	27,213	50.3		+ 5.4
		Burt, R.G.	LD	20,459	37.8		- 1.1
		Barber, P.J. Ms.	Lab	3,661	6.8		- 3.7
		Bovey, C.A.L. Ms.	UKIP	2,119	3.9	*	+ 0.7
		Victory, M.G.	Grn	641	1.2	*	- 1.2
2005: Con				6,754	12.5		

Workington [636]

59,607	65.9	Cunningham, T.A.*	Lab	17,865	45.5		- 6.5
		Pattinson, J.L. Ms.	Con	13,290	33.9		+ 4.8
		Collins, S.B.	LD	5,318	13.5		- 0.9
		Wingfield, M.	BNP	1,496	3.8	*	
		Lee, S.P.	UKIP	876	2.2	*	- 1.2
		Logan, I.R.L.	ED	414	1.1	*	
2005: Lab				4,575	11.7		

Worsley & Eccles South [637]

72,473	57.5	Keeley, B.M. Ms.*	Lab	17,892	42.9		-10.4
		Lindley, I.D.	Con	13,555	32.5		+ 4.8
		Gadsden, C.R.G.	LD	6,883	16.5		+ 3.6
		Townsend, A.	UKIP	2,037	4.9	*	- 1.2
		Whitelegg, P.A.	ED	1,334	3.2	*	
2005: Lab				4,337	10.4		

Worthing East & Shoreham [638]

74,001	65.4	Loughton, T.P.*	Con	23,458	48.5	+ 4.6
		Doyle, J.E.	LD	12,353	25.5	+ 1.2
		Benn, E.S.W. Ms.	Lab	8,087	16.7	- 8.8
		Glennon, M.J.	UKIP	2,984	6.2	+ 1.4
		Board, S.E. Ms.	Grn	1,126	2.3 *	
		Maltby, C.T.	ED	389	0.8 *	
2005: Con				11,105	22.9	

Worthing West [639]

75,945	64.7	Bottomley, P.J.*	Con	25,416	51.7	+ 4.1
		Thorpe, H.I. Ms.	LD	13,687	27.9	+ 1.1
		Ross, I.W.J.	Lab	5,800	11.8	- 7.4
		Wallace, J.R.	UKIP	2,924	6.0	+ 0.7
		Aherne, D.	Grn	996	2.0 *	
		Dearsley, S.	Ch P	300	0.6 *	
2005: Con				11,729	23.9	

Wrekin, The [640]

65,544	70.1	Pritchard, M.A.*	Con	21,922	47.7	+ 5.6
		Kalinauckas, P.	Lab	12,472	27.1	- 12.1
		Cameron-Daw, A.V. Ms.	LD	8,019	17.4	+ 2.4
		Hurst, M.W.	UKIP	2,050	4.5 *	+ 0.9
		Harwood, S. Ms.	BNP	1,505	3.3 *	
2005: Con				9,450	20.6	

Wrexham [641]

50,872	64.8	Lucas, I.C.*	Lab	12,161	36.9	- 9.2
		Rippeth, T.P.	LD	8,503	25.8	+ 2.2
		Hughes, G.B.	Con	8,375	25.4	+ 5.4
		Jones, A.	PC	2,029	6.2	+ 0.4
		Roberts, M.	BNP	1,134	3.4 *	+ 0.4
		Humberstone, J.M.	UKIP	774	2.3 *	
2005: Lab				3,658	11.1	

Wycombe [642]

74,175	64.9	Baker, S.J.	Con	23,423	48.6	+ 1.2
		Guy, S.	LD	13,863	28.8	+ 10.9
		Lomas, A.P.	Lab	8,326	17.3	- 12.8
		Wiseman, J.	UKIP	2,123	4.4 *	+ 0.5
		Khokar, M.A.	Ind	228	0.5 *	
		Fitton, D.A.H.	Ind	188	0.4 *	
2005: Con				9,560	19.9	

Wyre & Preston North [643]

70,201	73.1	Wallace, R.B.L.*	Con	26,877	52.4	- 2.3
		Gallagher, D.C.	LD	11,033	21.5	+ 5.4
		Smith, C.J. Ms.	Lab	10,932	21.3	- 5.9
		Cecil, N.A.V.	UKIP	2,466	4.8 *	+ 2.7
2005: Con				15,844	30.9	

Wyre Forest [644]

76,713	66.3	Garnier, M.R.T.	Con	18,793	36.9	+ 7.8
		Taylor, R.T.*	ICHC	16,150	31.7	
		Knowles, N.	Lab	7,298	14.3	- 8.2
		Farmer, N.M.	LD	6,040	11.9	+10.6
		Wrench, M.J.W.	UKIP	1,498	2.9 *	+ 0.6
		Howells, G.C.	BNP	1,120	2.2 *	
2005: IKHHC				2,643	5.2	

Wythenshawe & Sale East [645]

79,923	51.0	Goggins, P.*	Lab	17,987	44.1	- 8.0
		Clowes, J.C. Ms.	Con	10,412	25.6	+ 3.3
		Eakins, M.	LD	9,107	22.3	+ 0.9
		Todd, B.	BNP	1,572	3.9 *	
		Cassidy, C.	UKIP	1,405	3.4 *	+ 0.4
		Worthington, L. Ms.	TUSC	268	0.7 *	
2005: Lab				7,575	18.6	

Yeovil [646]

82,314	69.4	Laws, D.A.*	LD	31,843	55.7	+ 4.2
		Davis, K.J.	Con	18,807	32.9	- 1.2
		Skevington, L.	Lab	2,991	5.2	- 5.3
		Pearson, N.C.	UKIP	2,357	4.1 *	+ 0.3
		Baehr, R.W.	BNP	1,162	2.0 *	
2005: LD				13,036	22.8	

Ynys Mon [647]

50,075	68.8	Owen, A.*	Lab	11,490	33.4	- 1.3
		Rees, D.	PC	9,029	26.2	- 4.9
		Ridge-Newman, A.	Con	7,744	22.5	+11.4
		Wood, M.	LD	2,592	7.5	+ 0.7
		Rogers, P.	Ind	2,225	6.5	
		Gill, E. Ms.	UKIP	1,201	3.5 *	+ 2.5
		Owen, D.	Ch P	163	0.5 *	
2005: Lab				2,461	7.1	

York Central [648]

76,439	60.8	Bayley, H.*	Lab	18,573	40.0		- 8.9
		Wade Weeks, S. Ms.	Con	12,122	26.1		+ 3.2
		Vassie, C.	LD	11,694	25.2		+ 5.0
		Chase, A.D.	Grn	1,669	3.6	*	- 1.7
		Kelly, J.	BNP	1,171	2.5	*	
		Abbott, P.	UKIP	1,100	2.4	*	+ 0.3
		Vee, E.	MRLP	154	0.3	*	
2005: Lab				6,451	13.9		

York Outer [649]

75,939	70.2	Sturdy, J.C.	Con	22,912	43.0		+ 6.7
		Kirk, M.A. Ms.	LD	19,224	36.1		- 0.7
		Alexander, J.M.	Lab	9,108	17.1		- 9.9
		Morris, J.M. Ms.	UKIP	1,100	2.1	*	
		Smurthwaite, C. Ms.	BNP	956	1.8	*	
2005: LD				3,688	6.9		

Yorkshire East [650]

80,105	64.0	Knight, G.*	Con	24,328	47.5		+ 2.1
		Adamson, R.M.	LD	10,842	21.2		+ 2.2
		Rounding, P.A.	Lab	10,401	20.3		-11.8
		Daniels, C.	UKIP	2,142	4.2	*	+ 0.5
		Pudsey, G.S.	BNP	1,865	3.6	*	
		Allerston, R.	Soc Dem	914	1.8	*	
		Jackson, M.	Grn	762	1.5	*	
2005: Con				13,486	26.3		

4 List of tables

Table 1. Full Summary Results By Country

England	*Votes*	*Votes %*	*% ch*	*Candidates*	*Elected*	*Lost Dep*
Con	9,908,019	39.5	3.8	532	297	0
Lab	7,039,387	28.1	-7.4	532	191	5
LD	6,075,613	24.2	1.3	532	43	0
UKIP	866,564	3.5	0.9	490	0	392
BNP	532,323	2.1	1.3	306	0	235
Grn	258,950	1.0	-0.1	298	1	292
Ind	116,619	0.5	0.1	270	0	261
ED	64,826	0.3	0.2	107	0	106
Respect	33,251	0.1	-0.2	11	0	8
Speaker	22,860	0.1		1	1	0
ICHC	16,150	0.1	0.0	1	0	0
Ch P	15,840	0.1		62	0	62
ISGB	12,174	0.0		1	0	0
NF	10,400	0.0	0.0	16	0	16
BCD	10,331	0.0	1	0	0	
TUSC	8,042	0.0		25	0	25
MRLP	7,158	0.0	0.0	25	0	25
Lib	6,392	0.0	-0.1	4	0	3
CPA	6,276	0.0	0.0	17	0	17
M K	5,379	0.0	0.0	6	0	6
LIND	5,311	0.0		3	0	2
ND	4,723	0.0	0.0	23	0	23
Soc Lab	4,368	0.0	0.0	14	0	14
MIF	4,339	0.0		1	0	0
Soc Alt	3,298	0.0	0.0	4	0	4
Trust	2,699	0.0		1	0	1
MACI	2,590	0.0		1	0	0
BIC	2,182	0.0		1	0	1
LLPB	1,964	0.0		1	0	1
Soc Dem	1,551	0.0		2	0	2
AGS	1,454	0.0	0.0	5	0	5
BIB	1,424	0.0		1	0	1
Pirate	1,220	0.0		8	0	8
SIG	1,208	0.0		1	0	1
CSP	1,173	0.0		2	0	2
TF	1,078	0.0		1	0	1
SMRA	977	0.0		2	0	2
D Lab	842	0.0		1	0	1
EIP	803	0.0	0.0	1	0	1
D Nat	753	0.0		2	0	2
SKGP	746	0.0		1	0	1
WRP	738	0.0	0.0	7	0	7

England	*Votes*	*Votes %*	*% ch*	*Candidates*	*Elected*	*Lost Dep*
PPNV	737	0.0	0.0	3	0	3
IVH	722	0.0		1	0	1
APP	675	0.0		4	0	4
MEP	616	0.0		1	0	1
Ch M	598	0.0		2	0	2
Comm	572	0.0	0.0	4	0	4
IZB	545	0.0	0.0	1	0	1
UPS	494	0.0		1	0	1
Impact	477	0.0		3	0	3
MPEA	475	0.0		1	0	1
Best	474	0.0		2	0	2
JAC	427	0.0		2	0	2
Cor D	396	0.0		1	0	1
ISQM	393	0.0		1	0	1
Reform	379	0.0		1	0	1
Cam Soc	362	0.0		1	0	1
JBNF	333	0.0		1	0	1
CNPG	332	0.0		1	0	1
PNDP	331	0.0		1	0	1
NCDV	327	0.0		1	0	1
IFED	327	0.0		4	0	4
NSPS	325	0.0		1	0	1
You	319	0.0		2	0	2
EPA	319	0.0		2	0	2
CURE	317	0.0		4	0	4
CG	305	0.0	0.0	1	0	1
CITY	303	0.0		1	0	1
Poet	298	0.0		1	0	1
FFR	270	0.0		1	0	1
RRG	266	0.0		1	0	1
JP	265	0.0	0.0	1	0	1
IPT	265	0.0		1	0	1
YRDPL	264	0.0		3	0	3
GSOT	259	0.0		1	0	1
ILEU	236	0.0		1	0	1
Vote	233	0.0	0.0	1	0	1
IUK	230	0.0		1	0	1
C28	217	0.0	0.0	1	0	1
UV	209	0.0		1	0	1
FDP	207	0.0		1	0	1
DDP	202	0.0		1	0	1
Sci	197	0.0		1	0	1
NICF	196	0.0		1	0	1
IEAC	190	0.0		1	0	1

England	Votes	Votes %	% ch	Candidates	Elected	Lost Dep
Libert	182	0.0		2	0	2
MRP	173	0.0		1	0	1
SEP	170	0.0		2	0	2
PPBF	168	0.0		1	0	1
CIP	167	0.0		1	0	1
RTBP	153	0.0		1	0	1
AC	149	0.0		1	0	1
Soc	143	0.0	0.0	1	0	1
TOC	123	0.0		1	0	1
SMA	119	0.0		2	0	2
New	118	0.0		1	0	1
MCP	112	0.0		3	0	3
BP Elvis	112	0.0		1	0	1
Comm L	110	0.0		1	0	1
MEDI	109	0.0		1	0	1
AWP	109	0.0		1	0	1
CTDP	107	0.0		1	0	1
LTT	100	0.0		1	0	1
Youth	95	0.0		1	0	1
AD	95	0.0		1	0	1
Nat Lib	93	0.0		1	0	1
FAWG	91	0.0		1	0	1
VCCA	84	0.0	0.0	1	0	1
NFP	84	0.0		1	0	1
AWL	75	0.0		1	0	1
Nobody	73	0.0		1	0	1
Wessex Reg	62	0.0	0.0	1	0	1
Hum	50	0.0		1	0	1
Rest	45	0.0		1	0	1
PPE	35	0.0		1	0	1
BB	35	0.0		1	0	1
South	31	0.0		1	0	1
Blue	17	0.0		1	0	1

Total Vote 25,081,268

Electorate 38,300,110   65.5% **Turnout**

Scotland	Votes	Votes %	% ch	Candidates	Elected	Lost Dep
Lab	1,035,528	42.0	3.1	59	41	0
SNP	491,386	19.9	2.3	59	6	0
LD	465,471	18.9	-3.7	59	11	0
Con	412,905	16.7	0.9	59	1	2
UKIP	17,223	0.7	0.3	28	0	27
Grn	16,827	0.7	-0.4	20	0	19
BNP	8,910	0.4	0.3	13	0	13
Ind	6,479	0.3	0.1	16	0	15
TUSC	3,530	0.1		10	0	10
SSP	3,157	0.1	-1.7	10	0	10
Soc Lab	1,673	0.1	-0.2	5	0	5
Ch P	835	0.0		1	0	1
Trust	534	0.0		1	0	1
Lib	389	0.0	0.0	1	0	1
SJP	290	0.0		2	0	2
Comm	179	0.0	0.0	1	0	1
SACL	138	0.0		1	0	1
Pirate	128	0.0		1	0	1
Joy	93	0.0		1	0	1
Land	57	0.0		1	0	1
Comm L	48	0.0		1	0	1
Total Vote	2,465,780					
Electorate	3,863,042	63.8%	**Turnout**			

Wales	*Votes*	*Votes %*	*% ch*	*Candidates*	*Elected*	*Lost Dep*
Lab	531,602	36.2	-6.5	40	26	0
Con	382,730	26.1	4.7	40	8	0
LD	295,164	20.1	1.7	40	3	0
PC	165,394	11.3	-1.3	40	3	11
UKIP	35,684	2.4	1.0	40	0	40
BNP	23,088	1.6	1.5	19	0	18
Ind	15,212	1.0	0.4	15	0	12
BGPV	6,458	0.4		1	0	0
Grn	6,293	0.4	-0.1	13	0	13
Ch P	1,947	0.1		8	0	8
Soc Lab	1,155	0.1	0.0	4	0	4
Bean	558	0.0		1	0	1
NF	384	0.0		1	0	1
MRLP	352	0.0		2	0	2
TUSC	341	0.0		2	0	2
Comm	196	0.0	0.0	1	0	1
AGS	127	0.0		1	0	1
Total Vote	1,466,685					
Electorate	2,265,125	64.8%	**Turnout**			

Northern Ireland *Votes*		*Votes %*	*% ch*	*Candidates*	*Elected*	*Lost Dep*
SF	171,942	25.5	1.2	17	5	4
DUP	168,216	25.0	-8.7	16	8	0
SDLP	110,970	16.5	-1.0	18	3	2
UCUNF	102,361	15.2	-2.9	17	0	2
Ind	44,236	6.6	4.8	6	1	4
APNI	42,762	6.3	2.4	18	1	10
TUV	26,300	3.9		10	0	2
Grn	3,542	0.5		4	0	4
PBP	2,936	0.4		1	0	0
ND	606	0.1		1	0	1
Total Vote	673,871					
Electorate	1,169,184	57.6%	**Turnout**			

Table 2. Full Summary Results - Great Britain

Great Britain	*Votes*	*Votes%*	*%ch*	*Candidates*	*Elected*	*Lost Dep*
Con	10,703,654	36.9	3.7	631	306	2
Lab	8,606,517	29.7	-6.5	631	258	5
LD	6,836,248	23.6	0.9	631	57	0
UKIP	919,471	3.2	0.9	558	0	459
BNP	564,321	1.9	1.2	338	0	266
SNP	491,386	1.7	0.1	59	6	0
Grn	282,070	1.0	-0.1	331	1	324
PC	165,394	0.6	-0.1	40	3	11
Ind	138,310	0.5	0.1	301	0	288
ED	64,826	0.2	0.2	107	0	106
Respect	33,251	0.1	-0.1	11	0	8
Speaker	22,860	0.1	0.0	1	1	0
Ch P	18,622	0.1		71	0	71
ICHC	16,150	0.1	0.0	1	0	0
ISGB	12,174	0.0		1	0	0
TUSC	11,913	0.0		37	0	37
NF	10,784	0.0	0.0	17	0	17
BCD	10,331	0.0	1	0	0	
MRLP	7,510	0.0	0.0	27	0	27
Soc Lab	7,196	0.0	-0.1	23	0	23
Lib	6,781	0.0	0.0	5	0	4
BGPV	6,458	0.0		1	0	0
CPA	6,276	0.0	0.0	17	0	17
M K	5,379	0.0	0.0	6	0	6
LIND	5,311	0.0		3	0	2
ND	4,723	0.0	-0.1	23	0	23
MIF	4,339	0.0		1	0	0
Soc Alt	3,298	0.0	0.0	4	0	4
Trust	3,233	0.0		2	0	2
SSP	3,157	0.0	-0.2	10	0	10
MACI	2,590	0.0		1	0	0
BIC	2,182	0.0		1	0	1
LLPB	1,964	0.0		1	0	1
AGS	1,581	0.0	0.0	6	0	6
Soc Dem	1,551	0.0		2	0	2
BIB	1,424	0.0		1	0	1
Pirate	1,348	0.0		9	0	9
SIG	1,208	0.0		1	0	1
CSP	1,173	0.0		2	0	2
TF	1,078	0.0		1	0	1
SMRA	977	0.0		2	0	2
Comm	947	0.0	0.0	6	0	6

Great Britain	Votes	Votes%	%ch	Candidates	Elected	Lost Dep
D Lab	842	0.0		1	0	1
EIP	803	0.0	0.0	1	0	1
D Nat	753	0.0		2	0	2
SKGP	746	0.0		1	0	1
WRP	738	0.0	0.0	7	0	7
PPNV	737	0.0	0.0	3	0	3
IVH	722	0.0		1	0	1
APP	675	0.0		4	0	4
MEP	616	0.0		1	0	1
Ch M	598	0.0		2	0	2
Bean	558	0.0		1	0	1
IZB	545	0.0	0.0	1	0	1
UPS	494	0.0		1	0	1
Impact	477	0.0		3	0	3
MPEA	475	0.0		1	0	1
Best	474	0.0		2	0	2
JAC	427	0.0		2	0	2
Cor D	396	0.0		1	0	1
ISQM	393	0.0		1	0	1
Reform	379	0.0		1	0	1
Cam Soc	362	0.0		1	0	1
JBNF	333	0.0		1	0	1
CNPG	332	0.0		1	0	1
PNDP	331	0.0		1	0	1
NCDV	327	0.0		1	0	1
IFED	327	0.0		4	0	4
NSPS	325	0.0		1	0	1
You	319	0.0		2	0	2
EPA	319	0.0		2	0	2
CURE	317	0.0		4	0	4
CG	305	0.0	0.0	1	0	1
CITY	303	0.0		1	0	1
Poet	298	0.0		1	0	1
SJP	290	0.0		2	0	2
FFR	270	0.0		1	0	1
RRG	266	0.0		1	0	1
JP	265	0.0	0.0	1	0	1
IPT	265	0.0		1	0	1
YRDPL	264	0.0		3	0	3
GSOT	259	0.0		1	0	1
ILEU	236	0.0		1	0	1
Vote	233	0.0	0.0	1	0	1
IUK	230	0.0		1	0	1
C28	217	0.0	0.0	1	0	1

Great Britain	Votes	Votes%	%ch	Candidates	Elected	Lost Dep
UV	209	0.0		1	0	1
FDP	207	0.0		1	0	1
DDP	202	0.0		1	0	1
Sci	197	0.0		1	0	1
NICF	196	0.0		1	0	1
IEAC	190	0.0		1	0	1
Libert	182	0.0		2	0	2
MRP	173	0.0		1	0	1
SEP	170	0.0		2	0	2
PPBF	168	0.0		1	0	1
CIP	167	0.0		1	0	1
Comm L	158	0.0		2	0	2
RTBP	153	0.0		1	0	1
AC	149	0.0		1	0	1
Soc	143	0.0	0.0	1	0	1
SACL	138	0.0		1	0	1
TOC	123	0.0		1	0	1
SMA	119	0.0		2	0	2
New	118	0.0		1	0	1
MCP	112	0.0		3	0	3
BP Elvis	112	0.0		1	0	1
MEDI	109	0.0		1	0	1
AWP	109	0.0		1	0	1
CTDP	107	0.0		1	0	1
LTT	100	0.0		1	0	1
Youth	95	0.0		1	0	1
AD	95	0.0		1	0	1
Nat Lib	93	0.0		1	0	1
Joy	93	0.0		1	0	1
FAWG	91	0.0		1	0	1
VCCA	84	0.0	0.0	1	0	1
NFP	84	0.0		1	0	1
AWL	75	0.0		1	0	1
Nobody	73	0.0		1	0	1
Wessex Reg	62	0.0	0.0	1	0	1
Land	57	0.0		1	0	1
Hum	50	0.0		1	0	1
Rest	45	0.0		1	0	1
PPE	35	0.0		1	0	1
BB	35	0.0		1	0	1
South	31	0.0		1	0	1
Blue	17	0.0		1	0	1

Total Vote 29,013,733

Electorate 44,428,277   65.3% **Turnout**

Table 3.   Full Summary Results - United Kingdom (UK)

UK	Votes	Votes %	% ch	Candidates	Elected	Lost Dep
Con	10,703,654	36.1	3.7	631	306	2
Lab	8,606,517	29.0	-6.2	631	258	5
LD	6,836,248	23.0	1.0	631	57	0
UKIP	919,471	3.1	0.9	558	0	459
BNP	564,321	1.9	1.2	338	0	266
SNP	491,386	1.7	0.1	59	6	0
Grn	285,612	1.0	-0.1	335	1	328
Ind	182,546	0.6	0.2	307	1	292
SF	171,942	0.6	-0.1	17	5	4
DUP	168,216	0.6	-0.3	16	8	0
PC	165,394	0.6	-0.1	40	3	11
SDLP	110,970	0.4	-0.1	18	3	2
UCUNF	102,361	0.3	-0.1	17	0	2
ED	64,826	0.2	0.2	107	0	106
APNI	42,762	0.1	0.0	18	1	10
Respect	33,251	0.1	-0.1	11	0	8
TUV	26,300	0.1		10	0	2
Speaker	22,860	0.1	0.0	1	1	0
Ch P	18,622	0.1		71	0	71
ICHC	16,150	0.1	0.0	1	0	0
ISGB	12,174	0.0		1	0	0
TUSC	11,913	0.0		37	0	37
NF	10,784	0.0	0.0	17	0	17
BCD	10,331	0.0	1	0	1	
MRLP	7,510	0.0	0.0	27	0	27
Soc Lab	7,196	0.0	-0.1	23	0	23
Lib	6,781	0.0	0.0	5	0	4
BGPV	6,458	0.0		1	0	0
CPA	6,276	0.0	0.0	17	0	17
M K	5,379	0.0	0.0	6	0	6
ND	5,329	0.0	-0.1	24	0	24
LIND	5,311	0.0		3	0	2
MIF	4,339	0.0		1	0	0
Soc Alt	3,298	0.0	0.0	4	0	4
Trust	3,233	0.0		2	0	2
SSP	3,157	0.0	-0.1	10	0	10
PBP	2,936	0.0		1	0	0
MACI	2,590	0.0		1	0	0
BIC	2,182	0.0		1	0	1
LLPB	1,964	0.0		1	0	1
AGS	1,581	0.0	0.0	6	0	6
Soc Dem	1,551	0.0		2	0	2
BIB	1,424	0.0		1	0	1
Pirate	1,348	0.0		9	0	9
SIG	1,208	0.0		1	0	1
CSP	1,173	0.0		2	0	2

UK	Votes	Votes %	% ch	Candidates	Elected	Lost Dep
TF	1,078	0.0		1	0	1
SMRA	977	0.0		2	0	2
Comm	947	0.0	0.0	6	0	6
D Lab	842	0.0		1	0	1
EIP	803	0.0	0.0	1	0	1
D Nat	753	0.0		2	0	2
SKGP	746	0.0		1	0	1
WRP	738	0.0	0.0	7	0	7
PPNV	737	0.0	0.0	3	0	3
IVH	722	0.0		1	0	1
APP	675	0.0		4	0	4
MEP	616	0.0		1	0	1
Ch M	598	0.0		2	0	2
Bean	558	0.0		1	0	1
IZB	545	0.0	0.0	1	0	1
UPS	494	0.0		1	0	1
Impact	477	0.0		3	0	3
MPEA	475	0.0		1	0	1
Best	474	0.0		2	0	2
JAC	427	0.0		2	0	2
Cor D	396	0.0		1	0	1
ISQM	393	0.0		1	0	1
Reform	379	0.0		1	0	1
Cam Soc	362	0.0		1	0	1
JBNF	333	0.0		1	0	1
CNPG	332	0.0		1	0	1
PNDP	331	0.0		1	0	1
NCDV	327	0.0		1	0	1
IFED	327	0.0		4	0	4
NSPS	325	0.0		1	0	1
You	319	0.0		2	0	2
EPA	319	0.0		2	0	2
CURE	317	0.0		4	0	4
CG	305	0.0	0.0	1	0	1
CITY	303	0.0		1	0	1
Poet	298	0.0		1	0	1
SJP	290	0.0		2	0	2
FFR	270	0.0		1	0	1
RRG	266	0.0		1	0	1
JP	265	0.0	0.0	1	0	1
IPT	265	0.0		1	0	1
YRDPL	264	0.0		3	0	3
GSOT	259	0.0		1	0	1
ILEU	236	0.0		1	0	1
Vote	233	0.0	0.0	1	0	1
IUK	230	0.0		1	0	1

UK	Votes	Votes %	% ch	Candidates	Elected	Lost Dep
C28	217	0.0	0.0	1	0	1
UV	209	0.0		1	0	1
FDP	207	0.0		1	0	1
DDP	202	0.0		1	0	1
Sci	197	0.0		1	0	1
NICF	196	0.0		1	0	1
IEAC	190	0.0		1	0	1
Libert	182	0.0		2	0	2
MRP	173	0.0		1	0	1
SEP	170	0.0		2	0	2
PPBF	168	0.0		1	0	1
CIP	167	0.0		1	0	1
Comm L	158	0.0		2	0	2
RTBP	153	0.0		1	0	1
AC	149	0.0		1	0	1
Soc	143	0.0	0.0	1	0	1
SACL	138	0.0		1	0	1
TOC	123	0.0		1	0	1
SMA	119	0.0		2	0	2
New	118	0.0		1	0	1
MCP	112	0.0		3	0	3
BP Elvis	112	0.0		1	0	1
MEDI	109	0.0		1	0	1
AWP	109	0.0		1	0	1
CTDP	107	0.0		1	0	1
LTT	100	0.0		1	0	1
Youth	95	0.0		1	0	1
AD	95	0.0		1	0	1
Nat Lib	93	0.0		1	0	1
Joy	93	0.0		1	0	1
FAWG	91	0.0		1	0	1
VCCA	84	0.0	0.0	1	0	1
NFP	84	0.0		1	0	1
AWL	75	0.0		1	0	1
Nobody	73	0.0		1	0	1
Wessex Reg	62	0.0	0.0	1	0	1
Land	57	0.0		1	0	1
Hum	50	0.0		1	0	1
Rest	45	0.0		1	0	1
PPE	35	0.0		1	0	1
BB	35	0.0		1	0	1
South	31	0.0		1	0	1
Blue	17	0.0		1	0	1
Total Vote	29,687,604					
Electorate	45,597,461	65.1%	**Turnout**			

Table 4. Concise Summary Results

	Votes	Votes%	%ch	Candidates	Elected	Lost Dep
England						
Con	9,908,019	39.5	3.8	532	297	0
Lab	7,039,387	28.1	-7.4	532	191	5
LD	6,075,613	24.2	1.3	532	43	0
UKIP	866,564	3.5	0.9	490	0	392
BNP	532,323	2.1	1.3	306	0	235
Grn	258,950	1.0	-0.1	298	1	292
Others	400,412	1.6	0.2	735	1	714
Total Vote	25,081,268			3,425	533	1,638
Electorate	38,300,110	65.5%	**Turnout**			
Scotland						
Con	412,905	16.7	0.9	59	1	2
Lab	1,035,528	42.0	3.1	59	41	0
LD	465,471	18.9	-3.7	59	11	0
SNP	491,386	19.9	2.3	59	6	0
UKIP	17,223	0.7	0.3	28	0	27
BNP	8,910	0.4	0.3	13	0	13
Grn	16,827	0.7	-0.4	20	0	19
Others	17,530	0.7	-2.7	52	0	51
Total Vote	2,465,780			349	59	112
Electorate	3,863,042	63.8%	**Turnout**			
Wales						
Con	382,730	26.1	4.7	40	8	0
Lab	531,602	36.2	-6.5	40	26	0
LD	295,164	20.1	1.7	40	3	0
PC	165,394	11.3	-1.3	40	3	11
UKIP	35,684	2.4	1.0	40	0	40
BNP	23,088	1.6	1.5	19	0	18
Grn	6,293	0.4	-0.1	13	0	13
Others	26,730	1.8	-1.0	36	0	32
Total Vote	1,466,685			268	40	114
Electorate	2,265,125	64.8%	**Turnout**			

	Votes	*Votes%*	*%ch*	*Candidates*	*Elected*	*Lost Dep*
Northern Ireland						
SF	171,942	25.5	1.2	17	5	4
DUP	168,216	25.0	-8.7	16	8	0
SDLP	110,970	16.5	-1.0	18	3	2
UCUNF	102,361	15.2	-2.9	17	0	2
APNI	42,762	6.3	2.4	18	1	10
TUV	26,300	3.9		10	0	2
Grn	3,542	0.5		4	0	4
Others	47,778	7.1	4.7	8	1	5
Total Vote	673,871			108	18	29
Electorate	1,169,184	57.6%	**Turnout**			
Great Britain						
Con	10,703,654	36.9	3.7	631	306	2
Lab	8,606,517	29.7	-6.5	631	258	5
LD	6,836,248	23.6	0.9	631	57	0
UKIP	919,471	3.2	0.9	558	0	459
BNP	564,321	1.9	1.2	338	0	266
SNP	491,386	1.7	0.1	59	6	0
Grn	282,070	1.0	-0.1	331	1	324
PC	165,394	0.6	-0.1	40	3	11
Others	444,672	1.5	-0.1	823	1	797
Total Vote	29,013,733			4,042	632	1,864
Electorate	44,428,277	65.3%	**Turnout**			
UK						
Con	10,703,654	36.1	3.706	631	306	2
Lab	8,606,517	29.0	-6.196	631	258	5
LD	6,836,248	23.0	1.0	631	57	0
UKIP	919,471	3.1	0.9	558	0	459
BNP	564,321	1.9	1.2	338	0	266
SNP	491,386	1.7	0.1	59	6	0
Grn	285,612	1.0	-0.1	335	1	328
SF	171,942	0.6	-0.1	17	5	4
DUP	168,216	0.6	-0.3	16	8	0
PC	165,394	0.6	-0.1	40	3	11
Others	774,843	2.6	-0.1	894	6	818
Total Vote	29,687,604			4,150	650	189
Electorate	45,597,461	65.1%	**Turnout**			

Table 5. General Election Voting in the English Regions

	Con	Lab	LD	Others	Total
East Midlands					
votes	915,933	661,869	463,068	183,409	2,224,279
votes%	41.2	29.8	20.8	8.2	
votes% 2005	37.1	39.0	18.5	5.5	
change	4.1	-9.2	2.4	2.8	
seats	31	15	0	0	46
seats 2005	18	25	1	0	44
electorate					3,332,058
%turnout					66.8
%turnout2005					62.7
change					4.1
Eastern					
votes	1,356,680	564,581	692,932	264,804	2,878,997
votes%	47.1	19.6	24.1	9.2	
votes% 2005	43.3	29.8	21.8	5.0	
change	3.8	-10.2	2.2	4.2	
seats	52	2	4	0	58
seats 2005	40	13	3	0	56
electorate					4,257,453
%turnout					67.6
%turnout2005					64.0
change					3.7
London					
votes	1,174,477	1,245,625	751,613	229,553	3,401,268
votes%	34.5	36.6	22.1	6.7	
votes% 2005	31.9	38.9	21.9	7.3	
change	2.6	-2.3	0.2	-0.5	
seats	28	38	7	0	73
seats 2005	21	44	8	1	74
electorate					5,276,910
%turnout					64.5
%turnout2005					57.8
change					6.6
North East					
votes	282,347	518,263	280,468	108,847	1,189,925
votes%	23.7	43.6	23.6	9.1	
votes% 2005	19.5	52.9	23.3	4.3	
change	4.2	-9.3	0.2	4.9	
seats	2	25	2	0	29
seats 2005	1	28	1	0	30
electorate					1,948,281
%turnout					61.1
%turnout2005					57.4
change					3.6

	Con	*Lab*	*LD*	*Others*	*Total*
North West					
votes	1,038,767	1,289,934	707,774	236,515	3,272,990
votes%	31.7	39.4	21.6	7.2	
votes% 2005	28.7	45.1	21.4	4.9	
change	3.0	-5.7	0.3	2.4	
seats	22	47	6	0	75
seats 2005	9	61	6	0	76
electorate					5,255,192
%turnout					62.3
%turnout2005					57.3
change					4.9
South East					
votes	2,118,035	697,567	1,124,786	353,839	4,294,227
votes%	49.3	16.2	26.2	8.2	
votes% 2005	45.0	24.4	25.4	5.3	
change	4.4	-8.1	0.8	3.0	
seats	74	4	4	2	84
seats 2005	58	19	6	0	83
electorate					6,298,261
%turnout					68.2
%turnout2005					64.7
change					3.5
South West					
votes	1,187,637	426,910	962,954	195,942	2,773,443
votes%	42.8	15.4	34.7	7.1	
votes% 2005	38.6	22.8	32.6	6.0	
change	4.2	-7.4	2.2	1.0	
seats	36	4	15	0	55
seats 2005	22	13	16	0	51
electorate					4,020,915
%turnout					69.0
%turnout2005					66.5
change					2.5
West Midlands					
votes	1,044,081	808,101	540,280	248,110	2,640,572
votes%	39.5	30.6	20.5	9.4	
votes% 2005	35.0	38.7	18.6	7.7	
change	4.5	-8.1	1.9	1.7	
seats	33	24	2	0	59
seats 2005	16 .	39	3	1	59
electorate	.	.	.		4,084,007
%turnout	.	.	.		64.7
%turnout2005	.	.	.		60.7
change	.	.	.		4.0

	Con	Lab	LD	Other	Total
Yorkshire & The Humber					
votes	790,062	826,537	551,738	237,230	2,405,567
votes%	32.8	34.4	22.9	9.9	
votes% 2005	29.1	43.6	20.7	6.6	
change	3.7	-9.2	2.3	3.2	
seats	19	32	3	0	54
seats 2005	9	44	3	0	56
electorate	.	.	.		3,827,033
%turnout	.	.	.		62.9
%turnout2005	.	.	.		59.1
change	.	.	.		3.8

Table 6. General Election Voting in the English Counties

	Con	*Lab*	*LD*	*Other*	*Total*
Avon					
votes	197,886	128,118	192,030	34,422	552,456
votes%	35.8	23.2	34.8	6.2	
votes% 2005	31.9	31.8	30.9	5.4	
change	3.9	-8.6	3.8	0.9	
seats	6	2	3	0	11
seats 2005	2	5	3	0	10
electorate					794,040
%turnout					69.6
%turnout2005					67.4
change					2.2
Bedfordshire					
votes	130,233	79,123	59,184	23,019	291,559
votes%	44.7	27.1	20.3	7.9	
votes% 2005	40.6	34.2	20.3	4.9	
change	4.1	-7.1	0.0	3.0	
seats	4	2	0	0	6
seats 2005	3	3	0	0	6
electorate					430,323
%turnout					67.8
%turnout2005					62.3
change					5.4
Berkshire					
votes	209,400	74,613	104,133	25,672	413,818
votes%	50.6	18.0	25.2	6.2	
votes% 2005	43.5	24.0	27.4	5.0	
change	7.1	-6.0	-2.2	1.2	
seats	7	1	0	0	8
seats 2005	6	2	0	0	8
electorate					599,295
%turnout					69.1
%turnout2005					64.4
change					4.6
Buckinghamshire					
votes	161,323	56,389	75,881	70,210	363,803
votes%	44.3	15.5	20.9	19.3	
votes% 2005	47.8	25.9	21.2	5.0	
change	-3.5	-10.4	-0.4	14.3	
seats	6	0	0	1	7
seats 2005	6	1	0	0	7
electorate					541,314
%turnout					67.2
%turnout2005					64.4
change					2.8

	Con	Lab	LD	Other	Total
Cambridgeshire					
votes	169,389	60,983	109,159	36,797	376,328
votes%	45.0	16.2	29.0	9.8	
votes% 2005	42.8	25.8	26.9	4.5	
change	2.2	-9.6	2.1	5.3	
seats	6	0	1	0	7
seats 2005	6	0	1	0	7
electorate					552,672
%turnout					68.1
%turnout2005					63.5
Change					4.6
Cheshire					
votes	211,043	168,072	109,601	29,288	518,004
votes%	40.7	32.4	21.2	5.7	
votes% 2005	37.1	40.5	20.3	2.0	
change	3.6	-8.1	0.9	3.6	
seats	8	3	0	0	11
seats 2005	4	7	0	0	11
electorate					788,634
%turnout					65.7
%turnout2005					61.0
change					4.7
Cleveland					
votes	69,116	99,665	53,432	27,443	249,656
votes%	27.7	39.9	21.4	11.0	
votes% 2005	23.0	51.9	19.3	5.8	
change	4.7	-12.0	2.1	5.2	
seats	1	4	1	0	6
seats 2005	0	6	0	0	6
electorate					414,460
%turnout					60.2
%turnout2005					57.0
change					3.3
Cornwall					
votes	115,016	24,257	117,307	24,301	280,881
votes%	40.9	8.6	41.8	8.7	
votes% 2005	31.8	15.9	44.4	7.9	
change	9.1	-7.2	-2.7	0.7	
seats	3	0	3	0	6
seats 2005	0	0	5	0	5
electorate					416,114
%turnout					67.5
%turnout2005					65.8
change					1.7

	Con	*Lab*	*LD*	*Other*	*Total*
Cumbria					
votes	104,466	81,518	64,400	14,560	264,944
votes%	39.4	30.8	24.3	5.5	
votes% 2005	37.9	34.8	23.4	3.9	
change	1.5	-4.0	0.9	1.6	
seats	2	3	1	0	6
seats 2005	1	4	1	0	6
electorate					388,434
%turnout					68.2
%turnout2005					63.7
Change					4.5
Derbyshire					
votes	186,869	176,457	110,385	37,896	511,607
votes%	36.5	34.5	21.6	7.4	
votes% 2005	30.1	43.9	21.4	4.6	
change	6.4	-9.4	0.2	2.8	
seats	6	5	0	0	11
seats 2005	1	8	1	0	10
electorate					769,857
%turnout					66.5
%turnout2005					63.4
change					3.0
Devon					
votes	260,513	85,556	200,777	54,454	601,300
votes%	43.3	14.2	33.4	9.1	
votes% 2005	38.1	20.4	32.7	8.8	
change	5.3	-6.2	0.7	0.3	
seats	8	2	2	0	12
seats 2005	5	3	3	0	11
electorate					875,484
%turnout					68.7
%turnout2005					66.4
change					2.3
Dorset					
votes	188,973	47,594	128,322	26,222	391,111
votes%	48.3	12.2	32.8	6.7	
votes% 2005	44.1	18.3	32.8	4.7	
change	4.2	-6.2	0.0	2.0	
seats	7	0	1	0	8
seats 2005	6	1	1	0	8
electorate					573,008
%turnout					68.3
%turnout2005					66.7
change					1.5

	Con	Lab	LD	Other	Total
Durham					
votes	62,077	131,367	69,838	26,920	290,202
votes%	21.4	45.3	24.1	9.3	
votes% 2005	16.6	56.3	21.3	5.8	
change	4.8	-11.0	2.7	3.5	
seats	0	7	0	0	7
seats 2005	0	7	0	0	7
electorate					471,869
%turnout					61.5
%turnout2005					58.4
change					3.1
East Sussex					
votes	166,115	81,571	113,799	44,455	405,940
votes%	40.9	20.1	28.0	11.0	
votes% 2005	39.8	25.4	26.3	8.6	
change	1.2	-5.3	1.8	2.3	
seats	5	0	2	1	8
seats 2005	3	4	1	0	8
electorate					592,891
%turnout					68.5
%turnout2005					64.7
change					3.8
Essex					
votes	417,114	157,134	180,391	92,303	846,942
votes%	49.2	18.6	21.3	10.9	
votes% 2005	46.0	28.9	19.1	6.0	
change	3.3	-10.4	2.2	4.9	
seats	17	0	1	0	18
seats 2005	13	3	1	0	17
electorate					1,278,025
%turnout					66.3
%turnout2005					62.7
change					3.6
Gloucestershire					
votes	143,085	66,858	91,430	17,706	319,079
votes%	44.8	21.0	28.7	5.5	
votes% 2005	41.7	29.3	23.3	5.7	
change	3.2	-8.3	5.3	-0.2	
seats	5	0	1	0	6
seats 2005	3	2	1	0	6
electorate					458,408
%turnout					69.6
%turnout2005					66.2
change					3.4

	Con	*Lab*	*LD*	*Other*	*Total*
Greater Manchester					
votes	317,129	467,912	276,595	100,096	1,161,732
votes%	27.3	40.3	23.8	8.6	
votes% 2005	23.7	47.2	23.3	5.8	
change	3.6	-6.9	0.5	2.8	
seats	2	22	3	0	27
seats 2005	1	23	4	0	28
electorate					1,958,014
%turnout					59.3
%turnout2005					54.7
change					4.7
Hampshire					
votes	435,666	130,830	261,834	51,814	880,144
votes%	49.5	14.9	29.7	5.9	
votes% 2005	42.8	23.2	29.6	4.4	
change	6.7	-8.4	0.2	1.5	
seats	14	2	2	0	18
seats 2005	10	3	4	0	17
electorate					1,304,594
%turnout					67.5
%turnout2005					63.7
change					3.8
Hereford and Worcester					
votes	181,827	66,394	100,433	47,840	396,494
votes%	45.9	16.7	25.3	12.1	
votes% 2005	42.9	24.5	21.8	10.8	
change	2.9	-7.7	3.5	1.3	
seats	8	0	0	0	8
seats 2005	4	2	1	1	8
electorate					573,076
%turnout					69.2
%turnout2005					66.4
change					2.8
Hertfordshire					
votes	282,697	106,478	134,793	37,356	561,324
votes%	50.4	19.0	24.0	6.7	
votes% 2005	44.8	30.2	21.4	3.6	
change	5.6	-11.3	2.6	3.1	
seats	11	0	0	0	11
seats 2005	9	2	0	0	11
electorate					811,809
%turnout					69.1
%turnout2005					66.0
change					3.1

	Con	Lab	LD	Other	Total
Humberside					
votes	151,043	126,655	92,399	40,901	410,998
votes%	36.8	30.8	22.5	10.0	
votes% 2005	33.0	41.0	20.8	5.2	
change	3.8	-10.2	1.7	4.7	
seats	5	5	0	0	10
seats 2005	3	7	0	0	10
electorate					680,430
%turnout					60.4
%turnout2005					57.3
change					3.1
Isle of Wight					
votes	32,810	8,169	22,283	7,002	70,264
votes%	46.7	11.6	31.7	10.0	
votes% 2005	48.9	17.2	29.5	4.3	
change	-2.3	-5.6	2.2	5.6	
seats	1	0	0	0	1
seats 2005	1	0	0	0	1
electorate					109,922
%turnout					63.9
%turnout2005					62.0
change					1.9
Kent					
votes	418,077	174,599	173,176	62,210	828,062
votes%	50.5	21.1	20.9	7.5	
votes% 2005	45.8	32.4	17.3	4.4	
change	4.7	-11.4	3.6	3.1	
seats	17	0	0	0	17
seats 2005	10	7	0	0	17
electorate					1,233,869
%turnout					67.1
%turnout2005					65.3
change					1.8
Lancashire					
votes	276,408	251,017	129,101	57,078	713,604
votes%	38.7	35.2	18.1	8.0	
votes% 2005	35.0	41.4	17.0	6.5	
change	3.7	-6.3	1.1	1.5	
seats	9	6	1	0	16
seats 2005	3	12	0	0	15
electorate					1,107,553
%turnout					64.4
%turnout2005					60.3
change					4.2

	Con	*Lab*	*LD*	*Other*	*Total*
Leicestershire					
votes	208,448	140,367	118,341	41,130	508,286
votes%	41.0	27.6	23.3	8.1	
votes% 2005	37.4	36.1	20.8	5.8	
change	3.7	-8.5	2.5	2.3	
seats	7	3	0	0	10
seats 2005	5	5	0	0	10
electorate					747,287
%turnout					68.0
%turnout2005					63.6
change					4.4
Lincolnshire					
votes	174,729	68,043	70,827	37,509	351,108
votes%	49.8	19.4	20.2	10.7	
votes% 2005	46.8	29.5	17.4	6.3	
change	3.0	-10.1	2.8	4.4	
seats	7	0	0	0	7
seats 2005	6	1	0	0	7
electorate					530,372
%turnout					66.2
%turnout2005					62.5
change					3.7
London					
votes	1,174,477	1,245,625	751,613	229,553	3,401,268
votes%	34.5	36.6	22.1	6.7	
votes% 2005	31.9	38.9	21.9	7.3	
change	2.6	-2.3	0.2	-0.5	
seats	28	38	7	0	73
seats 2005	21	44	8	1	74
electorate					5,276,910
%turnout					64.5
%turnout2005					57.8
change					6.6
Merseyside					
votes	129,721	321,415	128,077	35,493	614,706
votes%	21.1	52.3	20.8	5.8	
votes% 2005	19.4	53.8	22.9	3.9	
change	1.7	-1.5	-2.0	1.9	
seats	1	13	1	0	15
seats 2005	0	15	1	0	16
electorate					1,012,557
%turnout					60.7
%turnout2005					54.1
change					6.6

	Con	Lab	LD	Other	Total
Norfolk					
votes	188,944	83,088	121,710	44,484	438,226
votes%	43.1	19.0	27.8	10.2	
votes% 2005	39.9	30.0	25.4	4.7	
change	3.2	-11.0	2.4	5.4	
seats	7	0	2	0	9
seats 2005	4	3	1	0	8
electorate					646,376
%turnout					67.8
%turnout2005					64.4
change					3.4
North Yorkshire					
votes	187,402	76,186	111,283	25,334	400,205
votes%	46.8	19.0	27.8	6.3	
votes% 2005	43.7	27.9	24.7	3.7	
change	3.2	-8.9	3.1	2.7	
seats	7	1	0	0	8
seats 2005	5	2	1	0	8
electorate					609,772
%turnout					65.6
%turnout2005					65.3
change					.4
Northamptonshire					
votes	163,036	88,535	65,676	26,891	344,138
votes%	47.4	25.7	19.1	7.8	
votes% 2005	43.1	37.5	15.2	4.2	
change	4.3	-11.8	3.9	3.7	
seats	7	0	0	0	7
seats 2005	4	2	0	0	6
electorate					502,134
%turnout					68.5
%turnout2005					65.1
change					3.4
Northumberland					
votes	46,037	48,018	50,818	13,888	158,761
votes%	29.0	30.2	32.0	8.7	
votes% 2005	25.6	39.4	33.7	1.3	
change	3.3	-9.2	-1.7	7.5	
seats	1	2	1	0	4
seats 2005	1	2	1	0	4
electorate					241,620
%turnout					65.7
%turnout2005					61.6
change					4.1

	Con	Lab	LD	Other	Total
Nottinghamshire					
votes	182,851	188,467	97,839	39,983	509,140
votes%	35.9	37.0	19.2	7.9	
votes% 2005	33.1	44.5	16.2	6.3	
change	2.8	-7.5	3.1	1.6	
seats	4	7	0	0	11
seats 2005	2	9	0	0	11
electorate					782,408
%turnout					65.1
%turnout2005					59.7
change					5.4
Oxfordshire					
votes	156,647	59,911	92,999	22,445	332,002
votes%	47.2	18.0	28.0	6.8	
votes% 2005	40.9	23.4	29.0	6.8	
change	6.3	-5.4	-0.9	0.0	
seats	5	1	0	0	6
seats 2005	4	1	1	0	6
electorate					485,085
%turnout					68.4
%turnout2005					65.5
change					2.9
Shropshire					
votes	112,643	52,039	56,622	19,620	240,924
votes%	46.8	21.6	23.5	8.1	
votes% 2005	41.8	30.8	23.0	4.4	
change	5.0	-9.2	0.5	3.7	
seats	4	1	0	0	5
seats 2005	4	1	0	0	5
electorate					351,613
%turnout					68.5
%turnout2005					66.0
Change					2.5
Somerset					
votes	118,756	22,163	129,153	16,207	286,279
votes%	41.5	7.7	45.1	5.7	
votes% 2005	41.4	14.9	40.1	3.6	
change	0.1	-7.1	5.0	2.0	
seats	1	0	4	0	5
seats 2005	2	0	3	0	5
electorate					407,981
%turnout					70.2
%turnout2005					67.2
change					3.0

	Con	Lab	LD	Other	Total
South Yorkshire					
votes	121,131	247,337	139,777	80,472	588,717
votes%	20.6	42.0	23.7	13.7	
votes% 2005	18.0	52.7	21.4	8.0	
change	2.6	-10.7	2.4	5.7	
seats	0	13	1	0	14
seats 2005	0	14	1	0	15
electorate					965,448
%turnout					61.0
%turnout2005					54.9
change					6.1
Staffordshire					
votes	224,879	168,302	97,026	50,560	540,767
votes%	41.6	31.1	17.9	9.3	
votes% 2005	35.2	41.4	15.5	7.8	
change	6.3	-10.3	2.4	1.5	
seats	8	4	0	0	12
seats 2005	3	9	0	0	12
electorate					838,167
%turnout					64.5
%turnout2005					58.2
change					6.3
Suffolk					
votes	168,303	77,775	87,695	30,845	364,618
votes%	46.2	21.3	24.1	8.5	
votes% 2005	41.7	31.8	20.6	6.0	
change	4.5	-10.4	3.4	2.5	
seats	7	0	0	0	7
seats 2005	5	2	0	0	7
electorate					538,248
%turnout					67.7
%turnout2005					65.2
change					2.5
Surrey					
votes	322,236	57,032	166,667	37,918	583,853
votes%	55.2	9.8	28.5	6.5	
votes% 2005	50.5	16.7	28.4	4.4	
change	4.7	-6.9	0.1	2.1	
seats	11	0	0	0	11
seats 2005	11	0	0	0	11
electorate					824,574
%turnout					70.8
%turnout2005					65.5
change					5.4

	Con	*Lab*	*LD*	*Other*	*Total*
Tyne and Wear					
votes	105,117	239,213	106,380	40,596	491,306
votes%	21.4	48.7	21.7	8.3	
votes% 2005	17.4	55.8	23.2	3.6	
change	4.0	-7.1	-1.5	4.7	
seats	0	12	0	0	12
seats 2005	0	13	0	0	13
electorate					820,332
%turnout					59.9
%turnout2005					55.8
change					4.0
Warwickshire					
votes	131,303	79,428	58,837	17,816	287,384
votes%	45.7	27.6	20.5	6.2	
votes% 2005	40.7	36.9	17.9	4.5	
change	5.0	-9.3	2.6	1.7	
seats	6	0	0	0	6
seats 2005	2	3	0	0	5
electorate					408,568
%turnout					70.3
%turnout2005					66.0
change					4.4
West Midlands					
votes	393,429	441,938	227,362	112,274	1,175,003
votes%	33.5	37.6	19.3	9.6	
votes% 2005	29.5	44.4	18.1	8.1	
change	4.0	-6.8	1.3	1.5	
seats	7	19	2	0	28
seats 2005	3	24	2	0	29
electorate					1,912,583
%turnout					61.4
%turnout2005					58.0
change					3.4
West Sussex					
votes	215,761	54,453	114,014	32,113	416,341
votes%	51.8	13.1	27.4	7.7	
votes% 2005	46.7	21.3	26.1	6.0	
change	5.1	-8.2	1.3	1.7	
seats	8	0	0	0	8
seats 2005	7	1	0	0	8
electorate					606,717
%turnout					68.6
%turnout2005					64.8
change					3.8

	Con	Lab	LD	Other	Total
West Yorkshire					
votes	330,486	376,359	208,279	90,523	1,005,647
votes%	32.9	37.4	20.7	9.0	
votes% 2005	27.8	45.9	18.6	7.7	
change	5.1	-8.5	2.1	1.3	
seats	7	13	2	0	22
seats 2005	1	21	1	0	23
electorate					1,571,383
%turnout					64.0
%turnout2005					60.1
change					3.9
Wiltshire					
votes	163,408	52,364	103,935	22,630	342,337
votes%	47.7	15.3	30.4	6.6	
votes% 2005	44.3	24.3	26.9	4.5	
change	3.5	-9.0	3.5	2.1	
seats	6	0	1	0	7
seats 2005	4	2	0	0	6
electorate					495,880
%turnout					69.0
%turnout2005					65.3
change					3.7

Table 8. General Election Voting within the Welsh Assembly Electoral Areas

	Con	*Lab*	*LD*	*PC*	*Other*	*Total*
Mid and West Wales						
votes	86,506	64,280	72,558	60,067	11,992	295,403
votes%	29.3	21.8	24.6	20.3	4.1	
votes% 2005	23.8	26.3	24.2	23.4	2.3	
change	5.4	-4.6	.4	-3.0	1.8	
seats 2010	3	1	2	2	0	8
seats 2005	1	2	3	2	0	8
Electorate						431,085
% turnout						68.5
% turnout 2005						67.2
change 05/10						1.3
North Wales						
votes	95,783	107,544	49,840	40,116	15,414	308,697
votes%	31.0	34.8	16.1	13.0	5.0	
votes% 2005	24.3	40.8	15.4	14.2	5.3	
change	6.8	-6.0	.8	-1.2	-.3	
seats 2010	2	6	0	1	0	9
seats 2005	1	7	0	1	0	9
Electorate						468,581
% turnout						65.9
% turnout 2005						62.9
change 05/10						3.0
South Wales Central						
votes	81,631	125,340	67,028	24,587	16,808	315,394
votes%	25.9	39.7	21.3	7.8	5.3	
votes% 2005	21.0	47.7	20.2	8.5	2.7	
change	4.9	-7.9	1.0	-.7	2.7	
seats 2010	2	5	1	0	0	8
seats 2005	0	7	1	0	0	8
Electorate						493,832
% turnout						63.9
% turnout 2005						62.1
change 05/10						1.8
South Wales East						
votes	66,923	123,448	55,492	19,056	31,255	296,174
votes%	22.6	41.7	18.7	6.4	10.6	
votes% 2005	20.3	48.9	13.7	7.1	10.0	
change	2.3	-7.2	5.1	-.7	.6	
seats 2010	1	7	0	0	0	8
seats 2005	1	6	0	0	1	8
Electorate						466,414
% turnout						63.5
% turnout 2005						61.6
change 05/10						1.9

	Con	Lab	LD	PC	Other	Total
South Wales West						
votes	51,887	110,990	50,246	21,568	16,326	251,017
votes%	20.7	44.2	20.0	8.6	6.5	
votes% 2005	16.8	50.4	18.9	9.6	4.4	
change	3.9	-6.2	1.1	-1.0	2.1	
seats 2010	0	7	0	0	0	7
seats 2005	0	7	0	0	0	7
Electorate						405,213
% turnout						61.9
% turnout 2005						59.3
change 05/10						2.6

Table 9. Seats That Changed Hands 2005– 2010

Conservative gains

From Labour

Aberconwy	Dorset South	Nuneaton
Amber Valley	Dover	Pendle
Basildon S. & Thurrock E.	Dudley South	Plymouth Sutton &
Battersea	Ealing Central & Acton	Devonport
Bedford	Elmet & Rothwell	Portsmouth North
Blackpool N. & Cleveleys	Erewash	Pudsey
Brentford & Isleworth	Gillingham & Rainham	Reading West
Brigg & Goole	Gloucester	Redditch
Brighton Kemptown	Great Yarmouth	Rossendale & Darwen
Bristol North West	Halesowen & Rowley Regis	Rugby
Broxtowe	Harlow	Sherwood
Burton	Harrow East	South Ribble
Bury North	Hastings & Rye	Stafford
Calder Valley	Hendon	Stevenage
Cannock Chase	High Peak	Stockton South
Cardiff North	Hove	Stourbridge
Carlisle	Ipswich	Stroud
Carmarthen W. &	Keighley	Swindon North
Pembrokeshire S.	Kingswood	Swindon South
Chester, City of	Lancaster & Fleetwood	Tamworth
Chatham & Aylesford	Leicestershire North West	Thurrock
Cleethorpes	Lincoln	Vale of Glamorgan
Colne Valley	Loughborough	Warrington South
Corby	Milton Keynes North	Warwick & Leamington
Crawley	Milton Keynes South	Warwickshire North
Crewe & Nantwich	Morecambe & Lunesdale	Watford
Croydon Central	Northampton North	Waveney
Dartford	Northampton South	Weaver Vale
Derbyshire South	Norwich North	Wolverhampton S. W.
Dewsbury		Worcester

From Liberal Democrats

Camborne & Redruth	Montgomeryshire	Romsey & Southampton N.
Cornwall South East	Newton Abbot	Truro & Falmouth
Harrogate & Knaresborough	Oxford West & Abingdon	Winchester
Hereford & Herefordshire S.	Richmond Park	York Outer

From ICHC

Wyre Forest

Labour gains

From Liberal Democrats	Chesterfield	
From No Label	Blaenau Gwent	
From Respect	Bethnal Green & Bow	
From Speaker	Glasgow North East	

Liberal Democrats gains

From Conservative	Eastbourne	
	Solihull	Wells
From Labour	Brent Central	Norwich South
Bradford East	Burnley	Redcar

Green gains

From Labour	Brighton Pavilion

Plaid Cymru gains

From Labour	Arfon

APNI gains

From DUP	Belfast East

Independent gains

From UUP	Down North

Speaker gains

From Con	Buckingham

Table 10. Candidates elected at By-elections during the 2005– 2010 Parliament

Candidate	Party	By-election constituency	By-election Date	Gen. Election constituency	Outcome
Mark Hunter	LD	Cheadle	15-Jul-05	Cheadle	Elected
Jim Devine	Lab	Livingston	29-Sep-05	Livingston	Did not stand (Lab held)
Willie Rennie	LD	Dunfermline & W Fife	09-Feb-06	Dunfermline & W Fife	Defeated
Dai Davies	Ind	Blaenau Gwent	29-Jun-06	Blaenau Gwent	Defeated
Robert Neill	Con	Bromley & Chislehurst	29-Jun-06	Bromley & Chislehurst	Elected
Virendra Sharma	Lab	Ealing, Southall	19-Jul-07	Ealing, Southall	Elected
Philip Wilson	Lab	Sedgefield	19-Jul-07	Sedgefield	Elected
Edward Timpson	Con	Crewe & Nantwich	22-May-08	Crewe & Nantwich	Elected
John Howell	Con	Henley	26-Jun-08	Henley	Elected
David Davis	Con	Haltemprice & Howden	10-Jul-08	Haltemprice & Howden	Elected
John Mason	SNP	Glasgow East	24-Jul-08	Glasgow East	Defeated
Lindsay Roy	Lab	Glenrothes	06-Nov-08	Glenrothes	Elected
Chloe Smith	Con	Norwich North	23-Jul-09	Norwich North	Elected
Willie Bain	Lab	Glasgow N. E.	12-Nov-09	Glasgow N. E.	Elected

*   Three 'old' constituencies -Leicestershire North West, Middlesbrough South and Cleveland East, and Strangford- were vacant at dissolution.

Table 11. Three Way Marginal Seats

Constituency	1st	%maj 1st over 2nd	2nd	%maj 1st over 3rd	3rd
Hampstead & Kilburn	Lab	0.1	Con	1.6	LD
Derby North	Lab	1.4	Con	5.0	LD
Oldham East & Saddleworth	Lab	0.2	LD	5.4	Con
Northampton North	Con	4.8	Lab	6.2	LD
Norwich South	LD	0.7	Lab	6.4	Con
Bradford East	LD	0.9	Lab	6.9	Con
Brighton Pavilion	Grn	2.4	Lab	7.6	Con
Watford	Con	2.6	LD	8.2	Lab
Warrington South	Con	2.8	Lab	8.3	LD
Birmingham Hall Green	Lab	7.8	Respect	8.3	LD
Argyll & Bute	LD	7.6	Con	8.9	Lab
Upper Bann	DUP	8.1	UCUNF	9.1	SF
Plymouth Sutton & Devonport	Con	2.6	Lab	9.6	LD
Great Grimsby	Lab	2.2	Con	10.3	LD
Ealing Central & Acton	Con	7.9	Lab	10.4	LD
Colne Valley	Con	8.7	LD	10.6	Lab
Ynys Mon	Lab	7.1	PC	10.9	Con
Wrexham	Lab	11.1	LD	11.5	Con
Ashfield	Lab	0.4	LD	11.5	Con
Bristol North West	Con	6.5	LD	12.0	Lab
Bristol East	Lab	8.3	Con	12.2	LD
Luton South	Lab	5.5	Con	12.2	LD
Edinburgh West	LD	8.2	Lab	12.7	Con
Edinburgh South	Lab	0.7	LD	13.2	Con
Carmarthen East & Dinefwr	PC	9.2	Lab	13.3	Con
Brentford & Isleworth	Con	3.6	Lab	13.6	LD
Bridgend	Lab	5.9	Con	13.8	LD
Swansea West	Lab	1.4	LD	13.8	Con
Newport East	Lab	4.8	LD	14.0	Con
Huddersfield	Lab	11.0	Con	14.1	LD
Hove	Con	3.7	Lab	14.2	LD
Calder Valley	Con	12.4	Lab	14.2	LD
Nottingham South	Lab	4.3	Con	14.2	LD
York Central	Lab	13.9	Con	14.8	LD
Cambridge	LD	13.5	Con	14.9	Lab
Derbyshire North East	Lab	5.2	Con	14.9	LD
Filton & Bradley Stoke	Con	14.3	Lab	15.5	LD
Bristol South	Lab	9.8	LD	15.5	Con
Lewisham West & Penge	Lab	12.9	LD	15.6	Con
Leicester West	Lab	11.2	Con	15.7	LD
Aberdeen South	Lab	8.1	LD	15.8	Con
Gordon	LD	13.8	SNP	15.9	Lab
Southampton Itchen	Lab	0.4	Con	15.9	LD
Darlington	Lab	7.9	Con	16.0	LD
Belfast East	APNI	4.4	DUP	16.0	UCUNF

Table 12. Seats in Rank Order of % Majority

	Constituency	%maj	maj 2nd		Constituency	%maj	maj 2nd
	Conservative seats				**Conservative seats**		
1	Warwickshire North	0.1	54 Lab	54	Wirral West	6.2	2,436 Lab
2	Camborne & Redruth	0.2	66 LD	55	Cornwall South East	6.5	3,220 LD
3	Thurrock	0.2	92 Lab	56	Bristol North West	6.5	3,274 LD
4	Hendon	0.2	106 Lab	57	Dorset West	6.8	3,923 LD
5	Oxford W. & Abingdon	0.3	176 LD	58	Richmond Park	6.9	4,091 LD
6	Cardiff North	0.4	194 Lab	59	York Outer	6.9	3,688 LD
7	Sherwood	0.4	214 Lab	60	Cannock Chase	7.0	3,195 Lab
8	Stockton South	0.7	332 Lab	61	Loughborough	7.1	3,744 Lab
9	Broxtowe	0.7	389 Lab	62	Harrow East	7.1	3,403 Lab
10	Lancaster & Fleetwood	0.8	333 Lab	63	Warwick & Leamington	7.2	3,513 Lab
11	Truro & Falmouth	0.9	435 LD	64	Swindon South	7.5	3,544 Lab
12	Newton Abbot	1.1	523 LD	65	Ealing Central & Acton	7.9	3,716 Lab
13	Amber Valley	1.2	536 Lab	66	Pendle	8.0	3,585 Lab
14	Waveney	1.5	769 Lab	67	Stevenage	8.0	3,578 Lab
15	Wolverhampton S. W.	1.7	691 Lab	68	Elmet & Rothwell	8.1	4,521 Lab
16	Harrogate & Knaresborough	2.0	1,039 LD	69	Carmarthen W. &		
17	Morecambe & Lunesdale	2.0	866 Lab		Pembrokeshire S.	8.5	3,423 Lab
18	Carlisle	2.0	853 Lab	70	Romsey & Southampton N.	8.5	4,156 LD
19	Stroud	2.2	1,299 Lab	71	Colne Valley	8.7	4,837 LD
20	Weaver Vale	2.3	991 Lab	72	Vale of Glamorgan	8.8	4,307 Lab
21	Lincoln	2.3	1,058 Lab	73	Dumfriesshire, Clydesdale		
22	Watford	2.6	1,425 LD		& Tweeddale	9.1	4,194 Lab
23	Plymouth Sutton &			74	Norwich North	9.2	3,901 Lab
	Devonport	2.6	1,149 Lab	75	Bosworth	9.3	5,032 LD
24	Dewsbury	2.8	1,526 Lab	76	High Peak	9.3	4,677 Lab
25	Warrington South	2.8	1,553 Lab	77	Chelmsford	9.4	5,110 LD
26	Bedford	3.0	1,353 Lab	78	Milton Keynes South	9.4	5,201 Lab
27	Brighton Kemptown	3.1	1,328 Lab	79	Rossendale & Darwen	9.5	4,493 Lab
28	Pudsey	3.4	1,659 Lab	80	Cleethorpes	9.6	4,298 Lab
29	Corby	3.5	1,895 Lab	81	Somerset North East	9.6	4,914 Lab
30	Montgomeryshire	3.5	1,184 LD	82	Great Yarmouth	9.9	4,276 Lab
31	Brentford & Isleworth	3.6	1,958 Lab	83	Dudley South	10.1	3,856 Lab
32	Hove	3.7	1,868 Lab	84	Totnes	10.3	4,927 LD
33	Enfield North	3.8	1,692 Lab	85	Cambridgeshire S. E.	10.3	5,946 LD
34	Hastings & Rye	4.0	1,993 Lab	86	Dover	10.5	5,274 Lab
35	St Albans	4.4	2,305 LD	87	South Ribble	10.8	5,554 Lab
36	Ipswich	4.4	2,079 Lab	88	Peterborough	10.8	4,861 Lab
37	Halesowen & Rowley Regis	4.6	2,023 Lab	89	Stafford	10.9	5,460 Lab
38	Nuneaton	4.6	2,069 Lab	90	Stourbridge	10.9	5,164 Lab
39	Gloucester	4.8	2,420 Lab	91	Harlow	11.2	4,925 Lab
40	Northampton North	4.8	1,936 Lab	92	Aberconwy	11.3	3,398 Lab
41	Bury North	5.0	2,243 Lab	93	Ilford North	11.5	5,404 Lab
42	Kingswood	5.1	2,445 Lab	94	Preseli Pembrokeshire	11.6	4,605 Lab
43	Weston-Super-Mare	5.1	2,691 LD	95	Tewkesbury	11.7	6,310 LD
44	Hereford & Herefordshire S.	5.1	2,481 LD	96	Brigg & Goole	11.7	5,147 Lab
45	Wyre Forest	5.2	2,643 other	97	Crewe & Nantwich	11.8	6,046 Lab
46	Erewash	5.2	2,501 Lab	98	Maidstone & The Weald	12.0	5,889 LD
47	Blackpool N. & Cleveleys	5.3	2,150 Lab	99	Battersea	12.2	5,977 Lab
48	Devon West & Torridge	5.4	2,957 LD	100	Canterbury	12.3	6,048 LD
49	Winchester	5.4	3,048 LD	101	Salisbury	12.3	5,966 LD
50	Chester, City of	5.5	2,583 Lab	102	Aldershot	12.3	5,586 LD
51	Croydon Central	5.8	2,879 Lab	103	Finchley & Golders Green	12.3	5,809 Lab
52	Worcester	6.1	2,982 Lab	104	Calder Valley	12.4	6,431 Lab
53	Keighley	6.2	2,940 Lab	105	Crawley	12.5	5,928 Lab

Constituency	%maj	maj 2nd		Constituency	%maj	maj 2nd
Conservative seats				**Conservative seats**		
106 Worcestershire West	12.5	6,754 LD		162 Horsham	20.5	11,460 LD
107 Reading West	12.6	6,004 Lab		163 Wrekin, The	20.6	9,450 Lab
108 Rugby	12.6	6,000 Lab		164 Rochester & Strood	20.7	9,953 Lab
109 Burton	12.7	6,304 Lab		165 Herefordshire North	20.8	9,887 LD
110 Woking	12.9	6,807 LD		166 Newbury	20.9	12,248 LD
111 Basildon S. & Thurrock E.	12.9	5,772 Lab		167 Bury St Edmunds	21.1	12,380 LD
112 Tamworth	13.1	6,090 Lab		168 Wiltshire South West	21.1	10,367 LD
113 Redditch	13.2	5,821 Lab		169 Spelthorne	21.2	10,019 LD
114 Sussex Mid	13.3	7,402 LD		170 Dartford	21.2	10,628 Lab
115 Cambridgeshire South	13.3	7,838 LD		171 Gainsborough	21.4	10,559 LD
116 Hexham	13.3	5,788 LD		172 Bromsgrove	21.9	11,308 Lab
117 Bournemouth West	13.4	5,583 LD		173 Monmouth	22.4	10,425 Lab
118 Somerset North	13.6	7,862 LD		174 Stratford-on-Avon	22.4	11,346 LD
119 Broadland	13.8	7,292 LD		175 New Forest East	22.6	11,307 LD
120 Chatham & Aylesford	13.9	6,069 Lab		176 Forest of Dean	22.7	11,064 Lab
121 Congleton	13.9	7,063 LD		177 Wellingborough	22.8	11,787 Lab
122 Guildford	14.0	7,782 LD		178 Worthing E. & Shoreham	22.9	11,105 LD
123 Swindon North	14.0	7,060 Lab		179 Harwich & Essex North	23.4	11,447 LD
124 Dorset North	14.1	7,625 LD		180 Cotswolds, The	23.5	12,864 LD
125 Derbyshire South	14.1	7,128 Lab		181 Altrincham & Sale W.	23.5	11,595 LD
126 Filton & Bradley Stoke	14.3	6,914 Lab		182 Chipping Barnet	23.6	11,927 Lab
127 Leicestershire N.W.	14.5	7,511 Lab		183 Bexhill & Battle	23.6	12,880 LD
128 Dorset South	14.8	7,443 Lab		184 Meon Valley	23.7	12,125 LD
129 Shrewsbury & Atcham	15.0	7,944 LD		185 Selby & Ainsty	23.7	12,265 Lab
130 Isle of Wight	15.0	10,527 LD		186 Aylesbury	23.7	12,618 LD
131 Reading East	15.2	7,605 LD		187 Haltemprice & Howden	23.8	11,602 LD
132 Staffordshire Moorlands	15.3	6,689 Lab		188 Derbyshire Mid	23.9	11,292 Lab
133 Wiltshire North	15.4	7,483 LD		189 Worthing West	23.9	11,729 LD
134 Northampton South	15.4	6,004 Lab		190 Macclesfield	23.9	11,959 LD
135 Poole	15.9	7,541 LD		191 Bexleyheath & Crayford	24.0	10,344 Lab
136 Scarborough & Whitby	16.5	8,130 Lab		192 Wantage	24.0	13,547 LD
137 Portsmouth North	16.5	7,289 Lab		193 Wimbledon	24.1	11,408 LD
138 Thanet South	16.6	7,617 Lab		194 Beverley & Holderness	24.4	12,987 LD
139 Suffolk Coastal	16.6	9,128 LD		195 Kensington	24.5	8,616 Lab
140 Milton Keynes North	16.6	8,961 Lab		196 Putney	24.6	10,053 Lab
141 Southend West	16.7	7,270 LD		197 Wokingham	24.7	13,492 LD
142 Clwyd West	16.8	6,419 Lab		198 Uxbridge & Ruislip S.	24.9	11,216 Lab
143 Suffolk South	16.9	8,689 LD		199 Penrith & The Border	24.9	11,241 LD
144 Castle Point	17.0	7,632 other		200 Rutland & Melton	25.4	14,000 LD
145 Bridgwater & Somerset W.	17.0	9,249 LD		201 Sittingbourne & Sheppey	25.5	12,383 Lab
146 Tiverton & Honiton	17.0	9,320 LD		202 Suffolk C.& Ipswich N.	25.8	13,786 LD
147 Devon Central	17.1	9,230 LD		203 Kenilworth & Southam	25.9	12,552 LD
148 Devon East	17.2	9,114 LD		204 Basingstoke	26.0	13,176 LD
149 Enfield Southgate	17.2	7,626 Lab		205 Hertfordshire S. W.	26.3	14,920 LD
150 Bournemouth East	17.6	7,728 LD		206 Hampshire East	26.3	13,497 LD
151 Harborough	17.8	9,797 LD		207 Yorkshire East	26.3	13,486 LD
152 Skipton & Ripon	18.2	9,950 LD		208 Rochford & Southend E.	26.5	11,050 Lab
153 Gillingham & Rainham	18.6	8,680 Lab		209 Norfolk South West	26.7	13,140 LD
154 Folkestone & Hythe	19.2	10,122 LD		210 Hemel Hempstead	27.1	13,406 LD
155 Kettering	19.2	9,094 Lab		211 Suffolk West	27.1	13,050 LD
156 Gravesham	19.7	9,312 Lab		212 Reigate	27.2	13,591 LD
157 Wycombe	19.9	9,560 LD		213 Norfolk Mid	27.3	13,856 LD
158 Norfolk South	19.9	10,940 LD		214 Louth & Horncastle	27.5	13,871 LD
159 Huntingdon	19.9	10,819 LD		215 Bedfordshire Mid	27.6	15,152 LD
160 Ludlow	20.0	9,749 LD		216 Havant	27.7	12,160 LD
161 Shipley	20.1	9,944 Lab		217 Hertford & Stortford	27.9	15,437 LD

Constituency	%maj	maj	2nd	Constituency	%maj	maj	2nd
Conservative seats				**Conservative seats**			
218 Bognor Regis &				271 Epping Forest	32.5	15,131	LD
Littlehampton	27.9	13,063	LD	272 Braintree	32.8	16,121	Lab
219 Hitchin & Harpenden	27.9	15,271	LD	273 Bedfordshire South West	32.8	16,649	LD
220 Chichester	28.0	15,877	LD	274 Staffordshire South	32.9	16,590	Lab
221 Clacton	28.0	12,068	Lab	275 Sleaford & N. Hykeham	33.4	19,905	LD
222 Saffron Walden	28.0	15,242	LD	276 Brentwood & Ongar	33.4	16,921	LD
223 Devizes	28.1	13,005	LD	277 Sutton Coldfield	33.6	17,005	Lab
224 Charnwood	28.1	15,029	LD	278 Esher & Walton	34.1	18,593	LD
225 Grantham & Stamford	28.1	14,826	LD	279 Bedfordshire North East	34.1	18,942	LD
226 Croydon South	28.1	15,818	LD	280 Northamptonshire South	34.2	20,478	LD
227 Stone	28.1	13,292	LD	281 Runnymede & Weybridge	34.3	16,509	LD
228 Ribble Valley	28.2	14,769	Lab	282 Lichfield	34.3	17,683	LD
229 Leicestershire South	28.4	15,524	LD	283 Old Bexley & Sidcup	34.9	15,857	Lab
230 Surrey South West	28.5	16,318	LD	284 Hampshire North West	34.9	18,583	LD
231 Cambridgeshire N. W.	28.6	16,677	LD	285 Hampshire North East	35.1	18,597	LD
232 Boston & Skegness	28.8	12,426	Lab	286 Orpington	35.2	17,200	LD
233 Mole Valley	28.8	15,653	LD	287 Tonbridge & Malling	35.4	18,178	LD
234 Eddisbury	29.2	13,255	LD	288 Sevenoaks	35.4	17,515	LD
235 Epsom & Ewell	29.4	16,134	LD	289 New Forest West	35.5	16,896	LD
236 Rushcliffe	29.5	15,811	LD	290 Welwyn Hatfield	35.6	17,423	Lab
237 Thirsk & Malton	29.6	11,281	LD	291 Romford	36.5	16,954	Lab
238 Derbyshire Dales	29.6	13,866	LD	292 Faversham & Kent Mid	36.6	17,088	LD
239 Basildon & Billericay	29.7	12,338	Lab	293 Daventry	37.1	19,188	LD
240 Arundel & South Downs	29.8	16,691	LD	294 Hertsmere	37.2	17,605	Lab
241 Cities of London &				295 Beckenham	37.3	17,784	LD
Westminster	30.0	11,076	Lab	296 Ruislip, Northwood &			
242 Chingford & Woodford				Pinner	38.0	19,060	Lab
Green	30.1	12,963	Lab	297 Windsor	38.4	19,054	LD
243 Bracknell	30.1	15,704	LD	298 Witney	39.4	22,740	LD
244 Hertfordshire North East	30.1	15,194	LD	299 Aldridge-Brownhills	39.5	15,266	Lab
245 Fylde	30.2	13,185	LD	300 Maldon	40.5	19,407	LD
246 Shropshire North	30.5	15,828	LD	301 Broxbourne	41.2	18,804	Lab
247 Hornchurch & Upminster	30.7	16,371	LD	302 Beaconsfield	41.5	21,782	LD
248 Gosport	30.7	14,413	LD	303 Chelsea & Fulham	42.0	16,722	Lab
249 Wyre & Preston North	30.9	15,844	LD	304 Rayleigh & Wickford	42.7	22,338	LD
250 Surrey East	30.9	16,874	LD	305 South Holland &			
251 Tunbridge Wells	31.0	15,576	LD	The Deepings	43.6	21,880	LD
252 Norfolk North West	31.0	14,810	LD	306 Richmond (Yorks)	43.7	23,336	LD
253 Henley	31.0	16,588	LD				
254 Worcestershire Mid	31.1	15,864	LD	**Labour seats**			
255 Meriden	31.2	16,253	Lab	1 Hampstead & Kilburn	0.1	42	
256 Christchurch	31.2	15,410	LD	2 Bolton West	0.2	92	
257 Thanet North	31.2	13,528	Lab	3 Oldham E. & Saddleworth	0.2	103	
258 Maidenhead	31.2	16,769	LD	4 Sheffield Central	0.4	165	
259 Wealden	31.3	17,179	LD	5 Ashfield	0.4	192	
260 Ashford	31.3	17,297	LD	6 Southampton Itchen	0.4	192	
261 Fareham	31.5	17,092	LD	7 Edinburgh South	0.7	316	
262 Newark	31.5	16,152	Lab	8 Chesterfield	1.2	549	
263 Cambridgeshire N. E.	31.5	16,425	LD	9 Wirral South	1.3	531	
264 Bromley & Chislehurst	31.6	13,900	LD	10 Derby North	1.4	613	
265 Surrey Heath	31.8	17,289	LD	11 Swansea West	1.4	504	
266 Devon South West	31.8	15,874	LD	12 Dudley North	1.7	649	
267 Chesham & Amersham	31.9	16,710	LD	13 Hull North	1.9	641	
268 Tatton	32.0	14,487	LD	14 Rochdale	1.9	889	
269 Banbury	32.4	18,227	LD	15 Great Grimsby	2.2	714	
270 Witham	32.4	15,196	LD	16 Morley & Outwood	2.3	1,101	

Constituency	%maj	maj 2nd	Constituency	%maj	maj 2nd
Labour seats			**Labour seats**		
17 Telford	2.4	978	72 Copeland	9.0	3,833
18 Walsall North	2.7	990	73 Lancashire West	9.0	4,343
19 Birmingham Edgbaston	3.1	1,274	74 Birmingham Erdington	9.2	3,277
20 Halifax	3.4	1,472	75 Bolton North East	9.4	4,084
21 Newcastle-under-Lyme	3.6	1,552	76 Leeds North East	9.6	4,545
22 Middlesbrough S. &			77 Feltham & Heston	9.6	4,658
Cleveland E.	3.6	1,677	78 Bristol South	9.8	4,734
23 Wakefield	3.6	1,613	79 Ellesmere Port & Neston	9.8	4,331
24 Edinburgh N. & Leith	3.6	1,724	80 Ochil & S. Perthshire	10.3	5,187
25 Plymouth Moor View	3.8	1,588	81 Stoke-on-Trent South	10.4	4,130
26 Gedling	3.9	1,859	82 Worsley & Eccles South	10.4	4,337
27 Eltham	4.0	1,663	83 Cardiff South & Penarth	10.6	4,709
28 Walsall South	4.3	1,755	84 Tynemouth	10.9	5,739
29 Nottingham South	4.3	1,772	85 Huddersfield	11.0	4,472
30 Newport East	4.8	1,650	86 Wrexham	11.1	3,658
31 Tooting	5.0	2,524	87 Dunfermline & Fife W.	11.2	5,470
32 Derbyshire North East	5.2	2,445	88 Leicester West	11.2	4,017
33 Exeter	5.2	2,721	89 Slough	11.6	5,523
34 Chorley	5.2	2,593	90 Cardiff West	11.6	4,751
35 Blackpool South	5.3	1,852	91 Workington	11.7	4,575
36 Westminster North	5.4	2,126	92 Newcastle upon Tyne E.	11.8	4,453
37 Southampton Test	5.5	2,413	93 Barrow & Furness	11.8	5,208
38 Luton South	5.5	2,329	94 Bradford South	12.2	4,622
39 Bridgend	5.9	2,263	95 Mansfield	12.4	6,012
40 Dagenham & Rainham	5.9	2,630	96 Rother Valley	12.5	5,866
41 Delyn	6.1	2,272	97 Llanelli	12.5	4,701
42 Gower	6.4	2,683	98 Merthyr Tydfil &		
43 Penistone & Stocksbridge	6.6	3,049	Rhymney	12.6	4,056
44 Durham, City of	6.6	3,067	99 Bishop Auckland	12.7	5,218
45 Birmingham Northfield	6.7	2,782	100 Poplar & Limehouse	12.9	6,030
46 Stalybridge & Hyde	6.7	2,744	101 Lewisham West & Penge	12.9	5,828
47 Harrow West	6.8	3,143	102 Heywood & Middleton	12.9	5,971
48 Bury South	6.8	3,292	103 Glasgow North	13.2	3,898
49 Scunthorpe	6.9	2,549	104 Erith & Thamesmead	13.4	5,703
50 Streatham	7.0	3,259	105 Coventry North West	13.5	6,288
51 Vale of Clwyd	7.1	2,509	106 Salford & Eccles	13.8	5,725
52 Wolverhampton N. E.	7.1	2,484	107 York Central	13.9	6,451
53 Ynys Mon	7.1	2,461	108 Bradford West	14.2	5,763
54 Hyndburn	7.2	3,090	109 Sheffield Heeley	14.2	5,807
55 Alyn & Deeside	7.3	2,919	110 Dumfries & Galloway	14.3	7,449
56 Birmingham Selly Oak	7.5	3,482	111 Hartlepool	14.4	5,509
57 Hammersmith	7.5	3,549	112 Derby South	14.9	6,122
58 Pontypridd	7.6	2,785	113 Lewisham East	14.9	6,216
59 Newcastle upon Tyne N.	7.8	3,414	114 Doncaster Central	14.9	6,229
60 Birmingham Hall Green	7.8	3,799	115 Warrington North	15.3	6,771
61 Darlington	7.9	3,388	116 Brent North	15.4	8,028
62 Sefton Central	8.0	3,862	117 Falkirk	15.4	7,843
63 Aberdeen South	8.1	3,506	118 West Bromwich West	15.6	5,651
64 Clwyd South	8.2	2,834	119 Sunderland Central	15.8	6,725
65 Islington S. & Finsbury	8.2	3,569	120 Leyton & Wanstead	16.0	6,416
66 Bristol East	8.3	3,722	121 Bassetlaw	16.6	8,215
67 Don Valley	8.3	3,595	122 Stockton North	16.9	6,676
68 Coventry South	8.4	3,845	123 Stoke-on-Trent Central	17.1	5,566
69 Batley & Spen	8.6	4,406	124 Blyth Valley	17.3	6,668
70 Oxford East	8.9	4,581	125 Stockport	17.3	6,784
71 Newport West	8.9	3,544	126 Durham North West	17.4	7,612

Constituency	%maj	maj 2nd	Constituency	%maj	maj 2nd
Labour seats			**Labour seats**		
127 Luton North	17.5	7,520	182 Manchester Central	26.1	10,439
128 Manchester Gorton	17.5	6,703	183 Doncaster North	26.3	10,909
129 West Bromwich East	17.6	6,696	184 Neath	26.3	9,775
130 Stirling	17.7	8,304	185 Midlothian	26.4	10,349
131 Leeds West	18.1	7,016	186 Kilmarnock & Loudoun	26.6	12,378
132 Holborn & St Pancras	18.2	9,942	187 Leigh	27.1	12,011
133 Hull West & Hessle	18.2	5,742	188 Coventry North East	27.1	11,775
134 Wansbeck	18.4	7,031	189 Leeds East	27.2	10,293
135 Edinburgh South West	18.6	8,447	190 Ayrshire Central	27.3	12,007
136 Wythenshawe & Sale E.	18.6	7,575	191 Tyneside North	27.8	12,884
137 Leicester South	18.7	8,808	192 Caerphilly	27.8	10,755
138 Liverpool Wavertree	18.9	7,167	193 Islington North	27.8	12,401
139 Wolverhampton S. E.	19.0	6,593	194 Rotherham	27.9	10,462
140 Dulwich & W. Norwood	19.4	9,365	195 Warley	28.1	10,756
141 Ealing North	19.5	9,301	196 Birmingham Ladywood	28.2	10,105
142 Dundee West	19.6	7,278	197 Birmingham Perry Barr	28.3	11,908
143 Stretford & Urmston	19.9	8,935	198 Leeds Central	28.5	10,645
144 Blaydon	20.3	9,117	199 East Kilbride, Strathaven		
145 Renfrewshire East	20.4	10,420	& Lesmahagow	28.5	14,503
146 Wallasey	20.4	8,507	200 Makerfield	28.5	12,490
147 Stoke-on-Trent North	20.5	8,235	201 Barnsley East	28.9	11,090
148 Nottingham East	21.0	6,969	202 Houghton & Sunderland S.	28.9	10,990
149 Ayrshire North & Arran	21.5	9,895	203 Lanark & Hamilton East	29.0	13,478
150 Ayr, Carrick & Cumnock	21.6	9,911	204 Leicester East	29.3	14,082
151 Sedgefield	21.6	8,696	205 St Helens North	29.4	13,101
152 Blackburn	21.7	9,856	206 Durham North	29.5	12,076
153 Ealing Southall	21.7	9,291	207 Barnsley Central	30.0	11,093
154 Oldham West & Royton	21.8	9,352	208 Lewisham Deptford	30.3	12,499
155 Bolton South East	21.8	8,634	209 South Shields	30.4	11,109
156 Newcastle upon Tyne C.	21.9	7,466	210 St Helens S. & Whiston	30.6	14,122
157 Ilford South	22.0	11,287	211 Washington &		
158 Aberdeen North	22.2	8,361	Sunderland West	30.7	11,458
159 Hemsworth	22.5	9,844	212 Hackney N.& Stoke		
160 Livingston	22.5	10,791	Newington	31.1	14,461
161 Bethnal Green & Bow	22.8	11,574	213 Mitcham & Morden	31.2	13,666
162 Edinburgh East	23.0	9,181	214 Glasgow South	31.6	12,658
163 Walthamstow	23.1	9,478	215 Croydon North	31.9	16,481
164 Ashton Under Lyne	23.7	9,094	216 Cynon Valley	32.2	9,617
165 Nottingham North	23.7	8,138	217 Blaenau Gwent	32.5	10,516
166 Normanton, Pontefract			218 Gateshead	32.8	12,549
& Castleford	23.7	10,979	219 Wentworth & Dearne	33.1	13,920
167 Wigan	23.8	10,487	220 Swansea East	33.2	10,838
168 Preston	23.8	7,733	221 Jarrow	33.3	12,908
169 Edmonton	23.8	9,613	222 Hackney S. & Shoreditch	33.3	14,288
170 Birmingham Hodge Hill	24.3	10,302	223 Cumbernauld, Kilsyth &		
171 Linlithgow & Falkirk E.	24.4	12,553	Kirkintilloch East	33.4	13,755
172 Greenwich & Woolwich	24.7	10,153	224 Glasgow Central	34.5	10,551
173 Vauxhall	24.7	10,651	225 Airdrie & Shotts	34.6	12,408
174 Torfaen	24.7	9,306	226 Paisley & Renfrewshire N.	35.0	15,280
175 East Lothian	24.9	12,258	227 Sheffield Brightside &		
176 Hull East	25.1	8,597	Hillsborough	35.0	13,632
177 Sheffield South East	25.4	10,505	228 Islwyn	35.2	12,215
178 Hayes & Harlington	25.4	10,824	229 Aberavon	35.7	11,039
179 Bolsover	25.4	11,182	230 Blackley & Broughton	36.0	12,303
180 Middlesbrough	26.0	8,689	231 Barking	36.5	16,555
181 Denton & Reddish	26.1	9,831	232 Liverpool Riverside	36.5	14,173

Constituency	%maj	maj 2nd		Constituency	%maj	maj 2nd

Labour seats

	Constituency	%maj	maj 2nd
233	Glasgow East	36.8	11,840
234	Camberwell & Peckham	36.8	17,187
235	Rhondda	37.2	11,553
236	Halton	37.5	15,504
237	Ogmore	38.2	13,246
238	Glasgow North West	38.3	13,611
239	Inverclyde	38.4	14,416
240	Garston & Halewood	39.4	16,877
241	Glenrothes	40.6	16,448
242	Dunbartonshire West	41.2	17,408
243	Paisley & Renfrewshire S.	41.5	16,614
244	Tottenham	41.6	16,931
245	Easington	42.9	14,982
246	Motherwell & Wishaw	43.0	16,806
247	Birkenhead	43.6	15,395
248	Rutherglen & Hamilton W.	44.7	21,002
249	Glasgow South West	46.2	14,671
250	West Ham	48.0	22,534
251	Coatbridge, Chryston & Bellshill	49.8	20,714
252	Kirkcaldy & Cowdenbeath	50.2	23,009
253	Bootle	51.3	21,181
254	Liverpool West Derby	51.6	18,467
255	Glasgow North East	54.2	15,942
256	East Ham	55.2	27,826
257	Knowsley	57.5	25,686
258	Liverpool Walton	57.7	19,818

Liberal Democrat seats

	Constituency	%maj	maj 2nd	
1	Solihull	0.3	175	Con
2	Dorset Mid & Poole N.	0.6	269	Con
3	Norwich South	0.7	310	Lab
4	Bradford East	0.9	365	Lab
5	Wells	1.4	800	Con
6	St Austell & Newquay	2.8	1,312	Con
7	Brent Central	3.0	1,345	Lab
8	Somerton & Frome	3.0	1,817	Con
9	Sutton & Cheam	3.3	1,608	Con
10	St Ives	3.7	1,719	Con
11	Manchester Withington	4.2	1,894	Lab
12	Burnley	4.3	1,818	Lab
13	Dunbartonshire East	4.6	2,184	Lab
14	Chippenham	4.7	2,470	Con
15	Cheadle	6.2	3,272	Con
16	Cornwall North	6.4	2,981	Con
17	Eastbourne	6.6	3,435	Con
18	Taunton Deane	6.9	3,993	Con
19	Berwick-upon-Tweed	7.0	2,690	Con
20	Eastleigh	7.2	3,864	Con
21	Birmingham Yardley	7.3	3,002	Lab
22	Argyll & Bute	7.6	3,431	Con
23	Aberdeenshire West & Kincardine	8.2	3,684	Con
24	Edinburgh West	8.2	3,803	Lab
25	Torbay	8.3	4,078	Con
26	Cheltenham	9.3	4,920	Con

Liberal Democrat seats

	Constituency	%maj	maj 2nd	
27	Brecon & Radnorshire	9.6	3,747	Con
28	Devon North	11.3	5,821	Con
29	Carshalton & Wallington	11.5	5,260	Con
30	Berwickshire, Roxburgh & Selkirk	11.6	5,675	Con
31	Redcar	12.4	5,214	Lab
32	Hornsey & Wood Green	12.5	6,875	Lab
33	Portsmouth South	12.6	5,200	Con
34	Cardiff Central	12.7	4,576	Lab
35	Kingston & Surbiton	13.2	7,560	Con
36	Cambridge	13.5	6,792	Con
37	Southport	13.8	6,024	Con
38	Gordon	13.8	6,748	SNP
39	Thornbury & Yate	14.8	7,116	Con
40	Colchester	15.1	6,982	Con
41	Hazel Grove	15.2	6,371	Con
42	Lewes	15.3	7,647	Con
43	Caithness, Sutherland & Easter Ross	16.8	4,826	Lab
44	Inverness, Nairn, Badenoch & Strathspey	18.6	8,765	Lab
45	Bermondsey & Old Southwark	19.1	8,530	Lab
46	Twickenham	20.3	12,140	Con
47	Bristol West	20.5	11,366	Lab
48	Leeds North West	20.9	9,103	Con
49	Ceredigion	21.8	8,324	PC
50	Fife North East	22.6	9,048	Con
51	Yeovil	22.8	13,036	Con
52	Norfolk North	23.4	11,626	Con
53	Westmorland & Lonsdale	23.8	12,264	Con
54	Bath	25.2	11,883	Con
55	Sheffield Hallam	29.9	15,284	Con
56	Ross, Skye & Lochaber	37.5	13,072	SNP
57	Orkney & Shetland	51.3	9,928	Lab

Scottish National seats

	Constituency	%maj	maj 2nd	
1	Dundee East	4.5	1,821	Lab
2	Angus	8.6	3,282	Con
3	Perth & North Perthshire	9.1	4,379	Con
4	Banff & Buchan	10.5	4,027	Con
5	Na h-Eileanan an Iar (Western Isles)	12.8	1,885	Lab
6	Moray	13.6	5,590	Con

Plaid Cymru seats

	Constituency	%maj	maj 2nd	
1	Arfon	5.6	1,455	Lab
2	Carmarthen E.& Dinefwr	9.2	3,481	Lab
3	Dwyfor Meirionnydd	22.0	6,367	Con

Speaker

	Constituency	%maj	maj 2nd	
1	Buckingham	25.9	12,529	Ind

Green seat

	Constituency	%maj	maj 2nd	
1	Brighton Pavilion	2.4	1,252	Lab

Constituency	%maj	maj	2nd
Independent seat			
1 Down North	42.9	14,364	UCUNF
Sinn Fein seats			
1 Fermanagh & S.Tyrone	0.0	4	Ind
2 Newry & Armagh	18.6	8,331	SDLP
3 Tyrone West	28.7	10,685	DUP
4 Ulster Mid	37.6	15,363	DUP
5 Belfast West	54.7	17,579	SDLP
Democratic Unionist seats			
1 Antrim South	3.5	1,183	UCUNF
2 Belfast North	6.0	2,224	SF
3 Upper Bann	8.1	3,361	UCUNF
4 Londonderry East	15.3	5,355	SF
5 Strangford	18.1	5,876	UCUNF
6 Antrim East	22.2	6,770	UCUNF
7 Lagan Valley	28.7	10,486	UCUNF
8 Antrim North	29.6	12,558	TUV
SDLP seats			
1 Foyle	12.7	4,824	SF
2 Belfast South	17.3	5,926	DUP
3 Down South	19.8	8,412	SF
APNI seats			
1 Belfast East	4.4	1,533	DUP

Table 13. Seats in Rank Order of % Majority by Region and Country

Constituency		%maj	maj 2nd		Constituency		%maj	maj 2nd
East Midlands					**Eastern**			
Conservative seats					**Conservative seats**			
7	Sherwood	0.4	214 Lab		3	Thurrock	0.2	92 Lab
9	Broxtowe	0.7	389 Lab		14	Waveney	1.5	769 Lab
13	Amber Valley	1.2	536 Lab		22	Watford	2.6	1,425 LD
21	Lincoln	2.3	1,058 Lab		26	Bedford	3.0	1,353 Lab
29	Corby	3.5	1,895 Lab		35	St Albans	4.4	2,305 LD
40	Northampton North	4.8	1,936 Lab		36	Ipswich	4.4	2,079 Lab
46	Erewash	5.2	2,501 Lab		67	Stevenage	8.0	3,578 Lab
61	Loughborough	7.1	3,744 Lab		74	Norwich North	9.2	3,901 Lab
75	Bosworth	9.3	5,032 LD		77	Chelmsford	9.4	5,110 LD
76	High Peak	9.3	4,677 Lab		82	Great Yarmouth	9.9	4,276 Lab
125	Derbyshire South	14.1	7,128 Lab		85	Cambridgeshire S. E.	10.3	5,946 LD
127	Leicestershire N. W.	14.5	7,511 Lab		88	Peterborough	10.8	4,861 Lab
134	Northampton South	15.4	6,004 Lab		91	Harlow	11.2	4,925 Lab
151	Harborough	17.8	9,797 LD		111	Basildon S. & Thurrock E.	12.9	5,772 Lab
155	Kettering	19.2	9,094 Lab		115	Cambridgeshire South	13.3	7,838 LD
171	Gainsborough	21.4	10,559 LD		119	Broadland	13.8	7,292 LD
177	Wellingborough	22.8	11,787 Lab		139	Suffolk Coastal	16.6	9,128 LD
188	Derbyshire Mid	23.9	11,292 Lab		141	Southend West	16.7	7,270 LD
200	Rutland & Melton	25.4	14,000 LD		143	Suffolk South	16.9	8,689 LD
214	Louth & Horncastle	27.5	13,871 LD		144	Castle Point	17.0	7,632 other
224	Charnwood	28.1	15,029 LD		158	Norfolk South	19.9	10,940 LD
225	Grantham & Stamford	28.1	14,826 LD		159	Huntingdon	19.9	10,819 LD
229	Leicestershire South	28.4	15,524 LD		167	Bury St Edmunds	21.1	12,380 LD
232	Boston & Skegness	28.8	12,426 Lab		179	Harwich & Essex North	23.4	11,447 LD
236	Rushcliffe	29.5	15,811 LD		202	Suffolk C.& Ipswich N.	25.8	13,786 LD
238	Derbyshire Dales	29.6	13,866 LD		205	Hertfordshire S. W.	26.3	14,920 LD
262	Newark	31.5	16,152 Lab		208	Rochford & Southend E.	26.5	11,050 Lab
275	Sleaford & N. Hykeham	33.4	19,905 LD		209	Norfolk South West	26.7	13,140 LD
280	Northamptonshire South	34.2	20,478 LD		210	Hemel Hempstead	27.1	13,406 LD
293	Daventry	37.1	19,188 LD		211	Suffolk West	27.1	13,050 LD
305	South Holland & The Deepings	43.6	21,880 LD		213	Norfolk Mid	27.3	13,856 LD
					215	Bedfordshire Mid	27.6	15,152 LD
					217	Hertford & Stortford	27.9	15,437 LD
Labour seats					219	Hitchin & Harpenden	27.9	15,271 LD
5	Ashfield	0.4	192 LD		221	Clacton	28.0	12,068 Lab
8	Chesterfield	1.2	549 LD		222	Saffron Walden	28.0	15,242 LD
10	Derby North	1.4	613 Con		231	Cambridgeshire N. W.	28.6	16,677 LD
26	Gedling	3.9	1,859 Con		239	Basildon & Billericay	29.7	12,338 Lab
29	Nottingham South	4.3	1,772 Con		244	Hertfordshire North East	30.1	15,194 LD
32	Derbyshire North East	5.2	2,445 Con		252	Norfolk North West	31.0	14,810 LD
88	Leicester West	11.2	4,017 Con		263	Cambridgeshire N. E.	31.5	16,425 LD
95	Mansfield	12.4	6,012 Con		270	Witham	32.4	15,196 LD
112	Derby South	14.9	6,122 Con		271	Epping Forest	32.5	15,131 LD
121	Bassetlaw	16.6	8,215 Con		272	Braintree	32.8	16,121 Lab
137	Leicester South	18.7	8,808 LD		273	Bedfordshire S. W.	32.8	16,649 LD
148	Nottingham East	21.0	6,969 LD		276	Brentwood & Ongar	33.4	16,921 LD
165	Nottingham North	23.7	8,138 Con		279	Bedfordshire N. E.	34.1	18,942 LD
179	Bolsover	25.4	11,182 Con		290	Welwyn Hatfield	35.6	17,423 Lab
204	Leicester East	29.3	14,082 Con		294	Hertsmere	37.2	17,605 Lab
					300	Maldon	40.5	19,407 LD
					301	Broxbourne	41.2	18,804 Lab
					304	Rayleigh & Wickford	42.7	22,338 LD

Constituency	%maj	maj 2nd

Eastern

Labour seats

38	Luton South	5.5	2,329 Con
127	Luton North	17.5	7,520 Con

Liberal Democrat seats

3	Norwich South	0.7	310 Lab
36	Cambridge	13.5	6,792 Con
40	Colchester	15.1	6,982 Con
52	Norfolk North	23.4	11,626 Con

London

Conservative seats

4	Hendon	0.2	106 Lab
31	Brentford & Isleworth	3.6	1,958 Lab
33	Enfield North	3.8	1,692 Lab
51	Croydon Central	5.8	2,879 Lab
58	Richmond Park	6.9	4,091 LD
62	Harrow East	7.1	3,403 Lab
65	Ealing Central & Acton	7.9	3,716 Lab
93	Ilford North	11.5	5,404 Lab
99	Battersea	12.2	5,977 Lab
103	Finchley & Golders Green	12.3	5,809 Lab
149	Enfield Southgate	17.2	7,626 Lab
182	Chipping Barnet	23.6	11,927 Lab
191	Bexleyheath & Crayford	24.0	10,344 Lab
193	Wimbledon	24.1	11,408 LD
195	Kensington	24.5	8,616 Lab
196	Putney	24.6	10,053 Lab
198	Uxbridge & Ruislip S.	24.9	11,216 Lab
226	Croydon South	28.1	15,818 LD
241	Cities of London & Westminster	30.0	11,076 Lab
242	Chingford & Woodford Green	30.1	12,963 Lab
247	Hornchurch & Upminster	30.7	16,371 Lab
264	Bromley & Chislehurst	31.6	13,900 LD
283	Old Bexley & Sidcup	34.9	15,857 Lab
286	Orpington	35.2	17,200 LD
291	Romford	36.5	16,954 Lab
295	Beckenham	37.3	17,784 LD
296	Ruislip, Northwood & Pinner	38.0	19,060 Lab
303	Chelsea & Fulham	42.0	16,722 Lab

Labour seats

1	Hampstead & Kilburn	0.1	42 Con
27	Eltham	4.0	1,663 Con
31	Tooting	5.0	2,524 Con
36	Westminster North	5.4	2,126 Con
40	Dagenham & Rainham	5.9	2,630 Con
47	Harrow West	6.8	3,143 Con
50	Streatham	7.0	3,259 LD

Constituency	%maj	maj 2nd

London

Labour seats

57	Hammersmith	7.5	3,549 Con
65	Islington S. & Finsbury	8.2	3,569 LD
77	Feltham & Heston	9.6	4,658 Con
100	Poplar & Limehouse	12.9	6,030 Con
101	Lewisham W. & Penge	12.9	5,828 LD
104	Erith & Thamesmead	13.4	5,703 Con
113	Lewisham East	14.9	6,216 LD
116	Brent North	15.4	8,028 Con
120	Leyton & Wanstead	16.0	6,416 LD
132	Holborn & St Pancras	18.2	9,942 LD
140	Dulwich & W. Norwood	19.4	9,365 LD
141	Ealing North	19.5	9,301 Con
153	Ealing Southall	21.7	9,291 Con
157	Ilford South	22.0	11,287 Con
161	Bethnal Green & Bow	22.8	11,574 LD
163	Walthamstow	23.1	9,478 LD
169	Edmonton	23.8	9,613 Con
172	Greenwich & Woolwich	24.7	10,153 Con
173	Vauxhall	24.7	10,651 LD
178	Hayes & Harlington	25.4	10,824 Con
193	Islington North	27.8	12,401 LD
208	Lewisham Deptford	30.3	12,499 LD
212	Hackney N. & Stoke Newington	31.1	14,461 LD
213	Mitcham & Morden	31.2	13,666 Con
215	Croydon North	31.9	16,481 Con
222	Hackney S. & Shoreditch	33.3	14,288 LD
231	Barking	36.5	16,555 Con
234	Camberwell & Peckham	36.8	17,187 LD
244	Tottenham	41.6	16,931 LD
250	West Ham	48.0	22,534 Con
256	East Ham	55.2	27,826 Con

Liberal Democrat seats

7	Brent Central	3.0	1,345 Lab
9	Sutton & Cheam	3.3	1,608 Con
29	Carshalton & Wallington	11.5	5,260 Con
32	Hornsey & Wood Green	12.5	6,875 Lab
35	Kingston & Surbiton	13.2	7,560 Con
45	Bermondsey & Old Southwark	19.1	8,530 Lab
46	Twickenham	20.3	12,140 Con

North East

Conservative seats

8	Stockton South	0.7	332 Lab
116	Hexham	13.3	5,788 LD

Labour seats

22	Middlesbrough S. & Cleveland E.	3.6	1,677 Con
44	Durham, City of	6.6	3,067 LD

Constituency	%maj	maj 2nd		Constituency	%maj	maj 2nd

North East

Labour seats

59	Newcastle upon Tyne N.	7.8	3,414 LD
61	Darlington	7.9	3,388 Con
84	Tynemouth	10.9	5,739 Con
92	Newcastle upon Tyne E.	11.8	4,453 LD
99	Bishop Auckland	12.7	5,218 Con
111	Hartlepool	14.4	5,509 Con
119	Sunderland Central	15.8	6,725 Con
122	Stockton North	16.9	6,676 Con
124	Blyth Valley	17.3	6,668 LD
126	Durham North West	17.4	7,612 LD
134	Wansbeck	18.4	7,031 LD
144	Blaydon	20.3	9,117 LD
151	Sedgefield	21.6	8,696 Con
156	Newcastle upon Tyne C.	21.9	7,466 LD
180	Middlesbrough	26.0	8,689 LD
191	Tyneside North	27.8	12,884 LD
202	Houghton & Sunderland S.	28.9	10,990 Con
206	Durham North	29.5	12,076 Con
209	South Shields	30.4	11,109 Con
211	Washington & Sunderland West	30.7	11,458 Con
218	Gateshead	32.8	12,549 LD
221	Jarrow	33.3	12,908 Con
245	Easington	42.9	14,982 LD

Liberal Democrat seats

19	Berwick-upon-Tweed	7.0	2,690 Con
31	Redcar	12.4	5,214 Lab

North West

Conservative seats

10	Lancaster & Fleetwood	0.8	333 Lab
17	Morecambe & Lunesdale	2.0	866 Lab
18	Carlisle	2.0	853 Lab
20	Weaver Vale	2.3	991 Lab
25	Warrington South	2.8	1,553 Lab
41	Bury North	5.0	2,243 Lab
47	Blackpool N. & Cleveleys	5.3	2,150 Lab
50	Chester, City of	5.5	2,583 Lab
54	Wirral West	6.2	2,436 Lab
66	Pendle	8.0	3,585 Lab
79	Rossendale & Darwen	9.5	4,493 Lab
87	South Ribble	10.8	5,554 Lab
97	Crewe & Nantwich	11.8	6,046 Lab
121	Congleton	13.9	7,063 LD
181	Altrincham & Sale West	23.5	11595 LD
190	Macclesfield	23.9	11,959 LD
199	Penrith & The Border	24.9	11,241 LD
228	Ribble Valley	28.2	14,769 Lab
234	Eddisbury	29.2	13,255 LD
245	Fylde	30.2	13,185 LD
249	Wyre & Preston North	30.9	15,844 LD
268	Tatton	32.0	14,487 LD

North West

Labour seats

2	Bolton West	0.2	92 Con
3	Oldham E. & Saddleworth	0.2	103 LD
9	Wirral South	1.3	531 Con
14	Rochdale	1.9	889 LD
34	Chorley	5.2	2,593 Con
35	Blackpool South	5.3	1,852 Con
46	Stalybridge & Hyde	6.7	2,744 Con
48	Bury South	6.8	3,292 Con
54	Hyndburn	7.2	3,090 Con
62	Sefton Central	8.0	3,862 Con
72	Copeland	9.0	3,833 Con
73	Lancashire West	9.0	4,343 Con
75	Bolton North East	9.4	4,084 Con
79	Ellesmere Port & Neston	9.8	4,331 Con
82	Worsley & Eccles South	10.4	4,337 Con
91	Workington	11.7	4,575 Con
93	Barrow & Furness	11.8	5,208 Con
102	Heywood & Middleton	12.9	5,971 Con
106	Salford & Eccles	13.8	5,725 LD
115	Warrington North	15.3	6,771 Con
125	Stockport	17.3	6,784 Con
128	Manchester Gorton	17.5	6,703 LD
136	Wythenshawe & Sale E.	18.6	7,575 Con
138	Liverpool Wavertree	18.9	7,167 LD
143	Stretford & Urmston	19.9	8,935 Con
146	Wallasey	20.4	8,507 Con
152	Blackburn	21.7	9,856 Con
154	Oldham W. & Royton	21.8	9,352 Con
155	Bolton South East	21.8	8,634 Con
164	Ashton Under Lyne	23.7	9,094 Con
167	Wigan	23.8	10,487 Con
168	Preston	23.8	7,733 LD
181	Denton & Reddish	26.1	9,831 Con
182	Manchester Central	26.1	10,439 LD
187	Leigh	27.1	12,011 Con
200	Makerfield	28.5	12,490 Con
205	St Helens North	29.4	13,101 Con
210	St Helens S. & Whiston	30.6	14,122 LD
230	Blackley & Broughton	36.0	12,303 Con
232	Liverpool Riverside	36.5	14,173 LD
236	Halton	37.5	15,504 Con
240	Garston & Halewood	39.4	16,877 LD
247	Birkenhead	43.6	15,395 Con
253	Bootle	51.3	21,181 LD
254	Liverpool West Derby	51.6	18,467 LD
257	Knowsley	57.5	25,686 LD
258	Liverpool Walton	57.7	19,818 LD

Liberal Democrat seats

11	Manchester Withington	4.2	1,894 Lab
12	Burnley	4.3	1,818 Lab
15	Cheadle	6.2	3,272 Con
37	Southport	13.8	6,024 Con
41	Hazel Grove	15.2	6,371 Con
53	Westmorland & Lonsdale	23.8	12,264 Con

	Constituency	%maj	maj 2nd
South East			
Conservative seats			
5	Oxford West & Abingdon	0.3	176 LD
27	Brighton Kemptown	3.1	1,328 Lab
32	Hove	3.7	1,868 Lab
34	Hastings & Rye	4.0	1,993 Lab
49	Winchester	5.4	3,048 LD
70	Romsey & Southampton N.	8.5	4,156 LD
78	Milton Keynes South	9.4	5,201 Lab
86	Dover	10.5	5,274 Lab
98	Maidstone & The Weald	12.0	5,889 LD
100	Canterbury	12.3	6,048 LD
102	Aldershot	12.3	5,586 LD
105	Crawley	12.5	5,928 Lab
107	Reading West	12.6	6,004 Lab
110	Woking	12.9	6,807 LD
114	Sussex Mid	13.3	7,402 LD
120	Chatham & Aylesford	13.9	6,069 Lab
122	Guildford	14.0	7,782 LD
130	Isle of Wight	15.0	10,527 LD
131	Reading East	15.2	7,605 LD
137	Portsmouth North	16.5	7,289 Lab
138	Thanet South	16.6	7,617 Lab
140	Milton Keynes North	16.6	8,961 Lab
153	Gillingham & Rainham	18.6	8,680 Lab
154	Folkestone & Hythe	19.2	10,122 LD
156	Gravesham	19.7	9,312 Lab
157	Wycombe	19.9	9,560 LD
162	Horsham	20.5	11,460 LD
164	Rochester & Strood	20.7	9,953 Lab
166	Newbury	20.9	12,248 LD
169	Spelthorne	21.2	10,019 LD
170	Dartford	21.2	10,628 Lab
175	New Forest East	22.6	11,307 LD
178	Worthing E. & Shoreham	22.9	11,105 LD
183	Bexhill & Battle	23.6	12,880 LD
184	Meon Valley	23.7	12,125 LD
186	Aylesbury	23.7	12,618 LD
189	Worthing West	23.9	11,729 LD
192	Wantage	24.0	13,547 LD
197	Wokingham	24.7	13,492 LD
201	Sittingbourne & Sheppey	25.5	12,383 Lab
204	Basingstoke	26.0	13,176 LD
206	Hampshire East	26.3	13,497 LD
212	Reigate	27.2	13,591 LD
216	Havant	27.7	12,160 LD
218	Bognor Regis & Littlehampton	27.9	13,063 LD
220	Chichester	28.0	15,877 LD
230	Surrey South West	28.5	16,318 LD
233	Mole Valley	28.8	15,653 LD
235	Epsom & Ewell	29.4	16,134 LD
240	Arundel & South Downs	29.8	16,691 LD
243	Bracknell	30.1	15,704 LD
248	Gosport	30.7	14,413 LD
250	Surrey East	30.9	16,874 LD

	Constituency	%maj	maj 2nd
South East			
Conservative seats			
251	Tunbridge Wells	31.0	15,576 LD
253	Henley	31.0	16,588 LD
257	Thanet North	31.2	13,528 Lab
258	Maidenhead	31.2	16,769 LD
259	Wealden	31.3	17,179 LD
260	Ashford	31.3	17,297 LD
261	Fareham	31.5	17,092 LD
265	Surrey Heath	31.8	17,289 LD
267	Chesham & Amersham	31.9	16,710 LD
269	Banbury	32.4	18,227 LD
278	Esher & Walton	34.1	18,593 LD
281	Runnymede & Weybridge	34.3	16,509 LD
284	Hampshire North West	34.9	18,583 LD
285	Hampshire North East	35.1	18,597 LD
287	Tonbridge & Malling	35.4	18,178 LD
288	Sevenoaks	35.4	17,515 LD
289	New Forest West	35.5	16,896 LD
292	Faversham & Kent Mid	36.6	17,088 LD
297	Windsor	38.4	19,054 LD
298	Witney	39.4	22,740 LD
302	Beaconsfield	41.5	21,782 LD
Labour seats			
6	Southampton Itchen	0.4	192 Con
37	Southampton Test	5.5	2,413 Con
70	Oxford East	8.9	4,581 LD
89	Slough	11.6	5,523 Con
Liberal Democrat seats			
17	Eastbourne	6.6	3,435 Con
20	Eastleigh	7.2	3,864 Con
33	Portsmouth South	12.6	5,200 Con
42	Lewes	15.3	7,647 Con
Speaker			
1	Buckingham	25.9	12,529 Ind
Green seat			
1	Brighton Pavilion	2.4	1,252 Lab
South West			
Conservative seats			
2	Camborne & Redruth	0.2	66 LD
11	Truro & Falmouth	0.9	435 LD
12	Newton Abbot	1.1	523 LD
19	Stroud	2.2	1,299 Lab
23	Plymouth Sutton & Devonport	2.6	1,149 Lab
39	Gloucester	4.8	2,420 Lab
42	Kingswood	5.1	2,445 Lab

Constituency	%maj	maj 2nd
South West		
Conservative seats		
43 Weston-Super-Mare	5.1	2,691 LD
48 Devon West & Torridge	5.4	2,957 LD
55 Cornwall South East	6.5	3,220 LD
56 Bristol North West	6.5	3,274 LD
57 Dorset West	6.8	3,923 LD
64 Swindon South	7.5	3,544 Lab
81 Somerset North East	9.6	4,914 Lab
84 Totnes	10.3	4,927 LD
95 Tewkesbury	11.7	6,310 LD
101 Salisbury	12.3	5,966 LD
117 Bournemouth West	13.4	5,583 LD
118 Somerset North	13.6	7,862 LD
123 Swindon North	14.0	7,060 Lab
124 Dorset North	14.1	7,625 LD
126 Filton & Bradley Stoke	14.3	6,914 Lab
128 Dorset South	14.8	7,443 Lab
133 Wiltshire North	15.4	7,483 LD
135 Poole	15.9	7,541 LD
145 Bridgwater & Somerset West	17.0	9,249 LD
146 Tiverton & Honiton	17.0	9,320 LD
147 Devon Central	17.1	9,230 LD
148 Devon East	17.2	9,114 LD
150 Bournemouth East	17.6	7,728 LD
168 Wiltshire South West	21.1	10,367 LD
176 Forest of Dean	22.7	11,064 Lab
180 Cotswolds, The	23.5	12,864 LD
223 Devizes	28.1	13,005 LD
256 Christchurch	31.2	15,410 LD
266 Devon South West	31.8	15,874 LD
Labour seats		
25 Plymouth Moor View	3.8	1,588 Con
33 Exeter	5.2	2,721 Con
66 Bristol East	8.3	3,722 Con
78 Bristol South	9.8	4,734 LD
Liberal Democrat seats		
2 Dorset Mid & Poole N,	0.6	269 Con
5 Wells	1.4	800 Con
6 St Austell & Newquay	2.8	1,312 Con
8 Somerton & Frome	3.0	1,817 Con
10 St Ives	3.7	1,719 Con
14 Chippenham	4.7	2,470 Con
16 Cornwall North	6.4	2,981 Con
18 Taunton Deane	6.9	3,993 Con
25 Torbay	8.3	4,078 Con
26 Cheltenham	9.3	4,920 Con
28 Devon North	11.3	5,821 Con
39 Thornbury & Yate	14.8	7,116 Con
47 Bristol West	20.5	11,366 Lab
51 Yeovil	22.8	13,036 Con
54 Bath	25.2	11,883 Con

Constituency	%maj	maj 2nd
West Midlands		
Conservative seats		
1 Warwickshire North	0.1	54 Lab
15 Wolverhampton S. W.	1.7	691 Lab
37 Halesowen & Rowley Regis	4.6	2,023 Lab
38 Nuneaton	4.6	2,069 Lab
44 Hereford & Herefordshire S.	5.1	2,481 LD
45 Wyre Forest	5.2	2,643 other
52 Worcester	6.1	2,982 Lab
60 Cannock Chase	7.0	3,195 Lab
63 Warwick & Leamington	7.2	3,513 Lab
83 Dudley South	10.1	3,856 Lab
89 Stafford	10.9	5,460 Lab
90 Stourbridge	10.9	5,164 Lab
106 Worcestershire West	12.5	6,754 LD
108 Rugby	12.6	6,000 Lab
109 Burton	12.7	6,304 Lab
112 Tamworth	13.1	6,090 Lab
113 Redditch	13.2	5,821 Lab
129 Shrewsbury & Atcham	15.0	7,944 LD
132 Staffordshire Moorlands	15.3	6,689 Lab
160 Ludlow	20.0	9,749 LD
163 Wrekin, The	20.6	9,450 Lab
165 Herefordshire North	20.8	9,887 LD
172 Bromsgrove	21.9	11,308 Lab
174 Stratford-on-Avon	22.4	11,346 LD
203 Kenilworth & Southam	25.9	12,552 LD
227 Stone	28.1	13,292 LD
246 Shropshire North	30.5	15,828 LD
254 Worcestershire Mid	31.1	15,864 LD
255 Meriden	31.2	16,253 Lab
274 Staffordshire South	32.9	16,590 Lab
277 Sutton Coldfield	33.6	17,005 Lab
282 Lichfield	34.3	17,683 LD
299 Aldridge-Brownhills	39.5	15,266 Lab
Labour seats		
12 Dudley North	1.7	649 Con
17 Telford	2.4	978 Con
18 Walsall North	2.7	990 Con
19 Birmingham Edgbaston	3.1	1,274 Con
21 Newcastle-under-Lyme	3.6	1,552 Con
28 Walsall South	4.3	1,755 Con
45 Birmingham Northfield	6.7	2,782 Con
52 Wolverhampton N. E.	7.1	2,484 Con
56 Birmingham Selly Oak	7.5	3,482 Con
60 Birmingham Hall Green	7.8	3,799 Resp
68 Coventry South	8.4	3,845 Con
74 Birmingham Erdington	9.2	3,277 Con
81 Stoke-on-Trent South	10.4	4,130 Con
105 Coventry North West	13.5	6,288 Con
118 West Bromwich West	15.6	5,651 Con
123 Stoke-on-Trent Central	17.1	5,566 LD
129 West Bromwich East	17.6	6,696 Con
139 Wolverhampton S. E.	19.0	6,593 Con

Constituency	%maj	maj	2nd

West Midlands

Labour seats

	Constituency	%maj	maj	2nd
147	Stoke-on-Trent North	20.5	8,235	Con
170	Birmingham Hodge Hill	24.3	10,302	LD
188	Coventry North East	27.1	11,775	Con
195	Warley	28.1	10,756	Con
196	Birmingham Ladywood	28.2	10,105	LD
197	Birmingham Perry Barr	28.3	11,908	LD

Liberal Democrat seats

	Constituency	%maj	maj	2nd
1	Solihull	0.3	175	Con
21	Birmingham Yardley	7.3	3,002	Lab

Yorkshire and the Humber

Conservative seats

	Constituency	%maj	maj	2nd
16	Harrogate & Knaresborough	2.0	1,039	LD
24	Dewsbury	2.8	1,526	Lab
28	Pudsey	3.4	1,659	Lab
53	Keighley	6.2	2,940	Lab
59	York Outer	6.9	3,688	LD
68	Elmet & Rothwell	8.1	4,521	Lab
71	Colne Valley	8.7	4,837	Lab
80	Cleethorpes	9.6	4,298	Lab
96	Brigg & Goole	11.7	5,147	Lab
104	Calder Valley	12.4	6,431	Lab
136	Scarborough & Whitby	16.5	8,130	Lab
152	Skipton & Ripon	18.2	9,950	LD
161	Shipley	20.1	9,944	Lab
185	Selby & Ainsty	23.7	12,265	Lab
187	Haltemprice & Howden	23.8	11,602	LD
194	Beverley & Holderness	24.4	12,987	LD
207	Yorkshire East	26.3	13,486	LD
237	Thirsk & Malton	29.6	11,281	LD
306	Richmond (Yorks)	43.7	23,336	LD

Labour seats

	Constituency	%maj	maj	2nd
4	Sheffield Central	0.4	165	LD
13	Hull North	1.9	641	LD
15	Great Grimsby	2.2	714	Con
16	Morley & Outwood	2.3	1,101	Con
20	Halifax	3.4	1,472	Con
23	Wakefield	3.6	1,613	Con
43	Penistone & Stocksbridge	6.6	3,049	Con
49	Scunthorpe	6.9	2,549	Con
67	Don Valley	8.3	3595	Con
69	Batley & Spen	8.6	4,406	Con
76	Leeds North East	9.6	4,545	Con
85	Huddersfield	11.0	4,472	Con
94	Bradford South	12.2	4,622	Con
96	Rother Valley	12.5	5,866	Con
107	York Central	13.9	6,451	Con
108	Bradford West	14.2	5,763	Con
109	Sheffield Heeley	14.2	5,807	LD
114	Doncaster Central	14.9	6,229	Con
131	Leeds West	18.1	7,016	LD
133	Hull West & Hessle	18.2	5,742	LD

Yorkshire and the Humber

Labour seats

	Constituency	%maj	maj	2nd
159	Hemsworth	22.5	9,844	Con
166	Normanton, Pontefract & Castleford	23.7	10,979	Con
176	Hull East	25.1	8,597	LD
177	Sheffield South East	25.4	10,505	LD
183	Doncaster North	26.3	10,909	Con
189	Leeds East	27.2	10,293	Con
194	Rotherham	27.9	10,462	Con
198	Leeds Central	28.5	10,645	LD
201	Barnsley East	28.9	11,090	LD
207	Barnsley Central	30.0	11,093	LD
219	Wentworth & Dearne	33.1	13,920	Con
227	Sheffield Brightside & Hillsborough	35.0	13,632	LD

Liberal Democrat seats

	Constituency	%maj	maj	2nd
4	Bradford East	0.9	365	Lab
48	Leeds North West	20.9	9,103	Con
55	Sheffield Hallam	29.9	15,284	Con

Scotland

Conservative seats

	Constituency	%maj	maj	2nd
73	Dumfriesshire, Clydesdale & Tweeddale	9.1	4,194	Lab

Labour seats

	Constituency	%maj	maj	2nd
7	Edinburgh South	0.7	316	LD
24	Edinburgh North & Leith	3.6	1,724	LD
63	Aberdeen South	8.1	3,506	LD
80	Ochil & South Perthshire	10.3	5,187	SNP
87	Dunfermline & Fife West	11.2	5,470	LD
103	Glasgow North	13.2	3,898	LD
110	Dumfries & Galloway	14.3	7,449	Con
117	Falkirk	15.4	7,843	SNP
130	Stirling	17.7	8,304	Con
135	Edinburgh South West	18.6	8,447	Con
142	Dundee West	19.6	7,278	SNP
145	Renfrewshire East	20.4	10,420	Con
149	Ayrshire North & Arran	21.5	9,895	SNP
150	Ayr, Carrick & Cumnock	21.6	9,911	Con
158	Aberdeen North	22.2	8,361	SNP
160	Livingston	22.5	10,791	SNP
162	Edinburgh East	23.0	9181	SNP
171	Linlithgow & Falkirk E.	24.4	12,553	SNP
175	East Lothian	24.9	12,258	Con
185	Midlothian	26.4	10,349	SNP
186	Kilmarnock & Loudoun	26.6	12,378	SNP
190	Ayrshire Central	27.3	12,007	Con
199	East Kilbride, Strathaven & Lesmahagow	28.5	14,503	SNP
203	Lanark & Hamilton E.	29.0	13,478	SNP
214	Glasgow South	31.6	12,658	SNP
223	Cumbernauld, Kilsyth & Kirkintilloch East	33.4	13,755	SNP

Constituency	%maj	maj 2nd
Scotland		
Labour seats		
224 Glasgow Central	34.5	10,551 SNP
225 Airdrie & Shotts	34.6	12,408 SNP
226 Paisley & Renfrewshire N.	35.0	15,280 SNP
233 Glasgow East	36.8	11,840 SNP
238 Glasgow North West	38.3	13,611 LD
239 Inverclyde	38.4	14,416 SNP
241 Glenrothes	40.6	16,448 SNP
242 Dunbartonshire West	41.2	17,408 SNP
243 Paisley & Renfrewshire S.	41.5	16,614 SNP
246 Motherwell & Wishaw	43.0	16,806 SNP
248 Rutherglen & Hamilton West	44.7	21,002 SNP
249 Glasgow South West	46.2	14,671 SNP
251 Coatbridge, Chryston & Bellshill	49.8	20,714 SNP
252 Kirkcaldy & Cowdenbeath	50.2	23,009 SNP
255 Glasgow North East	54.2	15,942 SNP
Liberal Democrat seats		
13 Dunbartonshire East	4.6	2,184 Lab
22 Argyll & Bute	7.6	3,431 Con
23 Aberdeenshire West & Kincardine	8.2	3,684 Con
24 Edinburgh West	8.2	3,803 Lab
30 Berwickshire, Roxburgh & Selkirk	11.6	5,675 Con
38 Gordon	13.8	6,748 SNP
43 Caithness, Sutherland & Easter Ross	16.8	4,826 Lab
44 Inverness, Nairn, Badenoch & Strathspey	18.6	8,765 Lab
50 Fife North East	22.6	9,048 Con
56 Ross, Skye & Lochaber	37.5	13,072 SNP
57 Orkney & Shetland	51.3	9,928 Lab
Scottish National seats		
1 Dundee East	4.5	1,821 Lab
2 Angus	8.6	3,282 Con
3 Perth & North Perthshire	9.1	4,379 Con
4 Banff & Buchan	10.5	4,027 Con
5 Na h-Eileanan an Iar (Western Isles)	12.8	1,885 Lab
6 Moray	13.6	5,590 Con

Constituency	%maj	maj 2nd
Wales		
Conservative seats		
6 Cardiff North	0.4	194 Lab
30 Montgomeryshire	3.5	1,184 LD
69 Carmarthen West & Pembrokeshire South	8.5	3,423 Lab
72 Vale of Glamorgan	8.8	4,307 Lab
92 Aberconwy	11.3	3,398 Lab
94 Preseli Pembrokeshire	11.6	4,605 Lab
142 Clwyd West	16.8	6,419 Lab
173 Monmouth	22.4	10,425 Lab
Labour seats		
11 Swansea West	1.4	504 LD
30 Newport East	4.8	1,650 LD
39 Bridgend	5.9	2,263 Con
41 Delyn	6.1	2,272 Con
42 Gower	6.4	2,683 Con
51 Vale of Clwyd	7.1	2,509 Con
53 Ynys Mon	7.1	2,461 PC
55 Alyn & Deeside	7.3	2,919 Con
58 Pontypridd	7.6	2,785 LD
64 Clwyd South	8.2	2,834 Con
71 Newport West	8.9	3,544 Con
83 Cardiff South & Penarth	10.6	4,709 Con
86 Wrexham	11.1	3,658 LD
90 Cardiff West	11.6	4,751 Con
97 Llanelli	12.5	4,701 PC
98 Merthyr Tydfil & Rhymney	12.6	4,056 LD
174 Torfaen	24.7	9,306 Con
184 Neath	26.3	9,775 PC
192 Caerphilly	27.8	10,755 Con
216 Cynon Valley	32.2	9,617 PC
217 Blaenau Gwent	32.5	10,516 other
220 Swansea East	33.2	10,838 LD
228 Islwyn	35.2	12,215 Con
229 Aberavon	35.7	11,039 LD
235 Rhondda	37.2	11,553 PC
237 Ogmore	38.2	13,246 Con
Liberal Democrat seats		
27 Brecon & Radnorshire	9.6	3,747 Con
34 Cardiff Central	12.7	4,576 Lab
49 Ceredigion	21.8	8,324 PC
Plaid Cymru seats		
1 Arfon	5.6	1,455 Lab
2 Carmarthen East & Dinefwr	9.2	3,481 Lab
3 Dwyfor Meirionnydd	22.0	6,367 Con

Constituency	%maj	maj	2nd
Northern Ireland			
Independent seat			
1 Down North	42.9	14,364	UCUNF
Sinn Fein seats			
1 Fermanagh & South Tyrone	0.0	4	Ind
2 Newry & Armagh	18.6	8,331	SDLP
3 Tyrone West	28.7	10,685	DUP
4 Ulster Mid	37.6	15,363	DUP
5 Belfast West	54.7	17,579	SDLP
Democratic Unionist seats			
1 Antrim South	3.5	1,183	UCUNF
2 Belfast North	6.0	2,224	SF
3 Upper Bann	8.1	3,361	UCUNF
4 Londonderry East	15.3	5,355	SF
5 Strangford	18.1	5,876	UCUNF
6 Antrim East	22.2	6,770	UCUNF
7 Lagan Valley	28.7	10,486	UCUNF
8 Antrim North	29.6	12,558	TUV
SDLP seats			
1 Foyle	12.7	4,824	SF
2 Belfast South	17.3	5,926	DUP
3 Down South	19.8	8,412	SF
APNI seat			
1 Belfast East	4.4	1,533	DUP

Table 14. Target lists for the main parties by rank order of swing to win (GB)

Target lists show for each party the swing it requires to gain the seat from the party which currently holds it. Where appropriate they take account of the need to overtake the second placed party.

Nat. rank	Constituency	1st Pty	Swing to gain	Nat. rank	Constituency	1st Pty	Swing to gain
Conservative target list				**Conservative target list**			
1	Hampstead & Kilburn	Lab	0.04	49	Taunton Deane	LD	3.4
2	Bolton West	Lab	0.1	50	Scunthorpe	Lab	3.4
3	Solihull	LD	0.2	51	Berwick-upon-Tweed	LD	3.5
4	Southampton Itchen	Lab	0.2	52	Vale of Clwyd	Lab	3.5
5	Dorset Mid & Poole North	LD	0.3	53	Oldham East & Saddleworth	Lab	3.5
6	Wirral South	Lab	0.7	54	Wolverhampton North East	Lab	3.6
7	Derby North	Lab	0.7	55	Eastleigh	LD	3.6
8	Wells	LD	0.7	56	Hyndburn	Lab	3.6
9	Dudley North	Lab	0.8	57	Alyn & Deeside	Lab	3.7
10	Great Grimsby	Lab	1.1	58	Birmingham Selly Oak	Lab	3.7
11	Morley & Outwood	Lab	1.1	59	Hammersmith	Lab	3.7
12	Telford	Lab	1.2	60	Argyll & Bute	LD	3.8
13	Walsall North	Lab	1.4	61	Darlington	Lab	3.9
14	St Austell & Newquay	LD	1.4	62	Sefton Central	Lab	4.0
15	Somerton & Frome	LD	1.5	63	Norwich South	LD	4.1
16	Birmingham Edgbaston	Lab	1.5	64	Aberdeenshire W. & Kincardine	LD	4.1
17	Sutton & Cheam	LD	1.7	65	Clwyd South	Lab	4.1
18	Halifax	Lab	1.7	66	Bristol East	Lab	4.1
19	Newcastle-under-Lyme	Lab	1.8	67	Don Valley	Lab	4.1
20	Middlesbrough South & Cleveland East	Lab	1.8	68	Torbay	LD	4.1
21	Wakefield	Lab	1.8	69	Coventry South	Lab	4.2
22	St Ives	LD	1.9	70	Bradford East	LD	4.3
23	Plymouth Moor View	Lab	1.9	71	Brighton Pavilion	Grn	4.3
24	Gedling	Lab	1.9	72	Batley & Spen	Lab	4.3
25	Eltham	Lab	2.0	73	Angus	SNP	4.3
26	Walsall South	Lab	2.1	74	Newport West	Lab	4.5
27	Nottingham South	Lab	2.2	75	Copeland	Lab	4.5
28	Chippenham	LD	2.4	76	Lancashire West	Lab	4.5
29	Tooting	Lab	2.5	77	Perth & North Perthshire	SNP	4.5
30	Derbyshire North East	Lab	2.6	78	Birmingham Erdington	Lab	4.6
31	Exeter	Lab	2.6	79	Cheltenham	LD	4.7
32	Chorley	Lab	2.6	80	Bolton North East	Lab	4.7
33	Blackpool South	Lab	2.6	81	Leeds North East	Lab	4.8
34	Westminster North	Lab	2.7	82	Feltham & Heston	Lab	4.8
35	Southampton Test	Lab	2.7	83	Brecon & Radnorshire	LD	4.8
36	Luton South	Lab	2.8	84	Ellesmere Port & Neston	Lab	4.9
37	Bridgend	Lab	3.0	85	Stoke-on-Trent South	Lab	5.2
38	Dagenham & Rainham	Lab	3.0	86	Worsley & Eccles South	Lab	5.2
39	Delyn	Lab	3.1	87	Banff & Buchan	SNP	5.2
40	Cheadle	LD	3.1	88	Cardiff South & Penarth	Lab	5.3
41	Cornwall North	LD	3.2	89	Ynys Mon	Lab	5.4
42	Gower	Lab	3.2	90	Tynemouth	Lab	5.4
43	Penistone & Stocksbridge	Lab	3.3	91	Huddersfield	Lab	5.5
44	Eastbourne	LD	3.3	92	Leicester West	Lab	5.6
45	Birmingham Northfield	Lab	3.3	93	Devon North	LD	5.7
46	Stalybridge & Hyde	Lab	3.4	94	Carshalton & Wallington	LD	5.7
47	Harrow West	Lab	3.4	95	Wrexham	Lab	5.7
48	Bury South	Lab	3.4	96	Slough	Lab	5.8

Nat. rank	*Constituency*	*1st Pty*	*Swing to gain*
Conservative target list			
97	Berwickshire, Roxburgh & Selkirk	LD	5.8
98	Cardiff West	Lab	5.8
99	Workington	Lab	5.8
100	Barrow & Furness	Lab	5.9
101	Bradford South	Lab	6.1
102	Mansfield	Lab	6.2
103	Rother Valley	Lab	6.3
104	Portsmouth South	LD	6.3
105	Bishop Auckland	Lab	6.3
106	Edinburgh West	LD	6.4
107	Poplar & Limehouse	Lab	6.5
108	Heywood & Middleton	Lab	6.5
109	Kingston & Surbiton	LD	6.6
110	Carmarthen East & Dinefwr	PC	6.6
111	Erith & Thamesmead	Lab	6.7
112	Coventry North West	Lab	6.8
113	Cambridge	LD	6.8
114	Moray	SNP	6.8
115	Southport	LD	6.9
116	York Central	Lab	6.9
117	Bradford West	Lab	7.1
118	Dumfries & Galloway	Lab	7.1
119	Hartlepool	Lab	7.2
120	Thornbury & Yate	LD	7.4
121	Derby South	Lab	7.4
122	Doncaster Central	Lab	7.5
123	Ashfield	Lab	7.5
124	Colchester	LD	7.6
125	Hazel Grove	LD	7.6
126	Lewes	LD	7.6
127	Warrington North	Lab	7.7
128	Brent North	Lab	7.7
129	Newport East	Lab	7.7
130	Bristol South	Lab	7.8
131	Lewisham West & Penge	Lab	7.8
132	West Bromwich West	Lab	7.8
133	Aberdeen South	Lab	7.9
134	Sunderland Central	Lab	7.9
135	Bassetlaw	Lab	8.3
136	Stockton North	Lab	8.5
137	Edinburgh South	Lab	8.5
138	Stockport	Lab	8.7
139	Gordon	LD	8.7
140	Ochil & South Perthshire	Lab	8.7
141	Luton North	Lab	8.7
142	Swansea West	Lab	8.8
143	West Bromwich East	Lab	8.8
144	Stirling	Lab	8.9
145	Stoke-on-Trent Central	Lab	8.9
146	Edinburgh South West	Lab	9.3
147	Wythenshawe & Sale East	Lab	9.3
148	Birmingham Hall Green	Lab	9.4
149	Wolverhampton South East	Lab	9.5
150	Lewisham East	Lab	9.7

Nat. rank	*Constituency*	*1st Pty*	*Swing to gain*
Conservative target list			
151	Ealing North	Lab	9.8
152	Salford & Eccles	Lab	9.8
153	Cardiff Central	LD	9.9
154	Stretford & Urmston	Lab	9.9
155	Twickenham	LD	10.2
156	Renfrewshire East	Lab	10.2
157	Wallasey	Lab	10.2
158	Stoke-on-Trent North	Lab	10.2
159	Leeds North West	LD	10.5
160	Leyton & Wanstead	Lab	10.7
161	Ayr, Carrick & Cumnock	Lab	10.8
162	Sedgefield	Lab	10.8
163	Blackburn	Lab	10.8
164	Nottingham East	Lab	10.8
165	Arfon	PC	10.8
166	Ealing Southall	Lab	10.9
167	Oldham West & Royton	Lab	10.9
168	Bolton South East	Lab	10.9
169	Dwyfor Meirionnydd	PC	11.0
170	Ilford South	Lab	11.0
171	Hull West & Hessle	Lab	11.1
172	Birmingham Yardley	LD	11.1
173	Durham North West	Lab	11.2
174	Hemsworth	Lab	11.2
175	Burnley	LD	11.3
176	Leeds West	Lab	11.3
177	Fife North East	LD	11.3
178	Yeovil	LD	11.4
179	Rochdale	Lab	11.5
180	Norfolk North	LD	11.7
181	Ashton Under Lyne	Lab	11.8
182	Nottingham North	Lab	11.9
183	Normanton, Pontefract & Castleford	Lab	11.9
184	Wigan	Lab	11.9
185	Edmonton	Lab	11.9
186	Westmorland & Lonsdale	LD	11.9
187	Leicester South	Lab	12.1
188	Dulwich & West Norwood	Lab	12.2
189	Greenwich & Woolwich	Lab	12.3
190	Torfaen	Lab	12.4
191	East Lothian	Lab	12.5
192	Islington South & Finsbury	Lab	12.5
193	Pontypridd	Lab	12.5
194	Newcastle upon Tyne North	Lab	12.6
195	Bath	LD	12.6
196	Sheffield Heeley	Lab	12.6
197	Hayes & Harlington	Lab	12.7
198	Bolsover	Lab	12.7
199	Oxford East	Lab	12.8
200	Holborn & St Pancras	Lab	12.9
201	Denton & Reddish	Lab	13.1
202	Doncaster North	Lab	13.1
203	Preston	Lab	13.2
204	Newcastle upon Tyne C.	Lab	13.3

Nat. rank	Constituency	1st Pty	Swing to gain
Conservative target list			
205	Leigh	Lab	13.5
206	Middlesbrough	Lab	13.6
207	Coventry North East	Lab	13.6
208	Dundee East	SNP	13.6
209	Leeds East	Lab	13.6
210	Ayrshire Central	Lab	13.7
211	Inverness, Nairn, Badenoch & Strathspey	LD	13.7
212	Edinburgh North & Leith	Lab	13.8
213	Caerphilly	Lab	13.9
214	Blyth Valley	Lab	13.9
215	Dunbartonshire East	LD	13.9
216	Rotherham	Lab	13.9
217	Streatham	Lab	14.0
218	Warley	Lab	14.1
219	Vauxhall	Lab	14.1
220	Wansbeck	Lab	14.2
221	Caithness, Sutherland & Easter Ross	LD	14.2
222	Makerfield	Lab	14.3
223	Houghton & Sunderland S.	Lab	14.5
224	Birmingham Perry Barr	Lab	14.5
225	Bethnal Green & Bow	Lab	14.5
226	Leeds Central	Lab	14.6
227	Llanelli	Lab	14.6
228	Leicester East	Lab	14.7
229	St Helens North	Lab	14.7
230	Durham North	Lab	14.7
231	Bristol West	LD	14.8
232	Sheffield Hallam	LD	14.9
233	Barnsley Central	Lab	15.0
234	Chesterfield	Lab	15.1
235	South Shields	Lab	15.2
236	Barnsley East	Lab	15.3
237	Washington & Sunderland W.	Lab	15.3
238	Newcastle upon Tyne East	Lab	15.4
239	Mitcham & Morden	Lab	15.6
240	Bermondsey & Old Southwark	LD	15.6
241	Sheffield South East	Lab	15.7
242	Hull East	Lab	15.7
243	Hornsey & Wood Green	LD	15.7
244	Ayrshire North & Arran	Lab	15.9
245	Croydon North	Lab	15.9
246	Aberdeen North	Lab	16.0
247	Tyneside North	Lab	16.2
248	Edinburgh East	Lab	16.2
249	Wentworth & Dearne	Lab	16.5
250	Neath	Lab	16.6
251	Jarrow	Lab	16.6
252	Hull North	Lab	16.7
253	Redcar	LD	16.8
254	Blaydon	Lab	16.9
255	Lanark & Hamilton East	Lab	17.5
256	St Helens South & Whiston	Lab	17.5
257	Midlothian	Lab	17.6

Nat. rank	Constituency	1st Pty	Swing to gain
Conservative target list			
258	Islwyn	Lab	17.6
259	Falkirk	Lab	17.8
260	Blackley & Broughton	Lab	18.0
261	Barking	Lab	18.3
262	Swansea East	Lab	18.4
263	Durham, City of	Lab	18.5
264	Halton	Lab	18.8
265	Aberavon	Lab	18.8
266	Livingston	Lab	18.8
267	Walthamstow	Lab	18.9
268	Linlithgow & Falkirk East	Lab	18.9
269	Ogmore	Lab	19.1
270	Kilmarnock & Loudoun	Lab	19.2
271	Ceredigion	LD	19.2
272	East Kilbride, Strathaven & Lesmahagow	Lab	19.3
273	Dundee West	Lab	19.6
274	Gateshead	Lab	19.6
275	Paisley & Renfrewshire North	Lab	19.7
276	Merthyr Tydfil & Rhymney	Lab	19.9
277	Lewisham Deptford	Lab	20.1
278	Islington North	Lab	20.1
279	Glasgow South	Lab	20.1
280	Birmingham Hodge Hill	Lab	20.2
281	Ross, Skye & Lochaber	LD	20.2
282	Hackney N. & Stoke Newington	Lab	20.2
283	Manchester Gorton	Lab	20.2
284	Manchester Central	Lab	20.5
285	Glasgow North	Lab	20.6
286	Sheffield Central	Lab	20.7
287	Manchester Withington	LD	21.0
288	Brent Central	LD	21.0
289	Hackney South & Shoreditch	Lab	21.1
290	Cynon Valley	Lab	21.2
291	Garston & Halewood	Lab	21.7
292	Sheffield Brightside & Hillsborough	Lab	21.8
293	Birkenhead	Lab	21.8
294	Birmingham Ladywood	Lab	21.9
295	Inverclyde	Lab	22.0
296	Glasgow North West	Lab	22.1
297	Tottenham	Lab	22.2
298	Glasgow Central	Lab	22.5
299	Dunfermline & Fife West	Lab	22.6
300	Easington	Lab	22.6
301	Blaenau Gwent	Lab	22.7
302	Camberwell & Peckham	Lab	23.1
303	Na h-Eileanan an Iar (Western Isles)	SNP	23.3
304	West Ham	Lab	24.0
305	Liverpool Wavertree	Lab	24.1
306	Liverpool Riverside	Lab	24.2
307	Rhondda	Lab	24.4
308	Cumbernauld, Kilsyth & Kirkintilloch East	Lab	24.5

Nat. rank	Constituency	1st Pty	Swing to gain	Nat. rank	Constituency	1st Pty	Swing to gain
Conservative target list				**Labour target list**			
309	Airdrie & Shotts	Lab	24.7	37	Halesowen & Rowley Regis	Con	2.3
310	Paisley & Renfrewshire S.	Lab	24.8	38	Nuneaton	Con	2.3
311	Rutherglen & Hamilton W.	Lab	25.6	39	Gloucester	Con	2.4
312	Orkney & Shetland	LD	25.7	40	Northampton North	Con	2.4
313	Motherwell & Wishaw	Lab	25.9	41	Bury North	Con	2.5
314	Dunbartonshire West	Lab	26.8	42	Kingswood	Con	2.6
315	Liverpool West Derby	Lab	27.4	43	Erewash	Con	2.6
316	Glenrothes	Lab	27.6	44	Blackpool North & Cleveleys	Con	2.6
317	East Ham	Lab	27.6	45	Chester, City of	Con	2.8
318	Kirkcaldy & Cowdenbeath	Lab	27.6	46	Arfon	PC	2.8
319	Glasgow South West	Lab	28.0	47	Croydon Central	Con	2.9
320	Glasgow East	Lab	28.5	48	Worcester	Con	3.0
321	Bootle	Lab	28.8	49	Keighley	Con	3.1
322	Coatbridge, Chryston & Bellshill	Lab	29.2	50	Wirral West	Con	3.1
323	Knowsley	Lab	31.0	51	Cannock Chase	Con	3.5
324	Glasgow North East	Lab	31.5	52	Loughborough	Con	3.5
325	Liverpool Walton	Lab	32.7	53	Harrow East	Con	3.5
				54	Warwick & Leamington	Con	3.6
Labour target list				55	Birmingham Yardley	LD	3.7
1	Warwickshire North	Con	0.06	56	Swindon South	Con	3.8
2	Thurrock	Con	0.1	57	Ealing Central & Acton	Con	3.9
3	Hendon	Con	0.1	58	Pendle	Con	4.0
4	Cardiff North	Con	0.2	59	Stevenage	Con	4.0
5	Sherwood	Con	0.2	60	Elmet & Rothwell	Con	4.1
6	Norwich South	LD	0.3	61	Edinburgh West	LD	4.1
7	Stockton South	Con	0.3	62	Carmarthen West & Pembrokeshire South	Con	4.2
8	Broxtowe	Con	0.4	63	Vale of Glamorgan	Con	4.4
9	Lancaster & Fleetwood	Con	0.4	64	Argyll & Bute	LD	4.4
10	Bradford East	LD	0.5	65	Dumfriesshire, Clydesdale & Tweeddale	Con	4.6
11	Amber Valley	Con	0.6	66	Carmarthen East & Dinefwr	PC	4.6
12	Waveney	Con	0.8	67	Norwich North	Con	4.6
13	Wolverhampton South West	Con	0.9	68	Watford	Con	4.6
14	Morecambe & Lunesdale	Con	1.0	69	High Peak	Con	4.6
15	Carlisle	Con	1.0	70	Milton Keynes South	Con	4.7
16	Stroud	Con	1.1	71	Rossendale & Darwen	Con	4.8
17	Weaver Vale	Con	1.1	72	Cleethorpes	Con	4.8
18	Lincoln	Con	1.2	73	Somerset North East	Con	4.8
19	Brighton Pavilion	Grn	1.2	74	Great Yarmouth	Con	5.0
20	Plymouth Sutton & Devonport	Con	1.3	75	Dudley South	Con	5.1
21	Dewsbury	Con	1.4	76	Dover	Con	5.2
22	Warrington South	Con	1.4	77	Colne Valley	Con	5.3
23	Brent Central	LD	1.5	78	South Ribble	Con	5.4
24	Bedford	Con	1.5	79	Peterborough	Con	5.4
25	Brighton Kemptown	Con	1.6	80	Stafford	Con	5.4
26	Pudsey	Con	1.7	81	Stourbridge	Con	5.5
27	Corby	Con	1.7	82	Harlow	Con	5.6
28	Brentford & Isleworth	Con	1.8	83	Aberconwy	Con	5.7
29	Hove	Con	1.9	84	Ilford North	Con	5.7
30	Enfield North	Con	1.9	85	Preseli Pembrokeshire	Con	5.8
31	Hastings & Rye	Con	2.0	86	Brigg & Goole	Con	5.9
32	Manchester Withington	LD	2.1	87	Crewe & Nantwich	Con	5.9
33	Burnley	LD	2.2	88	Bristol North West	Con	6.0
34	Ipswich	Con	2.2	89	Battersea	Con	6.1
35	Dundee East	SNP	2.2				
36	Dunbartonshire East	LD	2.3				

Nat. rank	Constituency	1st Pty	Swing to gain	Nat. rank	Constituency	1st Pty	Swing to gain
Labour target list				**Labour target list**			
90	Finchley & Golders Green	Con	6.2	142	Hexham	Con	12.1
91	Calder Valley	Con	6.2	143	Kensington	Con	12.3
92	Redcar	LD	6.2	144	Putney	Con	12.3
93	Crawley	Con	6.2	145	Perth & North Perthshire	SNP	12.4
94	Hornsey & Wood Green	LD	6.2	146	Uxbridge & Ruislip South	Con	12.4
95	Reading West	Con	6.3	147	Sittingbourne & Sheppey	Con	12.7
96	Rugby	Con	6.3	148	Beverley & Holderness	Con	13.0
97	Burton	Con	6.3	149	Leeds North West	LD	13.2
98	Cardiff Central	LD	6.3	150	Altrincham & Sale West	Con	13.3
99	Na h-Eileanan an Iar (Western Isles)	SNP	6.4	151	Rochford & Southend East	Con	13.3
100	Basildon S.& Thurrock E.	Con	6.5	152	Macclesfield	Con	13.3
101	Tamworth	Con	6.6	153	Wyre Forest	Con	13.3
102	Redditch	Con	6.6	154	Wimbledon	Con	13.4
103	Chatham & Aylesford	Con	6.9	155	Harwich & Essex North	Con	13.5
104	Swindon North	Con	7.0	156	Yorkshire East	Con	13.6
105	Derbyshire South	Con	7.1	157	Fife North East	LD	13.6
106	Filton & Bradley Stoke	Con	7.2	158	Aberdeenshire W. & Kincardine	LD	13.8
107	Leicestershire North West	Con	7.2	159	Clacton	Con	14.0
108	Dorset South	Con	7.4	160	St Albans	Con	14.0
109	Cambridge	LD	7.4	161	Bridgwater & Somerset West	Con	14.1
110	Staffordshire Moorlands	Con	7.6	162	Camborne & Redruth	Con	14.1
111	Northampton South	Con	7.7	163	Ribble Valley	Con	14.1
112	Gordon	LD	8.0	164	Leicestershire South	Con	14.3
113	Scarborough & Whitby	Con	8.2	165	Congleton	Con	14.4
114	Portsmouth North	Con	8.3	166	Boston & Skegness	Con	14.4
115	Thanet South	Con	8.3	167	Hemel Hempstead	Con	14.6
116	Milton Keynes North	Con	8.3	168	Castle Point	Con	14.7
117	Caithness, Sutherland & Easter Ross	LD	8.4	169	Bosworth	Con	14.7
118	Clwyd West	Con	8.4	170	Banff & Buchan	SNP	14.7
119	Reading East	Con	8.5	171	Basildon & Billericay	Con	14.8
120	Enfield Southgate	Con	8.6	172	Norfolk South West	Con	14.9
121	Gillingham & Rainham	Con	9.3	173	Stone	Con	14.9
122	Inverness, Nairn, Badenoch & Strathspey	LD	9.3	174	York Outer	Con	15.0
123	Bermondsey & Old Southwark	LD	9.6	175	Charnwood	Con	15.0
124	Kettering	Con	9.6	176	Cities of London & Westminster	Con	15.0
125	Gravesham	Con	9.8	177	Canterbury	Con	15.0
126	Shipley	Con	10.1	178	Chingford & Woodford Green	Con	15.0
127	Bristol West	LD	10.3	179	Eddisbury	Con	15.1
128	Wrekin, The	Con	10.3	180	Basingstoke	Con	15.1
129	Rochester & Strood	Con	10.4	181	Suffolk Coastal	Con	15.2
130	Dartford	Con	10.6	182	Dwyfor Meirionnydd	PC	15.2
131	Bromsgrove	Con	11.0	183	Rushcliffe	Con	15.2
132	Monmouth	Con	11.2	184	Spelthorne	Con	15.3
133	Moray	SNP	11.3	185	Hornchurch & Upminster	Con	15.3
134	Forest of Dean	Con	11.3	186	Bury St Edmunds	Con	15.4
135	Wellingborough	Con	11.4	187	Croydon South	Con	15.4
136	Shrewsbury & Atcham	Con	11.7	188	Wyre & Preston North	Con	15.5
137	Chipping Barnet	Con	11.8	189	Meriden	Con	15.6
138	Selby & Ainsty	Con	11.9	190	Thanet North	Con	15.6
139	Derbyshire Mid	Con	11.9	191	Wycombe	Con	15.7
140	Bexleyheath & Crayford	Con	12.0	192	Bournemouth West	Con	15.8
141	Angus	SNP	12.0	193	Newark	Con	15.8
				194	Worthing East & Shoreham	Con	15.9
				195	Norfolk Mid	Con	16.0

Nat. rank	Constituency	1st Pty	Swing to gain
Labour target list			
196	Grantham & Stamford	Con	16.1
197	Louth & Horncastle	Con	16.1
198	Fylde	Con	16.3
199	Southend West	Con	16.3
200	Derbyshire Dales	Con	16.4
201	Braintree	Con	16.4
202	Staffordshire South	Con	16.4
203	Bedfordshire South West	Con	16.6
204	Shropshire North	Con	16.7
205	Havant	Con	16.7
206	Suffolk South	Con	16.7
207	Cambridgeshire North West	Con	16.8
208	Sutton Coldfield	Con	16.8
209	Gainsborough	Con	16.8
210	Banbury	Con	16.8
211	Witham	Con	16.9
212	Cambridgeshire North East	Con	16.9
213	Broadland	Con	17.0
214	Portsmouth South	LD	17.3
215	Lichfield	Con	17.3
216	Haltemprice & Howden	Con	17.3
217	Suffolk C.l & Ipswich N.	Con	17.3
218	Sleaford & North Hykeham	Con	17.4
219	Gosport	Con	17.4
220	Old Bexley & Sidcup	Con	17.4
221	Bournemouth East	Con	17.6
222	Welwyn Hatfield	Con	17.8
223	Bracknell	Con	17.8
224	Poole	Con	17.9
225	Suffolk West	Con	17.9
226	Berwick-upon-Tweed	LD	18.0
227	Norfolk South	Con	18.1
228	Harborough	Con	18.2
229	Romford	Con	18.2
230	Isle of Wight	Con	18.4
231	Rutland & Melton	Con	18.4
232	Bromley & Chislehurst	Con	18.5
233	Hertfordshire North East	Con	18.5
234	Hertsmere	Con	18.6
235	Tatton	Con	18.7
236	Sheffield Hallam	LD	18.7
237	Bognor Regis & Littlehampton	Con	18.7
238	Ashford	Con	18.7
239	Colchester	LD	18.8
240	Ross, Skye & Lochaber	LD	18.8
241	Bedfordshire Mid	Con	18.9
242	Huntingdon	Con	18.9
243	Northamptonshire South	Con	19.0
244	Aldershot	Con	19.0
245	Ruislip, Northwood & Pinner	Con	19.0
246	Wantage	Con	19.0
247	Hazel Grove	LD	19.2
248	Devon East	Con	19.3
249	Folkestone & Hythe	Con	19.4
250	Berwickshire, Roxburgh & Selkirk	LD	19.6

Nat. rank	Constituency	1st Pty	Swing to gain
Labour target list			
251	Kenilworth & Southam	Con	19.6
252	Thirsk & Malton	Con	19.7
253	Aldridge-Brownhills	Con	19.8
254	Worcestershire Mid	Con	19.8
255	Aylesbury	Con	19.8
256	Faversham & Kent Mid	Con	19.8
257	Bexhill & Battle	Con	19.8
258	Bedfordshire North East	Con	19.8
259	Tewkesbury	Con	19.8
260	Epping Forest	Con	19.9
261	Worthing West	Con	20.0
262	Hertford & Stortford	Con	20.0
263	Wiltshire South West	Con	20.1
264	Penrith & The Border	Con	20.2
265	Chelmsford	Con	20.4
266	Daventry	Con	20.4
267	Cambridgeshire South	Con	20.4
268	Norfolk North West	Con	20.5
269	Hitchin & Harpenden	Con	20.5
270	Brecon & Radnorshire	LD	20.5
271	Fareham	Con	20.5
272	Weston-Super-Mare	Con	20.5
273	Broxbourne	Con	20.6
274	Somerset North	Con	20.9
275	Skipton & Ripon	Con	21.0
276	Chelsea & Fulham	Con	21.0
277	Stratford-on-Avon	Con	21.0
278	Reigate	Con	21.0
279	Oxford West & Abingdon	Con	21.0
280	Truro & Falmouth	Con	21.1
281	Cotswolds, The	Con	21.1
282	Runnymede & Weybridge	Con	21.3
283	Wokingham	Con	21.3
284	Hertfordshire South West	Con	21.4
285	Maidstone & The Weald	Con	21.5
286	New Forest East	Con	21.5
287	Montgomeryshire	Con	21.6
288	Rayleigh & Wickford	Con	21.7
289	Beckenham	Con	21.7
290	Devon South West	Con	21.8
291	St Ives	LD	21.8
292	Sevenoaks	Con	21.8
293	Tiverton & Honiton	Con	21.9
294	Epsom & Ewell	Con	22.1
295	Totnes	Con	22.2
296	Southport	LD	22.2
297	Eastleigh	LD	22.2
298	Ceredigion	LD	22.2
299	Chichester	Con	22.4
300	Devizes	Con	22.5
301	South Holland & The Deepings	Con	22.5
302	Kingston & Surbiton	LD	22.5
303	Carshalton & Wallington	LD	22.6
304	Solihull	LD	22.6
305	Hampshire North West	Con	22.6

Nat. rank	Constituency	1st Pty	Swing to gain
Labour target list			
306	Henley	Con	22.6
307	Tonbridge & Malling	Con	22.7
308	Tunbridge Wells	Con	22.7
309	St Austell & Newquay	LD	22.8
310	Herefordshire North	Con	22.9
311	Saffron Walden	Con	22.9
312	Witney	Con	22.9
313	Cheadle	LD	23.1
314	Cornwall South East	Con	23.2
315	Christchurch	Con	23.3
316	Horsham	Con	23.3
317	Cambridgeshire South East	Con	23.5
318	Wealden	Con	23.5
319	Brentwood & Ongar	Con	23.5
320	Maldon	Con	23.6
321	Salisbury	Con	23.6
322	Newton Abbot	Con	23.6
323	Surrey Heath	Con	23.7
324	Richmond (Yorks)	Con	23.8
325	Wells	LD	23.8
326	Surrey East	Con	23.9
327	Woking	Con	23.9
328	Devon Central	Con	24.0
329	Ludlow	Con	24.0
330	Esher & Walton	Con	24.1
331	Torbay	LD	24.2
332	Hereford & Herefordshire S.	Con	24.3
333	Devon North	LD	24.3
334	Chippenham	LD	24.3
335	Twickenham	LD	24.4
336	Hampshire East	Con	24.4
337	New Forest West	Con	24.5
338	Arundel & South Downs	Con	24.6
339	Beaconsfield	Con	24.7
340	Sutton & Cheam	LD	24.7
341	Wiltshire North	Con	24.8
342	Bath	LD	24.8
343	Worcestershire West	Con	24.9
344	Sussex Mid	Con	25.0
345	Thornbury & Yate	LD	25.0
346	Dorset West	Con	25.0
347	Devon West & Torridge	Con	25.1
348	Mole Valley	Con	25.3
349	Norfolk North	LD	25.3
350	Orpington	Con	25.4
351	Meon Valley	Con	25.4
352	Hampshire North East	Con	25.4
353	Windsor	Con	25.5
354	Harrogate & Knaresborough	Con	25.6
355	Orkney & Shetland	LD	25.7
356	Dorset North	Con	25.8
357	Dorset Mid & Poole North	LD	26.0
358	Yeovil	LD	26.0
359	Romsey & Southampton N.	Con	26.1
360	Eastbourne	LD	26.1

Nat. rank	Constituency	1st Pty	Swing to gain
Labour target list			
361	Maidenhead	Con	26.2
362	Lewes	LD	26.2
363	Surrey South West	Con	26.4
364	Winchester	Con	26.9
365	Taunton Deane	LD	27.0
366	Cornwall North	LD	27.1
367	Cheltenham	LD	27.1
368	Chesham & Amersham	Con	27.4
369	Richmond Park	Con	27.5
370	Guildford	Con	27.5
371	Somerton & Frome	LD	27.7
372	Newbury	Con	27.8
373	Westmorland & Lonsdale	LD	30.6
Liberal Democrat target list			
1	Camborne & Redruth	Con	0.1
2	Oldham East & Saddleworth	Lab	0.1
3	Oxford West & Abingdon	Con	0.2
4	Sheffield Central	Lab	0.2
5	Ashfield	Lab	0.2
6	Edinburgh South	Lab	0.4
7	Truro & Falmouth	Con	0.4
8	Newton Abbot	Con	0.5
9	Chesterfield	Lab	0.6
10	Swansea West	Lab	0.7
11	Hull North	Lab	1.0
12	Rochdale	Lab	1.0
13	Harrogate & Knaresborough	Con	1.0
14	Hampstead & Kilburn	Lab	1.0
15	Watford	Con	1.3
16	Montgomeryshire	Con	1.8
17	Edinburgh North & Leith	Lab	1.8
18	St Albans	Con	2.2
19	Newport East	Lab	2.4
20	Weston-Super-Mare	Con	2.6
21	Hereford & Herefordshire S.	Con	2.6
22	Devon West & Torridge	Con	2.7
23	Winchester	Con	2.7
24	Derby North	Lab	2.9
25	Northampton North	Con	3.1
26	Cornwall South East	Con	3.2
27	Bristol North West	Con	3.3
28	Durham, City of	Lab	3.3
29	Dorset West	Con	3.4
30	Richmond Park	Con	3.5
31	York Outer	Con	3.5
32	Streatham	Lab	3.5
33	Pontypridd	Lab	3.8
34	Newcastle upon Tyne N.	Lab	3.9
35	Aberdeen South	Lab	4.1
36	Islington South & Finsbury	Lab	4.1
37	Birmingham Hall Green	Lab	4.2
38	Romsey & Southampton N.	Con	4.2
39	Colne Valley	Con	4.4
40	Oxford East	Lab	4.4

Nat. rank	*Constituency*	*1st Pty*	*Swing to gain*	Nat. rank	*Constituency*	*1st Pty*	*Swing to gain*
Liberal Democrat target list				**Liberal Democrat target list**			
41	Warrington South	Con	4.6	96	Suffolk Coastal	Con	8.3
42	Bosworth	Con	4.6	97	Cardiff South & Penarth	Lab	8.3
43	Chelmsford	Con	4.7	98	Southend West	Con	8.3
44	Bristol South	Lab	4.9	99	Birmingham Selly Oak	Lab	8.4
45	Totnes	Con	5.1	100	Suffolk South	Con	8.4
46	Cambridgeshire S. E.	Con	5.2	101	Bridgwater & Somerset W.	Con	8.5
47	Ealing Central & Acton	Con	5.2	102	Tiverton & Honiton	Con	8.5
48	Plymouth Sutton & Devonport	Con	5.5	103	Devon Central	Con	8.6
49	Wrexham	Lab	5.5	104	Stoke-on-Trent Central	Lab	8.6
50	Dunfermline & Fife West	Lab	5.6	105	Devon East	Con	8.6
51	Tewkesbury	Con	5.8	106	Blyth Valley	Lab	8.6
52	Newcastle upon Tyne East	Lab	5.9	107	Durham North West	Lab	8.7
53	Maidstone & The Weald	Con	6.0	108	Heywood & Middleton	Lab	8.7
54	Bristol East	Lab	6.1	109	Manchester Gorton	Lab	8.7
55	Great Grimsby	Lab	6.1	110	Bournemouth East	Con	8.8
56	Canterbury	Con	6.1	111	Stockport	Lab	8.8
57	Salisbury	Con	6.2	112	Harborough	Con	8.9
58	Aldershot	Con	6.2	113	Penistone & Stocksbridge	Lab	8.9
59	Worcestershire West	Con	6.2	114	Southampton Test	Lab	8.9
60	Luton South	Lab	6.3	115	Leeds West	Lab	9.1
61	Merthyr Tydfil & Rhymney	Lab	6.3	116	Skipton & Ripon	Con	9.1
62	Woking	Con	6.4	117	Holborn & St Pancras	Lab	9.1
63	Lewisham West & Penge	Lab	6.5	118	Hull West & Hessle	Lab	9.1
64	Glasgow North	Lab	6.6	119	Dumfriesshire, Clydesdale & Tweeddale	Con	9.1
65	Sussex Mid	Con	6.6	120	Wansbeck	Lab	9.2
66	Cambridgeshire South	Con	6.6	121	Doncaster Central	Lab	9.3
67	Hexham	Con	6.7	122	Leicester South	Lab	9.3
68	Bournemouth West	Con	6.7	123	Liverpool Wavertree	Lab	9.5
69	Somerset North	Con	6.8	124	Somerset North East	Con	9.5
70	Salford & Eccles	Lab	6.9	125	Folkestone & Hythe	Con	9.6
71	Broadland	Con	6.9	126	High Peak	Con	9.6
72	Congleton	Con	7.0	127	Dulwich & West Norwood	Lab	9.7
73	Guildford	Con	7.0	128	Pendle	Con	9.8
74	Huddersfield	Lab	7.0	129	Wycombe	Con	9.9
75	Dorset North	Con	7.0	130	Norfolk South	Con	9.9
76	Sheffield Heeley	Lab	7.1	131	Huntingdon	Con	10.0
77	Calder Valley	Con	7.1	132	Ludlow	Con	10.0
78	Bridgend	Lab	7.2	133	Blaydon	Lab	10.1
79	York Central	Lab	7.4	134	Scarborough & Whitby	Con	10.2
80	Lewisham East	Lab	7.4	135	Exeter	Lab	10.2
81	Shrewsbury & Atcham	Con	7.5	136	Horsham	Con	10.3
82	Isle of Wight	Con	7.5	137	Peterborough	Con	10.4
83	Reading East	Con	7.6	138	Herefordshire North	Con	10.4
84	Wiltshire North	Con	7.7	139	Newbury	Con	10.5
85	Filton & Bradley Stoke	Con	7.8	140	Southampton Itchen	Lab	10.5
86	Brentford & Isleworth	Con	7.8	141	Nottingham East	Lab	10.5
87	Leicester West	Lab	7.9	142	Bury St Edmunds	Con	10.5
88	Poole	Con	7.9	143	Wiltshire South West	Con	10.6
89	Leyton & Wanstead	Lab	8.0	144	Spelthorne	Con	10.6
90	Darlington	Lab	8.0	145	Pudsey	Con	10.6
91	Nottingham South	Lab	8.0	146	Milton Keynes North	Con	10.7
92	Hove	Con	8.2	147	Northampton South	Con	10.7
93	Derbyshire North East	Lab	8.2	148	Gainsborough	Con	10.7
94	Aberconwy	Con	8.3	149	Lincoln	Con	10.8
95	Bishop Auckland	Lab	8.3				

Nat. rank	Constituency	1st Pty	Swing to gain	Nat. rank	Constituency	1st Pty	Swing to gain
Liberal Democrat target list				**Liberal Democrat target list**			
150	Gower	Lab	10.8	205	Ipswich	Con	12.5
151	Brighton Pavilion	Grn	10.9	206	Penrith & The Border	Con	12.5
152	Wythenshawe & Sale East	Lab	10.9	207	Forest of Dean	Con	12.5
153	Newcastle upon Tyne C.	Lab	10.9	208	Chester, City of	Con	12.5
154	Halifax	Lab	11.0	209	Weaver Vale	Con	12.5
155	Newcastle-under-Lyme	Lab	11.0	210	Bury South	Lab	12.5
156	Lancaster & Fleetwood	Con	11.0	211	Sedgefield	Lab	12.6
157	Dewsbury	Con	11.1	212	Hull East	Lab	12.6
158	Don Valley	Lab	11.1	213	Moray	SNP	12.6
159	Stratford-on-Avon	Con	11.2	214	Rossendale & Darwen	Con	12.6
160	New Forest East	Con	11.3	215	Carmarthen East & Dinefwr	PC	12.6
161	Worcester	Con	11.4	216	Cardiff North	Con	12.7
162	Clwyd South	Lab	11.4	217	Rutland & Melton	Con	12.7
163	Bethnal Green & Bow	Lab	11.4	218	Sheffield South East	Lab	12.7
164	Derby South	Lab	11.4	219	Hartlepool	Lab	12.7
165	Worthing East & Shoreham	Con	11.5	220	Cleethorpes	Con	12.7
166	Bradford South	Lab	11.5	221	Arfon	PC	12.8
167	Reading West	Con	11.5	222	Stalybridge & Hyde	Lab	12.8
168	Walthamstow	Lab	11.6	223	Milton Keynes South	Con	12.8
169	Mansfield	Lab	11.7	224	Erewash	Con	12.9
170	Harwich & Essex North	Con	11.7	225	Suffolk Central & Ipswich North	Con	12.9
171	Bedford	Con	11.7	226	Aberdeen North	Lab	12.9
172	Cotswolds, The	Con	11.7	227	Redditch	Con	12.9
173	Altrincham & Sale West	Con	11.7	228	Kenilworth & Southam	Con	13.0
174	Alyn & Deeside	Lab	11.8	229	Middlesbrough	Lab	13.0
175	Bexhill & Battle	Con	11.8	230	Basingstoke	Con	13.0
176	Rother Valley	Lab	11.8	231	Dorset South	Con	13.0
177	Stoke-on-Trent South	Lab	11.8	232	Coventry South	Lab	13.1
178	Norwich North	Con	11.8	233	Manchester Central	Lab	13.1
179	Meon Valley	Con	11.8	234	Cannock Chase	Con	13.1
180	Scunthorpe	Lab	11.9	235	Morley & Outwood	Lab	13.1
181	Aylesbury	Con	11.9	236	Hertfordshire South West	Con	13.1
182	Preston	Lab	11.9	237	Hampshire East	Con	13.2
183	Haltemprice & Howden	Con	11.9	238	Loughborough	Con	13.2
184	Cardiff West	Lab	11.9	239	Yorkshire East	Con	13.2
185	Worthing West	Con	11.9	240	Clwyd West	Con	13.2
186	Macclesfield	Con	11.9	241	Oldham West & Royton	Lab	13.2
187	Edinburgh East	Lab	12.0	242	Stoke-on-Trent North	Lab	13.3
188	Sefton Central	Lab	12.0	243	Norfolk South West	Con	13.4
189	Wantage	Con	12.0	244	Stockton North	Lab	13.4
190	Wimbledon	Con	12.0	245	Newport West	Lab	13.5
191	Bromsgrove	Con	12.0	246	Hemel Hempstead	Con	13.5
192	Rugby	Con	12.1	247	Suffolk West	Con	13.6
193	Portsmouth North	Con	12.1	248	Swindon South	Con	13.6
194	Birmingham Hodge Hill	Lab	12.1	249	Reigate	Con	13.6
195	Gloucester	Con	12.2	250	Stirling	Lab	13.6
196	Beverley & Holderness	Con	12.2	251	Norfolk Mid	Con	13.6
197	Leeds North East	Lab	12.2	252	Swindon North	Con	13.7
198	Plymouth Moor View	Lab	12.2	253	Rochford & Southend E.	Con	13.7
199	Brighton Kemptown	Con	12.3	254	Louth & Horncastle	Con	13.7
200	Vauxhall	Lab	12.3	255	Warwick & Leamington	Con	13.8
201	Warrington North	Lab	12.4	256	Bury North	Con	13.8
202	Wokingham	Con	12.4	257	Bedfordshire Mid	Con	13.8
203	Edinburgh South West	Lab	12.4	258	Stevenage	Con	13.8
204	Coventry North West	Lab	12.4	259	Havant	Con	13.8

Nat. rank	Constituency	1st Pty	Swing to gain	Nat. rank	Constituency	1st Pty	Swing to gain
Liberal Democrat target list				**Liberal Democrat target list**			
260	East Lothian	Lab	13.9	313	Elmet & Rothwell	Con	14.8
261	Tyneside North	Lab	13.9	314	Ynys Mon	Lab	14.9
262	Stourbridge	Con	13.9	315	Ribble Valley	Con	14.9
263	Derbyshire Mid	Con	13.9	316	Dudley South	Con	14.9
264	Islington North	Lab	13.9	317	Arundel & South Downs	Con	14.9
265	Hertford & Stortford	Con	13.9	318	Burton	Con	14.9
266	Bognor Regis & Littlehampton	Con	13.9	319	Poplar & Limehouse	Lab	14.9
				320	Leigh	Lab	14.9
267	Hitchin & Harpenden	Con	14.0	321	Brent North	Lab	14.9
268	Leicestershire North West	Con	14.0	322	Preseli Pembrokeshire	Con	15.0
269	Chichester	Con	14.0	323	Midlothian	Lab	15.0
270	Kingswood	Con	14.0	324	Wyre Forest	Con	15.0
271	Saffron Walden	Con	14.0	325	Walsall North	Lab	15.0
272	Devizes	Con	14.0	326	Barnsley Central	Lab	15.0
273	Charnwood	Con	14.0	327	Derbyshire South	Con	15.0
274	Grantham & Stamford	Con	14.0	328	Wirral West	Con	15.0
275	Croydon South	Con	14.0	329	Bracknell	Con	15.1
276	Gillingham & Rainham	Con	14.0	330	Hertfordshire North East	Con	15.1
277	Birmingham Erdington	Lab	14.0	331	Fylde	Con	15.1
278	Torfaen	Lab	14.1	332	Caerphilly	Lab	15.1
279	Stone	Con	14.1	333	Wrekin, The	Con	15.1
280	Wakefield	Lab	14.1	334	Perth & North Perthshire	SNP	15.2
281	Birmingham Ladywood	Lab	14.1	335	Carlisle	Con	15.2
282	Worsley & Eccles South	Lab	14.1	336	Lewisham Deptford	Lab	15.2
283	Uxbridge & Ruislip South	Con	14.2	337	Finchley & Golders Green	Con	15.2
284	Bolton West	Lab	14.2	338	Kensington	Con	15.3
285	Birmingham Perry Barr	Lab	14.2	339	Shropshire North	Con	15.3
286	Birmingham Northfield	Lab	14.2	340	Dover	Con	15.3
287	Staffordshire Moorlands	Con	14.2	341	St Helens South & Whiston	Lab	15.3
288	Leicestershire South	Con	14.2	342	Tamworth	Con	15.3
289	Leeds Central	Lab	14.2	343	Gosport	Con	15.4
290	Ochil & South Perthshire	Lab	14.2	344	Walsall South	Lab	15.4
291	Surrey South West	Con	14.2	345	Wyre & Preston North	Con	15.4
292	Shipley	Con	14.3	346	Surrey East	Con	15.4
293	Cambridgeshire North West	Con	14.3	347	Tunbridge Wells	Con	15.5
294	Chipping Barnet	Con	14.3	348	Norfolk North West	Con	15.5
295	Rotherham	Lab	14.3	349	Greenwich & Woolwich	Lab	15.5
296	Middlesbrough S. & Cleveland E.	Lab	14.4	350	Henley	Con	15.5
297	Mole Valley	Con	14.4	351	Croydon Central	Con	15.5
298	Barnsley East	Lab	14.4	352	Wellingborough	Con	15.6
299	Monmouth	Con	14.4	353	Makerfield	Lab	15.6
300	Sunderland Central	Lab	14.5	354	Hackney N. & Stoke Newington	Lab	15.6
301	Broxtowe	Con	14.5				
302	Eddisbury	Con	14.6	355	Worcestershire Mid	Con	15.6
303	Telford	Lab	14.7	356	Hastings & Rye	Con	15.6
304	Epsom & Ewell	Con	14.7	357	Christchurch	Con	15.6
305	Batley & Spen	Lab	14.7	358	Maidenhead	Con	15.6
306	Rushcliffe	Con	14.7	359	Wealden	Con	15.6
307	Stafford	Con	14.7	360	Stockton South	Con	15.7
308	Durham North	Lab	14.7	361	Ashford	Con	15.7
309	Vale of Glamorgan	Con	14.8	362	Neath	Lab	15.7
310	Delyn	Lab	14.8	363	Wirral South	Lab	15.7
311	Thirsk & Malton	Con	14.8	364	Fareham	Con	15.7
312	Derbyshire Dales	Con	14.8	365	Amber Valley	Con	15.7
				366	Nottingham North	Lab	15.7

Nat. rank	Constituency	1st Pty	Swing to gain
Liberal Democrat target list			
367	St Helens North	Lab	15.8
368	Bolton South East	Lab	15.8
369	Cambridgeshire North East	Con	15.8
370	Bromley & Chislehurst	Con	15.8
371	Cities of London & Westminster	Con	15.8
372	Birmingham Edgbaston	Lab	15.8
373	Stretford & Urmston	Lab	15.8
374	Selby & Ainsty	Con	15.8
375	Great Yarmouth	Con	15.9
376	Wolverhampton South West	Con	15.9
377	Normanton, Pontefract & Castleford	Lab	15.9
378	Surrey Heath	Con	15.9
379	Nuneaton	Con	15.9
380	Devon South West	Con	15.9
381	Chesham & Amersham	Con	15.9
382	Gedling	Lab	16.0
383	Blackpool South	Lab	16.0
384	Tatton	Con	16.0
385	Harrow West	Lab	16.0
386	Basildon S. & Thurrock E.	Con	16.0
387	Keighley	Con	16.0
388	Dwyfor Meirionnydd	PC	16.0
389	Halesowen & Rowley Regis	Con	16.1
390	Crawley	Con	16.1
391	Sherwood	Con	16.1
392	Hammersmith	Lab	16.1
393	Wolverhampton South East	Lab	16.2
394	Stroud	Con	16.2
395	Banbury	Con	16.2
396	Witham	Con	16.2
397	Doncaster North	Lab	16.2
398	Wolverhampton North East	Lab	16.2
399	Ilford South	Lab	16.2
400	Epping Forest	Con	16.2
401	Brigg & Goole	Con	16.2
402	Blackburn	Lab	16.3
403	Angus	SNP	16.3
404	Coventry North East	Lab	16.3
405	Bedfordshire South West	Con	16.4
406	Gateshead	Lab	16.4
407	Thanet South	Con	16.4
408	Banff & Buchan	SNP	16.4
409	Leeds East	Lab	16.4
410	Ellesmere Port & Neston	Lab	16.5
411	Rochester & Strood	Con	16.5
412	Carmarthen W. & Pembrokeshire S.	Con	16.5
413	Wigan	Lab	16.5
414	Denton & Reddish	Lab	16.6
415	Swansea East	Lab	16.6
416	Crewe & Nantwich	Con	16.6
417	Kettering	Con	16.6
418	Tynemouth	Lab	16.6

Nat. rank	Constituency	1st Pty	Swing to gain
Liberal Democrat target list			
419	Thanet North	Con	16.6
420	Hackney S. & Shoreditch	Lab	16.7
421	West Bromwich East	Lab	16.7
422	Dundee East	SNP	16.7
423	Feltham & Heston	Lab	16.7
424	Sleaford & North Hykeham	Con	16.7
425	Brentwood & Ongar	Con	16.7
426	West Bromwich West	Lab	16.8
427	Ashton Under Lyne	Lab	16.8
428	Sittingbourne & Sheppey	Con	16.8
429	Braintree	Con	16.9
430	Hemsworth	Lab	16.9
431	Newark	Con	16.9
432	Meriden	Con	16.9
433	Slough	Lab	17.0
434	Dartford	Con	17.0
435	Esher & Walton	Con	17.0
436	Bedfordshire North East	Con	17.0
437	Harlow	Con	17.1
438	Northamptonshire South	Con	17.1
439	Hyndburn	Lab	17.1
440	Runnymede & Weybridge	Con	17.1
441	Lichfield	Con	17.1
442	Llanelli	Lab	17.2
443	Blackpool N. & Cleveleys	Con	17.2
444	Bolsover	Lab	17.2
445	Wentworth & Dearne	Lab	17.3
446	South Ribble	Con	17.3
447	Chatham & Aylesford	Con	17.3
448	Corby	Con	17.3
449	Boston & Skegness	Con	17.3
450	Thurrock	Con	17.3
451	Castle Point	Con	17.4
452	Workington	Lab	17.4
453	Erith & Thamesmead	Lab	17.4
454	Vale of Clwyd	Lab	17.4
455	Hampshire North West	Con	17.4
456	Waveney	Con	17.4
457	Tooting	Lab	17.5
458	Sheffield Brightside & Hillsborough	Lab	17.5
459	Putney	Con	17.6
460	Hampshire North East	Con	17.6
461	Orpington	Con	17.6
462	Gravesham	Con	17.6
463	Battersea	Con	17.7
464	Tonbridge & Malling	Con	17.7
465	Washington & Sunderland W.	Lab	17.7
466	Jarrow	Lab	17.7
467	Bradford West	Lab	17.7
468	Sevenoaks	Con	17.7
469	New Forest West	Con	17.8
470	Chorley	Lab	17.8
471	Glasgow Central	Lab	17.8
472	Aberavon	Lab	17.8

Nat. rank	Constituency	1st Pty	Swing to gain	Nat. rank	Constituency	1st Pty	Swing to gain
Liberal Democrat target list				**Liberal Democrat target list**			
473	Ayrshire Central	Lab	17.9	528	Ruislip, Northwood & Pinner	Con	20.4
474	Harrow East	Con	17.9	529	Bassetlaw	Lab	20.6
475	Eltham	Lab	17.9	530	Beaconsfield	Con	20.7
476	Sutton Coldfield	Con	18.0	531	East Kilbride, Strathaven &		
477	Chingford & Woodford Green	Con	18.0		Lesmahagow	Lab	20.8
478	Enfield Southgate	Con	18.0	532	Tottenham	Lab	20.8
479	Lancashire West	Lab	18.1	533	Aldridge-Brownhills	Con	20.8
480	Morecambe & Lunesdale	Con	18.1	534	Copeland	Lab	20.9
481	Westminster North	Lab	18.2	535	Renfrewshire East	Lab	20.9
482	Dudley North	Lab	18.2	536	Croydon North	Lab	21.0
483	Ilford North	Con	18.2	537	Blaenau Gwent	Lab	21.1
484	Houghton & Sunderland S.	Lab	18.2	538	Na h-Eileanan an Iar		
485	Staffordshire South	Con	18.2		(Western Isles)	SNP	21.2
486	Liverpool Riverside	Lab	18.3	539	Inverclyde	Lab	21.3
487	Faversham & Kent Mid	Con	18.3	540	Rayleigh & Wickford	Con	21.3
488	Ealing Southall	Lab	18.3	541	Barrow & Furness	Lab	21.5
489	Camberwell & Peckham	Lab	18.4	542	Easington	Lab	21.5
490	Falkirk	Lab	18.5	543	Edmonton	Lab	21.6
491	Basildon & Billericay	Con	18.5	544	Paisley & Renfrewshire N.	Lab	21.8
492	Linlithgow & Falkirk East	Lab	18.5	545	South Holland & The		
493	Daventry	Con	18.5		Deepings	Con	21.8
494	Dundee West	Lab	18.5	546	Richmond (Yorks)	Con	21.8
495	Ealing North	Lab	18.6	547	Halton	Lab	21.9
496	Beckenham	Con	18.6	548	Birkenhead	Lab	22.0
497	Livingston	Lab	18.7	549	Romford	Con	22.0
498	Ayrshire North & Arran	Lab	18.7	550	Chelsea & Fulham	Con	22.1
499	Warley	Lab	18.7	551	Mitcham & Morden	Lab	22.3
500	Hornchurch & Upminster	Con	18.8	552	Rhondda	Lab	22.3
501	Bolton North East	Lab	18.8	553	Kilmarnock & Loudoun	Lab	22.6
502	Enfield North	Con	18.8	554	Broxbourne	Con	22.7
503	Bexleyheath & Crayford	Con	18.9	555	Hayes & Harlington	Lab	23.0
504	South Shields	Lab	18.9	556	Barking	Lab	23.1
505	Ayr, Carrick & Cumnock	Lab	18.9	557	Cumbernauld, Kilsyth &		
506	Warwickshire North	Con	19.0		Kirkintilloch East	Lab	23.8
507	Wallasey	Lab	19.1	558	Rutherglen & Hamilton W.	Lab	24.4
508	Glasgow North West	Lab	19.1	559	Airdrie & Shotts	Lab	25.0
509	Dagenham & Rainham	Lab	19.1	560	Paisley & Renfrewshire S.	Lab	25.0
510	Windsor	Con	19.2	561	West Ham	Lab	25.6
511	Ogmore	Lab	19.3	562	Motherwell & Wishaw	Lab	25.6
512	Hertsmere	Con	19.3	563	Bootle	Lab	25.7
513	Lanark & Hamilton East	Lab	19.3	564	Liverpool West Derby	Lab	25.8
514	Cynon Valley	Lab	19.3	565	Dunbartonshire West	Lab	26.6
515	Old Bexley & Sidcup	Con	19.4	566	Glasgow South West	Lab	26.7
516	Islwyn	Lab	19.4	567	Glenrothes	Lab	27.3
517	Luton North	Lab	19.6	568	Kirkcaldy & Cowdenbeath	Lab	27.6
518	Witney	Con	19.7	569	Glasgow East	Lab	28.3
519	Garston & Halewood	Lab	19.7	570	Knowsley	Lab	28.8
520	Leicester East	Lab	19.8	571	Liverpool Walton	Lab	28.9
521	Hendon	Con	19.9	572	Coatbridge, Chryston &		
522	Glasgow South	Lab	19.9		Bellshill	Lab	29.1
523	Dumfries & Galloway	Lab	20.0	573	East Ham	Lab	29.4
524	Blackley & Broughton	Lab	20.0	574	Glasgow North East	Lab	30.3
525	Clacton	Con	20.0				
526	Maldon	Con	20.3				
527	Welwyn Hatfield	Con	20.3				

Nat. rank	Constituency	1st Pty	Swing to gain
Green Party target list			
1	Norwich South	LD	9.41
2	Cambridge	LD	16.6
3	Argyll & Bute	LD	18.3
4	Gordon	LD	18.4
5	Leeds West	Lab	19.0
6	Edinburgh East	Lab	19.2
7	Huddersfield	Lab	19.8
8	Hove	Con	19.8
9	Inverness, Nairn, Badenoch & Strathspey	LD	19.8
10	York Central	Lab	20.1
11	Bethnal Green & Bow	Lab	20.6
12	Brighton Kemptown	Con	20.6
13	Bristol South	Lab	20.7
14	Leicester West	Lab	20.7
15	Lancaster & Fleetwood	Con	20.8
16	Stirling	Lab	20.9
17	Bristol East	Lab	21.0
18	Aberdeen South	Lab	21.0
19	Ochil & South Perthshire	Lab	21.0
20	Luton South	Lab	21.1
21	Edinburgh South West	Lab	21.1
22	Plymouth Sutton & Devonport	Con	21.1
23	Dewsbury	Con	21.3
24	Nottingham East	Lab	21.4
25	East Lothian	Lab	21.4
26	Northampton South	Con	21.5
27	Cardiff South & Penarth	Lab	21.6
28	Dumfriesshire, Clydesdale & Tweeddale	Con	21.6
29	Edinburgh South	Lab	21.6
30	Calder Valley	Con	21.6
31	Colne Valley	Con	21.7
32	Poplar & Limehouse	Lab	21.7
33	Bury St Edmunds	Con	21.8
34	Torfaen	Lab	21.8
35	Swansea West	Lab	21.9
36	Stockport	Lab	22.0
37	Northampton North	Con	22.0
38	Sheffield Heeley	Lab	22.0
39	Norwich North	Con	22.1
40	Scarborough & Whitby	Con	22.1
41	Lewisham West & Penge	Lab	22.1
42	Reading East	Con	22.2
43	Newcastle upon Tyne Central	Lab	22.2
44	Birmingham Selly Oak	Lab	22.3
45	Edinburgh North & Leith	Lab	22.3
46	Watford	Con	22.3
47	Cardiff Central	LD	22.3
48	Nottingham South	Lab	22.4
49	Cardiff West	Lab	22.4
50	Filton & Bradley Stoke	Con	22.4

Nat. rank	Constituency	1st Pty	Swing to gain
Scottish National Party target list			
1	Ochil & South Perthshire	Lab	5.14
2	Argyll & Bute	LD	6.3
3	Gordon	LD	6.9
4	Falkirk	Lab	7.7
5	Dundee West	Lab	9.8
6	Ayrshire North & Arran	Lab	10.7
7	Inverness, Nairn, Badenoch & Strathspey	LD	11.0
8	Aberdeen North	Lab	11.1
9	Caithness, Sutherland & Easter Ross	LD	11.1
10	Livingston	Lab	11.3
11	Edinburgh East	Lab	11.5
12	Linlithgow & Falkirk East	Lab	12.2
13	Stirling	Lab	12.2
14	Edinburgh West	LD	12.4
15	Aberdeenshire West & Kincardine	LD	12.4
16	Midlothian	Lab	13.2
17	Kilmarnock & Loudoun	Lab	13.3
18	Aberdeen South	Lab	13.7
19	East Kilbride, Strathaven & Lesmahagow	Lab	14.2
20	East Lothian	Lab	14.3
21	Ayrshire Central	Lab	14.3
22	Lanark & Hamilton East	Lab	14.5
23	Ayr, Carrick & Cumnock	Lab	14.6
24	Fife North East	LD	15.1
25	Dumfriesshire, Clydesdale & Tweeddale	Con	15.1
26	Edinburgh South West	Lab	15.3
27	Glasgow South	Lab	15.8
28	Cumbernauld, Kilsyth & Kirkintilloch East	Lab	16.7
29	Dunbartonshire East	LD	17.2
30	Glasgow Central	Lab	17.3
31	Airdrie & Shotts	Lab	17.3
32	Edinburgh North & Leith	Lab	17.3
33	Glasgow North	Lab	17.3
34	Paisley & Renfrewshire N.	Lab	17.5
35	Dumfries & Galloway	Lab	17.6
36	Edinburgh South	Lab	17.8
37	Glasgow East	Lab	18.4
38	Ross, Skye & Lochaber	LD	18.8
39	Inverclyde	Lab	19.2
40	Glasgow North West	Lab	19.4
41	Dunfermline & Fife West	Lab	20.0
42	Berwickshire, Roxburgh & Selkirk	LD	20.3
43	Glenrothes	Lab	20.3
44	Dunbartonshire West	Lab	20.6
45	Paisley & Renfrewshire S.	Lab	20.8
46	Renfrewshire East	Lab	21.2
47	Motherwell & Wishaw	Lab	21.5
48	Rutherglen & Hamilton West	Lab	22.4

Nat. rank	*Constituency*	*1st Pty*	*Swing to gain*
Scottish National Party target list			
49	Glasgow South West	Lab	23.1
50	Coatbridge, Chryston & Bellshill	Lab	24.9
51	Kirkcaldy & Cowdenbeath	Lab	25.1
52	Orkney & Shetland	LD	25.7
53	Glasgow North East	Lab	27.1
Plaid Cymru target list			
1	Ynys Mon	Lab	3.57
2	Llanelli	Lab	6.3
3	Aberconwy	Con	9.0
4	Ceredigion	LD	10.9
5	Clwyd West	Con	13.1
6	Neath	Lab	13.2
7	Caerphilly	Lab	14.1
8	Cynon Valley	Lab	16.1
9	Clwyd South	Lab	17.1
10	Wrexham	Lab	17.4
11	Carmarthen West & Pembrokeshire South	Con	17.6
12	Islwyn	Lab	18.1
13	Bridgend	Lab	18.3
14	Pontypridd	Lab	18.5
15	Preseli Pembrokeshire	Con	18.5
16	Rhondda	Lab	18.6
17	Cardiff West	Lab	19.0
18	Gower	Lab	19.1
19	Cardiff South & Penarth	Lab	19.6
20	Torfaen	Lab	19.7
21	Swansea West	Lab	19.9
22	Montgomeryshire	Con	20.9
23	Cardiff Central	LD	21.1
24	Vale of Glamorgan	Con	21.3
25	Alyn & Deeside	Lab	21.4
26	Merthyr Tydfil & Rhymney	Lab	21.5
27	Newport East	Lab	21.7
28	Delyn	Lab	21.8
29	Vale of Clwyd	Lab	21.9
30	Ogmore	Lab	22.1
31	Swansea East	Lab	22.4
32	Aberavon	Lab	22.4
33	Cardiff North	Con	22.6
34	Newport West	Lab	22.7
35	Monmouth	Con	22.9
36	Blaenau Gwent	Lab	24.1
37	Brecon & Radnorshire	LD	25.9

Table 15. Regional target lists (GB)

Nat rank	Constituency	1st Pty	Swing to gain	Nat rank	Constituency	1st Pty	Swing to gain
East Midlands				**Liberal Democrat target list**			
Conservative target list				5	Ashfield	Lab	0.2
				9	Chesterfield	Lab	0.6
7	Derby North	Lab	0.7	24	Derby North	Lab	2.9
24	Gedling	Lab	1.9	25	Northampton North	Con	3.1
27	Nottingham South	Lab	2.2	42	Bosworth	Con	4.6
30	Derbyshire North East	Lab	2.6	87	Leicester West	Lab	7.9
92	Leicester West	Lab	5.6	91	Nottingham South	Lab	8.0
102	Mansfield	Lab	6.2	93	Derbyshire North East	Lab	8.2
121	Derby South	Lab	7.4	112	Harborough	Con	8.9
123	Ashfield	Lab	7.5	122	Leicester South	Lab	9.3
135	Bassetlaw	Lab	8.3	126	High Peak	Con	9.6
164	Nottingham East	Lab	10.8	141	Nottingham East	Lab	10.5
182	Nottingham North	Lab	11.9	147	Northampton South	Con	10.7
187	Leicester South	Lab	12.1	148	Gainsborough	Con	10.7
198	Bolsover	Lab	12.7	149	Lincoln	Con	10.8
228	Leicester East	Lab	14.7	164	Derby South	Lab	11.4
234	Chesterfield	Lab	15.1	169	Mansfield	Lab	11.7
				217	Rutland & Melton	Con	12.7
Labour target list				224	Erewash	Con	12.9
				238	Loughborough	Con	13.2
5	Sherwood	Con	0.2	254	Louth & Horncastle	Con	13.7
8	Broxtowe	Con	0.4	263	Derbyshire Mid	Con	13.9
11	Amber Valley	Con	0.6	268	Leicestershire North West	Con	14.0
18	Lincoln	Con	1.2	273	Charnwood	Con	14.0
27	Corby	Con	1.7	274	Grantham & Stamford	Con	14.0
40	Northampton North	Con	2.4	288	Leicestershire South	Con	14.2
43	Erewash	Con	2.6	301	Broxtowe	Con	14.5
52	Loughborough	Con	3.5	306	Rushcliffe	Con	14.7
69	High Peak	Con	4.6	312	Derbyshire Dales	Con	14.8
105	Derbyshire South	Con	7.1	327	Derbyshire South	Con	15.0
107	Leicestershire North West	Con	7.2	352	Wellingborough	Con	15.6
111	Northampton South	Con	7.7	365	Amber Valley	Con	15.7
124	Kettering	Con	9.6	366	Nottingham North	Lab	15.7
135	Wellingborough	Con	11.4	382	Gedling	Lab	16.0
139	Derbyshire Mid	Con	11.9	391	Sherwood	Con	16.1
164	Leicestershire South	Con	14.3	417	Kettering	Con	16.6
166	Boston & Skegness	Con	14.4	424	Sleaford & North Hykeham	Con	16.7
169	Bosworth	Con	14.7	431	Newark	Con	16.9
175	Charnwood	Con	15.0	438	Northamptonshire South	Con	17.1
183	Rushcliffe	Con	15.2	444	Bolsover	Lab	17.2
193	Newark	Con	15.8	448	Corby	Con	17.3
196	Grantham & Stamford	Con	16.1	449	Boston & Skegness	Con	17.3
197	Louth & Horncastle	Con	16.1	493	Daventry	Con	18.5
200	Derbyshire Dales	Con	16.4	520	Leicester East	Lab	19.8
209	Gainsborough	Con	16.8	529	Bassetlaw	Lab	20.6
218	Sleaford & North Hykeham	Con	17.4	545	South Holland & The Deepings	Con	21.8
228	Harborough	Con	18.2				
231	Rutland & Melton	Con	18.4	**Green target list**			
243	Northamptonshire South	Con	19.0	14	Leicester West	Lab	20.7
266	Daventry	Con	20.4	24	Nottingham East	Lab	21.4
301	South Holland & The Deepings	Con	22.5	26	Northampton South	Con	21.5
				37	Northampton North	Con	22.0
				48	Nottingham South	Lab	22.4

Nat rank	Constituency	1st Pty	Swing to gain

East of England

Conservative target list

36	Luton South	Lab	2.8
63	Norwich South	LD	4.1
113	Cambridge	LD	6.8
124	Colchester	LD	7.6
141	Luton North	Lab	8.7
180	Norfolk North	LD	11.7

Labour target list

2	Thurrock	Con	0.1
6	Norwich South	LD	0.3
12	Waveney	Con	0.8
24	Bedford	Con	1.5
34	Ipswich	Con	2.2
59	Stevenage	Con	4.0
67	Norwich North	Con	4.6
68	Watford	Con	4.6
74	Great Yarmouth	Con	5.0
79	Peterborough	Con	5.4
82	Harlow	Con	5.6
100	Basildon S. & Thurrock E.	Con	6.5
109	Cambridge	LD	7.4
151	Rochford & Southend East	Con	13.3
155	Harwich & Essex North	Con	13.5
159	Clacton	Con	14.0
160	St Albans	Con	14.0
167	Hemel Hempstead	Con	14.6
168	Castle Point	Con	14.7
171	Basildon & Billericay	Con	14.8
172	Norfolk South West	Con	14.9
181	Suffolk Coastal	Con	15.2
186	Bury St Edmunds	Con	15.4
195	Norfolk Mid	Con	16.0
199	Southend West	Con	16.3
201	Braintree	Con	16.4
203	Bedfordshire South West	Con	16.6
206	Suffolk South	Con	16.7
207	Cambridgeshire North West	Con	16.8
211	Witham	Con	16.9
212	Cambridgeshire North East	Con	16.9
213	Broadland	Con	17.0
217	Suffolk C. & Ipswich N.	Con	17.3
222	Welwyn Hatfield	Con	17.8
225	Suffolk West	Con	17.9
227	Norfolk South	Con	18.1
233	Hertfordshire North East	Con	18.5
234	Hertsmere	Con	18.6
239	Colchester	LD	18.8
241	Bedfordshire Mid	Con	18.9
242	Huntingdon	Con	18.9
258	Bedfordshire North East	Con	19.8
260	Epping Forest	Con	19.9
262	Hertford & Stortford	Con	20.0
265	Chelmsford	Con	20.4

Labour target list

267	Cambridgeshire South	Con	20.4
268	Norfolk North West	Con	20.5
269	Hitchin & Harpenden	Con	20.5
273	Broxbourne	Con	20.6
284	Hertfordshire South West	Con	21.4
288	Rayleigh & Wickford	Con	21.7
311	Saffron Walden	Con	22.9
317	Cambridgeshire South East	Con	23.5
319	Brentwood & Ongar	Con	23.5
320	Maldon	Con	23.6
349	Norfolk North	LD	25.3

Liberal Democrat target list

15	Watford	Con	1.3
18	St Albans	Con	2.2
43	Chelmsford	Con	4.7
46	Cambridgeshire South East	Con	5.2
60	Luton South	Lab	6.3
66	Cambridgeshire South	Con	6.6
71	Broadland	Con	6.9
96	Suffolk Coastal	Con	8.3
98	Southend West	Con	8.3
100	Suffolk South	Con	8.4
130	Norfolk South	Con	9.9
131	Huntingdon	Con	10.0
137	Peterborough	Con	10.4
142	Bury St Edmunds	Con	10.5
170	Harwich & Essex North	Con	11.7
171	Bedford	Con	11.7
178	Norwich North	Con	11.8
205	Ipswich	Con	12.5
225	Suffolk C. & Ipswich N.	Con	12.9
236	Hertfordshire South West	Con	13.1
243	Norfolk South West	Con	13.4
246	Hemel Hempstead	Con	13.5
247	Suffolk West	Con	13.6
251	Norfolk Mid	Con	13.6
253	Rochford & Southend East	Con	13.7
257	Bedfordshire Mid	Con	13.8
258	Stevenage	Con	13.8
265	Hertford & Stortford	Con	13.9
267	Hitchin & Harpenden	Con	14.0
271	Saffron Walden	Con	14.0
293	Cambridgeshire North West	Con	14.3
330	Hertfordshire North East	Con	15.1
348	Norfolk North West	Con	15.5
369	Cambridgeshire North East	Con	15.8
375	Great Yarmouth	Con	15.9
386	Basildon S. & Thurrock E.	Con	16.0
396	Witham	Con	16.2
400	Epping Forest	Con	16.2
405	Bedfordshire South West	Con	16.4
425	Brentwood & Ongar	Con	16.7
429	Braintree	Con	16.9
436	Bedfordshire North East	Con	17.0

Nat rank	Constituency	1st Pty	Swing to gain

East of England

Liberal Democrat target list

Nat rank	Constituency	1st Pty	Swing to gain
437	Harlow	Con	17.1
450	Thurrock	Con	17.3
451	Castle Point	Con	17.4
456	Waveney	Con	17.4
491	Basildon & Billericay	Con	18.5
512	Hertsmere	Con	19.3
517	Luton North	Lab	19.6
525	Clacton	Con	20.0
526	Maldon	Con	20.3
527	Welwyn Hatfield	Con	20.3
540	Rayleigh & Wickford	Con	21.3
554	Broxbourne	Con	22.7

Green target list

Nat rank	Constituency	1st Pty	Swing to gain
1	Norwich South	LD	9.4
2	Cambridge	LD	16.6
20	Luton South	Lab	21.1
33	Bury St Edmunds	Con	21.8
39	Norwich North	Con	22.1
46	Watford	Con	22.3

London

Conservative target list

Nat rank	Constituency	1st Pty	Swing to gain
1	Hampstead & Kilburn	Lab	0.04
17	Sutton & Cheam	LD	1.7
25	Eltham	Lab	2.0
29	Tooting	Lab	2.5
34	Westminster North	Lab	2.7
38	Dagenham & Rainham	Lab	3.0
47	Harrow West	Lab	3.4
59	Hammersmith	Lab	3.7
82	Feltham & Heston	Lab	4.8
94	Carshalton & Wallington	LD	5.7
107	Poplar & Limehouse	Lab	6.5
109	Kingston & Surbiton	LD	6.6
111	Erith & Thamesmead	Lab	6.7
128	Brent North	Lab	7.7
131	Lewisham West & Penge	Lab	7.8
150	Lewisham East	Lab	9.7
151	Ealing North	Lab	9.8
155	Twickenham	LD	10.2
160	Leyton & Wanstead	Lab	10.7
166	Ealing Southall	Lab	10.9
170	Ilford South	Lab	11.0
185	Edmonton	Lab	11.9
188	Dulwich & West Norwood	Lab	12.2
189	Greenwich & Woolwich	Lab	12.3
192	Islington South & Finsbury	Lab	12.5
197	Hayes & Harlington	Lab	12.7
200	Holborn & St Pancras	Lab	12.9
217	Streatham	Lab	14.0
219	Vauxhall	Lab	14.1

Conservative target list

Nat rank	Constituency	1st Pty	Swing to gain
225	Bethnal Green & Bow	Lab	14.5
239	Mitcham & Morden	Lab	15.6
240	Bermondsey & Old Southwark	LD	15.6
243	Hornsey & Wood Green	LD	15.7
245	Croydon North	Lab	15.9
261	Barking	Lab	18.3
267	Walthamstow	Lab	18.9
277	Lewisham Deptford	Lab	20.1
278	Islington North	Lab	20.1
282	Hackney N. & Stoke Newington	Lab	20.2
288	Brent Central	LD	21.0
289	Hackney South & Shoreditch	Lab	21.1
297	Tottenham	Lab	22.2
302	Camberwell & Peckham	Lab	23.1
304	West Ham	Lab	24.0
317	East Ham	Lab	27.6

Labour target list

Nat rank	Constituency	1st Pty	Swing to gain
3	Hendon	Con	0.1
23	Brent Central	LD	1.5
28	Brentford & Isleworth	Con	1.8
30	Enfield North	Con	1.9
47	Croydon Central	Con	2.9
53	Harrow East	Con	3.5
57	Ealing Central & Acton	Con	3.9
84	Ilford North	Con	5.7
89	Battersea	Con	6.1
90	Finchley & Golders Green	Con	6.2
94	Hornsey & Wood Green	LD	6.2
120	Enfield Southgate	Con	8.6
123	Bermondsey & Old Southwark	LD	9.6
137	Chipping Barnet	Con	11.8
140	Bexleyheath & Crayford	Con	12.0
143	Kensington	Con	12.3
144	Putney	Con	12.3
146	Uxbridge & Ruislip South	Con	12.4
154	Wimbledon	Con	13.4
176	Cities of London & Westminster	Con	15.0
178	Chingford & Woodford Green	Con	15.0
185	Hornchurch & Upminster	Con	15.3
187	Croydon South	Con	15.4
220	Old Bexley & Sidcup	Con	17.4
229	Romford	Con	18.2
232	Bromley & Chislehurst	Con	18.5
245	Ruislip, Northwood & Pinner	Con	19.0
276	Chelsea & Fulham	Con	21.0
289	Beckenham	Con	21.7
302	Kingston & Surbiton	LD	22.5
303	Carshalton & Wallington	LD	22.6
335	Twickenham	LD	24.4
340	Sutton & Cheam	LD	24.7
350	Orpington	Con	25.4
369	Richmond Park	Con	27.5

Nat rank	Constituency	1st Pty	Swing to gain
Liberal Democrat target list			
14	Hampstead & Kilburn	Lab	1.0
30	Richmond Park	Con	3.5
32	Streatham	Lab	3.5
36	Islington South & Finsbury	Lab	4.1
47	Ealing Central & Acton	Con	5.2
63	Lewisham West & Penge	Lab	6.5
80	Lewisham East	Lab	7.4
86	Brentford & Isleworth	Con	7.8
89	Leyton & Wanstead	Lab	8.0
117	Holborn & St Pancras	Lab	9.1
127	Dulwich & West Norwood	Lab	9.7
163	Bethnal Green & Bow	Lab	11.4
168	Walthamstow	Lab	11.6
190	Wimbledon	Con	12.0
200	Vauxhall	Lab	12.3
264	Islington North	Lab	13.9
275	Croydon South	Con	14.0
283	Uxbridge & Ruislip South	Con	14.2
294	Chipping Barnet	Con	14.3
319	Poplar & Limehouse	Lab	14.9
321	Brent North	Lab	14.9
336	Lewisham Deptford	Lab	15.2
337	Finchley & Golders Green	Con	15.2
338	Kensington	Con	15.3
349	Greenwich & Woolwich	Lab	15.5
351	Croydon Central	Con	15.5
354	Hackney N.& Stoke Newington	Lab	15.6
370	Bromley & Chislehurst	Con	15.8
371	Cities of London & Westminster	Con	15.8
385	Harrow West	Lab	16.0
392	Hammersmith	Lab	16.1
399	Ilford South	Lab	16.2
420	Hackney South & Shoreditch	Lab	16.7
423	Feltham & Heston	Lab	16.7
453	Erith & Thamesmead	Lab	17.4
457	Tooting	Lab	17.5
459	Putney	Con	17.6
461	Orpington	Con	17.6
463	Battersea	Con	17.7
474	Harrow East	Con	17.9
475	Eltham	Lab	17.9
477	Chingford & Woodford Green	Con	18.0
478	Enfield Southgate	Con	18.0
481	Westminster North	Lab	18.2
483	Ilford North	Con	18.2
488	Ealing Southall	Lab	18.3
489	Camberwell & Peckham	Lab	18.4
495	Ealing North	Lab	18.6
496	Beckenham	Con	18.6
500	Hornchurch & Upminster	Con	18.8
502	Enfield North	Con	18.8
503	Bexleyheath & Crayford	Con	18.9
509	Dagenham & Rainham	Lab	19.1
515	Old Bexley & Sidcup	Con	19.4
521	Hendon	Con	19.9

Nat rank	Constituency	1st Pty	Swing to gain
Liberal Democrat target list			
528	Ruislip, Northwood & Pinner	Con	20.4
532	Tottenham	Lab	20.8
536	Croydon North	Lab	21.0
543	Edmonton	Lab	21.6
549	Romford	Con	22.0
550	Chelsea & Fulham	Con	22.1
551	Mitcham & Morden	Lab	22.3
555	Hayes & Harlington	Lab	23.0
556	Barking	Lab	23.1
561	West Ham	Lab	25.6
573	East Ham	Lab	29.4
Green target list			
11	Bethnal Green & Bow	Lab	20.6
32	Poplar & Limehouse	Lab	21.7
41	Lewisham West & Penge	Lab	22.1
58	Brentford & Isleworth	Con	22.6
62	Lewisham East	Lab	22.7
64	Ealing Central & Acton	Con	22.8
65	Leyton & Wanstead	Lab	22.8
66	Dulwich & West Norwood	Lab	22.8
69	Holborn & St Pancras	Lab	22.9
76	Hampstead & Kilburn	Lab	23.1
82	Greenwich & Woolwich	Lab	23.3
87	Chipping Barnet	Con	23.4
93	Lewisham Deptford	Lab	23.5
95	Croydon Central	Con	23.6
97	Uxbridge & Ruislip South	Con	23.6

North East

Conservative target list

Nat rank	Constituency	1st Pty	Swing to gain
20	Middlesbrough S. & Cleveland E.	Lab	1.8
51	Berwick-upon-Tweed	LD	3.5
61	Darlington	Lab	3.9
90	Tynemouth	Lab	5.4
105	Bishop Auckland	Lab	6.3
119	Hartlepool	Lab	7.2
134	Sunderland Central	Lab	7.9
136	Stockton North	Lab	8.5
162	Sedgefield	Lab	10.8
173	Durham North West	Lab	11.2
194	Newcastle upon Tyne North	Lab	12.6
204	Newcastle upon Tyne Central	Lab	13.3
206	Middlesbrough	Lab	13.6
214	Blyth Valley	Lab	13.9
220	Wansbeck	Lab	14.2
223	Houghton & Sunderland S.	Lab	14.5
230	Durham North	Lab	14.7
235	South Shields	Lab	15.2
237	Washington & Sunderland W.	Lab	15.3
238	Newcastle upon Tyne East	Lab	15.4

Nat rank	Constituency	1st Pty	Swing to gain

North East

Conservative target list

247	Tyneside North	Lab	16.2
251	Jarrow	Lab	16.6
253	Redcar	LD	16.8
254	Blaydon	Lab	16.9
263	Durham, City of	Lab	18.5
274	Gateshead	Lab	19.6
300	Easington	Lab	22.6

Labour target list

7	Stockton South	Con	0.3
92	Redcar	LD	6.2
142	Hexham	Con	12.1
226	Berwick-upon-Tweed	LD	18.0

Liberal Democrat target list

28	Durham, City of	Lab	3.3
34	Newcastle upon Tyne North	Lab	3.9
52	Newcastle upon Tyne East	Lab	5.9
67	Hexham	Con	6.7
90	Darlington	Lab	8.0
95	Bishop Auckland	Lab	8.3
106	Blyth Valley	Lab	8.6
107	Durham North West	Lab	8.7
120	Wansbeck	Lab	9.2
133	Blaydon	Lab	10.1
153	Newcastle upon Tyne Central	Lab	10.9
211	Sedgefield	Lab	12.6
219	Hartlepool	Lab	12.7
229	Middlesbrough	Lab	13.0
244	Stockton North	Lab	13.4
261	Tyneside North	Lab	13.9
296	Middlesbrough S. & Cleveland E.	Lab	14.4
300	Sunderland Central	Lab	14.5
308	Durham North	Lab	14.7
360	Stockton South	Con	15.7
406	Gateshead	Lab	16.4
418	Tynemouth	Lab	16.6
465	Washington & Sunderland W.	Lab	17.7
466	Jarrow	Lab	17.7
484	Houghton & Sunderland S.	Lab	18.2
504	South Shields	Lab	18.9

Green target list

542	Easington	Lab	21.5
43	Newcastle upon Tyne Central	Lab	22.2
88	Wansbeck	Lab	23.4
121	Newcastle upon Tyne North	Lab	24.2
166	South Shields	Lab	25.0
168	Newcastle upon Tyne East	Lab	25.0
215	Tynemouth	Lab	25.9
245	Gateshead	Lab	26.6

Nat rank	Constituency	1st Pty	Swing to gain

North West

Conservative target list

2	Bolton West	Lab	0.1
6	Wirral South	Lab	0.7
32	Chorley	Lab	2.6
33	Blackpool South	Lab	2.6
40	Cheadle	LD	3.1
46	Stalybridge & Hyde	Lab	3.4
48	Bury South	Lab	3.4
53	Oldham East & Saddleworth	Lab	3.5
56	Hyndburn	Lab	3.6
62	Sefton Central	Lab	4.0
75	Copeland	Lab	4.5
76	Lancashire West	Lab	4.5
80	Bolton North East	Lab	4.7
84	Ellesmere Port & Neston	Lab	4.9
86	Worsley & Eccles South	Lab	5.2
99	Workington	Lab	5.8
100	Barrow & Furness	Lab	5.9
108	Heywood & Middleton	Lab	6.5
115	Southport	LD	6.9
125	Hazel Grove	LD	7.6
127	Warrington North	Lab	7.7
138	Stockport	Lab	8.7
147	Wythenshawe & Sale East	Lab	9.3
152	Salford & Eccles	Lab	9.8
154	Stretford & Urmston	Lab	9.9
157	Wallasey	Lab	10.2
163	Blackburn	Lab	10.8
167	Oldham West & Royton	Lab	10.9
168	Bolton South East	Lab	10.9
175	Burnley	LD	11.3
179	Rochdale	Lab	11.5
181	Ashton Under Lyne	Lab	11.8
184	Wigan	Lab	11.9
186	Westmorland & Lonsdale	LD	11.9
201	Denton & Reddish	Lab	13.1
203	Preston	Lab	13.2
205	Leigh	Lab	13.5
222	Makerfield	Lab	14.3
229	St Helens North	Lab	14.7
256	St Helens South & Whiston	Lab	17.5
260	Blackley & Broughton	Lab	18.0
264	Halton	Lab	18.8
283	Manchester Gorton	Lab	20.2
284	Manchester Central	Lab	20.5
287	Manchester Withington	LD	21.0
291	Garston & Halewood	Lab	21.7
293	Birkenhead	Lab	21.8
305	Liverpool Wavertree	Lab	24.1
306	Liverpool Riverside	Lab	24.2
315	Liverpool West Derby	Lab	27.4
321	Bootle	Lab	28.8
323	Knowsley	Lab	31.0
325	Liverpool Walton	Lab	32.7

Nat rank	Constituency	1st Pty	Swing to gain
Labour target list			
9	Lancaster & Fleetwood	Con	0.4
14	Morecambe & Lunesdale	Con	1.0
15	Carlisle	Con	1.0
17	Weaver Vale	Con	1.1
22	Warrington South	Con	1.4
32	Manchester Withington	LD	2.1
33	Burnley	LD	2.2
41	Bury North	Con	2.5
44	Blackpool North & Cleveleys	Con	2.6
45	Chester, City of	Con	2.8
50	Wirral West	Con	3.1
58	Pendle	Con	4.0
71	Rossendale & Darwen	Con	4.8
78	South Ribble	Con	5.4
87	Crewe & Nantwich	Con	5.9
150	Altrincham & Sale West	Con	13.3
152	Macclesfield	Con	13.3
163	Ribble Valley	Con	14.1
165	Congleton	Con	14.4
179	Eddisbury	Con	15.1
188	Wyre & Preston North	Con	15.5
198	Fylde	Con	16.3
235	Tatton	Con	18.7
247	Hazel Grove	LD	19.2
264	Penrith & The Border	Con	20.2
296	Southport	LD	22.2
313	Cheadle	LD	23.1
373	Westmorland & Lonsdale	LD	30.6
Liberal Democrat target list			
2	Oldham East & Saddleworth	Lab	0.1
12	Rochdale	Lab	1.0
41	Warrington South	Con	4.6
70	Salford & Eccles	Lab	6.9
72	Congleton	Con	7.0
108	Heywood & Middleton	Lab	8.7
109	Manchester Gorton	Lab	8.7
111	Stockport	Lab	8.8
123	Liverpool Wavertree	Lab	9.5
128	Pendle	Con	9.8
152	Wythenshawe & Sale East	Lab	10.9
156	Lancaster & Fleetwood	Con	11.0
173	Altrincham & Sale West	Con	11.7
182	Preston	Lab	11.9
186	Macclesfield	Con	11.9
188	Sefton Central	Lab	12.0
201	Warrington North	Lab	12.4
206	Penrith & The Border	Con	12.5
208	Chester, City of	Con	12.5
209	Weaver Vale	Con	12.5
210	Bury South	Lab	12.5
214	Rossendale & Darwen	Con	12.6
222	Stalybridge & Hyde	Lab	12.8
233	Manchester Central	Lab	13.1
241	Oldham West & Royton	Lab	13.2

Nat rank	Constituency	1st Pty	Swing to gain
Liberal Democrat target list			
256	Bury North	Con	13.8
282	Worsley & Eccles South	Lab	14.1
284	Bolton West	Lab	14.2
302	Eddisbury	Con	14.6
315	Ribble Valley	Con	14.9
320	Leigh	Lab	14.9
328	Wirral West	Con	15.0
331	Fylde	Con	15.1
335	Carlisle	Con	15.2
341	St Helens South & Whiston	Lab	15.3
345	Wyre & Preston North	Con	15.4
353	Makerfield	Lab	15.6
363	Wirral South	Lab	15.7
367	St Helens North	Lab	15.8
368	Bolton South East	Lab	15.8
373	Stretford & Urmston	Lab	15.8
383	Blackpool South	Lab	16.0
384	Tatton	Con	16.0
402	Blackburn	Lab	16.3
410	Ellesmere Port & Neston	Lab	16.5
413	Wigan	Lab	16.5
414	Denton & Reddish	Lab	16.6
416	Crewe & Nantwich	Con	16.6
427	Ashton Under Lyne	Lab	16.8
439	Hyndburn	Lab	17.1
443	Blackpool North & Cleveleys	Con	17.2
446	South Ribble	Con	17.3
452	Workington	Lab	17.4
470	Chorley	Lab	17.8
479	Lancashire West	Lab	18.1
480	Morecambe & Lunesdale	Con	18.1
486	Liverpool Riverside	Lab	18.3
501	Bolton North East	Lab	18.8
507	Wallasey	Lab	19.1
519	Garston & Halewood	Lab	19.7
524	Blackley & Broughton	Lab	20.0
534	Copeland	Lab	20.9
541	Barrow & Furness	Lab	21.5
547	Halton	Lab	21.9
548	Birkenhead	Lab	22.0
563	Bootle	Lab	25.7
564	Liverpool West Derby	Lab	25.8
570	Knowsley	Lab	28.8
571	Liverpool Walton	Lab	28.9
Green target list			
15	Lancaster & Fleetwood	Con	20.8
36	Stockport	Lab	22.0
57	Macclesfield	Con	22.6
73	Stalybridge & Hyde	Lab	23.1
81	Bolton South East	Lab	23.3
92	Warrington South	Con	23.5

Nat rank	Constituency	1st Pty	Swing to gain

South East

Conservative target list

Nat rank	Constituency	1st Pty	Swing to gain
4	Southampton Itchen	Lab	0.2
35	Southampton Test	Lab	2.7
44	Eastbourne	LD	3.3
55	Eastleigh	LD	3.6
71	Brighton Pavilion	Grn	4.3
96	Slough	Lab	5.8
104	Portsmouth South	LD	6.3
126	Lewes	LD	7.6
199	Oxford East	Lab	12.8

Labour target list

Nat rank	Constituency	1st Pty	Swing to gain
19	Brighton Pavilion	Grn	1.2
25	Brighton Kemptown	Con	1.6
29	Hove	Con	1.9
31	Hastings & Rye	Con	2.0
70	Milton Keynes South	Con	4.7
76	Dover	Con	5.2
93	Crawley	Con	6.2
95	Reading West	Con	6.3
103	Chatham & Aylesford	Con	6.9
114	Portsmouth North	Con	8.3
115	Thanet South	Con	8.3
116	Milton Keynes North	Con	8.3
119	Reading East	Con	8.5
121	Gillingham & Rainham	Con	9.3
125	Gravesham	Con	9.8
129	Rochester & Strood	Con	10.4
130	Dartford	Con	10.6
147	Sittingbourne & Sheppey	Con	12.7
177	Canterbury	Con	15.0
180	Basingstoke	Con	15.1
184	Spelthorne	Con	15.3
190	Thanet North	Con	15.6
191	Wycombe	Con	15.7
194	Worthing East & Shoreham	Con	15.9
205	Havant	Con	16.7
210	Banbury	Con	16.8
214	Portsmouth South	LD	17.3
219	Gosport	Con	17.4
223	Bracknell	Con	17.8
230	Isle of Wight	Con	18.4
237	Bognor Regis & Littlehampton	Con	18.7
238	Ashford	Con	18.7
244	Aldershot	Con	19.0
246	Wantage	Con	19.0
249	Folkestone & Hythe	Con	19.4
255	Aylesbury	Con	19.8
256	Faversham & Kent Mid	Con	19.8
257	Bexhill & Battle	Con	19.8
261	Worthing West	Con	20.0
271	Fareham	Con	20.5
278	Reigate	Con	21.0
279	Oxford West & Abingdon	Con	21.0

Nat rank	Constituency	1st Pty	Swing to gain

Labour target list

Nat rank	Constituency	1st Pty	Swing to gain
282	Runnymede & Weybridge	Con	21.3
283	Wokingham	Con	21.3
285	Maidstone & The Weald	Con	21.5
286	New Forest East	Con	21.5
292	Sevenoaks	Con	21.8
294	Epsom & Ewell	Con	22.1
297	Eastleigh	LD	22.2
299	Chichester	Con	22.4
305	Hampshire North West	Con	22.6
306	Henley	Con	22.6
307	Tonbridge & Malling	Con	22.7
308	Tunbridge Wells	Con	22.7
312	Witney	Con	22.9
316	Horsham	Con	23.3
318	Wealden	Con	23.5
323	Surrey Heath	Con	23.7
326	Surrey East	Con	23.9
327	Woking	Con	23.9
330	Esher & Walton	Con	24.1
336	Hampshire East	Con	24.4
337	New Forest West	Con	24.5
338	Arundel & South Downs	Con	24.6
339	Beaconsfield	Con	24.7
344	Sussex Mid	Con	25.0
348	Mole Valley	Con	25.3
351	Meon Valley	Con	25.4
352	Hampshire North East	Con	25.4
353	Windsor	Con	25.5
359	Romsey & Southampton N.	Con	26.1
360	Eastbourne	LD	26.1
361	Maidenhead	Con	26.2
362	Lewes	LD	26.2
363	Surrey South West	Con	26.4
364	Winchester	Con	26.9
368	Chesham & Amersham	Con	27.4
370	Guildford	Con	27.5
372	Newbury	Con	27.8

Liberal Democrat target list

Nat rank	Constituency	1st Pty	Swing to gain
3	Oxford West & Abingdon	Con	0.2
23	Winchester	Con	2.7
38	Romsey & Southampton N.	Con	4.2
40	Oxford East	Lab	4.4
53	Maidstone & The Weald	Con	6.0
56	Canterbury	Con	6.1
58	Aldershot	Con	6.2
62	Woking	Con	6.4
65	Sussex Mid	Con	6.6
73	Guildford	Con	7.0
82	Isle of Wight	Con	7.5
83	Reading East	Con	7.6
92	Hove	Con	8.2
114	Southampton Test	Lab	8.9
125	Folkestone & Hythe	Con	9.6

Nat rank	Constituency	1st Pty	Swing to gain		Nat rank	Constituency	1st Pty	Swing to gain

Liberal Democrat target list

Nat rank	Constituency	1st Pty	Swing to gain
129	Wycombe	Con	9.9
136	Horsham	Con	10.3
139	Newbury	Con	10.5
140	Southampton Itchen	Lab	10.5
144	Spelthorne	Con	10.6
146	Milton Keynes North	Con	10.7
151	Brighton Pavilion	Grn	10.9
160	New Forest East	Con	11.3
165	Worthing East & Shoreham	Con	11.5
167	Reading West	Con	11.5
175	Bexhill & Battle	Con	11.8
179	Meon Valley	Con	11.8
181	Aylesbury	Con	11.9
185	Worthing West	Con	11.9
189	Wantage	Con	12.0
193	Portsmouth North	Con	12.1
199	Brighton Kemptown	Con	12.3
202	Wokingham	Con	12.4
223	Milton Keynes South	Con	12.8
230	Basingstoke	Con	13.0
237	Hampshire East	Con	13.2
249	Reigate	Con	13.6
259	Havant	Con	13.8
266	Bognor Regis & Littlehampton	Con	13.9
269	Chichester	Con	14.0
276	Gillingham & Rainham	Con	14.0
291	Surrey South West	Con	14.2
297	Mole Valley	Con	14.4
304	Epsom & Ewell	Con	14.7
317	Arundel & South Downs	Con	14.9
329	Bracknell	Con	15.1
340	Dover	Con	15.3
343	Gosport	Con	15.4
346	Surrey East	Con	15.4
347	Tunbridge Wells	Con	15.5
350	Henley	Con	15.5
356	Hastings & Rye	Con	15.6
358	Maidenhead	Con	15.6
359	Wealden	Con	15.6
361	Ashford	Con	15.7
364	Fareham	Con	15.7
378	Surrey Heath	Con	15.9
381	Chesham & Amersham	Con	15.9
390	Crawley	Con	16.1
395	Banbury	Con	16.2
407	Thanet South	Con	16.4
411	Rochester & Strood	Con	16.5
419	Thanet North	Con	16.6
428	Sittingbourne & Sheppey	Con	16.8
433	Slough	Lab	17.0
434	Dartford	Con	17.0
435	Esher & Walton	Con	17.0
440	Runnymede & Weybridge	Con	17.1
447	Chatham & Aylesford	Con	17.3
455	Hampshire North West	Con	17.4
460	Hampshire North East	Con	17.6

Liberal Democrat target list

Nat rank	Constituency	1st Pty	Swing to gain
462	Gravesham	Con	17.6
464	Tonbridge & Malling	Con	17.7
468	Sevenoaks	Con	17.7
469	New Forest West	Con	17.8
487	Faversham & Kent Mid	Con	18.3
510	Windsor	Con	19.2
518	Witney	Con	19.7
530	Beaconsfield	Con	20.7

Green target list

Nat rank	Constituency	1st Pty	Swing to gain
8	Hove	Con	19.8
12	Brighton Kemptown	Con	20.6
42	Reading East	Con	22.2
52	Southampton Test	Lab	22.5
53	Milton Keynes North	Con	22.5
77	Worthing East & Shoreham	Con	23.1
80	Portsmouth North	Con	23.3
90	Southampton Itchen	Lab	23.5
100	Milton Keynes South	Con	23.7

South West

Conservative target list

Nat rank	Constituency	1st Pty	Swing to gain
5	Dorset Mid & Poole North	LD	0.3
8	Wells	LD	0.7
14	St Austell & Newquay	LD	1.4
15	Somerton & Frome	LD	1.5
22	St Ives	LD	1.9
23	Plymouth Moor View	Lab	1.9
28	Chippenham	LD	2.4
31	Exeter	Lab	2.6
41	Cornwall North	LD	3.2
49	Taunton Deane	LD	3.4
66	Bristol East	Lab	4.1
68	Torbay	LD	4.1
79	Cheltenham	LD	4.7
93	Devon North	LD	5.7
120	Thornbury & Yate	LD	7.4
130	Bristol South	Lab	7.8
178	Yeovil	LD	11.4
195	Bath	LD	12.6
231	Bristol West	LD	14.8

Labour target list

Nat rank	Constituency	1st Pty	Swing to gain
16	Stroud	Con	1.1
20	Plymouth Sutton & Devonport	Con	1.3
39	Gloucester	Con	2.4
42	Kingswood	Con	2.6
56	Swindon South	Con	3.8
73	Somerset North East	Con	4.8
88	Bristol North West	Con	6.0
104	Swindon North	Con	7.0
106	Filton & Bradley Stoke	Con	7.2
108	Dorset South	Con	7.4

Nat rank	Constituency	1st Pty	Swing to gain

South West

Labour target list

127	Bristol West	LD	10.3
134	Forest of Dean	Con	11.3
161	Bridgwater & Somerset W.	Con	14.1
162	Camborne & Redruth	Con	14.1
192	Bournemouth West	Con	15.8
221	Bournemouth East	Con	17.6
224	Poole	Con	17.9
248	Devon East	Con	19.3
259	Tewkesbury	Con	19.8
263	Wiltshire South West	Con	20.1
272	Weston-Super-Mare	Con	20.5
274	Somerset North	Con	20.9
280	Truro & Falmouth	Con	21.1
281	Cotswolds, The	Con	21.1
290	Devon South West	Con	21.8
291	St Ives	LD	21.8
293	Tiverton & Honiton	Con	21.9
295	Totnes	Con	22.2
300	Devizes	Con	22.5
309	St Austell & Newquay	LD	22.8
314	Cornwall South East	Con	23.2
315	Christchurch	Con	23.3
321	Salisbury	Con	23.6
322	Newton Abbot	Con	23.6
325	Wells	LD	23.8
328	Devon Central	Con	24.0
331	Torbay	LD	24.2
333	Devon North	LD	24.3
334	Chippenham	LD	24.3
341	Wiltshire North	Con	24.8
342	Bath	LD	24.8
345	Thornbury & Yate	LD	25.0
346	Dorset West	Con	25.0
347	Devon West & Torridge	Con	25.1
356	Dorset North	Con	25.8
357	Dorset Mid & Poole North	LD	26.0
358	Yeovil	LD	26.0
365	Taunton Deane	LD	27.0
366	Cornwall North	LD	27.1
367	Cheltenham	LD	27.1
371	Somerton & Frome	LD	27.7

Liberal Democrat target list

1	Camborne & Redruth	Con	0.1
7	Truro & Falmouth	Con	0.4
8	Newton Abbot	Con	0.5
20	Weston-Super-Mare	Con	2.6
22	Devon West & Torridge	Con	2.7
26	Cornwall South East	Con	3.2
27	Bristol North West	Con	3.3
29	Dorset West	Con	3.4
44	Bristol South	Lab	4.9
45	Totnes	Con	5.1
48	Plymouth Sutton & Devonport	Con	5.5

Liberal Democrat target list

51	Tewkesbury	Con	5.8
54	Bristol East	Lab	6.1
57	Salisbury	Con	6.2
68	Bournemouth West	Con	6.7
69	Somerset North	Con	6.8
75	Dorset North	Con	7.0
84	Wiltshire North	Con	7.7
85	Filton & Bradley Stoke	Con	7.8
88	Poole	Con	7.9
101	Bridgwater & Somerset W.	Con	8.5
102	Tiverton & Honiton	Con	8.5
103	Devon Central	Con	8.6
105	Devon East	Con	8.6
110	Bournemouth East	Con	8.8
124	Somerset North East	Con	9.5
135	Exeter	Lab	10.2
143	Wiltshire South West	Con	10.6
172	Cotswolds, The	Con	11.7
195	Gloucester	Con	12.2
198	Plymouth Moor View	Lab	12.2
207	Forest of Dean	Con	12.5
231	Dorset South	Con	13.0
248	Swindon South	Con	13.6
252	Swindon North	Con	13.7
270	Kingswood	Con	14.0
272	Devizes	Con	14.0
357	Christchurch	Con	15.6
380	Devon South West	Con	15.9
394	Stroud	Con	16.2

Green target list

13	Bristol South	Lab	20.7
17	Bristol East	Lab	21.0
22	Plymouth Sutton & Devonport	Con	21.1
50	Filton & Bradley Stoke	Con	22.4
51	Forest of Dean	Con	22.5
60	Bristol West	LD	22.7
61	Exeter	Lab	22.7
68	Plymouth Moor View	Lab	22.9
75	Bristol North West	Con	23.1
89	Somerset North East	Con	23.4
91	Bridgwater & Somerset W.	Con	23.5

West Midlands

Conservative target list

3	Solihull	LD	0.2
9	Dudley North	Lab	0.8
12	Telford	Lab	1.2
13	Walsall North	Lab	1.4
16	Birmingham Edgbaston	Lab	1.5
19	Newcastle-under-Lyme	Lab	1.8
26	Walsall South	Lab	2.1
45	Birmingham Northfield	Lab	3.3

Nat rank	Constituency	1st Pty	Swing to gain
Conservative target list			
54	Wolverhampton North East	Lab	3.6
58	Birmingham Selly Oak	Lab	3.7
69	Coventry South	Lab	4.2
78	Birmingham Erdington	Lab	4.6
85	Stoke-on-Trent South	Lab	5.2
112	Coventry North West	Lab	6.8
132	West Bromwich West	Lab	7.8
143	West Bromwich East	Lab	8.8
145	Stoke-on-Trent Central	Lab	8.9
148	Birmingham Hall Green	Lab	9.4
149	Wolverhampton South East	Lab	9.5
158	Stoke-on-Trent North	Lab	10.2
172	Birmingham Yardley	LD	11.1
207	Coventry North East	Lab	13.6
218	Warley	Lab	14.1
224	Birmingham Perry Barr	Lab	14.5
280	Birmingham Hodge Hill	Lab	20.2
294	Birmingham Ladywood	Lab	21.9
Labour target list			
1	Warwickshire North	Con	0.1
13	Wolverhampton South West	Con	0.9
37	Halesowen & Rowley Regis	Con	2.3
38	Nuneaton	Con	2.3
48	Worcester	Con	3.0
51	Cannock Chase	Con	3.5
54	Warwick & Leamington	Con	3.6
55	Birmingham Yardley	LD	3.7
75	Dudley South	Con	5.1
80	Stafford	Con	5.4
81	Stourbridge	Con	5.5
96	Rugby	Con	6.3
97	Burton	Con	6.3
101	Tamworth	Con	6.6
102	Redditch	Con	6.6
110	Staffordshire Moorlands	Con	7.6
128	Wrekin, The	Con	10.3
131	Bromsgrove	Con	11.0
136	Shrewsbury & Atcham	Con	11.7
153	Wyre Forest	Con	13.3
173	Stone	Con	14.9
189	Meriden	Con	15.6
202	Staffordshire South	Con	16.4
204	Shropshire North	Con	16.7
208	Sutton Coldfield	Con	16.8
215	Lichfield	Con	17.3
251	Kenilworth & Southam	Con	19.6
253	Aldridge-Brownhills	Con	19.8
254	Worcestershire Mid	Con	19.8
277	Stratford-on-Avon	Con	21.0
304	Solihull	LD	22.6
310	Herefordshire North	Con	22.9
329	Ludlow	Con	24.0
332	Hereford & Herefordshire S.	Con	24.3
343	Worcestershire West	Con	24.9

Nat rank	Constituency	1st Pty	Swing to gain
Liberal Democrat target list			
21	Hereford & Herefordshire S.	Con	2.6
37	Birmingham Hall Green	Lab	4.2
59	Worcestershire West	Con	6.2
81	Shrewsbury & Atcham	Con	7.5
99	Birmingham Selly Oak	Lab	8.4
104	Stoke-on-Trent Central	Lab	8.6
132	Ludlow	Con	10.0
138	Herefordshire North	Con	10.4
155	Newcastle-under-Lyme	Lab	11.0
159	Stratford-on-Avon	Con	11.2
161	Worcester	Con	11.4
177	Stoke-on-Trent South	Lab	11.8
191	Bromsgrove	Con	12.0
192	Rugby	Con	12.1
194	Birmingham Hodge Hill	Lab	12.1
204	Coventry North West	Lab	12.4
227	Redditch	Con	12.9
228	Kenilworth & Southam	Con	13.0
232	Coventry South	Lab	13.1
234	Cannock Chase	Con	13.1
242	Stoke-on-Trent North	Lab	13.3
255	Warwick & Leamington	Con	13.8
262	Stourbridge	Con	13.9
277	Birmingham Erdington	Lab	14.0
279	Stone	Con	14.1
281	Birmingham Ladywood	Lab	14.1
285	Birmingham Perry Barr	Lab	14.2
286	Birmingham Northfield	Lab	14.2
287	Staffordshire Moorlands	Con	14.2
303	Telford	Lab	14.7
307	Stafford	Con	14.7
316	Dudley South	Con	14.9
318	Burton	Con	14.9
324	Wyre Forest	Con	15.0
325	Walsall North	Lab	15.0
333	Wrekin, The	Con	15.1
339	Shropshire North	Con	15.3
342	Tamworth	Con	15.3
344	Walsall South	Lab	15.4
355	Worcestershire Mid	Con	15.6
372	Birmingham Edgbaston	Lab	15.8
376	Wolverhampton South West	Con	15.9
379	Nuneaton	Con	15.9
389	Halesowen & Rowley Regis	Con	16.1
393	Wolverhampton South East	Lab	16.2
398	Wolverhampton North East	Lab	16.2
404	Coventry North East	Lab	16.3
421	West Bromwich East	Lab	16.7
426	West Bromwich West	Lab	16.8
432	Meriden	Con	16.9
441	Lichfield	Con	17.1
476	Sutton Coldfield	Con	18.0
482	Dudley North	Lab	18.2
485	Staffordshire South	Con	18.2
499	Warley	Lab	18.7
506	Warwickshire North	Con	19.0
533	Aldridge-Brownhills	Con	20.8

Nat rank	Constituency	1st Pty	Swing to gain

West Midlands

Green target list

Nat rank	Constituency	1st Pty	Swing to gain
44	Birmingham Selly Oak	Lab	22.3
84	Worcester	Con	23.3
85	Coventry North West	Lab	23.3
96	Shrewsbury & Atcham	Con	23.6

Yorkshire and The Humber

Conservative target list

Nat rank	Constituency	1st Pty	Swing to gain
10	Great Grimsby	Lab	1.1
11	Morley & Outwood	Lab	1.1
18	Halifax	Lab	1.7
21	Wakefield	Lab	1.8
43	Penistone & Stocksbridge	Lab	3.3
50	Scunthorpe	Lab	3.4
67	Don Valley	Lab	4.1
70	Bradford East	LD	4.3
72	Batley & Spen	Lab	4.3
81	Leeds North East	Lab	4.8
91	Huddersfield	Lab	5.5
101	Bradford South	Lab	6.1
103	Rother Valley	Lab	6.3
116	York Central	Lab	6.9
117	Bradford West	Lab	7.1
122	Doncaster Central	Lab	7.5
159	Leeds North West	LD	10.5
171	Hull West & Hessle	Lab	11.1
174	Hemsworth	Lab	11.2
176	Leeds West	Lab	11.3
183	Normanton, Pontefract & Castleford	Lab	11.9
196	Sheffield Heeley	Lab	12.6
202	Doncaster North	Lab	13.1
209	Leeds East	Lab	13.6
216	Rotherham	Lab	13.9
226	Leeds Central	Lab	14.6
232	Sheffield Hallam	LD	14.9
233	Barnsley Central	Lab	15.0
236	Barnsley East	Lab	15.3
241	Sheffield South East	Lab	15.7
242	Hull East	Lab	15.7
249	Wentworth & Dearne	Lab	16.5
252	Hull North	Lab	16.7
286	Sheffield Central	Lab	20.7
292	Sheffield Brightside & Hillsborough	Lab	21.8

Labour target list

Nat rank	Constituency	1st Pty	Swing to gain
10	Bradford East	LD	0.5
21	Dewsbury	Con	1.4
26	Pudsey	Con	1.7
49	Keighley	Con	3.1
60	Elmet & Rothwell	Con	4.1
72	Cleethorpes	Con	4.8

Labour target list

Nat rank	Constituency	1st Pty	Swing to gain
77	Colne Valley	Con	5.3
86	Brigg & Goole	Con	5.9
91	Calder Valley	Con	6.2
113	Scarborough & Whitby	Con	8.2
126	Shipley	Con	10.1
138	Selby & Ainsty	Con	11.9
148	Beverley & Holderness	Con	13.0
149	Leeds North West	LD	13.2
156	Yorkshire East	Con	13.6
174	York Outer	Con	15.0
216	Haltemprice & Howden	Con	17.3
236	Sheffield Hallam	LD	18.7
252	Thirsk & Malton	Con	19.7
275	Skipton & Ripon	Con	21.0
324	Richmond (Yorks)	Con	23.8
354	Harrogate & Knaresborough	Con	25.6

Liberal Democrat target list

Nat rank	Constituency	1st Pty	Swing to gain
4	Sheffield Central	Lab	0.2
11	Hull North	Lab	1.0
13	Harrogate & Knaresborough	Con	1.0
31	York Outer	Con	3.5
39	Colne Valley	Con	4.4
55	Great Grimsby	Lab	6.1
74	Huddersfield	Lab	7.0
76	Sheffield Heeley	Lab	7.1
77	Calder Valley	Con	7.1
79	York Central	Lab	7.4
113	Penistone & Stocksbridge	Lab	8.9
115	Leeds West	Lab	9.1
116	Skipton & Ripon	Con	9.1
118	Hull West & Hessle	Lab	9.1
121	Doncaster Central	Lab	9.3
134	Scarborough & Whitby	Con	10.2
145	Pudsey	Con	10.6
154	Halifax	Lab	11.0
157	Dewsbury	Con	11.1
158	Don Valley	Lab	11.1
166	Bradford South	Lab	11.5
176	Rother Valley	Lab	11.8
180	Scunthorpe	Lab	11.9
183	Haltemprice & Howden	Con	11.9
196	Beverley & Holderness	Con	12.2
197	Leeds North East	Lab	12.2
212	Hull East	Lab	12.6
218	Sheffield South East	Lab	12.7
220	Cleethorpes	Con	12.7
235	Morley & Outwood	Lab	13.1
239	Yorkshire East	Con	13.2
280	Wakefield	Lab	14.1
289	Leeds Central	Lab	14.2
292	Shipley	Con	14.3
295	Rotherham	Lab	14.3
298	Barnsley East	Lab	14.4
305	Batley & Spen	Lab	14.7
311	Thirsk & Malton	Con	14.8

Nat rank	Constituency	1st Pty	Swing to gain
Liberal Democrat target list			
313	Elmet & Rothwell	Con	14.8
326	Barnsley Central	Lab	15.0
374	Selby & Ainsty	Con	15.8
377	Normanton, Pontefract & Castleford	Lab	15.9
387	Keighley	Con	16.0
397	Doncaster North	Lab	16.2
401	Brigg & Goole	Con	16.2
409	Leeds East	Lab	16.4
430	Hemsworth	Lab	16.9
445	Wentworth & Dearne	Lab	17.3
458	Sheffield Brightside & Hillsborough	Lab	17.5
467	Bradford West	Lab	17.7
546	Richmond (Yorks)	Con	21.8
Green target list			
5	Leeds West	Lab	19.0
7	Huddersfield	Lab	19.8
10	York Central	Lab	20.1
23	Dewsbury	Con	21.3
30	Calder Valley	Con	21.6
31	Colne Valley	Con	21.7
38	Sheffield Heeley	Lab	22.0
40	Scarborough & Whitby	Con	22.1
70	Beverley & Holderness	Con	22.9
72	Yorkshire East	Con	23.0
86	Scunthorpe	Lab	23.3
98	Wakefield	Lab	23.7
99	Shipley	Con	23.7

Scotland

Nat rank	Constituency	1st Pty	Swing to gain
Conservative target list			
60	Argyll & Bute	LD	3.8
64	Aberdeenshire W. & Kincardine	LD	4.1
73	Angus	SNP	4.3
77	Perth & North Perthshire	SNP	4.5
87	Banff & Buchan	SNP	5.2
97	Berwickshire, Roxburgh & Selkirk	LD	5.8
106	Edinburgh West	LD	6.4
114	Moray	SNP	6.8
118	Dumfries & Galloway	Lab	7.1
133	Aberdeen South	Lab	7.9
137	Edinburgh South	Lab	8.5
139	Gordon	LD	8.7
140	Ochil & South Perthshire	Lab	8.7
144	Stirling	Lab	8.9
146	Edinburgh South West	Lab	9.3
156	Renfrewshire East	Lab	10.2
161	Ayr, Carrick & Cumnock	Lab	10.8
177	Fife North East	LD	11.3

Nat rank	Constituency	1st Pty	Swing to gain
Conservative target list			
191	East Lothian	Lab	12.5
208	Dundee East	SNP	13.6
210	Ayrshire Central	Lab	13.7
211	Inverness, Nairn, Badenoch & Strathspey	LD	13.7
212	Edinburgh North & Leith	Lab	13.8
215	Dunbartonshire East	LD	13.9
221	Caithness, Sutherland & Easter Ross	LD	14.2
244	Ayrshire North & Arran	Lab	15.9
246	Aberdeen North	Lab	16.0
248	Edinburgh East	Lab	16.2
255	Lanark & Hamilton East	Lab	17.5
257	Midlothian	Lab	17.6
259	Falkirk	Lab	17.8
266	Livingston	Lab	18.8
268	Linlithgow & Falkirk East	Lab	18.9
270	Kilmarnock & Loudoun	Lab	19.2
272	East Kilbride, Strathaven & Lesmahagow	Lab	19.3
273	Dundee West	Lab	19.6
275	Paisley & Renfrewshire N.	Lab	19.7
279	Glasgow South	Lab	20.1
281	Ross, Skye & Lochaber	LD	20.2
285	Glasgow North	Lab	20.6
295	Inverclyde	Lab	22.0
296	Glasgow North West	Lab	22.1
298	Glasgow Central	Lab	22.5
299	Dunfermline & Fife West	Lab	22.6
303	Na h-Eileanan an Iar (Western Isles)	SNP	23.3
308	Cumbernauld, Kilsyth & Kirkintilloch East	Lab	24.5
309	Airdrie & Shotts	Lab	24.7
310	Paisley & Renfrewshire S.	Lab	24.8
311	Rutherglen & Hamilton W.	Lab	25.6
312	Orkney & Shetland	LD	25.7
313	Motherwell & Wishaw	Lab	25.9
314	Dunbartonshire West	Lab	26.8
316	Glenrothes	Lab	27.6
318	Kirkcaldy & Cowdenbeath	Lab	27.6
319	Glasgow South West	Lab	28.0
320	Glasgow East	Lab	28.5
322	Coatbridge, Chryston & Bellshill	Lab	29.2
324	Glasgow North East	Lab	31.5
Labour target list			
35	Dundee East	SNP	2.2
36	Dunbartonshire East	LD	2.3
61	Edinburgh West	LD	4.1
64	Argyll & Bute	LD	4.4
65	Dumfriesshire, Clydesdale & Tweeddale	Con	4.6
99	Na h-Eileanan an Iar (Western Isles)	SNP	6.4

Nat rank	Constituency	1st Pty	Swing to gain
Scotland			
Labour target list			
112	Gordon	LD	8.0
117	Caithness, Sutherland & Easter Ross	LD	8.4
122	Inverness, Nairn, Badenoch & Strathspey	LD	9.3
133	Moray	SNP	11.3
141	Angus	SNP	12.0
145	Perth & North Perthshire	SNP	12.4
157	Fife North East	LD	13.6
158	Aberdeenshire W. & Kincardine	LD	13.8
170	Banff & Buchan	SNP	14.7
240	Ross, Skye & Lochaber	LD	18.8
250	Berwickshire, Roxburgh & Selkirk	LD	19.6
355	Orkney & Shetland	LD	25.7
Liberal Democrat target list			
6	Edinburgh South	Lab	0.4
17	Edinburgh North & Leith	Lab	1.8
35	Aberdeen South	Lab	4.1
50	Dunfermline & Fife West	Lab	5.6
64	Glasgow North	Lab	6.6
119	Dumfriesshire, Clydesdale & Tweeddale	Con	9.1
187	Edinburgh East	Lab	12.0
203	Edinburgh South West	Lab	12.4
213	Moray	SNP	12.6
226	Aberdeen North	Lab	12.9
250	Stirling	Lab	13.6
260	East Lothian	Lab	13.9
290	Ochil & South Perthshire	Lab	14.2
323	Midlothian	Lab	15.0
334	Perth & North Perthshire	SNP	15.2
403	Angus	SNP	16.3
408	Banff & Buchan	SNP	16.4
422	Dundee East	SNP	16.7
471	Glasgow Central	Lab	17.8
473	Ayrshire Central	Lab	17.9
490	Falkirk	Lab	18.5
492	Linlithgow & Falkirk East	Lab	18.5
494	Dundee West	Lab	18.5
497	Livingston	Lab	18.7
498	Ayrshire North & Arran	Lab	18.7
505	Ayr, Carrick & Cumnock	Lab	18.9
508	Glasgow North West	Lab	19.1
513	Lanark & Hamilton East	Lab	19.3
522	Glasgow South	Lab	19.9
523	Dumfries & Galloway	Lab	20.0
531	East Kilbride, Strathaven & Lesmahagow	Lab	20.8
535	Renfrewshire East	Lab	20.9
538	Na h-Eileanan an Iar (Western Isles)	SNP	21.2
539	Inverclyde	Lab	21.3

Nat rank	Constituency	1st Pty	Swing to gain
Liberal Democrat target list			
544	Paisley & Renfrewshire North	Lab	21.8
553	Kilmarnock & Loudoun	Lab	22.6
557	Cumbernauld, Kilsyth & Kirkintilloch East	Lab	23.8
558	Rutherglen & Hamilton W.	Lab	24.4
559	Airdrie & Shotts	Lab	25.0
560	Paisley & Renfrewshire S.	Lab	25.0
562	Motherwell & Wishaw	Lab	25.6
565	Dunbartonshire West	Lab	26.6
566	Glasgow South West	Lab	26.7
567	Glenrothes	Lab	27.3
568	Kirkcaldy & Cowdenbeath	Lab	27.6
569	Glasgow East	Lab	28.3
572	Coatbridge, Chryston & Bellshill	Lab	29.1
574	Glasgow North East	Lab	30.3
Green target list			
3	Argyll & Bute	LD	18.3
4	Gordon	LD	18.4
6	Edinburgh East	Lab	19.2
9	Inverness, Nairn, Badenoch & Strathspey	LD	19.8
16	Stirling	Lab	20.9
18	Aberdeen South	Lab	21.0
19	Ochil & South Perthshire	Lab	21.0
21	Edinburgh South West	Lab	21.1
25	East Lothian	Lab	21.4
28	Dumfriesshire, Clydesdale & Tweeddale	Con	21.6
29	Edinburgh South	Lab	21.6
45	Edinburgh North & Leith	Lab	22.3
63	Midlothian	Lab	22.7
67	Dundee East	SNP	22.8
78	Glasgow North	Lab	23.2
Scottish National Party target list			
1	Ochil & South Perthshire	Lab	5.1
2	Argyll & Bute	LD	6.3
3	Gordon	LD	6.9
4	Falkirk	Lab	7.7
5	Dundee West	Lab	9.8
6	Ayrshire North & Arran	Lab	10.7
7	Inverness, Nairn, Badenoch & Strathspey	LD	11.0
8	Aberdeen North	Lab	11.1
9	Caithness, Sutherland & Easter Ross	LD	11.1
10	Livingston	Lab	11.3
11	Edinburgh East	Lab	11.5
12	Linlithgow & Falkirk East	Lab	12.2
13	Stirling	Lab	12.2
14	Edinburgh West	LD	12.4
15	Aberdeenshire W. & Kincardine	LD	12.4

Nat rank	Constituency	1st Pty	Swing to gain
Scottish National Party target list			
16	Midlothian	Lab	13.2
17	Kilmarnock & Loudoun	Lab	13.3
18	Aberdeen South	Lab	13.7
19	East Kilbride, Strathaven & Lesmahagow	Lab	14.2
20	East Lothian	Lab	14.3
21	Ayrshire Central	Lab	14.3
22	Lanark & Hamilton East	Lab	14.5
23	Ayr, Carrick & Cumnock	Lab	14.6
24	Fife North East	LD	15.1
25	Dumfriesshire, Clydesdale & Tweeddale	Con	15.1
26	Edinburgh South West	Lab	15.3
27	Glasgow South	Lab	15.8
28	Cumbernauld, Kilsyth & Kirkintilloch East	Lab	16.7
29	Dunbartonshire East	LD	17.2
30	Glasgow Central	Lab	17.3
31	Airdrie & Shotts	Lab	17.3
32	Edinburgh North & Leith	Lab	17.3
33	Glasgow North	Lab	17.3
34	Paisley & Renfrewshire N.	Lab	17.5
35	Dumfries & Galloway	Lab	17.642
36	Edinburgh South	Lab	17.812
37	Glasgow East	Lab	18.406
38	Ross, Skye & Lochaber	LD	18.761
39	Inverclyde	Lab	19.215
40	Glasgow North West	Lab	19.396
41	Dunfermline & Fife West	Lab	20.026
42	Berwickshire, Roxburgh & Selkirk	LD	20.26
43	Glenrothes	Lab	20.306
44	Dunbartonshire West	Lab	20.593
45	Paisley & Renfrewshire S.	Lab	20.769
46	Renfrewshire East	Lab	21.156
47	Motherwell & Wishaw	Lab	21.478
48	Rutherglen & Hamilton W.	Lab	22.352
49	Glasgow South West	Lab	23.081
50	Coatbridge, Chryston & Bellshill	Lab	24.876
51	Kirkcaldy & Cowdenbeath	Lab	25.118
52	Orkney & Shetland	LD	25.708
53	Glasgow North East	Lab	27.104

Wales

Conservative target list

Nat rank	Constituency	1st Pty	Swing to gain
37	Bridgend	Lab	3.0
39	Delyn	Lab	3.1
42	Gower	Lab	3.2
52	Vale of Clwyd	Lab	3.5
57	Alyn & Deeside	Lab	3.7
65	Clwyd South	Lab	4.1
74	Newport West	Lab	4.5

Nat rank	Constituency	1st Pty	Swing to gain
Conservative target list			
83	Brecon & Radnorshire	LD	4.8
88	Cardiff South & Penarth	Lab	5.3
89	Ynys Mon	Lab	5.4
95	Wrexham	Lab	5.7
98	Cardiff West	Lab	5.8
110	Carmarthen East & Dinefwr	PC	6.6
129	Newport East	Lab	7.7
142	Swansea West	Lab	8.8
153	Cardiff Central	LD	9.9
165	Arfon	PC	10.8
169	Dwyfor Meirionnydd	PC	11.0
190	Torfaen	Lab	12.4
193	Pontypridd	Lab	12.5
213	Caerphilly	Lab	13.9
227	Llanelli	Lab	14.6
250	Neath	Lab	16.6
258	Islwyn	Lab	17.6
262	Swansea East	Lab	18.4
265	Aberavon	Lab	18.8
269	Ogmore	Lab	19.1
271	Ceredigion	LD	19.2
276	Merthyr Tydfil & Rhymney	Lab	19.9
290	Cynon Valley	Lab	21.2
301	Blaenau Gwent	Lab	22.7
307	Rhondda	Lab	24.4

Labour target list

Nat rank	Constituency	1st Pty	Swing to gain
4	Cardiff North	Con	0.2
46	Arfon	PC	2.8
62	Carmarthen West & Pembrokeshire South	Con	4.2
63	Vale of Glamorgan	Con	4.4
66	Carmarthen East & Dinefwr	PC	4.6
83	Aberconwy	Con	5.7
85	Preseli Pembrokeshire	Con	5.8
98	Cardiff Central	LD	6.3
118	Clwyd West	Con	8.4
132	Monmouth	Con	11.2
182	Dwyfor Meirionnydd	PC	15.2
270	Brecon & Radnorshire	LD	20.5
287	Montgomeryshire	Con	21.6
298	Ceredigion	LD	22.2

Liberal Democrat target list

Nat rank	Constituency	1st Pty	Swing to gain
10	Swansea West	Lab	0.7
16	Montgomeryshire	Con	1.8
19	Newport East	Lab	2.4
33	Pontypridd	Lab	3.8
49	Wrexham	Lab	5.5
61	Merthyr Tydfil & Rhymney	Lab	6.3
78	Bridgend	Lab	7.2
94	Aberconwy	Con	8.3
97	Cardiff South & Penarth	Lab	8.3
150	Gower	Lab	10.8

Nat rank	Constituency	1st Pty	Swing to gain
Wales			
Liberal Democrat target list			
162	Clwyd South	Lab	11.4
174	Alyn & Deeside	Lab	11.8
184	Cardiff West	Lab	11.9
215	Carmarthen East & Dinefwr	PC	12.6
216	Cardiff North	Con	12.7
221	Arfon	PC	12.8
240	Clwyd West	Con	13.2
245	Newport West	Lab	13.5
278	Torfaen	Lab	14.1
299	Monmouth	Con	14.4
309	Vale of Glamorgan	Con	14.8
310	Delyn	Lab	14.8
314	Ynys Mon	Lab	14.9
322	Preseli Pembrokeshire	Con	15.0
332	Caerphilly	Lab	15.1
362	Neath	Lab	15.7
388	Dwyfor Meirionnydd	PC	16.0
412	Carmarthen West & Pembrokeshire South	Con	16.5
415	Swansea East	Lab	16.6
442	Llanelli	Lab	17.2
454	Vale of Clwyd	Lab	17.4
472	Aberavon	Lab	17.8
511	Ogmore	Lab	19.3
514	Cynon Valley	Lab	19.3
516	Islwyn	Lab	19.4
537	Blaenau Gwent	Lab	21.1
552	Rhondda	Lab	22.3
Green target list			
27	Cardiff South & Penarth	Lab	21.6
34	Torfaen	Lab	21.8
35	Swansea West	Lab	21.9
47	Cardiff Central	LD	22.3
49	Cardiff West	Lab	22.4
59	Pontypridd	Lab	22.7
Plaid Cymru target list			
1	Ynys Mon	Lab	3.6
2	Llanelli	Lab	6.3
3	Aberconwy	Con	9.0
4	Ceredigion	LD	10.9
5	Clwyd West	Con	13.1
6	Neath	Lab	13.2
7	Caerphilly	Lab	14.1
8	Cynon Valley	Lab	16.1
9	Clwyd South	Lab	17.1
10	Wrexham	Lab	17.4
11	Carmarthen West & Pembrokeshire South	Con	17.6
12	Islwyn	Lab	18.1

Nat rank	Constituency	1st Pty	Swing to gain
Plaid Cymru target list			
13	Bridgend	Lab	18.3
14	Pontypridd	Lab	18.5
15	Preseli Pembrokeshire	Con	18.5
16	Rhondda	Lab	18.6
17	Cardiff West	Lab	19.0
18	Gower	Lab	19.1
19	Cardiff South & Penarth	Lab	19.6
20	Torfaen	Lab	19.7
21	Swansea West	Lab	19.9
22	Montgomeryshire	Con	20.9
23	Cardiff Central	LD	21.1
24	Vale of Glamorgan	Con	21.3
25	Alyn & Deeside	Lab	21.4
26	Merthyr Tydfil & Rhymney	Lab	21.5
27	Newport East	Lab	21.7
28	Delyn	Lab	21.8
29	Vale of Clwyd	Lab	21.9
30	Ogmore	Lab	22.1
31	Swansea East	Lab	22.4
32	Aberavon	Lab	22.4
33	Cardiff North	Con	22.6
34	Newport West	Lab	22.7
35	Monmouth	Con	22.9
36	Blaenau Gwent	Lab	24.1
37	Brecon & Radnorshire	LD	25.9

Table 16. Target lists for the main parties by rank order of swing to win (NI)

Nat. rank	*Constituency*	*1st Pty*	*Swing to gain*	Nat. rank	*Constituency*	*1st Pty*	*Swing to gain*
APNI target list				**Sinn Fein target list**			
1	Belfast South	SDLP	13.0	1	Belfast North	DUP	3.0
2	Londonderry East	DUP	14.6	2	Upper Bann	DUP	4.5
3	Antrim South	DUP	16.3	3	Foyle	SDLP	6.4
4	Antrim East	DUP	17.4	4	Londonderry East	DUP	7.7
5	Strangford	DUP	18.8	5	Down South	SDLP	9.9
6	Upper Bann	DUP	18.8	6	Antrim South	DUP	12.2
7	Lagan Valley	DUP	19.2	7	Antrim North	DUP	17.0
8	Newry & Armagh	SF	21.0	8	Antrim East	DUP	19.6
9	Belfast North	DUP	21.4	9	Belfast East	APNI	21.8
10	Antrim North	DUP	21.6	10	Strangford	DUP	22.2
11	Tyrone West	SF	23.1	11	Lagan Valley	DUP	22.9
12	Down South	SDLP	24.9	12	Down North	Ind	31.3
13	Foyle	SDLP	25.1	**TUV target list**			
14	Ulster Mid	SF	25.5	1	Londonderry East	DUP	13.6
15	Down North	Ind	28.8	2	Antrim North	DUP	14.8
16	Fermanagh & South Tyrone	SF	29.7	3	Antrim South	DUP	17.9
17	Belfast West	SF	34.6	4	Belfast East	APNI	19.7
Democratic Unionist target list				5	Antrim East	DUP	19.9
1	Belfast East	APNI	2.2	6	Lagan Valley	DUP	20.6
2	Belfast South	SDLP	8.7	7	Strangford	DUP	20.9
3	Tyrone West	SF	14.3	8	Ulster Mid	SF	22.3
4	Newry & Armagh	SF	14.6	9	Down South	SDLP	23.4
5	Foyle	SDLP	17.6	10	Down North	Ind	29.2
6	Ulster Mid	SF	18.8	**UCUNF target list**			
7	Down South	SDLP	20.0	1	Antrim South	DUP	1.7
8	Belfast West	SF	31.7	2	Upper Bann	DUP	4.1
Green target list				3	Londonderry East	DUP	8.4
7	Belfast South	SDLP	19.6	4	Strangford	DUP	9.0
90	Strangford	DUP	23.4	5	Belfast East	APNI	9.2
130	Down South	SDLP	24.3	6	Antrim East	DUP	11.1
330	Down North	Ind	30.1	7	Newry & Armagh	SF	11.5
SDLP target list				8	Belfast South	SDLP	11.9
1	Newry & Armagh	SF	9.3	9	Lagan Valley	DUP	14.3
2	Londonderry East	DUP	9.6	10	Tyrone West	SF	17.1
3	Upper Bann	DUP	11.5	11	Antrim North	DUP	17.7
4	Antrim South	DUP	15.7	12	Belfast North	DUP	19.6
5	Belfast North	DUP	16.5	13	Ulster Mid	SF	20.5
6	Tyrone West	SF	17.2	14	Down South	SDLP	20.9
7	Antrim North	DUP	18.8	15	Down North	Ind	21.5
8	Ulster Mid	SF	18.9	16	Foyle	SDLP	23.4
9	Antrim East	DUP	19.6	17	Belfast West	SF	34.0
10	Strangford	DUP	20.1				
11	Lagan Valley	DUP	22.4				
12	Belfast East	APNI	22.6				
13	Fermanagh & South Tyrone	SF	25.3				
14	Belfast West	SF	27.4				
15	Down North	Ind	30.6				

Table 17. Change of Vote Share 2005-2010 in Rank Order and Winning Party

	Constituency	%change	1st		Constituency	%change	1st
Conservative				**Conservative**			
1	Hartlepool	16.7	Lab	53	Orpington	8.5	Con
2	Montgomeryshire	13.8	Con	54	Cambridge	8.3	LD
3	Esher & Walton	13.2	Con	55	Sittingbourne & Sheppey	8.3	Con
4	Crewe & Nantwich	12.9	Con	56	Plymouth Moor View	8.3	Lab
5	Cardiff Central	12.3	LD	57	Kingswood	8.3	Con
6	Camborne & Redruth	12.0	Con	58	Warwick & Leamington	8.2	Con
7	Basingstoke	11.7	Con	59	Elmet & Rothwell	8.1	Con
8	St Ives	11.7	LD	60	Dwyfor Meirionnydd	8.1	PC
9	Devon South West	11.6	Con	61	Exeter	8.1	Lab
10	Ynys Mon	11.4	Lab	62	Warwickshire North	8.1	Con
11	Banff & Buchan	11.4	SNP	63	Derbyshire South	8.1	Con
12	Windsor	11.4	Con	64	Surrey South West	8.1	Con
13	Winchester	11.2	Con	65	Dudley South	8.1	Con
14	Aldridge-Brownhills	11.1	Con	66	Ipswich	8.0	Con
15	Ealing Southall	10.8	Lab	67	Tooting	8.0	Lab
16	Erewash	10.4	Con	68	Southampton Test	8.0	Lab
17	Meon Valley	10.4	Con	69	Newton Abbot	8.0	Con
18	Morley & Outwood	10.3	Lab	70	Slough	7.9	Lab
19	Richmond Park	10.1	Con	71	Blaydon	7.9	Lab
20	Cannock Chase	10.1	Con	72	Normanton, Pontefract & Castleford	7.9	Lab
21	Cornwall South East	10.1	Con	73	Jarrow	7.8	Lab
22	Norwich North	10.1	Con	74	Hampshire North West	7.8	Con
23	Truro & Falmouth	10.0	Con	75	Wyre Forest	7.8	Con
24	Harrogate & Knaresborough	9.9	Con	76	Devon Central	7.7	Con
25	Guildford	9.9	Con	77	Berwick-upon-Tweed	7.7	LD
26	Hemel Hempstead	9.9	Con	78	Ludlow	7.7	Con
27	Hampstead & Kilburn	9.8	Lab	79	Wimbledon	7.7	Con
28	Carmarthen W. & Pembrokeshire S.	9.8	Con	80	Keighley	7.7	Con
29	Hampshire East	9.7	Con	81	Dorset Mid & Poole North	7.7	LD
30	Birmingham Erdington	9.7	Lab	82	Maidenhead	7.6	Con
31	Shipley	9.7	Con	83	Dartford	7.6	Con
32	Putney	9.7	Con	84	Rochdale	7.6	Lab
33	Oxford West & Abingdon	9.6	Con	85	Mansfield	7.6	Lab
34	Reading West	9.6	Con	86	Penistone & Stocksbridge	7.5	Lab
35	Witney	9.4	Con	87	Battersea	7.5	Con
36	Bradford East	9.4	LD	88	Chesterfield	7.5	Lab
37	Chatham & Aylesford	9.4	Con	89	Leeds Central	7.5	Lab
38	Newcastle-under-Lyme	9.4	Lab	90	Somerset North	7.5	Con
39	Sedgefield	9.3	Lab	91	Hampshire North East	7.5	Con
40	Wakefield	9.1	Lab	92	Arundel & South Downs	7.4	Con
41	Dover	9.1	Con	93	Newbury	7.4	Con
42	Southampton Itchen	9.0	Lab	94	Welwyn Hatfield	7.4	Con
43	Wantage	8.9	Con	95	Chichester	7.4	Con
44	Derby South	8.7	Lab	96	Milton Keynes North	7.3	Con
45	Carmarthen E. & Dinefwr	8.7	PC	97	Bolsover	7.3	Lab
46	Oldham E. & Saddleworth	8.7	Lab	98	Burton	7.2	Con
47	Tamworth	8.7	Con	99	Hertfordshire South West	7.2	Con
48	Birmingham Yardley	8.6	LD	100	Dorset South	7.1	Con
49	Clacton	8.6	Con	101	Rossendale & Darwen	7.1	Con
50	Leicestershire North West	8.6	Con	102	Pendle	7.1	Con
51	Bromley & Chislehurst	8.5	Con	103	Alyn & Deeside	7.1	Lab
52	Delyn	8.5	Lab	104	Derbyshire North East	7.0	Lab

Constituency	%change	1st
Conservative		
105 Cardiff West	7.0	Lab
106 Gosport	7.0	Con
107 Beaconsfield	7.0	Con
108 Vauxhall	7.0	Lab
109 Greenwich & Woolwich	7.0	Lab
110 Walsall South	6.9	Lab
111 Reading East	6.9	Con
112 Brigg & Goole	6.9	Con
113 Waveney	6.9	Con
114 Washington & Sunderland W.	6.9	Lab
115 Weaver Vale	6.9	Con
116 Chesham & Amersham	6.8	Con
117 Ealing Central & Acton	6.8	Con
118 Walsall North	6.8	Lab
119 Stalybridge & Hyde	6.8	Lab
120 Thanet South	6.8	Con
121 Havant	6.8	Con
122 Aberconwy	6.8	Con
123 Basildon & Billericay	6.7	Con
124 Nottingham North	6.7	Lab
125 Chelmsford	6.7	Con
126 Huddersfield	6.7	Lab
127 York Outer	6.7	Con
128 Great Grimsby	6.7	Lab
129 South Ribble	6.6	Con
130 Romsey & Southampton N.	6.6	Con
131 West Bromwich West	6.6	Lab
132 Rochester & Strood	6.6	Con
133 Brentford & Isleworth	6.5	Con
134 Portsmouth North	6.5	Con
135 Gower	6.5	Lab
136 Harrow West	6.4	Lab
137 Preseli Pembrokeshire	6.4	Con
138 Stevenage	6.4	Con
139 Wirral South	6.3	Lab
140 Garston & Halewood	6.3	Lab
141 Thornbury & Yate	6.3	LD
142 Bognor Regis & Littlehampton	6.3	Con
143 Shrewsbury & Atcham	6.3	Con
144 Cornwall North	6.3	LD
145 Suffolk C.& Ipswich N.	6.2	Con
146 Kensington	6.2	Con
147 Nottingham South	6.2	Lab
148 Finchley & Golders Green	6.2	Con
149 Kettering	6.2	Con
150 Beverley & Holderness	6.2	Con
151 Surrey Heath	6.2	Con
152 Wealden	6.1	Con
153 Doncaster Central	6.1	Lab
154 West Bromwich East	6.1	Lab
155 Faversham & Kent Mid	6.1	Con
156 Harrow East	6.1	Con
157 Stoke-on-Trent North	6.0	Lab
158 Harborough	6.0	Con
159 Forest of Dean	6.0	Con

Constituency	%change	1st
Conservative		
160 Banbury	5.9	Con
161 Carlisle	5.9	Con
162 Bedfordshire North East	5.9	Con
163 Bedfordshire Mid	5.9	Con
164 Warrington North	5.9	Lab
165 Denton & Reddish	5.8	Lab
166 Scunthorpe	5.8	Lab
167 Burnley	5.8	LD
168 Sherwood	5.8	Con
169 Derby North	5.8	Lab
170 Crawley	5.8	Con
171 Wigan	5.8	Lab
172 Rugby	5.7	Con
173 Lichfield	5.7	Con
174 Swindon North	5.7	Con
175 St Helens S. & Whiston	5.7	Lab
176 Suffolk South	5.7	Con
177 Enfield Southgate	5.7	Con
178 Leeds West	5.6	Lab
179 Wolverhampton S. E.	5.6	Lab
180 Bournemouth West	5.6	Con
181 Derbyshire Dales	5.6	Con
182 Sunderland Central	5.6	Lab
183 Tunbridge Wells	5.6	Con
184 Wrekin, The	5.6	Con
185 Dudley North	5.6	Lab
186 Fareham	5.6	Con
187 Wellingborough	5.5	Con
188 Gillingham & Rainham	5.5	Con
189 Bury South	5.5	Lab
190 Bristol North West	5.5	Con
191 Hertfordshire North East	5.5	Con
192 Sevenoaks	5.5	Con
193 Staffordshire Moorlands	5.4	Con
194 Gainsborough	5.4	Con
195 Heywood & Middleton	5.4	Lab
196 Clwyd West	5.4	Con
197 Bridgend	5.4	Lab
198 Wrexham	5.4	Lab
199 Ribble Valley	5.4	Con
200 Darlington	5.4	Lab
201 Worcestershire West	5.4	Con
202 Bedford	5.4	Con
203 Basildon S. & Thurrock E.	5.3	Con
204 Glasgow North East	5.3	Lab
205 Rother Valley	5.3	Lab
206 Watford	5.3	Con
207 Filton & Bradley Stoke	5.3	Con
208 Gloucester	5.3	Con
209 Blackley & Broughton	5.3	Lab
210 Hendon	5.2	Con
211 Chelsea & Fulham	5.2	Con
212 Westminster North	5.2	Lab
213 Hereford & Herefordshire S.	5.2	Con
214 Houghton & Sunderland S.	5.2	Lab
215 Hitchin & Harpenden	5.2	Con

Constituency	%change	1st		Constituency	%change	1st
Conservative				**Conservative**		
216 Feltham & Heston	5.2	Lab		270 Norfolk North West	4.3	Con
217 Makerfield	5.2	Lab		271 Loughborough	4.3	Con
218 Norfolk South	5.2	Con		272 Cambridgeshire N. W.	4.3	Con
219 St Austell & Newquay	5.1	LD		273 Torfaen	4.2	Lab
220 Tonbridge & Malling	5.0	Con		274 Stoke-on-Trent South	4.2	Lab
221 Redditch	5.0	Con		275 Morecambe & Lunesdale	4.2	Con
222 Erith & Thamesmead	5.0	Lab		276 Bermondsey & Old		
223 Great Yarmouth	5.0	Con		Southwark	4.1	LD
224 Broxbourne	4.9	Con		277 Old Bexley & Sidcup	4.1	Con
225 Blackpool South	4.9	Lab		278 Worthing West	4.1	Con
226 Berwickshire, Roxburgh				279 Moray	4.1	SNP
& Selkirk	4.9	LD		280 Poole	4.1	Con
227 Bolton West	4.9	Lab		281 Harlow	4.1	Con
228 Swindon South	4.9	Con		282 Aberavon	4.1	Lab
229 Clwyd South	4.8	Lab		283 Leicestershire South	4.1	Con
230 Cleethorpes	4.8	Con		284 Colne Valley	4.1	Con
231 Gravesham	4.8	Con		285 Meriden	4.0	Con
232 Reigate	4.8	Con		286 Devizes	4.0	Con
233 Swansea West	4.8	Lab		287 Birmingham Perry Barr	4.0	Lab
234 Worsley & Eccles South	4.8	Lab		288 Hornsey & Wood Green	4.0	LD
235 Workington	4.8	Lab		289 Weston-Super-Mare	4.0	Con
236 Pudsey	4.8	Con		290 South Shields	4.0	Lab
237 Bradford South	4.8	Lab		291 Hornchurch & Upminster	3.9	Con
238 Gateshead	4.8	Lab		292 Bexleyheath & Crayford	3.9	Con
239 Eddisbury	4.8	Con		293 Rayleigh & Wickford	3.9	Con
240 Thanet North	4.7	Con		294 Cities of London &		
241 Plymouth Sutton &				Westminster	3.9	Con
Devonport	4.7	Con		295 Lewisham West & Penge	3.9	Lab
242 Stockton South	4.7	Con		296 Milton Keynes South	3.9	Con
243 Wolverhampton N. E.	4.7	Lab		297 Durham, City of	3.9	Lab
244 Stockton North	4.7	Lab		298 Brighton Kemptown	3.8	Con
245 Swansea East	4.7	Lab		299 Uxbridge & Ruislip South	3.8	Con
246 Amber Valley	4.7	Con		300 Aylesbury	3.8	Con
247 Stafford	4.7	Con		301 Chester, City of	3.8	Con
248 Blaenau Gwent	4.7	Lab		302 Wentworth & Dearne	3.8	Lab
249 Cambridgeshire N. E.	4.7	Con		303 Barnsley East	3.8	Lab
250 Dorset North	4.6	Con		304 Middlesbrough S. &		
251 Pontypridd	4.6	Lab		Cleveland E.	3.8	Lab
252 Saffron Walden	4.6	Con		305 Warrington South	3.7	Con
253 Wokingham	4.6	Con		306 Stoke-on-Trent Central	3.7	Lab
254 Nuneaton	4.6	Con		307 Edinburgh West	3.7	LD
255 Halesowen & Rowley Regis	4.6	Con		308 Barrow & Furness	3.7	Lab
256 Ashton Under Lyne	4.6	Lab		309 East Lothian	3.7	Lab
257 Leicester East	4.6	Lab		310 Northamptonshire South	3.7	Con
258 Worthing East & Shoreham	4.6	Con		311 Cotswolds, The	3.7	Con
259 Islington South & Finsbury	4.6	Lab		312 Durham North West	3.6	Lab
260 Leigh	4.5	Lab		313 Thurrock	3.6	Con
261 Bedfordshire South West	4.5	Con		314 Hertford & Stortford	3.6	Con
262 Blackpool N. & Cleveleys	4.5	Con		315 Calder Valley	3.6	Con
263 Runnymede & Weybridge	4.5	Con		316 Tiverton & Honiton	3.6	Con
264 Worcester	4.4	Con		317 Salford & Eccles	3.6	Lab
265 Northampton North	4.4	Con		318 Copeland	3.6	Lab
266 Vale of Glamorgan	4.4	Con		319 Chorley	3.6	Lab
267 Cardiff South & Penarth	4.4	Lab		320 Hull East	3.6	Lab
268 Harwich & Essex North	4.3	Con		321 High Peak	3.6	Con
269 Durham North	4.3	Lab		322 Aberdeen South	3.6	Lab

Constituency	%change	1st		Constituency	%change	1st
Conservative				**Conservative**		
323 Leicester South	3.6	Lab		377 Norfolk Mid	2.9	Con
324 Kingston & Surbiton	3.5	LD		378 Chipping Barnet	2.9	Con
325 Maldon	3.5	Con		379 Aberdeen North	2.9	Lab
326 Daventry	3.5	Con		380 New Forest West	2.9	Con
327 Birmingham Ladywood	3.5	Lab		381 Leeds North East	2.9	Lab
328 Vale of Clwyd	3.5	Lab		382 Solihull	2.9	LD
329 St Albans	3.5	Con		383 Eltham	2.9	Lab
330 Richmond (Yorks)	3.5	Con		384 Brentwood & Ongar	2.9	Con
331 St Helens North	3.5	Lab		385 Woking	2.9	Con
332 Blackburn	3.5	Lab		386 Kilmarnock & Loudoun	2.8	Lab
333 New Forest East	3.4	Con		387 Salisbury	2.8	Con
334 Rotherham	3.4	Lab		388 Mole Valley	2.8	Con
335 Newcastle upon Tyne N.	3.4	Lab		389 Coventry South	2.8	Lab
336 Stourbridge	3.4	Con		390 Newport West	2.8	Lab
337 Bury North	3.4	Con		391 Leicester West	2.8	Lab
338 Horsham	3.4	Con		392 Hertsmere	2.8	Con
339 Devon West & Torridge	3.4	Con		393 Broadland	2.8	Con
340 Grantham & Stamford	3.4	Con		394 Ruislip, Northwood &		
341 Norfolk South West	3.4	Con		Pinner	2.8	Con
342 Newark	3.4	Con		395 Newcastle upon Tyne C.	2.8	Lab
343 Bishop Auckland	3.4	Lab		396 Caithness, Sutherland &		
344 Chippenham	3.3	LD		Easter Ross	2.8	LD
345 Bristol South	3.3	Lab		397 Braintree	2.7	Con
346 Lincoln	3.3	Con		398 Blyth Valley	2.7	Lab
347 Wythenshawe & Sale E.	3.3	Lab		399 Ashford	2.7	Con
348 Coventry North East	3.3	Lab		400 Aldershot	2.7	Con
349 Dewsbury	3.3	Con		401 Don Valley	2.7	Lab
350 Hazel Grove	3.3	LD		402 Coventry North West	2.7	Lab
351 Haltemprice & Howden	3.2	Con		403 West Ham	2.6	Lab
352 Louth & Horncastle	3.2	Con		404 Poplar & Limehouse	2.6	Lab
353 Kenilworth & Southam	3.2	Con		405 Ealing North	2.6	Lab
354 Birmingham Northfield	3.2	Lab		406 Oldham West & Royton	2.6	Lab
355 Worcestershire Mid	3.2	Con		407 Wolverhampton S. W.	2.6	Con
356 Telford	3.2	Lab		408 Wansbeck	2.6	Lab
357 York Central	3.2	Lab		409 Bracknell	2.6	Con
358 Rushcliffe	3.1	Con		410 Staffordshire South	2.5	Con
359 Bournemouth East	3.1	Con		411 Wiltshire South West	2.5	Con
360 Camberwell & Peckham	3.1	Lab		412 Stroud	2.5	Con
361 Boston & Skegness	3.1	Con		413 Barnsley Central	2.5	Lab
362 Tatton	3.1	Con		414 Midlothian	2.5	Lab
363 Totnes	3.0	Con		415 Witham	2.5	Con
364 Northampton South	3.0	Con		416 Sussex Mid	2.5	Con
365 Charnwood	3.0	Con		417 Lancaster & Fleetwood	2.5	Con
366 Sheffield South East	3.0	Lab		418 Cheltenham	2.4	LD
367 Newcastle upon Tyne East	3.0	Lab		419 Dundee East	2.4	SNP
368 Hastings & Rye	3.0	Con		420 Hammersmith	2.4	Lab
369 Inverness, Nairn, Badenoch				421 Caerphilly	2.4	Lab
& Strathspey	3.0	LD		422 Ayr, Carrick & Cumnock	2.4	Lab
370 Easington	3.0	Lab		423 Birkenhead	2.4	Lab
371 East Kilbride, Strathaven &				424 Islington North	2.4	Lab
Lesmahagow	3.0	Lab		425 Middlesbrough	2.3	Lab
372 Islwyn	3.0	Lab		426 Selby & Ainsty	2.3	Con
373 Sheffield Heeley	3.0	Lab		427 Edmonton	2.3	Lab
374 Henley	3.0	Con		428 Fife North East	2.3	LD
375 Bolton South East	2.9	Lab		429 Corby	2.2	Con
376 Torbay	2.9	LD		430 Lancashire West	2.2	Lab

Constituency	%change	1st	Constituency	%change	1st
Conservative			**Conservative**		
431 Lanark & Hamilton East	2.2	Lab	483 Sutton Coldfield	1.4	Con
432 Brent North	2.2	Lab	484 Birmingham Selly Oak	1.4	Lab
433 Stone	2.2	Con	485 Manchester Central	1.3	Lab
434 Bolton North East	2.2	Lab	486 Cumbernauld, Kilsyth &		
435 Somerset North East	2.2	Con	Kirkintilloch East	1.3	Lab
436 Ross, Skye & Lochaber	2.2	LD	487 Falkirk	1.3	Lab
437 Hemsworth	2.2	Lab	488 Rutherglen & Hamilton W.	1.3	Lab
438 Ellesmere Port & Neston	2.1	Lab	489 Luton South	1.3	Lab
439 Eastleigh	2.1	LD	490 Epping Forest	1.2	Con
440 Yorkshire East	2.1	Con	491 Wycombe	1.2	Con
441 Lewes	2.1	LD	492 Barking	1.2	Lab
442 South Holland & The			493 Nottingham East	1.2	Lab
Deepings	2.1	Con	494 Dunbartonshire West	1.2	Lab
443 Streatham	2.0	Lab	495 Epsom & Ewell	1.2	Con
444 Bristol West	2.0	LD	496 Manchester Gorton	1.2	Lab
445 Penrith & The Border	2.0	Con	497 Bury St Edmunds	1.2	Con
446 Bethnal Green & Bow	2.0	Lab	498 Derbyshire Mid	1.1	Con
447 Ilford North	2.0	Con	499 Christchurch	1.1	Con
448 Hyndburn	1.9	Lab	500 Norwich South	1.1	LD
449 Altrincham & Sale West	1.9	Con	501 Taunton Deane	1.1	LD
450 Aberdeenshire W. &			502 Dorset West	1.1	Con
Kincardine	1.9	LD	503 Devon East	1.1	Con
451 Brecon & Radnorshire	1.9	LD	504 Sleaford & N. Hykeham	1.0	Con
452 Shropshire North	1.9	Con	505 Gordon	1.0	LD
453 Somerton & Frome	1.9	LD	506 Dundee West	1.0	Lab
454 Warley	1.9	Lab	507 Liverpool West Derby	1.0	Lab
455 Croydon North	1.9	Lab	508 Birmingham Hodge Hill	1.0	Lab
456 Batley & Spen	1.9	Lab	509 Liverpool Wavertree	1.0	Lab
457 Dumfriesshire, Clydesdale &			510 Thirsk & Malton	1.0	Con
Tweeddale	1.9	Con	511 Cardiff North	1.0	Con
458 Liverpool Riverside	1.9	Lab	512 Paisley & Renfrewshire N.	1.0	Lab
459 Wiltshire North	1.9	Con	513 Sheffield Central	1.0	Lab
460 Suffolk Coastal	1.8	Con	514 Edinburgh South West	1.0	Lab
461 Stockport	1.8	Lab	515 Cambridgeshire South	0.9	Con
462 Scarborough & Whitby	1.8	Con	516 Coatbridge, Chryston &		
463 Doncaster North	1.8	Lab	Bellshill	0.9	Lab
464 Inverclyde	1.8	Lab	517 Halifax	0.9	Lab
465 Broxtowe	1.8	Con	518 Rhondda	0.9	Lab
466 Sutton & Cheam	1.7	LD	519 Wallasey	0.9	Lab
467 Sheffield Brightside &			520 Dagenham & Rainham	0.9	Lab
Hillsborough	1.7	Lab	521 Hexham	0.8	Con
468 Twickenham	1.7	LD	522 Cambridgeshire S. E.	0.8	Con
469 Hayes & Harlington	1.7	Lab	523 Colchester	0.8	LD
470 Suffolk West	1.7	Con	524 Glasgow South West	0.8	Lab
471 Leeds East	1.6	Lab	525 Glasgow Central	0.8	Lab
472 Bootle	1.5	Lab	526 Lewisham Deptford	0.8	Lab
473 Paisley & Renfrewshire S.	1.5	Lab	527 Manchester Withington	0.8	LD
474 Neath	1.5	Lab	528 Preston	0.7	Lab
475 Oxford East	1.5	Lab	529 Wirral West	0.7	Con
476 Cynon Valley	1.5	Lab	530 Llanelli	0.7	Lab
477 Rochford & Southend E.	1.5	Con	531 Edinburgh East	0.6	Lab
478 Angus	1.5	SNP	532 Livingston	0.6	Lab
479 Monmouth	1.4	Con	533 Mitcham & Morden	0.6	Lab
480 East Ham	1.4	Lab	534 Surrey East	0.6	Con
481 Ogmore	1.4	Lab	535 Skipton & Ripon	0.6	Con
482 Tottenham	1.4	Lab	536 Renfrewshire East	0.5	Lab

Constituency	%change	1st
Conservative		
537 Argyll & Bute	0.5	LD
538 Arfon	0.5	PC
539 Cheadle	0.5	LD
540 Brighton Pavilion	0.4	Grn
541 Congleton	0.4	Con
542 Glasgow North West	0.4	Lab
543 Sefton Central	0.4	Lab
544 Canterbury	0.3	Con
545 Devon North	0.3	LD
546 Halton	0.3	Lab
547 Hove	0.3	Con
548 Gedling	0.3	Lab
549 Stratford-on-Avon	0.3	Con
550 Perth & North Perthshire	0.2	SNP
551 Bristol East	0.2	Lab
552 Ilford South	0.1	Lab
553 Birmingham Hall Green	0.1	Lab
554 Glenrothes	0.1	Lab
555 Linlithgow & Falkirk E.	0.1	Lab
556 Liverpool Walton	0.1	Lab
557 Motherwell & Wishaw	0.1	Lab
558 Bosworth	0.0	Con
559 Na h-Eileanan an Iar (Western Isles)	0.0	SNP
560 Hackney N. & Stoke Newington	0.0	Lab
561 Southend West	-0.1	Con
562 Bridgwater & Somerset W.	-0.1	Con
563 Rutland & Melton	-0.1	Con
564 Hull North	-0.2	Lab
565 Bradford West	-0.2	Lab
566 Hackney S. & Shoreditch	-0.2	Lab
567 Leeds North West	-0.3	LD
568 Tyneside North	-0.3	Lab
569 Portsmouth South	-0.4	LD
570 Chingford & Woodford Green	-0.4	Con
571 Luton North	-0.4	Lab
572 Newport East	-0.5	Lab
573 Holborn & St Pancras	-0.5	Lab
574 Bath	-0.5	LD
575 Hull West & Hessle	-0.5	Lab
576 Leyton & Wanstead	-0.5	Lab
577 Carshalton & Wallington	-0.6	LD
578 Herefordshire North	-0.7	Con
579 Lewisham East	-0.7	Lab
580 Enfield North	-0.8	Con
581 Ceredigion	-0.8	LD
582 Ochil & South Perthshire	-1.0	Lab
583 Tewkesbury	-1.0	Con
584 Dunbartonshire East	-1.0	LD
585 Croydon Central	-1.0	Con
586 Kirkcaldy & Cowdenbeath	-1.0	Lab
587 Wells	-1.0	LD
588 Stirling	-1.1	Lab
589 Croydon South	-1.1	Con

Constituency	%change	1st
Conservative		
590 Airdrie & Shotts	-1.1	Lab
591 Glasgow South	-1.1	Lab
592 Bassetlaw	-1.2	Lab
593 Southport	-1.2	LD
594 Yeovil	-1.2	LD
595 Stretford & Urmston	-1.4	Lab
596 Merthyr Tydfil & Rhymney	-1.4	Lab
597 Birmingham Edgbaston	-1.5	Lab
598 Romford	-1.7	Con
599 Glasgow North	-1.7	Lab
600 Ayrshire Central	-1.8	Lab
601 Beckenham	-1.8	Con
602 Huntingdon	-1.9	Con
603 Brent Central	-1.9	LD
604 Fylde	-2.1	Con
605 Ashfield	-2.2	Lab
606 Tynemouth	-2.2	Lab
607 Isle of Wight	-2.3	Con
608 Knowsley	-2.3	Lab
609 Wyre & Preston North	-2.3	Con
610 Dulwich & W. Norwood	-2.3	Lab
611 Eastbourne	-2.3	LD
612 Glasgow East	-2.4	Lab
613 Edinburgh South	-2.5	Lab
614 Bexhill & Battle	-2.6	Con
615 Macclesfield	-2.7	Con
616 Ayrshire North & Arran	-2.7	Lab
617 Orkney & Shetland	-2.8	LD
618 Peterborough	-2.9	Con
619 Spelthorne	-3.4	Con
620 Dunfermline & Fife West	-3.6	Lab
621 Edinburgh North & Leith	-3.7	Lab
622 Dumfries & Galloway	-3.7	Lab
623 Maidstone & The Weald	-3.8	Con
624 Norfolk North	-3.9	LD
625 Redcar	-4.1	LD
626 Walthamstow	-4.2	Lab
627 Castle Point	-4.3	Con
628 Folkestone & Hythe	-4.5	Con
629 Sheffield Hallam	-6.6	LD
630 Bromsgrove	-7.3	Con
631 Westmorland & Lonsdale	-8.1	LD
Labour		
1 Glasgow North East	68.3	Lab
2 Blaenau Gwent	20.1	Lab
3 East Ham	16.8	Lab
4 West Ham	10.9	Lab
5 Glenrothes	10.4	Lab
6 Dunbartonshire West	9.4	Lab
7 Edinburgh West	9.1	LD
8 Bethnal Green & Bow	8.5	Lab
9 Paisley & Renfrewshire N.	8.3	Lab
10 Paisley & Renfrewshire S.	7.0	Lab
11 Renfrewshire East	6.9	Lab

	Constituency	%change	1st		Constituency	%change	1st
Labour				**Labour**			
12	Oxford East	6.5	Lab	63	Garston & Halewood	1.6	Lab
13	Ochil & South Perthshire	6.5	Lab	64	Walthamstow	1.5	Lab
14	Kirkcaldy & Cowdenbeath	6.4	Lab	65	Midlothian	1.5	Lab
15	Leicester South	6.2	Lab	66	Edinburgh South	1.5	Lab
16	Hackney North & Stoke			67	Hammersmith	1.5	Lab
	Newington	6.0	Lab	68	Tottenham	1.4	Lab
17	Stirling	5.8	Lab	69	Ayrshire Central	1.3	Lab
18	Blackburn	5.7	Lab	70	Dunbartonshire East	1.0	LD
19	Bradford West	5.6	Lab	71	Holborn & St Pancras	1.0	Lab
20	Cumbernauld, Kilsyth &			72	Glasgow East	0.9	Lab
	Kirkintilloch East	5.4	Lab	73	Tooting	0.8	Lab
21	Kilmarnock & Loudoun	5.3	Lab	74	Luton North	0.7	Lab
22	Inverclyde	5.2	Lab	75	Ilford South	0.6	Lab
23	Rutherglen & Hamilton W.	5.2	Lab	76	Aberdeenshire West &		
24	Glasgow North	5.1	Lab		Kincardine	0.5	LD
25	Birmingham Hodge Hill	5.1	Lab	77	Staffordshire South	0.3	Con
26	Glasgow North West	4.9	Lab	78	Argyll & Bute	0.3	LD
27	Dumfries & Galloway	4.8	Lab	79	Liverpool Walton	0.2	Lab
28	Barking	4.7	Lab	80	Ross, Skye & Lochaber	0.2	LD
29	Poplar & Limehouse	4.7	Lab	81	Liverpool Riverside	0.0	Lab
30	Glasgow South	4.5	Lab	82	Gordon	-0.1	LD
31	Fife North East	4.4	LD	83	Aberdeen South	-0.2	Lab
32	Westminster North	4.0	Lab	84	Mitcham & Morden	-0.3	Lab
33	Birmingham Perry Barr	4.0	Lab	85	Slough	-0.4	Lab
34	Lanark & Hamilton East	3.9	Lab	86	Bolton North East	-0.4	Lab
35	Dundee West	3.9	Lab	87	Manchester Withington	-0.4	LD
36	Glasgow Central	3.8	Lab	88	Preston	-0.5	Lab
37	Caithness, Sutherland &			89	Cheadle	-0.5	LD
	Easter Ross	3.7	LD	90	Copeland	-0.7	Lab
38	Motherwell & Wishaw	3.6	Lab	91	Eltham	-0.7	Lab
39	Liverpool West Derby	3.6	Lab	92	Angus	-0.7	SNP
40	Liverpool Wavertree	3.6	Lab	93	Airdrie & Shotts	-0.9	Lab
41	Ayrshire North & Arran	3.5	Lab	94	Knowsley	-0.9	Lab
42	Ealing North	3.5	Lab	95	Dorset West	-1.1	Con
43	Edinburgh East	3.4	Lab	96	Dunfermline & Fife West	-1.2	Lab
44	Islington North	3.3	Lab	97	Ynys Mon	-1.3	Lab
45	Edinburgh North & Leith	3.2	Lab	98	Nottingham East	-1.3	Lab
46	East Lothian	3.1	Lab	99	Stroud	-1.5	Con
47	Edinburgh South West	3.0	Lab	100	Chesterfield	-1.6	Lab
48	Hackney S. & Shoreditch	3.0	Lab	101	Hayes & Harlington	-1.6	Lab
49	Birmingham Ladywood	3.0	Lab	102	Na h-Eileanan an Iar		
50	Orpington	3.0	Con		(Western Isles)	-1.6	SNP
51	Barrow & Furness	2.9	Lab	103	Newbury	-1.7	Con
52	East Kilbride, Strathaven &			104	Lewisham Deptford	-1.7	Lab
	Lesmahagow	2.8	Lab	105	Wirral South	-1.7	Lab
53	Croydon North	2.4	Lab	106	Sheffield Hallam	-1.7	LD
54	Islington South & Finsbury	2.4	Lab	107	Folkestone & Hythe	-1.8	Con
55	Dulwich & West Norwood	2.3	Lab	108	Carmarthen E. & Dinefwr	-1.8	PC
56	Glasgow South West	2.3	Lab	109	Surrey South West	-1.9	Con
57	Haltemprice & Howden	2.2	Con	110	Cardiff North	-1.9	Con
58	Linlithgow & Falkirk East	2.1	Lab	111	Vauxhall	-2.0	Lab
59	Coatbridge, Chryston &			112	Blaydon	-2.0	Lab
	Bellshill	2.1	Lab	113	Warley	-2.0	Lab
60	Banff & Buchan	2.0	SNP	114	Maidenhead	-2.1	Con
61	Aberdeen North	2.0	Lab	115	Leyton & Wanstead	-2.2	Lab
62	Ayr, Carrick & Cumnock	1.8	Lab	116	Edmonton	-2.3	Lab

Constituency	%change	1st

Labour

Constituency	%change	1st
117 Enfield North	-2.3	Con
118 Birkenhead	-2.3	Lab
119 Perth & North Perthshire	-2.3	SNP
120 Bermondsey & Old Southwark	-2.4	LD
121 New Forest East	-2.4	Con
122 Birmingham Edgbaston	-2.5	Lab
123 Brent North	-2.5	Lab
124 Birmingham Yardley	-2.5	LD
125 Bassetlaw	-2.5	Lab
126 Livingston	-2.6	Lab
127 Harrogate & Knaresborough	-2.7	Con
128 Wallasey	-2.7	Lab
129 St Helens S. & Whiston	-2.7	Lab
130 Stretford & Urmston	-2.8	Lab
131 Durham, City of	-2.9	Lab
132 Dundee East	-2.9	SNP
133 Oldham West & Royton	-2.9	Lab
134 Lancashire West	-2.9	Lab
135 Chingford & Woodford Green	-3.0	Con
136 Tynemouth	-3.0	Lab
137 Hereford & Herefordshire S.	-3.0	Con
138 Manchester Gorton	-3.0	Lab
139 Uxbridge & Ruislip South	-3.0	Con
140 Hendon	-3.0	Con
141 Leeds North East	-3.0	Lab
142 Batley & Spen	-3.1	Lab
143 Norfolk North	-3.1	LD
144 Cities of London & Westminster	-3.1	Con
145 Ealing Central & Acton	-3.2	Con
146 Greenwich & Woolwich	-3.3	Lab
147 Moray	-3.3	SNP
148 Dumfriesshire, Clydesdale & Tweeddale	-3.4	Con
149 Cornwall South East	-3.4	Con
150 Southport	-3.4	LD
151 Broxtowe	-3.4	Con
152 Arfon	-3.5	PC
153 Orkney & Shetland	-3.5	LD
154 Hampstead & Kilburn	-3.5	Lab
155 Hastings & Rye	-3.5	Con
156 Newport West	-3.6	Lab
157 Cardiff West	-3.6	Lab
158 Vale of Clwyd	-3.6	Lab
159 Hazel Grove	-3.6	LD
160 Twickenham	-3.7	LD
161 Devon North	-3.7	LD
162 Preseli Pembrokeshire	-3.7	Con
163 Sefton Central	-3.7	Lab
164 Worcestershire West	-3.7	Con
165 Mole Valley	-3.7	Con
166 Doncaster North	-3.8	Lab
167 Kingston & Surbiton	-3.8	LD
168 Thornbury & Yate	-3.8	LD

Labour

Constituency	%change	1st
169 Winchester	-3.9	Con
170 Dudley North	-3.9	Lab
171 Chester, City of	-3.9	Con
172 Wirral West	-4.0	Con
173 Exeter	-4.0	Lab
174 Ludlow	-4.0	Con
175 Carmarthen W. & Pembrokeshire S.	-4.0	Con
176 Gower	-4.0	Lab
177 Croydon South	-4.0	Con
178 Coventry South	-4.0	Lab
179 Ellesmere Port & Neston	-4.1	Lab
180 Camberwell & Peckham	-4.1	Lab
181 Brighton Kemptown	-4.1	Con
182 Henley	-4.1	Con
183 Sunderland Central	-4.1	Lab
184 Kensington	-4.1	Con
185 Streatham	-4.2	Lab
186 Dorset Mid & Poole N.	-4.2	LD
187 Richmond Park	-4.2	Con
188 Meon Valley	-4.2	Con
189 Dorset North	-4.2	Con
190 Hornsey & Wood Green	-4.3	LD
191 Lewes	-4.3	LD
192 Newton Abbot	-4.4	Con
193 St Ives	-4.4	LD
194 Corby	-4.4	Con
195 Tiverton & Honiton	-4.4	Con
196 Saffron Walden	-4.5	Con
197 Llanelli	-4.5	Lab
198 Brecon & Radnorshire	-4.5	LD
199 Hove	-4.5	Con
200 Wolverhampton S. W.	-4.5	Con
201 Feltham & Heston	-4.5	Lab
202 Ruislip, Northwood & Pinner	-4.5	Con
203 Rochdale	-4.5	Lab
204 Halifax	-4.5	Lab
205 Romsey & Southampton N.	-4.6	Con
206 Lewisham East	-4.6	Lab
207 Bootle	-4.6	Lab
208 Hyndburn	-4.6	Lab
209 Newcastle upon Tyne C.	-4.6	Lab
210 Devon Central	-4.7	Con
211 Totnes	-4.7	Con
212 Wakefield	-4.8	Lab
213 Peterborough	-4.8	Con
214 Guildford	-4.8	Con
215 Beckenham	-4.9	Con
216 Wokingham	-4.9	Con
217 Sutton & Cheam	-4.9	LD
218 Delyn	-4.9	Lab
219 Jarrow	-4.9	Lab
220 Brentwood & Ongar	-4.9	Con
221 Leicester East	-5.0	Lab
222 Harrow West	-5.0	Lab
223 Swansea East	-5.1	Lab

Constituency	%change	1st
Labour		
224 Falkirk	-5.1	Lab
225 Montgomeryshire	-5.2	Con
226 Coventry North West	-5.2	Lab
227 Lewisham West & Penge	-5.2	Lab
228 Sheffield Central	-5.2	Lab
229 Berwick-upon-Tweed	-5.2	LD
230 Oxford West & Abingdon	-5.2	Con
231 Devon West & Torridge	-5.3	Con
232 Bournemouth East	-5.3	Con
233 Wiltshire North	-5.3	Con
234 Yeovil	-5.3	LD
235 Richmond (Yorks)	-5.3	Con
236 Ilford North	-5.4	Con
237 Brentford & Isleworth	-5.4	Con
238 Finchley & Golders Green	-5.4	Con
239 Halton	-5.4	Lab
240 Sutton Coldfield	-5.5	Con
241 Gedling	-5.5	Lab
242 Cardiff Central	-5.5	LD
243 Isle of Wight	-5.6	Con
244 Westmorland & Lonsdale	-5.6	LD
245 Battersea	-5.6	Con
246 St Helens North	-5.6	Lab
247 Berwickshire, Roxburgh & Selkirk	-5.7	LD
248 Aylesbury	-5.7	Con
249 Bedford	-5.7	Con
250 Wiltshire South West	-5.7	Con
251 Southampton Test	-5.7	Lab
252 Ealing Southall	-5.8	Lab
253 Christchurch	-5.8	Con
254 Surrey East	-5.8	Con
255 Wyre & Preston North	-5.9	Con
256 Fylde	-5.9	Con
257 Bexhill & Battle	-5.9	Con
258 Stratford-on-Avon	-6.0	Con
259 Eastbourne	-6.0	LD
260 Staffordshire Moorlands	-6.0	Con
261 Newark	-6.0	Con
262 Penrith & The Border	-6.1	Con
263 Swindon South	-6.2	Con
264 Pendle	-6.2	Con
265 Sussex Mid	-6.2	Con
266 Ceredigion	-6.3	LD
267 Derbyshire Dales	-6.3	Con
268 Neath	-6.3	Lab
269 Somerton & Frome	-6.4	LD
270 Surrey Heath	-6.5	Con
271 Workington	-6.5	Lab
272 Tatton	-6.5	Con
273 Bridgend	-6.6	Lab
274 Manchester Central	-6.6	Lab
275 St Austell & Newquay	-6.6	LD
276 Harborough	-6.6	Con
277 Waveney	-6.6	Con
278 Bury North	-6.6	Con

Constituency	%change	1st
Labour		
279 Denton & Reddish	-6.7	Lab
280 Cheltenham	-6.7	LD
281 Loughborough	-6.7	Con
282 Rushcliffe	-6.7	Con
283 New Forest West	-6.7	Con
284 Solihull	-6.7	LD
285 Hampshire North East	-6.8	Con
286 Crawley	-6.8	Con
287 Clwyd South	-6.8	Lab
288 Watford	-6.8	Con
289 Bolton West	-6.8	Lab
290 Chelsea & Fulham	-6.9	Con
291 Somerset North East	-7.0	Con
292 Taunton Deane	-7.0	LD
293 Altrincham & Sale West	-7.0	Con
294 Bradford South	-7.0	Lab
295 Wealden	-7.1	Con
296 Burnley	-7.1	LD
297 Lancaster & Fleetwood	-7.1	Con
298 Ogmore	-7.1	Lab
299 Epping Forest	-7.2	Con
300 Swansea West	-7.2	Lab
301 Plymouth Moor View	-7.2	Lab
302 Gateshead	-7.3	Lab
303 Warwickshire North	-7.3	Con
304 Warrington North	-7.3	Lab
305 Huntingdon	-7.4	Con
306 Penistone & Stocksbridge	-7.4	Lab
307 Worthing West	-7.4	Con
308 Newcastle-under-Lyme	-7.4	Lab
309 Filton & Bradley Stoke	-7.4	Con
310 Devon East	-7.5	Con
311 Blackpool South	-7.5	Lab
312 Brighton Pavilion	-7.5	Grn
313 Bath	-7.5	LD
314 Croydon Central	-7.5	Con
315 Huddersfield	-7.6	Lab
316 Chorley	-7.6	Lab
317 Coventry North East	-7.6	Lab
318 Bedfordshire Mid	-7.7	Con
319 Bexleyheath & Crayford	-7.7	Con
320 Cardiff South & Penarth	-7.7	Lab
321 Erith & Thamesmead	-7.7	Lab
322 Harlow	-7.7	Con
323 Weston-Super-Mare	-7.7	Con
324 Newcastle upon Tyne East	-7.7	Lab
325 Hampshire North West	-7.7	Con
326 Beaconsfield	-7.8	Con
327 Shropshire North	-7.8	Con
328 Ribble Valley	-7.8	Con
329 Dwyfor Meirionnydd	-7.8	PC
330 Vale of Glamorgan	-7.8	Con
331 Bromley & Chislehurst	-7.9	Con
332 Cotswolds, The	-7.9	Con
333 Torbay	-7.9	LD
334 Harrow East	-7.9	Con

Constituency	%change	1st		Constituency	%change	1st
Labour				**Labour**		
335 Luton South	-7.9	Lab		391 Enfield Southgate	-8.8	Con
336 Broxbourne	-7.9	Con		392 Worthing E. & Shoreham	-8.8	Con
337 Colchester	-7.9	LD		393 Inverness, Nairn, Badenoch		
338 Louth & Horncastle	-8.0	Con		& Strathspey	-8.8	LD
339 Sevenoaks	-8.0	Con		394 Charnwood	-8.9	Con
340 Chesham & Amersham	-8.0	Con		395 York Central	-8.9	Lab
341 Wythenshawe & Sale E.	-8.0	Lab		396 Dagenham & Rainham	-8.9	Lab
342 Windsor	-8.0	Con		397 Brent Central	-8.9	LD
343 Thanet South	-8.1	Con		398 Bristol East	-8.9	Lab
344 Stoke-on-Trent South	-8.1	Lab		399 Banbury	-8.9	Con
345 Bournemouth West	-8.1	Con		400 Keighley	-9.0	Con
346 Chichester	-8.1	Con		401 Hartlepool	-9.0	Lab
347 Epsom & Ewell	-8.1	Con		402 Stone	-9.0	Con
348 Hull East	-8.1	Lab		403 Bristol West	-9.0	LD
349 Aberavon	-8.1	Lab		404 Newcastle upon Tyne N.	-9.0	Lab
350 Wells	-8.1	LD		405 Amber Valley	-9.0	Con
351 Bromsgrove	-8.1	Con		406 Plymouth Sutton &		
352 Cambridge	-8.2	LD		Devonport	-9.0	Con
353 Heywood & Middleton	-8.2	Lab		407 Derby North	-9.0	Lab
354 Ipswich	-8.2	Con		408 Colne Valley	-9.0	Con
355 Skipton & Ripon	-8.2	Con		409 Norfolk South	-9.0	Con
356 Newport East	-8.2	Lab		410 Worcestershire Mid	-9.1	Con
357 Blackley & Broughton	-8.2	Lab		411 Bedfordshire North East	-9.1	Con
358 Wyre Forest	-8.2	Con		412 Wrexham	-9.2	Lab
359 Warrington South	-8.3	Con		413 Horsham	-9.2	Con
360 Woking	-8.3	Con		414 West Bromwich East	-9.2	Lab
361 Bolton South East	-8.3	Lab		415 Southend West	-9.2	Con
362 Birmingham Selly Oak	-8.3	Lab		416 Blackpool N. & Cleveleys	-9.2	Con
363 Cornwall North	-8.3	LD		417 Alyn & Deeside	-9.2	Lab
364 Morley & Outwood	-8.4	Lab		418 Hertfordshire South West	-9.3	Con
365 Hitchin & Harpenden	-8.4	Con		419 Warwick & Leamington	-9.3	Con
366 Hertsmere	-8.4	Con		420 Wansbeck	-9.3	Lab
367 Dewsbury	-8.4	Con		421 Northampton North	-9.4	Con
368 Worcester	-8.4	Con		422 Witney	-9.4	Con
369 Herefordshire North	-8.4	Con		423 Stockton South	-9.4	Con
370 Reading East	-8.5	Con		424 Leeds East	-9.4	Lab
371 Lincoln	-8.5	Con		425 Truro & Falmouth	-9.4	Con
372 Bridgwater & Somerset W.	-8.5	Con		426 Weaver Vale	-9.4	Con
373 Aberconwy	-8.5	Con		427 Shipley	-9.4	Con
374 Milton Keynes South	-8.6	Con		428 Birmingham Hall Green	-9.4	Lab
375 Hampshire East	-8.6	Con		429 Telford	-9.5	Lab
376 Carshalton & Wallington	-8.6	LD		430 Cambridgeshire South	-9.5	Con
377 Chipping Barnet	-8.6	Con		431 High Peak	-9.5	Con
378 Nottingham South	-8.6	Lab		432 Sleaford & N. Hykeham	-9.5	Con
379 Cambridgeshire N. W.	-8.7	Con		433 Morecambe & Lunesdale	-9.5	Con
380 Macclesfield	-8.7	Con		434 Romford	-9.5	Con
381 Norwich South	-8.7	LD		435 Walsall South	-9.5	Lab
382 Arundel & South Downs	-8.7	Con		436 Carlisle	-9.6	Con
383 Tewkesbury	-8.7	Con		437 Thurrock	-9.6	Con
384 West Bromwich West	-8.7	Lab		438 South Ribble	-9.6	Con
385 Old Bexley & Sidcup	-8.7	Con		439 Tunbridge Wells	-9.6	Con
386 Portsmouth South	-8.7	LD		440 Aldershot	-9.6	Con
387 Tyneside North	-8.7	Lab		441 Runnymede & Weybridge	-9.6	Con
388 Esher & Walton	-8.8	Con		442 Wigan	-9.6	Lab
389 South Shields	-8.8	Lab		443 Stockport	-9.6	Lab
390 Leicestershire South	-8.8	Con		444 Halesowen & Rowley Regis	-9.7	Con

Constituency	%change	1st	Constituency	%change	1st
Labour			**Labour**		
445 Basildon S. & Thurrock E.	-9.7	Con	500 Boston & Skegness	-10.9	Con
446 Stevenage	-9.7	Con	501 Leeds North West	-10.9	LD
447 Ashford	-9.7	Con	502 Clacton	-10.9	Con
448 Nuneaton	-9.8	Con	503 Harwich & Essex North	-10.9	Con
449 Leigh	-9.8	Lab	504 Bognor Regis &		
450 Broadland	-9.8	Con	Littlehampton	-11.0	Con
451 Derby South	-9.8	Lab	505 Dudley South	-11.0	Con
452 Thirsk & Malton	-9.8	Con	506 Salisbury	-11.0	Con
453 Chippenham	-9.9	LD	507 Havant	-11.0	Con
454 York Outer	-9.9	Con	508 Bishop Auckland	-11.1	Lab
455 Poole	-10.0	Con	509 Milton Keynes North	-11.1	Con
456 Wantage	-10.0	Con	510 Monmouth	-11.1	Con
457 Birmingham Northfield	-10.1	Lab	511 Middlesbrough S. &		
458 Ashton Under Lyne	-10.1	Lab	Cleveland E.	-11.1	Lab
459 Derbyshire North East	-10.1	Lab	512 Bracknell	-11.1	Con
460 Suffolk Coastal	-10.1	Con	513 Birmingham Erdington	-11.1	Lab
461 Stalybridge & Hyde	-10.1	Lab	514 Thanet North	-11.1	Con
462 Suffolk South	-10.1	Con	515 Wentworth & Dearne	-11.2	Lab
463 Bristol South	-10.1	Lab	516 Kenilworth & Southam	-11.2	Con
464 Reigate	-10.2	Con	517 Walsall North	-11.2	Lab
465 Putney	-10.2	Con	518 Bradford East	-11.3	LD
466 Derbyshire Mid	-10.2	Con	519 Rochford & Southend E.	-11.3	Con
467 Stafford	-10.2	Con	520 Tonbridge & Malling	-11.3	Con
468 Leeds Central	-10.2	Lab	521 Clwyd West	-11.3	Con
469 Burton	-10.2	Con	522 Doncaster Central	-11.3	Lab
470 Tamworth	-10.3	Con	523 Mansfield	-11.4	Lab
471 Pudsey	-10.3	Con	524 Hexham	-11.4	Con
472 Hornchurch & Upminster	-10.3	Con	525 Dorset South	-11.4	Con
473 Barnsley Central	-10.4	Lab	526 Elmet & Rothwell	-11.4	Con
474 Worsley & Eccles South	-10.4	Lab	527 Northamptonshire S.	-11.4	Con
475 Stourbridge	-10.4	Con	528 Norfolk South West	-11.4	Con
476 Blyth Valley	-10.5	Lab	529 Fareham	-11.4	Con
477 Gainsborough	-10.5	Con	530 Sheffield Heeley	-11.5	Lab
478 Hertford & Stortford	-10.5	Con	531 Eastleigh	-11.5	LD
479 Congleton	-10.5	Con	532 Maldon	-11.5	Con
480 Erewash	-10.5	Con	533 Derbyshire South	-11.5	Con
481 Bury South	-10.5	Lab	534 Stoke-on-Trent North	-11.5	Lab
482 Eddisbury	-10.5	Con	535 Southampton Itchen	-11.5	Lab
483 South Holland & The			536 Calder Valley	-11.5	Con
Deepings	-10.5	Con	537 Sheffield South East	-11.6	Lab
484 Caerphilly	-10.5	Lab	538 Durham North West	-11.6	Lab
485 Cynon Valley	-10.5	Lab	539 Houghton & Sunderland S.	-11.7	Lab
486 Sherwood	-10.6	Con	540 Middlesbrough	-11.7	Lab
487 Nottingham North	-10.6	Lab	541 Basildon & Billericay	-11.7	Con
488 Kingswood	-10.6	Con	542 Meriden	-11.7	Con
489 Rother Valley	-10.6	Lab	543 Yorkshire East	-11.8	Con
490 Bedfordshire South West	-10.6	Con	544 Dover	-11.8	Con
491 Rutland & Melton	-10.6	Con	545 Devon South West	-11.8	Con
492 Somerset North	-10.6	Con	546 Hertfordshire N. E.	-11.9	Con
493 Oldham E. & Saddleworth	-10.7	Lab	547 Hemsworth	-11.9	Lab
494 Bury St Edmunds	-10.7	Con	548 Wolverhampton S. E.	-12.0	Lab
495 Rossendale & Darwen	-10.7	Con	549 Canterbury	-12.0	Con
496 Portsmouth North	-10.8	Con	550 Stockton North	-12.0	Lab
497 Cleethorpes	-10.8	Con	551 Rayleigh & Wickford	-12.0	Con
498 Braintree	-10.8	Con	552 Scarborough & Whitby	-12.0	Con
499 Spelthorne	-10.8	Con	553 Daventry	-12.1	Con

Constituency	%change	1st

Labour

	Constituency	%change	1st
554	Wrekin, The	-12.1	Con
555	Rugby	-12.1	Con
556	Torfaen	-12.1	Lab
557	Basingstoke	-12.2	Con
558	Bristol North West	-12.2	Con
559	Devizes	-12.2	Con
560	Suffolk C.l & Ipswich N.	-12.3	Con
561	Easington	-12.4	Lab
562	Great Yarmouth	-12.4	Con
563	Lichfield	-12.4	Con
564	Forest of Dean	-12.4	Con
565	Camborne & Redruth	-12.4	Con
566	Leicester West	-12.4	Lab
567	Gloucester	-12.4	Con
568	Faversham & Kent Mid	-12.5	Con
569	Scunthorpe	-12.5	Lab
570	Hull West & Hessle	-12.6	Lab
571	Maidstone & The Weald	-12.6	Con
572	Kettering	-12.7	Con
573	Brigg & Goole	-12.7	Con
574	Chatham & Aylesford	-12.7	Con
575	Rhondda	-12.8	Lab
576	Norfolk Mid	-12.8	Con
577	Cambridgeshire N. E.	-12.8	Con
578	Wycombe	-12.8	Con
579	Darlington	-12.9	Lab
580	Aldridge-Brownhills	-12.9	Con
581	Rochester & Strood	-13.1	Con
582	Gillingham & Rainham	-13.1	Con
583	Hull North	-13.1	Lab
584	Rotherham	-13.1	Lab
585	Grantham & Stamford	-13.2	Con
586	Wolverhampton N. E.	-13.3	Lab
587	Gravesham	-13.4	Con
588	Wimbledon	-13.4	Con
589	Redditch	-13.4	Con
590	Shrewsbury & Atcham	-13.5	Con
591	Durham North	-13.6	Lab
592	Stoke-on-Trent Central	-13.6	Lab
593	Beverley & Holderness	-13.6	Con
594	Cambridgeshire S. E.	-13.8	Con
595	Sedgefield	-13.9	Lab
596	Leeds West	-13.9	Lab
597	Witham	-13.9	Con
598	Suffolk West	-14.2	Con
599	Great Grimsby	-14.4	Lab
600	Crewe & Nantwich	-14.4	Con
601	Reading West	-14.5	Con
602	Gosport	-14.5	Con
603	Swindon North	-14.6	Con
604	Sheffield Brightside & Hillsborough	-14.6	Lab
605	Makerfield	-14.8	Lab
606	Welwyn Hatfield	-14.9	Con
607	Ashfield	-15.0	Lab
608	Islwyn	-15.1	Lab

Labour

	Constituency	%change	1st
609	Bolsover	-15.2	Lab
610	Salford & Eccles	-15.3	Lab
611	Leicestershire N.W.	-15.4	Con
612	Pontypridd	-15.4	Lab
613	Dartford	-15.5	Con
614	Norwich North	-15.7	Con
615	Castle Point	-15.7	Con
616	Bosworth	-15.9	Con
617	Chelmsford	-16.0	Con
618	Wellingborough	-16.0	Con
619	Northampton South	-16.1	Con
620	Washington & Sunderland West	-16.2	Lab
621	St Albans	-16.7	Con
622	Merthyr Tydfil & Rhymney	-16.8	Lab
623	Sittingbourne & Sheppey	-17.1	Con
624	Normanton, Pontefract & Castleford	-17.1	Lab
625	Selby & Ainsty	-17.1	Con
626	Cannock Chase	-17.9	Con
627	Norfolk North West	-18.3	Con
628	Don Valley	-18.6	Lab
629	Redcar	-18.6	LD
630	Hemel Hempstead	-18.9	Con
631	Barnsley East	-23.9	Lab

Liberal Democrat

	Constituency	%change	1st
1	Redcar	25.0	LD
2	Ashfield	19.5	Lab
3	Merthyr Tydfil & Rhymney	17.0	Lab
4	Dunfermline & Fife W.	14.9	Lab
5	Westmorland & Lonsdale	14.1	LD
6	Ceredigion	13.5	LD
7	Maidstone & The Weald	13.2	Con
8	Brent Central	13.1	LD
9	Burnley	12.0	LD
10	Bosworth	11.7	Con
11	Hull North	11.3	Lab
12	Pontypridd	11.2	Lab
13	Bath	11.2	LD
14	Cheltenham	11.1	LD
15	Canterbury	11.1	Con
16	St Albans	11.0	Con
17	Wycombe	10.9	Con
18	Leeds North West	10.6	LD
19	Wyre Forest	10.6	Con
20	Orkney & Shetland	10.5	LD
21	Salisbury	10.0	Con
22	Sheffield Central	9.5	Lab
23	Bristol West	9.0	LD
24	Spelthorne	8.8	Con
25	Newport East	8.5	Lab
26	Norfolk North West	8.5	Con

	Constituency	%change	1st		Constituency	%change	1st
Liberal Democrat				**Liberal Democrat**			
27	Lewisham East	8.3	Lab	82	Normanton, Pontefract &		
28	Eastleigh	8.2	LD		Castleford	5.3	Lab
29	Sedgefield	8.2	Lab	83	Torbay	5.2	LD
30	Carshalton & Wallington	7.9	LD	84	Braintree	5.2	Con
31	Bethnal Green & Bow	7.8	Lab	85	Durham North West	5.0	Lab
32	Selby & Ainsty	7.7	Con	86	York Central	5.0	Lab
33	Glasgow North East	7.7	Lab	87	Congleton	5.0	Con
34	Suffolk Coastal	7.7	Con	88	Darlington	5.0	Lab
35	Hertford & Stortford	7.5	Con	89	Birmingham Selly Oak	4.9	Lab
36	Ashford	7.2	Con	90	Bristol S.	4.9	Lab
37	Rutland & Melton	7.2	Con	91	Daventry	4.9	Con
38	Tewkesbury	7.1	Con	92	Rugby	4.9	Con
39	Sheffield Hallam	7.1	LD	93	Chipping Barnet	4.9	Con
40	Sheffield Heeley	7.0	Lab	94	Shipley	4.8	Con
41	Sheffield Brightside &			95	Makerfield	4.8	Lab
	Hillsborough	6.9	Lab	96	Caerphilly	4.7	Lab
42	Herefordshire N.	6.9	Con	97	Bristol East	4.7	Lab
43	Wimbledon	6.8	Con	98	Suffolk C. & Ipswich N.	4.7	Con
44	Leeds West	6.8	Lab	99	Forest of Dean	4.7	Con
45	Morley & Outwood	6.7	Lab	100	Devizes	4.7	Con
46	Bury St Edmunds	6.7	Con	101	Rochford & Southend E.	4.7	Con
47	Bristol North West	6.6	Con	102	Taunton Deane	4.7	LD
48	Monmouth	6.6	Con	103	Edinburgh N. & Leith	4.6	Lab
49	Chelmsford	6.6	Con	104	Witham	4.6	Con
50	Scarborough & Whitby	6.5	Con	105	Dartford	4.6	Con
51	Sheffield South East	6.4	Lab	106	Hove	4.6	Con
52	Streatham	6.3	Lab	107	Leicestershire N. W.	4.6	Con
53	Calder Valley	6.3	Con	108	Walsall S.	4.6	Lab
54	Fylde	6.2	Con	109	Bromsgrove	4.6	Con
55	Suffolk West	6.2	Con	110	Preston	4.5	Lab
56	Cambridgeshire S. E.	6.2	Con	111	Horsham	4.5	Con
57	Wells	6.1	LD	112	Eddisbury	4.5	Con
58	Shrewsbury & Atcham	6.1	Con	113	Bracknell	4.5	Con
59	Hemel Hempstead	6.0	Con	114	Thirsk & Malton	4.5	Con
60	Northampton S.	5.9	Con	115	Derbyshire Mid	4.5	Con
61	Blaenau Gwent	5.9	Lab	116	Gosport	4.5	Con
62	Skipton & Ripon	5.8	Con	117	Beckenham	4.5	Con
63	Cambridgeshire S.	5.8	Con	118	Rushcliffe	4.4	Con
64	Aldridge-Brownhills	5.8	Con	119	Swindon North	4.4	Con
65	Cornwall North	5.7	LD	120	Leicester West	4.4	Lab
66	Grantham & Stamford	5.7	Con	121	Woking	4.3	Con
67	Bridgwater & Somerset W.	5.7	Con	122	Swansea West	4.3	Lab
68	Eastbourne	5.6	LD	123	Harwich & Essex N.	4.3	Con
69	Kenilworth & Southam	5.6	Con	124	Maldon	4.3	Con
70	Manchester Central	5.6	Lab	125	Reading West	4.3	Con
71	Wellingborough	5.6	Con	126	Yeovil	4.2	LD
72	Gloucester	5.6	Con	127	Hexham	4.2	Con
73	Aldershot	5.5	Con	128	Stoke-on-Trent N.	4.2	Lab
74	Somerset North	5.5	Con	129	Lichfield	4.2	Con
75	Wyre & Preston N.	5.4	Con	130	Portsmouth S.	4.2	LD
76	Lewisham Deptford	5.4	Lab	131	Tiverton & Honiton	4.2	Con
77	Southend West	5.4	Con	132	Barnsley East	4.1	Lab
78	Boston & Skegness	5.4	Con	133	New Forest W.	4.1	Con
79	Hornchurch & Upminster	5.4	Con	134	Dulwich & W. Norwood	4.0	Lab
80	Epsom & Ewell	5.3	Con	135	Erewash	4.0	Con
81	Bexhill & Battle	5.3	Con	136	Rochester & Strood	3.9	Con

Constituency	%change	1st		Constituency	%change	1st
Liberal Democrat				**Liberal Democrat**		
137 Northamptonshire S.	3.9	Con		192 Reading East	3.0	Con
138 Glasgow N.	3.9	Lab		193 Cambridgeshire N. E.	3.0	Con
139 Bradford East	3.9	LD		194 Cannock Chase	3.0	Con
140 Thanet N.	3.8	Con		195 Keighley	3.0	Con
141 Stone	3.8	Con		196 Peterborough	2.9	Con
142 Bradford S.	3.8	Lab		197 Banbury	2.9	Con
143 Runnymede & Weybridge	3.8	Con		198 Leyton & Wanstead	2.9	Lab
144 Somerton & Frome	3.8	LD		199 Broadland	2.9	Con
145 Colne Valley	3.7	Con		200 Thanet S.	2.9	Con
146 Kettering	3.6	Con		201 Wolverhampton S. E.	2.9	Lab
147 Sittingbourne & Sheppey	3.6	Con		202 Faversham & Kent Mid	2.9	Con
148 Altrincham & Sale W.	3.6	Con		203 Gillingham & Rainham	2.8	Con
149 Worsley & Eccles S.	3.6	Lab		204 Nuneaton	2.8	Con
150 Stockport	3.6	Lab		205 Basildon S. & Thurrock E.	2.8	Con
151 Romford	3.6	Con		206 Twickenham	2.7	LD
152 Macclesfield	3.5	Con		207 Somerset N. E.	2.7	Con
153 Salford & Eccles	3.5	Lab		208 Enfield Southgate	2.7	Con
154 Berwickshire, Roxburgh &				209 Pudsey	2.7	Con
Selkirk	3.5	LD		210 Penrith & The Border	2.6	Con
155 Warrington S.	3.5	Con		211 Basingstoke	2.6	Con
156 Lancaster & Fleetwood	3.5	Con		212 South Holland & The		
157 Solihull	3.5	LD		Deepings	2.6	Con
158 Cleethorpes	3.5	Con		213 Hull East	2.6	Lab
159 Devon W. & Torridge	3.4	Con		214 Gravesham	2.6	Con
160 Epping Forest	3.4	Con		215 Birmingham Edgbaston	2.6	Lab
161 Burton	3.4	Con		216 Wolverhampton S. W.	2.5	Con
162 Birmingham Northfield	3.3	Lab		217 Poole	2.5	Con
163 Chippenham	3.3	LD		218 Aberavon	2.5	Lab
164 Great Yarmouth	3.3	Con		219 Milton Keynes S.	2.5	Con
165 Staffordshire S.	3.3	Con		220 Basildon & Billericay	2.5	Con
166 Southport	3.3	LD		221 Nottingham East	2.5	Lab
167 Dorset S.	3.3	Con		222 Heywood & Middleton	2.5	Lab
168 Hull W. & Hessle	3.2	Lab		223 Cardiff S. & Penarth	2.4	Lab
169 Redditch	3.2	Con		224 Warwick & Leamington	2.4	Con
170 Rossendale & Darwen	3.2	Con		225 Wrekin, The	2.4	Con
171 Charnwood	3.2	Con		226 High Peak	2.4	Con
172 Dewsbury	3.2	Con		227 Suffolk S.	2.4	Con
173 Havant	3.2	Con		228 Croydon S.	2.4	Con
174 Ashton Under Lyne	3.2	Lab		229 Carmarthen E. & Dinefwr	2.4	PC
175 Bedfordshire S. W.	3.2	Con		230 Norfolk S. W.	2.4	Con
176 Hornsey & Wood Green	3.2	LD		231 Manchester Withington	2.4	LD
177 Worcester	3.2	Con		232 Halesowen & Rowley Regis	2.3	Con
178 Great Grimsby	3.1	Lab		233 Chesham & Amersham	2.3	Con
179 Easington	3.1	Lab		234 Huntingdon	2.3	Con
180 Devon East	3.1	Con		235 Warley	2.3	Lab
181 Weston-Super-Mare	3.1	Con		236 Norfolk N.	2.3	LD
182 Worcestershire Mid	3.1	Con		237 Welwyn Hatfield	2.2	Con
183 Hertfordshire N. E.	3.1	Con		238 Norwich N.	2.2	Con
184 Stoke-on-Trent C.	3.1	Lab		239 Yorkshire East	2.2	Con
185 Reigate	3.1	Con		240 Chelsea & Fulham	2.2	Con
186 Derbyshire S.	3.0	Con		241 Isle of Wight	2.2	Con
187 Stretford & Urmston	3.0	Lab		242 Richmond (Yorks)	2.2	Con
188 Beverley & Holderness	3.0	Con		243 Wrexham	2.2	Lab
189 Dudley S.	3.0	Con		244 Warrington N.	2.1	Lab
190 Tonbridge & Malling	3.0	Con		245 Fareham	2.1	Con
191 Norfolk Mid	3.0	Con				

Constituency	%change	1st
Liberal Democrat		
246 Middlesbrough S. & Cleveland E.	2.1	Lab
247 Tamworth	2.1	Con
248 Amber Valley	2.1	Con
249 Plymouth Sutton & Devonport	2.1	Con
250 Stafford	2.0	Con
251 Surrey East	2.0	Con
252 Vale of Glamorgan	2.0	Con
253 Leicestershire S.	2.0	Con
254 Cities of London & Westminster	2.0	Con
255 Camberwell & Peckham	1.9	Lab
256 Bury N.	1.9	Con
257 Clwyd West	1.9	Con
258 Durham N.	1.9	Lab
259 Wolverhampton N. E.	1.9	Lab
260 Lincoln	1.9	Con
261 Gainsborough	1.8	Con
262 Wiltshire N.	1.8	Con
263 Sussex Mid	1.8	Con
264 West Bromwich W.	1.8	Lab
265 Derbyshire N. E.	1.8	Lab
266 Holborn & St Pancras	1.8	Lab
267 Edinburgh S.	1.7	Lab
268 Clwyd South	1.7	Lab
269 Stratford-on-Avon	1.7	Con
270 Corby	1.7	Con
271 Bognor Regis & Littlehampton	1.6	Con
272 Louth & Horncastle	1.6	Con
273 Walthamstow	1.6	Lab
274 Newark	1.6	Con
275 Cynon Valley	1.6	Lab
276 Camborne & Redruth	1.6	Con
277 Denton & Reddish	1.6	Lab
278 Gedling	1.5	Lab
279 Old Bexley & Sidcup	1.5	Con
280 Preseli Pembrokeshire	1.5	Con
281 Stroud	1.5	Con
282 Cotswolds, The	1.5	Con
283 Newcastle upon Tyne E.	1.5	Lab
284 Milton Keynes N.	1.4	Con
285 Arundel & S. Downs	1.4	Con
286 Sherwood	1.4	Con
287 Brigg & Goole	1.4	Con
288 Stalybridge & Hyde	1.4	Lab
289 Telford	1.4	Lab
290 Mansfield	1.4	Lab
291 Bedfordshire Mid	1.4	Con
292 Sutton Coldfield	1.4	Con
293 Brecon & Radnorshire	1.3	LD
294 West Ham	1.3	Lab
295 Dwyfor Meirionnydd	1.3	PC
296 Scunthorpe	1.2	Lab
297 Halifax	1.2	Lab

Constituency	%change	1st
Liberal Democrat		
298 Christchurch	1.2	Con
299 Shropshire N.	1.2	Con
300 Rother Valley	1.2	Lab
301 Middlesbrough	1.2	Lab
302 Worthing E. & Shoreham	1.2	Con
303 Broxbourne	1.1	Con
304 Watford	1.1	Con
305 Worthing West	1.1	Con
306 Bury South	1.1	Lab
307 Brighton Kemptown	1.1	Con
308 Hackney S. & Shoreditch	1.1	Lab
309 Meriden	1.0	Con
310 Wansbeck	1.0	Lab
311 Lewisham W. & Penge	1.0	Lab
312 Northampton N.	1.0	Con
313 Wallasey	0.9	Lab
314 Devon N.	0.9	LD
315 Tottenham	0.9	Lab
316 Alyn & Deeside	0.9	Lab
317 Tyneside N.	0.9	Lab
318 Wythenshawe & Sale E.	0.9	Lab
319 Washington & Sunderland W.	0.9	Lab
320 Torfaen	0.9	Lab
321 East Ham	0.8	Lab
322 W. Bromwich E.	0.8	Lab
323 Bedfordshire N. E.	0.8	Con
324 Stoke-on-Trent S.	0.8	Lab
325 Hackney N. & Stoke Newington	0.8	Lab
326 Broxtowe	0.8	Con
327 Walsall N.	0.8	Lab
328 Tatton	0.8	Con
329 Vale of Clwyd	0.7	Lab
330 Enfield N.	0.7	Con
331 Bermondsey & Old Southwark	0.7	LD
332 Ynys Mon	0.7	Lab
333 Sefton Central	0.7	Lab
334 Harlow	0.7	Con
335 Brentford & Isleworth	0.7	Con
336 Newcastle-under-Lyme	0.7	Lab
337 Folkestone & Hythe	0.7	Con
338 Huddersfield	0.6	Lab
339 Neath	0.6	Lab
340 Gower	0.6	Lab
341 Swindon South	0.6	Con
342 Putney	0.6	Con
343 Gateshead	0.6	Lab
344 Don Valley	0.6	Lab
345 Wealden	0.6	Con
346 Derby N.	0.5	Lab
347 Bridgend	0.5	Lab
348 Cardiff West	0.5	Lab
349 Ogmore	0.5	Lab
350 Lewes	0.5	LD

Constituency	%change	1st		Constituency	%change	1st
Liberal Democrat				**Liberal Democrat**		
351 Dumfries & Galloway	0.5	Lab		403 Na h-Eileanan an Iar		
352 Wirral West	0.5	Con		(Western Isles)	-0.5	SNP
353 Loughborough	0.4	Con		404 Lancashire West	-0.5	Lab
354 Batley & Spen	0.4	Lab		405 Coventry N. West	-0.5	Lab
355 Stourbridge	0.4	Con		406 Dumfriesshire, Clydesdale		
356 Inverness, Nairn, Badenoch				& Tweeddale	-0.5	Con
& Strathspey	0.4	LD		407 Oldham E. & Saddleworth	-0.5	Lab
357 Coventry South	0.4	Lab		408 South Ribble	-0.6	Con
358 Croydon Central	0.4	Con		409 Liverpool Riverside	-0.6	Lab
359 Birmingham Erdington	0.3	Lab		410 Kensington	-0.6	Con
360 Colchester	0.3	LD		411 Clacton	-0.6	Con
361 Devon South West	0.3	Con		412 Houghton & Sunderland S.	-0.6	Lab
362 Ruislip, Northwood &				413 Norwich South	-0.6	LD
Pinner	0.3	Con		414 Ellesmere Port & Neston	-0.7	Lab
363 Wantage	0.3	Con		415 York Outer	-0.7	Con
364 Leeds East	0.3	Lab		416 Blackpool South	-0.7	Lab
365 Battersea	0.3	Con		417 Exeter	-0.7	Lab
366 Wiltshire South West	0.3	Con		418 St Helens N.	-0.7	Lab
367 Aberconwy	0.2	Con		419 Cheadle	-0.7	LD
368 Hitchin & Harpenden	0.2	Con		420 Leeds Central	-0.7	Lab
369 Rhondda	0.2	Lab		421 Bassetlaw	-0.7	Lab
370 Luton South	0.1	Lab		422 Chorley	-0.7	Lab
371 Sleaford & N. Hykeham	0.1	Con		423 Doncaster N.	-0.8	Lab
372 Southampton Itchen	0.1	Lab		424 Erith & Thamesmead	-0.8	Lab
373 Harrow East	0.1	Con		425 Sevenoaks	-0.8	Con
374 Coventry N. E.	0.1	Lab		426 Dundee East	-0.8	SNP
375 Sunderland Central	0.1	Lab		427 Staffordshire Moorlands	-0.8	Con
376 Newcastle upon Tyne N.	0.1	Lab		428 Dorset N.	-0.9	Con
377 Dudley N.	0.0	Lab		429 Chingford & Woodford		
378 Dover	0.0	Con		Green	-0.9	Con
379 Tunbridge Wells	0.0	Con		430 Workington	-0.9	Lab
380 Birkenhead	-0.1	Lab		431 Manchester Gorton	-0.9	Lab
381 Finchley & Golders				432 Castle Point	-0.9	Con
Green	-0.1	Con		433 Henley	-0.9	Con
382 Wentworth & Dearne	-0.1	Lab		434 Leigh	-0.9	Lab
383 Truro & Falmouth	-0.1	Con		435 Stockton South	-1.0	Con
384 Hastings & Rye	-0.1	Con		436 Elmet & Rothwell	-1.0	Con
385 Tynemouth	-0.2	Lab		437 Hertsmere	-1.0	Con
386 Portsmouth N.	-0.2	Con		438 Carlisle	-1.0	Con
387 Chatham & Aylesford	-0.2	Con		439 Cambridgeshire N. W.	-1.0	Con
388 Bournemouth West	-0.2	Con		440 Crawley	-1.1	Con
389 Chichester	-0.3	Con		441 Ilford N.	-1.1	Con
390 Morecambe & Lunesdale	-0.3	Con		442 Worcestershire W.	-1.1	Con
391 Nottingham N.	-0.3	Lab		443 Hayes & Harlington	-1.1	Lab
392 Rayleigh & Wickford	-0.3	Con		444 Weaver Vale	-1.1	Con
393 Blackpool N. & Cleveleys	-0.4	Con		445 Dorset West	-1.2	Con
394 Thurrock	-0.4	Con		446 Sutton & Cheam	-1.2	LD
395 Bexleyheath & Crayford	-0.4	Con		447 Kingswood	-1.2	Con
396 Bournemouth E.	-0.4	Con		448 Bishop Auckland	-1.3	Lab
397 Cardiff N.	-0.4	Con		449 Kingston & Surbiton	-1.3	LD
398 Aylesbury	-0.4	Con		450 Newport West	-1.3	Lab
399 Knowsley	-0.4	Lab		451 Norfolk South	-1.3	Con
400 Rotherham	-0.4	Lab		452 Glasgow Central	-1.4	Lab
401 Nottingham South	-0.4	Lab		453 Bootle	-1.4	Lab
402 Dagenham & Rainham	-0.4	Lab		454 Edmonton	-1.5	Lab
				455 Hazel Grove	-1.5	LD

Constituency	%change	1st		Constituency	%change	1st
Liberal Democrat				**Liberal Democrat**		
456 Totnes	-1.5	Con		511 Barking	-2.6	Lab
457 Greenwich & Woolwich	-1.5	Lab		512 Doncaster Central	-2.6	Lab
458 Hampshire N. W.	-1.5	Con		513 Uxbridge & Ruislip S.	-2.7	Con
459 Wigan	-1.5	Lab		514 Liverpool West Derby	-2.7	Lab
460 Hampshire N. E.	-1.6	Con		515 Chester, City of	-2.7	Con
461 Oxford East	-1.6	Lab		516 Liverpool Walton	-2.7	Lab
462 Arfon	-1.7	PC		517 Hemsworth	-2.8	Lab
463 Stevenage	-1.7	Con		518 Poplar & Limehouse	-2.8	Lab
464 Hendon	-1.7	Con		519 Ipswich	-2.9	Con
465 Mole Valley	-1.7	Con		520 Feltham & Heston	-2.9	Lab
466 Bromley & Chislehurst	-1.8	Con		521 New Forest East	-3.0	Con
467 Bolton West	-1.8	Lab		522 Pendle	-3.0	Con
468 Southampton Test	-1.8	Lab		523 Ealing C. & Acton	-3.0	Con
469 Waveney	-1.8	Con		524 Surrey Heath	-3.0	Con
470 Islwyn	-1.8	Lab		525 Dundee West	-3.0	Lab
471 Swansea East	-1.8	Lab		526 Edinburgh S. West	-3.0	Lab
472 Birmingham Hall Green	-1.8	Lab		527 Hammersmith	-3.0	Lab
473 Derbyshire Dales	-1.9	Con		528 Bolton N. E.	-3.1	Lab
474 Ochil & S. Perthshire	-1.9	Lab		529 Dunbartonshire E.	-3.1	LD
475 Warwickshire N.	-1.9	Con		530 Filton & Bradley Stoke	-3.1	Con
476 Birmingham Ladywood	-1.9	Lab		531 Witney	-3.1	Con
477 Bedford	-2.0	Con		532 Halton	-3.2	Lab
478 Banff & Buchan	-2.0	SNP		533 Islington N.	-3.2	Lab
479 Bolsover	-2.0	Lab		534 Croydon N.	-3.2	Lab
480 Barnsley Central	-2.0	Lab		535 Ealing Southall	-3.3	Lab
481 Ribble Valley	-2.1	Con		536 Airdrie & Shotts	-3.4	Lab
482 Carmarthen W. &				537 Brentwood & Ongar	-3.4	Con
Pembrokeshire S.	-2.1	Con		538 Newcastle upon Tyne C.	-3.4	Lab
483 Mitcham & Morden	-2.1	Lab		539 Harborough	-3.5	Con
484 Plymouth Moor View	-2.1	Lab		540 Hampshire East	-3.5	Con
485 Hertfordshire S. W.	-2.1	Con		541 Coatbridge, Chryston &		
486 Vauxhall	-2.1	Lab		Bellshill	-3.6	Lab
487 Leeds N. E.	-2.1	Lab		542 Ilford S.	-3.6	Lab
488 Durham, City of	-2.1	Lab		543 Inverclyde	-3.6	Lab
489 Birmingham Hodge Hill	-2.1	Lab		544 Newton Abbot	-3.6	Con
490 Oldham W. & Royton	-2.1	Lab		545 Penistone & Stocksbridge	-3.7	Lab
491 Saffron Walden	-2.2	Con		546 Crewe & Nantwich	-3.7	Con
492 Slough	-2.2	Lab		547 Leicester S.	-3.7	Lab
493 Motherwell & Wishaw	-2.2	Lab		548 Derby S.	-3.7	Lab
494 Brighton Pavilion	-2.2	Grn		549 Kirkcaldy & Cowdenbeath	-3.7	Lab
495 Bolton S. E.	-2.2	Lab		550 Glasgow N. W.	-3.7	Lab
496 Leicester East	-2.3	Lab		551 Copeland	-3.7	Lab
497 Hereford & Herefordshire S.	-2.3	Con		552 Perth & N. Perthshire	-3.8	SNP
498 Romsey & Southampton N.	-2.4	Con		553 Kilmarnock & Loudoun	-3.8	Lab
499 Delyn	-2.4	Lab		554 Richmond Park	-3.8	Con
500 Thornbury & Yate	-2.4	LD		555 Blyth Valley	-3.9	Lab
501 Beaconsfield	-2.4	Con		556 Hampstead & Kilburn	-4.0	Lab
502 Llanelli	-2.5	Lab		557 Guildford	-4.0	Con
503 Wakefield	-2.5	Lab		558 Jarrow	-4.0	Lab
504 Birmingham Yardley	-2.5	LD		559 Oxford W. & Abingdon	-4.1	Con
505 Brent N.	-2.5	Lab		560 Birmingham Perry Barr	-4.1	Lab
506 Linlithgow & Falkirk E.	-2.5	Lab		561 Ayrshire Central	-4.1	Lab
507 Harrow West	-2.5	Lab		562 Islington S. & Finsbury	-4.2	Lab
508 Hyndburn	-2.6	Lab		563 Livingston	-4.3	Lab
509 Stockton N.	-2.6	Lab		564 Devon Central	-4.4	Con
510 Glasgow S. W.	-2.6	Lab		565 Luton N.	-4.5	Lab

Constituency	%change	1st

Liberal Democrat

566	St Austell & Newquay	-4.5	LD
567	Wokingham	-4.7	Con
568	Moray	-4.7	SNP
569	Windsor	-4.7	Con
570	Esher & Walton	-4.7	Con
571	Eltham	-4.7	Lab
572	Tooting	-4.8	Lab
573	Ayr, Carrick & Cumnock	-4.8	Lab
574	Dorset Mid & Poole N.	-4.9	LD
575	Argyll & Bute	-4.9	LD
576	Blackley & Broughton	-4.9	Lab
577	South Shields	-5.0	Lab
578	Edinburgh East	-5.0	Lab
579	Glenrothes	-5.0	Lab
580	Wirral South	-5.0	Lab
581	Aberdeen South	-5.1	Lab
582	Cumbernauld, Kilsyth & Kirkintilloch E.	-5.3	Lab
583	Aberdeen N.	-5.3	Lab
584	Blackburn	-5.4	Lab
585	Cambridge	-5.6	LD
586	Falkirk	-5.7	Lab
587	Westminster N.	-5.7	Lab
588	Ealing N.	-6.0	Lab
589	Ross, Skye & Lochaber	-6.1	LD
590	Rochdale	-6.1	Lab
591	Stirling	-6.2	Lab
592	Dunbartonshire W.	-6.3	Lab
593	Rutherglen & Hamilton W.	-6.4	Lab
594	Ayrshire N. & Arran	-6.4	Lab
595	Liverpool Wavertree	-6.4	Lab
596	St Helens S. & Whiston	-6.6	Lab
597	East Kilbride, Strathaven & Lesmahagow	-6.6	Lab
598	Angus	-6.7	SNP
599	Glasgow East	-6.8	Lab
600	Winchester	-7.0	Con
601	Newbury	-7.1	Con
602	Glasgow South	-7.2	Lab
603	Lanark & Hamilton E.	-7.4	Lab
604	Bradford West	-7.4	Lab
605	Paisley & Renfrewshire N.	-7.7	Lab
606	Barrow & Furness	-7.8	Lab
607	Fife N. E.	-7.8	LD
608	Aberdeenshire W. & Kincardine	-7.9	LD
609	Ludlow	-7.9	Con
610	East Lothian	-8.0	Lab
611	Maidenhead	-8.0	Con
612	Paisley & Renfrewshire S.	-8.1	Lab
613	Cornwall South East	-8.1	Con
614	Harrogate & Knaresborough	-8.3	Con
615	Cardiff Central	-8.4	LD
616	Meon Valley	-8.4	Con
617	Blaydon	-8.5	Lab
618	Berwick-upon-Tweed	-8.9	LD

Liberal Democrat

619	Gordon	-9.0	LD
620	Renfrewshire East	-9.0	Lab
621	Caithness, Sutherland & Easter Ross	-9.1	LD
622	St Ives	-9.1	LD
623	Midlothian	-9.1	Lab
624	Chesterfield	-9.1	Lab
625	Surrey South West	-9.2	Con
626	Garston & Halewood	-9.9	Lab
627	Haltemprice & Howden	-10.0	Con
628	Montgomeryshire	-12.5	Con
629	Hartlepool	-13.3	Lab
630	Edinburgh West	-13.6	LD
631	Orpington	-15.9	Con

Scottish National

1	Falkirk	8.9	Lab
2	Ayrshire N. & Arran	8.0	Lab
3	Glasgow East	7.7	Lab
4	Glasgow South	7.5	Lab
5	Ayrshire Central	7.5	Lab
6	Airdrie & Shotts	7.0	Lab
7	Gordon	6.2	LD
8	Perth & N. Perthshire	5.9	SNP
9	Angus	5.9	SNP
10	Caithness, Sutherland & Easter Ross	5.8	LD
11	Ross, Skye & Lochaber	5.5	LD
12	Inverness, Nairn, Badenoch & Strathspey	5.2	LD
13	East Kilbride, Strathaven & Lesmahagow	5.1	Lab
14	Ayr, Carrick & Cumnock	4.9	Lab
15	Dunbartonshire East	4.7	LD
16	Stirling	4.7	Lab
17	Aberdeenshire W. & Kincardine	4.4	LD
18	Livingston	4.4	Lab
19	Edinburgh West	4.1	LD
20	Fife North East	3.8	LD
21	Midlothian	3.7	Lab
22	Argyll & Bute	3.4	LD
23	Edinburgh East	3.4	Lab
24	Coatbridge, Chryston & Bellshill	3.3	Lab
25	Lanark & Hamilton E.	3.2	Lab
26	Moray	3.1	SNP
27	East Lothian	2.9	Lab
28	Glasgow Central	2.7	Lab
29	Rutherglen & Hamilton W.	2.2	Lab
30	Renfrewshire East	2.0	Lab
31	Aberdeen South	2.0	Lab
32	Linlithgow & Falkirk E.	1.9	Lab
33	Motherwell & Wishaw	1.7	Lab
34	Dumfriesshire, Clydesdale & Tweeddale	1.6	Con

Constituency	%change	1st
Scottish National		
35 Cumbernauld, Kilsyth & Kirkintilloch E.	1.6	Lab
36 Edinburgh South West	1.6	Lab
37 Glasgow North West	1.5	Lab
38 Edinburgh South	1.5	Lab
39 Glasgow South West	1.0	Lab
40 Na h-Eileanan an Iar (Western Isles)	0.8	SNP
41 Dundee East	0.6	SNP
42 Berwickshire, Roxburgh & Selkirk	0.6	LD
43 Paisley & Renfrewshire S.	0.5	Lab
44 Paisley & Renfrewshire N.	0.2	Lab
45 Orkney & Shetland	0.2	LD
46 Dumfries & Galloway	0.2	Lab
47 Aberdeen North	-0.1	Lab
48 Kirkcaldy & Cowdenbeath	-0.2	Lab
49 Edinburgh N. & Leith	-0.5	Lab
50 Glasgow North	-1.0	Lab
51 Dundee West	-1.2	Lab
52 Glenrothes	-1.6	Lab
53 Dunbartonshire W.	-1.6	Lab
54 Kilmarnock & Loudoun	-1.7	Lab
55 Inverclyde	-2.0	Lab
56 Ochil & S. Perthshire	-2.3	Lab
57 Glasgow North East	-3.5	Lab
58 Dunfermline & Fife W.	-8.3	Lab
59 Banff & Buchan	-9.9	SNP
Plaid Cymru		
1 Cynon Valley	6.8	Lab
2 Clwyd West	4.5	Con
3 Arfon	3.9	PC
4 Aberconwy	3.8	Con
5 Llanelli	3.5	Lab
6 Neath	2.8	Lab
7 Rhondda	2.2	Lab
8 Blaenau Gwent	1.7	Lab
9 Montgomeryshire	1.3	Con
10 Islwyn	0.6	Lab
11 Monmouth	0.6	Con
12 Wrexham	0.4	Lab
13 Vale of Glamorgan	0.3	Con
14 Alyn & Deeside	0.2	Lab
15 Cardiff Central	-0.1	LD
16 Swansea East	-0.2	Lab
17 Ogmore	-0.6	Lab
18 Newport West	-0.8	Lab
19 Clwyd South	-0.8	Lab
20 Torfaen	-0.9	Lab
21 Cardiff North	-0.9	Con
22 Bridgend	-1.0	Lab
23 Cardiff South & Penarth	-1.1	Lab
24 Brecon & Radnorshire	-1.1	LD
25 Gower	-1.2	Lab

Constituency	%change	1st
Plaid Cymru		
26 Vale of Clwyd	-1.4	Lab
27 Caerphilly	-1.4	Lab
28 Newport East	-1.7	Lab
29 Delyn	-2.4	Lab
30 Swansea West	-2.5	Lab
31 Preseli Pembrokeshire	-3.3	Con
32 Pontypridd	-3.7	Lab
33 Aberavon	-4.7	Lab
34 Merthyr Tydfil & Rhymney	-4.9	Lab
35 Ynys Mon	-4.9	Lab
36 Carmarthen W.& Pembrokeshire S.	-5.1	Con
37 Cardiff West	-5.9	Lab
38 Dwyfor Meirionnydd	-6.4	PC
39 Ceredigion	-7.6	LD
40 Carmarthen E. & Dinefwr	-10.2	PC
Democratic Unionist		
1 Tyrone West	2.0	SF
2 Foyle	-2.5	SDLP
3 Belfast West	-3.0	SF
4 Upper Bann	-3.7	DUP
5 Antrim East	-3.8	DUP
6 Antrim South	-4.3	DUP
7 Belfast South	-4.7	SDLP
8 Lagan Valley	-4.9	DUP
9 Newry & Armagh	-5.5	SF
10 Belfast North	-5.6	DUP
11 Londonderry East	-8.3	DUP
12 Antrim North	-8.4	DUP
13 Ulster Mid	-9.1	SF
14 Down South	-9.7	SDLP
15 Strangford	-10.6	DUP
16 Belfast East	-16.4	APNI
APNI		
1 Belfast East	25.1	APNI
2 Belfast South	8.7	SDLP
3 Belfast North	3.5	DUP
4 Londonderry East	2.9	DUP
5 Lagan Valley	1.3	DUP
6 Upper Bann	0.8	DUP
7 Antrim North	0.3	DUP
8 Down South	0.0	SDLP
9 Strangford	-0.3	DUP
10 Antrim South	-1.0	DUP
11 Down North	-2.0	Ind
12 Antrim East	-4.3	DUP

Contd..../

Constituency	%change	1st
SDLP		
1 Belfast South	8.7	SDLP
2 Tyrone West	4.9	SF
3 Down South	3.7	SDLP
4 Belfast West	1.8	SF
5 Antrim East	1.3	DUP
6 Strangford	-0.1	DUP
7 Upper Bann	-0.2	DUP
8 Lagan Valley	-1.1	DUP
9 Down North	-1.1	Ind
10 Foyle	-1.6	SDLP
11 Londonderry East	-1.7	DUP
12 Belfast East	-1.7	APNI
13 Newry & Armagh	-1.7	SF
14 Ulster Mid	-3.2	SF
15 Antrim North	-3.3	DUP
16 Antrim South	-3.7	DUP
17 Belfast North	-3.9	DUP
18 Fermanagh & S. Tyrone	-7.2	SF
UCUNF (vs. UUP+Con, 2005)		
1 Tyrone West	7.3	SF
2 Newry & Armagh	5.2	SF
3 Strangford	2.6	DUP
4 Antrim South	1.3	DUP
5 Belfast West	0.9	SF
6 Foyle	0.8	SDLP
7 Belfast North	0.6	DUP
8 Ulster Mid	0.4	SF
9 Upper Bann	0.1	DUP
10 Lagan Valley	-0.4	DUP
11 Down South	-2.6	SDLP
12 Antrim East	-3.0	DUP
13 Londonderry East	-3.3	DUP
14 Antrim North	-3.5	DUP
15 Belfast South	-5.4	SDLP
16 Belfast East	-10.3	APNI
17 Down North	-32.6	Ind

Table 18. Seats in Rank Order of Party Highest Share of Vote

	Constituency	%share		Constituency	%share
Conservative			**Labour**		
1	Richmond (Yorks)	62.8	1	Liverpool Walton	72.0
2	Beaconsfield	61.1	2	Knowsley	70.9
3	Windsor	60.8	3	East Ham	70.4
4	Hampshire North East	60.6	4	Glasgow North East	68.3
5	Chelsea & Fulham	60.5	5	Coatbridge, Chryston & Bellshill	66.6
6	Chesham & Amersham	60.4	6	Bootle	66.4
7	Maldon	59.8	7	Kirkcaldy & Cowdenbeath	64.5
8	Orpington	59.7	8	Liverpool West Derby	64.1
9	Maidenhead	59.5	9	West Ham	62.7
10	Aldridge-Brownhills	59.3	10	Birkenhead	62.5
11	South Holland & The Deepings	59.1	11	Glasgow South West	62.5
12	Esher & Walton	58.9	12	Glenrothes	62.3
13	New Forest West	58.8	13	Glasgow East	61.6
14	Witney	58.8	14	Dunbartonshire West	61.3
15	Broxbourne	58.8	15	Motherwell & Wishaw	61.1
16	Surrey South West	58.7	16	Rutherglen & Hamilton West	60.8
17	Hampshire North West	58.3	17	Paisley & Renfrewshire South	59.6
18	Tonbridge & Malling	57.9	18	Garston & Halewood	59.5
19	Beckenham	57.9	19	Tottenham	59.3
20	Rayleigh & Wickford	57.8	20	Liverpool Riverside	59.3
21	Arundel & South Downs	57.8	21	Camberwell & Peckham	59.2
22	Surrey Heath	57.6	22	Easington	58.9
23	Mole Valley	57.5	23	Airdrie & Shotts	58.2
24	Ruislip, Northwood & Pinner	57.5	24	Halton	57.7
25	Welwyn Hatfield	57.0	25	Cumbernauld, Kilsyth & Kirkintilloch East	57.2
26	Brentwood & Ongar	56.9	26	Mitcham & Morden	56.4
27	Sevenoaks	56.8	27	Croydon North	56.0
28	Hampshire East	56.8	28	Inverclyde	56.0
29	Surrey East	56.7	29	Hackney South & Shoreditch	55.7
30	Wealden	56.6	30	Birmingham Ladywood	55.7
31	Daventry	56.5	31	Rhondda	55.3
32	Christchurch	56.4	32	Hackney North & Stoke Newington	55.0
33	Newbury	56.4	33	Sheffield Brightside & Hillsborough	55.0
34	Tunbridge Wells	56.2	34	Hayes & Harlington	54.8
35	Meon Valley	56.2	35	Islington North	54.5
36	Faversham & Kent Mid	56.2	36	Barking	54.3
37	Epsom & Ewell	56.2	37	Blackley & Broughton	54.3
38	Henley	56.2	38	Gateshead	54.1
39	Hertsmere	56.0	39	Glasgow North West	54.1
40	Romford	56.0	40	Paisley & Renfrewshire North	54.0
41	Devon South West	56.0	41	Jarrow	53.9
42	Runnymede & Weybridge	55.9	42	Ogmore	53.8
43	Bedfordshire North East	55.8	43	Leicester East	53.8
44	Saffron Walden	55.5	44	Lewisham Deptford	53.7
45	Chichester	55.3	45	Edmonton	53.7
46	Fareham	55.3	46	Liverpool Wavertree	53.1
47	Northamptonshire South	55.2	47	Warley	52.9
48	Devizes	55.1	48	St Helens South & Whiston	52.9
49	Hitchin & Harpenden	54.6	49	Manchester Central	52.7
50	Tatton	54.6	50	Kilmarnock & Loudoun	52.5

Constituency	%share	Constituency	%share
Liberal Democrat		**UKIP**	
1 Orkney & Shetland	62.0	1 Buckingham	17.4
2 Westmorland & Lonsdale	60.0	2 Boston & Skegness	9.5
3 Bath	56.6	3 Christchurch	8.5
4 Yeovil	55.7	4 Spelthorne	8.5
5 Norfolk North	55.5	5 Dudley North	8.5
6 Twickenham	54.4	6 Walsall South	8.4
7 Sheffield Hallam	53.4	7 Cambridgeshire North West	8.3
8 Ross, Skye & Lochaber	52.6	8 Dudley South	8.2
9 Lewes	52.0	9 Devon East	8.2
10 Thornbury & Yate	51.9	10 Staffordshire Moorlands	8.2
11 Cheltenham	50.5	11 Wentworth & Dearne	8.1
12 Ceredigion	50.0	12 Newcastle-under-Lyme	8.1
13 Kingston & Surbiton	49.8	13 Hull East	8.0
14 Southport	49.6	14 Wolverhampton South East	7.7
15 Taunton Deane	49.1	15 Plymouth Moor View	7.7
16 Hazel Grove	48.8	16 Thurrock	7.4
17 Bermondsey & Old Southwark	48.4	17 Devon North	7.2
18 Carshalton & Wallington	48.3	18 Bournemouth West	7.2
19 Cornwall North	48.1	19 Cleethorpes	7.1
20 Bristol West	48.0	20 Suffolk South	7.1
21 Colchester	48.0	21 Hartlepool	7.0
22 Somerton & Frome	47.5	22 Surrey East	6.9
23 Leeds North West	47.5	23 Bournemouth East	6.9
24 Devon North	47.4	24 Warley	6.8
25 Eastbourne	47.3	25 Chichester	6.8
26 Cheadle	47.1	26 Aylesbury	6.8
27 Torbay	47.0	27 Peterborough	6.7
28 Eastleigh	46.5	28 Ribble Valley	6.7
29 Hornsey & Wood Green	46.5	29 Thirsk & Malton	6.6
30 Brecon & Radnorshire	46.2	30 Runnymede & Weybridge	6.5
31 Portsmouth South	45.9	31 Witham	6.5
32 Chippenham	45.8	32 Thanet North	6.5
33 Sutton & Cheam	45.7	33 Plymouth Sutton & Devonport	6.5
34 Berwickshire, Roxburgh & Selkirk	45.4	34 Bognor Regis & Littlehampton	6.5
35 Redcar	45.2	35 South Holland & The Deepings	6.5
36 Dorset Mid & Poole North	45.1	36 Halesowen & Rowley Regis	6.4
37 Manchester Withington	44.7	37 Suffolk West	6.4
38 Fife North East	44.3	38 Newton Abbot	6.4
39 Brent Central	44.2	39 Orkney & Shetland	6.3
40 Wells	44.0	40 Surrey Heath	6.3
41 Harrogate & Knaresborough	43.8	41 Norfolk South West	6.2
42 Berwick-upon-Tweed	43.7	42 Cornwall South East	6.2
43 Winchester	43.1	43 Great Grimsby	6.2
44 Solihull	42.9	44 Devon South West	6.2
45 Richmond Park	42.8	45 Stoke-on-Trent North	6.2
46 St Austell & Newquay	42.7	46 Mansfield	6.2
47 St Ives	42.7	47 Worthing East & Shoreham	6.2
48 Oxford West & Abingdon	42.0	48 Bootle	6.1
49 Newton Abbot	41.9	49 Totnes	6.0
50 Cardiff Central	41.4	50 Wealden	6.0
51 Caithness, Sutherland & Easter Ross	41.4		

	Constituency	%share		Constituency	%share
BNP			**Scottish National**		
1	Barking	14.6	1	Na h-Eileanan an Iar (Western Isles)	45.7
2	Dagenham & Rainham	11.2	2	Banff & Buchan	41.3
3	Rotherham	10.4	3	Moray	39.7
4	Stoke-on-Trent South	9.4	4	Perth & North Perthshire	39.6
5	West Bromwich West	9.4	5	Angus	39.6
6	Burnley	9.0	6	Dundee East	37.8
7	Barnsley Central	8.9	7	Falkirk	30.3
8	Barnsley East	8.6	8	Dundee West	28.9
9	Normanton, Pontefract & Castleford	8.4	9	Ochil & South Perthshire	27.6
10	Leeds Central	8.2	10	Kilmarnock & Loudoun	26.0
11	Walsall North	8.1	11	Ayrshire North & Arran	25.9
12	Stoke-on-Trent North	8.0	12	Livingston	25.9
13	Thurrock	7.9	13	Linlithgow & Falkirk East	25.4
14	Leeds East	7.8	14	Glasgow East	24.7
15	Sheffield Brightside & Hillsborough	7.8	15	Cumbernauld, Kilsyth & Kirkintilloch East	23.8
16	Rother Valley	7.7	16	Airdrie & Shotts	23.5
17	Stoke-on-Trent Central	7.7	17	East Kilbride, Strathaven & Lesmahagow	23.0
18	Ashton Under Lyne	7.6	18	Aberdeen North	22.2
19	Wentworth & Dearne	7.6	19	Gordon	22.2
20	Makerfield	7.4	20	Glenrothes	21.7
21	Morley & Outwood	7.2	21	Lanark & Hamilton East	21.0
22	Blackley & Broughton	7.2	22	Midlothian	20.6
23	Batley & Spen	7.2	23	Edinburgh East	20.4
24	Oldham West & Royton	7.1	24	Glasgow South	20.1
25	Heywood & Middleton	7.0	25	Dunbartonshire West	20.1
26	Jarrow	7.0	26	Caithness, Sutherland & Easter Ross	19.2
27	Hemsworth	7.0	27	Paisley & Renfrewshire North	19.1
28	Bradford South	7.0	28	Ayrshire Central	19.0
29	Amber Valley	7.0	29	Argyll & Bute	18.9
30	Doncaster North	6.8	30	Inverness, Nairn, Badenoch & Strathspey	18.7
31	Newcastle upon Tyne Central	6.7	31	Motherwell & Wishaw	18.2
32	Easington	6.6	32	Paisley & Renfrewshire South	18.1
33	Wolverhampton North East	6.6	33	Ayr, Carrick & Cumnock	18.0
34	Leicestershire North West	6.5	34	Inverclyde	17.5
35	South Shields	6.5	35	Glasgow Central	17.5
36	Pendle	6.4	36	Stirling	17.3
37	Hornchurch & Upminster	6.4	37	Coatbridge, Chryston & Bellshill	16.8
38	Salford & Eccles	6.3	38	Glasgow South West	16.3
39	Halifax	6.3	39	Rutherglen & Hamilton West	16.1
40	Nuneaton	6.3	40	East Lothian	16.0
41	Leigh	6.1	41	Aberdeenshire West & Kincardine	15.7
42	Leeds West	6.1	42	Glasgow North West	15.3
43	Dewsbury	6.0	43	Ross, Skye & Lochaber	15.1
44	Leicester West	6.0	44	Kirkcaldy & Cowdenbeath	14.3
45	Bolsover	6.0	45	Fife North East	14.2
46	Middlesbrough	5.8	46	Glasgow North East	14.1
47	Charnwood	5.8	47	Edinburgh West	13.2
48	West Bromwich East	5.8	48	Dumfries & Galloway	12.3
49	Wakefield	5.8	49	Edinburgh South West	12.2
50	Ashfield	5.8			

Constituency	%share	Constituency	%share

Green

1	Brighton Pavilion	31.3
2	Norwich South	14.9
3	Cambridge	7.6
4	Lewisham Deptford	6.7
5	Brighton Kemptown	5.5
6	Hove	5.2
7	Edinburgh East	5.1
8	Leeds West	4.7
9	Hackney North & Stoke Newington	4.6
10	Lancaster & Fleetwood	4.4
11	Bury St Edmunds	4.3
12	Witney	4.1
13	Huddersfield	4.0
14	Bristol West	3.8
15	Sheffield Central	3.8
16	York Central	3.6
17	Liverpool Riverside	3.5
18	Hackney South & Shoreditch	3.5
19	Herefordshire North	3.2
20	Glasgow North	3.2
21	Down North	3.1
22	Belfast South	3.0
23	Witham	3.0
24	Islington North	3.0
25	Shipley	3.0
26	Norwich North	2.9
27	Camberwell & Peckham	2.9
28	Norfolk Mid	2.9
29	St Ives	2.8
30	Richmond (Yorks)	2.8
31	Nottingham East	2.8
32	Manchester Gorton	2.7
33	Suffolk Central & Ipswich North	2.7
34	Holborn & St Pancras	2.7
35	Stroud	2.7
36	Dulwich & West Norwood	2.6
37	Glasgow Central	2.6
38	Ilford South	2.6
39	Greenwich & Woolwich	2.6
40	Wealden	2.5
41	Bristol South	2.5
42	Henley	2.5
43	Glasgow North West	2.5
44	Totnes	2.5
45	Sheffield Heeley	2.4
46	Tottenham	2.4
47	Birmingham Ladywood	2.4
48	Glasgow South	2.4
49	Oxford East	2.4
50	Bath	2.4

Plaid Cymru

1	Dwyfor Meirionnydd	44.3
2	Arfon	36.0
3	Carmarthen East & Dinefwr	35.6
4	Llanelli	29.9
5	Ceredigion	28.3
6	Ynys Mon	26.2
7	Cynon Valley	20.3
8	Neath	19.9
9	Rhondda	18.1
10	Aberconwy	17.8
11	Caerphilly	16.7
12	Clwyd West	15.4
13	Islwyn	13.0
14	Carmarthen West & Pembrokeshire South	10.4
15	Ogmore	9.6
16	Preseli Pembrokeshire	9.2
17	Clwyd South	8.7
18	Montgomeryshire	8.3
19	Pontypridd	7.3
20	Aberavon	7.1
21	Cardiff West	7.0
22	Swansea East	6.7
23	Gower	6.6
24	Wrexham	6.2
25	Bridgend	5.9
26	Vale of Clwyd	5.8
27	Vale of Glamorgan	5.5
28	Torfaen	5.3
29	Merthyr Tydfil & Rhymney	5.1
30	Delyn	5.0
31	Cardiff South & Penarth	4.2
32	Blaenau Gwent	4.1
33	Swansea West	4.0
34	Alyn & Deeside	3.9
35	Cardiff Central	3.4
36	Cardiff North	3.3
37	Newport West	2.8
38	Monmouth	2.7
39	Brecon & Radnorshire	2.5
40	Newport East	2.1

English Democrat

1	Doncaster North	5.2
2	Rochester & Strood	4.5
3	Doncaster Central	4.4
4	Dartford	4.3
5	Rayleigh & Wickford	4.2
6	Don Valley	4.0
7	Worsley & Eccles South	3.2
8	Haltemprice & Howden	3.0
9	West Bromwich East	3.0
10	Stockton North	2.9
11	Hull West & Hessle	2.8

Constituency	%share	Constituency	%share
English Democrat		**Christian**	
12 Chesterfield	2.6	1 Inverness, Nairn, Badenoch &	
13 Cambridgeshire North West	2.4	Strathspey	1.8
14 Portsmouth North	2.4	2 Birmingham Perry Barr	1.2
15 Daventry	2.3	3 Walsall South	1.2
16 Ashfield	2.3	4 Ealing Southall	1.2
17 Gravesham	2.1	5 Croydon North	1.1
18 Hull East	2.1	6 Brent Central	1.1
19 Kettering	2.0	7 Greenwich & Woolwich	1.1
20 Havant	1.8	8 Barking	1.1
21 Isle of Wight	1.8	9 Slough	1.0
22 Peterborough	1.7	10 Aldridge-Brownhills	1.0
23 East Ham	1.6	11 Hackney South & Shoreditch	1.0
24 Sevenoaks	1.6	12 Pontypridd	1.0
25 Northampton South	1.6	13 Ealing North	0.9
26 Salford & Eccles	1.5	14 Edmonton	0.9
27 Rossendale & Darwen	1.4	15 Leyton & Wanstead	0.9
28 Hampshire East	1.4	16 Horsham	0.8
29 Broxbourne	1.4	17 Preston	0.8
30 Gosport	1.3	18 Buckingham	0.8
31 Lincoln	1.3	19 Dagenham & Rainham	0.7
32 Selby & Ainsty	1.3	20 Manchester Gorton	0.7
33 Romford	1.3	21 Tottenham	0.6
34 Bedfordshire Mid	1.3	22 Hackney North & Stoke Newington	0.6
35 Chester, City of	1.3	23 Cardiff South & Penarth	0.6
36 Bristol North West	1.3	24 Cardiff North	0.6
37 Southend West	1.3	25 Clwyd West	0.6
38 Northamptonshire South	1.2	26 Ealing Central & Acton	0.6
39 Dewsbury	1.2	27 Worthing West	0.6
40 Sheffield Hallam	1.1	28 Birmingham Erdington	0.6
41 Old Bexley & Sidcup	1.1	29 Walthamstow	0.6
42 Fareham	1.1	30 Stockton South	0.6
43 Meon Valley	1.1	31 Thurrock	0.6
44 Bosworth	1.1	32 Brecon & Radnorshire	0.6
45 Gloucester	1.1	33 Croydon Central	0.5
46 Erith & Thamesmead	1.1	34 Bath	0.5
47 Hayes & Harlington	1.1	35 Hornchurch & Upminster	0.5
48 Bexleyheath & Crayford	1.1	36 Aldershot	0.5
49 Penistone & Stocksbridge	1.1	37 Tamworth	0.5
50 Workington	1.1	38 Streatham	0.5
		39 Wimbledon	0.5
Respect		40 Sheffield Hallam	0.5
		41 Vale of Glamorgan	0.5
1 Birmingham Hall Green	25.1	42 Oldham East & Saddleworth	0.5
2 Poplar & Limehouse	17.5	43 Ynys Mon	0.5
3 Bethnal Green & Bow	16.8	44 Blackley & Broughton	0.5
4 Bradford West	3.1	45 Vauxhall	0.5
5 Blackley & Broughton	2.9	46 Aberconwy	0.5
6 Oldham West & Royton	1.5	47 Filton & Bradley Stoke	0.4
7 Manchester Gorton	1.3	48 Walsall North	0.4
8 Garston & Halewood	0.6	49 Stretford & Urmston	0.4
9 Croydon North	0.5	50 Ruislip, Northwood & Pinner	0.4
10 Brent Central	0.5		
11 Enfield Southgate	0.4		

Constituency	%share		Constituency	%share

TUSC

1	Glasgow South West	2.9
2	Tottenham	2.6
3	Salford & Eccles	1.8
4	Sheffield Brightside & Hillsborough	1.7
5	Motherwell & Wishaw	1.6
6	Colne Valley	1.3
7	Bootle	1.1
8	Glasgow North	1.0
9	Dundee West	1.0
10	Carlisle	0.9
11	Manchester Gorton	0.9
12	Glasgow South	0.9
13	Huddersfield	0.8
14	Gateshead	0.7
15	Edinburgh East	0.7
16	Walthamstow	0.7
17	Wythenshawe & Sale East	0.7
18	Greenwich & Woolwich	0.6
19	Glasgow North East	0.6
20	Liverpool Walton	0.6
21	Swansea West	0.5
22	Edinburgh North & Leith	0.5
23	Wellingborough	0.5
24	Hull West & Hessle	0.5
25	Brighton Kemptown	0.5
26	Cardiff Central	0.4
27	Leicester West	0.4
28	Doncaster North	0.4
29	Bristol South	0.4
30	Midlothian	0.4
31	Stoke-on-Trent Central	0.4
32	Bristol East	0.4
33	Southampton Itchen	0.4
34	Spelthorne	0.4
35	Portsmouth North	0.3
36	Redcar	0.3
37	Inverness, Nairn, Badenoch & Strathspey	0.3

National Front

1	Rochdale	4.9
2	Hull East	2.6
3	West Ham	2.3
4	Rossendale & Darwen	2.3
5	Ruislip, Northwood & Pinner	1.8
6	Hayes & Harlington	1.3
7	Maidstone & The Weald	1.3
8	Tyneside North	1.3
9	Faversham & Kent Mid	1.2
10	Montgomeryshire	1.1
11	Tonbridge & Malling	1.0
12	Birmingham Yardley	0.9
13	Birmingham Erdington	0.6
14	Uxbridge & Ruislip South	0.6
15	Bradford East	0.5

MRLP

1	Buckingham	1.8
2	Huntingdon	1.0
3	Cheltenham	0.9
4	Faversham & Kent Mid	0.9
5	Surrey East	0.8
6	Sittingbourne & Sheppey	0.7
7	Esher & Walton	0.6
8	Wokingham	0.6
9	Tewkesbury	0.6
10	Amber Valley	0.6
11	Brecon & Radnorshire	0.5
12	Blackpool North & Cleveleys	0.5
13	Derbyshire Dales	0.5
14	Sussex Mid	0.5
15	Derbyshire Mid	0.5
16	Kingston & Surbiton	0.4
17	Witney	0.4
18	Dorset North	0.4
19	Cardiff Central	0.4
20	Hackney North & Stoke Newington	0.4
21	Croydon Central	0.4
22	Ludlow	0.4
23	Old Bexley & Sidcup	0.3
24	York Central	0.3
25	Sheffield Hallam	0.3
26	Milton Keynes North	0.3
27	Barking	0.2

Socialist Labour

1	Liverpool West Derby	1.7
2	Barnsley East	1.6
3	Birmingham Perry Barr	1.3
4	Pontypridd	1.2
5	Dunbartonshire West	1.2
6	Blaenau Gwent	1.2
7	St Helens North	1.1
8	Ayrshire North & Arran	1.0
9	Wolverhampton North East	1.0
10	Barnsley Central	1.0
11	Ayrshire Central	1.0
12	Merthyr Tydfil & Rhymney	0.6
13	Glasgow North East	0.5
14	Derbyshire South	0.5
15	Liverpool Wavertree	0.5
16	Plymouth Moor View	0.5
17	Camborne & Redruth	0.4
18	Camberwell & Peckham	0.4
19	Manchester Central	0.4
20	Newport East	0.4
21	Edinburgh North & Leith	0.3
22	Brighton Pavilion	0.3
23	Plymouth Sutton & Devonport	0.3

	Constituency	%share		Constituency	%share
Liberal			**Sinn Fein**		
1	Liverpool West Derby	9.3	15	Strangford	3.6
2	Thirsk & Malton	3.7	16	Belfast East	2.4
3	Exeter	2.1	17	Down North	.7
4	Hackney South & Shoreditch	1.3			
5	Edinburgh North & Leith	0.8	**Democratic Unionist**		
			1	Lagan Valley	49.8
CPA			2	Antrim North	46.4
			3	Strangford	45.9
1	West Ham	2.8	4	Antrim East	45.9
2	Hyndburn	1.9	5	Belfast North	40.0
3	Lewisham Deptford	1.2	6	Londonderry East	34.6
4	Ilford North	1.0	7	Antrim South	33.9
5	Erith & Thamesmead	0.9	8	Upper Bann	33.8
6	Liverpool Walton	0.9	9	Belfast East	32.8
7	Cambridgeshire South East	0.8	10	Belfast South	23.7
8	Suffolk West	0.8	11	Tyrone West	19.8
9	Lewisham West & Penge	0.7	12	Ulster Mid	14.4
10	Bolton South East	0.5	13	Newry & Armagh	12.8
11	Milton Keynes South	0.4	14	Foyle	11.8
12	Dover	0.4	15	Down South	8.6
13	Kingston & Surbiton	0.4	16	Belfast West	7.6
14	Milton Keynes North	0.4			
15	Richmond Park	0.2	**SDLP**		
16	Brentford & Isleworth	0.2			
17	Sutton & Cheam	0.1	1	Down South	48.5
			2	Foyle	44.7
SSP			3	Belfast South	41.0
			4	Newry & Armagh	23.4
1	Glasgow East	1.4	5	Belfast West	16.4
2	Glasgow Central	1.2	6	Londonderry East	15.4
3	Cumbernauld, Kilsyth &		7	Ulster Mid	14.3
	Kirkintilloch East	1.2	8	Tyrone West	14.0
4	Paisley & Renfrewshire South	0.9	9	Upper Bann	12.7
5	Aberdeen North	0.7	10	Belfast North	12.3
6	Edinburgh South West	0.7	11	Antrim North	8.8
7	Dundee East	0.6	12	Antrim South	8.7
8	Glasgow North East	0.6	13	Fermanagh & South Tyrone	7.6
9	Paisley & Renfrewshire North	0.5	14	Strangford	6.7
10	Livingston	0.5	15	Antrim East	6.6
			16	Lagan Valley	5.0
Sinn Fein			17	Down North	2.0
			18	Belfast East	1.1
1	Belfast West	71.1			
2	Ulster Mid	52.0	**UCUNF**		
3	Tyrone West	48.4			
4	Fermanagh & South Tyrone	45.5	1	Antrim South	30.4
5	Newry & Armagh	42.0	2	Strangford	27.8
6	Belfast North	34.0	3	Upper Bann	25.7
7	Foyle	31.9	4	Antrim East	23.7
8	Down South	28.7	5	Belfast East	21.2
9	Upper Bann	24.7	6	Lagan Valley	21.1
10	Londonderry East	19.3	7	Down North	20.4
11	Antrim South	13.9	8	Newry & Armagh	19.1
12	Antrim North	12.4	9	Londonderry East	17.8
13	Antrim East	6.8	10	Belfast South	17.3
14	Lagan Valley	4.0			

Constituency		%share

UCUNF

11	Tyrone West	14.2
12	Ulster Mid	11.0
13	Antrim North	10.9
14	Belfast North	7.7
15	Down South	7.3
16	Foyle	3.2
17	Belfast West	3.1

APNI

1	Belfast East	37.2
2	Belfast South	15.0
3	Lagan Valley	11.4
4	Antrim East	11.1
5	Strangford	8.7
6	Antrim South	7.7
7	Down North	5.6
8	Londonderry East	5.5
9	Belfast North	4.9
10	Antrim North	3.2
11	Upper Bann	3.0
12	Tyrone West	2.3
13	Belfast West	1.9
14	Down South	1.3
15	Newry & Armagh	1.2
16	Ulster Mid	1.0
17	Fermanagh & South Tyrone	.9
18	Foyle	.6

TUV

1	Antrim North	16.8
2	Lagan Valley	8.6
3	Londonderry East	7.4
4	Ulster Mid	7.3
5	Antrim East	6.0
6	Strangford	5.6
7	Belfast East	5.4
8	Antrim South	5.4
9	Down North	4.9
10	Down South	3.5

Table 19. Seats in Rank Order of Winning Party's Share of Vote

	Constituency	%share	1st		Constituency	%share	1st
1	Liverpool Walton	72.0	Lab	53	Cumbernauld, Kilsyth &		
2	Belfast West	71.1	SF		Kirkintilloch E.	57.2	Lab
3	Knowsley	70.9	Lab	54	Welwyn Hatfield	57.0	Con
4	East Ham	70.4	Lab	55	Brentwood & Ongar	56.9	Con
5	Glasgow North East	68.3	Lab	56	Sevenoaks	56.8	Con
6	Coatbridge, Chryston &			57	Hampshire East	56.8	Con
	Bellshill	66.6	Lab	58	Surrey East	56.7	Con
7	Bootle	66.4	Lab	59	Bath	56.6	LD
8	Kirkcaldy & Cowdenbeath	64.5	Lab	60	Wealden	56.6	Con
9	Liverpool West Derby	64.1	Lab	61	Daventry	56.5	Con
10	Down North	63.3	Ind	62	Mitcham & Morden	56.4	Lab
11	Richmond (Yorks)	62.8	Con	63	Christchurch	56.4	Con
12	West Ham	62.7	Lab	64	Newbury	56.4	Con
13	Birkenhead	62.5	Lab	65	Tunbridge Wells	56.2	Con
14	Glasgow South West	62.5	Lab	66	Meon Valley	56.2	Con
15	Glenrothes	62.3	Lab	67	Faversham & Kent Mid	56.2	Con
16	Orkney & Shetland	62.0	LD	68	Epsom & Ewell	56.2	Con
17	Glasgow East	61.6	Lab	69	Henley	56.2	Con
18	Dunbartonshire West	61.3	Lab	70	Croydon North	56.0	Lab
19	Motherwell & Wishaw	61.1	Lab	71	Hertsmere	56.0	Con
20	Beaconsfield	61.1	Con	72	Romford	56.0	Con
21	Windsor	60.8	Con	73	Devon South West	56.0	Con
22	Rutherglen & Hamilton W.	60.8	Lab	74	Inverclyde	56.0	Lab
23	Hampshire North East	60.6	Con	75	Runnymede & Weybridge	55.9	Con
24	Chelsea & Fulham	60.5	Con	76	Bedfordshire North East	55.8	Con
25	Chesham & Amersham	60.4	Con	77	Hackney South & Shoreditch	55.7	Lab
26	Westmorland & Lonsdale	60.0	LD	78	Yeovil	55.7	LD
27	Maldon	59.8	Con	79	Birmingham Ladywood	55.7	Lab
28	Orpington	59.7	Con	80	Norfolk North	55.5	LD
29	Paisley & Renfrewshire S.	59.6	Lab	81	Saffron Walden	55.5	Con
30	Garston & Halewood	59.5	Lab	82	Chichester	55.3	Con
31	Maidenhead	59.5	Con	83	Rhondda	55.3	Lab
32	Aldridge-Brownhills	59.3	Con	84	Fareham	55.3	Con
33	Tottenham	59.3	Lab	85	Northamptonshire South	55.2	Con
34	Liverpool Riverside	59.3	Lab	86	Devizes	55.1	Con
35	Camberwell & Peckham	59.2	Lab	87	Hackney N. & Stoke		
36	South Holland & The				Newington	55.0	Lab
	Deepings	59.1	Con	88	Sheffield Brightside &		
37	Easington	58.9	Lab		Hillsborough	55.0	Lab
38	Esher & Walton	58.9	Con	89	Hayes & Harlington	54.8	Lab
39	New Forest West	58.8	Con	90	Hitchin & Harpenden	54.6	Con
40	Witney	58.8	Con	91	Tatton	54.6	Con
41	Broxbourne	58.8	Con	92	Worcestershire Mid	54.5	Con
42	Surrey South West	58.7	Con	93	Islington North	54.5	Lab
43	Hampshire North West	58.3	Con	94	Lichfield	54.4	Con
44	Airdrie & Shotts	58.2	Lab	95	Twickenham	54.4	LD
45	Tonbridge & Malling	57.9	Con	96	Barking	54.3	Lab
46	Beckenham	57.9	Con	97	Blackley & Broughton	54.3	Lab
47	Rayleigh & Wickford	57.8	Con	98	Hertfordshire South West	54.2	Con
48	Arundel & South Downs	57.8	Con	99	Norfolk North West	54.2	Con
49	Halton	57.7	Lab	100	Ashford	54.1	Con
50	Surrey Heath	57.6	Con	101	Gateshead	54.1	Lab
51	Mole Valley	57.5	Con	102	Old Bexley & Sidcup	54.1	Con
52	Ruislip, Northwood & Pinner	57.5	Con	103	Glasgow North West	54.1	Lab

Constituency	%share	1st	Constituency	%share	1st
104 Paisley & Renfrewshire North	54.0	Lab	160 Thornbury & Yate	51.9	LD
105 Epping Forest	54.0	Con	161 Walthamstow	51.8	Lab
106 Sutton Coldfield	54.0	Con	162 Wallasey	51.8	Lab
107 Jarrow	53.9	Lab	163 Herefordshire North	51.8	Con
108 Newark	53.9	Con	164 Gosport	51.8	Con
109 Hertford & Stortford	53.8	Con	165 Worthing West	51.7	Con
110 Ogmore	53.8	Lab	166 Glasgow South	51.7	Lab
111 Leicester East	53.8	Lab	167 St Helens North	51.7	Lab
112 Lewisham Deptford	53.7	Lab	168 Eddisbury	51.7	Con
113 Edmonton	53.7	Lab	169 Meriden	51.7	Con
114 Kenilworth & Southam	53.6	Con	170 Wiltshire South West	51.7	Con
115 Hertfordshire North East	53.5	Con	171 Sleaford & North Hykeham	51.6	Con
116 Bromley & Chislehurst	53.5	Con	172 Cambridgeshire North East	51.6	Con
117 Sheffield Hallam	53.4	LD	173 Wiltshire North	51.6	Con
118 Reigate	53.4	Con	174 Bexhill & Battle	51.6	Con
119 Penrith & The Border	53.4	Con	175 Stratford-on-Avon	51.5	Con
120 Guildford	53.3	Con	176 Ealing Southall	51.5	Lab
121 Staffordshire South	53.2	Con	177 East Kilbride, Strathaven &		
122 Liverpool Wavertree	53.1	Lab	Lesmahagow	51.5	Lab
123 Clacton	53.0	Con	178 Devon Central	51.5	Con
124 Cotswolds, The	53.0	Con	179 Swansea East	51.5	Lab
125 Warley	52.9	Lab	180 Shropshire North	51.5	Con
126 Thirsk & Malton	52.9	Con	181 Hornchurch & Upminster	51.4	Con
127 St Helens South & Whiston	52.9	Lab	182 Bognor Regis & Littlehampton	51.4	Con
128 New Forest East	52.8	Con	183 Rushcliffe	51.2	Con
129 Banbury	52.8	Con	184 Rutland & Melton	51.1	Con
130 Bedfordshire South West	52.8	Con	185 Havant	51.1	Con
131 Ludlow	52.8	Con	186 Dorset North	51.1	Con
132 Chingford & Woodford Green	52.8	Con	187 Denton & Reddish	51.0	Lab
133 Manchester Central	52.7	Lab	188 Croydon South	50.9	Con
134 Basildon & Billericay	52.7	Con	189 Suffolk C. & Ipswich N.	50.8	Con
135 Horsham	52.7	Con	190 Renfrewshire East	50.8	Lab
136 Wokingham	52.7	Con	191 Sussex Mid	50.7	Con
137 Thanet North	52.7	Con	192 Tyneside North	50.7	Lab
138 Braintree	52.6	Con	193 Wentworth & Dearne	50.6	Lab
139 Ross, Skye & Lochaber	52.6	LD	194 Skipton & Ripon	50.6	Con
140 Kilmarnock & Loudoun	52.5	Lab	195 Stone	50.6	Con
141 Washington & Sunderland W.	52.5	Lab	196 Suffolk West	50.6	Con
142 Bedfordshire Mid	52.5	Con	197 Durham North	50.5	Lab
143 Cynon Valley	52.5	Lab	198 Basingstoke	50.5	Con
144 Bracknell	52.4	Con	199 Cheltenham	50.5	LD
145 Blaenau Gwent	52.4	Lab	200 Cambridgeshire North West	50.5	Con
146 Wyre & Preston North	52.4	Con	201 Bexleyheath & Crayford	50.5	Con
147 Fylde	52.2	Con	202 Bassetlaw	50.5	Lab
148 Witham	52.2	Con	203 Leeds East	50.4	Lab
149 Aylesbury	52.2	Con	204 Ealing North	50.4	Lab
150 Cities of London &			205 Houghton & Sunderland S.	50.3	Lab
Westminster	52.2	Con	206 Worcestershire West	50.3	Con
151 Derbyshire Dales	52.1	Con	207 Tiverton & Honiton	50.3	Con
152 Putney	52.0	Con	208 Woking	50.3	Con
153 Glasgow Central	52.0	Lab	209 Ribble Valley	50.3	Con
154 South Shields	52.0	Lab	210 Grantham & Stamford	50.3	Con
155 Lewes	52.0	LD	211 Birmingham Perry Barr	50.3	Lab
156 Ulster Mid	52.0	SF	212 Haltemprice & Howden	50.2	Con
157 Birmingham Hodge Hill	52.0	Lab	213 Manchester Gorton	50.1	Lab
158 Wantage	52.0	Con	214 Kensington	50.1	Con
159 Aberavon	51.9	Lab	215 Sittingbourne & Sheppey	50.0	Con

Constituency	%share	1st		Constituency	%share	1st
216 Ceredigion	50.0	LD		273 Norfolk South West	48.3	Con
217 Bolsover	50.0	Lab		274 Derbyshire Mid	48.3	Con
218 Hemel Hempstead	50.0	Con		275 Carshalton & Wallington	48.3	LD
219 Lanark & Hamilton East	50.0	Lab		276 Monmouth	48.3	Con
220 Linlithgow & Falkirk East	49.8	Lab		277 Uxbridge & Ruislip South	48.3	Con
221 Lagan Valley	49.8	DUP		278 Wellingborough	48.2	Con
222 Kingston & Surbiton	49.8	LD		279 Normanton, Pontefract &		
223 Vauxhall	49.8	Lab		Castleford	48.2	Lab
224 Romsey & Southampton N.	49.7	Con		280 Preston	48.2	Lab
225 Richmond Park	49.7	Con		281 Barrow & Furness	48.1	Lab
226 Blaydon	49.6	Lab		282 Cornwall North	48.1	LD
227 Louth & Horncastle	49.6	Con		283 Bristol West	48.0	LD
228 Southport	49.6	LD		284 Leigh	48.0	Lab
229 Charnwood	49.6	Con		285 Maidstone & The Weald	48.0	Con
230 Norfolk Mid	49.5	Con		286 Colchester	48.0	LD
231 Leicestershire South	49.5	Con		287 Thanet South	48.0	Con
232 Boston & Skegness	49.4	Con		288 Cambridgeshire South East	48.0	Con
233 Folkestone & Hythe	49.4	Con		289 Hull East	47.9	Lab
234 Enfield Southgate	49.4	Con		290 Blackburn	47.8	Lab
235 Ilford South	49.4	Lab		291 Suffolk South	47.7	Con
236 Selby & Ainsty	49.4	Con		292 Ayrshire Central	47.7	Lab
237 Norfolk South	49.3	Con		293 Wrekin, The	47.7	Con
238 Leeds Central	49.3	Lab		294 Dorset West	47.6	Con
239 Coventry North East	49.3	Lab		295 Wolverhampton South East	47.6	Lab
240 Somerset North	49.3	Con		296 Bury St Edmunds	47.5	Con
241 Gainsborough	49.3	Con		297 Somerton & Frome	47.5	LD
242 Luton North	49.3	Lab		298 Poole	47.5	Con
243 Salisbury	49.2	Con		299 Leeds North West	47.5	LD
244 Islwyn	49.2	Lab		300 Yorkshire East	47.5	Con
245 Rochester & Strood	49.2	Con		301 Bolton South East	47.4	Lab
246 Greenwich & Woolwich	49.2	Lab		302 Cambridgeshire South	47.4	Con
247 Kettering	49.1	Con		303 Ayrshire North & Arran	47.4	Lab
248 Wimbledon	49.1	Con		304 Devon North	47.4	LD
249 Taunton Deane	49.1	LD		305 Battersea	47.3	Con
250 Harborough	48.9	Con		306 Doncaster North	47.3	Lab
251 Altrincham & Sale West	48.9	Con		307 Eastbourne	47.3	LD
252 Huntingdon	48.9	Con		308 Buckingham	47.3	
253 Chipping Barnet	48.8	Con		Speaker		
254 Hazel Grove	48.8	LD		309 Makerfield	47.3	Lab
255 Dartford	48.8	Con		310 Barnsley Central	47.3	Lab
256 Sheffield South East	48.7	Lab		311 Tewkesbury	47.2	Con
257 Wycombe	48.6	Con		312 Ayr, Carrick & Cumnock	47.1	Lab
258 Stretford & Urmston	48.6	Lab		313 Beverley & Holderness	47.1	Con
259 Shipley	48.6	Con		314 Cheadle	47.1	LD
260 Nottingham North	48.6	Lab		315 Spelthorne	47.1	Con
261 Winchester	48.5	Con		316 Barnsley East	47.0	Lab
262 Gravesham	48.5	Con		317 Midlothian	47.0	Lab
263 Wigan	48.5	Lab		318 Torbay	47.0	LD
264 Down South	48.5	SDLP		319 Macclesfield	47.0	Con
265 Worthing East & Shoreham	48.5	Con		320 Harwich & Essex North	46.9	Con
266 Dundee West	48.5	Lab		321 Brent North	46.9	Lab
267 Livingston	48.5	Lab		322 Forest of Dean	46.9	Con
268 Bournemouth East	48.4	Con		323 Rochford & Southend East	46.9	Con
269 Tyrone West	48.4	SF		324 Hemsworth	46.8	Lab
270 Ashton Under Lyne	48.4	Lab		325 Aldershot	46.7	Con
271 Bermondsey & Old Southwark	48.4	LD		326 Isle of Wight	46.7	Con
272 Devon East	48.3	Con		327 Dulwich & West Norwood	46.6	Lab

Constituency	%share	1st	Constituency	%share	1st
328 Eastleigh	46.5	LD	383 Sedgefield	45.1	Lab
329 West Bromwich East	46.5	Lab	384 Dorset Mid & Poole North	45.1	LD
330 Hornsey & Wood Green	46.5	LD	385 Dorset South	45.1	Con
331 Suffolk Coastal	46.4	Con	386 Newcastle upon Tyne East	45.0	Lab
332 Antrim North	46.4	DUP	387 West Bromwich West	45.0	Lab
333 Neath	46.3	Lab	388 Caerphilly	44.9	Lab
334 Dunfermline & Fife West	46.3	Lab	389 Erith & Thamesmead	44.9	Lab
335 Hereford & Herefordshire S.	46.2	Con	390 Harlow	44.9	Con
336 Gillingham & Rainham	46.2	Con	391 Brigg & Goole	44.9	Con
337 Broadland	46.2	Con	392 Canterbury	44.8	Con
338 Chatham & Aylesford	46.2	Con	393 Crawley	44.8	Con
339 Chelmsford	46.2	Con	394 Torfaen	44.8	Lab
340 Brecon & Radnorshire	46.2	LD	395 Foyle	44.7	SDLP
341 Holborn & St Pancras	46.1	Lab	396 Manchester Withington	44.7	LD
342 Southend West	46.1	Con	397 Harrow East	44.7	Con
343 Copeland	46.0	Lab	398 Ellesmere Port & Neston	44.6	Lab
344 Finchley & Golders Green	46.0	Con	399 Rotherham	44.6	Lab
345 Newcastle upon Tyne C.	45.9	Lab	400 East Lothian	44.6	Lab
346 Strangford	45.9	DUP	401 Leicestershire North West	44.6	Con
347 Bolton North East	45.9	Lab	402 Swindon North	44.6	Con
348 Sunderland Central	45.9	Lab	403 Burton	44.5	Con
349 Dumfries & Galloway	45.9	Lab	404 Glasgow North	44.5	Lab
350 Middlesbrough	45.9	Lab	405 Blyth Valley	44.5	Lab
351 Antrim East	45.9	DUP	406 Aberdeen North	44.4	Lab
352 Totnes	45.9	Con	407 Fife North East	44.3	LD
353 Portsmouth South	45.9	LD	408 Dwyfor Meirionnydd	44.3	PC
354 Wansbeck	45.8	Lab	409 Stoke-on-Trent North	44.3	Lab
355 Crewe & Nantwich	45.8	Con	410 Durham, City of	44.3	Lab
356 Slough	45.8	Lab	411 Weston-Super-Mare	44.3	Con
357 Congleton	45.8	Con	412 Portsmouth North	44.3	Con
358 Tamworth	45.8	Con	413 Brent Central	44.2	LD
359 Chippenham	45.8	LD	414 Wythenshawe & Sale East	44.1	Lab
360 Harrogate & Knaresborough	45.7	Con	415 Rugby	44.0	Con
361 Ilford North	45.7	Con	416 Dover	44.0	Con
362 Falkirk	45.7	Lab	417 Castle Point	44.0	Con
363 Na h-Eileanan an Iar			418 Wells	44.0	LD
(Western Isles)	45.7	SNP	419 Shrewsbury & Atcham	43.9	Con
364 Sutton & Cheam	45.7	LD	420 Stafford	43.9	Con
365 Devon West & Torridge	45.7	Con	421 Westminster North	43.9	Lab
366 Leicester South	45.6	Lab	422 Basildon S & Thurrock E.	43.9	Con
367 Warrington North	45.5	Lab	423 Hammersmith	43.9	Lab
368 Fermanagh & South Tyrone	45.5	SF	424 Berwick-upon-Tweed	43.7	LD
369 Workington	45.5	Lab	425 Bromsgrove	43.7	Con
370 Derbyshire South	45.5	Con	426 Merthyr Tydfil & Rhymney	43.7	Lab
371 South Ribble	45.5	Con	427 Feltham & Heston	43.6	Lab
372 Oldham West & Royton	45.5	Lab	428 Harrow West	43.6	Lab
373 Nottingham East	45.4	Lab	429 Leyton & Wanstead	43.6	Lab
374 Berwickshire, Roxburgh &			430 Tooting	43.5	Lab
Selkirk	45.4	LD	431 Redditch	43.5	Con
375 Bradford West	45.3	Lab	432 Milton Keynes North	43.5	Con
376 Tynemouth	45.3	Lab	433 Edinburgh East	43.4	Lab
377 Bridgwater & Somerset West	45.3	Con	434 Derby South	43.3	Lab
378 Staffordshire Moorlands	45.2	Con	435 Chorley	43.2	Lab
379 Redcar	45.2	LD	436 Hexham	43.2	Con
380 Bournemouth West	45.1	Con	437 Reading West	43.2	Con
381 Lancashire West	45.1	Lab	438 Great Yarmouth	43.1	Con
382 Cornwall South East	45.1	Con	439 Dudley South	43.1	Con

Constituency	%share	1st		Constituency	%share	1st
440 Lewisham East	43.1	Lab		497 Caithness, Sutherland &		
441 Newton Abbot	43.0	Con		Easter Ross	41.4	LD
442 York Outer	43.0	Con		498 Montgomeryshire	41.3	Con
443 Bethnal Green & Bow	42.9	Lab		499 Sheffield Central	41.3	Lab
444 Worsley & Eccles South	42.9	Lab		500 Bradford South	41.3	Lab
445 Solihull	42.9	LD		501 Somerset North East	41.3	Con
446 Stockton North	42.8	Lab		502 Newport West	41.3	Lab
447 Edinburgh South West	42.8	Lab		503 Banff & Buchan	41.3	SNP
448 Scarborough & Whitby	42.8	Con		504 Cardiff West	41.2	Lab
449 Coventry North West	42.8	Lab		505 Halesowen & Rowley Regis	41.2	Con
450 Preseli Pembrokeshire	42.8	Con		506 Gedling	41.1	Lab
451 Streatham	42.8	Lab		507 Carmarthen West &		
452 St Austell & Newquay	42.7	LD		Pembrokeshire South	41.1	Con
453 St Ives	42.7	LD		508 Hastings & Rye	41.1	Con
454 Leeds North East	42.7	Lab		509 Lewisham West & Penge	41.1	Lab
455 Stockport	42.7	Lab		510 Hyndburn	41.1	Lab
456 Stourbridge	42.7	Con		511 Blackpool South	41.1	Lab
457 Elmet & Rothwell	42.6	Con		512 Belfast South	41.0	SDLP
458 Bosworth	42.6	Con		513 Rother Valley	40.9	Lab
459 Sheffield Heeley	42.6	Lab		514 High Peak	40.9	Con
460 Warwick & Leamington	42.6	Con		515 Newcastle upon Tyne North	40.8	Lab
461 Reading East	42.6	Con		516 Stroud	40.8	Con
462 Hartlepool	42.5	Lab		517 Northampton South	40.8	Con
463 Llanelli	42.5	Lab		518 Wirral South	40.8	Lab
464 Wirral West	42.5	Con		519 Delyn	40.8	Lab
465 Oxford East	42.5	Lab		520 Filton & Bradley Stoke	40.8	Con
466 Hull West & Hessle	42.5	Lab		521 St Albans	40.8	Con
467 Hendon	42.3	Con		522 Inverness, Nairn, Badenoch &		
468 Oxford West & Abingdon	42.3	Con		Strathspey	40.7	LD
469 Durham North West	42.3	Lab		523 Wolverhampton South West	40.7	Con
470 Enfield North	42.3	Con		524 Birmingham Edgbaston	40.6	Lab
471 Leeds West	42.3	Lab		525 Chester, City of	40.6	Con
472 Islington South & Finsbury	42.3	Lab		526 Norwich North	40.6	Con
473 Vale of Clwyd	42.3	Lab		527 Bury South	40.4	Lab
474 Corby	42.2	Con		528 Kingswood	40.4	Con
475 Batley & Spen	42.2	Lab		529 Peterborough	40.4	Con
476 Cleethorpes	42.1	Con		530 Birmingham Northfield	40.3	Lab
477 Newry & Armagh	42.0	SF		531 Dagenham & Rainham	40.3	Lab
478 Keighley	41.9	Con		532 Waveney	40.2	Con
479 Sefton Central	41.9	Lab		533 Bury North	40.2	Con
480 Birmingham Erdington	41.8	Lab		534 Warwickshire North	40.2	Con
481 Coventry South	41.8	Lab		535 Heywood & Middleton	40.1	Lab
482 Vale of Glamorgan	41.8	Con		536 Cannock Chase	40.1	Con
483 Blackpool North & Cleveleys	41.8	Con		537 Salford & Eccles	40.1	Lab
484 Rossendale & Darwen	41.8	Con		538 Belfast North	40.0	DUP
485 Swindon South	41.8	Con		539 Poplar & Limehouse	40.0	Lab
486 Stirling	41.8	Lab		540 York Central	40.0	Lab
487 Truro & Falmouth	41.7	Con		541 Gloucester	39.9	Con
488 Milton Keynes South	41.6	Con		542 Doncaster Central	39.7	Lab
489 Loughborough	41.6	Con		543 Moray	39.7	SNP
490 Clwyd West	41.5	Con		544 Walsall South	39.7	Lab
491 Morecambe & Lunesdale	41.5	Con		545 Perth & North Perthshire	39.6	SNP
492 Nuneaton	41.5	Con		546 Stalybridge & Hyde	39.6	Lab
493 Eltham	41.5	Lab		547 Alyn & Deeside	39.6	Lab
494 Cardiff Central	41.4	LD		548 Angus	39.6	SNP
495 Stevenage	41.4	Con		549 Birmingham Yardley	39.6	LD
496 Wolverhampton North East	41.4	Lab		550 Scunthorpe	39.5	Lab

Constituency	%share	1st
551 Worcester	39.5	Con
552 Erewash	39.5	Con
553 Croydon Central	39.4	Con
554 Calder Valley	39.4	Con
555 Darlington	39.4	Lab
556 Carlisle	39.3	Con
557 Wakefield	39.3	Lab
558 Middlesbrough South & Cleveland East	39.2	Lab
559 Sherwood	39.2	Con
560 Hull North	39.2	Lab
561 Cambridge	39.1	LD
562 Ipswich	39.1	Con
563 Broxtowe	39.0	Con
564 Chesterfield	39.0	Lab
565 Bishop Auckland	39.0	Lab
566 Stockton South	38.9	Con
567 Cardiff South & Penarth	38.9	Lab
568 Bedford	38.9	Con
569 Pendle	38.9	Con
570 Stoke-on-Trent Central	38.8	Lab
571 Huddersfield	38.8	Lab
572 Pontypridd	38.8	Lab
573 Stoke-on-Trent South	38.8	Lab
574 Mansfield	38.7	Lab
575 Dunbartonshire East	38.7	LD
576 Telford	38.7	Lab
577 Dudley North	38.7	Lab
578 Amber Valley	38.6	Con
579 Birmingham Selly Oak	38.5	Lab
580 Weaver Vale	38.5	Con
581 Bolton West	38.5	Lab
582 Southampton Test	38.5	Lab
583 Pudsey	38.5	Con
584 Bristol South	38.4	Lab
585 Gower	38.4	Lab
586 Aberdeenshire W. & Kincardine	38.4	LD
587 Clwyd South	38.4	Lab
588 Leicester West	38.4	Lab
589 Exeter	38.2	Lab
590 Derbyshire North East	38.2	Lab
591 Dumfriesshire, Clydesdale & Tweeddale	38.0	Con
592 Ealing Central & Acton	38.0	Con
593 Bristol North West	38.0	Con
594 Brighton Kemptown	38.0	Con
595 Newcastle-under-Lyme	38.0	Lab
596 Don Valley	37.9	Lab
597 Ochil & South Perthshire	37.9	Lab
598 Dundee East	37.8	SNP
599 Penistone & Stocksbridge	37.8	Lab
600 Morley & Outwood	37.6	Lab
601 Camborne & Redruth	37.6	Con
602 Lincoln	37.5	Con
603 Cardiff North	37.5	Con
604 Edinburgh North & Leith	37.5	Lab

Constituency	%share	1st
605 Halifax	37.4	Lab
606 Nottingham South	37.3	Lab
607 Brentford & Isleworth	37.2	Con
608 Belfast East	37.2	APNI
609 Plymouth Moor View	37.2	Lab
610 Newport East	37.0	Lab
611 Walsall North	37.0	Lab
612 Colne Valley	37.0	Con
613 Wyre Forest	36.9	Con
614 Wrexham	36.9	Lab
615 Thurrock	36.8	Con
616 Southampton Itchen	36.8	Lab
617 Hove	36.7	Con
618 Bristol East	36.6	Lab
619 Aberdeen South	36.5	Lab
620 Rochdale	36.4	Lab
621 Bridgend	36.3	Lab
622 Lancaster & Fleetwood	36.1	Con
623 Gordon	36.0	LD
624 Arfon	36.0	PC
625 Edinburgh West	35.9	LD
626 Aberconwy	35.8	Con
627 Warrington South	35.8	Con
628 Burnley	35.7	LD
629 Carmarthen East & Dinefwr	35.6	PC
630 Dewsbury	35.0	Con
631 Watford	34.9	Con
632 Luton South	34.9	Lab
633 Edinburgh South	34.7	Lab
634 Swansea West	34.7	Lab
635 Londonderry East	34.6	DUP
636 Plymouth Sutton & Devonport	34.3	Con
637 Northampton North	34.1	Con
638 Antrim South	33.9	DUP
639 Upper Bann	33.8	DUP
640 Bradford East	33.7	LD
641 Ashfield	33.7	Lab
642 Ynys Mon	33.4	Lab
643 Derby North	33.0	Lab
644 Birmingham Hall Green	32.9	Lab
645 Hampstead & Kilburn	32.8	Lab
646 Great Grimsby	32.7	Lab
647 Oldham East & Saddleworth	31.9	Lab
648 Argyll & Bute	31.6	LD
649 Brighton Pavilion	31.3	Grn
650 Norwich South	29.4	LD

Table 20. Seats in Rank Order of Percentage Turnout and Winning Party

	Constituency	*%turnout*	*1st*		*Constituency*	*%turnout*	*1st*
1	Renfrewshire East	77.3	Lab	56	Keighley	72.4	Con
2	Westmorland & Lonsdale	76.9	LD	57	Dorset Mid & Poole North	72.4	LD
3	Richmond Park	76.2	Con	58	Sussex Mid	72.4	Con
4	Winchester	75.8	Con	59	Warwick & Leamington	72.3	Con
5	Devon Central	75.7	Con	60	Solihull	72.3	LD
6	Somerset North East	75.4	Con	61	Orpington	72.2	Con
7	St Albans	75.4	Con	62	Kingswood	72.2	Con
8	Kenilworth & Southam	75.2	Con	63	Norfolk South	72.2	Con
9	Thornbury & Yate	75.2	LD	64	Wimbledon	72.1	Con
10	Dunbartonshire East	75.2	LD	65	Guildford	72.1	Con
11	Mole Valley	75.1	Con	66	Monmouth	72.1	Con
12	Somerset North	75.0	Con	67	Hexham	72.0	Con
13	Surrey South West	74.8	Con	68	Beckenham	72.0	Con
14	Cambridgeshire South	74.8	Con	69	Horsham	72.0	Con
15	Dorset West	74.6	Con	70	Bedfordshire Mid	71.9	Con
16	Chesham & Amersham	74.6	Con	71	Salisbury	71.9	Con
17	Somerton & Frome	74.3	LD	72	Charnwood	71.9	Con
18	Sheffield Hallam	74.3	LD	73	Wealden	71.8	Con
19	Worcestershire West	74.3	Con	74	Romsey & Southampton N.	71.8	Con
20	Twickenham	74.1	LD	75	Sefton Central	71.8	Lab
21	Hitchin & Harpenden	74.1	Con	76	Elmet & Rothwell	71.8	Con
22	Stroud	74.1	Con	77	Christchurch	71.8	Con
23	Newbury	74.0	Con	78	Suffolk Coastal	71.7	Con
24	Derbyshire Dales	73.8	Con	79	Derbyshire Mid	71.6	Con
25	Edinburgh South	73.8	Lab	80	Fareham	71.6	Con
26	Maidenhead	73.7	Con	81	Rutland & Melton	71.5	Con
27	Rushcliffe	73.6	Con	82	Wirral West	71.5	Con
28	Wiltshire North	73.4	Con	83	Saffron Walden	71.5	Con
29	Dorset North	73.4	Con	84	Woking	71.5	Con
30	Witney	73.3	Con	85	Tonbridge & Malling	71.5	Con
31	Hampshire North East	73.3	Con	86	Tiverton & Honiton	71.5	Con
32	Cheadle	73.3	LD	87	Cotswolds, The	71.5	Con
33	Henley	73.2	Con	88	Devon West & Torridge	71.4	Con
34	Norfolk North	73.2	LD	89	Derbyshire South	71.4	Con
35	Broxtowe	73.2	Con	90	Newark	71.4	Con
36	Ludlow	73.1	Con	91	Wokingham	71.4	Con
37	Wyre & Preston North	73.1	Con	92	Windsor	71.3	Con
38	Shipley	73.0	Con	93	Edinburgh West	71.3	LD
39	Northamptonshire South	73.0	Con	94	Forest of Dean	71.3	Con
40	Brentwood & Ongar	73.0	Con	95	Leicestershire South	71.2	Con
41	Leicestershire North West	72.9	Con	96	Bedfordshire North East	71.2	Con
42	Lewes	72.9	LD	97	Wirral South	71.1	Lab
43	Arundel & South Downs	72.9	Con	98	Cambridgeshire North East	71.1	Con
44	Sutton & Cheam	72.8	LD	99	Surrey East	71.1	Con
45	Broadland	72.7	Con	100	Stafford	71.1	Con
46	Stratford-on-Avon	72.7	Con	101	Harrogate & Knaresborough	71.1	Con
47	Meon Valley	72.7	Con	102	Herefordshire North	71.1	Con
48	Cardiff North	72.7	Con	103	Selby & Ainsty	71.1	Con
49	Chippenham	72.6	LD	104	Lichfield	71.0	Con
50	Devon East	72.6	Con	105	Hampshire East	71.0	Con
51	Carmarthen East & Dinefwr	72.6	PC	106	Sevenoaks	71.0	Con
52	Hertfordshire South West	72.5	Con	107	Suffolk South	70.9	Con
53	Brecon & Radnorshire	72.5	LD	108	Stirling	70.9	Lab
54	Daventry	72.5	Con	109	Pudsey	70.9	Con
55	Esher & Walton	72.4	Con	110	Ruislip, Northwood & Pinner	70.8	Con

Constituency	%turnout	1st		Constituency	%turnout	1st
111 Skipton & Ripon	70.7	Con		167 Harwich & Essex North	69.3	Con
112 Bromsgrove	70.7	Con		168 Old Bexley & Sidcup	69.2	Con
113 Bath	70.6	LD		169 Rayleigh & Wickford	69.2	Con
114 Worcestershire Mid	70.6	Con		170 Delyn	69.2	Lab
115 Hertford & Stortford	70.6	Con		171 Enfield Southgate	69.1	Con
116 Harborough	70.5	Con		172 Braintree	69.1	Con
117 Staffordshire Moorlands	70.5	Con		173 Truro & Falmouth	69.1	Con
118 Suffolk C. & Ipswich N.	70.5	Con		174 Colne Valley	69.1	Con
119 Taunton Deane	70.5	LD		175 Halesowen & Rowley Regis	69.0	Con
120 High Peak	70.4	Con		176 Carshalton & Wallington	69.0	LD
121 Stone	70.4	Con		177 Preseli Pembrokeshire	69.0	Con
122 Chelmsford	70.4	Con		178 Cornwall North	68.9	LD
123 Devon South West	70.4	Con		179 Fermanagh & South Tyrone	68.9	SF
124 Kingston & Surbiton	70.4	LD		180 Rugby	68.9	Con
125 Totnes	70.4	Con		181 Devon North	68.9	LD
126 Tewkesbury	70.4	Con		182 Dumfriesshire, Clydesdale &		
127 Wells	70.3	LD		Tweeddale	68.9	Con
128 Shrewsbury & Atcham	70.3	Con		183 Maidstone & The Weald	68.9	Con
129 Congleton	70.3	Con		184 Ynys Mon	68.8	Lab
130 Bosworth	70.2	Con		185 Devizes	68.8	Con
131 Sleaford & North Hykeham	70.2	Con		186 Epsom & Ewell	68.8	Con
132 York Outer	70.2	Con		187 Kettering	68.8	Con
133 Dover	70.1	Con		188 New Forest East	68.7	Con
134 Wrekin, The	70.1	Con		189 Paisley & Renfrewshire North	68.6	Lab
135 Chorley	70.1	Lab		190 Tooting	68.6	Lab
136 Brighton Pavilion	70.0	Grn		191 St Ives	68.6	LD
137 Wantage	70.0	Con		192 Dorset South	68.6	Con
138 Leeds North East	70.0	Lab		193 Sherwood	68.5	Con
139 Beaconsfield	70.0	Con		194 Bristol North West	68.5	Con
140 Filton & Bradley Stoke	70.0	Con		195 Edinburgh South West	68.5	Lab
141 Dumfries & Galloway	70.0	Lab		196 Dewsbury	68.4	Con
142 Witham	69.9	Con		197 Edinburgh North & Leith	68.4	Lab
143 Penrith & The Border	69.9	Con		198 Wiltshire South West	68.4	Con
144 Hornsey & Wood Green	69.9	LD		199 Altrincham & Sale West	68.4	Con
145 Hertfordshire North East	69.8	Con		200 Erewash	68.4	Con
146 Reigate	69.8	Con		201 Aberdeenshire West &		
147 Carmarthen West &				Kincardine	68.4	LD
Pembrokeshire South	69.7	Con		202 Norfolk Mid	68.4	Con
148 Newton Abbot	69.7	Con		203 Watford	68.3	Con
149 Maldon	69.6	Con		204 Staffordshire South	68.3	Con
150 New Forest West	69.6	Con		205 Aylesbury	68.3	Con
151 Chichester	69.6	Con		206 Wolverhampton South West	68.2	Con
152 Tynemouth	69.6	Lab		207 Loughborough	68.2	Con
153 Surrey Heath	69.6	Con		208 Tunbridge Wells	68.1	Con
154 Cornwall South East	69.5	Con		209 Stockton South	68.1	Con
155 Corby	69.5	Con		210 Harrow East	68.1	Con
156 Hampshire North West	69.5	Con		211 Gedling	68.0	Lab
157 Hove	69.5	Con		212 Hemel Hempstead	68.0	Con
158 Yeovil	69.4	LD		213 Hornchurch & Upminster	68.0	Con
159 Montgomeryshire	69.4	Con		214 Welwyn Hatfield	68.0	Con
160 Haltemprice & Howden	69.4	Con		215 Berwick-upon-Tweed	67.9	LD
161 Cambridgeshire South East	69.3	Con		216 Penistone & Stocksbridge	67.9	Lab
162 Vale of Glamorgan	69.3	Con		217 Sutton Coldfield	67.9	Con
163 Bury St Edmunds	69.3	Con		218 Ashford	67.9	Con
164 Warrington South	69.3	Con		219 South Ribble	67.9	Con
165 Eastleigh	69.3	LD		220 Faversham & Kent Mid	67.8	Con
166 Croydon South	69.3	Con		221 Stourbridge	67.8	Con

Constituency	%turnout	1st
222 Pendle	67.8	Con
223 Bracknell	67.8	Con
224 Tatton	67.8	Con
225 Copeland	67.8	Lab
226 Exeter	67.7	Lab
227 Folkestone & Hythe	67.7	Con
228 Grantham & Stamford	67.7	Con
229 Na h-Eileanan an Iar (Western Isles)	67.6	SNP
230 Gower	67.5	Lab
231 Gainsborough	67.5	Con
232 Warwickshire North	67.4	Con
233 Gravesham	67.4	Con
234 Hazel Grove	67.4	LD
235 Chipping Barnet	67.4	Con
236 Bexhill & Battle	67.4	Con
237 Bury North	67.3	Con
238 Calder Valley	67.3	Con
239 Llanelli	67.3	Lab
240 Argyll & Bute	67.3	LD
241 Bromley & Chislehurst	67.3	Con
242 Harrow West	67.3	Lab
243 Worcester	67.2	Con
244 Wellingborough	67.2	Con
245 Ribble Valley	67.2	Con
246 Ross, Skye & Lochaber	67.2	LD
247 Aberdeen South	67.2	Lab
248 Aberconwy	67.2	Con
249 Durham, City of	67.2	Lab
250 Ochil & South Perthshire	67.2	Lab
251 Ealing Central & Acton	67.2	Con
252 Hereford & Herefordshire S.	67.2	Con
253 Weston-Super-Mare	67.2	Con
254 Spelthorne	67.1	Con
255 Basingstoke	67.1	Con
256 Cambridge	67.1	LD
257 Enfield North	67.1	Con
258 Beverley & Holderness	67.1	Con
259 Eltham	67.0	Lab
260 East Lothian	67.0	Lab
261 Eastbourne	67.0	LD
262 Castle Point	66.9	Con
263 Perth & North Perthshire	66.9	SNP
264 Bristol West	66.9	LD
265 Cheltenham	66.8	LD
266 Bolton West	66.7	Lab
267 Chester, City of	66.7	Con
268 Reading East	66.7	Con
269 Finchley & Golders Green	66.7	Con
270 Banbury	66.7	Con
271 Norfolk South West	66.6	Con
272 Batley & Spen	66.6	Lab
273 East Kilbride, Strathaven & Lesmahagow	66.6	Lab
274 Burton	66.5	Con
275 Dunfermline & Fife West	66.5	Lab
276 Ellesmere Port & Neston	66.5	Lab

Constituency	%turnout	1st
277 Chingford & Woodford Green	66.5	Con
278 Leeds North West	66.5	LD
279 Gordon	66.4	LD
280 Camborne & Redruth	66.4	Con
281 Mitcham & Morden	66.4	Lab
282 Bexleyheath & Crayford	66.4	Con
283 Macclesfield	66.4	Con
284 Berwickshire, Roxburgh & Selkirk	66.4	LD
285 Canterbury	66.4	Con
286 Runnymede & Weybridge	66.4	Con
287 Wyre Forest	66.3	Con
288 Bedfordshire South West	66.3	Con
289 Bridgwater & Somerset West	66.3	Con
290 Richmond (Yorks)	66.3	Con
291 Fylde	66.3	Con
292 Blaydon	66.2	Lab
293 Dulwich & West Norwood	66.2	Lab
294 Bognor Regis & Littlehampton	66.2	Con
295 Redditch	66.1	Con
296 Gillingham & Rainham	66.1	Con
297 Reading West	65.9	Con
298 Derbyshire North East	65.9	Lab
299 Workington	65.9	Lab
300 South Holland & The Deepings	65.8	Con
301 Nuneaton	65.8	Con
302 Bedford	65.8	Con
303 Clwyd West	65.8	Con
304 Leicester East	65.8	Lab
305 Hampstead & Kilburn	65.7	Lab
306 Shropshire North	65.7	Con
307 Norwich North	65.7	Con
308 Dartford	65.7	Con
309 Battersea	65.7	Con
310 Lancashire West	65.7	Lab
311 Bury South	65.6	Lab
312 Cambridgeshire North West	65.6	Con
313 Hammersmith	65.6	Lab
314 Aldridge-Brownhills	65.6	Con
315 Thanet South	65.6	Con
316 Luton North	65.5	Lab
317 Alyn & Deeside	65.5	Lab
318 Amber Valley	65.5	Con
319 Newcastle upon Tyne North	65.5	Lab
320 Edinburgh East	65.4	Lab
321 Islington North	65.4	Lab
322 Worthing East & Shoreham	65.4	Con
323 Weaver Vale	65.4	Con
324 Norfolk North West	65.4	Con
325 Milton Keynes North	65.4	Con
326 Paisley & Renfrewshire S.	65.4	Lab
327 Bridgend	65.3	Lab
328 Oxford West & Abingdon	65.3	Con
329 Poole	65.3	Con
330 Scarborough & Whitby	65.3	Con
331 Crawley	65.3	Con
332 Lewisham West & Penge	65.2	Lab

Constituency	%turnout	1st		Constituency	%turnout	1st
333 Morley & Outwood	65.2	Lab		387 Gloucester	64.0	Con
334 Cardiff West	65.2	Lab		388 Yorkshire East	64.0	Con
335 Ealing North	65.2	Lab		389 Dunbartonshire West	64.0	Lab
336 Romford	65.2	Con		390 Broxbourne	64.0	Con
337 Southend West	65.2	Con		391 Newport West	64.0	Lab
338 Brigg & Goole	65.1	Con		392 Peterborough	63.9	Con
339 Waveney	65.1	Con		393 Midlothian	63.9	Lab
340 Southport	65.1	LD		394 Milton Keynes South	63.9	Con
341 Northampton North	65.1	Con		395 Isle of Wight	63.9	Con
342 Croydon Central	65.1	Con		396 Coventry North West	63.9	Lab
343 Rochester & Strood	65.0	Con		397 Ceredigion	63.9	LD
344 Louth & Horncastle	65.0	Con		398 Ealing Southall	63.8	Lab
345 Ilford North	65.0	Con		399 Fife North East	63.8	LD
346 Huntingdon	64.9	Con		400 Chesterfield	63.8	Lab
347 Harlow	64.9	Con		401 Dwyfor Meirionnydd	63.7	PC
348 Inverness, Nairn, Badenoch & Strathspey	64.9	LD		402 Vale of Clwyd	63.7	Lab
				403 Birmingham Hall Green	63.6	Lab
349 Wycombe	64.9	Con		404 Middlesbrough S. & Cleveland E.	63.6	Lab
350 Bradford West	64.9	Lab				
351 Swindon South	64.9	Con		405 Linlithgow & Falkirk East	63.6	Lab
352 Wrexham	64.8	Lab		406 Hendon	63.6	Con
353 Bristol East	64.8	Lab		407 Aldershot	63.5	Con
354 Bassetlaw	64.8	Lab		408 Telford	63.5	Lab
355 Neath	64.8	Lab		409 Walsall South	63.5	Lab
356 Stevenage	64.8	Con		410 Hyndburn	63.5	Lab
357 Bolton North East	64.7	Lab		411 Dudley North	63.5	Lab
358 Luton South	64.7	Lab		412 Basildon & Billericay	63.4	Con
359 Hertsmere	64.7	Con		413 Meriden	63.4	Con
360 Brighton Kemptown	64.7	Con		414 Walthamstow	63.4	Lab
361 Worthing West	64.7	Con		415 Dagenham & Rainham	63.4	Lab
362 Hastings & Rye	64.7	Con		416 Lancaster & Fleetwood	63.4	Con
363 Carlisle	64.7	Con		417 Inverclyde	63.4	Lab
364 Suffolk West	64.7	Con		418 Uxbridge & Ruislip South	63.3	Con
365 Norwich South	64.6	LD		419 Arfon	63.3	PC
366 Torbay	64.5	LD		420 Lewisham East	63.3	Lab
367 Epping Forest	64.5	Con		421 Newport East	63.3	Lab
368 Clwyd South	64.5	Lab		422 Stretford & Urmston	63.3	Lab
369 Tamworth	64.5	Con		423 Ulster Mid	63.2	SF
370 Gosport	64.5	Con		424 Islwyn	63.2	Lab
371 Chatham & Aylesford	64.5	Con		425 Leyton & Wanstead	63.2	Lab
372 Buckingham	64.5	Speaker		426 Wallasey	63.2	Lab
373 Islington South & Finsbury	64.4	Lab		427 Edmonton	63.2	Lab
374 Putney	64.4	Con		428 Thanet North	63.2	Con
375 Rossendale & Darwen	64.4	Con		429 Holborn & St Pancras	63.1	Lab
376 Brentford & Isleworth	64.4	Con		430 Livingston	63.1	Lab
377 Cumbernauld, Kilsyth & Kirkintilloch East	64.3	Lab		431 Derby North	63.1	Lab
				432 Oxford East	63.1	Lab
378 Ayrshire Central	64.2	Lab		433 Havant	63.0	Con
379 Boston & Skegness	64.2	Con		434 Dudley South	63.0	Con
380 Rother Valley	64.2	Lab		435 Pontypridd	63.0	Lab
381 Clacton	64.2	Con		436 Eddisbury	63.0	Con
382 Swindon North	64.2	Con		437 Darlington	62.9	Lab
383 Crewe & Nantwich	64.1	Con		438 Blackburn	62.9	Lab
384 Cleethorpes	64.0	Con		439 Greenwich & Woolwich	62.9	Lab
385 Sittingbourne & Sheppey	64.0	Con		440 Hackney North & Stoke Newington	62.9	Lab
386 Barrow & Furness	64.0	Lab				
				441 Streatham	62.8	Lab

	Constituency	%turnout	1st		Constituency	%turnout	1st
442	Burnley	62.8	LD	499	Warley	61.0	Lab
443	Kilmarnock & Loudoun	62.8	Lab	500	Tyrone West	61.0	SF
444	Wakefield	62.8	Lab	501	Aberavon	60.9	Lab
445	St Austell & Newquay	62.7	LD	502	Caithness, Sutherland &		
446	Warrington North	62.7	Lab		Easter Ross	60.9	LD
447	Portsmouth North	62.7	Con	503	York Central	60.8	Lab
448	Ayr, Carrick & Cumnock	62.6	Lab	504	Erith & Thamesmead	60.8	Lab
449	Redcar	62.5	LD	505	Hayes & Harlington	60.7	Lab
450	Bethnal Green & Bow	62.4	Lab	506	Durham North	60.7	Lab
451	Morecambe & Lunesdale	62.4	Con	507	Liverpool Wavertree	60.6	Lab
452	Ogmore	62.4	Lab	508	Croydon North	60.6	Lab
453	Coventry South	62.4	Lab	509	Birmingham Edgbaston	60.6	Lab
454	Brent North	62.3	Lab	510	West Bromwich East	60.6	Lab
455	Sheffield Heeley	62.3	Lab	511	Manchester Withington	60.5	LD
456	Poplar & Limehouse	62.3	Lab	512	Nottingham South	60.5	Lab
457	Colchester	62.3	LD	513	Bolsover	60.5	Lab
458	Kirkcaldy & Cowdenbeath	62.3	Lab	514	Mansfield	60.4	Lab
459	Ashfield	62.3	Lab	515	Newry & Armagh	60.4	SF
460	Caerphilly	62.3	Lab	516	Angus	60.4	SNP
461	Durham North West	62.3	Lab	517	Rhondda	60.3	Lab
462	Lanark & Hamilton East	62.3	Lab	518	Jarrow	60.3	Lab
463	Birmingham Selly Oak	62.2	Lab	519	Cardiff South & Penarth	60.2	Lab
464	Basildon S. & Thurrock E.	62.2	Con	520	Plymouth Sutton &		
465	Stockport	62.2	Lab		Devonport	60.2	Con
466	Newcastle-under-Lyme	62.2	Lab	521	Bishop Auckland	60.2	Lab
467	Moray	62.2	SNP	522	Down South	60.2	SDLP
468	Lincoln	62.2	Con	523	Chelsea & Fulham	60.2	Con
469	Sedgefield	62.1	Lab	524	Garston & Halewood	60.1	Lab
470	Ayrshire North & Arran	62.1	Lab	525	Halton	60.0	Lab
471	Bradford East	62.1	LD	526	Feltham & Heston	59.9	Lab
472	Falkirk	62.0	Lab	527	Banff & Buchan	59.8	SNP
473	Dundee East	62.0	SNP	528	Don Valley	59.8	Lab
474	Ipswich	62.0	Con	529	Glenrothes	59.8	Lab
475	Wansbeck	61.9	Lab	530	Bradford South	59.8	Lab
476	Bournemouth East	61.9	Con	531	Tyneside North	59.7	Lab
477	Halifax	61.9	Lab	532	Southampton Itchen	59.6	Lab
478	Blaenau Gwent	61.8	Lab	533	Coatbridge, Chryston &		
479	Northampton South	61.8	Con		Bellshill	59.4	Lab
480	Sheffield South East	61.7	Lab	534	St Helens North	59.4	Lab
481	Slough	61.6	Lab	535	Coventry North East	59.4	Lab
482	Glasgow South	61.6	Lab	536	Ilford South	59.4	Lab
483	Bristol South	61.6	Lab	537	Camberwell & Peckham	59.3	Lab
484	Torfaen	61.5	Lab	538	Westminster North	59.3	Lab
485	Rutherglen & Hamilton W.	61.5	Lab	539	Oldham West & Royton	59.3	Lab
486	Blackpool N. & Cleveleys	61.5	Con	540	Makerfield	59.3	Lab
487	Lewisham Deptford	61.5	Lab	541	Wolverhampton North East	59.2	Lab
488	Southampton Test	61.4	Lab	542	Stalybridge & Hyde	59.2	Lab
489	Sheffield Central	61.4	Lab	543	Stockton North	59.2	Lab
490	Barking	61.4	Lab	544	Tottenham	59.1	Lab
491	Oldham E. & Saddleworth	61.4	Lab	545	Cardiff Central	59.1	LD
492	Blyth Valley	61.3	Lab	546	St Helens South & Whiston	59.1	Lab
493	Great Yarmouth	61.2	Con	547	Rotherham	59.0	Lab
494	Brent Central	61.2	LD	548	Cynon Valley	59.0	Lab
495	Cannock Chase	61.1	Con	549	Birmingham Perry Barr	59.0	Lab
496	Huddersfield	61.1	Lab	550	Thurrock	58.9	Con
497	Leicester South	61.1	Lab	551	Dundee West	58.9	Lab
498	Plymouth Moor View	61.0	Lab	552	Hackney S. & Shoreditch	58.8	Lab

Constituency	%turnout	1st
553 Portsmouth South	58.7	LD
554 Scunthorpe	58.7	Lab
555 Newcastle upon Tyne East	58.7	Lab
556 Merthyr Tydfil & Rhymney	58.6	Lab
557 Birmingham Northfield	58.6	Lab
558 Stoke-on-Trent South	58.6	Lab
559 Wigan	58.5	Lab
560 Orkney & Shetland	58.5	LD
561 Motherwell & Wishaw	58.5	Lab
562 Belfast East	58.4	APNI
563 Leeds East	58.4	Lab
564 Leigh	58.4	Lab
565 Glasgow North West	58.3	Lab
566 Rochford & Southend East	58.3	Con
567 Aberdeen North	58.2	Lab
568 Rochdale	58.1	Lab
569 Bournemouth West	58.1	Con
570 Hemsworth	58.0	Lab
571 Swansea West	58.0	Lab
572 Derby South	58.0	Lab
573 Wentworth & Dearne	58.0	Lab
574 Wolverhampton South East	58.0	Lab
575 Doncaster North	57.9	Lab
576 Antrim North	57.8	DUP
577 Bootle	57.8	Lab
578 Vauxhall	57.7	Lab
579 Foyle	57.5	SDLP
580 Worsley & Eccles South	57.5	Lab
581 Gateshead	57.5	Lab
582 Heywood & Middleton	57.5	Lab
583 Bermondsey & Old Southwark	57.5	LD
584 Glasgow North	57.5	Lab
585 Airdrie & Shotts	57.5	Lab
586 Leeds West	57.5	Lab
587 Sheffield Brightside & Hillsborough	57.4	Lab
588 Belfast South	57.4	SDLP
589 Doncaster Central	57.2	Lab
590 Sunderland Central	57.0	Lab
591 Bolton South East	57.0	Lab
592 South Shields	57.0	Lab
593 Ashton Under Lyne	56.8	Lab
594 Denton & Reddish	56.7	Lab
595 Liverpool West Derby	56.7	Lab
596 Birmingham Hodge Hill	56.6	Lab
597 Walsall North	56.5	Lab
598 Birmingham Yardley	56.5	LD
599 Belfast North	56.5	DUP
600 Barnsley Central	56.5	Lab
601 Newcastle upon Tyne Central	56.5	Lab
602 Nottingham East	56.4	Lab
603 Birkenhead	56.3	Lab
604 Normanton, Pontefract & Castleford	56.2	Lab
605 Knowsley	56.1	Lab
606 Barnsley East	56.1	Lab
607 Lagan Valley	56.0	DUP

Constituency	%turnout	1st
608 Blackpool South	55.8	Lab
609 Stoke-on-Trent North	55.8	Lab
610 West Bromwich West	55.8	Lab
611 East Ham	55.6	Lab
612 Hartlepool	55.5	Lab
613 Upper Bann	55.4	DUP
614 Houghton & Sunderland S.	55.3	Lab
615 Londonderry East	55.3	DUP
616 Cities of London & Westminster	55.2	Con
617 Leicester West	55.2	Lab
618 Down North	55.2	Ind
619 West Ham	55.0	Lab
620 Salford & Eccles	55.0	Lab
621 Hull West & Hessle	55.0	Lab
622 Liverpool Walton	54.8	Lab
623 Easington	54.7	Lab
624 Swansea East	54.6	Lab
625 Glasgow South West	54.6	Lab
626 Nottingham North	54.2	Lab
627 Washington & Sunderland W.	54.2	Lab
628 Belfast West	54.0	SF
629 Antrim South	53.9	DUP
630 Great Grimsby	53.8	Lab
631 Strangford	53.7	DUP
632 Birmingham Erdington	53.5	Lab
633 Kensington	53.3	Con
634 Stoke-on-Trent Central	53.2	Lab
635 Preston	53.1	Lab
636 Liverpool Riverside	52.1	Lab
637 Glasgow East	52.0	Lab
638 Hull North	52.0	Lab
639 Middlesbrough	51.4	Lab
640 Wythenshawe & Sale East	51.0	Lab
641 Glasgow Central	50.9	Lab
642 Antrim East	50.7	DUP
643 Hull East	50.6	Lab
644 Manchester Gorton	50.5	Lab
645 Thirsk & Malton	49.9	Con
646 Blackley & Broughton	49.2	Lab
647 Glasgow North East	49.1	Lab
648 Birmingham Ladywood	48.7	Lab
649 Leeds Central	46.0	Lab
650 Manchester Central	44.3	Lab

Table 21. Seats in Rank Order of Change in Percentage Turnout 2005-2010*

	Constituency	%change	1st		Constituency	%change	1st
1	Staffordshire South	30.7	Con	54	Hornsey & Wood Green	8.1	LD
2	Hackney North & Stoke			55	Cambridge	8.1	LD
	Newington	13.5	Lab	56	Liverpool Walton	8.1	Lab
3	Barking	13.1	Lab	57	Newark	8.1	Con
4	Liverpool Wavertree	12.8	Lab	58	Chorley	8.0	Lab
5	Poplar & Limehouse	12.2	Lab	59	Bradford East	8.0	LD
6	Feltham & Heston	12.0	Lab	60	Runnymede & Weybridge	8.0	Con
7	Cambridgeshire North East	12.0	Con	61	Croydon North	8.0	Lab
8	Brentford & Isleworth	11.5	Con	62	East Ham	8.0	Lab
9	Islington North	11.5	Lab	63	Northampton North	7.9	Con
10	Tottenham	11.3	Lab	64	Lewisham West & Penge	7.8	Lab
11	Ealing Central & Acton	11.2	Con	65	Chesham & Amersham	7.8	Con
12	Liverpool West Derby	11.0	Lab	66	Warrington South	7.8	Con
13	Sefton Central	11.0	Lab	67	Slough	7.7	Lab
14	Streatham	11.0	Lab	68	Birmingham Hall Green	7.7	Lab
15	Bethnal Green & Bow	10.9	Lab	69	Brighton Pavilion	7.7	Grn
16	Luton South	10.9	Lab	70	Lancashire West	7.6	Lab
17	Islington South & Finsbury	10.8	Lab	71	Chelsea & Fulham	7.6	Con
18	Hampshire North East	10.7	Con	72	Filton & Bradley Stoke	7.5	Con
19	Lewisham Deptford	10.6	Lab	73	Hackney South & Shoreditch	7.5	Lab
20	Hull West & Hessle	10.3	Lab	74	Nottingham East	7.5	Lab
21	Bolton North East	10.2	Lab	75	Sheffield Brightside &		
22	West Ham	10.2	Lab		Hillsborough	7.5	Lab
23	Esher & Walton	10.1	Con	76	Warrington North	7.4	Lab
24	Holborn & St Pancras	9.9	Lab	77	Camberwell & Peckham	7.3	Lab
25	Hampstead & Kilburn	9.9	Lab	78	Barnsley East	7.3	Lab
26	Wyre & Preston North	9.8	Con	79	Windsor	7.2	Con
27	Weaver Vale	9.8	Con	80	Bury South	7.1	Lab
28	Greenwich & Woolwich	9.6	Lab	81	Leigh	7.1	Lab
29	Makerfield	9.6	Lab	82	Glasgow North	7.1	Lab
30	Salford & Eccles	9.5	Lab	83	Erith & Thamesmead	7.1	Lab
31	Liverpool Riverside	9.4	Lab	84	Cardiff West	7.1	Lab
32	Dulwich & West Norwood	9.3	Lab	85	Sheffield South East	7.0	Lab
33	Vauxhall	9.3	Lab	86	Bootle	7.0	Lab
34	Leyton & Wanstead	9.3	Lab	87	Hammersmith	7.0	Lab
35	Chelmsford	9.3	Con	88	Glasgow Central	7.0	Lab
36	Tooting	9.2	Lab	89	Fylde	7.0	Con
37	Dewsbury	9.2	Con	90	Crawley	6.9	Con
38	Nottingham South	9.1	Lab	91	Nuneaton	6.9	Con
39	Ealing Southall	8.9	Lab	92	St Albans	6.9	Con
40	Bradford West	8.9	Lab	93	Beaconsfield	6.8	Con
41	Walthamstow	8.8	Lab	94	Harrow East	6.8	Con
42	Bermondsey & Old Southwark	8.8	LD	95	Garston & Halewood	6.8	Lab
43	Barnsley Central	8.8	Lab	96	Maldon	6.8	Con
44	Luton North	8.6	Lab	97	Morley & Outwood	6.8	Lab
45	Eltham	8.6	Lab	98	Washington & Sunderland West	6.8	Lab
46	Westminster North	8.5	Lab	99	Enfield North	6.8	Con
47	Lewisham East	8.5	Lab	100	Sherwood	6.7	Con
48	Ruislip, Northwood & Pinner	8.5	Con	101	Hove	6.7	Con
49	Broadland	8.3	Con	102	Beckenham	6.7	Con
50	Stockport	8.2	Lab	103	Dunfermline & Fife West	6.6	Lab
51	Reading East	8.2	Con	104	Dagenham & Rainham	6.6	Lab
52	Tewkesbury	8.2	Con	105	Cambridgeshire South	6.6	Con
53	Woking	8.1	Con	106	Warwick & Leamington	6.6	Con

Constituency	%change	1st		Constituency	%change	1st
107 Rother Valley	6.5	Lab		164 Glasgow South	5.6	Lab
108 Battersea	6.5	Con		165 Norwich South	5.6	LD
109 Wigan	6.5	Lab		166 Oxford East	5.6	Lab
110 Don Valley	6.5	Lab		167 Copeland	5.6	Lab
111 Harborough	6.4	Con		168 Yeovil	5.6	LD
112 Halton	6.4	Lab		169 Sutton & Cheam	5.5	LD
113 Sheffield Hallam	6.4	LD		170 Wealden	5.5	Con
114 Sheffield Central	6.4	Lab		171 Jarrow	5.5	Lab
115 Witham	6.4	Con		172 Bolton West	5.5	Lab
116 Birkenhead	6.3	Lab		173 Delyn	5.5	Lab
117 Bradford South	6.3	Lab		174 Hitchin & Harpenden	5.4	Con
118 Sunderland Central	6.3	Lab		175 Southampton Test	5.4	Lab
119 Hampshire East	6.3	Con		176 Leeds North East	5.4	Lab
120 South Shields	6.3	Lab		177 Northamptonshire South	5.4	Con
121 Derbyshire Dales	6.3	Con		178 Wallasey	5.4	Lab
122 Rutland & Melton	6.2	Con		179 Henley	5.4	Con
123 Basingstoke	6.2	Con		180 Hayes & Harlington	5.4	Lab
124 Carlisle	6.1	Con		181 Romsey & Southampton N.	5.4	Con
125 Congleton	6.1	Con		182 Newport East	5.4	Lab
126 Leicestershire North West	6.1	Con		183 Stalybridge & Hyde	5.3	Lab
127 Westmorland & Lonsdale	6.1	LD		184 Oldham West & Royton	5.3	Lab
128 Burton	6.1	Con		185 Durham North	5.3	Lab
129 Hazel Grove	6.1	LD		186 Boston & Skegness	5.3	Con
130 Edinburgh North & Leith	6.0	Lab		187 Doncaster North	5.2	Lab
131 Coventry North East	6.0	Lab		188 Blackburn	5.2	Lab
132 Reading West	6.0	Con		189 Ashton Under Lyne	5.2	Lab
133 Leicestershire South	6.0	Con		190 Surrey Heath	5.2	Con
134 Brighton Kemptown	5.9	Con		191 Aberconwy	5.2	Con
135 Halesowen & Rowley Regis	5.9	Con		192 Ashfield	5.2	Lab
136 Swindon South	5.9	Con		193 Wolverhampton South West	5.2	Con
137 St Helens South & Whiston	5.9	Lab		194 Rayleigh & Wickford	5.2	Con
138 Penistone & Stocksbridge	5.9	Lab		195 Surrey East	5.2	Con
139 Aylesbury	5.9	Con		196 Ellesmere Port & Neston	5.2	Lab
140 Hull North	5.9	Lab		197 Manchester Withington	5.2	LD
141 Croydon South	5.8	Con		198 Doncaster Central	5.2	Lab
142 Devon Central	5.8	Con		199 Sutton Coldfield	5.2	Con
143 Batley & Spen	5.8	Lab		200 Loughborough	5.1	Con
144 Alyn & Deeside	5.8	Lab		201 Birmingham Perry Barr	5.1	Lab
145 Caerphilly	5.8	Lab		202 Bracknell	5.1	Con
146 Erewash	5.8	Con		203 Renfrewshire East	5.1	Lab
147 York Outer	5.8	Con		204 Derbyshire Mid	5.1	Con
148 Ilford South	5.8	Lab		205 Birmingham Erdington	5.1	Lab
149 Chippenham	5.8	LD		206 Aberdeen South	5.1	Lab
150 Nottingham North	5.8	Lab		207 Cambridgeshire South East	5.1	Con
151 Colchester	5.8	LD		208 Blyth Valley	5.1	Lab
152 Hastings & Rye	5.7	Con		209 Brentwood & Ongar	5.1	Con
153 Brent Central	5.7	LD		210 Somerton & Frome	5.1	LD
154 Edmonton	5.7	Lab		211 Barrow & Furness	5.1	Lab
155 Ribble Valley	5.7	Con		212 Arfon	5.1	PC
156 Bury North	5.7	Con		213 Ealing North	5.1	Lab
157 Enfield Southgate	5.7	Con		214 Kenilworth & Southam	5.0	Con
158 Wolverhampton South East	5.7	Lab		215 Guildford	5.0	Con
159 Bolton South East	5.7	Lab		216 Sevenoaks	5.0	Con
160 Mitcham & Morden	5.6	Lab		217 Croydon Central	4.9	Con
161 Stockton South	5.6	Con		218 Pudsey	4.9	Con
162 Charnwood	5.6	Con		219 Shipley	4.9	Con
163 Bridgend	5.6	Lab		220 Braintree	4.9	Con

Constituency	%change	1st	Constituency	%change	1st
221 Lincoln	4.9	Con	278 Walsall North	4.3	Lab
222 Rotherham	4.9	Lab	279 South Holland & The		
223 Stoke-on-Trent North	4.9	Lab	Deepings	4.3	Con
224 Peterborough	4.9	Con	280 High Peak	4.3	Con
225 Eastleigh	4.9	LD	281 Tyneside North	4.3	Lab
226 Horsham	4.9	Con	282 Bolsover	4.3	Lab
227 Solihull	4.9	LD	283 Torbay	4.3	LD
228 Surrey South West	4.9	Con	284 Lichfield	4.3	Con
229 Telford	4.8	Lab	285 Witney	4.3	Con
230 Aberdeenshire W. & Kincardine	4.8	LD	286 Wimbledon	4.3	Con
231 Southampton Itchen	4.8	Lab	287 Worcestershire West	4.3	Con
232 Carshalton & Wallington	4.8	LD	288 Scunthorpe	4.3	Lab
233 Uxbridge & Ruislip South	4.7	Con	289 Wrekin, The	4.2	Con
234 Manchester Gorton	4.7	Lab	290 Cotswolds, The	4.2	Con
235 Grantham & Stamford	4.7	Con	291 Broxtowe	4.2	Con
236 Broxbourne	4.7	Con	292 Denton & Reddish	4.2	Lab
237 Derbyshire North East	4.7	Lab	293 Hartlepool	4.2	Lab
238 Hendon	4.7	Con	294 Bournemouth West	4.2	Con
239 Newport West	4.7	Lab	295 Crewe & Nantwich	4.2	Con
240 Hyndburn	4.7	Lab	296 Wolverhampton North East	4.2	Lab
241 Hornchurch & Upminster	4.7	Con	297 Stafford	4.1	Con
242 Plymouth Sutton & Devonport	4.7	Con	298 West Bromwich West	4.1	Lab
243 Leeds West	4.7	Lab	299 Pendle	4.1	Con
244 Fareham	4.7	Con	300 Gedling	4.1	Lab
245 Chipping Barnet	4.7	Con	301 Orkney & Shetland	4.1	LD
246 Gordon	4.6	LD	302 Dorset North	4.1	Con
247 Berwick-upon-Tweed	4.6	LD	303 Southport	4.1	LD
248 Bromley & Chislehurst	4.6	Con	304 Cities of London &		
249 Sheffield Heeley	4.6	Lab	Westminster	4.1	Con
250 Devon East	4.6	Con	305 Hertford & Stortford	4.1	Con
251 Reigate	4.6	Con	306 Bishop Auckland	4.0	Lab
252 Livingston	4.6	Lab	307 Bassetlaw	4.0	Lab
253 Skipton & Ripon	4.6	Con	308 Old Bexley & Sidcup	4.0	Con
254 Oldham East & Saddleworth	4.6	Lab	309 Worcestershire Mid	4.0	Con
255 Norfolk South West	4.6	Con	310 Southend West	4.0	Con
256 Daventry	4.6	Con	311 Blaydon	4.0	Lab
257 Putney	4.6	Con	312 Truro & Falmouth	4.0	Con
258 Cheadle	4.6	LD	313 Thanet North	4.0	Con
259 Bosworth	4.6	Con	314 Newcastle-under-Lyme	4.0	Lab
260 Derbyshire South	4.5	Con	315 Winchester	3.9	Con
261 Stoke-on-Trent Central	4.5	Lab	316 Somerset North East	3.9	Con
262 Redcar	4.5	LD	317 Corby	3.9	Con
263 Glasgow South West	4.5	Lab	318 Stourbridge	3.9	Con
264 Warwickshire North	4.5	Con	319 Stroud	3.9	Con
265 Huddersfield	4.5	Lab	320 Macclesfield	3.9	Con
266 Suffolk Coastal	4.5	Con	321 Kirkcaldy & Cowdenbeath	3.9	Lab
267 Edinburgh East	4.5	Lab	322 Wiltshire North	3.9	Con
268 Cornwall North	4.4	LD	323 Finchley & Golders Green	3.9	Con
269 South Ribble	4.4	Con	324 Blackpool North & Cleveleys	3.9	Con
270 Thurrock	4.4	Con	325 Lancaster & Fleetwood	3.9	Con
271 Chichester	4.4	Con	326 Suffolk West	3.9	Con
272 Durham North West	4.4	Lab	327 Brent North	3.9	Lab
273 Harrogate & Knaresborough	4.4	Con	328 Tatton	3.9	Con
274 Stoke-on-Trent South	4.4	Lab	329 Leicester East	3.9	Lab
275 Spelthorne	4.4	Con	330 Newcastle upon Tyne North	3.8	Lab
276 Cheltenham	4.4	LD	331 Gateshead	3.8	Lab
277 Edinburgh South	4.4	Lab	332 Ilford North	3.8	Con

Constituency	%change	1st		Constituency	%change	1st
333 Chesterfield	3.8	Lab		389 Workington	3.4	Lab
334 Chatham & Aylesford	3.8	Con		390 Exeter	3.4	Lab
335 Glasgow East	3.8	Lab		391 Glasgow North East	3.4	Lab
336 Norwich North	3.8	Con		392 Swindon North	3.4	Con
337 Bedford	3.8	Con		393 Salisbury	3.4	Con
338 Wiltshire South West	3.8	Con		394 Blackley & Broughton	3.4	Lab
339 Colne Valley	3.8	Con		395 Leicester South	3.4	Lab
340 Coventry North West	3.8	Lab		396 Birmingham Edgbaston	3.3	Lab
341 Paisley & Renfrewshire North	3.8	Lab		397 Meriden	3.3	Con
342 Norfolk North West	3.8	Con		398 Clwyd South	3.3	Lab
343 Hertfordshire South West	3.8	Con		399 Bristol West	3.3	LD
344 Eastbourne	3.8	LD		400 Burnley	3.3	LD
345 Warley	3.8	Lab		401 Worsley & Eccles South	3.2	Lab
346 Maidstone & The Weald	3.7	Con		402 Tonbridge & Malling	3.2	Con
347 Hemsworth	3.7	Lab		403 Keighley	3.2	Con
348 St Helens North	3.7	Lab		404 Romford	3.2	Con
349 Leeds North West	3.7	LD		405 Bedfordshire Mid	3.2	Con
350 Cannock Chase	3.7	Con		406 Banff & Buchan	3.2	SNP
351 Durham, City of	3.7	Lab		407 Camborne & Redruth	3.2	Con
352 Mole Valley	3.7	Con		408 Penrith & The Border	3.2	Con
353 Hemel Hempstead	3.7	Con		409 Lanark & Hamilton East	3.2	Lab
354 Heywood & Middleton	3.7	Lab		410 Gosport	3.2	Con
355 Wentworth & Dearne	3.6	Lab		411 Somerset North	3.2	Con
356 Glenrothes	3.6	Lab		412 Hertfordshire North East	3.2	Con
357 Rushcliffe	3.6	Con		413 Merthyr Tydfil & Rhymney	3.2	Lab
358 Worthing East & Shoreham	3.6	Con		414 Lewes	3.1	LD
359 Tynemouth	3.6	Lab		415 East Kilbride, Strathaven &		
360 Birmingham Ladywood	3.5	Lab		Lesmahagow	3.1	Lab
361 Wokingham	3.5	Con		416 Montgomeryshire	3.1	LD
362 New Forest West	3.5	Con		417 Bromsgrove	3.1	Con
363 Stratford-on-Avon	3.5	Con		418 Linlithgow & Falkirk East	3.1	Lab
364 Chingford & Woodford Green	3.5	Con		419 Glasgow North West	3.1	Lab
365 Blackpool South	3.5	Lab		420 Norfolk South	3.1	Con
366 Wansbeck	3.5	Lab		421 Rutherglen & Hamilton W.	3.1	Lab
367 Walsall South	3.5	Lab		422 Argyll & Bute	3.0	LD
368 Edinburgh South West	3.5	Lab		423 Coventry South	3.0	Lab
369 Bedfordshire South West	3.5	Con		424 Hull East	3.0	Lab
370 Darlington	3.5	Lab		425 Kingswood	3.0	Con
371 Mansfield	3.5	Lab		426 Bognor Regis & Littlehampton	3.0	Con
372 Sussex Mid	3.5	Con		427 Brecon & Radnorshire	3.0	LD
373 Devizes	3.5	Con		428 Richmond Park	3.0	Con
374 Sleaford & North Hykeham	3.4	Con		429 Perth & North Perthshire	3.0	SNP
375 Tamworth	3.4	Con		430 Islwyn	3.0	Lab
376 Birmingham Northfield	3.4	Lab		431 Basildon S. & Thurrock E.	3.0	Con
377 Stone	3.4	Con		432 Moray	3.0	SNP
378 Hampshire North West	3.4	Con		433 Edinburgh West	3.0	LD
379 Wycombe	3.4	Con		434 Bournemouth East	2.9	Con
380 Cumbernauld, Kilsyth &				435 Harrow West	2.9	Lab
Kirkintilloch East	3.4	Lab		436 Northampton South	2.9	Con
381 Suffolk C. & Ipswich N.	3.4	Con		437 Beverley & Holderness	2.9	Con
382 Maidenhead	3.4	Con		438 Ogmore	2.9	Lab
383 Wirral South	3.4	Lab		439 Epping Forest	2.9	Con
384 Hexham	3.4	Con		440 Gainsborough	2.8	Con
385 Llanelli	3.4	Lab		441 Normanton, Pontefract &		
386 Wirral West	3.4	Con		Castleford	2.8	Lab
387 Watford	3.4	Con		442 Easington	2.8	Lab
388 Newcastle upon Tyne East	3.4	Lab		443 Dundee West	2.8	Lab

Constituency	%change	1st	Constituency	%change	1st
444 Dover	2.8	Con	498 Cambridgeshire North West	2.3	Con
445 Worcester	2.8	Con	499 Neath	2.3	Lab
446 Norfolk Mid	2.8	Con	500 East Lothian	2.3	Lab
447 Yorkshire East	2.8	Con	501 Banbury	2.2	Con
448 Louth & Horncastle	2.8	Con	502 Cardiff North	2.2	Con
449 Airdrie & Shotts	2.8	Lab	503 Torfaen	2.2	Lab
450 Dudley South	2.8	Con	504 Na h-Eileanan an Iar		
451 Bedfordshire North East	2.8	Con	(Western Isles)	2.2	SNP
452 Rochford & Southend East	2.8	Con	505 Devon South West	2.2	Con
453 Rossendale & Darwen	2.8	Con	506 Dudley North	2.2	Lab
454 Plymouth Moor View	2.7	Lab	507 Stevenage	2.1	Con
455 Staffordshire Moorlands	2.7	Con	508 Selby & Ainsty	2.1	Con
456 Middlesbrough South &			509 Suffolk South	2.1	Con
Cleveland East	2.7	Lab	510 Gower	2.1	Lab
457 Worthing West	2.7	Con	511 Houghton & Sunderland S.	2.1	Lab
458 Stirling	2.7	Lab	512 Great Grimsby	2.1	Lab
459 Saffron Walden	2.7	Con	513 Arundel & South Downs	2.1	Con
460 Middlesbrough	2.7	Lab	514 Dunbartonshire East	2.1	LD
461 Kingston & Surbiton	2.7	LD	515 Tunbridge Wells	2.1	Con
462 Dunbartonshire West	2.7	Lab	516 Gillingham & Rainham	2.1	Con
463 Rochester & Strood	2.6	Con	517 Aldridge-Brownhills	2.0	Con
464 Wells	2.6	LD	518 Elmet & Rothwell	2.0	Con
465 New Forest East	2.6	Con	519 Cardiff South & Penarth	2.0	Lab
466 Portsmouth North	2.6	Con	520 Birmingham Yardley	2.0	LD
467 Leicester West	2.6	Lab	521 Milton Keynes North	2.0	Con
468 Ross, Skye & Lochaber	2.6	LD	522 Coatbridge, Chryston &		
469 Harlow	2.6	Con	Bellshill	2.0	Lab
470 Bristol South	2.6	Lab	523 Wantage	1.9	Con
471 Faversham & Kent Mid	2.6	Con	524 Birmingham Selly Oak	1.9	Lab
472 Epsom & Ewell	2.6	Con	525 Isle of Wight	1.9	Con
473 Havant	2.5	Con	526 Ipswich	1.9	Con
474 Manchester Central	2.5	Lab	527 Cornwall South East	1.9	Con
475 Redditch	2.5	Con	528 Herefordshire North	1.8	Con
476 Ashford	2.5	Con	529 Motherwell & Wishaw	1.8	Lab
477 Bury St Edmunds	2.5	Con	530 Twickenham	1.8	LD
478 Inverclyde	2.5	Lab	531 Bristol East	1.8	Lab
479 Carmarthen West &			532 Bexleyheath & Crayford	1.8	Con
Pembrokeshire South	2.5	Con	533 Carmarthen East & Dinefwr	1.8	PC
480 Milton Keynes South	2.5	Con	534 Richmond (Yorks)	1.7	Con
481 Paisley & Renfrewshire S.	2.4	Lab	535 Scarborough & Whitby	1.7	Con
482 Falkirk	2.4	Lab	536 Hertsmere	1.7	Con
483 Cleethorpes	2.4	Con	537 Fife North East	1.7	LD
484 Aberdeen North	2.4	Lab	538 Leeds Central	1.7	Lab
485 Shropshire North	2.4	Con	539 Clacton	1.6	Con
486 Dartford	2.4	Con	540 Thornbury & Yate	1.6	LD
487 Brigg & Goole	2.4	Con	541 Gravesham	1.6	Con
488 Wyre Forest	2.4	Con	542 Ayrshire North & Arran	1.6	Lab
489 Chester, City of	2.4	Con	543 Caithness, Sutherland &		
490 West Bromwich East	2.4	Lab	Easter Ross	1.5	LD
491 Knowsley	2.3	Lab	544 Wrexham	1.5	Lab
492 Berwickshire, Roxburgh &			545 Meon Valley	1.5	Con
Selkirk	2.3	LD	546 Bath	1.5	LD
493 Huntingdon	2.3	Con	547 Gloucester	1.5	Con
494 Leeds East	2.3	Lab	548 Aberavon	1.5	Lab
495 Harwich & Essex North	2.3	Con	549 Waveney	1.5	Con
496 Dwyfor Meirionnydd	2.3	PC	550 Weston-Super-Mare	1.5	Con
497 Bridgwater & Somerset W.	2.3	Con	551 Rugby	1.5	Con

Constituency	%change	1st		Constituency	%change	1st
552 Amber Valley	1.5	Con		607 Pontypridd	-0.2	Lab
553 Kensington	1.5	Con		608 Wythenshawe & Sale East	-0.2	Lab
554 Christchurch	1.4	Con		609 Welwyn Hatfield	-0.2	Con
555 Newbury	1.4	Con		610 Orpington	-0.2	Con
556 Wellingborough	1.4	Con		611 Sedgefield	-0.2	Lab
557 Poole	1.3	Con		612 Bristol North West	-0.3	Con
558 Swansea West	1.3	Lab		613 Strangford	-0.3	DUP
559 Portsmouth South	1.3	LD		614 Kettering	-0.4	Con
560 Wakefield	1.3	Lab		615 Dundee East	-0.5	SNP
561 Calder Valley	1.3	Con		616 Stretford & Urmston	-0.6	Lab
562 Midlothian	1.3	Lab		617 Dorset South	-0.8	Con
563 Ynys Mon	1.3	Lab		618 Preseli Pembrokeshire	-1.0	Con
564 Taunton Deane	1.2	LD		619 Folkestone & Hythe	-1.0	Con
565 Ochil & South Perthshire	1.2	Lab		620 Preston	-1.1	Lab
566 Great Yarmouth	1.2	Con		621 Haltemprice & Howden	-1.1	Con
567 Basildon & Billericay	1.2	Con		622 Sittingbourne & Sheppey	-1.2	Con
568 Inverness, Nairn, Badenoch &				623 Cynon Valley	-1.3	Lab
Strathspey	1.1	LD		624 Monmouth	-1.3	Con
569 Ludlow	1.1	Con		625 Rhondda	-1.5	Lab
570 Hereford & Herefordshire S.	1.1	Con		626 Belfast North	-1.7	DUP
571 Stockton North	1.1	Lab		627 Oxford West & Abingdon	-1.7	Con
572 Ayrshire Central	1.1	Lab		628 Dorset West	-1.8	Con
573 Tiverton & Honiton	1.0	Con		629 Vale of Clwyd	-2.1	Lab
574 Swansea East	1.0	Lab		630 Eddisbury	-2.1	Con
575 Shrewsbury & Atcham	1.0	Con		631 St Austell & Newquay	-2.2	LD
576 Rochdale	0.9	Lab		632 Antrim South	-3.1	DUP
577 Morecambe & Lunesdale	0.9	Con		633 Buckingham	-3.8	Speaker
578 Halifax	0.9	Lab		634 Belfast South	-3.9	SDLP
579 Birmingham Hodge Hill	0.9	Lab		635 Ceredigion	-4.1	LD
580 St Ives	0.8	LD		636 Antrim East	-4.1	DUP
581 Vale of Glamorgan	0.8	Con		637 Antrim North	-4.3	DUP
582 Down North	0.8	Ind		638 Blaenau Gwent	-4.4	Lab
583 Newton Abbot	0.7	Con		639 Fermanagh & South Tyrone	-4.5	SF
584 Clwyd West	0.7	Con		640 Lagan Valley	-4.6	DUP
585 Ayr, Carrick & Cumnock	0.7	Lab		641 Londonderry East	-5.4	DUP
586 Totnes	0.7	Con		642 Down South	-5.7	SDLP
587 Kilmarnock & Loudoun	0.6	Lab		643 Upper Bann	-6.6	DUP
588 Altrincham & Sale West	0.6	Con		644 Derby South	-6.7	Lab
589 Devon North	0.6	LD		645 Foyle	-8.8	SDLP
590 Derby North	0.6	Lab		646 Ulster Mid	-9.9	SF
591 Bexhill & Battle	0.5	Con		647 Newry & Armagh	-10.2	SF
592 Thanet South	0.5	Con		648 Belfast West	-10.5	SF
593 Norfolk North	0.5	LD		649 Tyrone West	-11.7	SF
594 Forest of Dean	0.4	Con		650 Thirsk & Malton	-15.9	Con
595 Dumfries & Galloway	0.4	Lab				
596 Dumfriesshire, Clydesdale &						
Tweeddale	0.3	Con				
597 Castle Point	0.3	Con				
598 Dorset Mid & Poole North	0.3	LD				
599 Devon West & Torridge	0.2	Con				
600 York Central	0.2	Lab				
601 Belfast East	0.2	APNI				
602 Canterbury	0.0	Con				
603 Cardiff Central	-0.1	LD				
604 Newcastle upon Tyne Central	-0.1	Lab				
605 Angus	-0.1	SNP				
606 Aldershot	-0.1	Con				

* For constituencies with boundary changes the calculation has been made by reference to a 'notional' turnout for 2005.

Table 22. Seats in Rank Order of Winning Party's Share of Electorate

	Constituency	%share	1st		Constituency	%share	1st
1	Westmorland & Lonsdale	46.1	LD	54	Aldridge-Brownhills	38.9	Con
2	Chesham & Amersham	45.0	Con	55	South Holland & The		
3	Hampshire North East	44.4	Con		Deepings	38.9	Con
4	Surrey South West	43.9	Con	56	Welwyn Hatfield	38.7	Con
5	Maidenhead	43.8	Con	57	Yeovil	38.7	LD
6	Windsor	43.4	Con	58	Lichfield	38.6	Con
7	Mole Valley	43.2	Con	59	Epsom & Ewell	38.6	Con
8	Witney	43.1	Con	60	Ludlow	38.6	Con
9	Orpington	43.1	Con	61	Chichester	38.5	Con
10	Beaconsfield	42.7	Con	62	Worcestershire Mid	38.5	Con
11	Esher & Walton	42.7	Con	63	Derbyshire Dales	38.5	Con
12	Arundel & South Downs	42.1	Con	64	Newark	38.5	Con
13	Newbury	41.8	Con	65	Guildford	38.4	Con
14	Beckenham	41.7	Con	66	Bootle	38.4	Lab
15	Maldon	41.7	Con	67	Belfast West	38.4	SF
16	Richmond (Yorks)	41.6	Con	68	Tunbridge Wells	38.3	Con
17	Brentwood & Ongar	41.5	Con	69	Wyre & Preston North	38.3	Con
18	Tonbridge & Malling	41.4	Con	70	Faversham & Kent Mid	38.1	Con
19	Henley	41.1	Con	71	Hertford & Stortford	38.0	Con
20	New Forest West	40.9	Con	72	Horsham	38.0	Con
21	Daventry	40.9	Con	73	Lewes	37.9	LD
22	Meon Valley	40.9	Con	74	Cotswolds, The	37.9	Con
23	Ruislip, Northwood & Pinner	40.7	Con	75	Richmond Park	37.9	Con
24	Wealden	40.6	Con	76	Devizes	37.9	Con
25	Norfolk North	40.6	LD	77	Wiltshire North	37.9	Con
26	Hampshire North West	40.5	Con	78	Bedfordshire Mid	37.8	Con
27	Christchurch	40.5	Con	79	Rushcliffe	37.7	Con
28	Hitchin & Harpenden	40.4	Con	80	Wokingham	37.6	Con
29	Surrey East	40.3	Con	81	Broxbourne	37.6	Con
30	Sevenoaks	40.3	Con	82	Mitcham & Morden	37.5	Lab
31	Northamptonshire South	40.3	Con	83	Dorset North	37.5	Con
32	Hampshire East	40.3	Con	84	Old Bexley & Sidcup	37.5	Con
33	Twickenham	40.3	LD	85	Stratford-on-Avon	37.5	Con
34	Kenilworth & Southam	40.3	Con	86	Hertfordshire North East	37.4	Con
35	Kirkcaldy & Cowdenbeath	40.2	Lab	87	Rutherglen & Hamilton W.	37.4	Lab
36	Surrey Heath	40.1	Con	88	Worcestershire West	37.4	Con
37	Rayleigh & Wickford	40.0	Con	89	Penrith & The Border	37.3	Con
38	Bath	40.0	LD	90	Reigate	37.3	Con
39	Knowsley	39.8	Lab	91	Glenrothes	37.3	Lab
40	Sheffield Hallam	39.7	LD	92	Runnymede & Weybridge	37.1	Con
41	Bedfordshire North East	39.7	Con	93	Paisley & Renfrewshire North	37.1	Lab
42	Saffron Walden	39.7	Con	94	Tatton	37.0	Con
43	Coatbridge, Chryston &			95	Somerset North	36.9	Con
	Bellshill	39.6	Lab	96	Winchester	36.8	Con
44	Fareham	39.6	Con	97	Herefordshire North	36.8	Con
45	Liverpool Walton	39.5	Lab	98	Cumbernauld, Kilsyth &		
46	Devon South West	39.4	Con		Kirkintilloch East	36.8	Lab
47	Hertfordshire South West	39.3	Con	99	Ashford	36.8	Con
48	Renfrewshire East	39.2	Lab	100	Sussex Mid	36.7	Con
49	Dunbartonshire West	39.2	Lab	101	Cambridgeshire North East	36.7	Con
50	East Ham	39.1	Lab	102	Sutton Coldfield	36.7	Con
51	Thornbury & Yate	39.1	LD	103	Rutland & Melton	36.6	Con
52	Paisley & Renfrewshire S.	39.0	Lab	104	Witham	36.5	Con
53	Devon Central	39.0	Con	105	Romford	36.5	Con

Constituency	%share	1st	Constituency	%share	1st
106 Wantage	36.4	Con	162 Harborough	34.5	Con
107 Braintree	36.4	Con	163 Cheadle	34.5	LD
108 Liverpool West Derby	36.4	Lab	164 West Ham	34.5	Lab
109 Chelsea & Fulham	36.4	Con	165 East Kilbride, Strathaven &		
110 Staffordshire South	36.3	Con	Lesmahagow	34.3	Lab
111 New Forest East	36.3	Con	166 Enfield Southgate	34.2	Con
112 Hertsmere	36.2	Con	167 Glasgow South West	34.1	Lab
113 Orkney & Shetland	36.2	LD	168 Grantham & Stamford	34.0	Con
114 Sleaford & North Hykeham	36.2	Con	169 Clacton	34.0	Con
115 Bromley & Chislehurst	36.0	Con	170 Bognor Regis &		
116 Woking	36.0	Con	Littlehampton	34.0	Con
117 Tiverton & Honiton	36.0	Con	171 Hemel Hempstead	34.0	Con
118 Suffolk C. & Ipswich N.	35.8	Con	172 Croydon North	34.0	Lab
119 Skipton & Ripon	35.8	Con	173 Basingstoke	33.9	Con
120 Garston & Halewood	35.7	Lab	174 Edmonton	33.9	Lab
121 Motherwell & Wishaw	35.7	Lab	175 Suffolk South	33.9	Con
122 Romsey & Southampton N.	35.7	Con	176 Norfolk Mid	33.8	Con
123 Charnwood	35.7	Con	177 Shropshire North	33.8	Con
124 Islington North	35.6	Lab	178 Ribble Valley	33.8	Con
125 Aylesbury	35.6	Con	179 Kettering	33.8	Con
126 Stone	35.6	Con	180 Cheltenham	33.7	LD
127 Norfolk South	35.6	Con	181 Broadland	33.6	Con
128 Bracknell	35.5	Con	182 Glasgow North East	33.6	Lab
129 Dorset West	35.5	Con	183 Ogmore	33.6	Lab
130 Shipley	35.5	Con	184 Bexleyheath & Crayford	33.5	Con
131 Inverclyde	35.5	Lab	185 Putney	33.5	Con
132 Norfolk North West	35.5	Con	186 Altrincham & Sale West	33.5	Con
133 Cambridgeshire South	35.4	Con	187 Folkestone & Hythe	33.5	Con
134 Wimbledon	35.4	Con	188 Worthing West	33.5	Con
135 Salisbury	35.4	Con	189 Basildon & Billericay	33.5	Con
136 Ross, Skye & Lochaber	35.4	LD	190 Brecon & Radnorshire	33.5	LD
137 Leicester East	35.4	Lab	191 Wrekin, The	33.4	Con
138 Wiltshire South West	35.3	Con	192 Airdrie & Shotts	33.4	Lab
139 Somerton & Frome	35.3	LD	193 Forest of Dean	33.4	Con
140 Croydon South	35.3	Con	194 Gosport	33.4	Con
141 Leicestershire South	35.2	Con	195 Carshalton & Wallington	33.3	LD
142 Banbury	35.2	Con	196 Barking	33.3	Lab
143 Birkenhead	35.2	Lab	197 Rhondda	33.3	Lab
144 Camberwell & Peckham	35.1	Lab	198 Hayes & Harlington	33.3	Lab
145 Selby & Ainsty	35.1	Con	199 Thanet North	33.3	Con
146 Devon East	35.1	Con	200 Suffolk Coastal	33.3	Con
147 Chingford & Woodford Green	35.1	Con	201 Gainsborough	33.3	Con
148 Tottenham	35.1	Lab	202 Cambridgeshire South East	33.3	Con
149 Kingston & Surbiton	35.0	LD	203 Chippenham	33.2	LD
150 Bedfordshire South West	35.0	Con	204 Sutton & Cheam	33.2	LD
151 Hornchurch & Upminster	35.0	Con	205 Tewkesbury	33.2	Con
152 Down North	34.9	Ind	206 Cornwall North	33.1	LD
153 Haltemprice & Howden	34.9	Con	207 Cambridgeshire North West	33.1	Con
154 Epping Forest	34.8	Con	208 Maidstone & The Weald	33.1	Con
155 Monmouth	34.8	Con	209 Lewisham Deptford	33.0	Lab
156 Bexhill & Battle	34.7	Con	210 Kilmarnock & Loudoun	33.0	Lab
157 Halton	34.6	Lab	211 Bury St Edmunds	32.9	Con
158 Fylde	34.6	Con	212 Ealing Southall	32.9	Lab
159 Derbyshire Mid	34.6	Con	213 Walthamstow	32.9	Lab
160 Taunton Deane	34.6	LD	214 Blaydon	32.9	Lab
161 Hackney N. & Stoke			215 Hazel Grove	32.9	LD
Newington	34.6	Lab	216 Ulster Mid	32.9	SF

Constituency	%share	1st	Constituency	%share	1st
217 Chipping Barnet	32.9	Con	273 Cornwall South East	31.4	Con
218 Ealing North	32.9	Lab	274 St Helens S. & Whiston	31.2	Lab
219 Hackney S. & Shoreditch	32.8	Lab	275 Stafford	31.2	Con
220 Meriden	32.8	Con	276 Copeland	31.2	Lab
221 Wallasey	32.7	Lab	277 Macclesfield	31.2	Con
222 Gravesham	32.7	Con	278 Gateshead	31.1	Lab
223 Bassetlaw	32.7	Lab	279 Hexham	31.1	Con
224 Suffolk West	32.7	Con	280 Somerset North East	31.1	Con
225 Dorset Mid & Poole North	32.6	LD	281 Islwyn	31.1	Lab
226 Devon North	32.6	LD	282 Lanark & Hamilton East	31.1	Lab
227 Devon West & Torridge	32.6	Con	283 Battersea	31.1	Con
228 Eddisbury	32.6	Con	284 Hereford & Herefordshire S.	31.1	Con
229 Chelmsford	32.5	Con	285 Poole	31.0	Con
230 Harwich & Essex North	32.5	Con	286 Solihull	31.0	LD
231 Harrogate & Knaresborough	32.5	Con	287 Cynon Valley	31.0	Lab
232 Hornsey & Wood Green	32.5	LD	288 Greenwich & Woolwich	30.9	Lab
233 Leicestershire North West	32.5	Con	289 Wells	30.9	LD
234 Jarrow	32.5	Lab	290 Shrewsbury & Atcham	30.9	Con
235 Derbyshire South	32.5	Con	291 Dorset South	30.9	Con
236 Wellingborough	32.4	Con	292 Bromsgrove	30.9	Con
237 Blaenau Gwent	32.4	Lab	293 Dover	30.9	Con
238 Southport	32.3	LD	294 Na h-Eileanan an Iar		
239 Totnes	32.3	Con	(Western Isles)	30.9	SNP
240 Luton North	32.3	Lab	295 South Ribble	30.9	Con
241 Louth & Horncastle	32.3	Con	296 Liverpool Riverside	30.9	Lab
242 Warley	32.3	Lab	297 Dulwich & West Norwood	30.8	Lab
243 Eastleigh	32.2	LD	298 Warwick & Leamington	30.8	Con
244 Easington	32.2	Lab	299 Barrow & Furness	30.8	Lab
245 Norfolk South West	32.2	Con	300 Dunfermline & Fife West	30.8	Lab
246 Havant	32.2	Con	301 Stretford & Urmston	30.7	Lab
247 Liverpool Wavertree	32.2	Lab	302 St Albans	30.7	Con
248 Congleton	32.2	Con	303 St Helens North	30.7	Lab
249 Bristol West	32.1	LD	304 Finchley & Golders Green	30.7	Con
250 Dumfries & Galloway	32.1	Lab	305 Ayrshire Central	30.7	Lab
251 Sittingbourne & Sheppey	32.1	Con	306 Durham North	30.6	Lab
252 Dartford	32.0	Con	307 Elmet & Rothwell	30.6	Con
253 Rochester & Strood	32.0	Con	308 Livingston	30.6	Lab
254 Glasgow East	32.0	Lab	309 Uxbridge & Ruislip South	30.6	Con
255 Ceredigion	32.0	LD	310 Gillingham & Rainham	30.5	Con
256 Glasgow South	31.9	Lab	311 Buckingham	30.5	Speaker
257 Staffordshire Moorlands	31.9	Con	312 Harrow East	30.4	Con
258 Boston & Skegness	31.7	Con	313 Wirral West	30.4	Con
259 Huntingdon	31.7	Con	314 Yorkshire East	30.4	Con
260 Worthing East & Shoreham	31.7	Con	315 Keighley	30.4	Con
261 Linlithgow & Falkirk East	31.7	Lab	316 Torbay	30.3	LD
262 Eastbourne	31.7	LD	317 Rugby	30.3	Con
263 Aberavon	31.6	Lab	318 Chorley	30.3	Lab
264 Beverley & Holderness	31.6	Con	319 Tyneside North	30.3	Lab
265 Sheffield Brightside &			320 Stroud	30.2	Con
Hillsborough	31.6	Lab	321 Bolsover	30.2	Lab
266 Spelthorne	31.6	Con	322 York Outer	30.2	Con
267 Leeds North West	31.6	LD	323 Berwickshire, Roxburgh &		
268 Wycombe	31.6	Con	Selkirk	30.1	LD
269 Glasgow North West	31.5	Lab	324 Sefton Central	30.1	Lab
270 Tynemouth	31.5	Lab	325 Sheffield South East	30.1	Lab
271 Thanet South	31.5	Con	326 Blackburn	30.1	Lab
272 Fermanagh & South Tyrone	31.4	SF	327 Midlothian	30.1	Lab

Constituency	%share	1st
328 Bridgwater & Somerset W.	30.0	Con
329 Southend West	30.0	Con
330 Bournemouth East	30.0	Con
331 Workington	30.0	Lab
332 Neath	30.0	Lab
333 Newton Abbot	30.0	Con
334 Bosworth	29.9	Con
335 Colchester	29.9	LD
336 East Lothian	29.9	Lab
337 Leeds North East	29.9	Lab
338 Isle of Wight	29.8	Con
339 Tooting	29.8	Lab
340 Durham, City of	29.8	Lab
341 Chatham & Aylesford	29.8	Con
342 Weston-Super-Mare	29.8	Con
343 Canterbury	29.7	Con
344 Bolton North East	29.7	Lab
345 Ilford North	29.7	Con
346 Berwick-upon-Tweed	29.7	LD
347 Ellesmere Port & Neston	29.7	Lab
348 Aldershot	29.7	Con
349 Birmingham Perry Barr	29.7	Lab
350 South Shields	29.6	Lab
351 Lancashire West	29.6	Lab
352 Burton	29.6	Con
353 Stirling	29.6	Lab
354 Preseli Pembrokeshire	29.5	Con
355 Tyrone West	29.5	SF
356 Tamworth	29.5	Con
357 Ayr, Carrick & Cumnock	29.5	Lab
358 Leeds East	29.5	Lab
359 Ayrshire North & Arran	29.5	Lab
360 Castle Point	29.4	Con
361 Bradford West	29.4	Lab
362 Birmingham Hodge Hill	29.4	Lab
363 Crewe & Nantwich	29.4	Con
364 Wentworth & Dearne	29.4	Lab
365 Ilford South	29.3	Lab
366 Edinburgh South West	29.3	Lab
367 Harrow West	29.3	Lab
368 Corby	29.3	Con
369 St Ives	29.3	LD
370 Coventry North East	29.3	Lab
371 Brigg & Goole	29.2	Con
372 Brent North	29.2	Lab
373 Crawley	29.2	Con
374 Kingswood	29.2	Con
375 Down South	29.2	SDLP
376 Harlow	29.1	Con
377 Holborn & St Pancras	29.1	Lab
378 Dunbartonshire East	29.1	LD
379 Wirral South	29.0	Lab
380 Vale of Glamorgan	29.0	Con
381 Stourbridge	28.9	Con
382 Denton & Reddish	28.9	Lab
383 Truro & Falmouth	28.8	Con

Constituency	%share	1st
384 Cities of London & Westminster	28.8	Con
385 High Peak	28.8	Con
386 Hammersmith	28.8	Lab
387 Redditch	28.7	Con
388 Vauxhall	28.7	Lab
389 Montgomeryshire	28.7	Con
390 Carmarthen West & Pembrokeshire South	28.7	Con
391 Llanelli	28.6	Lab
392 Swindon North	28.6	Con
393 Broxtowe	28.6	Con
394 Warrington North	28.6	Lab
395 Dundee West	28.6	Lab
396 Filton & Bradley Stoke	28.5	Con
397 Washington & Sunderland W.	28.5	Lab
398 Reading West	28.5	Con
399 Halesowen & Rowley Regis	28.4	Con
400 Milton Keynes North	28.4	Con
401 Edinburgh East	28.4	Lab
402 Wansbeck	28.4	Lab
403 Reading East	28.4	Con
404 Wigan	28.4	Lab
405 Enfield North	28.4	Con
406 Loughborough	28.3	Con
407 Falkirk	28.3	Lab
408 Fife North East	28.3	LD
409 Dwyfor Meirionnydd	28.3	PC
410 Slough	28.2	Lab
411 Redcar	28.2	LD
412 Delyn	28.2	Lab
413 West Bromwich East	28.2	Lab
414 Swansea East	28.1	Lab
415 Batley & Spen	28.1	Lab
416 Leigh	28.1	Lab
417 Makerfield	28.0	Lab
418 Sedgefield	28.0	Lab
419 Caerphilly	28.0	Lab
420 Gedling	28.0	Lab
421 Scarborough & Whitby	28.0	Con
422 Lagan Valley	27.9	DUP
423 Houghton & Sunderland S.	27.8	Lab
424 Leicester South	27.8	Lab
425 Eltham	27.8	Lab
426 Bermondsey & Old Southwark	27.8	LD
427 Wolverhampton South West	27.8	Con
428 Portsmouth North	27.8	Con
429 Oxford West & Abingdon	27.7	Con
430 Wolverhampton South East	27.6	Lab
431 Leyton & Wanstead	27.6	Lab
432 Torfaen	27.5	Lab
433 Ashton Under Lyne	27.5	Lab
434 Doncaster North	27.4	Lab
435 Coventry North West	27.4	Lab
436 Clwyd West	27.3	Con
437 Nuneaton	27.3	Con
438 Basildon S.& Thurrock E.	27.3	Con

Constituency	%share	1st	Constituency	%share	1st
439 Rochford & Southend East	27.3	Con	494 Pendle	26.4	Con
440 Erith & Thamesmead	27.3	Lab	495 Durham North West	26.4	Lab
441 Blyth Valley	27.3	Lab	496 Rotherham	26.3	Lab
442 Pudsey	27.3	Con	497 Nottingham North	26.3	Lab
443 Lewisham East	27.3	Lab	498 Rother Valley	26.3	Lab
444 Cardiff North	27.2	Con	499 Cambridge	26.3	LD
445 Islington South & Finsbury	27.2	Lab	500 Aberdeenshire West &		
446 Dudley South	27.2	Con	Kincardine	26.3	LD
447 Hemsworth	27.1	Lab	501 Bournemouth West	26.2	Con
448 Swindon South	27.1	Con	502 Dumfriesshire, Clydesdale &		
449 Birmingham Ladywood	27.1	Lab	Tweeddale	26.2	Con
450 Chester, City of	27.1	Con	503 Waveney	26.2	Con
451 Warwickshire North	27.1	Con	504 Sunderland Central	26.2	Lab
452 Normanton, Pontefract &			505 Feltham & Heston	26.1	Lab
Castleford	27.1	Lab	506 Hyndburn	26.1	Lab
453 Bury North	27.1	Con	507 Coventry South	26.1	Lab
454 Brent Central	27.0	LD	508 Westminster North	26.0	Lab
455 Manchester Withington	27.0	LD	509 Bristol North West	26.0	Con
456 Bolton South East	27.0	Lab	510 Gower	26.0	Lab
457 Erewash	27.0	Con	511 Alyn & Deeside	25.9	Lab
458 Cleethorpes	27.0	Con	512 Newcastle upon Tyne Central	25.9	Lab
459 Oldham West & Royton	27.0	Lab	513 Morecambe & Lunesdale	25.9	Con
460 Portsmouth South	26.9	LD	514 Carmarthen East & Dinefwr	25.9	PC
461 Vale of Clwyd	26.9	Lab	515 Exeter	25.8	Lab
462 Hendon	26.9	Con	516 Aberdeen North	25.8	Lab
463 Cardiff West	26.9	Lab	517 Peterborough	25.8	Con
464 Sherwood	26.9	Con	518 Bolton West	25.7	Lab
465 Rossendale & Darwen	26.9	Con	519 Foyle	25.7	SDLP
466 Streatham	26.9	Lab	520 Blackpool North & Cleveleys	25.7	Con
467 Antrim North	26.8	DUP	521 Penistone & Stocksbridge	25.6	Lab
468 Stevenage	26.8	Con	522 Edinburgh North & Leith	25.6	Lab
469 St Austell & Newquay	26.8	LD	523 Edinburgh South	25.6	Lab
470 Bethnal Green & Bow	26.8	Lab	524 Croydon Central	25.6	Con
471 Lewisham West & Penge	26.8	Lab	525 Preston	25.6	Lab
472 Oxford East	26.8	Lab	526 Edinburgh West	25.6	LD
473 Newcastle upon Tyne North	26.7	Lab	527 Bedford	25.6	Con
474 Blackley & Broughton	26.7	Lab	528 Merthyr Tydfil & Rhymney	25.6	Lab
475 Barnsley Central	26.7	Lab	529 Glasgow North	25.6	Lab
476 Kensington	26.7	Con	530 Nottingham East	25.6	Lab
477 Norwich North	26.7	Con	531 Gloucester	25.6	Con
478 Milton Keynes South	26.6	Con	532 Ealing Central & Acton	25.5	Con
479 Worcester	26.6	Con	533 Dagenham & Rainham	25.5	Lab
480 Hastings & Rye	26.6	Con	534 Colne Valley	25.5	Con
481 Stockport	26.6	Lab	535 Hove	25.5	Con
482 Sheffield Heeley	26.5	Lab	536 Ochil & South Perthshire	25.5	Lab
483 Bury South	26.5	Lab	537 Carlisle	25.4	Con
484 Calder Valley	26.5	Con	538 Newry & Armagh	25.4	SF
485 Stockton South	26.5	Con	539 Sheffield Central	25.4	Lab
486 Perth & North Perthshire	26.5	SNP	540 Stockton North	25.4	Lab
487 Glasgow Central	26.5	Lab	541 Manchester Gorton	25.3	Lab
488 Inverness, Nairn, Badenoch &			542 Amber Valley	25.3	Con
Strathspey	26.4	LD	543 Northampton South	25.2	Con
489 Newcastle upon Tyne East	26.4	Lab	544 Weaver Vale	25.2	Con
490 Great Yarmouth	26.4	Con	545 Caithness, Sutherland &		
491 Thirsk & Malton	26.4	Con	Easter Ross	25.2	LD
492 Barnsley East	26.4	Lab	546 Walsall South	25.2	Lab
493 Newport West	26.4	Lab	547 Derby South	25.1	Lab

Constituency	%share	1st	Constituency	%share	1st
548 Derbyshire North East	25.1	Lab	604 Hull West & Hessle	23.4	Lab
549 West Bromwich West	25.1	Lab	605 Lincoln	23.3	Con
550 Camborne & Redruth	25.0	Con	606 Antrim East	23.2	DUP
551 Middlesbrough South &			607 Scunthorpe	23.2	Lab
Cleveland East	25.0	Lab	608 Halifax	23.1	Lab
552 Poplar & Limehouse	24.9	Lab	609 Heywood & Middleton	23.1	Lab
553 Chesterfield	24.9	Lab	610 Ynys Mon	22.9	Lab
554 Warrington South	24.8	Con	611 Blackpool South	22.9	Lab
555 Darlington	24.8	Lab	612 Lancaster & Fleetwood	22.9	Con
556 Clwyd South	24.8	Lab	613 Arfon	22.8	PC
557 Stoke-on-Trent North	24.7	Lab	614 Stoke-on-Trent South	22.7	Lab
558 Worsley & Eccles South	24.7	Lab	615 Doncaster Central	22.7	Lab
559 Moray	24.7	SNP	616 Don Valley	22.7	Lab
560 Banff & Buchan	24.7	SNP	617 Leeds Central	22.7	Lab
561 Bradford South	24.7	Lab	618 Plymouth Moor View	22.7	Lab
562 Strangford	24.7	DUP	619 Belfast North	22.6	DUP
563 Wakefield	24.6	Lab	620 Luton South	22.6	Lab
564 Birmingham Edgbaston	24.6	Lab	621 Nottingham South	22.6	Lab
565 Brighton Kemptown	24.6	Con	622 Wythenshawe & Sale East	22.5	Lab
566 Aberdeen South	24.6	Lab	623 Burnley	22.4	LD
567 Telford	24.6	Lab	624 Birmingham Erdington	22.4	Lab
568 Dudley North	24.5	Lab	625 Birmingham Yardley	22.3	LD
569 Morley & Outwood	24.5	Lab	626 Northampton North	22.2	Con
570 Cannock Chase	24.5	Con	627 Salford & Eccles	22.1	Lab
571 Wolverhampton North East	24.5	Lab	628 Brighton Pavilion	21.9	Grn
572 Wyre Forest	24.5	Con	629 Southampton Itchen	21.9	Lab
573 Cardiff Central	24.5	LD	630 Belfast East	21.8	APNI
574 Pontypridd	24.4	Lab	631 Thurrock	21.7	Con
575 York Central	24.3	Lab	632 Hampstead & Kilburn	21.6	Lab
576 Leeds West	24.3	Lab	633 Argyll & Bute	21.3	LD
577 Hull East	24.3	Lab	634 Leicester West	21.2	Lab
578 Ipswich	24.2	Con	635 Rochdale	21.2	Lab
579 Aberconwy	24.1	Con	636 Ashfield	21.0	Lab
580 Birmingham Selly Oak	24.0	Lab	637 Birmingham Hall Green	20.9	Lab
581 Brentford & Isleworth	24.0	Con	638 Bradford East	20.9	LD
582 Dewsbury	23.9	Lab	639 Walsall North	20.9	Lab
583 Gordon	23.9	LD	640 Derby North	20.8	Lab
584 Wrexham	23.9	Lab	641 Stoke-on-Trent Central	20.7	Lab
585 Angus	23.9	SNP	642 Plymouth Sutton & Devonport	20.6	Con
586 Watford	23.9	Con	643 Hull North	20.4	Lab
587 Bridgend	23.7	Lab	644 Swansea West	20.1	Lab
588 Bristol East	23.7	Lab	645 Oldham East & Saddleworth	19.6	Lab
589 Huddersfield	23.7	Lab	646 Londonderry East	19.1	DUP
590 Bristol South	23.7	Lab	647 Norwich South	19.0	LD
591 Southampton Test	23.6	Lab	648 Upper Bann	18.7	DUP
592 Newcastle-under-Lyme	23.6	Lab	649 Antrim South	18.3	DUP
593 Birmingham Northfield	23.6	Lab	650 Great Grimsby	17.6	Lab
594 Hartlepool	23.6	Lab			
595 Belfast South	23.6	SDLP			
596 Middlesbrough	23.6	Lab			
597 Dundee East	23.4	SNP			
598 Bishop Auckland	23.4	Lab			
599 Stalybridge & Hyde	23.4	Lab			
600 Mansfield	23.4	Lab			
601 Cardiff South & Penarth	23.4	Lab			
602 Newport East	23.4	Lab			
603 Manchester Central	23.4	Lab			

Table 23. Gender of Candidates by Party

	Female	%	Male	%		Female	%	Male	%
Lab	191	30.3	440	69.7	CIP	0	.0	1	100.0
Con	153	24.2	478	75.8	CITY	0	.0	1	100.0
LD	134	21.2	497	78.8	CNPG	0	.0	1	100.0
Grn	108	32.2	227	67.8	Comm	0	.0	6	100.0
UKIP	82	14.7	476	85.3	Cor D	0	.0	1	100.0
BNP	57	16.9	281	83.1	CSP	0	.0	2	100.0
Ind	27	8.8	280	91.2	CTDP	0	.0	1	100.0
Ch P	20	28.2	51	71.8	D Lab	0	.0	1	100.0
SNP	17	28.8	42	71.2	D Nat	0	.0	2	100.0
ED	11	10.3	96	89.7	DDP	0	.0	1	100.0
TUSC	9	24.3	28	75.7	DUP	0	.0	16	100.0
PC	7	17.5	33	82.5	EIP	0	.0	1	100.0
APNI	6	33.3	12	66.7	EPA	0	.0	2	100.0
Soc Lab	6	26.1	17	73.9	FAWG	0	.0	1	100.0
SDLP	5	27.8	13	72.2	FDP	0	.0	1	100.0
UCUNF	4	23.5	13	76.5	FFR	0	.0	1	100.0
Respect	3	27.3	8	72.7	Fiche	0	.0	1	100.0
CPA	3	17.6	14	82.4	GSOT	0	.0	1	100.0
SF	3	17.6	14	82.4	Hum	0	.0	1	100.0
APP	2	50.0	2	50.0	ICHC	0	.0	1	100.0
Soc Alt	2	50.0	2	50.0	IEAC	0	.0	1	100.0
AGS	2	33.3	4	66.7	IFED	0	.0	4	100.0
MK	2	33.3	4	66.7	ILEU	0	.0	1	100.0
SSP	2	20.0	8	80.0	Impact	0	.0	3	100.0
ND	2	8.3	22	91.7	IPT	0	.0	1	100.0
AWL	1	100.0	0	.0	ISGB	0	.0	1	100.0
BIB	1	100.0	0	.0	ISQM	0	.0	1	100.0
IVH	1	100.0	0	.0	IUK	0	.0	1	100.0
LTT	1	100.0	0	.0	IZB	0	.0	1	100.0
MRP	1	100.0	0	.0	JAC	0	.0	2	100.0
TOC	1	100.0	0	.0	JBNF	0	.0	1	100.0
Comm L	1	50.0	1	50.0	Joy	0	.0	1	100.0
SJP	1	50.0	1	50.0	JP	0	.0	1	100.0
SMRA	1	50.0	1	50.0	Land	0	.0	1	100.0
You	1	50.0	1	50.0	Lib	0	.0	5	100.0
LIND	1	33.3	2	66.7	Libert	0	.0	2	100.0
MCP	1	33.3	2	66.7	LLPB	0	.0	1	100.0
PPNV	1	33.3	2	66.7	MACI	0	.0	1	100.0
CURE	1	25.0	3	75.0	MEDI	0	.0	1	100.0
WRP	1	14.3	6	85.7	MEP	0	.0	1	100.0
TUV	1	10.0	9	90.0	MIF	0	.0	1	100.0
AC	0	.0	1	100.0	MPEA	0	.0	1	100.0
AD	0	.0	1	100.0	MRLP	0	.0	27	100.0
AWP	0	.0	1	100.0	Nat Lib	0	.0	1	100.0
BB	0	.0	1	100.0	NCDV	0	.0	1	100.0
BCD	0	.0	1	100.0	New	0	.0	1	100.0
Best	0	.0	2	100.0	NF	0	.0	17	100.0
BGPV	0	.0	1	100.0	NFP	0	.0	1	100.0
BIC	0	.0	1	100.0	NICF	0	.0	1	100.0
Blue	0	.0	1	100.0	Nobody	0	.0	1	100.0
BP Elvis	0	.0	1	100.0	NSPS	0	.0	1	100.0
C28	0	.0	1	100.0	PBP	0	.0	1	100.0
Cam Soc	0	.0	1	100.0	Pirate	0	.0	9	100.0
CG	0	.0	1	100.0	PNDP	0	.0	1	100.
Ch M	0	.0	2	100.0	Poet	0	.0	1	100.0

Table 23. Gender of Candidates by Party (Contd.)

	Female	%	Male	%
PPBF	0	.0	1	100.0
PPE	0	.0	1	100.0
Reform	0	.0	1	100.0
Rest	0	.0	1	100.0
RRG	0	.0	1	100.0
RTBP	0	.0	1	100.0
SACL	0	.0	1	100.0
Sci	0	.0	1	100.0
SEP	0	.0	2	100.0
SIG	0	.0	1	100.0
SKGP	0	.0	1	100.0
SMA	0	.0	2	100.0
Soc	0	.0	1	100.0
Soc Dem	0	.0	2	100.0
South	0	.0	1	100.0
Speaker	0	.0	1	100.0
T F	0	.0	1	100.0
Trust	0	.0	2	100.0
UPS	0	.0	1	100.0
UV	0	.0	1	100.0
VCCA	0	.0	1	100.0
Vote	0	.0	1	100.0
Wessex Reg	0	.0	1	100.0
Youth	0	.0	1	100.0
YRDPL	0	.0	3	100.0
Total	**874**	**21.1**	**3276**	**78.9**

Table 24. Gender of Winning Canditates by Party

	Female	%	Male	%
Lab	81	31.4	177	68.6
Con	49	16.0	257	84.0
LD	7	12.3	50	87.7
Ind	1	100.0	0	.0
Grn	1	100.0	0	.0
APNI	1	100.0	0	.0
SDLP	1	33.3	2	66.7
SF	1	20.0	4	80.0
SNP	1	16.7	5	83.3
Speaker	0	.0	1	100.0
PC	0	.0	3	100.0
DUP	0	.0	8	100.0
Total	**143**	**22.0**	**507**	**78.0**

5   Index of General Election Candidates

(# = candidate who contested more than one constituency)

Candidate Name	Party	PA
Aalders-Dunthorne, Andrew Paul	LD	547
ab Elis, Rhys Gwyn	PC	576
Abbott, Carolyn	Con	144
Abbott, Diane Julie	Lab	280
Abbott, James Edward	Grn	626
Abbott, Paul	UKIP	648
Abercorn, Annesley George	Con	301
Above, None of the	Ind	146
Abrahams, Debbie Angela	Lab	158
Abrams, Robert Edward	ED	143
Ackland, Rod	LD	173
Adams, Christopher Mark	UKIP	22
Adams, Derek George	BNP	68
Adams, Eddie	AGS	340
Adams, Gerry	SF	48
Adams, John Paul	Lab	177
Adams, Martin Paul	Ind	308
Adams, Nigel	Con	501
Adams, Peter	UKIP	345
Adams, Ray	UKIP	236
Adamson, Clare	SNP	348
Adamson, Robert Moray	LD	650
Adamson-Ross, Alison	Con	374
Adcock, Stephen	BNP	260
Addams, Fungus	ED	299
Addison, Keith Philip	BNP	488
Adeeko, Oluyemi	Ch P	292
Adegoke, Kemi	Con	206
Adeleye, Edward Adegboyega	Ch P	278
Adkin, Mark	UKIP	41
Adlard, Rob	Con	531
Adshead, Mark Stephen	MRLP	505
Afriyie, Adam	Con	623
Afzal, Qassim	LD	388
Agarwal, Victor	Lab	560
Agbogun-Toko, Grace	Ind	614
Agnew, John Stuart	UKIP	103
Agnew, Steven	Grn	202
Aherne, David	Grn	639
Ahmed, Abul Monsur Ohid	Lab	550
Ahmed, Farid	LD	595
Aiken, Martyn David	UKIP	221
Ainger, Nick	Lab	132
Ainsworth, Bob	Lab	165
Aitken, Victoria Anne	Con	324
Ajderian, Harriet Joy	Lab	36
Akaki, Sam	IEAC	218
Akhtar, Ruby	Ch P	484
Akinoshun, Abideen	ND	242
Alagaratnam, Rathy	Ind	399
Alcantara, Gene	Ind	290
Alcock, Mark	LD	440
Alden, Deirdre Caroline	Con	57
Alden, Robert James Cambray	Con	58
Alderson, Jacqueline Lesley	LD	633
Aldous, Peter	Con	605
Aldridge, Harry Christopher	UKIP	319

Candidate Name	Party	PA
Alexander, Danny	LD	331
Alexander, David	SNP	269
Alexander, David James	UKIP	302
Alexander, Douglas Garven	Lab	446
Alexander, Heidi	Lab	364
Alexander, James Martin	Lab	649
Ali, Arshad	Respect	87
Ali, Asghar Javed	LD	336
Ali, Itrat	Con	385
Ali, Junab	Lab	187
Ali, Kashif	Con	439
Ali, Richard	Con	109
Ali, Rushanara	Lab	52
Ali, Shahar	Grn	90
Ali, Zulfiqar	LD	539
Alingham, Tammy	Ind	278
Allan, Cherry Theodora	Grn	554
Allcock, Barry Stephen	UKIP	392
Allen, Bernard Adrian	BNP	513
Allen, Caroline Jane	Grn	328
Allen, Denis Graham	UKIP	565
Allen, Edward Thomas	T F	152
Allen, Gareth	Ind	426
Allen, Graham William	Lab	433
Allen, Karen	Con	522
Allen, Karen	BNP	320
Allen, Kathleen	Lab	556
Allen, Lori	Grn	425
Allen, Michael John	Ind	395
Allen, Peter Duncan	Grn	314
Allen, Valerie Margaret	Con	493
Allerston, Ray	Soc Dem	650
Allie, James Borbor	LD	91
Allison, Stephen	UKIP	296
Allister, Jim	TUV	14
Allnatt, Philip George	Ind	619
Allott, Philip David	Con	283
Allsebrook, Lewis Richard	BNP	184
Al-Samerai, Anood	LD	329
Alves, Anthony Joseph	ND	314
Ambroze, George	Ch P	460
Amess, David Anthony Andrew	Con	525
Amor, Michael John	UKIP	189
Andersen, Kai	Soc Lab	373
Anderson, Barry John	Con	352
Anderson, David	Lab	72
Anderson, Hazel	Con	259
Anderson, Janet	Lab	480
Anderson, Martina	SF	255
Anderson, Philip Andrew	UKIP	479
Andras, Peter	LD	603
Andrew, Kenneth	Con	133
Andrew, Steven John	Comm	507
Andrew, Stuart	Con	461
Andrewartha, Dennis Allan	LD	546
Andrewes, Timothy Howard	Grn	494
Andrews, Liz	UKIP	196

Candidate Name	Party	PA
Andrews, Mick	UKIP	195
Angus, Keith	LD	280
Anil, Mehboob	Ch P	220
Ankers, Paul John	LD	76
Annand, Hugh Martin Charles	LD	309
Anselmi, Simon Peter	UKIP	297
Anstis, Elizabeth	Grn	248
Anwar, Bobby	UKIP	67
Anwar, Mohammed Afzal	LD	447
Appleby, Andrew Jeffery	Ind	550
Appleby, John Christopher	LD	582
Appleby, Tom	LD	337
Araba, Arinola Ibiyemi	Ch P	571
Arakelian, Cath	Lab	146
Arbuthnot, James Norwich	Con	288
Archer, Gordon	SNP	469
Archer, Timothy John	Con	456
Archibald, Finlay	Pirate	262
Archibald, Susan	Ind	345
Argar, Edward John Comport	Con	443
Armitage, Alan Edmund	LD	597
Armston, Norma	You	76
Armstrong, Irwin	UCUNF	14
Armstrong, Paul	MCP	581
Arnott, Charlotte Elizabeth	UKIP	506
Arnott, Jonathan William	UKIP	507
Arrowsmith, Anna Imogen	LD	275
Arthur, David	Grn	137
Arthur, Michael James	UKIP	211
Asghar, Ali	LD	356
Ash, Juliette Katherine Christie	Con	174
Ashburner, Mike	BNP	31
Ashington, James	UKIP	600
Ashwell, Mark Austin	Ind	629
Aslam, Farida Tasleem	PC	128
Aspinall, Denise Margaret Elizabeth	LD	234
Astley, Grace Christine	Ind	67
Aston, Bernie	ED	194
Athow, Anna Christine	WRP	237
Atkins, Charlotte Jean Scott	Lab	529
Atkins, Madeleine Christine	Grn	294
Atkinson, Anthony Neville Graham	UKIP	5
Atkinson, John Clarke	UKIP	131
Atkinson, Ralph Steven	UKIP	170
Atreides, Leo	ND	98
Attfield, Danny	ND	93
Attwood, Alex	SDLP	48
Austin, Ian	Lab	204
Avery, Tony	BNP	237
Avis, Jane	Lab	172
Awan, Shazia	Con	361
Ayesh, Ala'eddin S S	LD	360
Ayling, Victoria Carolyn	Con	276
Bacon, Richard Michael	Con	424
Baddeley, Derek	UKIP	282
Baddeley, Melanie Jane	BNP	538

Candidate Name	Party	PA
Badrick, Mark	BNP	483
Badzak, Jasna	UKIP	615
Baehr, Robert William	BNP	646
Bage, Ronnie	BNP	296
Bagnall, Doug	You	78
Bagshawe, Louise Daphne	Con	161
Bahaijoub, Ali	Ind	615
Bailey, Adrian Edward	Lab	613
Bailey, Jeremy	Grn	39
Bailey, Malcolm	Grn	42
Bailey, Mark	BNP	241
Bailey, Robert William	BNP	477
Bailey, Shaun	Con	286
Bain, Willie	Lab	265
Baird, Shiona Elizabeth	Grn	211
Baird, Vera	Lab	466
Baker, Helen Lesley	Con	94
Baker, Jon	ED	102
Baker, Michael John Morton	UKIP	422
Baker, Nicholas Paul	BNP	192
Baker, Norman John	LD	362
Baker, Peter Charles John	UKIP	488
Baker, Steven John	Con	642
Bakhai, Nigel	LD	220
Bakht, Farid	Grn	52
Baldry, Antony Brian	Con	26
Baldry, Michael Richard	Ind	225
Baldwin, Harriett Mary Morison	Con	635
Baldwin, Tom	TUSC	101
Baldwin, William George	BNP	611
Ball, Chas	Grn	158
Ball, David Peter	ED	291
Ball, Jon Timothy Ashby	LD	218
Ball, Timothy Simon	LD	433
Ballance, Alisan Rowena Henderson	Grn	208
Balls, Ed	Lab	405
Banks, Gordon Raymond	Lab	436
Barber, Penelope Jane	Lab	635
Barber, Peter John	Grn	534
Barber, Stephen David	LD	148
Barclay, Stephen Paul	Con	120
Bardell, Lis	SNP	374
Barfe, Louis Frederick	Ind	605
Barker, Granville	UKIP	327
Barker, Gregory Leonard George	Con	54
Barker, Jo	Con	59
Barker, Malcolm Tom	Grn	143
Barker, Mike	LD	176
Barlow, Celia	Lab	321
Barlow, Mark Harry	UKIP	539
Barlow, Paul Thomas	UKIP	324
Barlow, Roger John	LD	382
Barnard, Steve	Grn	505
Barnbrook, Michael John	BNP	175
Barnecutt, Jessica	Grn	93
Barnes, Dawn Carol	LD	627
Barnes, Richard	BNP	393

Candidate Name	Party	PA
Baron, John Charles	Con	32
Baron, Quentin	Ind	39
Barraclough, Leopold Dominic	Lab	226
Barrenger, Darren Michael	Lab	297
Barrett, Peter Anthony	LD	450
Barrie, Jim	SNP	212
Barron, Allyson Margret	Lab	103
Barron, Kevin Charles	LD	608
Barron, Kevin John	Lab	481
Barry, Raymond John	EPA	632
Barschak, Aaron Alexander	Ind	627
Barter, Murray Paul	UKIP	84
Bartlett, Mark Franklin	Lab	274
Bartolotti, Philippa Jane	Grn	418
Bartos, Martin	Grn	264
Barwell, Gavin Laurence	Con	170
Basarik, Erol	Reform	233
Basnett, Neil William	Ind	543
Basu, Suneil	Grn	220
Bate, Clive Stanley	Ch P	128
Bateman, Alan	BNP	559
Bateman, Irene Lillian	BNP	32
Bateman, Julia	LD	260
Bateman, Michael Richard	BNP	139
Bates, Nicola Suzanne	Con	505
Bates, Reginald John	BNP	560
Bates, Tom	BNP	283
Batey, David Robert	LD	182
Batten, Bob	NF	583
Batten, Gerard Joseph	UKIP	477
Baugh, Alan James	UKIP	277
Baum, Richard	LD	111
Bavage, Trevor Anthony John	AGS	354
Baxendale, Eileen Janet Gladys	LD	265
Baxter, Ashley John	Grn	520
Baxter, Ian Gerard	Grn	396
Bayley, Hugh	Lab	648
Baynes, Jake	UKIP	609
Baynes, Simon Robert Maurice	Con	217
Beacham, Thomas Edgar Roy	IFED	570
Beadle, Ronald Walter Alexander Leslie	LD	416
Beamish, Claudia Hamilton	Lab	208
Beany, Captain	Bean	1
Beasley, Raymond J	BNP	427
Beatson, John Winston	BNP	506
Beattie, Colin	SNP	396
Beaumont, Lynne	LD	253
Bebb, Guto Ap Owain	Con	2
Beck, Peter Charles	Grn	61
Beckett, Margaret Mary	Lab	182
Beckett, Mike	LD	204
Beddow, Alan Charles	LD	601
Beech, Mark William	MRLP	126
Beeley, James Malcolm	UKIP	209
Beer, Jeffrey Stuart	UKIP	577
Beg, Aktar	Lab	478
Begg, Anne	Lab	4

Candidate Name	Party	PA
Barnett, John Ewan	LD	212
Beirne, John	LD	492
Beith, Alan James	LD	50
Bell, Daniel Brian	CPA	123
Bell, Jacqueline Dianne	LD	536
Bell, John	Con	154
Bell, Mike	LD	617
Bell, Roger Alwyn	Ind	513
Bell, Ronald	Con	70
Bell, Stuart	Lab	394
Bellamy, Caroline	Comm L	231
Bellin, Ioan Rhys	PC	454
Bellingham, Henry Campbell	Con	423
Belmore, Alan	LD	303
Belsey, Anne Emily Jane	MRP	125
Benn, Emily Sophia Wedgwood	Lab	638
Benn, Hilary James	Lab	351
Bennett, Barry John Sinclair	BNP	272
Bennett, Charles Anselm	UKIP	619
Bennett, Clive	BNP	558
Bennett, Derek	UKIP	594
Bennett, Jack Henry Alsop	UKIP	633
Bennett, Natalie Louise	Grn	316
Bennett, Nigel Andrew	LD	549
Bennett-Spencer, Alan	ED	178
Bennion, Roger Phillip	LD	565
Benson, Daisy	LD	465
Benson, Mark	UKIP	310
Bent, Nick	Lab	600
Bentley, Alexander Michael	LD	246
Bentley, David James	UKIP	439
Bentley, Neil Darren	LD	37
Benton, Joseph Edward	Lab	79
Benyon, Richard Henry Ronald	Con	412
Benzing, Heidi Caroline	Lab	93
Bercow, John Simon	Speaker	108
Beresford, Paul	Con	400
Bergan, Ruth	Grn	531
Berger, Luciana Clare	Lab	372
Berhanu, Alex	LD	328
Berrill-Cox, Adrian Leigh	Con	334
Berrington, Jim	Soc Lab	265
Berry, Jake	Con	480
Berry, Roger Leslie	Lab	344
Best, Nic	Grn	596
Bettney, John	BNP	195
Betts, Clive James Charles	Lab	507
Bevan, David Maybery	UKIP	454
Bevan, James	UKIP	408
Beverley, Chris	BNP	405
Beverley, Joanna	BNP	355
Beverley, Scott	Ch P	467
Bews, John Roger	BNP	305
Bex, Colin Roland	WR	627
Bhandari, Samrat	Ind	41
Bhansali, Vikrant Rahoul	Con	544
Bhatia, Catriona Judith Steel	LD	208

Candidate Name	Party	PA
Boaden, Michael William	Lab	130
Board, Susan Elizabeth	Grn	638
Boater, Dennis Henry	BNP	332
Boddington, Juliet Marie	AGS	497
Bodsworth, Stuart Andrew	LD	534
Boethe, Nahid	LD	294
Boles, Nicholas Edward Coleridge	Con	274
Bolter, Jeffrey Warner	UKIP	172
Bolton, Barry George	Grn	525
Bolton, Charles Nicholas	Grn	101
Bonar, Stuart Andrew	LD	452
Bonavia, Kevin Andrew Martin	Lab	476
Bone, Edward	ED	157
Bone, Jennifer	Lab	44
Bone, Peter William	Con	608
Bonson, Nigel Stuart	Con	507
Boot, David Thomas	Lab	555
Boote, Samuel John	LD	432
Booth, Christopher	UKIP	61
Booth, Ken	BNP	414
Booth, Martin Joseph	Cam Soc	119
Booth, Steph	Lab	116
Borrow, David Stanley	Lab	521
Borrowman, Duncan Keith	LD	438
Borthwick, John Hamilton	UKIP	62
Boswell, Andrew Philip	Grn	422
Bottomley, Peter James	Con	639
Boudier, Richard	Lab	135
Boulding, Stephen Christopher	Grn	511
Boulton, Ian Michael	Lab	251
Bourke, Joseph Gerald	LD	175
Boutle, Toby Jefferson	Con	329
Bovey, Caroline Anne Louise	UKIP	635
Bowen, Mark	Con	248
Bower, Michael John	APNI	584
Bower, Stuart Nicholas	UKIP	18
Bowers, Christopher Alan	LD	606
Bowler, Maxine	TUSC	503
Bowley, David John	Ind	358
Bowman, Peter	UKIP	141
Boyce, Harry	BNP	609
Boyd, Donald MacLeod	Ch P	331
Boyle, Christopher Peter	LD	320
Boyle, Erin Margaret	Con	264
Bradbury, Farel	Ind	580
Bradbury, Neil	LD	72
Bradbury, Norman Alec	Ind	361
Bradley, David Alexander	Lab	617
Bradley, Dominic	SDLP	419
Bradley, John	Con	262
Bradley, Karen Anne	Con	529
Bradnock, David	BNP	530
Bradshaw, Benjamin Peter James	Lab	244
Bradshaw, Paula Jane	UCUNF	47
Brady, Graham Stuart	Con	9
Braid, David Oswald	C28	349
Brake, Thomas Anthony	LD	133

Candidate Name	Party	PA
Bramall, Christopher Ashley	LD	541
Bramall, Jon	LD	205
Brandon, Ian	Grn	604
Braney, Peter Barrie Temple	UKIP	536
Bray, Angie	Con	218
Bray, Prue	LD	629
Brazier, Julian William Hendy	Con	125
Brazil, Julian Charles Martin	LD	577
Brean, Vaughan	Grn	191
Breeze, Mark	Ind	539
Breeze, Paul Derrick	Ind	537
Brennan, Kevin Denis	Lab	129
Brennan, Stephen	Ind	286
Brereton, William Dacre	LD	179
Brice, Chris	LD	222
Bridgen, Andrew	Con	359
Bridger, Rodney Wayne	ED	298
Brier, Jeremy Marc	Con	380
Brierley, Robert	Ind	385
Brigden, John Gerard	LD	201
Briggs, Melissa Louise	Ind	74
Briggs, Miles	Con	250
Brighton, Paul John	LD	10
Brighton, Richard Adrian	LD	557
Brimicombe, Juliana	Ch P	7
Brindley, Simon David	BNP	433
Brine, Steve	Con	622
Brinson, David Charles	Lab	225
Brinton, Sal Virginia	LD	604
Brison, Bill	Ind	111
Bristow, Paul	Con	395
Briton, Christopher	Grn	609
Britton, Michael Kenneth	Lab	567
Broad, Alan David	UKIP	32
Broad, Clive Herbert	UKIP	571
Broadhurst, Stephen John	LD	180
Brock, Bob	UKIP	238
Brodie, Chic	SNP	23
Brodie, Richard John	LD	207
Brodie, Sophie Rebecca	Con	196
Brokenshire, James Peter	Con	438
Brolly, Owen Gerard Matthew	UKIP	40
Brons, Andrew Henry William	BNP	338
Brooke, Annette Lesley	LD	197
Brooke, Dorothy	BNP	582
Brooks, Michael Edward	Sci	81
Brooks, Patrick	Ind	52
Brooks, Rowland John	BNP	438
Brooks-Gordon, Belinda Margaret	LD	550
Broomfield, Paul James	UKIP	178
Brophy, Jane Elisabeth	LD	9
Brothers, David John	UKIP	66
Broughton, Kevin	BNP	466
Brown, Adam	UKIP	393
Brown, Andrew	Ind	109
Brown, Anthony Murray	Grn	453
Brown, Colin David	UKIP	380

Candidate Name	Party	PA
Brown, Darren Adrian	Lab	197
Brown, Edward Martin	Lab	43
Brown, Ernest Andrew	Ind	276
Brown, Gordon	Lab	345
Brown, Graeme Harold	Con	204
Brown, John	LD	30
Brown, Keith	BNP	468
Brown, Lyn	Lab	614
Brown, Nicholas Hugh	Lab	415
Brown, Paul	Grn	555
Brown, Robert Hamilton	UKIP	121
Brown, Russell Leslie	Lab	207
Brown, Trevor David	BNP	352
Browne, Christopher Alan	UKIP	527
Browne, Jeremy Richard	LD	564
Browne, John Kenneth	UKIP	434
Bruce, Fiona Claire	Con	159
Bruce, Malcolm Gray	LD	271
Brunskill, Elaine	TUSC	259
Bryan, Gordon Craig	ND	261
Bryan, Kevin Alistair	NF	480
Bryant, Christopher John	Lab	470
Bryant, David John	Lab	159
Bryant, Patricia Anne	UKIP	187
Buchan, Jimmy	Con	27
Buchanan, Thomas Ernest	DUP	584
Buck, Karen Patricia	Lab	615
Buckland, Jayne Cecelia	Lab	608
Buckland, Robert James	Con	561
Buckley, Karen Elizabeth	Con	327
Bucklitsch, Peter James	LD	568
Bull, Charlotte Elizabeth	UKIP	176
Bull, Richard Edward	LD	185
Bullion, Alan James	LD	502
Bullman, Ken	UKIP	9
Bulmer, Geoffrey James	BNP	354
Bulmer, Martin Gordon	UKIP	466
Bunney, Michael	Lab	198
Burberry, Rob James	UKIP	628
Burden, Richard	Lab	62
Burden, Sam	Lab	105
Burgess, Brian	Ind	412
Burgess, Jeff	UKIP	64
Burgess, Simon	Lab	97
Burgess, Steve	Grn	230
Burke, George	Ind	128
Burke, Mark Alexander	BNP	84
Burkinshaw, Peter	UKIP	119
Burley, Aidan	Con	124
Burn, James	Grn	64
Burnham, Andrew Murray	Lab	361
Burns, Conor	Con	83
Burns, Jonathan Harold	Con	576
Burns, Simon Hugh McGuigan	Con	139
Burrowes, David John Barrington	Con	238
Burrows, Greg	UKIP	116
Burrows, John	BNP	583

Candidate Name	Party	PA
Candeland, Brian	Grn	389
Cann, Mark Michael Robert	Lab	190
Cann, Rodney Sheridan	Ind	190
Cannon, Barbara Ann	Lab	449
Cannon, Graham Geoffrey	UKIP	447
Cantrill, Roderick Giles	LD	44
Capell, Brian	UKIP	43
Caplan, Darren Spencer	Con	280
Capstick, Ken	Soc Lab	30
Carbin, Trevor William	LD	620
Care, Lucy Helen	LD	181
Carew, Adam Sebastian	LD	287
Carey, Michael John	BNP	344
Carlyle, Robert	BNP	316
Carman, Dominic Simon Evelyn	LD	28
Carmichael, Alexander Morrison	LD	441
Carmichael, William Neil	Con	546
Carr, Errol Weston Ellis	Ind	578
Carr, James Wilson	Lab	246
Carr, Ray	ED	100
Carr, Sarah Jane	LD	306
Carr-Brown, Sharon Lesley	Lab	83
Carroll, Peter	LD	384
Carswell, John Douglas Wilson	Con	152
Carter, Julie	UKIP	218
Carter, Nigel David	UKIP	98
Cartwright, John	Ind	387
Cartwright, John Sydney	MRLP	170
Carvath, Richard	Ind	495
Cash, Bill	Con	540
Cash, Joanne Catherine	Con	615
Cashley, Calum Peter	SNP	229
Cassidy, Chris	UKIP	645
Cassidy, David Paul	Ind	512
Cassidy, Michael William	ED	324
Castle, Michael Max	Ind	170
Castle, Michael Victor	Lab	424
Caton, Martin Philip	Lab	273
Caulfield, Maria Colette	Con	114
Cawsey, Ian Arthur	Lab	96
Cecil, Nigel Anthony Valencourt	UKIP	643
Cecil, Victoria Patricia Elizabeth	UKIP	313
Chadwick, Gary Charles	BNP	361
Chadwick, Paul	UKIP	112
Chaggar, Sati	ED	220
Chamberlain, Andrew Scott	LD	24
Chamberlain, Phillip Christopher	Grn	619
Chamberlain-Webber, James	UKIP	97
Chambers, Glyn Edward	Con	590
Chambers, Pamela	BNP	196
Chance, Tom	Grn	49
Chaney, Sidney Albert	BNP	157
Chapman, Douglas	SNP	345
Chapman, Jenny	Lab	176
Chapman, John	Ind	316
Chapman, Kristian Thomas	LD	3
Chapman, Mark Richard	LD	527

Candidate Name	Party	PA
Chappell, David Edward	LD	113
Charalambous, Andrew	Con	233
Charalambous, Bambos	Lab	238
Charles, Hilary	Grn	436
Charlton, Peter Albert	UKIP	362
Charlton, William McKnight	Ind	607
Chase, Andrew David	Grn	648
Chase, Derek	Grn	151
Chatfield, Jonathan Peter	LD	123
Chaudhary, Sunil	Ch P	515
Cheeseman, Daniel Paul	ED	40
Cheeseman, Elaine Frances	ED	438
Cheeseman, Jonathan David	ED	104
Cheeseman, Peter	BNP	181
Chidsey, Colin Richard	BNP	101
Chilvers, Karen Louise	LD	317
Chinners,	MRLP	243
Chisholm, Oliver Marshall	UKIP	200
Chisholm-Benli, Judith	UKIP	595
Chishti, Atta-ur-Rehman	Con	261
Chiverton, Mark Hammond	Lab	333
Chope, Christopher Robert	Con	150
Choudhry, Aqila	LD	353
Choudhury, Faruk	Ind	381
Choudhury, Mahmood	Ind	52
Chowdhry, Wilson	Grn	329
Christian-Brookes, Andrew James	Ind	633
Christofi, Kim	Ch P	332
Churchman, Stephen William	LD	217
Chytry, Anthony Brian	Ind	476
Clack, Helyn	Con	593
Clamp, Jonathan Charles William Da Silva	Con	364
Clapp, Susan Irene	BNP	120
Clappison, James	Con	311
Clare, John Dominic William	Grn	326
Clark, Christopher Robert	Lab	20
Clark, Danny	PC	437
Clark, David Robert	CPA	201
Clark, Derek Roland	UKIP	428
Clark, Gary Philip	TUSC	228
Clark, Geoffrey	UKIP	275
Clark, Gregory David	Con	580
Clark, John Samuel	Lib	569
Clark, Jonathan Thomas	PC	401
Clark, Katy	Lab	25
Clark, Paul Gordon	Lab	261
Clark, Reg	LD	296
Clarke, Anthony R	Ind	428
Clarke, Charles Rodway	Lab	431
Clarke, Craig Stuart	ED	101
Clarke, Jeff	Con	624
Clarke, John James	BNP	556
Clarke, John Nobby	Ind	166
Clarke, Kenneth Harry	Con	486
Clarke, Mark Adrian	Con	574
Clarke, Michael John	BNP	11
Clarke, Owen	Grn	576

Candidate Name	Party	PA
Clarke, Raymond Patrick	UKIP	132
Clarke, Thomas	Lab	156
Clayton, James Alexander	BNP	69
Clayton, Michael Paul	BNP	514
Clayton, Philip Gerald	Ind	148
Clayton, Richard Mark	LD	618
Clayton, Sam Matthew	BNP	235
Clayworth, Andrew William	Lab	486
Clegg, Nick	LD	505
Clein, Richard	LD	500
Cleland, Sheena Margaret	SNP	232
Clement-Jones, Simon William	LD	506
Clements, Anthony George Ashbee	ND	570
Clift, Jim	BNP	366
Clifton-Brown, Geoffrey Robert	Con	164
Clowes, Janet Christine	Con	645
Clucas, Helen Flora	LD	346
Cluer, Dilys Vine	Grn	497
Clutton, James Raymond	UKIP	169
Clwyd, Ann	Lab	174
Clynch, Geoffrey	BNP	333
Coad, Diana	Con	515
Coaker, Vernon Rodney	Lab	260
Coates, Chris	Grn	404
Coates, Sam	Grn	126
Coats, Sarah Naomi Annie	APP	391
Cobain, Fred	UCUNF	46
Cobb, Christopher Paul	UKIP	107
Coburn, David Adam	UKIP	438
Cockrill, Garry Lee	UKIP	525
Coffey, Ann	Lab	534
Coffey, Therese Anne	Con	548
Coghill-Marshall, Nigel Revell	UKIP	214
Coke, Richard Toby	UKIP	421
Colbourne, Nick	Lab	402
Cole, Harry	CURE	581
Cole, Richard Michael	MK	491
Cole, Tim	Ind	116
Cole-Hamilton, Gillian	LD	25
Coleman, Chris	LD	254
Coleman, Ernest Charles	ED	368
Coleman, Michael	BNP	539
Coleman, Ruth	LD	355
Coleman, Terry George	UKIP	19
Coleshill, Gail Marie	LD	518
Coley, Peter	LD	358
Colgate, Emma Louise	BNP	571
Collett, Adrian Paul	LD	7
Collignon, Bernard Michael	UKIP	243
Collings, Jonathan Charles	Ind	214
Collins, Damian Noel	Con	253
Collins, Jane Maria	UKIP	498
Collins, Melanie Jane	Grn	317
Collins, Michael John David	LD	164
Collins, Philip John	UKIP	99
Collins, Scott Jon	LD	429
Collins, Stanley Bernard	LD	636

Candidate Name	Party	PA
Collins, William Shane	Grn	206
Colvile, Oliver Newton	Con	453
Coman, Lesley Diana	LD	399
Conalty, Jim	Lab	526
Condon, Jim	UKIP	73
Congdon, Tim	UKIP	254
Connarty, Michael	Lab	369
Connolly, Matthew Brendan	CPA	556
Connor, Cathy Diane	Grn	572
Connor, Rodney	Ind	249
Conroy, Jennifer Elizabeth	LD	520
Conway, Ann Patricia	BNP	575
Conway, Thomas	SDLP	376
Coogan, Michael	SF	542
Cook, Francis	Ind	535
Cook, John	Lab	430
Cook, John Patrick Mervyn	Ind	627
Cook, Richard Elliot	Con	469
Cook, Roy	BNP	452
Cooke, John	UKIP	531
Cooke, Steve	LD	545
Cooksley, Michael John	Ind	607
Coombe, Nic	Libert	187
Cooney, Clare	Grn	231
Cooney, Paul Francis	TUSC	322
Cooper, Andrew Varah	Grn	322
Cooper, Daisy	LD	548
Cooper, Hannah	Lab	412
Cooper, John	ED	42
Cooper, Julie Elizabeth	Lab	109
Cooper, Mark	Lab	441
Cooper, Roger	ED	587
Cooper, Rosemary Elizabeth	Lab	349
Cooper, Yvette	Lab	426
Coote, Mark Steven	Con	141
Corazzo, Paul Anthony	Lab	178
Corby, Edward David Patrick	Ind	333
Corbyn, Jeremy Bernard	Lab	334
Cordle, Sidney Clifford	CPA	242
Cornell, James Edward	BNP	284
Costa, Alberto Castrenze	Con	12
Costard, Ian Edward	NF	484
Costello, Liam	SMA	428
Cotterell, Priscilla Marie	Grn	364
Couchman, Paul Dennis	TUSC	527
Coulson, Denzil	LD	288
Courtenay, Roland Basil	NICF	140
Cowan, John Lessels	Lab	123
Cowdell, Alan Brian	Soc Lab	393
Cowen, Andrew	MPEA	39
Cowles, Mark Anthony	ED	612
Cox, Anthea Jane	Lab	326
Cox, Antonia Mary	Con	335
Cox, Charles Geoffrey	Con	192
Cox, David	Ind	532
Cox, Michael Francis	LD	587
Coyle, Michael Andrew	BNP	267

Candidate Name	Party	PA
Coyle, Sophia	SNP	6
Crabb, Stephen	Con	459
Craig, Jim	Grn	285
Craig, Lucy	Grn	146
Craig, Neil	D Nat	87
Craig, Robert Irving	South	36
Crampton, Anne	Con	506
Cranie, Peter Andrew	Grn	349
Crausby, David Anthony	Lab	76
Crawford, Keith Montgomery	UKIP	244
Crawford, Moira	Grn	266
Crawford, Richard	Grn	275
Crawford, Roger Martin	EPA	443
Crawshaw, Wayne	ED	196
Creagh, Mary Helen	Lab	591
Creagh-Osborne, Roger Michael	Grn	163
Creasy, Jillian	Grn	504
Creasy, Stella	Lab	595
Crew, Jason Richard	UKIP	336
Crichton, Vanessa	UKIP	286
Crick, Andrew Edward	LD	305
Cripps, Andrew Mark	NF	300
Critchlow, Tracy	Con	390
Crockart, Mike	LD	232
Crocker, Henry Frederick	UKIP	234
Crockett, Barney	Lab	271
Crockford, John Kennedy	FDP	177
Croft, John Anthony	UKIP	292
Crofts, Paul James	TUSC	608
Croll, Ian Phillip	LD	511
Crompton, Geoffrey Allan	BNP	458
Crone, Thomas Martin	Grn	370
Cross, Fiona Claire	PC	417
Crossman, Herbert Winford	UKIP	295
Crotty, Jo	LD	600
Crouch, Tracey Elizabeth Anne	Con	137
Crowd, Gary Alan	EIP	7
Crowther, David	LD	385
Crowther, Edith	BNP	103
Crowther, Stephen James	UKIP	190
Cruddas, Jon	Lab	175
Cruden, Adrian Hugh	Grn	193
Cryer, John Robert	Lab	366
Cubitt, Lyle	ND	14
Cudlipp, William Robert	Ind	95
Cullens, Alan	Con	149
Cullinane, Jim	Ind	601
Cullip, Martin James	Libert	556
Culnane, Mary Theresa	BNP	442
Cummings, Leslie Peter	JAC	458
Cummins, Susan	UKIP	252
Cunliffe, Alexander Martin	LD	242
Cunningham, Alexander	Lab	535
Cunningham, David Benedict	ED	92
Cunningham, Jim	Lab	167
Cunningham, Thomas Anthony	Lab	636
Curran, Frances	SSP	263

Candidate Name	Party	PA
Curran, Margaret Patricia	Lab	263
Curran, Susan	Grn	103
Curry, Stephen	BNP	615
Curtis, Chris	Ind	149
Curtis, Ian James	UKIP	326
Curtis, Katie Elizabeth	Lab	239
Curtis, Martin John	Con	433
Cuthbert, Ian Malcolm	Con	603
Cuthbert-Murray, Michael Andrew	UKIP	620
Cuthbertson, Ian Michael	LD	448
Cutter, Timothy George Frederick	TUSC	523
Dainty, Terence	Ind	361
Dakers, Andrew Stuart	LD	92
Dakin, Nicholas	Lab	498
D'Albert, Vic	LD	112
Dale-Mills, Colin	MRLP	108
Dalrymple, Robert Hamilton	Con	533
Damerell-O'Connor, Miriel Joyce	UKIP	162
Danczuk, Simon Christopher	Lab	474
Daniel, David	UKIP	405
Daniels, Chris	UKIP	650
Daniels, Gonul	Ind	237
Daramy, John Noneoftheabove	Ind	144
Darby, Peter	BNP	462
Darby, Simon	BNP	537
Darling, Alistair	Lab	231
Dartnell, Alice Sakura	Ind	275
Darwood, Thomas Faithful	Ind	28
Davey, Edward Jonathon	LD	343
Davey, Ian Arthur	Grn	321
David, Annajoy	Lab	497
David, Kay	LD	114
David, Wayne	Lab	114
Davidson, Christopher	BNP	449
Davidson, George Henry	Lab	629
Davidson, Hairy Knorm	MRLP	247
Davidson, Ian	Lab	268
Davidson, Michael	NF	614
Davidson, Ruth	Con	265
Davies, Alana Elizabeth	Lab	589
Davies, Allan Robert	Lab	32
Davies, Antony John	MRLP	69
Davies, Byron	Con	273
Davies, Dafydd Trystan	PC	174
Davies, David Clifford	BGPV	71
Davies, David Thomas Charles	Con	401
Davies, Gareth Mark	Con	195
Davies, Geraint Rhys	PC	470
Davies, Geraint Richard	Lab	559
Davies, Glyn	Con	402
Davies, Janet Marion	PC	89
Davies, Julia Mary	LD	532
Davies, Keith	LD	1
Davies, Martin	UKIP	414
Davies, Michael Francis	AGS	352
Davies, Myfanwy	PC	375

Candidate Name	Party	PA
Davies, Patrick	Lab	622
Davies, Paul Martin	Comm L	281
Davies, Philip Andrew	Con	509
Davies, Phillip Leslie	Lab	625
Davies, Rhodri	PC	71
Davies, Roy Richard	BNP	161
Davies, Stephanie	Grn	600
Davies, Susan Margaret	UKIP	126
Davies, Suzy	Con	89
Davies-Green, Helene Yvette	UKIP	122
Davis, Anne Veronica	UKIP	467
Davis, Carys	LD	571
Davis, David Michael	Con	284
Davis, Jean	LD	407
Davis, Kevin John	Con	646
Davis, Malcolm	UKIP	204
Davison, Ian	Grn	601
Davison, Ian James	UKIP	512
Dawber, Howard	Lab	55
Dawe, Hazel Frances	Grn	580
Dawe, Steve	Grn	573
Dawes, Timothy Morgan	Grn	458
Dawkins, Nigel Douglas	Con	64
Day, Cameron	Lab	232
Day, Francis Rowland	UKIP	133
Day, Mike	LD	273
Day, Peter Anthony	UKIP	409
D'Cruz, Brendan Thomas	LD	134
de Bois, Nick	Con	237
de Botton, Oliver Toby	Lab	315
de Freitas, Andrew	LD	276
De La Haye, Denny	Ind	281
de Piero, Gloria	Lab	19
De Roche, Stephane Michel	Ind	318
de Whalley, Andrew Michael	Grn	423
De Wulverton, Ian	UKIP	219
Deacon, Katrina Jean	Grn	398
Dean, Alan	LD	605
Dean, Mudasir Ahmed	Con	474
Deane, Martin John	Grn	324
Dearsley, Stuart	Ch P	639
Deboo, Richard James	AC	335
Deedman, Derek Roger	LD	18
Deeks, Robert William Ian	Lab	150
Delderfield, Dennis William	Ind	151
Delves, Nicholas Charles Elsworth	MRLP	183
Dempsey, Mark Edward	Lab	164
Denby, Colin	UKIP	474
Denham, John Yorke	Lab	523
Dennis, Jeff	Ind	180
Denny, Douglas Ernest	UKIP	74
Detheridge, Charlene Angela	Ch P	562
Devenney, Maurice	DUP	255
Devoy, Eddie	Ind	30
Devoy, Tony	Ind	29
Dewick, William James	BNP	41
Dews, David Alan	UKIP	461

Candidate Name	Party	PA
Dhall, Sushila Devi	Grn	443
Dhanda, Parmjit Singh	Lab	270
Dharamsey, Abby Jan	Ind	615
Dhindsa, Hardyal Singh	Lab	184
Dickens, Geoffrey William	BNP	291
Dinenage, Caroline Julia	Con	272
Diouf, Alexis Saliou	LD	186
Dismore, Andrew	Lab	304
Dixey, Dave	Grn	357
Dixon, Clifford	ED	300
Dixon, Emma Louise	Grn	334
Dixon, John	PC	132
Dixon, John Leslie	LD	127
Dixon, Mike	LD	62
Dixon, Paul	LD	551
Dixon, Peter Alexander	Lab	139
Djanogly, Jonathan Simon	Con	326
Dobbie, David Paul	LD	35
Dobbin, James	Lab	313
Dobson, Craig	LD	53
Dobson, Frank	Lab	316
Dobson, Ruaraidh	LD	445
Dobson, Tim	Pirate	388
Docherty, Thomas	Lab	213
Docker, Daniel Marcus	UKIP	606
Dodds, Anneliese Jane	Lab	464
Dodds, John	ED	335
Dodds, John Benjamin	ED	556
Dodds, Nigel	DUP	46
Dodman, Charles William Henry	UKIP	227
Doggett, Peter John	Grn	246
Doherty, Pat	SF	584
Doig, Andy	SNP	446
Donald, Martin	Con	228
Donaldson, Gary Alan	Ind	608
Donaldson, Jeffrey	DUP	347
Donaldson, Lynda	Con	481
Donelan, Michelle Emma May Elizabeth	Con	611
Donnelly, John	BNP	248
Donohoe, Brian Harold	Lab	24
Doran, Frank	Lab	3
Dorrell, Stephen James	Con	136
Dorries, Nadine Vanessa	Con	42
Doughty, Rodger	UKIP	514
Doughty, Susan Kathleen	LD	279
Douglas, Stuart	LD	406
Dove, James Frances	Lab	400
Dow, George Thomas	Grn	133
Dowd, James Patrick	Lab	365
Dowdall, Tina Charisse	UKIP	481
Dowding, Gina	Grn	350
Dowdney, Neil Francis	UKIP	344
Dowling, Christopher David	MRLP	28
Downes, Nikki	Soc Alt	166
Downey, Richard Michael	Con	258
Dowson, Lancelot Edgar	Ind	314
Doyle, Gemma	Lab	210

Candidate Name	Party	PA
Doyle, George	Ind	17
Doyle, James Edward	LD	638
Doyle-Price, Jacqueline	Con	571
Drax, Richard	Con	199
Drew, David Elliott	Lab	546
Drew, Simon Brooksby	Ind	577
Drinkall, Jeremy Brian	AWP	590
Driver, Eileen	Lab	472
Dromey, Jack	Lab	58
Drummond, Felicia Jane Beatrix	Con	458
Drury, Spencer	Con	278
Duale, Abdi	Respect	90
DuCane, Ian Arthur	ED	458
Duckworth, Will	Grn	541
Duddridge, James	Con	476
Duffen, Graham Michael	UKIP	65
Duffett, Helen Angela	LD	477
Duffield, Andrew	LD	312
Duffin, Ruth Lynda	UKIP	288
Duffy, Catherine Ann Marie	BNP	136
Duggan, Jim	PPNV	319
Dugher, Michael	Lab	30
Dul, Peter Jan	UKIP	473
Duncan, Alan James Carter	Con	488
Duncan, Ben	Grn	97
Duncan, Peter John	Con	207
Duncan, William Campbell	TUSC	396
Duncan Smith, Iain	Con	146
Dundas, Charles	LD	374
Dunford, John William	UKIP	55
Dunleavy, Deborah Jayne	Con	76
Dunlop, Jayne	APNI	14
Dunn, Alex	Grn	100
Dunn, Cheryl Ann	BNP	221
Dunn, Gareth	UKIP	576
Dunne, David James	Con	346
Dunne, Frank	Ind	372
Dunne, Philip Martin	Con	379
Dunsire, Ian Malcolm	ED	333
Durance, Ross Scott	UKIP	331
Durant, David Warren	Ind	317
Durkan, Mark	SDLP	255
Durrance, Terry John	UKIP	526
Duthie, David Shaw	UKIP	480
Duxbury, David Thomas	UKIP	521
Dyer, Shaun	Pirate	358
Dynamite, Napoleon	MRLP	438
Dyson, Mark Henry	LD	332
Eades, Philip Michael	LD	455
Eagle, Angela	Lab	592
Eagle, Maria	Lab	258
Eakins, Martin	LD	645
Eardley, Graham	UKIP	604
Earwicker, Raymond William	LD	84
Easter, Mike	NF	573
Easton, Clive Gwennap	UKIP	89

Candidate Name	Party	PA
Evans, Christopher	Lab	336
Evans, Dave William	UKIP	197
Evans, Graham Thomas	Con	607
Evans, Guy	Grn	38
Evans, Jerry	LD	59
Evans, Jonathan Peter	Con	127
Evans, Judy	LD	453
Evans, Karsten	Ind	561
Evans, Nigel Martin	Con	471
Evans, Robin James	BNP	67
Evans, Sarah	Lab	289
Evans, Stephen Michael	UKIP	111
Evemy, Michael Stephen	LD	619
Evennett, Antony William	BNP	463
Evennett, David Anthony	Con	55
Everitt, Richard	Lab	438
Evetts, Luke	Con	135
Ewing, Annabelle	SNP	436
Exley, David Antony	BNP	37
Exley-Moore, Tania Chantelle	LD	497
Fabricant, Michael Louis David	Con	367
Fairbairn, Steve	BNP	73
Fairman, Richard Geoffrey	UKIP	520
Fairweather, David Sebastian	UKIP	26
Faithfull, Matthew	UKIP	486
Fajardo, Gabriela	Ch P	615
Falconer, Andrew Graham	LD	485
Fallon, Michael Cathel	Con	502
Fanthom, Gordon Edward	UKIP	631
Farage, Nigel Paul	UKIP	108
Farmer, Howard Malcolm	UKIP	125
Farmer, Marcus	Ind	389
Farmer, Neville Mackenzie	LD	644
Farmer, Robert David	BNP	244
Farrant, Susan Rietta	LD	200
Farrelly, Paul	Lab	413
Farron, Tim	LD	616
Farry, Stephen	APNI	202
Faulkner, Michael Patrick	UKIP	494
Fazal, Nadia	LD	593
Feakes, Alexander David	LD	365
Featherstone, Lynne	LD	318
Featonby-Warren, Pauline	UKIP	551
Fekri, Nader	LD	338
Fellows, Marion	SNP	406
Fellows, Sarah Jane	LD	530
Felse, Michael James	ED	193
Fenn, Stephen John	LD	149
Fensome, Matthew	MRLP	397
Ferguson, Jim	Con	331
Ferguson, Michael Stewart	BNP	394
Fernandes, Suzanne	Ch P	218
Fernando, Charith Harsha	Ch P	57
Ferrett, John	Lab	458
Field, Frank	Lab	56
Field, Mark Christopher	Con	151

Candidate Name	Party	PA
Field, Russell David	LD	165
Finch, Raymond Terence	UKIP	226
Findlay, Rebecca	Grn	544
Findley, Martyn Russell	BNP	435
Finlay, Stephen	BNP	596
Finnie, John	SNP	331
Finnie, Joseph T	BNP	263
Firth, Rachel	BNP	322
Fisher, John Malcolm	LD	538
Fisher, Peter	LD	521
Fitter, Nick	Grn	319
Fitton, David Arthur Haydn	Ind	642
Fitton, James	BNP	491
Fitzgerald, Michael Richard Ducie	UKIP	457
Fitzharris, Sally Ann	LD	344
Fitzpatrick, Barney	APNI	376
Fitzpatrick, Eamonn	Ind	427
Fitzpatrick, James	Lab	456
Fitzpatrick, Martin	Ind	505
Flannery, Sarah Catherine	Ind	563
Flello, Robert Charles Douglas	Lab	539
Fleming, David Alexander	BNP	423
Fleming, Malcolm	SNP	267
Fletcher, Derek	Nobody	467
Fletcher, Lee Charles	Grn	241
Fletcher, Mark	Grn	187
Fletcher, Samantha	Grn	147
Flint, Caroline Louise	Lab	194
Fluss, James Gordon	UKIP	148
Flux, Barry Malcolm	Con	73
Flynn, Helen Catherine	LD	513
Flynn, Michael	Ch P	596
Flynn, Paul Phillip	Lab	418
Flynn, Sian Pamela	Con	162
Flynn, Tom	Lab	525
Foden, John Boyd	UKIP	377
Foley, Ben	Grn	41
Follows, Terence	SIG	539
Foote, Celia Elizabeth	AGS	353
Foote-Wood, Chris	LD	394
Forbes, Christopher	UKIP	165
Forbes, Jayne Elizabeth	Grn	28
Forbes, Peter Martin	Grn	383
Ford, David Michael	Grn	87
Ford, Malcolm John	UKIP	613
Ford, Michael	UKIP	88
Ford, Shirley Florence	Grn	522
Ford, Steven	Ind	312
Fordham, Ed	LD	290
Formosa, Mark Anthony	Con	564
Forrest, Alistair	UKIP	374
Forrest, Maya Henderson	Con	268
Forse, Geoff	Grn	358
Forster, Christopher Walter Charles	BNP	300
Foster, Amanda Marie	BNP	176
Foster, Donald Michael Ellison	LD	36
Foster, Hannah Margaret	Con	244

Candidate Name	Party	PA
Foster, Kevin John	Con	167
Foster, Michael Jabez	Lab	298
Foster, Michael John	Lab	633
Foster, Nick	Grn	344
Foster, Paul Andrew	Lab	471
Fovargue, Yvonne Helen	Lab	385
Fowke, Steve	UKIP	182
Fowler, Barry	BNP	158
Fowler, Sherry Melinda	UKIP	51
Fowler, Steven	UKIP	602
Fox, Bridget Caroline	LD	335
Fox, Christopher James	Grn	297
Fox, Colin Anthony	SSP	231
Fox, Frances Agnes	UKIP	451
Fox, Joseph B	UKIP	468
Fox, Liam	Con	517
Fox, Thomas William	Ind	38
Foy, Maria Teresa	UKIP	58
France, Mark Anthony	Ind	105
Francis, Alan Herbert	Grn	397
Francis, Decima Shamona	Ind	117
Francis, Hywel	Lab	1
Francis, Martin	Grn	91
Francois, Mark Gino	Con	463
Fraser, Kit	Joy	331
Fraser, Leah	Con	592
Fraser, Stephanie Mary	Con	173
Frazer, William	Ind	419
Freedman, Maxwell Oliver	Lab	343
Freeman, Alan	UKIP	618
Freeman, George	Con	421
Freeman, Stephen	ND	49
Freer, Mike	Con	252
French, Chris	UKIP	168
French, Grant	UKIP	448
Freshwater, Roy Andrew	UKIP	233
Fryer, Jonathan Harold	LD	456
Fulcher, Rachel	Grn	548
Fullbrook, Lorraine	Con	521
Fuller, Richard Quentin	Con	41
Fulton, David Edward	UKIP	94
Furness, David Robert	BNP	219
Fychan, Heledd	PC	402
Fyfe, Stephen	BNP	276
Fyvie, Ian Christopher	Soc Lab	98
Gadsden, Charles Richard George	LD	637
Gain, Stan	CPA	614
Gajadharsingh, Anthony George	Lab	142
Galbraith, Mary	Lab	209
Gale, Christopher George	Lib	244
Gale, David	Ind	181
Gale, Roger James	Con	567
Gallagher, Daniel Charles	LD	643
Gallagher, William Edmund	Con	10
Galletley, Ian Percival	Con	535
Galloway, George	Respect	456

Candidate Name	Party	PA
Galloway, Tamara Eileen	Grn	442
Gandy, Kim Elizabeth	UKIP	614
Gann, Thomas George	Lab	496
Gapes, Michael John	Lab	329
Gardiner, Barry	Lab	91
Gardner, Andrew	Ind	59
Garg, Sidharath	Lab	587
Garnett, Andrew David	Con	372
Garnett, Martin Charles	LD	241
Garnier, Edward Henry	Con	291
Garnier, Mark Robert Timothy	Con	644
Garrett, Ann Christine	Grn	40
Garrett, Ian Anthony George	LD	612
Gaskell, Pat	UKIP	370
Gasper, Julia Margaret	UKIP	443
Gasson, Emily Jane	LD	198
Gaszczak, Susan	LD	463
Gates, Deirdre Anne	BNP	310
Gatley, Shaun	BNP	395
Gatt, Donald	UKIP	403
Gauci, Rosalind Christella	BNP	521
Gauke, David Michael	Con	310
Geddes, Stewart	Con	232
Geddis, Sean Anthony	Ind	36
Gell, Keith Vernon	Ind	225
George, Andrew Henry	LD	494
Geraghty, David	Pirate	181
German, Veronica Kathleen	LD	418
Gerrish, Brian John	Ind	453
Ghafoor, Kamran	Con	440
Ghai, Ashay	LD	446
Ghani, Nusrat Munir	Con	61
Gibb, Ian	Con	219
Gibb, Nicolas John	Con	74
Gibson, Ian	BNP	461
Gibson, John Philip Robson	LD	349
Gibson, Keith Allan	TUSC	325
Gibson, Michael George	Poet	563
Gibson, Patricia	SNP	25
Gibson, Terry	BNP	416
Gidley, Sandra Julia	LD	478
Gilbert, Andrew Norman	Con	56
Gilbert, Brian Patrick	UKIP	581
Gilbert, Stephen David John	LD	491
Gildernew, Michelle	SF	249
Giles, Graham William	Lab	272
Gill, Christopher John Fred	UKIP	379
Gill, Elaine	UKIP	647
Gill, Parmjit Singh	LD	357
Gill, Steven Daniel	BNP	293
Gillan, Cheryl Elise Kendall	Con	142
Gillard, Karen	LD	163
Gilligan, Dylan	Youth	513
Gilmore, Colin Roger	BNP	356
Gilmore, Sheila	Lab	228
Gilroy, Linda	Lab	453
Gilroy, Patsy	Con	406

Candidate Name	Party	PA
Gimson, Sally Louise	Lab	360
Girling, Keith Frank	Con	35
Girvan, Deborah	APNI	542
Gitau, James Kamau Naaman	Ch P	170
Gittins, Paul Steven	ND	499
Gittos, Tim	UKIP	140
Glackin, Jamie	Lab	450
Gladwin, Tony	BNP	525
Glass, Pat	Lab	216
Glen, John Philip	Con	496
Glenn, Stephen	LD	369
Glennon, Michael Joseph	UKIP	638
Glindon, Mary Theresa	Lab	583
Glover, Peter	TUSC	79
Glover, Philip	UKIP	83
Glover, Timothy Richard	Grn	332
Glynn, Graham Michael	ED	501
Goddard, Stephen Howard	LD	443
Godsiff, Roger Duncan	Lab	59
Goggins, Paul	Lab	645
Golberg, Bernice Clare	Grn	170
Gold, David Stanley	Con	236
Goldberg, Joseph Daniel	Lab	627
Golden, Beverley Joan	Grn	409
Golden, Maurice Charles	Con	24
Goldfinch, Jessica	Grn	430
Goldie, Brian	UKIP	245
Golding, Paul Anthony	BNP	502
Goldsmith, Zac	Con	473
Goldspink, Stephen Kenneth Savill	ED	121
Goldsworthy, Julia Anne	LD	118
Gollins, James Grimshaw	Impact	510
Golton, Stewart	LD	235
Gonzalez, Lee Grant	Con	454
Goodall, Chris	Grn	444
Goodall, David Ian	LD	523
Goode, Roy	UKIP	528
Goodman, Helen Catherine	Lab	66
Goodwill, Robert	Con	497
Goodwin, Roy	BNP	70
Goodyer, Eric	Lab	136
Gordon, Katy	LD	264
Gordon, Stephen Joseph	LD	425
Gore, John Shaw	CIP	527
Gormley, Kerry	Grn	327
Gorrie, Angela	SSP	211
Gossage, John Richard	LD	132
Gough, John	Con	31
Gould, Gareth David	Lab	520
Gould, Jenny Nancy	Grn	485
Gove, Michael Andrew	Con	553
Gower, Tom	BNP	165
Grady, Patrick	SNP	264
Graham, Alastair	Con	115
Graham, Andrew	Ind	236
Graham, David	Lab	17
Graham, Richard Michael John Ogilvie	Con	270

Candidate Name	Party	PA
Griffiths, David Jason	Grn	129
Griffiths, David Philip	Ch P	155
Griffiths, John Henry	ED	55
Griffiths, Judy	Soc Alt	167
Griffiths, Kenneth John	BNP	204
Griffiths, Philip William Barrington	UKIP	625
Griffiths, Robert David	Comm	128
Groves, Matthew Paul	Con	452
Gruffydd, Llyr Huws	PC	155
Grunsell, Jackie	TUSC	158
Grunshaw, Clive	Lab	350
Guest, Marlene	BNP	482
Guiver, Ian	UKIP	183
Gummer, Benedict Michael	Con	332
Gunnion, Ray	TUSC	406
Gunstock, Ashley	Grn	366
Gurney, Sam	Lab	340
Gutfreund-Walmsley, Robert	UKIP	389
Guy, Steve	LD	642
Gwynn, Lawrence Douglas	UKIP	127
Gwynne, Andrew John	Lab	180
Gwyther, Christine	Lab	131
Gyimah, Sam	Con	552
Hacking, Belinda	Con	213
Hadden, Jason Mark	Con	171
Hague, William Jefferson	Con	472
Haig, Barbara	Grn	542
Haigh, Andrew Martin	UKIP	179
Haigh, Ann Mary	LD	239
Hain, Peter	Lab	408
Haines, Gerald Leslie	Grn	477
Halden, Stephen Frank	UKIP	560
Haley, Darren	UKIP	501
Halfon, Robert Henry	Con	292
Hall, Bill	UKIP	42
Hall, Craig Ian	Ind	327
Hall, Glenn	Con	72
Hall, Joe	Ind	381
Hall, Justine	Grn	388
Hall, Pamela Theresa	Con	373
Hall, Patrick	Lab	41
Hall, Simon	Grn	380
Hall, Sylvia	UKIP	314
Hallam, Robert George	CNPG	364
Hallas, David Matthew	LD	580
Hall-Matthews, David Nicholas John	LD	87
Hames, Duncan John	LD	147
Hamilton, Andrea	UKIP	35
Hamilton, David	Lab	396
Hamilton, David	UKIP	390
Hamilton, Fabian	Lab	353
Hamilton, Harry	UCUNF	586
Hamilton, Helen Jane	BNP	554
Hamilton, Karen	LD	63
Hamilton, Richard James Munro	BNP	397
Hamilton, Walter	BNP	265

Candidate Name	Party	PA
Harston, Jonathan Graham	LD	503
Hart, Brian	Ind	272
Hart, Simon Anthony	Con	132
Hartigan, Christopher N	BNP	507
Harvey, Celia Jane	Con	358
Harvey, Martin	UKIP	106
Harvey, Nicholas Barton	LD	190
Harvey, Nigel	UKIP	598
Harvie, Amanda	Con	4
Harwood, Susan	BNP	640
Haselhurst, Alan	Con	489
Haslam, Kenneth	BNP	385
Havard, Dai	Lab	393
Hawkins, Julie Marie	Grn	428
Hawkins, Miriam	Grn	591
Hawkins, Quentin John	BNP	312
Hawkins, Robert James	Soc Lab	118
Hawkins, Robert Oliver	Soc Lab	453
Hawksworth, Denise Elizabeth	LD	75
Hay, Bruce Alexander	UKIP	465
Hayball, Anna T	Grn	198
Haycocks, Daniel John	SMA	84
Hayes, John Henry	Con	520
Hayles, Arthur	Grn	236
Hayman, Sue	Lab	282
Haynes, Adrian John	UKIP	608
Hayter, John	ED	463
Hazelgrove, Claire	Lab	513
Hazell, Dirk	LD	140
Hazell, Elizabeth Anne	UKIP	593
Heading, Brendan Joseph	APNI	586
Heading, Brian	SDLP	347
Heald, Adrian	Lab	382
Heald, Oliver	Con	309
Healey, John	Lab	611
Healy, Caroline Frances	Con	388
Healy, Denis Gerard	LD	324
Healy, Joseph	Grn	590
Heasley, Evan	UKIP	424
Heath, Christopher Derek Landen	UKIP	502
Heath, David William St John	LD	519
Heathcoat-Amory, David	Con	609
Heather, Gary Frederick John	Lab	580
Heather, Leonard Alfred	BNP	431
Heatley, Brian	Grn	199
Heaton-Harris, Christopher	Con	178
Hein, John	Lib	229
Hemingway, Martin Francis	Grn	354
Hemming, John Alexander Melvin	LD	65
Hemming-Clark, John Stanley Charles David	ISQM	438
Hemsted, Andy	Con	595
Henderson, Gordon	Con	512
Henderson, Ivan John	Lab	152
Henderson, Juliet Mary	Con	470
Henderson, Margaret Adams	Ind	315
Hendon, Warren	UKIP	353
Hendrick, Mark Phillip	Lab	460

Candidate Name	Party	PA
Hodgson, Sharon	Lab	603
Hoey, Catherine Letitia	Lab	590
Hogan, Bruce Alan	Lab	254
Hogan, Kevin Matthew Joseph Christopher	Ind	30
Hogan, Nick	UKIP	149
Hogbin, Martin	MRLP	552
Holden, Bill	Ind	430
Holder, Nick	Con	414
Holland, Andrew Miles	Ch P	430
Holland, Rowena Emma	Con	434
Holland, Simon	Lab	145
Holland, Stephen Alan	Con	534
Holliday, Christian John	Con	558
Holliman, Carrie	APP	326
Hollingbery, George	Con	391
Hollings, Peter George	UKIP	95
Hollister, Adrian Oakley	Grn	412
Hollobone, Philip Thomas	Con	341
Holloway, Adam James Harold	Con	275
Hollowell, Francis Graeme	LD	160
Holly, Michael Charles	Con	313
Holme, John	Ind	496
Holmes, Edward	BNP	19
Holmes, Hugh David	BNP	455
Holmes, Jason	BNP	602
Holmes, Paul Robert	LD	144
Holmes, Roger Graeme	MK	163
Holt, Doreen	LD	70
Holt, Ian	BNP	262
Holtom, Ann Lesley	LD	58
Holvey, Tom	LD	501
Hood, Jim	Lab	348
Hood, Mark	Lab	250
Hookem, Michael	UKIP	323
Hooks, Paul Stephen	BNP	88
Hooper, Jacqueline Mary	UKIP	420
Hooper, Peter John	Ind	623
Hooton, Damon John	LD	561
Hope, Alan	MRLP	627
Hope, Beverley	LD	228
Hope, Jill Susan	LD	397
Hope, Philip Ian	Lab	161
Hopkins, Kelvin	Lab	380
Hopkins, Kris	Con	338
Hoppe, Damon Leroy	Grn	540
Hopwood, Roy Graham	UKIP	69
Hopwood, Stephen	Ind	577
Hoque, Mohammed Aminul	Ind	456
Hordon, Kenneth William	UKIP	325
Horn, Mark Philip Malcolm	LIND	274
Hornby, Fiona Clare	LD	187
Horne, Graeme	SNP	487
Hornett, Jonathan Terence	Grn	608
Horsfield, Andy	UKIP	53
Horton, Toby	UKIP	569
Horwood, Martin Charles	LD	141
Hosie, Stewart	SNP	211

Candidate Name	Party	PA
Hossack, Yvonne	Ind	536
Hossain, Reza	Grn	489
Houlden, Martin James	Ind	187
Houston, Fiona	Con	156
Houston, John	Ind	223
Howard, Frances Mary	UKIP	496
Howard, William Geoffrey	Ind	108
Howarth, George Edward	Lab	346
Howarth, James Gerald Douglas	Con	7
Howat, Sandy	SNP	230
Howe, Adrian Michael	PNDP	276
Howe, Jacqueline Ann	LD	424
Howe, Peter Phillip	ND	130
Howe, Philip	Ind	470
Howell, John Michael	Con	305
Howell, Philip David	BNP	134
Howell, Stella Hermione	UKIP	34
Howells, Gordon Clifford	BNP	644
Howitt, Hugh Alexander	UKIP	70
Howlett, John Edward	UKIP	113
Howson, James William	UKIP	10
Hoyle, Lindsay Harvey	Lab	149
Hubner, Andrew Patrick	Ind	168
Huddleston, Nigel Paul	Con	381
Hudson, Grahame Francis Grenville	LD	488
Hudson, Henry Richard	UKIP	276
Hudson, Linda	UKIP	603
Hudson, Neil	Con	230
Huggins, Steven	Ind	358
Hughes, David Norman	UKIP	82
Hughes, Elizabeth Patricia	Lab	421
Hughes, Frank Roger Wynne	UKIP	174
Hughes, Gareth Bryn	Con	641
Hughes, Jason Philip	Lab	619
Hughes, John Valentine	Grn	560
Hughes, Laurence	UKIP	305
Hughes, Louise	Ind	217
Hughes, Neil	LD	130
Hughes, Ron	Ind	53
Hughes, Ronald Arvon	Lab	2
Hughes, Simon Henry Ward	LD	49
Huhne, Christopher Murray Paul	LD	226
Hull, Robert	Lab	468
Hulme, Janet Elizabeth	Lab	162
Humberstone, John Malcolm	UKIP	641
Humphrey, Christopher Alan	Ind	152
Humphrey, Steven John	Ind	82
Humphrey, William	DUP	48
Humphreys, Alice	LD	400
Humphreys, Alwyn	Lab	217
Humphreys, James William	Grn	335
Hunt, Anthony John	Lab	379
Hunt, Jane Marion	Con	356
Hunt, Jeremy	Con	554
Hunt, John Geoffrey	Grn	92
Hunt, Jon	LD	124
Hunt, Richard	Con	594

Candidate Name	Party	PA
Hunt, Tristram Julian William	Lab	537
Hunter, Mark James	LD	138
Huppert, Julian Leon	LD	119
Hurd, Nicholas Richard	Con	484
Hurds, Lucy Ann	LD	307
Hurll, Martyn John	LD	150
Hurne, Janice Carol	Lab	410
Hurst, Chris	BNP	581
Hurst, Malcolm William	UKIP	640
Hurst, Natalie	Grn	498
Hussain, Ashiq	Lab	8
Hussain, Qurban	LD	381
Hussain, Raja Sakhawat	Ind	85
Hussey, Ross	UCUNF	584
Hutchens, Kevin	Lab	12
Hutchings, Maria	Con	226
Hutchinson, Andrew	LD	193
Hutton, Donna Elizabeth	Lab	155
Hutton, Simon	LD	330
Hutty, Philip Andrew	LD	188
Huxtable, Keely Susan	Con	62
Hyde, Philip Joseph	Ind	477
Hyden, Steve	Lab	367
Hylands, Robert Leonard	LD	272
Hynd, Roland Thomas	BNP	528
Hynes, Sarah Anne	BNP	154
Illingworth, Jamie	UKIP	86
Illsley, Andrew	UKIP	540
Illsley, Eric	Lab	29
Ingall, Stephen Michael	UKIP	358
Inglis, Otto	UKIP	213
Ingram, Andy	BNP	467
Inman, Kevin	NF	204
Innes, Jayne Elisabeth	Lab	435
Iqbal, Khizar	Ind	193
Iqbal, Zahid	Con	87
Ireland, Daren Andrew	TUSC	371
Irfanullah, Bushra	BIB	67
Irranca-Davies, Huw	Lab	437
Irvine, Tom	UKIP	411
Irwin, William George	DUP	419
Islam, Mohammed Sarul	PC	129
Ison, John Paul	UKIP	516
Ivory, Trevor Charles Colin	Con	422
Jack, Linda Anne	LD	42
Jackman, James Daniel Morris	BNP	447
Jackson, Chris	NF	474
Jackson, Derek Leslie	Land	345
Jackson, Glenda	Lab	290
Jackson, Ian Andrew	LD	367
Jackson, Michael	Grn	650
Jackson, Neil Playle	BNP	54
Jackson, Richard Adam	Lab	563
Jackson, Stewart James	Con	451
Jacob, Samuel Augusten	Ch P	545
Jacobsen, David	Soc Lab	229

Candidate Name	Party	PA
Johnson, Michael	ED	480
Johnson, Neil Duncan	UKIP	76
Johnson, Peter Frank	Soc Dem	60
Johnson, Ruth Marion	Ch P	251
Johnston, Robert	Lab	543
Johnstone, Alex	Con	5
Joines, David Paul	BNP	440
Jonas, David	Grn	606
Jones, Adrian	BNP	273
Jones, Andrew Hanson	Con	293
Jones, Anthony David	BNP	531
Jones, Arfon	PC	641
Jones, Barry	Lab	288
Jones, Ben	Con	285
Jones, Brian Arthur	UKIP	566
Jones, Caroline Yvonne	Con	1
Jones, Darren Paul	Lab	192
Jones, David Ian	Con	155
Jones, Debi	Con	500
Jones, Dic	PC	558
Jones, Elise Mary	BNP	271
Jones, Elizabeth Eirwen	UKIP	206
Jones, George Albert	BNP	543
Jones, Glyndwr Cennydd	PC	393
Jones, Graham Peter	Lab	327
Jones, Helen Mary	Lab	599
Jones, Helen Michele	LD	155
Jones, Hilary Jane	UKIP	373
Jones, Jacqueline Ann Crawford	UKIP	597
Jones, Jenny	Grn	117
Jones, Jimmy	Ind	78
Jones, Keith Martin	BNP	417
Jones, Kevan David	Lab	215
Jones, Leigh	UKIP	400
Jones, Leslie	LD	404
Jones, Madge	UKIP	237
Jones, Marcus Charles	Con	435
Jones, Maurice	PC	10
Jones, Michael Gerard	Lab	74
Jones, Nick	UKIP	146
Jones, Nigel	LD	413
Jones, Peter Maxwell	LD	398
Jones, Roy David	BNP	3
Jones, Simon Andrew Peter	Con	175
Jones, Susan Elan	Lab	154
Jones-Davies, Henry Ellis	PC	459
Jones-Evans, Angela	Con	129
Jordan, Debra	Ind	120
Joshi, Bhavna	Lab	547
Jowell, Tessa Jane Helen	Lab	206
Joyce, Eric	Lab	245
Joyce, Rachel	Con	295
Juby, Geoffrey William	LD	475
Judge, Andrew John	Lab	621
Jug, Lord Toby	MRLP	326
Julian, Robin	UKIP	192
Juniper, Anthony Thomas	Grn	119

Candidate Name	Party	PA
Kadara, Abimbola	Ch P	578
Kaikavoosi, Siamak	Ind	522
Kalinauckas, Paul	Lab	640
Kamble, Vasundhara	APNI	249
Kane, Gareth	LD	414
Kapetanos, James	APP	590
Kapur, Rohen	Ind	318
Kara, Soraya Anne	CURE	98
Kasab, Onay Mustafa	TUSC	278
Kaufman, Gerald Bernard	Lab	388
Kawczynski, Daniel Robert	Con	510
Kay, Tony	UKIP	184
Kayes, Ros	LD	199
Keal, Howard	LD	569
Kearsley, Mike	ED	243
Keating, Edward	LD	598
Keats, Robert Jeffrey	Grn	333
Keaveney, Paula	LD	258
Kebbell, Alan John	UKIP	523
Keeble, Sally Curtis	Lab	427
Keeley, Barbara Mary	Lab	637
Keen, Alan	Lab	248
Keen, Ann	Lab	92
Kelley, Claire Elizabeth	LD	293
Kelly, Chris	Con	205
Kelly, Christine Ann	BNP	421
Kelly, Dolores	SDLP	586
Kelly, Gerry	SF	46
Kelly, Jeff	BNP	648
Kelly, Lynnette Catherine	Lab	65
Kelly, Mike	UKIP	534
Kelly, Stuart Edward	LD	56
Kemp, Graham	NF	247
Kemp, Penelope Anne	Grn	253
Kendall, David John	LD	93
Kendall, Gareth Anthony	UKIP	384
Kendall, Liz	Lab	358
Kennedy, Charles Peter	LD	479
Kennedy, Danny	UCUNF	419
Kennedy, Gordon	Ind	175
Kennedy, Seema Louise Ghiassi	Con	21
Kennet, Miriam Frances	Grn	515
Kenny, Paul Robert	Lab	80
Kent, Debra	BNP	350
Kerevan, George	SNP	228
Kerr, Duncan Alistair	Grn	144
Kerr, Jimmy	SSP	446
Kerrin, Gary J	UKIP	299
Khaira, Asa Singh	Ind	248
Khalsa, Satnam Kaur	LD	300
Khan, Arshad	JP	168
Khan, Ayoub	LD	61
Khan, Gulzaman	Ch P	594
Khan, Hamira	Con	263
Khan, Johar	LD	238
Khan, Karrar	LD	486
Khan, Maryam	Lab	111

Candidate Name	Party	PA
Khan, Sadiq Aman	Lab	574
Khan, Shafiqui Islam	Lab	133
Khan, Shasha	Grn	171
Khan, Tariq Ayoub	LD	60
Khan, Zakir Hussain	Con	52
Khokar, Mudassar Aziz	Ind	642
Kidd, Heather Mary	LD	379
Kidney, David Neil	Lab	528
Kiersch, Leila	Grn	135
Kilbane-Dawe, Iarla Jonathan	LD	233
Kilpatrick, Kaye	TUV	202
Kindersley, Sebastian Gerald Molesworth	LD	122
King, Andrew	Lab	483
King, Anthony David John	BNP	71
King, Edward John	Ind	307
King, Marietta Eve Neild	UKIP	291
King, Michael	UKIP	281
King, Nicholas Percy Robert	Con	197
King, Robert John	ED	451
King, Stuart Thomas	Lab	462
Kinzett, Rene Harwood	Con	559
Kirby, Christopher Charles Andrew	Lab	104
Kirby, Simon Gerard	Con	97
Kirby, Spencer Lee	BNP	633
Kirk, Alastair James	Ch P	561
Kirk, Madeleine Anne	LD	649
Kirkby, Alan Dennis	Ind	49
Kirkman, David Thomas	Lab	309
Kirkwood, Andy	Vote	199
Kirwan, David Stanley	Ind	625
Kissach, Derek Alan	Ind	319
Kitchen, Ian Ashley	BNP	303
Kitcher, Amy	LD	393
Klein, Sonia Nabila	Lab	328
Knapp, Knigel	MRLP	280
Knight, David John	ED	457
Knight, Gregory	Con	650
Knight, Jenny	UKIP	570
Knight, Jim	Lab	199
Knight, John Anthony	Grn	382
Knight, John William	UKIP	251
Knight, Lesley Anne	Grn	190
Knight, Mark Andrew	UKIP	404
Knight, Ricky	Grn	102
Knowles, Nigel	Lab	644
Knox, Allan McLean	LD	471
Knox, Patricia Lineve	ND	117
Kocan, Michael Karl	UKIP	71
Koundarjian, Hratche	Lab	362
Krakowiak, Peter John	Grn	238
Kramer, Susan Veronica	LD	473
Krishna-Das, Arjuna	Grn	311
Kriss, Adrian David	BIC	105
Kulka, Jane N	LD	468
Kushlick, Danny	Ind	102
Kwarteng, Kwasi Alfred Addo	Con	527

Candidate Name	Party	PA
Lear, Andy	Best	243
Lebar, Ron	Ch M	165
Lee, Andrew	Con	504
Lee, Christine Mary	Ind	313
Lee, David	LD	552
Lee, George	Con	316
Lee, Graham John	Grn	484
Lee, Jessica Katherine	Con	241
Lee, Jessica Marian	Grn	300
Lee, Joseph	LD	278
Lee, Phillip James	Con	84
Lee, Stephen Peter	UKIP	636
Leech, John	LD	389
Lee-Delisle, Edward George	Ind	201
Leeder, Adam James	Lab	548
Leeds, Samuel Luke	Ch P	64
Lees, Christopher	UKIP	102
Lees, Jonathan	LD	240
Leff, Jonty	WRP	387
Leffman, Liz	LD	391
Lefroy, Jeremy	Con	528
Legard, Edward	Con	176
Leigh, Andrew Michael	UKIP	453
Leigh, Edward Julian Egerton	Con	257
Leighton, Luke Kenneth Casson	Pirate	554
LeMay, Debbie	ED	106
Lennon, Dominic Joseph	UKIP	334
Lennon, John Francis	CPA	397
Lenton, Christopher	UKIP	601
Leon-Smith, Grahame	IFED	527
Lepper, Paul Robert	WRP	544
Leppert, Julian Peter	BNP	146
Leslie, Charlotte Ann	Con	100
Leslie, Christopher Michael	Lab	432
Leslie, George	SNP	342
Le-Surf, Michael	Lab	463
Letwin, Oliver	Con	200
Levin, Martin	IFED	366
Levy, Martin Richard	Comm	415
Lewin, Andrew Alan	LD	308
Lewin, Terence John	BNP	612
Lewis, Brandon Kenneth	Con	277
Lewis, Charlotte	BNP	133
Lewis, Ivan	Lab	112
Lewis, James	Lab	235
Lewis, Jo	Lab	540
Lewis, Julian Murray	Con	409
Lewis, Peter Michael	UKIP	510
Lewis, Steffan	PC	336
Lewthwaite, James Graham	D Nat	86
Liddell-Grainger, Ian Richard	Con	95
Lidington, David Roy	Con	22
Light, Barbara Ann	Lab	489
Lightwing, Stuart William	UKIP	395
Lilley, Peter Bruce	Con	315
Lindley, Iain David	Con	637
Lindley, Ian Paul	LD	215

Candidate Name	Party	PA
Lindsay, Alison Jean	SNP	533
Lindsey, Corinne Jane	Grn	420
Ling, Philip	LD	105
Linley, Matt	WRP	248
Linsley, Howard Jeremy	Lab	391
Linton, Bill	Grn	237
Linton, Martin	Lab	38
List, Sandra Ann	UKIP	511
Lister, Kevin John	Grn	164
Lithgow, Jane Alison	Grn	614
Little, Antony Daniel	Con	431
Little, Frank	LD	408
Littlejohn, Graeme	LD	436
Littlewood, Hugh Rodney Andrew	Best	527
Litwin, Craig Jason	UKIP	175
Liversuch, Paul Amos	Soc Lab	186
Livingstone, Marc	Comm	266
Ljubisic, Petar	Ch P	219
Llewellyn, Dominic Robin Crofts	Con	415
Llewelyn, Alun	PC	408
Lloyd, Christopher	Lab	89
Lloyd, David Ronald	BNP	362
Lloyd, Joan Rose	Ind	464
Lloyd, Jon	UKIP	224
Lloyd, Stephen Anthony Christopher	LD	225
Lloyd, Tony	Lab	387
Lloyd, Trevor Sidney	BNP	57
Lloyd Davies, Mark Thomas	Con	101
Llwyd, Elfyn	PC	217
Lo, Anna	APNI	47
Loakes, Clyde William	Lab	428
Lobley, Matthew	Con	353
Lochmuller, Anthony James	Grn	427
Lochner, Wayne	UKIP	456
Lock, Kathleen Jane	LD	560
Locke, Geoffrey Lewis Edward	UKIP	538
Logan, Ian Robert Lennox	ED	636
Logan, Kevin	CPA	327
Logan, Liam	SDLP	202
Lomas, Alan Ernest	Ind	546
Lomas, Andrew Philip	Lab	642
Lomas, David George	BNP	21
Lomax, David William	LD	563
Long, Naomi	APNI	45
Longley, Graham Edwin	LD	476
Lopresti, Jack	Con	251
Lord, Jonathan George Caladine	Con	628
Lord, Roger Gordon	UKIP	489
Lorriman, Duncan	BNP	501
Loughton, John	LD	223
Loughton, Timothy Paul	Con	638
Lovatt, Carol	UKIP	537
Love, Andy	Lab	233
Love, John	LD	6
Love, Nicholas	LD	611
Lovell, Gregory Stewart	Lab	147
Low, Keith	Nat Lib	226

Candidate Name	Party	PA
Low, Sheila	Con	269
Loynes, Christopher	Grn	31
Lucas, Caroline	Grn	98
Lucas, Chris	LD	219
Lucas, Christopher John	UKIP	357
Lucas, Eric Paul	Grn	36
Lucas, Ian Colin	Lab	641
Lucas, Jon	Grn	251
Lucas, Melwyn	TUV	15
Luff, Peter James	Con	634
Lumby, Richard John	BNP	60
Lumby, Tanya Jane	BNP	65
Lumley, Karen Elizabeth	Con	467
Lunn, Robin Christopher	Lab	634
Lunn, Trevor	APNI	347
Lunnon, Tim	Lab	18
Lury, Martin	LD	145
Lyburn, Peter James	Con	450
Lynch, Gerry	APNI	13
Lynch, Rae	TUSC	99
Lynn, Peter James	Grn	157
Lyon, Martin Edward	UKIP	410
Lyon, Steve	Ch P	319
Lyven, Donald Edmund	Grn	252
Macarthur, Malcolm	UKIP	427
Macaskill, Malcolm	Con	487
Macaulay, Lesley Ann	UCUNF	376
MacDonald, Christopher Peter	UKIP	38
MacDonald, George	TUSC	331
Macdonald, Gordon	LD	469
Macdonald, Moira	Lab	188
Macdonald, Stuart	Grn	627
Macharia, Geoffrey Wangombe	Ch P	544
Maciejowska, Judy	Grn	222
MacIntyre, Cameron James	Ind	229
Mack, Paul	Ind	446
Mackay, Christine Ann	Con	323
MacKay, Donald Murdo	UKIP	469
Mackay, John	Lab	115
Mackenzie, Bruce William	Grn	462
Mackenzie, Charlotte	Lab	579
Mackenzie, James Neil Grant	Grn	224
Mackie, Katie	Con	245
Mackintosh, Fred	LD	230
MacLaren, Mags	SNP	445
MacLaren of MacLaren, Donald	Ind	345
Maclennan, Iain Ross	Grn	457
Macleod, Donnie	Grn	331
Macleod, Mary	Con	92
MacNeil, Angus Brendan	SNP	407
Macpherson, James Stephen	BNP	535
MacShane, Denis	Lab	482
MacSween, Donald John	Lab	407
Mactaggart, Fiona Margaret	Lab	515
Mad, Cap'n Tom	Ind	151
Maginness, Alban Alphonsus	SDLP	46

Candidate Name	Party	PA
Maguire, Jonathan Paul	ED	147
Mahapatra, Neil	Con	499
Mahfouz, Bassam	Lab	218
Mahmood, Khalid	Lab	63
Mahmood, Shabana	Lab	61
Mahmud, Kabir	Ind	456
Mahoney, Barry Joseph	UKIP	429
Mahoney, Kevin	UKIP	589
Mailer, Peter William	BNP	50
Main, Anne Margaret	Con	490
Main, Thomas	BNP	264
Mainland, John	LD	345
Mainprize, Jonathan Patrick	BNP	324
Mair, Colin Edward Daniel	ED	378
Majorowicz, Terence	BNP	124
Malakounides, Mal	ND	238
Malik, Ahmed Abdul	Ind	52
Malik, Atiq	Ind	91
Malik, Kamran	Ind	614
Malik, Shahid	Lab	193
Mall, Ashar Javid	Ch P	595
Mallaber, Judy	Lab	11
Mallender, Richard	Grn	486
Maloney, Francis Thomas	UKIP	28
Maltby, Clive Trend	ED	638
Mander, John Malcolm	UKIP	616
Mann, Harry	Lab	310
Mann, John	Lab	35
Mann, Keith James	APP	444
Mann, Rachel Elizabeth	Grn	78
Mann, Simon Edgar	Ind	422
Manson, Gareth Thomas	Lab	189
Manwaring, Bill	UCUNF	48
Manwell, John Desmond	CPA	371
Manzoor, Mazhar	UKIP	279
Marbrow, Richard	LD	370
Marchant, Patricia Anne	Grn	261
Marchant, Simon Philip	Grn	475
Marchesi, David Terence	Soc Lab	452
Marcus, Simon Joel Solomon	Con	28
Marjoram, Joseph William	Con	355
Marriott, Irenea	UKIP	433
Marris, Robert	Lab	632
Marsden, Adam	Con	371
Marsden, Gordon	Lab	70
Marsh, Colin Bernard	BNP	607
Marshall, Andrew Ieuan	UKIP	375
Marshall, David Malcolm	UKIP	260
Marshall, Gary Leon	BNP	190
Marshall, Jan	Lab	501
Marshall, Jeffrey Christopher	BNP	52
Marten, Danny	Lab	284
Martin, Christopher David Everest	UKIP	458
Martin, David Lee	Ch P	621
Martin, Deborah Vivien	Ind	108
Martin, Edward Stephen	LD	602
Martin, Fiona Margaret	LD	378

Candidate Name	Party	PA
Martin, Larna Jane	Ch P	590
Martin, Lee	Con	551
Martin, Malcolm Kershaw	CPA	363
Martin, Paul St John	MEP	333
Martin, Penelope Ann	Lab	69
Martin, Tony Lee	BNP	399
Martins, Rabi	LD	380
Masih, Richard Eric	Ch P	447
Mason, John	SNP	263
Mason, Marion Ann	UKIP	532
Mason-Apps, Peter William	UKIP	515
Masroor, Ajmal	LD	52
Mastin, Steven James	Con	466
Matcham, Victor Peter	UKIP	201
Mather, Charles Edward	BNP	618
Mather, John Mark	Ind	385
Mathew, Brian	LD	517
Mathias, Alun John	Ind	126
Matthews, Colin Robert	Grn	188
Matthews, Gordon Elton	Grn	634
Matthews, Jamie	LD	461
Matthews, John	Grn	454
Matthys, Jennifer Alice	BNP	179
Maude, Francis Anthony Aylmer	Con	319
Maude, John	BNP	111
Maunder, Karen	UKIP	367
Mawer, Peter	ED	325
May, Anthony James	CPA	343
May, Matthew John	Lab	429
May, Peter Nicholas	LD	559
May, Susan Jane	CPA	473
May, Theresa Mary	Con	383
Maynard, Paul Christopher	Con	69
McAleer, Mark Thomas	UKIP	621
McAllister, Billy	SNP	265
McAllister, Francis	NF	587
McAlpine, Janette	Con	342
McAskie, Pete	Grn	318
McAuley, Martin	Ind	46
McBride, Andrew	BNP	580
McBride, Andy	Ind	212
McBride, David	LD	442
McCabe, Steve	Lab	64
McCaffrey, John Vincent	BNP	551
McCall, Joe	SNP	213
McCallister, John	UCUNF	203
McCamphill, Justin	SDLP	13
McCann, Eamonn Joseph	PBP	255
McCann, Michael	Lab	223
McCann, Thomas Diamond	LD	289
McCarthy, Kerry	Lab	99
McCarthy-Fry, Sarah Louise	Lab	457
McCarthy-Stewart, Colin James	BNP	137
McCartney, Jason Alexander	Con	158
McCartney, Karl Ian	Con	368
McCaskill, Gordon Alexander	Con	446
McCastree, Dean	Ind	90

Candidate Name	Party	PA
McClean, Ciaran Martin	Ind	584
McCleery, George	Ind	396
McClintock, John Henry Conyngham	LD	137
McCloy, Ian Anthon	Ind	559
McClymont, Gregg	Lab	173
McCole, Steve	BNP	106
McConnell, Ivor	TUV	203
McCormick, Angela	TUSC	264
McCormick, Thomas Graeme	SNP	210
McCrea, Ian	DUP	585
McCrea, Robert Thomas William	DUP	15
McCune, Rodney James	UCUNF	13
McDaid, James	Soc Lab	24
McDaid, Louise	Soc Lab	25
McDonagh, Siobhain Ann	Lab	399
McDonald, Andrew	UKIP	216
McDonald, Anita Grace	Lab	484
McDonald, Brian	BNP	140
McDonald, Ian	BNP	603
McDonald, Mark	SNP	4
McDonald, Patrick Sarchfield	Lab	383
McDonald, Rose-Marie	UKIP	335
McDonald, Strachan David	UKIP	574
McDonnell, Alasdair	SDLP	47
McDonnell, John Martin	Lab	300
McDougall, Simon Edward	LD	74
McElduff, Kevin David	Lab	530
McEllenborough, Steven	BNP	372
McEnhill, Paul Henry Adrian	ED	448
McFadden, Patrick Bosco	Lab	631
McFarlane, Duncan Malcolm	Ind	348
McFarlane, Jim	TUSC	212
McFarlane, Keith	BNP	72
McGavigan, Colin	Con	348
McGavigan, Katharine Mary	Soc Lab	210
McGeechan, John	Ind	6
McGibbon, Adam Mark James	Grn	47
McGill, Iain	Con	229
McGlade, Fred	UKIP	350
McGlinchey, Frances Monica	SNP	156
McGlynn, Christopher George	LD	178
McGough, Michael Jack	UKIP	93
McGovern, Alison	Lab	624
McGovern, Jim	Lab	212
McGrellis, Keith	APNI	255
McGuinness, George Hugh	UKIP	287
McGuinness, Martin	SF	585
McGuire, Anne Catherine	Lab	533
McGuirk, Kathleen	Lab	317
McHugh, Kevin	BNP	58
McIntosh, Anne	Con	569
McIntosh, Sally Ann	LD	184
McIntyre, Martyn Anthony	Con	210
McIntyre, Tony	UKIP	564
McIsaac, Shona	Lab	153
McKay, Daithi	SF	14
McKay, Timothy Charles	LD	231

Candidate Name	Party	PA
McKeane, Steven	UKIP	208
McKechin, Ann	Lab	264
McKee, Natalie	LD	266
McKee, Vincent	LD	166
McKeever, Gareth	Con	616
McKeever, Kevin Martin Joseph	Lab	291
McKendrick, John Dempster	Lab	479
McKenna, Francis James	UKIP	253
McKenna, John	SNP	223
McKenzie, Malcolm Keith	UKIP	124
McKenzie, Michael	SNP	17
McKenzie, Richard Mark	Lab	305
McKenzie, Winston Truman	UKIP	578
McKinnell, Catherine	Lab	416
McKinney, Fearghal	SDLP	249
McLaughlan, Ian Philip	Lab	511
McLaughlin, Mitchel	SF	15
McLean, David Alexander	Ind	233
Mclean, Scott	BNP	266
McLoughlin, Patrick Allen	Con	183
McMahon, Jamie	Lab	257
McManus, Angela	UKIP	21
McMullan, Oliver	SF	13
McNally, John	SNP	245
McNamee, Colin	UKIP	101
McNaughton, Karl Raymond	Grn	8
McNerney, Kevin John	Lab	293
McNulty, Tony	Lab	294
McPartland, Stephen Anthony	Con	532
McPhee, Euan Cuthbertson	Grn	118
McTigue, Joan	Ind	394
McVey, Esther	Con	625
McVey, Kevin	SSP	265
McWilliam, Stephanie	UKIP	163
Meacher, Michael Hugh	Lab	440
Meaden, Geoffery Jasper	Grn	125
Meale, Joseph Alan	Lab	390
Mearns, Ian	Lab	259
Medway, Clive	UKIP	491
Meegan, George Geoffrey	MEDI	261
Meek, Iain	Ind	316
Meekins, Roger	UKIP	554
Meeson, Kevin	BNP	351
Melia, Tony	Impact	480
Meller, Ian	BNP	359
Meloy, Bryan John	Grn	270
Meltzer, Robin Mark	LD	340
Menzies, Mark Andrew	Con	256
Mercer, Patrick	Con	411
Meredith, Lawrence	LD	472
Meropoulos, John	UKIP	478
Merrick, Patricia Anne	Lab	227
Merrill, Sarah-Jane	Lab	516
Merriman, Huw William	Con	185
Merrin, Richard James	Con	318
Merron, Gillian Joanna	Lab	368
Merryfield, Andy	Lab	609

Candidate Name	Party	PA
Metcalfe, John	TUSC	130
Metcalfe, Stephen	Con	33
Miah, Abjol	Respect	52
Miah, Shahid	Respect	440
Michael, Alun Edward	Lab	128
Michaluk, Gerald Robert Gilmer	Con	436
Micklethwait, Anthony Robert	UKIP	485
Milburn, Jeff	Con	337
Mildren, Malcolm K	Ind	427
Miles, Jeff	UKIP	355
Miles, Jennifer Anne	Grn	561
Miles, Jeremy	Lab	39
Miles, Rollo	Grn	286
Milford, Barry David West	UKIP	483
Miliband, David	Lab	522
Miliband, Ed	Lab	196
Millam, Bernadette	LD	98
Millar, Robin John	Con	16
Millar, Walter Ernest	TUV	585
Miller, Andrew Peter	Lab	234
Miller, Ian	Lab	51
Miller, Maria Frances Lewis	Con	34
Miller, Martin	Lab	138
Miller, Thomas Arthur Clifford	Lab	628
Miller, Wendy Margaret	Grn	452
Mills, Andrew Thomas	UKIP	399
Mills, James Rodney	UKIP	513
Mills, Nigel John	Con	11
Mills, Roma Ann Clare	Lab	490
Millson, Steve	Grn	401
Milne, Galen	LD	27
Milton, Anne Frances	Con	279
Milton, Nicholas David	Lab	339
Milton, Philip James	Con	190
Miney, Neil Lawrence	UKIP	372
Minihane, Stuart Alan	BNP	555
Mitchell, Andrew John Bower	Con	557
Mitchell, Austin Vernon	Lab	276
Mitchell, Christine Margaret	BNP	489
Mitchell, David	Grn	107
Mitchell, Helen Mary	BNP	424
Mitchell, Jonathan Stuart	LD	206
Mitchell, Philip Anthony	Grn	256
Mitchell, Steven Paul	Lab	597
Mobberley, Amanda	UKIP	632
Moelwyn Hughes, Hugh	UKIP	418
Moffat, Andrew John	BNP	74
Mohindra, Gagan	Con	583
Mold, Stephen	Con	181
Mole, Christopher David	Lab	332
Mollet, Richard James	Lab	554
Molloy, Pete	BNP	215
Moloney, Patrick	LD	371
Monaghan, James	LD	405
Moncrieff, Andrew	UKIP	145
Monk, Andy	UKIP	123
Monksummers, Roger John	MRLP	198

Candidate Name	Party	PA
Montgomery, Craig	Lab	240
Montgomery, Marc Desmond	UKIP	555
Moon, Madeleine	Lab	94
Moore, Alison	Lab	252
Moore, Emma Sophie	Con	437
Moore, John David	UKIP	339
Moore, John Hamilton	UKIP	285
Moore, Kevin	LD	508
Moore, Michael Kevin	LD	51
Moore, Suzanne Lynne	ND	280
Moore, Tony	UKIP	138
Moore, Victoria	BNP	290
Moran, Layla Michelle	LD	38
Mordaunt, Penelope Mary	Con	457
Morden, Jessica Elizabeth	Lab	417
Morgan, Andrew David	Con	131
Morgan, Andrew Philip	Con	77
Morgan, David Paul	LD	576
Morgan, John	Lab	488
Morgan, Julie	Lab	127
Morgan, Nicola Ann	Con	377
Morgan, Stephen Richard	Lab	442
Morgan, Wayne	LD	94
Morland, Malcolm	LD	153
Morrice, Graeme	Lab	374
Morris, Andrew George	Ind	530
Morris, Anne Marie	Con	420
Morris, Carl Anthony Graham	Lab	571
Morris, David	Con	404
Morris, Grahame Mark	Lab	221
Morris, James George	Con	282
Morris, John Hugh	PPNV	279
Morris, Judith Mary	UKIP	649
Morris, Margaret	LTT	277
Morris, Paul	BNP	93
Morris, Paul Edward	NF	65
Morris, Stephen	ED	495
Morris, Valerie	ED	112
Morris, Virginia	Con	614
Morrish, Jacqueline Mary	Grn	379
Morrison, Clive	Ch P	233
Morrison, Elaine	Grn	17
Morrison, Loanna	Con	49
Morrison, Sammy	TUV	13
Morson, Steven William	UKIP	105
Morton, Wendy	Con	582
Mosley, Stephen James	Con	143
Moss, Colin John	Ind	312
Moss, Simon Alexander	Grn	575
Moulton, Jeremy Richard	Con	524
Mountain, Patrick William	Lab	378
Mountford, Jill	AWL	117
Mowat, David John	Con	600
Mowat, John Ross	SNP	441
Moyies, James William	UKIP	476
Mozar, Lynne	BNP	108
Mudie, George	Lab	352

Candidate Name	Party	PA
Nesbitt, Mike	UCUNF	542
Nettleship, Roger	FAWG	522
Nevols, Keith Stuart	LD	512
Newby, Andrew John	Grn	304
Newell, Jordan Alexander	Lab	157
Newman, David Ian	LD	421
Newman, Godfrey	LD	319
Newman, Martin John	UKIP	44
Newmark, Brooks	Con	88
Newton, Sarah Louise	Con	579
Newton, Stephen William	UKIP	137
Nicholas, Alun Reginald	Ind	541
Nicholls-Jones, Paul	PC	1
Nicholson, Christopher Alan	LD	544
Nicholson, Warwick Joseph	UKIP	155
Nieboer, Jeremy Christopher Savill	UKIP	198
Nielsen, Magnus	UKIP	290
Nixon, David Earnest	UKIP	413
Nixon, Richard Alan	LD	96
Noble, Garryck Henry Summers	PPE	157
Noble, Jennie	BNP	576
Nokes, Caroline Fiona Ellen	Con	478
Nolan, Christopher	Ind	235
Nolan, Mark	Con	209
Noonan, Hazel	Con	165
Noone, Denis Eamon	UKIP	349
Norman, Alexander Jesse	Con	306
Norman, Felicity Mary	Grn	307
Normington, James Adam	Lab	514
Norquay, Sheena	Con	407
Norrie, Gordon	UKIP	396
Norris, Dan	Lab	518
North, James David	BNP	508
Northover, Ed	Con	366
Northover, Ian Donald	Ind	455
Northover, Lisa Jacqueline Emma	LD	82
Norton, William Guy Darrell	Con	63
Noyce, Christopher David	LD	295
Nti, Suzanne Maria	CPA	398
Nugent, Joseph	UKIP	371
Nunn, Jack Stephen	Pirate	151
Nurse, Patricia Margaret	UKIP	378
Nuttall, David John	Con	111
Nuttall, Paul Andrew	UKIP	79
O hOisin, Cathal Joseph Martin	SF	376
Oakensen, David Alan	Lab	519
Oakes, Graham John	LD	244
Oakes, Shan	Grn	284
Oakley, Robert Nigel	UKIP	261
Oakton, Jonathan Paul	UKIP	307
O'Brien, Michael	Lab	602
O'Brien, Shannon Francis	BNP	392
O'Brien, Stephen Rothwell	Con	227
O'Connell, Alyson	Soc Lab	71
O'Connor, Barry	ED	222
O'Connor, Patrick Joseph	LD	257

Candidate Name	Party	PA
Palmer, Matthew James Steven	Con	86
Palmer, Nicholas Douglas	Lab	107
Palmer, Richard Frank	UKIP	177
Palmer, Rory	Lab	81
Pandya, Abhijit Pradip Gajanan	UKIP	294
Papworth, Thomas James	LD	484
Parekh, Shailesh	Con	60
Parish, Neil Quentin Gordon	Con	572
Park, Diane	IVH	283
Park, Mags	SNP	266
Parker, Margot	UKIP	508
Parker, Nigel Richard	Ind	610
Parker, Robert	UKIP	394
Parker, Rosamund Mary	UKIP	567
Parker, Stephen Andrew	UKIP	546
Parker, Vincent	SF	202
Parkin, Gordon Howard	UKIP	535
Parkinson, Stephen Graeme	Con	416
Parmar, Jasbir Singh	Con	598
Parramore, Lawrence Edward	ED	195
Parrott, Eluned Sian	LD	589
Parrott, Julien Henry	UKIP	575
Parry, Dawn	Con	417
Parry-Hearn, Steven Charles	Lab	517
Parsley, Ian James	UCUNF	202
Parsons, Brett Roger	UKIP	543
Parsons, Mike	Ind	169
Parsons, Peryn Walter	BNP	617
Parsons, Simon	Soc Lab	454
Parton, Adam Robert	Ind	159
Partridge, Simon James	LD	277
Pascoe, Anna Kerensa	LD	191
Passey, Carolyn Anne	UKIP	437
Patel, Harshadbhai	Con	91
Patel, Priti	Con	626
Paterson, James	LD	403
Paterson, Lindsay	Con	345
Paterson, Owen William	Con	511
Patten, Simon Geoffrey	BNP	630
Pattinson, Judith Lorraine	Con	636
Pattisson, Peter	LD	364
Patton, Brian David	LD	167
Paul, Shereen Hanook	Ch P	574
Pavey, Sharon	Grn	189
Pawsey, Mark Julian Francis	Con	483
Paxton, Wesley	LD	481
Payne, Natasha Rose	UKIP	582
Payne, Richard Kenneth	BNP	27
Payton, Alexander C B L	LD	299
Pearce, Dennis	BNP	425
Pearce, Kathryn Elizabeth	Lab	95
Pearce, Susan	Grn	62
Pearce, Teresa	Lab	242
Pearcey, Jackie	LD	78
Pearson, Caroline	UKIP	340
Pearson, Gary	Ind	445
Pearson, John	Grn	414

Candidate Name	Party	PA
Pearson, Nigel Charles	UKIP	646
Pearson, Steven	UKIP	257
Pedrick-Friend, David	Lab	575
Pelling, Andrew John	Ind	170
Pendragon, Arthur Uther	Ind	496
Penketh, Stuart Philip	Con	234
Penlington, Paul Alan	LD	588
Penn-Bull, Jocelyn Fortnum Derry	UKIP	622
Penning, Mike	Con	302
Penrose, John David	Con	617
Pepper, Simon Benjamin	Grn	239
Pepperell, Funda	Lab	34
Percy, Andrew	Con	96
Perkins, Toby	Lab	144
Perrett, Daniel Philip	Grn	595
Perrin, Pamela Marjorie	UKIP	242
Perrin, Paul William	UKIP	321
Perry, Claire Louise	Con	187
Perry, Jillian Barbara	Grn	160
Perry, Nicholas David Stanford	LD	298
Perschke, Jack	Con	182
Peverelle, Charles John	ED	617
Pewsey, Tony Stephen	ED	226
Phelps, Margaret Mary	LD	626
Phillips, Christopher William Stuart	Con	365
Phillips, David	UKIP	144
Phillips, Francis Patrick Strain	Ind	108
Phillips, Kay Anne	Respect	68
Phillips, Michael Sheridan	UKIP	397
Phillips, Peter Fraser	BNP	623
Phillips, Stephen James	Con	514
Phillips, Stephen John	NCDV	532
Phillips, Terry	ED	525
Phillipson, Bridget	Lab	320
Philp, Chris	Con	290
Philpot, Roy Bernard	UKIP	547
Phoenix, Romayne Alison Geraldine	Grn	365
Piasecki, John Stefan	Lab	84
Pickles, David John	UKIP	556
Pickles, Eric Jack	Con	93
Pickles, Nick	Con	426
Pickles, Scott Andrew	Ind	195
Pidgeon, Caroline Valerie	LD	590
Pidgeon, Cheryl Jacqueline	Lab	241
Pierce, Martin	LD	614
Pillai, Evangeline	CPA	92
Pincher, Christopher	Con	562
Pinkett, Jennifer	LD	562
Pinto, Joseph Francis Anthony Philip	UKIP	398
Pitfield, Adrian Bruce William	UKIP	464
Pitfield, Spencer	Con	448
Pitt, Mike	LD	43
Pitt, Steve	LD	592
Pitts, John	UKIP	157
Plaskitt, James Andrew	Lab	601
Platt, Alan Arthur	ED	270
Platt, David Steven	UKIP	610

Candidate Name	Party	PA
Platts, Nancy	Lab	98
Plummer, Michael Ian	LD	410
Plumstead, David	Ind	253
Pocock, Robert Leonard	Lab	557
Polenceus, Janus	ED	544
Pollard, Luke	Lab	191
Polley, Gabriel Alexander Clark	WRP	431
Pontey, Jason Anthony	UKIP	484
Poole, Neil	LD	498
Pope, Peter Ronald	MRLP	343
Pope-De-Locksley, Jack	MCP	280
Popham, Mike	LD	99
Popham, Tony	Ind	243
Popple, Peter George	Ind	497
Porter, Brenda	Con	526
Porter, Colin	BNP	30
Porter, Malcolm Douglas	BNP	257
Potter, John James	LD	531
Poulter, Colin	BNP	225
Poulter, Daniel Leonard James	Con	547
Pound, Steve	Lab	219
Povey, Stephen Francis	UKIP	529
Powell, Alan Jeffrey	MRLP	379
Powell, Lucy	Lab	389
Powell, Michael John	LD	454
Powell, Nicolas Edwin	UKIP	154
Powell, William Denston	LD	131
Powley, Marek Daniel Alexander	Grn	242
Poynton, Neville	BNP	85
Pratt, Sandy	Ind	552
Prentice, Gordon	Lab	447
Preston, Paul Micheal	BNP	360
Price, Arthur Stephen	ND	554
Price, Darren	PC	273
Price, Janet Dorothy	BNP	302
Priestley, Michael Alfred	LD	2
Primarolo, Dawn	Lab	101
Prince, Nicholas Adrian Paul	BNP	298
Prior, Peter Herbert	FFR	383
Prisk, Michael Mark	Con	308
Pritchard, Mark Andrew	Con	640
Procter, Alan	ED	354
Procter, Dave	Ind	351
Prosser, Gwynfor Mathews	Lab	201
Proud, Ian	UKIP	416
Pryke, Jesse Clifford	UKIP	386
Psallidas, Stephen Anthony	LD	522
Pudsey, Gary Stephen	BNP	650
Pugh, Alun John	Lab	16
Pugh, John David	LD	526
Purdy, Jean Margaret	BNP	112
Quar, Graeme Brian	Ind	391
Quince, William James	Con	157
Quinn, Tony	SDLP	585
Quinton, Nigel Alan	LD	315
Qureshi, Farooq	LD	366

Candidate Name	Party	PA
Qureshi, Sohail	Con	79
Qureshi, Yasmin	Lab	77
Raab, Dominic	Con	243
Rabone, Barry Maciek	LD	31
Raby, Diana Linda	Respect	258
Radcliffe, David Stephen	LD	64
Radford, Jackie	LD	437
Radford, Martin David	BNP	75
Radford, Nicholas Michael Hector	LD	496
Radford, Stephen	Lib	373
Radic, Fiona Jane	Grn	451
Rae, Ben	Lib	281
Rafiq, Waheed	UKIP	60
Rahuja, Suhail	Con	387
Raikes, Gary	BNP	5
Rait, Timothy Sylvester	BNP	383
Rajput, Sachin	Con	90
Ralfe, Brian	Ind	321
Ralph, Andrew James	YRDPL	532
Ralph, David John	YRDPL	309
Rammell, William Ernest	Lab	292
Ramsay, Adrian Philip	Grn	431
Ramsbottom, Marc Steven	LD	387
Randall, Alexander John	Con	587
Randle-Jolliffe, Paul David	Ind	333
Rankin, Davena Monica	Con	267
Rankine, Andrew	LD	327
Ransome, Elizabeth Lucy Claire	UKIP	181
Ransome, Felicity Elizabeth Ellen	UKIP	356
Ransome, Sue	UKIP	11
Rantzen, Esther	Ind	381
Rathbone, Jennifer Ann	Lab	126
Raval, Dave	LD	281
Raven, James Russell	LD	297
Ravenscroft, Brian Christian	BNP	261
Rawcliffe, Bill	TUSC	196
Raynsford, Nick	Lab	278
Read, Charles Derek Edward	Ind	272
Reardon, John Bernard	Grn	130
Reckless, Mark John	Con	475
Reddall, Philip Richard	BNP	511
Redfern, Andy	Grn	259
Redfern, John Phillip	LD	537
Redgrave, Ernest Arthur	Ind	399
Redmond, Tom	BNP	353
Redwood, John Alan	Con	629
Reed, Andrew John	Lab	377
Reed, Graham Richard	LD	533
Reed, Jamieson Ronald	Lab	160
Reed, Roderick Andrew	UKIP	364
Reed, Simon John	MK	494
Reed, Simon Luke	LD	596
Reekie, Rhonda	Grn	4
Rees, Dave	Ind	336
Rees, Dylan	PC	647
Rees, Jeff	PC	418

Candidate Name	Party	PA
Rees, Mari	Lab	459
Rees-Mogg, Annunziata Mary	Con	519
Rees-Mogg, Jacob William	Con	518
Reevell, Simon Justin	Con	193
Reeves, David Paul	Lab	42
Reeves, Rachel Jane	Lab	355
Rehal, Ash	Lab	247
Reichardt, James Philip Campbell	Ind	309
Reid, Alan	LD	17
Reid, Bruce Robertson	UKIP	215
Reid, Christopher Anthony	ED	327
Reid, Jeff	LD	73
Reid, Julia	UKIP	147
Reid, Laurence	BNP	114
Reid, Malcolm	Ind	596
Reisdorf, Peter Timothy Clifford	LD	625
Reissmann, Karen Joanna	TUSC	388
Remfry, Paul Martin	UKIP	607
Rendel, David Digby	LD	412
Rennie, Willie	LD	213
Rennison, Rebecca Louise	Lab	620
Reynolds, Emma Elizabeth	Lab	630
Reynolds, Gary	BNP	358
Reynolds, Glen	Lab	27
Reynolds, Jonathan	Lab	531
Reynolds, Paul	LD	359
Reynolds, Thomas Patrick Christopher	Ind	607
Rhodes, Stephen	Ind	381
Rhys, Llywelyn ab Owain	PC	127
Riaz, Mohammed	Con	85
Rice, Andrew Julian	UKIP	272
Rich, Loic Joachim	MK	579
Richards, Janet Elizabeth	Grn	410
Richards, Steven Andrew	UKIP	246
Richardson, Patricia Hazel	BNP	239
Richardson, Thomas Leonard	BNP	430
Richter, Fabian Felix	Con	36
Riddle, Matthew Robert	Con	570
Ridge-Newman, Anthony	Con	647
Ridgeon, George Frederick	MRLP	566
Ridley, Gary Christopher	Con	166
Rifkind, Malcolm Leslie	Con	340
Rigby, Bill	Grn	53
Rigby, Peter Edward	Ind	315
Righton, Caroline Anne	Con	491
Riley, Keith	Ind	350
Ringland, Trevor	UCUNF	45
Riordan, Linda June	Lab	283
Rippeth, Thomas Philip	LD	641
Ritchie, Margaret	SDLP	203
Ritchie, Stuart	LD	224
Rix, Simon	LD	172
Robathan, Andrew Robert George	Con	360
Robathan, David Paull	LD	189
Robb, Kirsten	Grn	223
Robb, Mike	Lab	331
Robbins, Steven	Ind	117

Candidate Name	Party	PA
Rose, James Hugh Sjoerd	ED	364
Rose, Shelley	BNP	380
Roseman, Edward	ED	615
Roseman, Frank	ED	151
Roseman, George	ED	140
Rosindell, Andrew Richard	Con	477
Ross, Adrian Norman	Grn	55
Ross, Colin Andrew	LD	630
Ross, Douglas Gordon	Con	403
Ross, Gordon Halliday	Grn	172
Ross, Ian William James	Lab	639
Ross, Keith Malcolm	Grn	559
Ross, Michael James	LD	325
Ross, Susan	BNP	4
Ross, Tom Williams	Lab	9
Ross, William	TUV	376
Rotheram, Steven	Lab	371
Rothwell, Paul	ND	159
Rounding, Paul Alec	Lab	650
Rowe, Derek James	UKIP	401
Rowe, Leslie Anthony	Grn	472
Rowe, Philip Andrew	UKIP	205
Rowen, Paul John	LD	474
Rowlands, Anthony Francis	LD	311
Rowlands, David John	UKIP	417
Rowlands, David William Lloyd	UKIP	402
Rowley, Alexandra Margaret	LD	634
Rowley, Lee Benjamin	Con	75
Rowntree, David Alexander De Horne	Lab	151
Roxburgh, Julie	PPNV	628
Roy, Frank	Lab	406
Roy, Lindsay Allan	Lab	269
Roy, Smarajit	Grn	399
Royston, James William	Lab	54
Ruane, Caitriona	SF	203
Ruane, Christopher Shaun	Lab	588
Rudd, Amber	Con	298
Ruddock, Joan	Lab	363
Ruffley, David Laurie	Con	113
Rukin, Joe	Ind	339
Rundle, Anthony John	UKIP	346
Rundle, David George	LD	26
Rush, Chris	LD	426
Rush, Stephen Peter	UKIP	471
Rushton, James Stuart	Con	539
Ruskell, Mark Christopher	Grn	533
Russell, Christine Margaret	Lab	143
Russell, Robert Edward	LD	157
Russell, Sam	Lab	311
Rust, Jason Geoffrey	Con	231
Rustem, Lawrence	BNP	278
Rutley, David Henry	Con	382
Rutter, David	UKIP	311
Ryan, Joan Marie	Lab	237
Ryan, Michael Gerard	Lab	170
Ryde, John Edward	BNP	81
Ryder, Janet	PC	154

Candidate Name	Party	PA
Scott, Eleanor Roberta	Grn	479
Scott, Jack	Lab	505
Scott, Karelia	LD	55
Scott, Kevin	BNP	259
Scott, Lee	Con	328
Scott, Patricia Ann	BNP	497
Scott-Hayward, Mike	UKIP	250
Screen, Elizabeth Anne	Soc Lab	417
Scriven, Paul James	LD	504
Scriven, Terence Graham	LD	409
Seabeck, Alison Jane	Lab	452
Seabrook, Danny	BNP	311
Seaman-Digby, Scott Michael	Con	300
Searle, James	BNP	286
Searle, Julie	Con	180
Sedgwick, Robert Philip	Grn	400
Sedgwick-Jell, Simon David Francis	Grn	123
Seeby, Ian John	BNP	43
Seeff, Geoffrey Michael	LD	146
Seerius, R U	MRLP	184
Seeruthun, Rav	Lab	384
Sellwood, Matthew William	Grn	280
Selous, Andrew Edmund Armstrong	Con	44
Sen, Nusret	DDP	281
Senior, Ian	BNP	591
Sephton, Matthew Joseph	Con	495
Serter, Jonathan Nicholas	UKIP	171
Seunarine, Kris	UKIP	269
Sexton, Richard Graham	Ch P	147
Seyed Mohamed, Mohamed Bazeer	Ind	171
Shadbolt, Jerry	UKIP	248
Shaer, Paul Martin	Ind	280
Shafi, Adeela	Con	99
Shahzad, Aneel	Ch P	300
Shaikh, Mohommad	Respect	171
Shakir, Babar	Ch P	593
Shand, Timothy John Cairns	Lab	279
Shannon, Jim	DUP	542
Shapcott, David	BNP	327
Shapps, Grant	Con	610
Sharkey, Margaret Mary	Soc Lab	117
Sharma, Alok Kumar	Con	465
Sharma, Virendra Kumar	Lab	220
Sharp, Andrew	SNP	224
Sharp, Janis	Ind	67
Sharp, John	Con	503
Sharp, Keith Haberfield	Ind	420
Sharpley, Rosie	LD	628
Shaw, Jeffrey Stephen	UKIP	504
Shaw, Jo	LD	316
Shaw, John Daniel	LD	34
Shaw, Jonathan Rowland	Lab	137
Shaw, Paul Russell	ND	157
Shaw, Robert Henry	ED	272
Shaw, William Brooke	UKIP	194
Shawcross, Valerie	Lab	49
Shea, Paul Simon	Con	222

Candidate Name	Party	PA
Sheehan, Shaista	LD	621
Sheerman, Barry John	Lab	322
Sheffield, Bob	LD	480
Shelbrooke, Alec	Con	235
Sheldon, John	BNP	503
Shepherd, Richard Charles Scrimgeour	Con	8
Sheppard, Edward John	BNP	166
Sheridan, Jim	Lab	445
Sheridan, Tommy	TUSC	268
Sherman, Benjamin John	RTBP	139
Shields, Peter Timothy	Ind	85
Shing, Stephen Sai Hung	Ind	225
Shone, Mike	Grn	528
Shonk, Trevor Leslie	UKIP	568
Shore, Michael Patrick	BNP	107
Shore, Reg	LD	368
Shores, Gary Colin	Con	325
Shuker, Gavin	Lab	381
Sibley, Leslie Frederick	Lab	26
Sidaway, Ian David	UKIP	77
Siddall-Jones, Edward	UKIP	557
Siddorn, Gareth John	Lab	502
Sidford, Matthew John	Grn	566
Sidhu, William	Ch M	166
Sijuwola, Dapo	Rest	28
Sills, Kevin John	ED	428
Silver, David William	UKIP	29
Simmonds, Heidi Ann-Marie	Ch P	384
Simmonds, Mark Jonathan Mortlock	Con	80
Simmons, Cathrine Hannah	Grn	192
Simpkins, Michael	BNP	147
Simpson, Andrew Stuart John	LD	427
Simpson, Daniel Anthony	LIND	378
Simpson, David	DUP	586
Simpson, Edwin Herbert	LD	194
Simpson, Graham	Con	223
Simpson, Keith Robert	Con	103
Simpson, Liz	LD	573
Simpson, Mike	LD	554
Simpson, Phil	Grn	57
Sinclair, Ron	Soc Lab	387
Sinclair, William Neil	BNP	536
Sinclaire, Nikki	SMRA	392
Singh, Gurcharan	Con	220
Singh, Marsha	Lab	87
Singleton, Kim	Soc Lab	372
Sinha, Murli	LD	594
Si'Ree, Ian John	BNP	588
Sivieri, Mike	Ind	480
Skelton, David James	Con	215
Skelton, Robert	SEP	387
Skevington, Lee	Lab	646
Skidmore, Chris	Con	344
Skinner, Clive Richard	BNP	341
Skinner, Dennis Edward	Lab	75
Skudder, Andrew Clifford	Lab	319
Slater, Jonathan	Lab	7

Candidate Name	Party	PA
Slater, Simon Clive	LD	392
Slaughter, Andy	Lab	286
Slaughter, Lee William	UKIP	159
Slavin, Jim	Ind	374
Sleigh, John	LD	4
Small, Janice Ann	Con	37
Smeeth, Ruth Lauren	Lab	110
Smith, Andrea Claire Harte	Grn	272
Smith, Andrew David	Lab	443
Smith, Andrew George	UKIP	239
Smith, Angela	Lab	448
Smith, Angela Evans	Lab	33
Smith, Anthony Bernard Frederick	UKIP	298
Smith, Brian	TUSC	267
Smith, Catherine Jane	Lab	643
Smith, Chloe Rebecca	Con	430
Smith, Christopher David	Grn	456
Smith, David George William Gilbert	Ind	272
Smith, David Stewart	LD	591
Smith, Edward Ian	Ind	19
Smith, Gail	LD	507
Smith, Geraldine	Lab	404
Smith, Henry Edward Millar	Con	168
Smith, Ian Jonathan	UKIP	550
Smith, Jacqueline Mary	UKIP	382
Smith, Jacqui	Lab	467
Smith, Jason Paul	UKIP	87
Smith, John Norman	UKIP	31
Smith, Julian Richard	Con	513
Smith, Kathryn Anne	Lab	275
Smith, Kerry James Daryl Luke	UKIP	33
Smith, Matthew Garrett	LD	71
Smith, Maureen Irene	Ch P	137
Smith, Michael John	UKIP	270
Smith, Naomi	LD	151
Smith, Nicholas Desmond John	Lab	71
Smith, Nick	UKIP	368
Smith, Owen	Lab	454
Smith, Paul	Lab	102
Smith, Paul D	LD	237
Smith, Paul Winston	UKIP	562
Smith, Peter David	Lab	425
Smith, Peter Edward	D Lab	593
Smith, Philip Ashley	LD	80
Smith, Philip Peter	Grn	168
Smith, Robert	LD	5
Smith, Robert J	Lab	299
Smith, Robert Watt	UKIP	441
Smith, Robin	Ind	629
Smith, Royston Matthew	Con	523
Smith, Sadie Laureina	LD	613
Smith, Steven	NF	338
Smith, Tam	SNP	369
Smith, Tracey	BNP	504
Smith, Tristan James Law	Grn	615
Smith, Valentine James	UKIP	306
Smurthwaite, Cathy	BNP	649

Candidate Name	Party	PA
Smyth, Adrianne Fairfax	UKIP	309
Snape, Christopher Kay	ED	442
Snare, Robert Thomas Fredrick	UKIP	7
Sneddon, Clive Roderick	LD	211
Snelgrove, Anne Christine	Lab	561
Snowden, Derek Martin	UKIP	592
Snowdon, Tom	LD	11
Soames, Nicholas	Con	555
Sodey, David	UKIP	308
Somerville, Lydia Helen	Grn	577
Sood, Manish Acharya	Lab	423
Sopowski, Peter William Joseph	Lab	409
Sorbie, Mitchell	UKIP	210
Soubry, Anna Mary	Con	107
Soucek, Ondrej	Ind	362
Soulsby, Peter Alfred	Lab	357
Southall, Christopher John	Grn	152
Spademan, John	Lab	626
Sparling, Michael Harry	Lab	163
Speht, Rob	LD	558
Spellar, John Francis	Lab	598
Spelman, Caroline Alice	Con	392
Spence, Alan	BNP	415
Spenceley, Lorna Helen	LD	120
Spencer, Brian Thomas	LD	493
Spencer, Mark	Con	508
Spencer, Max	UKIP	316
Spencer, Paul David	UKIP	617
Spencer, Philip Wiiliam	BNP	565
Spencer, Terence Albert William	ED	608
Spencer Nairn, Christopher Frank	Con	441
Spickernell, Godfrey	Blue	140
Spink, Robert Michael	ISGB	134
Spink, Sheila Mary	BNP	77
Spinks, Michael John	Ind	281
Spottiswoode, John Charles Thomas	Grn	523
Spratt, Jimmy	DUP	47
Stafford, Kevan	BNP	377
Stafford, Paul Brandy	BNP	130
Stafford, Peter	BNP	371
Stafford, Peter James	BNP	370
Stamp, Andrew	LD	261
Stamp, Barry	LD	528
Stanbury, Daryl Phillip	UKIP	572
Stanley, John Paul	Con	573
Stanton, Elinor Claire Ruth	Grn	392
Stanyer, John Brian	UKIP	449
Starkey, Jonathan Charles	Ind	234
Starkey, Phyllis Margaret	Lab	398
Starkey, Timothy Luke	LD	142
Startin, Nicholas James	Grn	496
Staveley, Peter	UKIP	365
Steel, James Alexander Drummond	Ind	164
Stelling, Watts	Ind	216
Stephen, Alasdair MacGregor	SNP	479
Stephen, John David	LD	430
Stephen, Louis Joseph Shay	Grn	633

Candidate Name	Party	PA
Stephens, Chris	SNP	268
Stephens, Matt	Con	194
Stephenson, Andrea	Con	369
Stephenson, Andrew	Con	447
Stephenson, Jeff	Ind	291
Stephenson, Julia Caroline	Grn	140
Stevens, Alan Peter	UKIP	142
Stevens, Alistair John	LD	314
Stevens, John Christopher Courtenay	BCD	108
Stevens, Richard Michael	Lab	444
Stevenson, Andrew John	Con	130
Stevenson, Ben	Comm	171
Stevenson, Elizabeth Elaine	Con	71
Stevenson, John Bernard	Ind	249
Stevenson, Mark Christopher	Grn	305
Stewart, Charles	BNP	79
Stewart, Colin	Con	212
Stewart, Iain Aitken	Con	398
Stewart, Kaukab	SNP	231
Stewart, Michael	BNP	216
Stewart, Robert Alexander	Con	40
Stewart, Rory	Con	449
Stockell, Josh	Grn	183
Stocker, John Francis	UKIP	490
Stockton, John Robert	Lab	607
Stokes, David	Lab	82
Stokoe, Linda-Lee	UKIP	596
Stone, David Robert	Ind	226
Storey, Campbell	Con	596
Storier, Miles Elliott	UKIP	136
Story, Alex	Con	591
Stott, Alwyn	BNP	439
Stranack, Andrew Jeremy	Con	117
Strathdee, Joanna Jane	SNP	3
Straw, Jack	Lab	67
Streatfield, Christopher James	UKIP	332
Streeter, Gary Nicholas	Con	191
Strickland, Alan	Lab	50
Stride, Melvyn John	Con	188
Strike, Edward Albert	Ch P	536
Stringer, Andrew George	Grn	547
Stringer, Graham	Lab	68
Strobridge, Geoff	BNP	476
Stroud, Mark	UKIP	553
Stroud, Philippa Claire	Con	556
Strutt, Simon John	CTDP	108
Stuart, Gisela Gschaider	Lab	57
Stuart, Graham Charles	Con	53
Stunell, Andrew	LD	301
Sturdy, Julian Charles	Con	649
Sturgess, Jeremy Bruce	BB	238
Sturman, David Lorrimer	Ind	477
Sugarman, Jason Ashley	Con	362
Sullivan, Pat	UKIP	503
Sullivan, Richard Alan	Con	266
Sullivan, Sean	Con	578
Summers, William Duncan	LD	423

Candidate Name	Party	PA
Sumner, John Patrick	UKIP	493
Susperregi, Mikel	ED	316
Sutcliffe, Gerry	Lab	86
Sutton, Ian	BNP	29
Sutton, Jenny	TUSC	578
Sutton, Jodie Louise	UKIP	241
Sutton, Sharon	BNP	86
Sutton, Tony Bernard	LD	434
Swabey, John Charles Merttins	UKIP	186
Swaddle, Andy	BNP	337
Swales, Ian Cameron	LD	466
Swallow, John Paul	Ind	451
Swan, Russ	Ind	508
Swansborough, Paul James	Ind	467
Swayne, Desmond Angus	Con	410
Sweeney, Frank	WRP	381
Sweeny, Kate	Grn	116
Swindell, Colin	Lab	183
Swinglehurst, Ian Addison	Ind	527
Swinson, Jo	LD	209
Swire, Hugo George William	Con	189
Syed, Navaid	CPA	77
Symons, Adam James	LD	192
Syms, Robert Andrew Raymond	Con	455
Taaffe, Nancy	TUSC	595
Tailor, Arvind Ambelai	ED	91
Tait, Matthew Robert James	BNP	398
Takhar, Harry	Impact	57
Talbot, Robin Lee	UKIP	120
Tames, Lawrence Albert	BNP	512
Tami, Mark Richard	Lab	10
Tandy, Jonathan	Lab	510
Tann, Bosco Lemore	BNP	277
Tansley, Kate	Grn	148
Tappy, Tony	ED	429
Tapsell, Peter Hannay Bailey	Con	378
Tarrant, Michael Norman Alan	UKIP	333
Taylor, Andrew Anthony	BNP	285
Taylor, Dari Jean	Lab	536
Taylor, Douglas Samuel	Trust	450
Taylor, James Charles	BNP	152
Taylor, James Kirk	LD	23
Taylor, Jonathan Christopher	Ind	83
Taylor, Mark	UKIP	167
Taylor, Mick	LD	351
Taylor, Mo	Grn	356
Taylor, Paul	Ind	336
Taylor, Rebecca Elisabeth	LD	482
Taylor, Richard Thomas	ICHC	644
Taylor, Sharon Jane	Lab	532
Taylor, Susan Elizabeth	UKIP	517
Taylor, Wendy Barbara	LD	415
Tayya, Krishna Murth	Ind	460
Tealby-Watson, Elfreda Drusilla Sarah	LD	386
Tear, Andrew Paul	LD	352
Teather, Sarah Louise	LD	90

Candidate Name	Party	PA
Tempest, Michelle Elizabeth	Con	216
Tempest, Piers	Con	29
Temple, Owen	LD	216
Temple, Ruth	MCP	628
Tennant, John	UKIP	259
Terry, Andrew	BNP	516
Terry, Stephen	Lab	308
Teverson, Terrye Lynn	LD	579
Thacker, Lee Nigel	LD	174
Thacker, Rajeev Kumar	Grn	621
Thackeray, Arthur Misty	UKIP	263
Thackray, Mark Anthony	UKIP	354
Thewlis-Hardy, Graham Gordon	BNP	426
Thing, Sam	MRLP	11
Thirlwall, Peter	Ind	482
Thomas, Daniel	Con	336
Thomas, Deborah Helen	Con	581
Thomas, Derek Gordon	Con	494
Thomas, Gareth	Lab	295
Thomas, Howard	CSP	465
Thomas, Jane	Lab	338
Thomas, Kay	BNP	437
Thomas, Nicholas Huw	PC	94
Thomas, Rhodri Hugh	Grn	589
Thompson, Alan	LD	499
Thompson, Alistair John	Con	612
Thompson, Derek George	Ind	282
Thompson, Robert James	LD	227
Thompson, Sheik Gerald Logos	Ind	578
Thompson, Victor	ND	522
Thompson Bates, Peter Mervyn Paul	Ind	297
Thomson, Angela Joan	Grn	139
Thomson, Derek Leslie	Ch P	127
Thomson, Richard Gordon	SNP	271
Thomson, Ross	Con	271
Thornberry, Emily	Lab	335
Thornton, James Douglas	Ind	456
Thornton, Peter Carlyle	LD	449
Thorogood, Peter Brian	ED	477
Thorp, Howard Geoffrey	Grn	607
Thorpe, Hazel Irene	LD	639
Throup, Margaret Ann	Con	516
Thunderclap, Baron Von	MRLP	555
Thurso, John Archibald	LD	115
Tibbetts, Philip Stephen	LD	282
Tibby, Mike	ED	236
Ticher, Peter	RRG	240
Tierney, Serena	LD	555
Tilbrook, Claire Elizabeth	ED	139
Tilbrook, Robin Charles William	ED	93
Timms, Stephen	Lab	222
Timpson, Anthony Edward	Con	169
Tindame, Stephane	Ind	177
Tingey, Robin Howard	UKIP	561
Tingle, Glenn Stuart	UKIP	430
Tinker, Christine Mary	LD	540
Tinnion, Antoine	Lab	312

Candidate Name	Party	PA
Tisi, Julian Peter	LD	623
Tod, Martin	LD	622
Todd, Bernard	BNP	645
Todd, Jonathan William	Lab	616
Tolman, Mark Charles	BNP	44
Tolstoy-Miloslavsky, Nikolai	UKIP	627
Tombs, Sebastian Martineau	LD	342
Tomkins, Tony	Ind	58
Tomlinson, Brian	Lab	581
Tomlinson, Justin Paul	Con	560
Tonks, Roger William	BNP	40
Took, Christopher James	LD	20
Toole, Steven Thomas	LD	236
Toseland, Erwin	BNP	194
Tosh, Michael Ian	TUSC	457
Tovey, Clive	Ind	393
Townend, Sam	Lab	100
Townsend, Andrew	UKIP	637
Townsend, Charles Edward	LD	417
Townsend, Christopher	LD	310
Townsend, Gemma Rose	Con	363
Townsend, Matthew John	Grn	128
Treanor, Donna	BNP	95
Trebilcock, Tony	BNP	387
Tredinnick, David	Con	81
Tregoning, Nick	LD	459
Trevelyan, Anne-Marie Belinda	Con	50
Trevitt, William Herbert	Ind	547
Trickett, Jon Hedley	Lab	303
Triggs, Gordon Wilfred	UKIP	273
Trimble, Daphne	UCUNF	347
Tripathi, Dharmendra Pati	Ind	248
Trower, Richard James	BNP	168
Truss, Elizabeth Mary	Con	425
Tucker, Chris	LD	515
Tuckett, Jane Carol	Ind	281
Tun, Si Thu	IUK	70
Tunnicliffe, Eleanor	Lab	473
Turberville, Michael Jeffrey	Ind	464
Turner, Andrew John	Con	333
Turner, Karl	Lab	323
Turner, Martin Marshall	LD	543
Turner, Michael Henry	BNP	577
Turner, Nicola	LD	158
Turner, Thomas Philip	UKIP	588
Turner-Thomas, Richard Jeffries	Ind	576
Turtill, Peter Edward	Ind	332
Turville, Ron	Ind	124
Tutton, Andrew	Ind	1
Tweed, Karen	Con	322
Twigg, Derek	Lab	285
Twigg, Stephen	Lab	373
Twigger, Paul	LD	373
Twine, Adam	Grn	597
Tyler, Jack Anthony	UKIP	605
Tyler, Stephen John	BNP	49
Tyler-Moore, Adam	Lab	527

Candidate Name	Party	PA
Tyrie, Andrew	Con	145
Tyrrell, John	Soc Lab	63
Tyzack, Peter Laurence	LD	251
Umunna, Chuka Harrison	Lab	544
Uncles, Louise Ann	ED	502
Uncles, Steven Thomas	ED	275
Underwood, Jonathan William Rowland	LD	572
Upex, John Randle	UKIP	293
Uppal, Paul Singh	Con	632
Upton, Robert	UKIP	100
Urch, Brian Morgan	BNP	94
Urquhart, Jean	SNP	115
Urquhart, Ramsay	UKIP	262
Uttley, Joseph	NF	323
Vaizey, Ed	Con	597
Valdmanis, Paul	UKIP	630
Valentine, Tim	Grn	247
Vamadeva, Jannen	JBNF	91
van der Stighelen, Henri	UKIP	328
Van Terheyden, Alexander Rene	Pirate	52
Vance, David	TUV	45
Vann, Henry Paul	LD	41
Vanneck-Surplice, Teresa Millicent	Ind	92
Vara, Shailesh Lakhman	Con	121
Varga, Karen Tracy	Grn	543
Varley, Nick	Con	214
Varnham, Sean Michael	ED	137
Varnsverry, Paul David	LD	428
Varrall, Mary Elizabeth	LD	54
Vass, Richard Anthony	New	547
Vassie, Christian	LD	648
Vaughan, Andrew John	Grn	476
Vaz, Keith	Lab	356
Vaz, Valerie	Lab	594
Vee, Eddie	MRLP	648
Veitch, Michael George	Con	224
Vel, Dr	Ind	525
Veldhuizen, Dutch	UKIP	81
Vere, Charlotte	Con	98
Vickers, Charles Jeremy	ED	532
Vickers, Martin John	Con	153
Vickery, Albert Roy	Grn	574
Victory, Malcolm Gordon	Grn	635
Vidler, Nigel Brian	ED	190
Villiers, Theresa	Con	148
Vincent, John William	LD	168
Vines, Caven	UKIP	482
Voisey, John Roderick	BNP	336
Voizey, Guy Stuart Bennett	LD	125
Voller, Rachel Alexandra	Lab	477
von Ruhland, Christopher John	Grn	127
Vowles, Glenn Royston	Grn	99
Vyas, Anant Manishanker	Ind	397

Candidate Name	Party	PA
Wade Weeks, Susan	Con	648
Wadsworth, Gerard Mark	UKIP	587
Wainman, Sally	Ind	332
Wainwright, Elizabeth Jane	BNP	105
Wakefield, Colin	Ind	320
Wakeham, Bill	UKIP	452
Walker, Adam	BNP	66
Walker, Charles Ashley Rupert	Con	106
Walker, Christopher John	Grn	343
Walker, Gary Robert	Ind	368
Walker, John Andrew	BNP	10
Walker, Mark	BNP	499
Walker, Marshall Robert	BNP	608
Walker, Neil Albert	Ind	537
Walker, Robin Caspar	Con	633
Walkington, Alexander Stuart Burnett	LD	490
Wall, Derek Norman	Grn	623
Wallace, Elizabeth	UKIP	240
Wallace, John Richard	UKIP	639
Wallace, Robert Ben Lobban	Con	643
Waller, David Leonard	UKIP	573
Walley, Joan Lorraine	Lab	538
Walsh, John Patrick Peter	Con	394
Walter, Hannah Ruth	TUSC	466
Walter, Robert J	Con	198
Walters, Michael Philip	ED	201
Walters, Mike	Ind	124
Waltho, Lynda	Lab	541
Walton, David	Ch P	259
Warburton, Paul	Ind	595
Ward, Brian	CITY	537
Ward, Claire Margaret	Lab	604
Ward, David	LD	85
Ward, Douglas Neil	BNP	498
Ward, Kevin	LD	263
Ward, Melvin John	UKIP	63
Ward, Stephen John	BNP	96
Wareham, Frederick Hugo Joel	UKIP	462
Wareham, Jill Louise	LD	333
Ware-Lane, Julian Gabriel St John	Lab	134
Warleigh-Lack, Christopher Byron	Grn	219
Warner, Duncan Noel	BNP	534
Warner-O'Neill, Nerissa Eilis	Con	460
Warnes, Kevin Robert	Grn	509
Warrender, Ernest John Valentine	UKIP	36
Warry, Timothy Niall	ILEU	519
Warville, Danny	BNP	328
Warwick, Greville James Guy	UKIP	57
Wasley, Paul James	LD	470
Waterson, Nigel Christopher	Con	225
Watkins, Elwyn	LD	439
Watkinson, Angela Eileen	Con	317
Watson, Donald William Edward	Ch P	454
Watson, Donna	BNP	522
Watson, Michael	Lab	106
Watson, Neville Kenneth	IPT	578

Candidate Name	Party	PA
Watson, Paula Denise	Ch P	175
Watson, Thomas Anthony	Lab	612
Watson, Tony	UKIP	30
Watt, Helen Dorothy	LD	210
Watts, Anthony	Ind	108
Watts, David Kenneth	LD	107
Watts, David Leonard	Lab	492
Watts, Neill John	SMRA	516
Waudby, Adrian	BNP	357
Weald, Ben	ED	238
Weald, Raquel	ED	237
Weale, Robert	BNP	541
Weatherill, Nicola	UKIP	387
Weatheritt, Mick	UKIP	50
Weatherley, Mike	Con	321
Webb, Billy	APNI	46
Webb, Lawrence James	UKIP	317
Webb, Steven John	LD	570
Webb, Sunita	UKIP	91
Webb, Timothy Stephen Daniel	Ch P	427
Webb, Victor Charles	UKIP	580
Webber, Sam Dunning	LD	104
Webber-Jones, Robin	LD	136
Weddell, Allan Andrew James	UKIP	143
Wedon, Kenneth Alfred Ernest	UKIP	139
Weir, Michael Fraser	SNP	12
Welch, Peter	LD	525
Welfare, Damien	Lab	148
Wells, Anthony Brian	UKIP	274
Wells, Jim	DUP	203
Wellstead, Nicholas James	UKIP	455
Wesson, Paul Gerald	Ind	627
West, Charles Archibald	LD	510
West, Robert Malcolm Brian	BNP	368
Westbrook, Margaret Emily	Grn	545
Weston, Paul Martin Laurence	UKIP	151
Weston, Pauline Jill	Grn	610
Westrop, Maddy	UKIP	541
Wharton, James Stephen	Con	536
Whately, Helen Olivia Bicknell	Con	343
Whatham, Stephen Benjamin	Soc Lab	492
Wheatley, Ken	Ind	105
Wheeler, Heather Kay	Con	186
Wheeler, John Stuart	Trust	54
Wheelhouse, Paul Richard William	SNP	51
Whelpley, William Thomas	BNP	317
Whiffen, Stephen John	Grn	178
White, Alastair Theodore	Grn	26
White, Allan	ED	73
White, Barry Jack	Ind	146
White, Chris	Con	601
White, David Charles	LD	292
White, Iain Richard	SNP	209
White, John	UKIP	634
White, Kathryn	Lab	22
White, Kevin	Grn	467
White, Robert James	Grn	464

Candidate Name	Party	PA
Whiteford, Eilidh	SNP	27
Whitehead, Alan Patrick Vincent	Lab	524
Whitehead, John Michael	Ind	474
Whitehouse, Richard Fredrick	LD	631
Whitehurst, Grahame Michael	Ind	35
Whitelam, Neil	BNP	53
Whitelaw, Alastair	Grn	262
Whitelegg, Paul Anthony	ED	637
Whiteley, Jacqueline	Con	482
Whiteside, Christopher John	Con	160
Whiteside, Martin John	Grn	546
Whitfield, Ruth	Con	6
Whiting, Arthur Dennis	BNP	201
Whitlock, Vernon Charles	Lab	572
Whittaker, Craig	Con	116
Whittaker, James Alan	Grn	510
Whittaker, John	UKIP	301
Whittall, James	BNP	510
Whittingdale, John Flasby Lawrance	Con	386
Whittingham, John Parton	Ind	143
Whittle, Lindsay	PC	114
Whitty, Carole Ann	Lab	577
Whyte, Stewart Norman Gunn	Con	3
Wicks, Malcolm Hunt	Lab	171
Wieteska, Michael Barry	UKIP	2
Wiggin, Christopher James	LD	29
Wiggin, William David	Con	307
Wight, Kenneth John	UKIP	383
Wignall, John	UKIP	109
Wilcock, Jeremy David	LD	323
Wilcock, Peter Anthony	LD	489
Wildgoose, David Basil	ED	505
Wildgust, Fred	Ind	576
Wilkes, Mark Ashley	LD	66
Wilkins, Kevin	LD	121
Wilkins, Luke Samuel O'Neill	Ind	241
Wilkins, Nicholas John Eric	Grn	142
Wilkinson, Graham Peter	UKIP	315
Wilkinson, John	UKIP	611
Wilkinson, Sharon	BNP	109
Willcott, Joanne	Grn	424
Willescroft, Bob	UKIP	68
Willett, Joanie Mary Anna	MK	162
Willetts, David L	Con	299
Willey, Matthew James	Lab	553
Williams, Alessandra	Ind	280
Williams, Alex	Con	545
Williams, Anthony	Ch P	237
Williams, Christopher John	PC	126
Williams, David Andrew	Lab	169
Williams, David John	UKIP	150
Williams, Derek Anthony	CURE	195
Williams, Edmund Morys	Lab	392
#Williams, Elwyn	UKIP	16
#Williams, Elwyn Watkin	UKIP	135
Williams, Errol Ainsworth	Ch P	90
Williams, Geoff	LD	33

Candidate Name	Party	PA
Williams, Greg	Lab	5
Williams, Harry H J	BNP	253
Williams, Hugh Martyn	UKIP	191
Williams, Hywel	PC	16
Williams, John	Ch P	281
Williams, John Graham	UKIP	360
Williams, Juliet	LD	97
Williams, Laurence	ED	242
Williams, Mark Fraser	LD	135
Williams, Martin	Ind	194
Williams, Matthew Robert	Con	418
Williams, Matthew Stuart	ED	287
Williams, Novlette Louise	Ch P	171
Williams, Paul John	UKIP	444
Williams, Philip	BNP	169
Williams, Rob	TUSC	559
Williams, Roger	Ind	248
Williams, Roger Hugh	LD	89
Williams, Stephen Roy	LD	102
Williams, Susan	Con	78
Williams, Terry	NF	58
Williams, Terry	TUV	542
Williamson, Chris	Lab	181
Williamson, Gavin Alexander	Con	530
Willis, James Martin	LD	177
Willis, Michael John	LD	377
Willmott, Ross	Lab	359
Willott, Jennifer Nancy	LD	126
Wills, Harry	LD	269
Willsher, Kevin Robert John	Ind	428
Wilson, David	Con	330
Wilson, Elisabeth Mary	LD	283
Wilson, Munira Hassam	LD	248
Wilson, Patrick John	LD	195
Wilson, Peter Henry	Ind	80
Wilson, Phil	Lab	499
Wilson, Portia Christine	LD	161
Wilson, Robert	Con	464
Wilson, Sammy	DUP	13
Windisch, Adrian	Grn	465
Windsor, Helena	UKIP	552
Windsor, Timothy John	BNP	418
Wingfield, Martin	BNP	636
Wingfield, Tina Dorothy-Rose	BNP	495
Winlow, William	LD	256
Winnett, Paul	BNP	92
Winnick, David Julian	Lab	593
Winstanley, James Thomas	BNP	493
Winstanley, Michael William	Con	618
Winterton, Rosie	Lab	195
Wise, Richard Lionel	Grn	315
Wiseman, John	UKIP	642
Wiseman, Michelle Jacqueline	Con	112
Wishart, Pete	SNP	450
Witherick, Allan Siao Ming	LD	106
Witheridge, Sean	BNP	496
Wolfe, Patricia Ann	UKIP	432

Candidate Name	Party	PA
Young, Michael John	MRLP	512
Young, Mick	Ind	302
Young, Tony	Grn	558
Younger-Ross, Richard Alan	LD	420
Zadrozny, Jason Bernard	LD	19
Zahawi, Nadhim	Con	543
Zair, Samuel	LLPB	66
Zalzala, Yasmin	Ind	389
Zaman, Shafiq-Uz	Ch P	68
Zebedee, Ann Patricia	UKIP	629
Zeichner, Daniel Stephen	Lab	119
Zeigler, Simon Christopher David	UKIP	128
Zero None of the Above, Vote	ND	251
Zukowskyj, Paul Mark	LD	610
Zulfikar, Mohammed	Respect	388

6 Projection of seats

Projection of seats in the House of Commons for a range of shares of the vote

The 'ready reckoner' grid on the following pages converts vote shares into House of Commons seats assuming uniform change. The starting point is the share of the vote actually won by the two main parties at the 2010 general election in Great Britain – Labour 29.7%; the Conservatives 36.9%. It is then simply a matter of adding or subtracting vote share for the two main parties. For example, if we wish to see the outcome if Labour gets 35% of the vote and the Conservatives 35%, then for each constituency we would add 5.3% to Labour's vote share and subtract 1.9% from that of the Conservatives. That leaves 'other parties' and the Liberal Democrats to take into consideration. We have assumed that votes for 'others' will remain constant with the 2010 outcome unchanged. The Liberal Democrat vote share is calculated as: 100% minus (new Conservative share + new Labour share + 'others' share). As before, the vote share for the Liberal Democrats is adjusted in each constituency to take account of the new pattern of voting for Conservative and Labour. If voters are switching to both Labour and the Conservatives then obviously the vote share for the Liberal Democrats must decline. Should the vote share for both the two main parties decline, then that for the Liberal Democrats is bound to rise as a consequence.

The next stage of the operation is straightforward. Once we have added or subtracted vote share for the different parties we can then calculate which party would now 'win' each seat. These 'wins' are then summed to give a composition for the 650 seat House of Commons, with 326 or more seats required for an overall majority. No adjustments have been made to the 18 Northern Ireland seats which together form a fixed number of, in effect, 'others'. Two other seats also fall into this residual category – Brighton Pavilion (Green) and Buckingham (Speaker). Since nation-wide opinion polls rarely report support for the nationalist parties, we have made no separate calculations for Plaid Cymru and the Scottish National Party. The number of seats likely to be won by the nationalists for any given configuration of vote shares may be calculated as 650 minus the sum of Conservative, Labour, Liberal Democrat and Other (20) seats.

A simple example should illustrate how the grid works in practice. Consider what would happen if the share of the vote between the two main parties was divided so that Labour received 40% and the Conservative 35%. Locate the column headed 40, indicating Labour's share. Next, find the row marked 35, indicating the Conservative share. Find the cell where column and row intersect. The result shows that, assuming uniform change in each constituency, the Conservatives would win 240 seats, Labour 355 seats and Liberal Democrats 31 seats. This sums to 626 seats. Adding the 18 seats in Northern Ireland and the two 'others' to this total takes us to 646 seats, leaving the Nationalists with 4 seats. The shaded areas on the ready reckoner denote which party, if any, would capture an overall majority for any given distribution of vote shares.

KEY:
Con
Lab

Labour % share of vote

Con \ Lab	25	26	27	28	29	30	31	32	33	34	35	36	37	38	39	40	41	42	43	44	45	46
25	C111 L207 D302	C133 L218 D269	C140 L240 D240	C148 L267 D205	C147 L286 D187	C157 L296 D168	C153 L314 D154	C150 L324 D147	C157 L330 D134	C160 L336 D125	C160 L336 D125	C158 L359 D107	C163 L365 D96	C162 L370 D92	C162 L376 D87	C166 L379 D80	C169 L383 D73	C169 L392 D65	C165 L396 D65	C165 L401 D60	C161 L409 D56	C159 L415 D52
26	C143 L214 D263	C153 L226 D241	C156 L249 D215	C171 L271 D178	C171 L283 D166	C166 L296 D159	C171 L308 D142	C167 L324 D130	C165 L331 D125	C166 L335 D120	C166 L335 D120	C166 L360 D98	C169 L363 D92	C172 L370 D82	C176 L374 D75	C178 L379 D68	C177 L380 D68	C176 L387 D63	C174 L393 D59	C170 L399 D57	C171 L405 D50	C165 L414 D47
27	C163 L213 D244	C178 L235 D207	C181 L258 D181	C179 L274 D167	C186 L281 D153	C186 L295 D140	C181 L308 D132	C180 L316 D125	C178 L329 D114	C177 L339 D105	C178 L350 D95	C181 L355 D88	C180 L366 D78	C185 L368 D71	C183 L373 D69	C183 L376 D66	C183 L382 D60	C182 L384 D60	C183 L390 D53	C179 L396 D51	C178 L403 D45	C176 L407 D43
28	C193 L218 D209	C192 L238 D190	C196 L260 D164	C197 L272 D151	C197 L282 D141	C197 L291 D133	C198 L305 D118	C194 L314 D113	C193 L321 D107	C189 L341 D91	C192 L348 D83	C194 L354 D76	C192 L361 D71	C187 L369 D68	C190 L372 D63	C188 L374 D63	C190 L379 D56	C188 L384 D54	C190 L387 D49	C193 L393 D45	C183 L400 D45	C180 L404 D42
29	C211 L224 D185	C214 L241 D165	C212 L258 D150	C209 L271 D140	C213 L280 D127	C211 L291 D119	C211 L299 D111	C210 L309 D102	C210 L321 D90	C210 L332 D79	C200 L346 D77	C199 L354 D71	C199 L359 D66	C197 L363 D64	C194 L372 D59	C195 L375 D55	C196 L377 D52	C196 L383 D47	C193 L387 D46	C193 L390 D43	C191 L395 D40	C188 L400 D38
30	C225 L227 D168	C226 L243 D151	C230 L254 D136	C226 L267 D127	C223 L278 D119	C225 L290 D106	C227 L297 D97	C228 L303 D90	C221 L320 D80	C217 L328 D76	C215 L337 D71	C205 L353 D66	C206 L357 D61	C204 L362 D58	C205 L365 D55	C200 L375 D50	C200 L376 D49	C199 L381 D46	C199 L385 D42	C199 L389 D38	C199 L391 D36	C195 L396 D35
31	C244 L229 D147	C242 L241 D137	C240 L253 D127	C242 L263 D115	C242 L275 D103	C240 L287 D94	C236 L294 D91	C234 L304 D83	C234 L314 D73	C227 L322 D72	C225 L335 D63	C220 L343 D61	C213 L355 D56	C212 L359 D53	C209 L366 D50	C208 L368 D49	C203 L378 D44	C206 L380 D40	C206 L384 D36	C204 L386 D36	C204 L389 D33	C203 L393 D30
32	C257 L226 D137	C258 L240 D122	C260 L250 D110	C259 L259 D102	C253 L272 D95	C250 L282 D89	C247 L290 D84	C243 L304 D74	C243 L311 D67	C240 L316 D65	C236 L329 D58	C231 L338 D55	C225 L346 D53	C216 L356 D52	C215 L363 D47	C215 L367 D43	C215 L371 D39	C208 L381 D37	C211 L382 D33	C210 L384 D32	C209 L387 D30	C208 L394 D26
33	C275 L226 D119	C276 L236 D108	C269 L247 D104	C269 L257 D94	C266 L267 D87	C260 L277 D84	C259 L288 D74	C253 L301 D67	C252 L306 D63	C249 L315 D57	C245 L322 D56	C239 L332 D53	C234 L340 D50	C231 L349 D44	C223 L360 D42	C220 L366 D39	C220 L370 D35	C219 L375 D32	C213 L382 D31	C215 L382 D29	C217 L388 D23	C217 L393 D21
34	C282 L227 D111	C284 L235 D101	C284 L242 D84	C278 L255 D87	C279 L261 D80	C273 L271 D77	C270 L286 D65	C265 L295 D61	C259 L303 D59	C256 L310 D55	C252 L319 D52	C251 L326 D45	C246 L333 D45	C239 L343 D42	C236 L351 D38	C227 L363 D35	C225 L369 D32	C224 L373 D29	C226 L375 D25	C220 L385 D23	C222 L389 D20	C221 L391 D19
35	C293 L227 D100	C291 L234 D95	C294 L242 D84	C292 L248 D80	C288 L258 D74	C286 L267 D68	C279 L281 D61	C274 L288 D59	C269 L299 D53	C265 L306 D50	C263 L314 D46	C257 L322 D45	C256 L329 D39	C250 L336 D38	C244 L347 D34	C240 L355 D31	C234 L367 D25	C233 L370 D23	C232 L374 D22	C232 L379 D20	C225 L389 D17	C226 L389 D16
36	C305 L224 D91	C302 L232 D86	C301 L242 D77	C301 L246 D73	C298 L251 D71	C292 L268 D61	C290 L274 D57	C285 L283 D53	C281 L292 D48	C274 L300 D47	C270 L311 D42	C267 L316 D41	C262 L325 D37	C260 L330 D34	C257 L341 D28	C252 L350 D24	C247 L357 D22	C240 L367 D21	C239 L373 D19	C237 L378 D16	C237 L380 D14	C229 L390 D13

Conservative % share of vote